赵敏寿文集

燕山大学知名学者学术文库

赵敏寿 著

燕山大学出版社
2020·秦皇岛

图书在版编目(CIP)数据

赵敏寿文集/赵敏寿著. —秦皇岛:燕山大学出版社,2020.8
(燕山大学知名学者学术文库)
ISBN 978-7-5761-0026-6

Ⅰ. ①赵…　Ⅱ. ①赵…　Ⅲ. ①有色金属冶金—文集　Ⅳ. ①TF8-53

中国版本图书馆 CIP 数据核字(2020)第 130526 号

赵敏寿文集

赵敏寿　著

总 策 划:唐志国
责任编辑:孙志强
封面设计:吴　波
出版发行:燕山大学出版社 YANSHAN UNIVERSITY PRESS
地　　址:河北省秦皇岛市河北大街西段 438 号
邮政编码:066004
电　　话:0335-8387555
印　　刷:中国标准出版社秦皇岛印刷厂
经　　销:全国新华书店

开　　本:787 mm×1092 mm　1/16　**印　　张**:31.25　**字　　数**:640 千字
版　　次:2020 年 8 月第 1 版　**印　　次**:2020 年 8 月第 1 次印刷
书　　号:ISBN 978-7-5761-0026-6
定　　价:135.00 元

作 者 简 介

赵敏寿，男，1941 年 8 月 5 日生，籍贯安徽省颍上县。

1960.9—1965.7，合肥工业大学化学工程系稀有元素专业学习。

1965.9—1968.7，中国科学院长春应用化学研究所熔盐电化学专业研究生阶段学习。

1965.9—2004.12，中国科学院长春应用化学研究所工作。

1980.10，助理研究员。

1986.10，副研究员。

1990.10，研究员。

1997.10，博士生导师。

2001.7，作为学科带头人引进，在燕山大学环境与化学工程学院任教授、博士生导师。

曾任中国有色金属学会第三届理事、第四届常务理事，有色金属学会成立以来，任历届冶金物理化学专业学术委员，现为名誉委员。曾任有色金属学会熔融盐委员会副主任，现任委员。两届中国金属学会冶金物理化学专业学术委员，现为名誉委员。1986 年 4 月—1995 年 5 月任长春应化所熔融盐和合金实验室主任。

20 世纪 90 年代以前，主要从事稀土熔盐电化学和合金、金属间化合物研究。

自 1997 年以来，主要从事电化学和新能源材料化学研究。具体对象为 MH-Ni 电池新型负极材料研究，2008 年开展锂离子电池新型正极和负极材料研究工作。在 MH-Ni 电池低温负极材料研究方面取得当时国内外未见报道的结果。

承担“六五”“七五”“九五”国家攻关项目、中国科学院“八五”重大项目、国家自然科学基金项目、中国科学院创新项目、总装备部军事预先研究项目、吉林省科委项目等。

以项目负责人或主要参与者身份获得国家科技进步二等奖(1985 年)，国家发明四等奖(1989 年)，中科院科技进步一等奖 2 项(1983 年，1991 年)、二等奖(1987 年)、三等奖 2 项(1990 年，1995 年)、中科院自然科学二等奖(1994 年)，中国有色金属工业总公司科技进步二等奖(1988 年)，计 9 项。作为第一发明人获国家发明专利 8 项。

先后去日本京都大学工学部、美国新奥尔良大学先进材料研究中心进行合作研究。去日本、苏联和朝鲜讲学。

在国内外学术杂志发表论文 180 多篇，参与 3 部专著《熔盐化学原理和应用》《稀土新材料和流程进展》和《当代无机化学前沿》部分章节的撰写。

获得政府特殊津贴(1992 年)，吉林省人民政府授予有突出贡献的中青年专家称号(1997 年)。

总　　序

这是一所底蕴深厚的高等学府，在全国各类大学排行榜中均名列百强，学府的工程学、材料科学两个学科进入 ESI 全球排名前 1%。她出身名门，历经九十余载的风风雨雨，两次白手起家，从荆棘中走出了一条属于自己的高水平大学建设之路。她，就是燕山大学。

燕山大学源于哈尔滨工业大学，始建于 1920 年。1958 年哈尔滨工业大学重型机械系及相关专业成建制迁至工业重镇齐齐哈尔市富拉尔基区，组建了哈尔滨工业大学重型机械学院。1960 年独立办学，定名为东北重型机械学院，1978 年被确定为全国重点高等院校。1985 年开始在河北省秦皇岛市创办分校，1997 年学校整体南迁到秦皇岛。1997 年1 月经国家教委批准，更名为燕山大学。1998 年，由机械工业部划转到河北省，实行中央与地方共建，以河北省管理为主。2006 年，国防科工委和河北省共建燕山大学。2010 年，国家国防科工局和河北省共建燕山大学。2014 年，河北省、教育部、工信部和国家国防科工局四方共建燕山大学。

不论是在松花江畔的哈尔滨，嫩江红岸的齐齐哈尔，还是在渤海之滨的秦皇岛，燕大人一直用自己的勤劳和智慧践行着"厚德、博学、求是"的校训精神，推动学校实现了跨越式发展。艰苦奋斗、知难而上、不畏艰辛、勇于创新的拓荒精神在燕大人中代代相传，这是学校历经九十余载而生生不息、发展壮大的根本原因，是燕大人倍感骄傲、弥足珍贵的精神财富，是学校各项事业快速发展的力量源泉。

大学之大，不在于大楼，而在于大师。燕大严谨治学品格的养成，依赖于我校知名学者的身体力行、言传身教。他们崇尚学术、追求真理、潜心育人的敬业精神，对科学孜孜以求的探索历程，已成为燕大人宝贵的精神财富，对青年师生的成长极具启迪意义，并将永远激励着一代又一代的燕大人为建设特色鲜明的一流大学奋勇前进。

鉴往知新。为了牢记传承，弘扬燕大精神，展现成果，燕山大学出版社策划了《燕山大学知名学者学术文库》系列图书，作为燕山大学建设一流大学文化的重要组成部分，先期邀请了我校十余位知名学者将他们几十年来厚积薄发的学术思想及人生感悟、代表性学术论文编撰成系列文集，付梓出版，冀望以此启迪来者，激励后人，在学术与人生道路上立志向学，诚意为学，孜孜拳拳，奋进有成。

燕山大学校长　刘宏民

2017 年 3 月 12 日

前　言

我 1941 年 8 月 5 日出生在安徽省颍上县东十八里铺东赵庄一个农民家庭，祖辈务农。父母亲和大哥都是文盲，二哥小学毕业。1954 年升入初中时，父母领着我和两个妹妹生活。家乡处在淮河边上，经常闹水灾，家境很贫穷，是人民助学金使我得以完成初中、高中到大学的学业。1965 年7 月大学毕业并考取中国科学院长春应用化学研究所"熔融盐电化学"专业研究生。"国家和人民培养了我"是我的肺腑之言。刻苦学习、努力工作报答父母养育之恩、报答国家和人民培养之恩是我终生的信条。

个人的经历总是和国家的命运紧密相连。在我刚完成研究生的外语学习时，1966 年 6 月初，"文化大革命"开始了，学位论文工作停止，在"文化大革命"的 10 年时间里，我在参加研究组的"军工"任务的同时，还要到部队农场劳动锻炼。1976 年打倒"四人帮"之后，特别是 1978 年改革开放后，科研工作逐步正常开展起来。

把失去的 10 年补回来，是当时时代的要求，也是个人工作的动力。20 世纪 90 年代以前，我结合当时国民经济需要的稀土熔融盐电化学及金属间化合物和合金开展工作，并且多项科研成果获奖。

从 1997 年至最后一位研究生毕业的 2014 年 7 月，我主要进行了新能源材料化学和电化学的教学、科研工作。

本论文集收集的 51 篇文章是和我一起工作的长春应化所的同事、硕士、博士研究生，以及燕山大学环化学院的同事、硕士、博士研究生共同辛勤劳动的代表性学术论文。在论文集出版之时，特向在近 50 年工作中一起拼博的同事、硕士、博士研究生们表示衷心的祝贺和诚挚的谢意。特别感谢我的妻子孙长英女士，为支持我工作，她承担了几乎全部家务，在 Ni-MH 电池低温负极材料研究中做出了突出贡献。

"勤能补拙"是我近 50 年工作的基本体会；昂扬向上、孜孜以求是我的工作状态；勤于思考、严谨治学是我的工作态度；立足国家需要、在学科前沿上探索是我的不懈追求。

衷心感谢燕山大学的领导对论文集出版的关心和支持，感谢学校出版社编辑人员的辛勤劳动。

承蒙指出论文中的错误或不足，致以诚挚的感谢。

赵敏寿

2019 年 12 月 22 日于燕山大学

目　录

第一部分
工作经历和成就

一、科研工作

自1966年6月，结束中科院研究生英语和俄语的学习回到长春应化所后，参加课题组的科研工作，主要涉及如下方向：

1. 碱金属的熔盐化学和电化学。

2. 稀土元素在熔盐介质中的物理化学性质。

3. 稀土功能材料，稀土-铝合金的制备、性能和应用。

4. 新能源材料化学（Ni-MH电池和锂离子电池正、负极材料）。

二、人才培养

培养硕士27名，博士9名，博士后2名。这些毕业的硕士、博士和博士后，绝大多数活跃在科学研究的前沿，已经成为研究单位的科研骨干、学术带头人和高等学校的科研和教学骨干，也有的走上科研教学的领导岗位。

张英珊，1988年硕士毕业，在国内一级化学杂志发表4篇论文，在山东大学威海分校任教。

王立民，1992年硕士毕业后，2000年于日本东北大学博士毕业。现任中科院长春应用化学研究所研究员、博士生导师，中科院百人计划，新能源材料化学学术带头人之一。

张新波，2005年硕博连读毕业后，在日本国立产业技术综合研究中心做博士后4年。现任中科院长春应用化学研究所研究员、博士生导师，稀土资源利用国家重点实验室主任。国家杰出青年科学基金获得者，国家万人计划科技创新领军人才，国家万人计划青年拔尖人才，国家优秀青年科学基金获得者，是中科院锂－空电池项目的负责人，新能源材料化学学术带头人之一。

唐金魁，1998年硕士毕业，2014年于南开大学博士毕业，现任中科院长春应用化学研究所研究员、博士生导师。国家杰出青年科学基金获得者，国家万人计划科技创新领军人才，先进磁功能材料的分子基础和材料设计研究学术带头人。荣获2014年吉林省自然科学奖一等奖，2015年度中国科学院杰出科技成就奖。

柴玉俊，2005年博士毕业后，在日本产业技术研究所做博士后1年。现任河北师范大学副教授。先后主持国家自然科学基金（2009—2012年）和河北省自然基金项目（2012—2014年），从事Li－Na电池和制氢的研究与教学工作。

韩树民，2003年博士毕业，现任燕山大学教授、博士生导师，从事新能源材料化学研究和教学工作。

乔玉卿，2003年博士毕业，现任燕山大学教授，从事新能源材料化学研究和教学工作。

王艳芝，2009年博士毕业，现任燕山大学教授，从事新能源材料化学研究和教学工作。

李书存，2008年博士毕业，现任燕山大学副教授，目前在加拿大进修，从事新能源材料化学研究和教学工作。

刘广田，2009年博士毕业，现任燕山大学副教授，从事有机化学研究和教学工作。

翟静，2010年博士毕业，现任燕山大学副研究员，从事新能源材料化学研究和实验教学工作。

李佳，2006年硕士毕业，2010年在中国科学院上海微系统与信息技术研究所博士毕业。先后任上海电气集团股份有限公司中央研究院高级主任工程师、上海电气一国轩新能源科技有限公司技术副总经理。

侯春平，2006 年硕士毕业，2018 年于西北工业大学博士毕业。现任北方民族大学副教授，从事锂电池负极材料和碳基功能材料的研究和教学工作。

苏静，2004 年硕士毕业，先后任燕山大学建筑工程与力学学院、艺术与设计学院党委副书记兼副院长。

三、获奖情况

以课题负责人或课题主要工作人员，获国家、中科院和部级科研成果奖励

8 项：

1. 较低温度下熔盐电解制备稀土-铝合金研究，获中国科学院科技进步一等奖（1983 年）。

2. 工业铝电解槽添加稀土氧氯化物或稀土碳酸盐直接生产稀土铝合金及其应用，获国家科技进步二等奖（1985 年）。

3. 稀土-6063 变形铝合金挤压型材制备工艺，获国家发明四等奖（1989 年）。

4. 稀土在有色金属中的应用，获中国科学院科技进步一等奖（1991 年）。

5. 稀土元素熔盐电化学研究，获中国科学院自然科学二等奖（1994 年）。

6. 75 千安旁插铝电解槽直接生产稀土-铝合金，获中国科学院科技进步二等奖（1987 年）。

7. 铸锭法铝锂-1 合金研制，获中国科学院科技进步三等奖（1993 年）。

8. 铝基稀土中间合金工业实验，获中国有色金属工业总公司科技进步二等奖（1988 年）。

1992 年 10 月获"政府特殊津贴"。

1997 年 12 月吉林省人民政府授予“有突出贡献的中青年专业技术人才”称号。

《科技日报》和《长春日报》，分别在 2000 年 7 月 10 日和 2001 年 5 月 31 日，在第 1 版通篇位置报道我们研制成功"低温镍氢电池"的消息。

四、主持项目

1. 新型多晶巨磁阻化合物研究，国家自然科学基金委前沿探索项目（1997—1998 年）。

2. 超高强度变型铝合金研制，中国科学院重点项目（1997—1999 年）。

3. 稀土-6063 变形铝合金挤压型材研究，国家“七五”攻关项目。

4. 高纯稀土金属制备及应用，中国科学院“八五”重大项目。

5. 熔融碳酸盐燃料电池中国科学院创新项目，新型阳极材料，国家“九五”攻关项目（1997—1999 年）。

6. 中国科学院国防创新项目（2001 年）。

7. 总装备部军事预先研究项目（2001—2003 年）。

8. 吉林省科委项目（2000—2001 年）。

五、国家发明专利

以第一发明人获得国家发明专利 8 项：

1. 赵敏寿，柴玉俊；ZL 2004 1 0011202.2；钛-矾基固溶体氢化物合金电极的制备方法。

2. 赵敏寿，孙长英；ZL 02101347.0；镍-氢电池超低温负极合金材料的制备方法。

3. 赵敏寿，张新波；ZL 021 17955.7；

镍-金属氢化物负极合金材料的制备方法。

4. 赵敏寿，孙长英，吴耀明；ZL 00 1 1896. X；镍一氢电池新型负极合金材料的制备方法。

5. 赵敏寿，于先进，吴耀明，苏锵；ZL 99 1 09925.7；镍一氢电池稀土拉维斯相合金负极材料的制备方法。

6. 赵敏寿，吴耀明，孙长英；ZL 00 1 14823.0；镍-氢电池低温负极合金材料的制备方法。

7. 赵敏寿，孙长英；ZL 00 1 33098. 5；熔溶碳酸盐燃料电池新型阳极材料的制备方法。

8. 赵敏寿，梁金，马先锋，唐金魁，严学伟，赵伟，孙长英；ZL 98 1 04695.9；镧拉维斯相金属间化合物的合成方法。

六、专著

1.《熔盐化学——原理和应用》，冶金工业出版社 1990 年 2 月第 1 版。

2.《稀土新材料及新流程进展》，科学出版社 1998 年 7 月第 1 版。

七、媒体报道

千里冰封何所惧　寒流滚滚仍从容
可抗低温的镍氢电池在长研制成功[①]

本报讯（记者王智卿 通讯员徐海 石明山） 能量大、寿命长、无污染，且能在恶劣低温环境下使用的电池，一直是很多从事特殊工作的人梦寐以求的。日前，这样的电池终于在中国率先问世。中科院长春应化所稀土化学与物理开放实验室成功研制出的可在零下 40 摄氏度应用的镍氢电池，填补了我国乃至世界能源领域的一个空白。

使电池能在低温环境下使用的技术关键是解决负极材料问题。长春应化所从 1997 年开始从事镍氢电池负极材料的研制，他们大胆提出了新的合金成分设计思想，先后研制出 3 种新型负极材料，它们在零下 40 摄氏度的低温条件下，放电容量是普通负极材料的 14 倍～17 倍。在充分掌握负极材料和低温电池制备关键技术与工艺的基础上，他们委托深圳格瑞普电池有限公司成功制作出 AA 型和 D 型两种低温电池。经检测，AA 型电池在室温充电，在零下 40 摄氏度的环境下搁置 8 小时以后，其电池容量为室温容量的一半以上，完全可满足使用要求，而同等温度条件下的普通 MH-Ni 电池容量仅为室温的 1/10。D 型电池的低温性能正在检测当中。

据介绍，这种新型电池可满足航空、航天及多种军事、民用领域对电源的特殊需要，具有广阔的市场前景。目前，长春应化所已就该项研究申请了 4 项国家发明专利。

① 选自《长春日报》2001-05-31，第 1 版。

低温镍氢电池即将问世
我国“镍氢电池负极材料”研究获重大突破①

本报讯　记者张兆军报道：中科院长春应用化学研究所稀土化学和物理开放实验室，在“镍氢电池负极材料”研制方面取得重大突破，他们研制的新型负极材料与传统负极材料相比具有特别显著的低温性能。在6月11日—15日召开的“第十三届世界氢能会议”上，他们的4篇相关论文引起了与会代表的高度关注，下届世界氢能大会主席、加拿大著名科学家萨瓦多格教授当即向他们发出了参加第十四届世界氢能大会的邀请。

中科院稀土化学和物理开放实验室“镍氢电池研究课题组”研制的镍氢电池新型负极材料，与目前市场主流采用的“AB5型镍氢电池负极材料”相比，在摄氏零下28度的低温情况下，60 mA/g电流放电时，新型负极材料的放电容量是传统材料的1.5倍；在300mA/g电流放电时，是传统材料的14倍；在600mA/g电流放电情况下，新型负极材料的放电容量为65mAh/g，而传统负极材料的放电容量几乎等于零。在摄氏零下40度的低温情况下，新型负极材料的放电容量超过传统负极材料的3.5倍以上。

镍氢电池新型负极材料的研制成功，无疑将促使低温镍氢电池早日问世，为航空、航天以及寒带地区民用和军用带来福音。

① 选自《科技日报》2000-07-10，第1版。

第二部分
学术思想及人生感悟

应用化学50年——我的中国梦

1965年9月3日，我满怀梦想，进入中国科学院长春应用化学研究所，成为一名“熔融电化学”专业研究生，开启了美好梦想的应用化学工作。然而，行将结束在北京中国科学技术大学学习英语和俄语时，那场1966年6月开始的十年“文革”，改变了当时一代年轻人的命运，我的研究生学位论文工作也成为泡影。但我是幸运的，被分派到一个承担国防绝密任务的课题组工作。当时所内一般科研几乎完全停顿，我所在的课题组仍然日夜倒班地工作。虽然研究生的论文工作不能开展，参加集体的科研工作对于毫无科研经验的我是绝好的学习锻炼机遇。

从1965年9月3日开始至2014年8月我脱离研究工作，转瞬间半个世纪过去了。而今，我已近耄耋之年，抚今追昔，感慨万千，借文集出版之机，把一些人生的感悟和经历与读者特别是年轻读者分享。

一、抓紧“革命运动”的空隙和周日自学电化学基础知识

我大学的专业是稀有元素化学工程，只是从物理化学课本中学到一些电化学的入门知识，对于专门从事电化学研究工作真是杯水车薪，只能利用“革命运动”的空隙和周日自学电化学。鉴于当时尚未见国内出版的电化学基础书籍，只能阅读Glasstone的电化学名著《Introduction To Electrochemistry》，进而阅读Delahay的《New Instrumental Methods in Electrochemistry》的重点章节。通过上述阅读，既提高了英文的阅读能力，又逐步学习了电化学知识。

20世纪80年代初，我拜托所内去美国进修的同志，复印了Allen J. Bard和Larry R. Faulkner的电化学权威著作《Electrochemical Methods——Fundamental and Application 1980》的部分章节。其后，买到了谷林瑛等4位先生的中文译本，更是经常翻阅学习。

1977年我参加了厦门大学田召武先生举办的电化学培训班，较系统地学习了电化学基础知识和田先生发明的“电化学综合测试仪”的使用，受益匪浅。

二、做实际应用工作必须先做应用基础研究

我国稀土资源世界第一，开展其在国民经济和国防军工中的应用研究，是中国“熔融电化学”工作者责无旁贷的重任。20世纪80年代中期，结合当时铝工业和国家输电工程的发展，我们及国内许多研究结果都证实：某些稀土元素在铝中作用机理被阐明，对铝材诸多性能有明显改善。要满足大规模应用的需求，必须研究出工业生产铝-稀土合金的方法。

稀土元素氧化物的“标准生成自由能”绝对值远大于氧化铝的，稀土元素的“标准电极电位”值也是远大于铝的。因此，在通常情况下，利用铝金属还原稀土氧化物或者稀土元素与铝金属共电沉积是不能实现的。我曾测定多种稀土元素在铝及多种液体金属上的沉积电位。结果表明：由于强烈的合金化作用，使其沉积电位明显向正方向偏移。在铝电解用

冰晶石熔体中，铝金属可以还原稀土氧化物生成铝-稀土合金也为我们的实验首先证实。这样在冰晶石熔体中，铝金属和稀土元素可以共电沉积和稀土氧化物可以被铝金属还原两方面的应用基础研究结果，构成了工业铝电解槽添加稀土氧化物直接生产铝-稀土合金的理论基础。该工作获1985年国家科学技术进步二等奖。

三、紧跟国民经济发展和科学技术前沿确立新的科研方向，在浩如烟海的工作中做出自己的特色

20世纪90年代中期，我们紧跟国民经济发展和国际科研的新动向，开展镍金属-氢化物电池（Ni-MH）新型负极材料研究。

当时，国内外对Ni-MH负极材料已经进行了大量研究，具体从何处着手是首先要解决的问题。大量的文献和国内外实际调研发现：军工部门为某地导弹更换电源需要－40℃下的0.2C放电的Ni-MH，要求放电容量是常温的40%。显然，研制超低温的新型负极材料是技术关键。我们从金属（包括合金）储氢的基本原理——压力-浓度-温度等温曲线（*P-C-T*）出发，所有文献中的*P-C-T*曲线都是常温的，根本没有低温的，更不用说－40℃的了，但是常温的*P-C-T*曲线仍然是工作的理论基础，必须深刻理解其本质才能加以应用。

Ni-MH电池的充/放电过程中，H^+是电荷载体。在超低温下，H的解吸附是影响放电过程的关键因素。*P-C-T*曲线告诉我们：提高负极材料在超低温下的平衡压力才能有更多的H被解吸附。据此，运用某些稀土元素特性和非化学计量比原理，制备出低温新型负极材料，组装8Ah容量的Ni-MH，－40℃下0.2C放电，达到室温容量80%以上。此工作在军事预研项目验收时，被评为超额完成任务的创新成果。我曾应邀在乌克兰、法国巴黎和日本横滨召开的储氢和Ni-MH电池国际会议上作报告，受到广泛的关注。

在21世纪初，众多新能源电池中，锂离子电池（LIB）呈现异军突起、最接近在交通工具上应用的态势。但是，研究得最多的正极$LiCoO_2$体系仍然存在着安全问题，国内外都时有手机用LIB电池爆炸的事件，在改进$LiCoO_2$体系性能的同时，开展新体系的研究势在必行。

$LiFePO_4$是美国Goodenough研究组1997年提出的LIB电池新型正极材料，具有放电电压稳定、安全性好、Fe较Co资源丰富等优点。但是电导率低和Li离子扩散系数低是其固有的缺点。减小颗粒（纳米化）、掺杂、与C复合等方法综合运用是克服其缺点的有效方法。必须深刻认识$LiFePO_4$中的Fe是＋2价的并在制备过程中防止其氧化是一个技术关键。掺杂的元素应遵从离子半径尽可能与被取代元素相近的原则。我们开展LIB电池正极材料研究的时间不是很长，但受到了国内外同行的关注，应邀在印度出版的《Current Topics in Electrochemistry》一书中发表综述评论文章《Supervalent doping of $LiFePO_4$ with special rare earth ions》。

随着国内外关于能量存储和转换研究工作的蓬勃发展，我们又开展了电化学超级电容器材料的研究，水热法合成了多孔Mn_3O_4，自1995年1月发表以来，国际上已引用了几十次。

四、广泛进行国内、国际学术交流，跟上世界科技发展的脚步

20 世纪 80 年代初，日方学术振兴会资助我去考察和学习“熔融盐电化学”研究情况，历时 3 个月。其后，我参加了每两年一次在中、日轮流举行的“中日双边熔盐化学会”(10 次)；在日本京都大学(1 年)、名古屋大学(1 个月)和美国新奥尔良大学(1 个月)进行合作研究；去美国、法国(2 次)、德国、加拿大、澳大利亚、日本、丹麦、乌克兰、韩国(2 次)参加国际学术会议；应邀去苏联、日本和朝鲜讲学。国内举行的与我们研究工作密切相关的学术会议我更是尽可能参与。参加上述这些学术活动，对于了解国内外学术动态和发展趋势，跟上本学科世界科技发展的脚步，拓宽自己的学术思想，分享他人的成功和失败，我受益良多。

以上几点是我从事应用化学 50 年的粗浅体会，错误之处颇多，敬请读者斧正。

赵敏寿
2017 年 11 月 20 日

第三部分
代表性论文

一、新能源材料化学和电化学

（一）锂离子电池(LIB)正极材料

Supervalent Doping of $LiFePO_4$ with Special Rare Earth Ions: A Review①

Minshou Zhao[a,c], Xian Zhao[b], Yuqing Qiao[a]

([a] College of Environmental and Chemical Engineering, Yanshan University, Qinhuangdao 066004, China)

([b] College of Chemistry and Chemical Engineering, Shanghai Jiaotong University, Shanghai 200240, China)

([c] State Key Laboratory of Metastable Material Science and Technology, Yanshan University, Qinhuangdao, Hebei 066004, China)

Abstract: The review addresses the work on supervalent doping of $LiFePO_4$ with Nd, Gd, Sm, Eu and Yb ions carried out in our group. The dopant choice, the preparation of $LiFe_xM_{1-x}PO_4$, and the effect of supervalent doping with special rare earth ions on electrochemical performance are emphasized.

Key words: Cathode Material; Doping; Rare earth element; Lithium iron phosphate

Introduction

The scope of application of lithium ion battery with $LiFePO_4$ as cathode material is currently expanding from mobile electronic devices to electric vehicles (EVs), power tools and hybrid-electric vehicles (HEVs), and it also has attractive prospects in space and military fields. This kind of lithium-ion battery is considered as a high-capacity and high-power battery because $LiFePO_4$ has a higher theoretical capacity of 170 mAh • g^{-1} and a flat discharge voltage of 3.4 V vs lithium, and has high safety characteristics and a long life cycle. $LiFePO_4$ also has high thermal and chemical stability and offers economic and environmental advantages, being a low cost and non-toxic material [1, 2, 3]. However, inherent poor electrical conductivity and slow lithium ion diffusivity are its obvious shortcomings [4], which result in poor dischargeability rate, and these factors restrict its practical use. Therefore, many approaches are used to improve its electrochemical performance to meet the demands in various fields. Currently, the main methods to overcome the disadvantages mentioned above are the following:

① Current Topics in Electrochemistry, 2012(17): 53-64.

improving the synthesis process to reduce the product particle size[5] and carbon-doping[6,7] or bulk-doping of metal ions [8], which can enhance the comprehensive performance of the resultant product. Recently doping approaches have become a hot research area.

This review addresses the research results of the recent work on $LiFePO_4$ carried out in our group.

1 Why some special rare earth ions?

1. According to M. Saiful Islam *et al.* [9], the energy of dopant substitution or "solution" reaction can be calculated by combining appropriate defect and lattice energy. The calculated result shows that the lowest energy for Nd^{3+} ion is found at Fe site for all aliovalent cations.

2. Among all the rare earth elements, only Gd has 7 electrons in the outermost shell which is referred to as "half full 4f electron shell". The special electronic structure itself provokes interest.

3. Among all the rare earth elements, three elements, Sm, Eu, and Yb, are well known abnormal elements. They often present stable 3 valence in their compounds, but also stable 2 valence in some reductive environments.

4. Aliovalent doping or substitution for Fe site in $LiFePO_4$ will create many defects, which enhance electrochemical activity of $LiFePO_4$, and then improve the electrochemical performance.

5. Aliovalent doping or substitution for Fe site seems to result in non-balance of charge in $LiFePO_4$. However, aliovalent dopant charge is balanced by lithium vacancies, with the total charge on the iron site being $+2.000(\pm 0.006)$ [10].

Therefore, it is expected that doping $LiFePO_4$ with these special rare earth ions mentioned above may improve the comprehensive performance of $LiFePO_4$ and its special electrochemical properties.

2 Preparation of $LiFe_{1-x}M_xPO_4/C$ composite

$LiFe_{1-x}M_xPO_4$ (M = Nd, Gd, Sm, Eu and Yb; $x = 0, 0.01, 0.02, 0.04, 0.06, 0.08$) compounds were synthesized by two-step heating solid-state reaction. $CH_3COOLi \cdot 2H_2O$ (AR), $FeC_2O_4 \cdot 2H_2O$(AR), $NH_4H_2PO_4$ (AR) and M_2O_3 (purity of 99.9 mass %) were mixed according to the stoichiometric amount of $LiFePO_4$, using 5 mass % glucose as the reductive agent and carbon source. Milling (ball-to-powder weight ratio of 15 : 1) was carried out for 8 hr, using anhydrous ethanol as dispersing agent under the argon atmosphere. The powder material was ground and compressed into a pellet after the anhydrous ethanol was evaporated. It was preheated at 400 ℃ for 6 hr and then calcined at 700 ℃ for 16 hr in the series resistance furnace. All these heat treatments were carried out under nitrogen atmosphere.

3 Sample characterization

Thermogravimetric analysis of all

kinds of precursors was conducted in a Pyris Diamond TG/DSC apparatus in the temperature range from 40 ℃ to 810 ℃. The structure of all kinds of powder samples was analyzed by X-ray diffraction (XRD) in RIGAKU D/max-2500/pc. The sample morphology was observed by a field-emission scanning electron microscope (FE-SEM) in S-4800 FE-SEM equipped with an energy dispersive spectroscopy (EDS), which was used to analyze the elemental composition. The distribution of the material particle size was measured by ZetaPAL laser particle size analyzer. The electrochemical performance has been measured using galvanostatic charge/discharge and EIS methods. The magnetic measurement of $LiFePO_4$/C sample was performed by SQUID on a Magnetic Property Measurement System (SQUID) XL-7.

4 Cathode preparation, cell assembly and charge/discharge test

The electrode was prepared by dispersing 80 mass % active material, 15 mass % acetylene black and 5 mass % polyvinylidene fluoride (PVdF) in 1-methyl-2-pyrrolidinone (NMP) to form a slurry. The slurry was then coated onto an Al foil substrate (the electro-active material of about 1.5 mg · cm^{-2}), dried under the infrared light, cut into pieces and weighted, and finally dried at 120 ℃ for 16 hr in a vacuum drying oven. The cells were assembled in an argon-filled glove box, and the cathode film and the lithium metal foil anode were separated by a microporous polypropylene (Celgard 2400) separator containing a liquid electrolyte of 1M $LiPF_6$ in 1 : 1 (vol.) EC/DMC. The cells were charged and discharged on electrochemical testing BTS-5V 10 mA, and the voltage range was between 4.2 V and 2.5 V.

5 Aliovalent doping with Neodymium or substitution for Fe sites

Hu *et al.* [11] reported that the discharge capacity and electric conductivity of $LiFePO_4$ have been improved significantly after doping with neodymium ion, which was synthesized by hydrothermal method and mixed with glucose as carbon source. Doping some ions in $LiFePO_4$ bulk to enhance the electric conductivity gave rise to much controversy. As recognized, coating carbon on the particle surface of $LiFePO_4$ can increase the electric conductivity. Zhao *et al.* recently reported in detail the effect of neodymium aliovalent substitution on the structure and electrochemical performance of $LiFePO_4$ [12].

5.1 TG-DSC analysis

Fig. 1 shows three obvious weight loss regions. The first one between 150 ℃ and 230 ℃ is related to the dehydration of the hydrates. The second one between 230 ℃ and 300 ℃ is related to the anaerobic thermal decomposition of glucose and the decomposition of FeC_2O_4 and $NH_4H_2PO_4$. The third one between 470 ℃ and 560 ℃ should concern complete decomposition of residual glucose, FeC_2O_4 and $NH_4H_2PO_4$. The corresponding DSC curve shows a smaller endothermic peak at 192.89 ℃ and two exothermic peaks. The obvious one locates at 268.10 ℃ which is related to the formation of $LiFePO_4$ compound, and the other smaller one is between 470 ℃ and 560 ℃ where a new solid-state reaction with the transformation of crystalline structure occurs, as indicated in literature[13]. Therefore, the choice of temperature higher than 600 ℃ to synthesize the target product is reasonable and feasible.

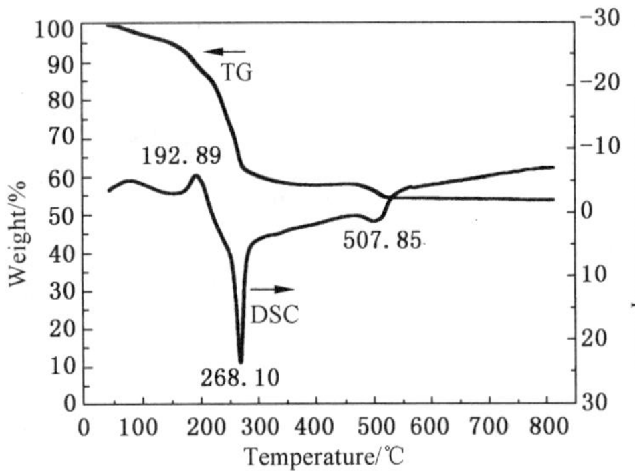

Fig. 1　TG-DSC analysis curve of $LiFe_{0.94}Nd_{0.06}PO_4/C$ precursor

Oxidation of Fe^{2+} ion into Fe^{3+} ion should be avoided and the content of Fe^{3+} ion in $LiFePO_4$ should be decreased as much as possible during the experiment process, because the existence of Fe^{3+} ion would seriously affect the electrochemical performance of $LiFePO_4/C$. Therefore, it is imperative to explore the appropriate synthesis process. In our group, SQUID is used to measure the magnetic property of Fe^{3+} in the sample. Fig. 2 shows the measured magnetization curve of $LiFePO_4/C$ by us. The curve is a straight line if the impurity phases, which are ferromagnetic or ferrimagnetic do not exist, whereas, non-linear behaviour will be observed at low-magnetic field if the impurity phases that are ferromagnetic or ferromagnetic exist[14, 15]. That is to say that the non-linear extent reflects the content of the impurity phases. Therefore, it is concluded from Fig. 2 that the sample B, which was calcined at 700 ℃ for 16 hr, contains less content of the impurity phases than the sample A, which was calcined at 700 ℃ for 16 hr. Here, the synthesis process used for sample B is preferable.

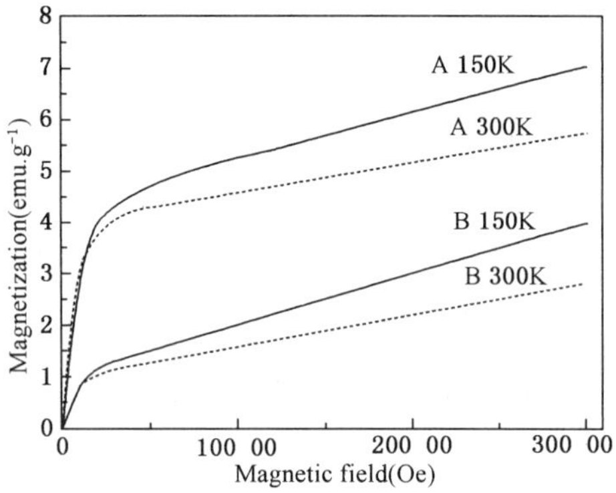

Fig. 2　Magnetization curve of $LiFePO_4/C$

5.2　XRD pattern

The diffraction peak position and relative intensity of the $LiFe_{0.94}Nd_{0.06}PO_4/C$ sample is almost the same as $LiFePO_4$, as shown in Fig. 3 and no impurity peak is observed, which suggests that the small amount of Nd^{3+}-doped does not change the olivine crystal structure of $LiFePO_4$. In addition, carbon diffraction peak is not observed in Fig. 4, which implies that the addition of micro-carbon also does not affect the crystal structure of $LiFePO_4$.

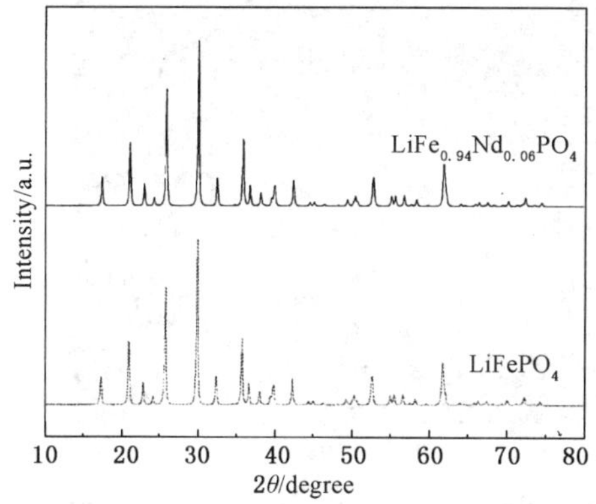

Fig. 3 XRD images of $LiFePO_4$ and $LiFe_{0.94}Nd_{0.06}PO_4/C$

5.3 FE-SEM and EDS analysis

Fig. 4 is FE-SEM image of $LiFePO_4$, $LiFePO_4/C$ and $LiFe_{0.94}Nd_{0.06}PO_4/C$. It can be seen from (a)and(b)that the particle size is refined after adding a small amount of glucose which can be completely decomposed in the calcination process. During calcination process carbon is generated and can inhibit the generation of Fe^{3+} and can be coated on $LiFePO_4$ to prevent it from conglomeration. It is apparent from Fig. 4(b)and (c) that the particle size of $LiFe_{0.94}Nd_{0.06}PO_4/C$ (about 150 nm) is significantly smaller than that of $LiFePO_4/C$ (about 400 nm), which indicates that doping small amount of Nd^{3+} ion can effectively reduce the particle size of $LiFePO_4$.

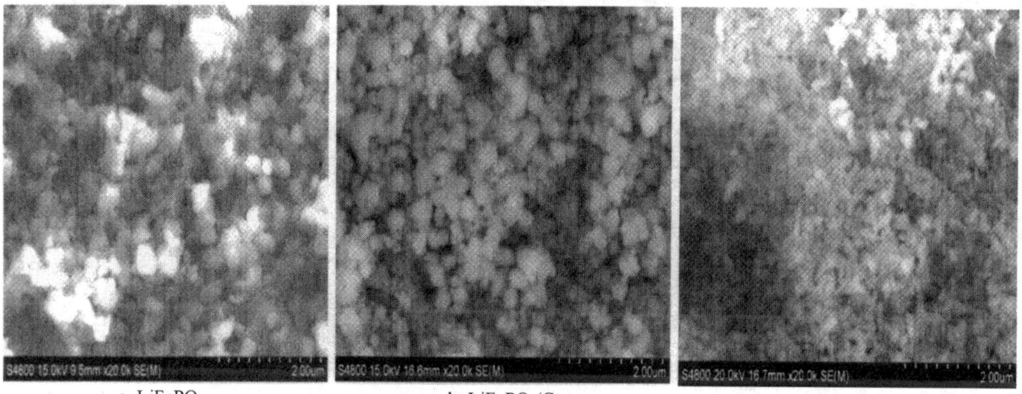

a $LiFePO_4$ b $LiFePO_4/C$ c $LiFe_{0.94}Nd_{0.06}PO_4/C$

Fig. 4 FE-SEM image of $LiFePO_4$, $LiFePO_4/C$ and $LiFe_{0.94}Nd_{0.06}PO_4/C$

The EDS analysis image of $LiFe_{0.94}Nd_{0.06}PO_4/C$ is shown in Fig. 5. The compositions of substation element are listed in Table 1.

Combined with XRD, these results indicate that Nd^{3+} occupies Fe site in $LiFePO_4$ or has been dissolved into the $LiFePO_4$.

5.4 Electrochemical performance

As shown in Fig. 6, 7 and 8, $LiFe_{0.96}Nd_{0.06}PO_4$ delivers the maximum discharge capacity of 165.2 mAh • g^{-1}, 146.8 mAh • g^{-1}, 125.7 mAh • g^{-1}, 114.8 mAh • g^{-1} at 0.2 C, 1 C, 2 C, 5 C rates, respectively, and the capacity retention rate is 92.8% after 100 cycles. Fig. 9 indicates that using PZS as carbon source for coating on the surface of $LiFePO_4$ is more beneficial for the cycle stability than glucose.

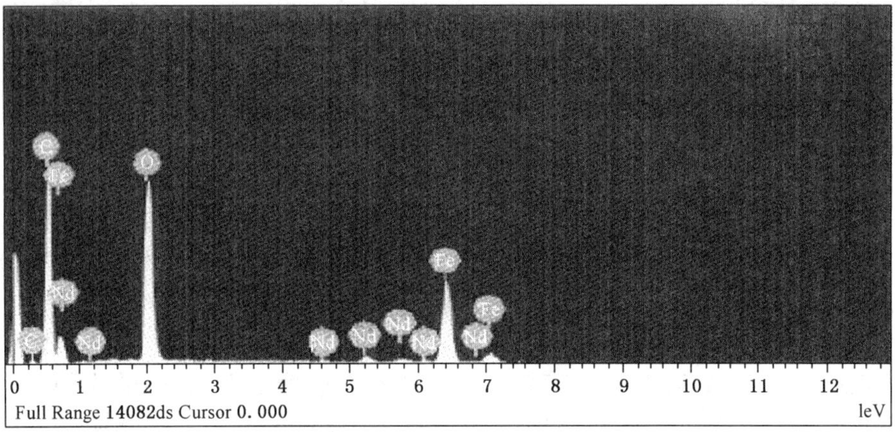

Fig. 5　EDS image of $LiFe_{0.94}Nd_{0.06}PO_4/C$

Table 1　Composition of substation element in $LiFe_{0.94}Nd_{0.06}PO_4/C$

Elt	C K	O K	P K	Fe K	Nd L	Total
W/%	6.07	46.75	17.14	25.98	4.07	100.00
A/%	11.29	65.31	12.37	10.40	0.63	100.00

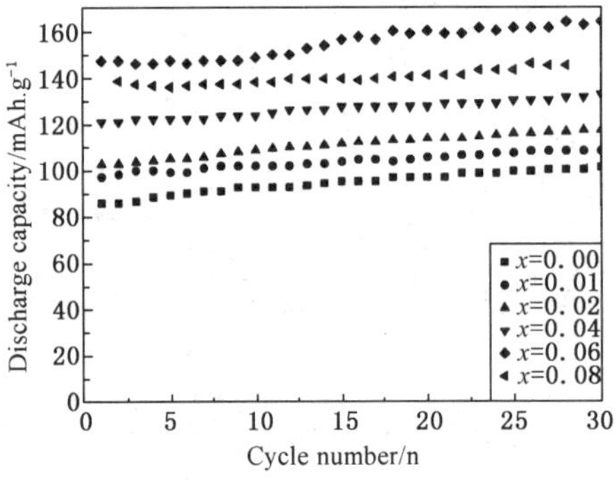

Fig. 6　Discharge capacity as a function of cycle number for $LiFe_{1-x}Nd_xPO_4/C$ ($x=0\sim0.08$) at 0. 2 C rate

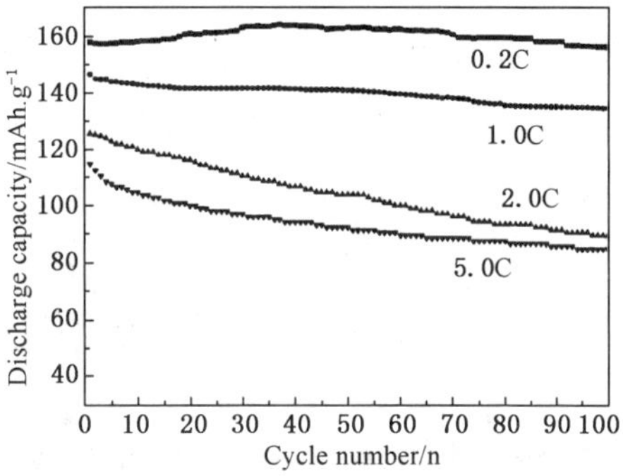

Fig. 7　Discharge capacity as a function of cycle number for $LiFe_{0.04}Nd_{0.06}PO_4/C$ at different rates

6　Aliovalent doping gadolinium or substitution for Fe site

6. 1　XRD

Fig. 10A and Fig. 10B show the XRD pattern of $LiFePO_4/C$ composite and Rietveld refinement of the XRD pattem for $LiFe_{0.93}Gd_{0.07}PO_4/C$ composite[16], respectively. The observed pattern and calculated pattern match well in Fig. 10B. The crystal phases of two samples are olivine structures indexed by orthorhombic Pnma. These results suggest that a small amount of Gd^{3+} ion-doped does not affect the olivine structure of $LiFePO_4$. In addition, a carbon diffraction peak is not observed in Fig. 10A and Fig. 10B, which implies that the micro-carbon coating does not affect the structure of $LiFePO_4$ also.

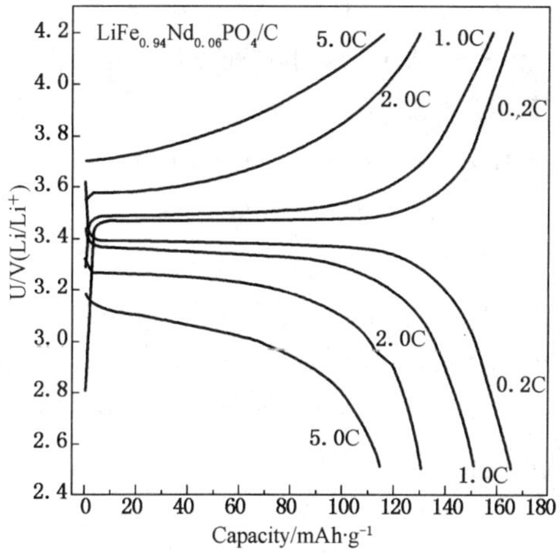

Fig. 8 Initial charge-discharge curve of $LiFe_{0.94}Nd_{0.06}PO_4/C$ of at different rates

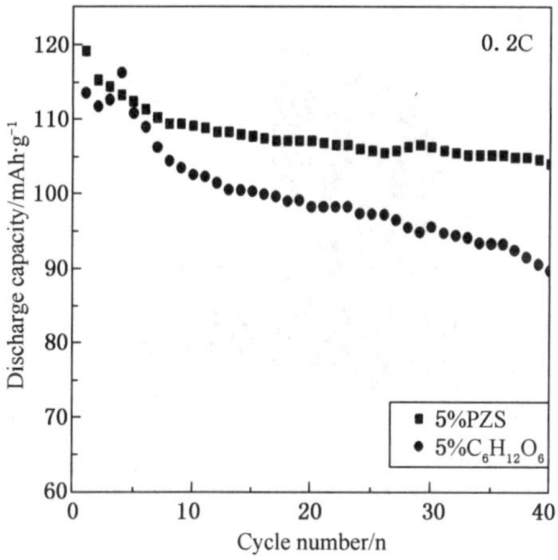

Fig. 9 Influence of different carbon source on cycle stability $LiFePO_4/C$ at a rate of 0.2C

However, XRD pattern of Gd-doped $LiFePO_4$ shows more Bragg reflections than Gd-free $LiFePO_4$ because the ionic radius of Gd^{3+} ion doped (0.093 8 nm) is larger than that of Fe^{2+} ion (0.078 nm), leading to bigger unit cell parameters, as shown in Table 2. Table 2 lists the unit cell parameter obtained from Rietveld refinement of the XRD for $LiFe_{0.93}Gd_{0.07}PO_4/C$ and unit cell parameter of $LiFePO_4/C$.

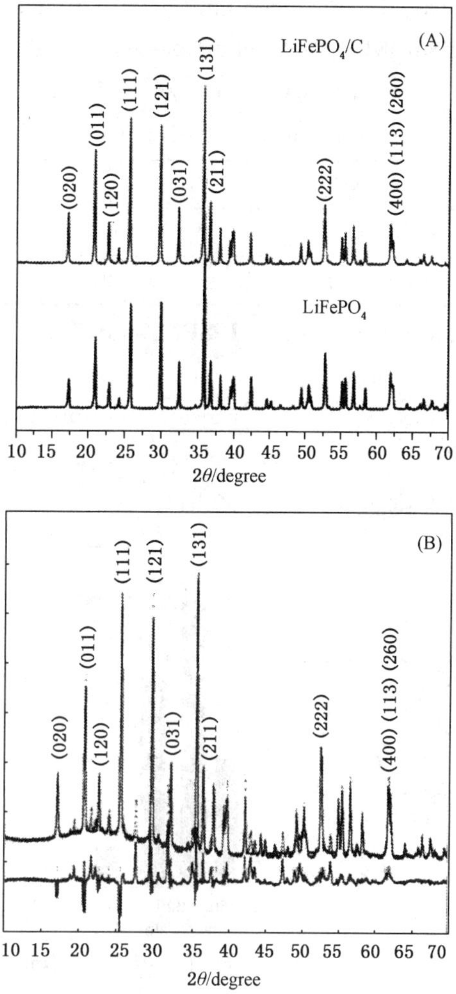

Fig. 10 (A) XRD of $LiFePO_4$ and $LiFePO_4/C$ and (B) Rietveld refinement of XRD for $LiFe_{0.93}Gd_{0.07}PO_4/C$

Results of Rietveld refinement confirm that Gd^{3+} ion has been successfully doped into the $LiFePO_4/C$. Clearly, doping a small amount of Gd^{3+} ion has little effect on the cell parameters of $LiFePO_4$, and the dopant of a larger ionic radius perhaps creates more defects in $LiFePO_4$, which is beneficial for the electrochemical catalytic activity of the electrode.

Table 2　Unit cell parameter obtained from XRD Rietveld refinement of XRD for $LiFe_{0.93}Gd_{0.07}PO_4/C$ and unit cell parameter of $LiFePO_4/C$

Sample	a/nm	b/nm	c/nm
$LiFePO_4/C$	1.032 4	0.600 7	0.469 5
$LiFe_{0.93}Gd_{0.07}PO_4/C$	1.047 1	0.609 2	0.475 8

6.2　Particle size, FE-SEM and EDS

The grain size of samples can be described by particle size distribution. Fig. 11 presents the particle size distribution histogram of $LiFePO_4/C$ sample and $LiFe_{0.93}Gd_{0.07}PO_4/C$ sample, respectively. Fig. 12 depicts the FE-SEM images of $LiFePO_4/C$ and $LiFe_{0.93}Gd_{0.07}PO_4/C$, respectively. It is apparent from Fig. 11 and Fig. 12 that the particle size of $LiFe_{0.93}Gd_{0.07}PO_4/C$ sample is significantly smaller than that of $LiFePO_4/C$ sample, and the particle scale is uniform after doping Gd^{3+} ion, which indicates that doping a small amount of Gd^{3+} can effectively reduce the particle size of $LiFePO_4/C$ and make it more uniform.

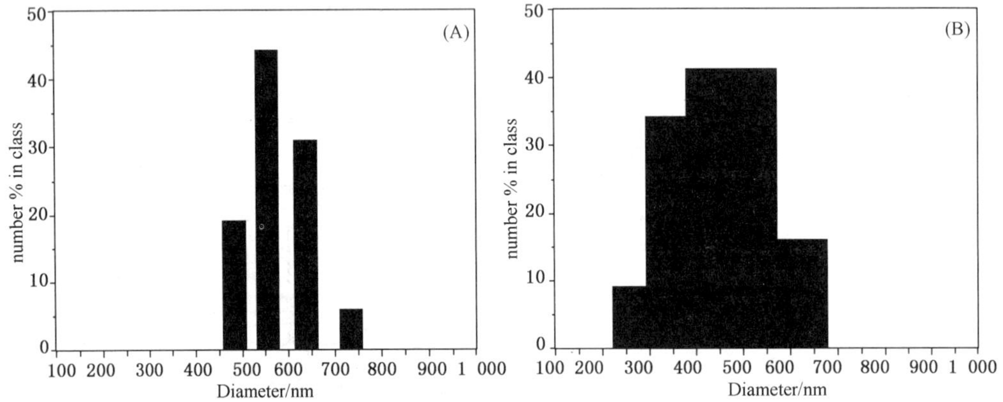

Fig. 11　(A) particle size distributions of $LiFePO_4/C$ and (B) particle size distributions of $LiFe_{0.93}Gd_{0.07}PO_4/C$

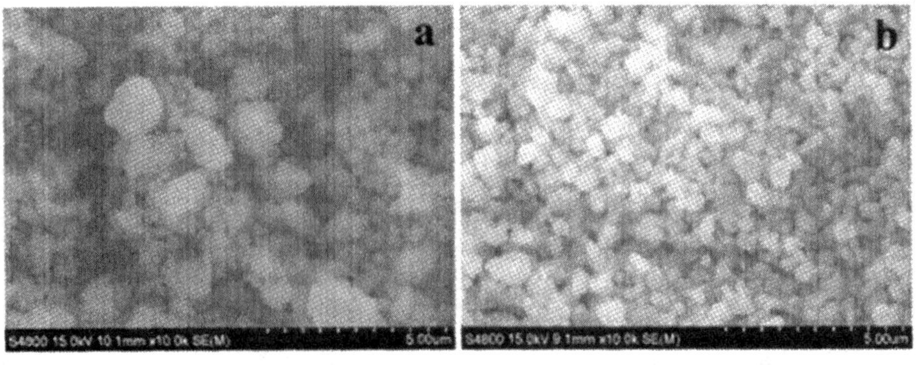

Fig. 12　FE-SEM images of $LiFePO_4/C$(a) and $LiFe_{0.93}Gd_{0.07}PO_4/C$(b)

The EDS image of $LiFe_{0.93}Gd_{0.07}PO_4/C$ is shown in Fig. 13. The compositions of the substituent elements are listed in Table 3. The result shows the atomic ratio of Fe, Gd, P and O is 0.981 : 0.067 : 1 : 4.858 in $LiFe_{0.93}Gd_{0.07}PO_4/C$ sample, essentially coinciding with $LiFe_{0.93}Gd_{0.07}PO_4/C$. The supervalent-cation dopant in $LiFePO_4$ is studied by combining neutron and X-ray diffraction. The results showed that low levels of dopants were indeed soluble in the olivine lattice up to the extent of 3 mol %. Therefore, we infer that Gd^{3+} ion occupies Fe^{2+} ion site in $LiFePO_4/C$ or has been dissolved into $LiFePO_4/C$ to form a solid solution.

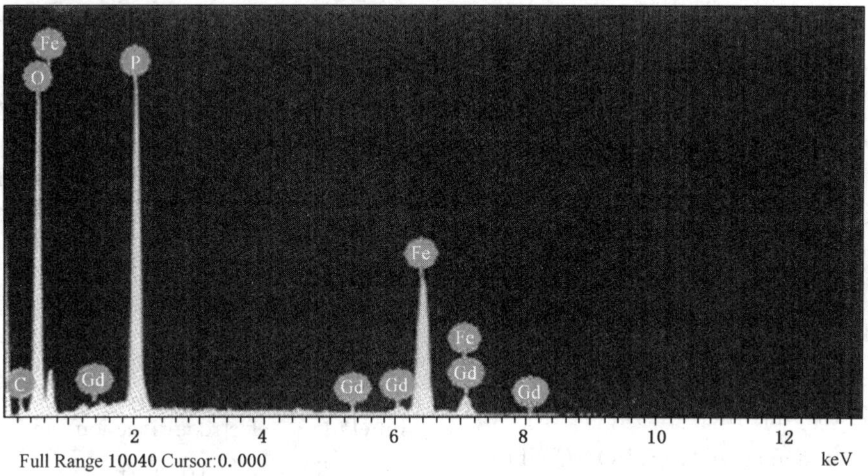

Fig. 13 EDS image of $LiFe_{0.93}Gd_{0.07}PO_4/C$

Table 3 Element composition in $LiFe_{0.93}Gd_{0.07}PO_4/C$

Elt	C K	O K	P K	Fe K	Gd L	Total
W/%	5.40	42.23	16.83	29.77	5.77	100.00
A/%	10.71	62.81	12.93	12.68	0.87	100.00

6.3 Electrochemical performance

The cycle performance of $LiFe_{0.93}Gd_{0.07}PO_4/C$ sample at various rates is shown in Fig. 14(A). The maximum discharge capacity is 150.7 mAh · g^{-1}, 125.9 mAh · g^{-1}, 106.0 mAh · g^{-1} and 81.3 mAh · g^{-1} at rates of 0.2 C, 1 C, 5 C and 10 C, respectively. Fig. 14(B) shows the discharge curves of $LiFe_{0.93}Gd_{0.07}PO_4/C$ sample at various rates. It is concluded that doping an appropriate amount of Gd^{3+} ion can improve the high-rate discharge performance of $LiFePO_4/C$ composite.

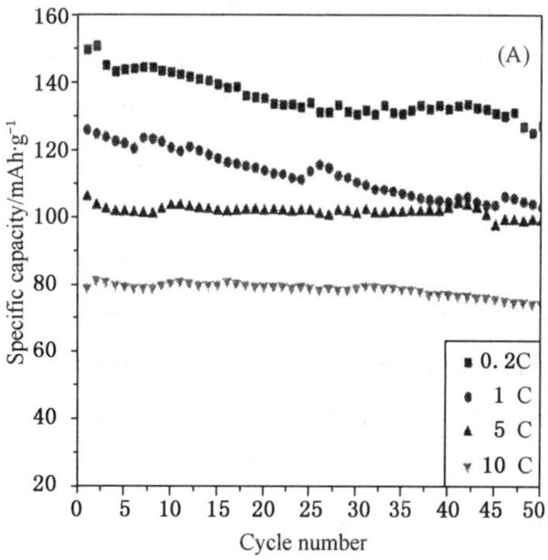

Fig. 14 (A) Discharge capacity as a function of cycle number for $LiFe_{0.93}Gd_{0.07}PO_4/C$ at various rates

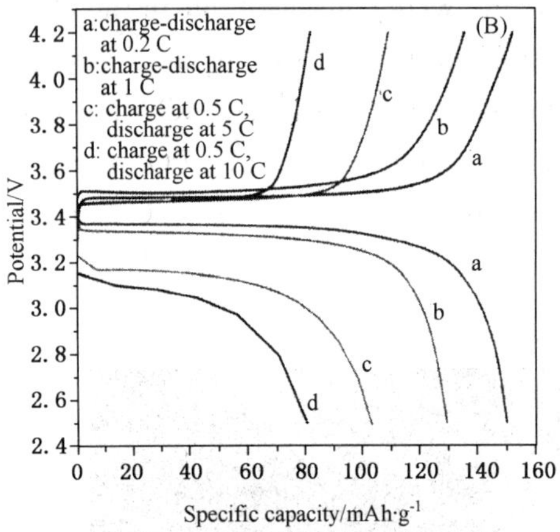

Fig. 14 (B) Second charge-discharge curves of $LiFe_{0.93}Gd_{0.07}PO_4/C$ at various rates

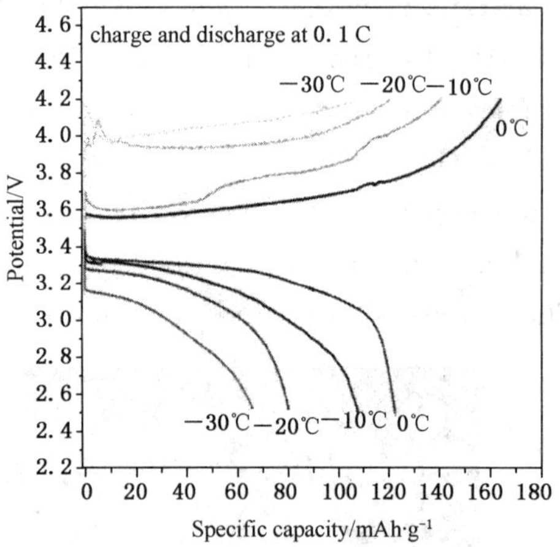

Fig. 15 Initial charge-discharge curves of $LiFe_{0.93}Gd_{0.07}PO_4/C$ at various temperatures

It is inferred that doping Gd^{3+} ion can reduce the particle size of $LiFePO_4$/C, shorten the transport path of Li^+ ion, increase the disorder of the lattice and create the defect in $LiFePO_4$/C. These factors would improve the electrochemical performance of $LiFePO_4$/C composite.

The electrochemical measurements have also been carried out at lower temperatures, as shown in Fig. 15. And at 0.1 C rate, the initial discharge capacity is 122.2 mAh · g^{-1}, 107.7 mAh · g^{-1}, 80.4 mAh · g^{-1} and 66.3 mAh · g^{-1} at 0 ℃, −10 ℃, −20 ℃ and −30 ℃, respectively. The discharge capacity monotonously sharply decreases with decreasing temperature, just as expected. At lower temperature the transport speed of Li^+ ion slows down and ohmic polarization influence becomes more dominant. These perhaps are key issues to influence discharge capability.

EIS was used to further analyze the effect of doping Gd^{3+} ion on the electrode reaction impedance. Fig. 16 shows EIS of $LiFePO_4$/C electrode reaction and $LiFe_{0.93}Gd_{0.07}PO_4$/C electrode reaction at 15 ℃. The results were obtained using Zview software and are listed in Table 4. The ohmic resistance (Rs) almost does not change for two samples, because the same electrolyte was used. As expected, charge-transfer impedance obviously decreases in the charge-discharge process because of the addition of Gd^{3+} ion. The charge transfer resistance (Rct) for $LiFePO_4$/C electrode reaction and $LiFe_{0.93}Gd_{0.07}PO_4$/C electrode reaction is 692.6 Ω and 241.3 Ω, respectively. This great decrease in the impedance will benefit to overcome the restriction of kinetics in the charge-discharge process and improve the cycling performance of the material.

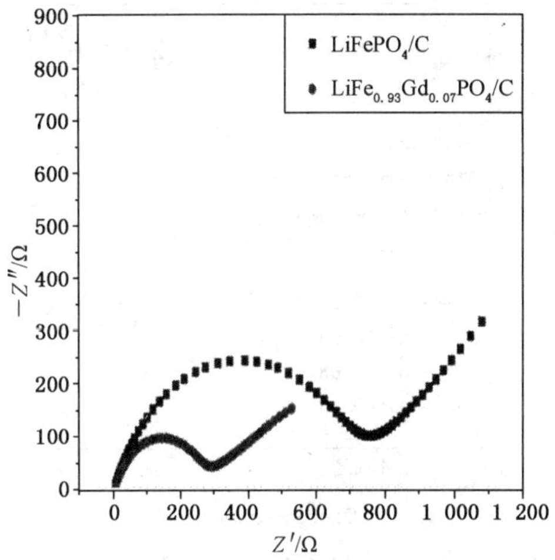

Fig. 16　EIS for $LiFePO_4/C$ and $LiFe_{0.93}Gd_{0.07}PO_4/C$ electrode after 3 cycles

Table 4　Electrochemical impedance and exchange current density

Sample	$Rs(\Omega)$	$Rct(\Omega)$	I_0 $(mA \cdot g^{-1})$
$LiFePO_4/C$	3.406	692.6	26.3
$LiFe_{0.93}Gd_{0.07}PO_4/C$	3.288	241.3	128.5

An apparent exchange current density(I_0)can be often used to sign the catalytic activity of electrode, which is an important parameter of kinetics for an electrochemical reaction. When overpotential is very small, it can be calculated using Formula(1)[17] and the results are also listed in Table 4.

$$I_0 = R \cdot T/nRct \cdot F \qquad (1)$$

where R is gas constant, T is absolute temperature, F is Faraday constant, n is charge-transfer number and Rct is charge-transfer resistance.

7　Aliovalent doping abnormal rare earth (Sm, Eu, Yb) or substitution for Fe site in $LiFePO_4$

Compared with other rare earth elements, Sm, Eu and Yb have some unique characteristics and are often called as abnormal rare earth elements. Based on results of Nd and Gd as dopants in $LiFePO_4$, doping Sm, Eu and Yb were also carried out via the same experimental procedures as above mentioned[18,19].

As expected, the effect of respective doping Sm, Eu and Yb in $LiFePO_4$ on the electrochemical performances has almost the same results and trend. The experimental results of doping Sm as a representative element have been given below.

7.1　Electrochemical performance

The cycle performance of $LiFe_{1-x}Sm_xPO_4/C$ sample and initial charge-discharge curves are shown in Fig. 17(left) and(right), respectively, It is concluded from Fig. 17 that due to doping Sm, the discharge capacity increases and the difference of plateau gap between the charge/discharge curves become narrow, and the polarization becomes small. The rate performance has been improved because of doping Sm in $LiFePO_4$, just like as influence on discharge capacity.

Fig. 18 shows EIS for $LiFe_{1-x}Sm_xPO_4/C$(x=0, 0.06, 0.08, 0.10) electrode reaction. When x equals 0.08, Rct has lowest value, 199 Ω, much lower than that without doping Sm, 1 211 Ω.

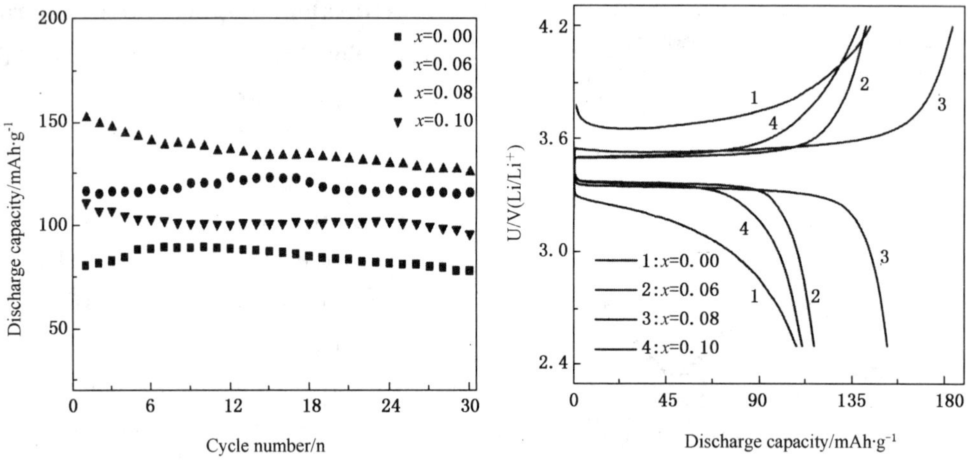

Fig. 17　Cycle performances(left)and initial charge-discharge curve of $LiFe_{1-x}Sm_xPO_4/C$(right)

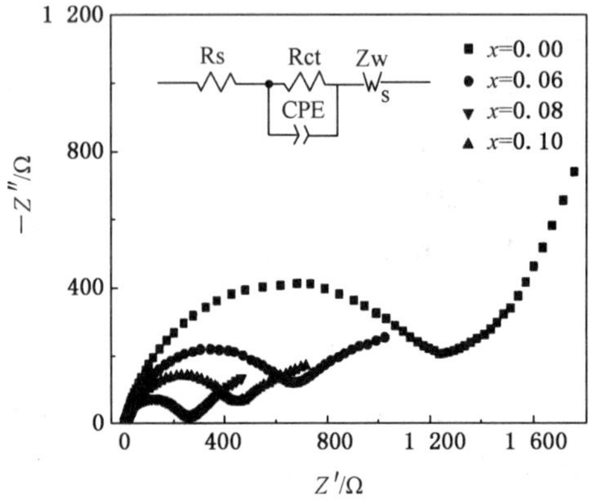

Fig. 18　EIS for $LiFe_{1-x}Sm_xPO_4/C$ ($x=0,0.06,0.08,0.10$)

7.2　Temperature effect

The effect of temperature on the discharge capacity has been carried out for doping Sm at the range of −20 ℃ to 60 ℃, as shown in Fig. 19. The relation between discharge capacity and temperature is as expected. The discharge capacity monotonously sharply decreases both at higher or lower temperature than ambient temperature.

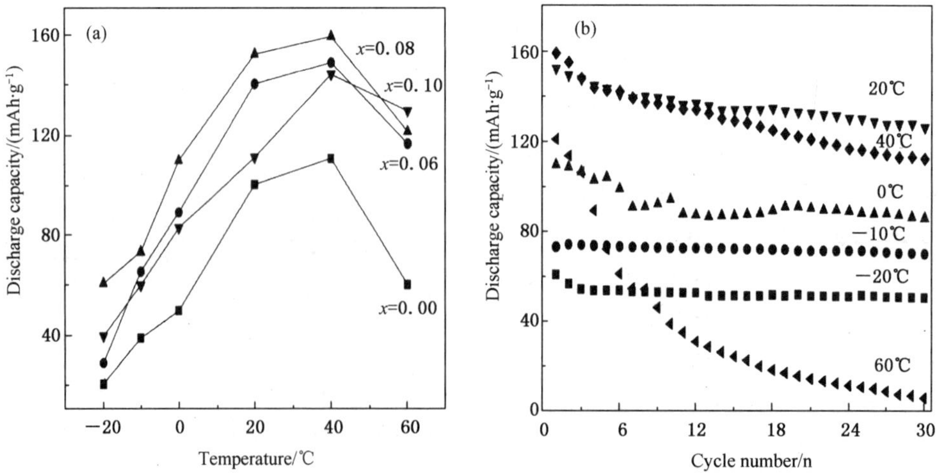

Fig. 19　(a)Discharge capacity of $LiFe_{1-x}Sm_xPO_4/C$ and(b)cycle performances of sample with $x=0.08$ at various temperature

8 There are many problems to be further investigated on doping in olivine $LiFePO_4$

Since 1997, more than thousand papers on $LiFePO_4$ cathode material for Li-ion battery have been published, and the application of $LiFePO_4$ as cathode material is moving forward fast and has seen the first light in commercialization. Doping some elements in $LiFePO_4$ is a very effective approach for the improvement of performances for $LiFePO_4$ However, there are some academic problems to be investigated in future. More accurate experimental methods and compelling results are needed.

1. There are ambivalent viewpoints on dopant state in olivine lattice. Islam *et al*. reported that "on energetic ground, $LiFePO_4$ is not tolerant to aliovalent doping(e. g. , Al, Ga, Zr, Ti, Nb, Ta) on either Li(M1) or Fe(M2) sites." However, Wagemaker *et al*. stated that "low levels of dopants are indeed soluble in the olivine lattice up to the extent of 3 mol % (in bulk materials)."

2. How does the dopant exist in $LiFePO_4$? and by substitution in Li site or Fe site or by forming solid solution in $LiFePO_4$?

3. Why is it that a small amount of dopant can greatly improve the electrochemical performances of $LiFePO_4$? Is it due to the creation of more defects in lattice or enhancing electrochemical activity?

4. Appropriate doping of some ions in $LiFePO_4$ can improve the electrochemical performance, which is a well known essential fact. However, what is the dependable mechanism?

References

[1] Pier Paolo Prosini, Daniela Zane and Mauro Pasquali. 2001, Electrochim. Acta, 46 (23), 3517.

[2] Navet, N. , Chouinard, Y. , Magnan, J. F. , Besner, S. , Gauthier, M. and Armand, M. 2001, J. Power Sources, 97-98, 503.

[3] Padhi, A. K. , Nanjundaswamy, K. S. and Goodenough, J. B. 1997, J. Electrochem. Soc. , 144, 1188.

[4] Kwon, S. J. , Kim, C. W. , Jeong, W. T. and Lee, K. S. 2004, J. Power Sources, 137 (1), 93.

[5] Yamada, A. , Chung, S. C. and Kinokuma, K. 2001, J. Electrechem. Soc. , 148(3), A224.

[6] Zhao, C. H. and Dahn, J. R. 2002, J. Electrochem. Soc. , 149(9), A 1184-1189.

[7] Tang, Z. Y. and Ruan, Y. L. 2005, Acta Chimica Sinica (Huaxue Xuebao), 63 (16), 1500.

[8] Chung, S. Y. , Jason, T. B. and Chiang, Y. M. 2002, Nature Materials, 1(2), 123.

[9] Saiful Islam, M. , Daniel J. Driscoll, Craig A. J. Fisher, and Peter R. Slater, 2005, Chem. Mater. , 17(20), 5085.

[10] Marnix Wagemaker, Brian L. Ellis, Drik Lutzenkirchen-Hecht, Fokko M. Mulder, and Linda F. Nazar, 2008, Chem. Mater. , 20(20), 6313.

[11] Jiezi Hu, jian Xie, Xinbing Zhao, Hongming Yu, Xin Zhou, gaoshao Cao, and Jiangping Tu, 2009, J. Mater. Sci. Technol. , 25 (3), 405.

[12] Xian Zhao, Xiaozhen Tang, Li Zhang, Minshou Zhao, and Jing Zhai, 2010, Electrochimica Acta, 55, 5899.

[13] Yu Boling, and Jiang Jiaodong, 1990, Applied Thermal Analysis, Textile Industry Press, Beijing, 114-120.

[14] Salah, A. A., Mauger, A., Julien, C. M. and Gendron, F. 2006, Mater. Sci. Eng. B, 129, 232.

[15] Zaghib, K., Ravet, N., Gauthier, M., Gendron, F., Manger, A., Goodenough, J. B. and Julien, C. M. 2006, J. Power Sources, 163, 560.

[16] Lijuan Pang, Minshou Zhao, Xian Zhao, and Yujun Chai, 2012, J. Power Sources, 201, 253.

[17] Bard, A. J. and Faulker, L. R., Electrochemical methods-fundamental and applications, Gu, L. Y., Lu, M. X. and Song, S. Z. Chinese Version, Chemical Industry Publishing Company, pp. 121.

[18] Qiouming Zhang, Yuqing Qiao, Minshou Zhao, and Limin Wang, 2012, Chinese J. Inorganic Chemistry, 28(1), 67-73.

[19] Qiouming Zhang, Yuqing Qiao, Minshou Zhao, and Limin Wang, 2012, J. the Chinese Society of Rare Earth, 30(1), 78-85.

Preparation and Electrochemical Performance of Gd-doped $LiFePO_4$/C Composites①

Lijuan Pang[a], Minshou Zhao[a,c], Xian Zhao[b], Yujun Chai[d]
([a] College of Environmental and Chemical Engineering, Yanshan University, Qinhuangdao 066004, China)
([b] College of Chemistry and Chemical Engineering, Shanghai Jiaotong University, Shanghai 200240, China)
([c] State Key Laboratory of Metastable Material Science and Technology, Yanshan University, Qinhuangdao 066004, China)
([d] Department of Chemistry and Materials Science, Heibei Normal University, Shijiazhuang 050016, China)

Abstract: In this paper, $LiFe_{1-x}Gd_xPO_4$/C composites (x=0, 0.02, 0.04, 0.06, 0.07, 0.08) are synthesized via a high-temperature solid phase reaction. The structure and electrochemical behavior of the materials are investigated using a wide range of techniques such as X-ray diffraction (XRD), scanning electron micro-scope (SEM), energy dispersive spectroscopy (EDS), particle size analysis, galvanostatic charge/discharge and electrochemical impedance spectroscopy (EIS). It is found that the maximum discharge capacity of the as-prepared $LiFe_{0.93}Gd_{0.07}PO_4$/C composite can reach up to 150.7mAh g^{-1}, 125.9 mAh g^{-1}, 106.0 mAh g^{-1} and 81.3 mAh g^{-1} at rates of 0.2 C, 1 C, 5 C and 10 C, respectively. And at 0.1 C rate, the initial discharge capacity of the composite monotonically increases with temperature from 66.3 to 122.2 mAh g^{-1} in the range of −30 to 0 ℃. It is also demonstrated that the presence of a small amount of Gd^{3+} ion in the sample prepared in this work can reduce the charge-transfer resistance, resulting in the enhanced electrochemical catalytic activity.

Key words: Lithium ion battery; Lithium iron phosphate; Gadolinium ion doped; Electrochemical performance; Low temperature

1 Introduction

Since the pioneering work of Padhi and coworkers in 1997[1], $LiFePO_4$, one of the most attractive cathode material, has received an extensive interests over the past decade due to cell safety, low cost, low toxicity, stable voltage platform and long cycle life. For pure $LiFePO_4$, the intrinsic disadvantages of poor electronic conductivity and slow diffusion coeficient of lithium ion[1,2] has been demonstrated to be the predominant restriction to the high rate performance of cell, which

① Journal of Power Sources, 2012(201): 253-258.

is open to address all around the world.

Up to the present, two techniques have been proposed to improve the electrochemical performance of $LiFePO_4$. One is coating carbon on its surface [3]. Huang et al. [4] reported that $LiFePO_4/C$ composite demonstrated excellent electrochemical property. The discharge capacity was 150 and 120 mAh g^{-1} at a rate of 0.2 C and 5 C, respectively. Chen and Dahn [5] reported that the capacity of $LiFePO_4/C$ reached 160 mAh g^{-1} at 0.1 C rate, which was closed to the theoretical capacity.

The second method is to dope metal ion, which has been considered as an efficient way for the enhancement of the electrochemical performance of $LiFePO_4$. Many elements have been used to dope $LiFePO_4$ as $Li_{1-x}M_xFePO_4$ [6-10] or $LiFe_{1-x}M_xPO_4$ [11] ($x=0-1$). However, the electrochemical performance of $LiFePO_4$ needs improvement to meet the requirement for practical lithium ion batteries as power or energy storage sources in the future. It has been reported that Cho et al. [12] synthesized $LiFe_{1-x}La_xPO_4/C$ by a solid state reaction. It was indicated that these La ion dopants had no effect on the structure of the material. Instead, it considerably improved its rate capacity performance and cyclic stability. Among the materials, $LiFe_{0.99}La_{0.01}PO_4/C$ presented the best electrochemical behavior, with a discharge capacity of 156 mAh g^{-1} at a rate of 0.2 C. Zhao et al. [13] synthesized $LiFe_{1-x}Nd_xPO_4/C$ ($x=0-0.08$), and $LiFe_{0.96}Nd_{0.06}PO_4/C$ delivered the highest discharge capacity of 165.2 mAh g^{-1}, 146.8 mAh g^{-1}, 125.7 mAh g^{-1} and 114.8 mAh g^{-1} at rates of 0.2 C, 1 C, 2 C and 5 C, respectively. According to Saiful Islam et al. [14], the energy of dopant substitution or the "solution" reaction can be calculated by combining the appropriate defect and lattice energy. The calculated results showed that for all trivalent dopants on Fe, the lowest energy was found for Nd^{3+} ion.

Demonstrated mentioned above, doping appropriate metal ions into $LiFePO_4$ is a very effective method to improve the performances of $LiFePO_4$.

Gd element has a special electronic structure (4f electron shell of half full), and we expected that doping Gd^{3+} ion will be beneficial for enhancing performances of $LiFePO_4$. In this paper, we have synthesized $LiFe_{1-x}Gd_xPO_4/C$ sample by a high temperature solid-phase reaction and its electrochemical performance has been characterized first time.

2 Experimental

$LiFe_{1-x}Gd_xPO_4/C$ composites ($x=0, 0.02, 0.04, 0.06, 0.07, 0.08$) were synthesized using $CH_3COOLi \cdot 2H_2O$(AR), $FeC_2O_4 \cdot 2H_2O$(AR), $NH_4H_2PO_4$(AR) and Gd_2O_3 (99.9%) as the raw materials in the mole ratio based on the formula of $LiFePO_4$. The starting materials, with added 5 wt.% glucose and a proper amount of anhydrous ethanol, were milled by ball-milling(ball to powder weight ratio of 15 : 1) for 12 h and dried using a hair driver. Then, the precursors were heat-treated at 350 ℃ for 6 h and 700 ℃ for 16 h under N_2 atmosphere, respectively.

The thermal behavior of precursor was analyzed using The mogravimetric apparatus (Pyris Diamond, PerkinElmer Thermal Analysis) under nitrogen flow. The sample was heated from ambient temperature to 800 ℃ at the rate of 10 ℃ min^{-1}. To identify the structure of the sample, the structure of the powder was performed with XRD on a Rigaku D/max-2500/pc. Laser particle size analyzer was applied to analyze the particle size of the sample. The morphology of sample was observed using a field-emission scanning electron microscope(FE-SEM) on S-4800 FE-SEM. The S-4800 FE-SEM is equipped with EDS, which is used to analyze the elemental composition.

The electrochemical performance of the sample was measured in a simulative cell with a lithium metal as anode electrode. The working electrode was produced by dispersing 80 wt. % active material, 15 wt. % acetylene black and 5 wt. % polyvinylidene fluoride (PVDF) binder in N-methylpyrrolidine(NMP) solvent to form a uniform slurry. The slurry was coated on Al foil and dried in a vacuum at 120 ℃ for 12 h. Celgard 2400 was used as a separator. The electrolyte was 1M $LiPF_6$/EC + DEC (1 : 1, v/v). The cell was tested over the voltage range 2.5—4.2 V.

3 Result and discussion

Fig. 1 shows the TG-DTA curves of $LiFe_{0.93}Gd_{0.07}PO_4$/C composite. The weight loss at 81 ℃ corresponds to the loss of remaining ethanol and adsorbed water in the precursor. The weight loss in the temperature region of 81—155 ℃ is related to the dehydration $CH_3COOLi \cdot 2H_2O$ and $FeC_2O_4 \cdot 2H_2O$. The main weight loss in the temperature ranges of 190—280 ℃ and 280—430 ℃ are described to the decomposition of $NH_4H_2PO_4$ and FeC_2O_4, respectively. The DTA curve shows a small endothermic peak at 177.45 ℃ and two exothermic peaks, which is located at 266.76 ℃ and 494.47 ℃ respectively. The obvious peak, located at 266.76 ℃, is related to the formation of $LiFePO_4$ compound, and the other smaller peak is located at 494.47 ℃, where a new solid-state reaction occurs with the transformation of crystalline material[15]. While further enhancing up temperature, the TG curve almost keeps a constant value until 800 ℃. Therefore, the temperature for synthesizing $LiFe_{0.93}Gd_{0.07}PO_4$/C should be higher than 500 ℃.

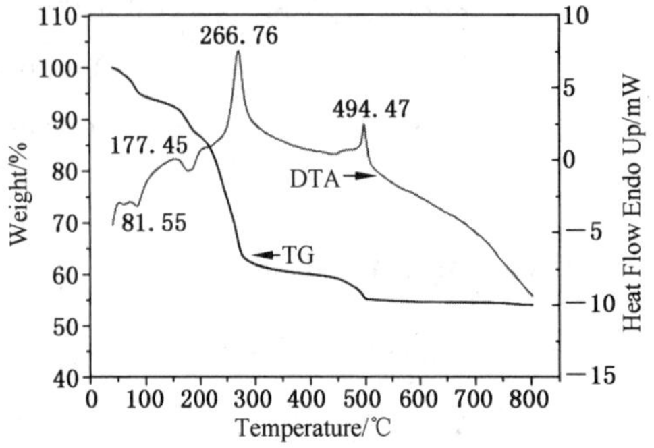

Fig. 1　TG-DTA curves of $LiFe_{0.93}Gd_{0.07}PO_4/C$ precursor

Fig. 2 A and B shows the XRD pattern of $LiFePO_4/C$ composite and Rietveld refinement of the XRD pattern for $LiFe_{0.93}Gd_{0.07}PO_4/C$ composite, respectively. The observed pattern and calculated pattern match well in Fig. 2B. The crystal phases of two samples are olivine structure indexed by orthorhombic Pnma. These results suggest that a small amount of Gd^{3+} ion-doped does not affect the olivine structure of $LiFePO_4$. In addition, a carbon diffraction peak does not be observed in Fig. 2A and B, which implies that the micro-carbon coating does not also affect the structure of $LiFePO_4$. However, XRD pattern of Gd-doped $LiFePO_4$ shows more Bragg reflections than Gd-free $LiFePO_4$ because the ionic radius of Gd^{3+} ion doped(0.093 8 nm) is larger than that of Fe^{2+} ion(0.078 nm), leading to bigger unit cell parameters, as shown in Table 1. Table 1 lists the unit cell parameters obtained from Rietveld refinement of the XRD for $LiFe_{0.93}Gd_{0.07}PO_4/C$ and unit cell parameters of $LiFePO_4/C$. Results of Rietveld refinement confirm that Gd^{3+} ion has been successfully doped into $LiFePO_4/C$. Clearly, doping a small amount of Gd^{3+} ion has little effect on the cell parameters of $LiFePO_4$. However, the dopant of a larger ionic radius perhaps creates the more defects in $LiFePO_4$, which is beneircial for the electrochemical catalytic activity of the electrode.

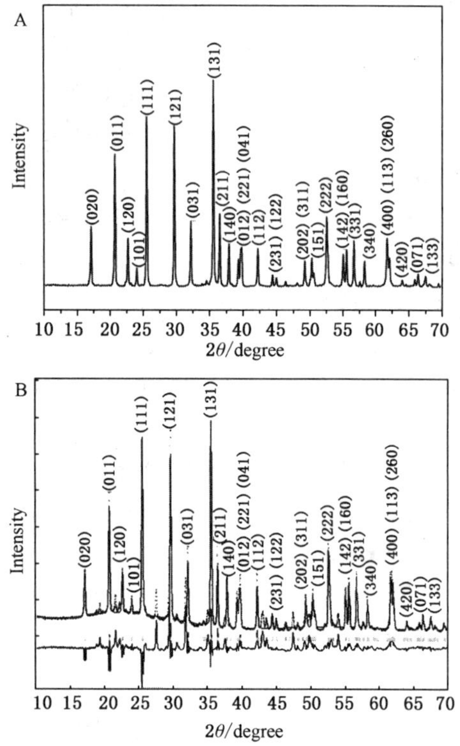

Fig. 2　(A) XRD pattern for $LiFePO_4/C$ composite. (B) Rietveld refinement of XRD pattern for $LiFe_{0.93}Gd_{0.07}PO_4/C$ composite

Table 1　Unit cell parameters obtained from Rietveld refinement of XRD for $LiFe_{0.93}Gd_{0.07}PO_4/C$ and unit cell parameters of $LiFePO_4/C$

Sample	a/nm	b/nm	c/nm
$LiFePO_4/C$	1.032 4	0.600 7	0.469 5
$LiFe_{0.93}Gd_{0.07}PO_4/C$	1.047 1	0.609 2	0.475 8

Table 2 Element composition in $LiFe_{0.93}Gd_{0.07}PO_4/C$

Element	C/K	O/K	P/K	Fe/K	Gd/L	Total
W%	5.40	42.23	16.83	29.77	5.77	100.00
A%	10.71	62.81	12.93	12.68	0.87	100.00

The grain size of samples can be described by particle size distribution. Fig. 3 presents the particle size distributions of $LiFePO_4/C$ sample and $LiFe_{0.93}Gd_{0.07}PO_4/C$ sample, respectively. Fig. 4 depicts the FE-SEM images of $LiFePO_4/C$ sample and $LiFe_{0.93}Gd_{0.07}PO_4/C$ sample, respectively. It is apparent from Figs. 3 and 4 that the particle size of $LiFe_{0.93}Gd_{0.07}PO_4/C$sample is signiircantly smaller than that of $LiFePO_4/C$ sample, and the particle scale is uniform after doping Gd^{3+} ion, which indicates that doping a small amount of Gd^{3+} can effectively reduce the particle size of $LiFePO_4/C$ and make it more uniform.

The EDS image of $LiFe_{0.93}Gd_{0.07}PO_4/C$ is shown in Fig. 5. The compositions of the substituent elements are listed in Table 2. The result shows the atomic ratio of Fe, Gd, P and O is 0.981 : 0.067 : 1 : 4.858 in $LiFe_{0.93}Gd_{0.07}PO_4/C$ sample, essentially coinciding with $LiFe_{0.93}Gd_{0.07}PO_4/C$. Wagemaker et al. [16] studied the supervalent-cation dopant in $LiFePO_4$ by combining neutron and X-ray diffraction. The results showed that low levels of dopants were indeed soluble in the olivine lattice up to the extent of 3 mol%. Therefore, we infer that Gd^{3+} ion occupies Fe^{2+} ion site in $LiFePO_4/C$ or has been dissolved into $LiFePO_4/C$ to form a solid solution.

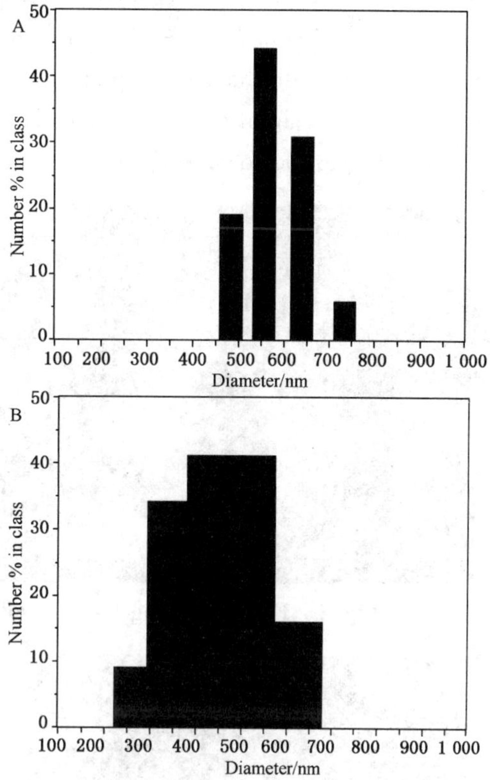

Fig. 3 A Particle size distribution of $LiFePO_4/C$. (B) Particle size distribution of $LiFe_{0.93}Gd_{0.07}PO_4/C$

The cycle performance of $LiFe_{1-x}Gd_xPO_4/C$ samples ($x = 0, 0.02, 0.04, 0.06, 0.07, 0.08$) at a rate of 0.2 C is shown in Fig. 6A. With increasing amount of Gd^{3+} ion doped, the discharge capacity becomes higher, but the discharge capacity decreases when the doping amount is 8%. We conclude that the sample has the best electrochemical performance when the amount of Gd^{3+} ion doped is 7%. Fig. 6B shows the charge-discharge curves of $LiFePO_4/C$ sample and $LiFe_{0.93}Gd_{0.07}PO_4/C$ sample at 0.2 C rate, respectively, which shows a wider voltage platform and a smaller gap between the charge and discharge curves after doping Gd^{3+} ion. This result indicates that the charge-discharge efficiency and reversibility are significantly improved.

The cycle performance of $LiFe_{0.93}Gd_{0.07}PO_4/C$ sample at various rates is shown in Fig. 7A. The maximum discharge capacity is 150.7 mAh g^{-1}, 125.9 mAh g^{-1}, 106.0 mAh g^{-1} and 81.3 mAh g^{-1} at rates of 0.2 C, 1 C, 5 C and 10 C, respectively.

Fig. 4　FE-SEM images of $LiFePO_4/C$(a) and $LiFe_{0.93}Gd_{0.07}PO_4/C$(b)

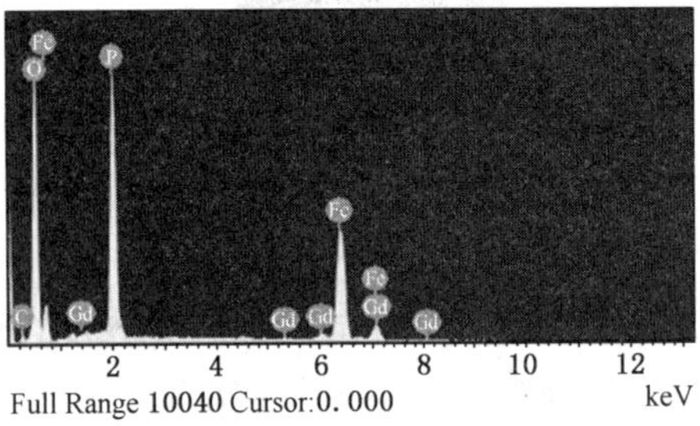

Fig. 5　EDS image of $LiFe_{0.93}Gd_{0.07}PO_4/C$

Fig. 7B shows the discharge curves of $LiFe_{0.93}Gd_{0.07}PO_4/C$ sample at various rates. It is concluded that doping an appropriate amount of Gd^{3+} ion can improve the high-rate discharge performance of $LiFePO_4/C$ composite.

It is inferred that doping Gd^{3+} ion can reduce the particle size of $LiFePO_4/C$, shorten the transport path of Li^+ ion, increase the disorder of the lattice and create the defect in $LiFePO_4/C$. These factors would improve the electrochemical performance of $LiFePO_4/C$ composite.

The electrochemical measurements have also been carried out at lower temperatures, as shown in Fig. 8. And at 0.1 C rate, the initial discharge capacity is 122.2 mAh g^{-1}, 107.7 mAh g^{-1}, 80.4 mAh g^{-1} and 66.3 mAh g^{-1} at 0 ℃, −10 ℃, −20 ℃ and −30 ℃ respectively. The discharge capacity monotonously sharply decreases with decreasing temperature, just as expected. At lower temperature the transport speed of Li^+ ion slows down and polarization influence becomes more dominant. These perhaps are key issues.

EIS was used to further analyze the effect of doping Gd^{3+} ion on the electrode reaction impedance. Before EIS tests, the electrodes were cycled galvanostatically for three cycles. Fig. 9 shows EIS of $LiFePO_4/C$ electrode reaction and $LiFe_{0.93}Gd_{0.07}PO_4/C$ electrode reaction at 15 ℃. An equivalent circuit model (Fig. 10) was constructured to analyze the impedance spectra. In Fig. 9, EIS is composed of two partially overlapped circles at high frequency

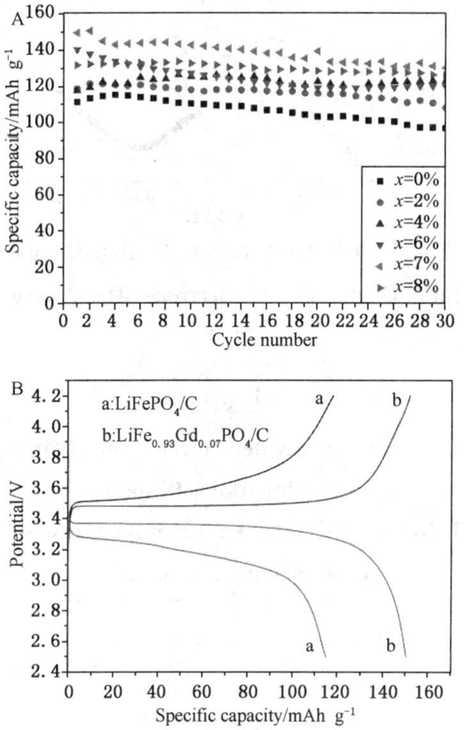

Fig. 6　(A) Discharge capacity as a function of cycle number for $LiFePO_4/C$ and $LiFe_{1-x}Gd_xPO_4/C$(x=0−0.08) at a rate of 0.2 C. (B) Second charge-discharge curves of $LiFePO_4/C$ and $LiFe_{0.93}Gd_{0.07}PO_4/C$ at a rate of 0.2 C

region and a straight line at low frequency region. An intercept at Z_{real} axis at high frequency represents the ohmic resistance (Rs), which consists of the resistances of the electrolyte and electrode. The semicircle at high frequency region represents the migration of Li^+ ion at the electrode/electrolyte interface via the SEI layer and the semicircle at middle frequency range indicates the charge-transfer resistance, which corresponds to Rct in the equivalent circuit, as shown in Fig. 10. The straight line in low frequency region is ascribed to the diffusion of Li^+ ion in the electrode material and called Warburg impedance, which corresponds to Zw in Fig. 10. In Fig. 10, a constant phase element (CPE) represents the double layer capacitance and passivation film capacitance[17].

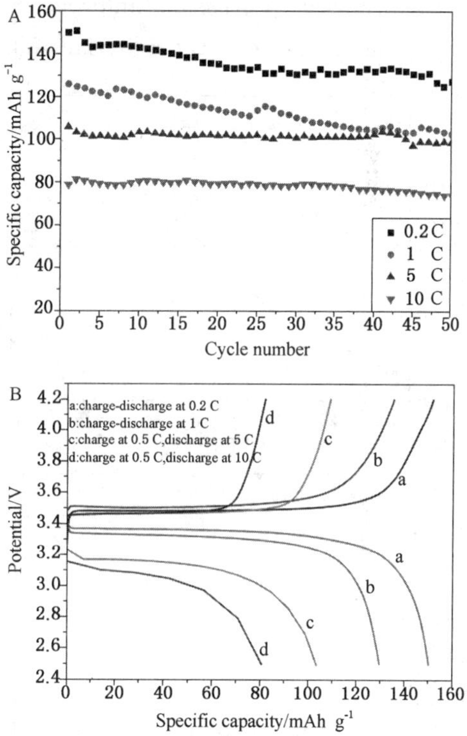

Fig. 7　A Discharge capacity as a function of cycle number for $LiFe_{0.93}Gd_{0.07}PO_4/C$ at various rates. (B) Second charge-discharge curves of $LiFe_{0.93}Gd_{0.07}PO_4/C$ at various rates

The results were obtained using Zview software and are listed in Table 3. The ohmic resistance (Rs) does not almost change for two samples, because the same electrolyte was used when the simulative cells were assembled. As expected, charge-transfer impedance obviously decreases in the charge-discharge process because of the addition of Gd^{3+} ion. The charge transfer resistance (Rct) for $LiFePO_4/C$ electrode reaction and $LiFe_{0.93}Gd_{0.07}PO_4/C$ electrode reaction is 692.6 and 241.3, respectively. This great decrease in the impedance will benefit to overcome the restriction of kinetics in the charge-discharge process and improve the cycling performance of the material[18].

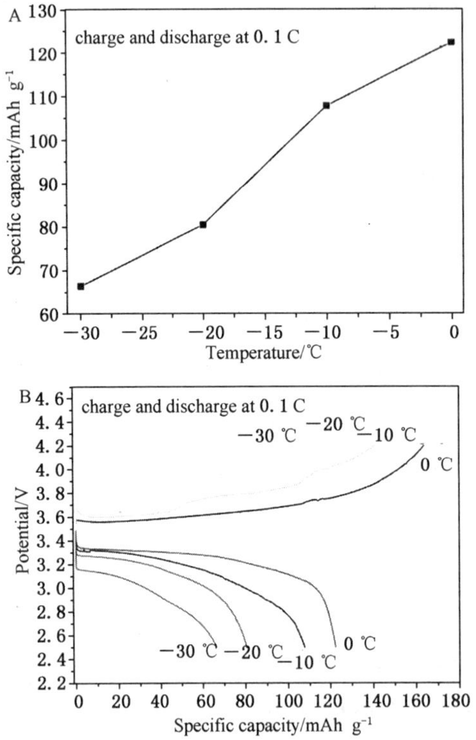

Fig. 8　A Initial discharge capacity for $LiFe_{0.93}Gd_{0.07}PO_4/C$ at various temperatures. (B) Initial charge-discharge curves of $LiFe_{0.93}Gd_{0.07}PO_4/C$ at various temperatures

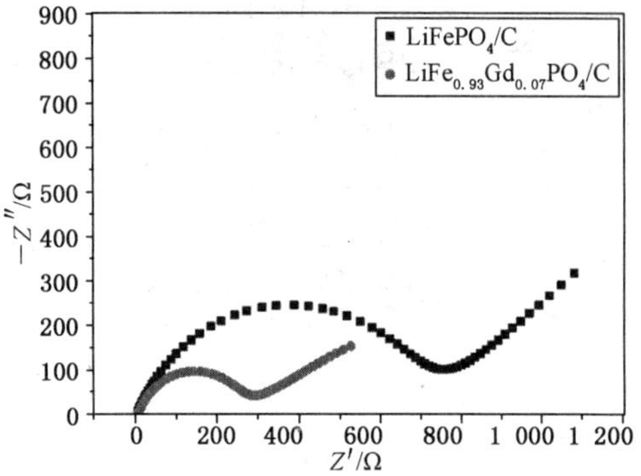

Fig. 9　EIS for $LiFePO_4/C$ electrode and $LiFe_{0.93}Gd_{0.07}PO_4/C$ electrode after 3 cycles

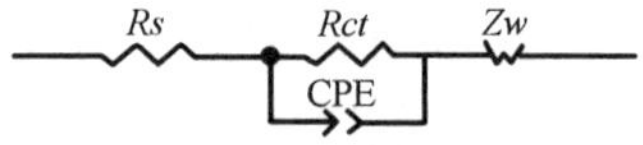

Fig. 10　Equivalent circuit for fitting experimental EIS data

Table 3　Electrochemical impedance and exchange current density

Sample	Rs/Ω	Rct/Ω	I_0 /mA g^{-1}
$LiFePO_4/C$	3.406	692.6	26.3
$LiFe_{0.93}Gd_{0.07}PO_4/C$	3.288	241.3	128.5

An apparent exchange current density (I_0) can be often used to sign the catalytic activity of electrode, which is an important parameter of kinetics for an electrochemical reaction. It can be calculated using Formula (1) [19] when overpotential is very small, and the results are also listed in Table 3.

$$I_0 = \frac{R \cdot T}{nRct \cdot F} \tag{1}$$

where R is gas constant, T is absolute temperature, F is Faraday constant, n is charge-transfer number and Rct is charge-transfer resistance.

I_0 for $LiFePO_4/C$ electrode and $LiFe_{0.93}Gd_{0.07}PO_4/C$ electrode is 26.3

mA g^{-1} and 128.5 mA g^{-1}, respectively. This result implies that the catalytic activity of the $LiFe_{0.93}Gd_{0.07}PO_4/C$ electrode is higher than that of $LiFePO_4/C$ electrode, which is why $LiFe_{0.93}Gd_{0.07}PO_4/C$ composite has better electrochemical performance. EIS results indicate that doping an appropriate amount of Gd^{3+} ion can improve the electrochemical activity of $LiFePO_4/C$ composite.

4 Conclusions

Olivine structured $LiFe_{1-x}Gd_xPO_4/C$ composites ($x=0, 0.02, 0.04, 0.06, 0.07, 0.08$) have been synthesized by a high temperature solid-state reaction. The electrochemical test results show that $LiFe_{0.93}Gd_{0.07}PO_4/C$ sample demonstrates excellent electrochemical performance with the maximum discharge capacity of 150.7 mAh g^{-1}, 125.9 mAh g^{-1}, 106.0 mAh g^{-1} and 81.3 mAh g^{-1} at rates of 0.2 C, 1 C, 5 C and 10 C, respectively. And at 0.1 C rate, the initial discharge capacity is 122.2 mAh g^{-1}, 107.7 mAh g^{-1}, 80.4 mAh g^{-1} and 66.3 mAh g^{-1} at 0 ℃, −10 ℃, −20 ℃ and −30 ℃ respectively. EIS results indicate that the charge-transfer resistance of electrode reaction greatly decreases by doping an appropriate amount of Gd^{3+} ion. It is inferred that Gd^{3+} ion occupies Fe^{2+} ion site in $LiFePO_4/C$ or has been dissolved into $LiFePO_4/C$ to form a solid solution.

Acknowledgement

This work was financially supported by the Natural Science Foundation of Hebei Province (grant number: B2011203074).

References

[1] A. K. Padhi, K. S. Nanjundaswamy, J. B. Goodenough, J. Electrochem. Soc. 144 (1997)1188-1194.
[2] S. J. Kwon, C. W. Kim, T. J. Woon, K. S. Lee, J. Power Sources 137(2004)93-99.
[3] N. Raver, Y. Chouinard, J. E. Magnan, S. Besner, M. Gauthier, M. Armand, J. Power Sources 97-98 (2001) 503-507.
[4] H. Huang, S. C. Yin, L. F. Nazar, Solid State Lett. 4 (2001) A170-A172.
[5] Z. H. Chen, J. R. Dahn, J. Electrochem. Soc. 149 (2002) A1184-A1189.
[6] K. F. Hsu, S. Y. Tsay, B. J. Hwang, J. Power Sources 146 (2005) 529-533.
[7] J. Yao, K. Konstantinov, G. X. Wang, H. K. Liu, J. Solid State Electrochem. 11 (2007) 177-185.
[8] G. X. Wang, S. L Bewlay, K. Konstantinov, H. K. Liu, S. X. Dou, J. H. Ahn, Electrochim. Acta 50 (2004) 443-447.
[9] X. Yin, K. Huang, S. Liu, H. Wang, H. Wang, J. Power Sources 195 (2010) 4308-4312.
[10] G. Wang, Y. Cheng, M. Yan, Z. Jiang, J Solid State Electrochem. 11 (2007) 457-462.
[11] D. Wang, Li S H., S. Shi, X. Huang, Chen S L., Electrochim. Acta 50 (2005) 2955-2958.
[12] Y.-D. Cho, G. T.-K. Fey, H.-M. Kao, J. Solid State Electrochem. 12 (2008) 815-823.
[13] X. Zhao, X. Tang, L Zhang, M. Zhao, J. Zhai, Electrochim. Acta 55 (20) (2010) 5899-5904.
[14] M. Saiful Islam, D. J. Driscoll, C. A. J.

Fisher, P. R. Slater, Chem. Mater. 17 (2005) 5085-5092.
[15] B. L. Yu, J. D. Jiang, Applied Thermal Analysis, Textile Industry Press, Beijing, 1990, p. 114.
[16] M. Wagemaker, L. E. Brian, D. Lützenkirchen-Hecht, F. M. Mulder, L. F. Nazar, Chem. Mater. 20 (2008) 6313-6315.
[17] G. X. Wang, L. Yanga, Y. Chena, J. Z. Wanga, S. Bewlaya, H. K. Liua, Electrochim. Acta 50 (2005) 4649-4654.
[18] S. T. Yang, Y. X. Liu, Y. H. Yin, H. Wang, T. Wang, Chin. J. Inorg. Chem. 23 (2007) 1165-1168.
[19] A. J. Bard, L. R. Faulker, Electrochemical methods-fundamental and applications, L. Y. Gu, M. X. Lu, S. Z. Song, Chinese Version, Chemical Industry Publishing Company, 1986, p. 121.

Effects of Neodymium Aliovalent Substitution on the Structure and Electrochemical Performance of $LiFePO_4$①

Xian Zhao[a], Xiaozhen Tang[a], Li Zhang[b], Minshou Zhao[b,c], Jing Zhai[b]

([a] College of Chemistry and Chemical Engineering, Shanghai Jiaotong University, Shanghai 200240, China)

([b] College of Environmental and Chemical Engineering, Yanshan University, Qinhuangdao 066004, China)

([c] State Key Laboratory of Metastable Material Science and Technology, Yanshan University, Qinhuangdao, Hebei 066004, China)

Abstract: $LiFe_{1-x}Nd_xPO_4/C$ ($x=0-0.08$) cathode material was synthesized using a solid-state reaction. The synthesis conditions were optimized by thermal analysis of the precursor and magnetic properties of $LiFePO_4/C$. The structure and electrochemical performances of the material were studied using XRD, FE-SEM, EDS, electrochemical impedance spectroscopy and galvanostatic charge-discharge. The results show that a small amount of aliovalent Nd^{3+} ion dopant substitution on Fe^{2+} ions can effectively reduce the particle size of $LiFePO_4/C$. Cell parameters of $LiFe_{1-x}Nd_xPO_4$ ($x=0.04-0.08$) were calculated, and the results showed that $LiFe_{1-x}Nd_x PO_4/C$ had the same olivine structure as $LiFePO_4$. $LiFe_{0.4}Nd_{0.6}PO_4/C$ delivers the discharge capacity of 165.2 mAh g^{-1} at rate of 0.2 C and the capacity retention rate is 92.8% after 100 cycles. Charge-transfer resistance decreases with the addition of glucose and Nd^{3+} ions. Poly(cyclotriphosphazene-co-4,4′-sulfonyldiphenol) (PZS) was synthesized and PZS nanorods were used as a carbon source to coat $LiFePO_4$. All of the results show that aliovalent doping substitution of Fe in $LiFePO_4$ is well tolerated.

Key words: Lithium-ion battery; Cathode material; Lithium iron phosphate; Neodymium ion-doped; Electrochemical performance

1 Introduction

Lithium-ion batteries that use $LiFePO_4$ as the cathode material can be used in electric vehicles (EVs) and hybrid-electric vehicles (HEVs). These batteries are also attractive for use in military and space applications. $LiFePO_4$ is the most promising candidate as alternative for $LiCoO_2$ because it has excellent thermal and chemical stability, a high theoretical capacity of 170 mAh g^{-1}, and it offers economic and environmental advantages because it is less expensive and less toxic

① ElectrochimicaActa, 2010(55): 5899-5904.

material [1-3]. However, it has inherently poor electrical conductivity, slow lithium ion diffusivity [4], and is not suitable for high-current charge-discharge. These factors limit its use in practical applications. If these problems could be resolved, $LiFePO_4$ would be a realistic alternative to $LiCoO_2$. Therefore, the direction of current research is to improve the elec-trochemical performance of $LiFePO_4$. Currently, the main solutions include improving the synthesis process to refine the material particle [5], and the carbon-doped [6,7] or bulk-doped metal ions [8,9], both of which can enhance the electrical conductivity of $LiFePO_4$ and shorten lithium ion transport path.

Recently, great progress has been made in the synthesis of $LiFePO_4$, and the electrochemical performance of $LiFePO_4$ has significantly improved. Hu et al. [10] reported that $LiFePO_4$ is curently synthesized using a hydrothermal method, and that Nd ion doping has significantly improved the discharge capacity. A highenergy ball milling method combined with a spray-drying method has been developed to synthesize $LiFePO_4$/C composite that has long-term cyclability [11,12]. $LiFePO_4$ nanorods have also been successfully prepared [13]. The report of ultra-fast charge/discharge battery materials is a new milestone in the development process of $LiFePO_4$ [14], however, this material is controversial [15,16]. The synthetic procedures used for lithium iron phosphate powder have been reviewed [17].

According to Islam et al. [18], the energy of dopant substitution or the "solution" reaction can be calculated by combining the appropriate defect and lattice energy. The calculated results showed that out of all trivalent dopants, the lowest energy occurred with Nd^{3+} ion substitution for Fe. In this paper, the Nd^{3+} ion is substituted for the Fe site in $LiFePO_4$. Our aim was to improve the electrochemical properties of $LiFePO_4$, especially its rate discharge performance.

2 Experimental

2.1 Material synthesis

$LiFe_{1-x}Nd_xPO_4$ ($x = 0, 0.01, 0.02, 0.04, 0.06, 0.08$) powders were synthesized using two-step heating solid-state reaction. $CH_3COOLi \cdot 2H_2O$, $FeC_2O_4 \cdot 2H_2O$, $NH_4H_2PO_4$ (Shanghai Chemical Reagents Corp.) and Nd_2O_3 (99.9 mass%) were mixed the stoichio-metrically based on the desired amount of $LiFePO_4$, and 5 mass% glucose was used as the reducing agent and carbon source. Mixing was accomplished using a ball milling (ball to powder weight ratio of 15 : 1) for 8 h. Anhydrous ethanol under an argon atmosphere was used as the dispersing agent.

After the anhydrous ethanol was evaporated, the powders were ground and compressed into pellets, heated to 400 ℃ for 6 h, and then calcined at 700 ℃ for 16 h in a series-resistance furnace, and all of the heating treatments were performed under a nitrogen atmosphere.

Poly (cyclotriphosphazene-co-4, 4′-sulfonyldiphenol) (PZS) was synthesized using the following procedure [24]: triethylamine (0.87 g) was added to the solution of hexachlorocyclotriphosp-hazene (HCCP) (0.50 g) (Aldrich) and 4,4′-sulfonyldiphenol (BPS) (1.08 g) in acetone (100 ml). The resultant solution was stirred at 30 ℃ in an ultrasonic bath (100 W, 80 kHz) for approximately 4 h. The produced particles were obtained by centrifugation and then washed with tetrahydrofuran (Shanghai Chemical Reagents Corp.) three times. Finally, the resultant product was dried under vacuum to yield PZS as a white powder, which was used as reducing agent and carbon source like as glucose.

PZS was mixed with the chemical reagent mentioned above in agate mortar, instead of ball milling, to avoid expensive HCCP loss. Glucose was mixed using the same procedure and compared with PZS as the carbon source on cycle stability. We found that the mix might not be adequate, and therefore, would not improve the performance of $LiFePO_4$.

2.2 Sample characterization

Thermogravimetric analysis of the precursor was investigated using a Pyris Diamond TG/DSC apparatus with a temperature range from 40 ℃ to 810 ℃ (10 ℃/min) under a nitrogen atmosphere. The magnetic measurements of $LiFePO_4/C$ samples were performed using SQUID on a Magnetic Property Measurement System XL-7. The structure of the powder was analyzed using X-ray diffraction (XRD) on a RIGAKU D/max-2500/pc. The sample morphology was determined using a field-emission scanning electron microscope (FE-SEM) on a S-4800 FE-SEM. The S-4800 FE-SEM is equipped with an energy dispersive spectroscopy (EDS), which was used to analyze the elemental composition.

2.3 Cell assembly and electrochemical test

The electrode was prepared by dispersing 80 mass% active material, 15 mass% acetylene black and 5 mass% polyvinylidene fluoride (PVdF) in 1-methyl-2-pyrrolidinone (NMP) to form the slurry. The slurry was used to coat an Al foil substrate (1.5—2.0 mg cm^{-2}) and was dried under an infrared light. The substrate was then cut into pieces and weighted, and then dried at 120 ℃ for 16 h in a vacuum drying oven to obtain the cathode film. The cells were assembled in an argon-filled glove box. The cathode film and the lithium metal foil anode were separated by a microporous polypropylene (Celgard 2400) separator that contained a liquid electrolyte with a concentration of 1 M $LiPF_6$ in 1 : 1 EC/DMC. The cells were charged and discharged on electrochemical testing BTS-5 V10 mA, and the voltage range was between 4.2 V and 2.5 V.

The mass of active material was determined for every piece of the cathode film by calculating the difference between the mass of slurry coated Al foil and the mass of pristine Al foil. This amount was then multiplied 80%.

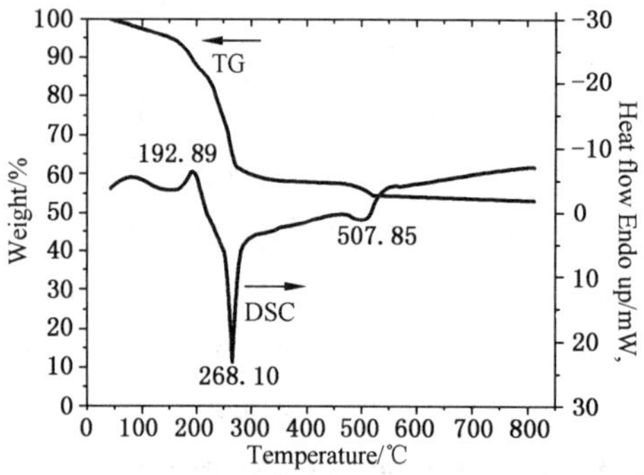

Fig. 1　TG-DSC curve of $LiFe_{0.94}Nd_{0.06}PO_4/C$ precursor

3　Results and discussion

3.1　TG-DSC analysis

In order to determine the pre-treatment and the second calcination temperature, TG-DSC analysis of $LiFePO_4/C$ precursor sample was performed. The results are shown in Fig. 1. These results indicate three significant weight loss regions. The first region (150—230 ℃) is related to the dehydration of the hydrates. The second region (230—300 ℃) is related to the anaerobic thermal decomposition of glucose, FeC_2O_4 and $NH_4H_2PO_4$. The third region (470-560 ℃) should be related to complete decomposition of residual glucose, FeC_2O_4 and $NH_4H_2PO_4$. The corresponding DSC curve shows a smaller endothermic peak at 192. 89 ℃ and two exothermic peaks. The obvious peak, locates at 268. 10 ℃, is related to the formation of $LiFePO_4$ compound, and the other smaller peak is between 470 ℃ and 560 ℃, which is where a new solidstate reaction occurs with the transformation of crystalline material[19]. Therefore, a temperature higher than 600 ℃, is reasonable to synthesis the target product.

3.2　Magnetic property analysis of $LiFePO_4/C$

Oxidizing Fe^{2+} ion into Fe^{3+} ion should be avoided or the content of Fe^{3+} ion in the sample should be decreased as much as possible during the experiment process, because of the Fe^{3+} ion would seriously affect the electrochemical performances of $LiFePO_4/C$. Therefore, it is imperative to determine an appropriate synthesis process. SQUID was used to measure the magnetic properties of $LiFePO_4/C$. Fig. 2 shows the magnetization curve of $LiFePO_4/C$. The curve is a straight line if the impurity phases, which are ferromagnetic or ferrimagnetic, do not exist. In contrast, non-linear behavior will be observed at low-magneticfields if the impurity phases that are ferromagnetic or ferrimagnetic exist [20,21]. The extent of non-linearity reflects the content of the impurity phases. Therefore, it is concluded from Fig. 2 that the sample B, which was calcined at 700 ℃ for 16 h, contains less content of the impurity phases than does sample A, which was calcined at 750 ℃ for 16 h. Hence, the synthetic procedure used to prepare sample B is preferable.

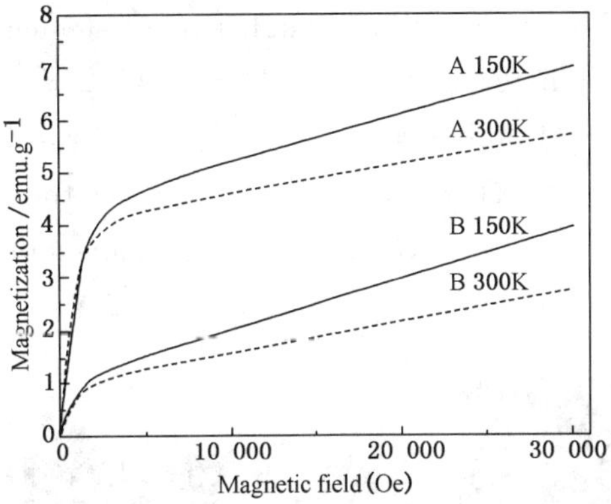

Fig. 2　Magnetization curve of $LiFePO_4$/C

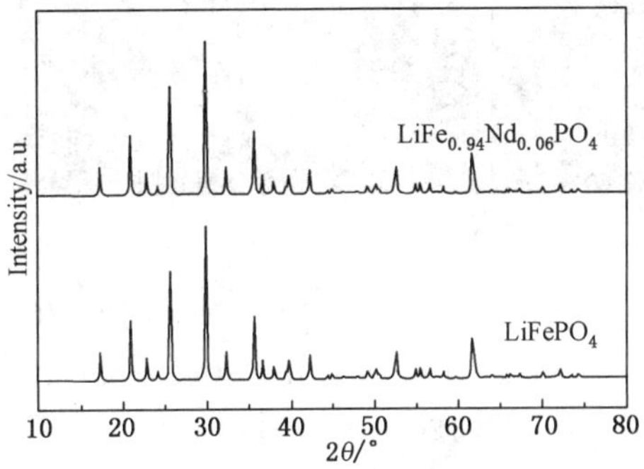

Fig. 3　XRD pattern for $LiFePO_4$ and $LiFe_{0.94}Nd_{0.06}PO_4$/C

3.3　XRD analysis

Fig. 3 shows the X-ray diffraction (XRD) patterns of $LiFe_{0.94}Nd_{0.06}PO_4$/C and $LiFePO_4$. The positive diffraction peak and relative intensity of the $LiFe_{0.94}Nd_{0.06}PO_4$/C sample are the same as those of $LiFePO_4$ and no impurity peak is observed. This suggests that the small amount of Nd^{3+} ion-doped does not change the olivine crystal structure of $LiFePO_4$. In addition, a carbon diffraction peak is not be observed in Fig. 3, which implies that the micro-carbon coating also does not affect the crystal structure of $LiFePO_4$. Table 1 shows the unit cell parameters of $LiFePO_4$ and $LiFe_{1-x}Nd_xPO_4$ (x=0.04, 0.06, 0.08), which were calculated using a Si internal standard. Clearly, a small amount of Nd^{3+} ion-doped has a small effect on $LiFePO_4$ cell parameters, and the lattice constants increase slightly after doping with 0.04 and 0.06 moles of Nd^{3+} ion. The reason might be that a small amount of the dopant cannot greatly change the cell structure, however, the dopant has a larger ionic radius and causes the more defects in $LiFePO_4$. According to Chung's report of doping ions[22], taking into account of the effective ionic radius and the lowest energy of "solution" reaction for Nd^{3+} ion on the Fe site [18], the radius of the Nd^{3+} ion (99.5 pm) is more similar to the Fe^{2+} ion (74 pm) than to the Li^+ ion (68 pm). Therefore, we infer that Nd^{3+} ions are much more inclined to replace the Fe site.

3.4　FE-SEM and EDS analysis

The particle size of the cathode material is an extremely important factor in the performance of the battery [22]. Fig. 4 shows the FE-SEM image of $LiFePO_4$, $LiFePO_4$/C and $LiFe_{0.94}Nd_{0.06}PO_4$/C. It is clearly shown that the particle size is refined after adding a small amount of glucose, which can be completely decomposed in the calcination process. During calcination process carbon is generated that can inhibit the generation of Fe^{3+} ion and can be coated on $LiFePO_4$ to prevent from its conglomeration. It is apparent from Fig. 4(b) and (c) that the particle size of $LiFe_{0.94}Nd_{0.06}PO_4/C$ (about 150 nm) is significantly smaller than that of $LiFePO_4/C$ (about 400 nm), which indicates that a small amount of Nd^{3+} ion doping can effectively reduce the particle size of $LiFePO_4$. The EDS image of $LiFe_{0.94}Nd_{0.06}PO_4/C$ is shown in Fig. 5. The compositions of substituent elements are listed in Table 2.

Combined with XRD, these results indicate that the Nd^{3+} ion occupies the Fe site in $LiFePO_4$ or has been dissolved into $LiFePO_4$.

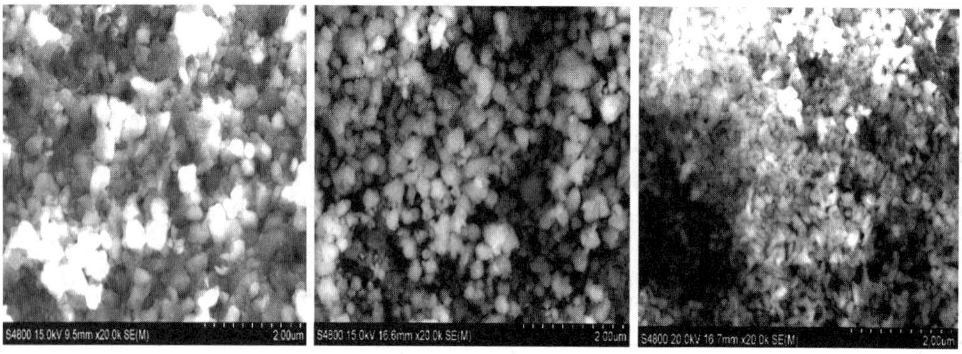

(a) (b) (c)

Fig. 4 FE-SEM image of (a) $LiFePO_4$ (b) $LiFePO_4/C$ and (c) $LiFe_{0.94}Nd_{0.06}PO_4/C$

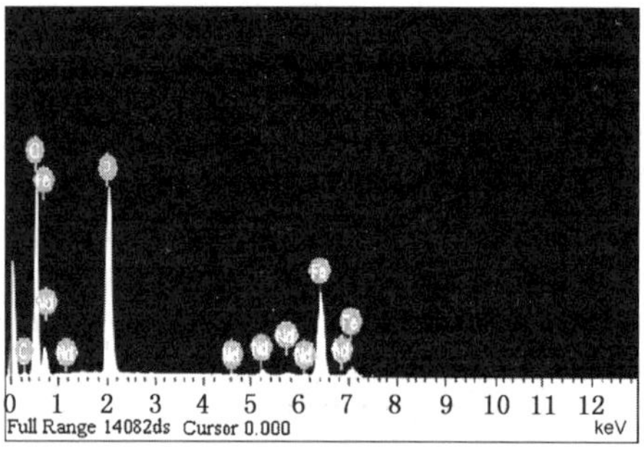

Fig. 5 EDS image of $LiFe_{0.94}Nd_{0.06}PO_4/C$

Table 1 Unit cell parameter of $LiFePO_4$ and $LiFe_{1-x}Nd_xPO_4$

Sample	a/nm	b/nm	c/nm	V/nm^3
$LiFePO_4$	1.032 0	0.601 2	0.469 9	0.291 5
$LiFe_{0.96}Nd_{0.04}PO_4$	1.034 4	0.602 1	0.471 1	0.293 4
$LiFe_{0.94}Nd_{0.06}PO_4$	1.033 7	0.601 6	0.470 38	0.292 5
$LiFe_{0.92}Nd_{0.08}PO_4$	1.033 4	0.601 5	0.470 43	0.292 4

Table 2 Composition of element in $LiFe_{0.94}Nd_{0.06}PO_4/C$

Elt	C K	O K	P K	Fe K	Nd L	Total
W/%	6.07	46.75	17.14	25.98	4.07	100.00
A/%	11.29	65.31	12.37	10.40	0.63	100.00

3.5 Electrochemical property

Fig. 6 shows the cycle performance of $LiFe_{1-x}Nd_xPO_4/C$ at a rate of 0.2 C. The discharge capacity is improved with an increase of the dopant, but it decreases when the doping amount is 8%. We concluded that the sample has the best electrochemical performance when the amount of Nd^{3+} doped ions is 6%. Fig. 7 shows the cycle performance of $LiFe_{0.94}Nd_{0.06}PO_4/C$ at various charge-discharge rates. At 1 C the discharge capacity of the composite cathode slightly decreases from 146.8 mAh g^{-1} at the first cycle to 138.7 mAh g^{-1} at the 100th cycle, demonstrating an excellent cycling stability. However, the discharge capacity gradually decreases with an increasing in the discharge rate. The highest discharge capacities were 125.7 mAh g^{-1} and 114.8 mAh g^{-1} at 2 and 5 C rates, respectively. We concluded that a small amount of Nd^{3+} ion doping could improve the high-rate discharge performance of $LiFePO_4/C$ because Nd^{3+} ion doping refined the grain size of $LiFePO_4/C$ and shortened the transport path of Li^+ and improved its transfer. In addition, Nd^{3+} ions and Fe^{2+} ions have similar electronegativities. This is more useful to promote Nd^{3+} ions for doping into $LiFePO_4/C$, which can increase the disorder of the lattice and create the defects in $LiFePO_4/C$. These factors would improve the delivering current performance of $LiFePO_4/C$.

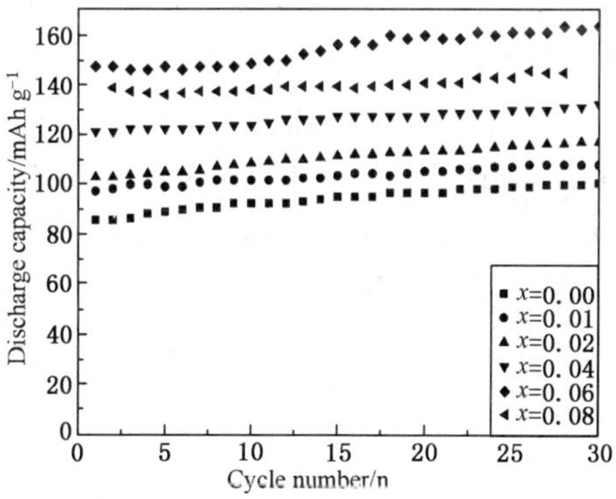

Fig. 6 Discharge capacity as a function of cycle number for $Life_{1-x}Nd_xPO_4/C$ ($x=0-0.08$) at a rate of 0.2 C

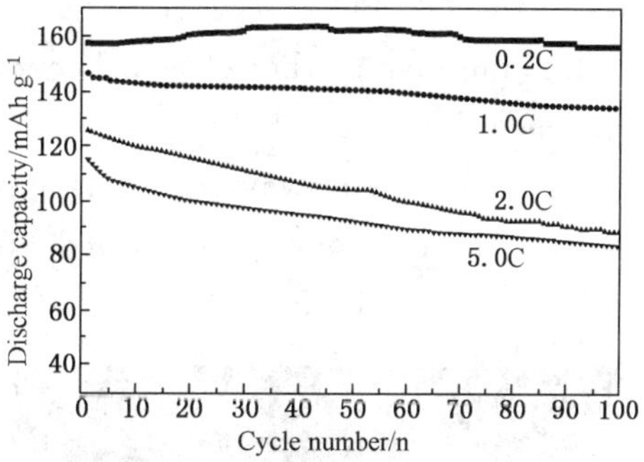

Fig. 7 Discharge capacity as a function of cycle number for $LiFe_{0.94}Nd_{0.06}PO_4/C$ at different rates

PZS was synthesized and characterized by TG-DSC, XRD, FE-SEM and EDS according to a previously reported procedure [23]. All the results demonstrate that PZS nanorods and spherical PZS were formed as shown in Fig. 8(a) and (b), respectively. This is the first report of the use of synthesized PZS nanorods to coat $LiFePO_4$ as a reducing agent and carbon source. The effect of carbon coated $LiFePO_4/C$, came from different carbon sources, on cycle stability, is shown in Fig. 9. Even although the $LiFePO_4/C$ with PZS as the reducing agent and carbon source delivers a higher discharge capacity, the difference between both the initial capacities of $LiFePO_4/C$ with different carbon sources is clearly very small, however, the effect of different carbon sources on the cycle stability of carbon coated $LiFePO_4/C$ is critical. PZS becomes nanoscale carbon when it is calcined at 700 ℃, but glucose becomes μ scale carbon at the same calcination temperature [23]. Nanoscale carbon easily forms a net framework between the particles of the $LiFePO_4/C$, which is beneficial for improving the electrochemical performances of the $LiFePO_4/C$. Further investigation is underway regarding how different carbon sources influence the performances of $LiFePO_4/C$.

Fig. 8　(a) PZS nanorods image; (b) spherical PZS image

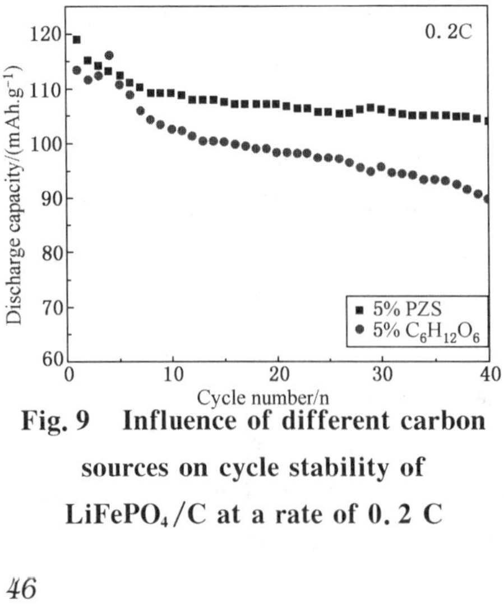

Fig. 9　Influence of different carbon sources on cycle stability of $LiFePO_4/C$ at a rate of 0.2 C

Fig. 10(a) shows the initial charge-discharge curve of $LiFePO_4/C$ and $LiFe_{0.94}Nd_{0.06}PO_4/C$ at a rate of 0.2 C, which shows a wider voltage platform and a smaller space between the charge and discharge curves after Nd^{3+} ion is doped. This indicates that the charge-discharge efficiency and reversibility is significantly improved. Fig. 10(b) shows the initial charge-discharge curves of $LiFe_{0.94}Nd_{0.06}PO_4/C$ at different rates. It is apparent that with an increase in discharge rate, the distance between charge and discharge curves becomes larger and the voltage platform becomes narrow, and even disappears. This phenomenon might have occurred because the polarization could become larger and the structure of $LiFePO_4$ might be destroyed with an increase in discharge current density, which would seriously affect the charge-discharge efficiency and reversibility. Fig. 11 shows the electrochemical impedance spectra (EIS) of the bare $LiFePO_4$, $LiFePO_4/C$ and $LiFe_{0.94}Nd_{0.06}PO_4/C$ after 10 cycles. The EIS is composed of two partially overlapped circles in the high frequency region and a sloping line in the low frequency region.

The semicircle in the high frequency region represents the migration of the Li^+ ions at the electrode/electrolyte interface through the SEI layer and it corresponds to the R_f in the equivalent circuit, as shown in Fig. 12. The semicircle in middle frequency range corresponds to the charge-transfer resistance and corresponds to the R_{ct}, in the equivalent circuit. The sum of R_f and R_{ct} corresponds to the diameter of the semicircle. The straight line in the low frequency region is attributed to the diffusion of the lithium ions in the bulk of the electrode material or socalled Warburg impedance, which is represented by Z_w in Fig. 12. A constant phase element (CPE) represents the double layer capacitance and passivation film capacitance [24]. The capacitance resistance is so small that it is negligible. The fitting results were obtained using Zview-Impedance 2.80 software and are listed in Table 3. The resistance of the solvent (R_e) did not change for the three kinds of samples because the same electrolyte is used when the test cell is assembled. However, the impedance obviously decreases in the charge-discharge process with the addition of glucose and Nd^{3+} ions. This decrease in impedance will benefit to overcome the restriction of kinetics in the charge-discharge process, inhibit the capacity fade and improve the cycling performance of the material [25]. An apparent exchange current density (I_0) can be used to measure the catalytic activity of electrodes, which is an important parameter of kinetics for an electrochemical reaction. It can be calculated using the following formula [26] and also the results are listed in Table 3:

$$I_0 = \frac{R \cdot T}{nR_{ct} \cdot F}$$

where R is the gas constant, T is the absolute temperature, F is the Faraday constant, n is the charge-transfer number and R_{ct} is the charge-transfer resistance.

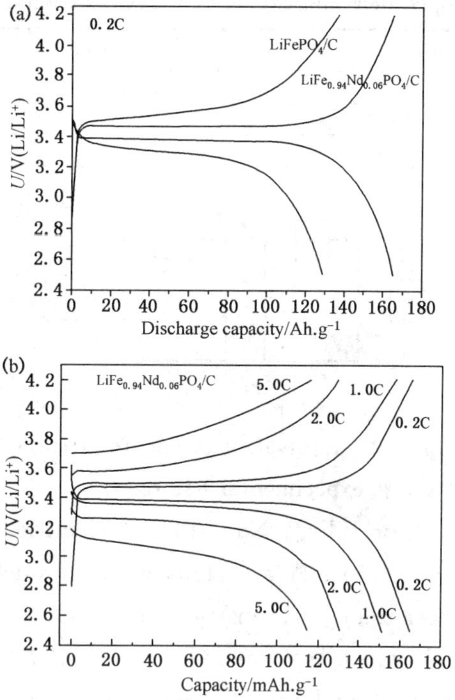

Fig. 10　(a) Initial charge-discharge curve of $LiFePO_4/C$ and $LiFe_{0.94}Nd_{0.06}PO_4/C$ at a rate of 0.2 C; (b) initial charge-discharge curve of $LiFe_{0.94}Nd_{0.06}PO_4/C$ at different rate

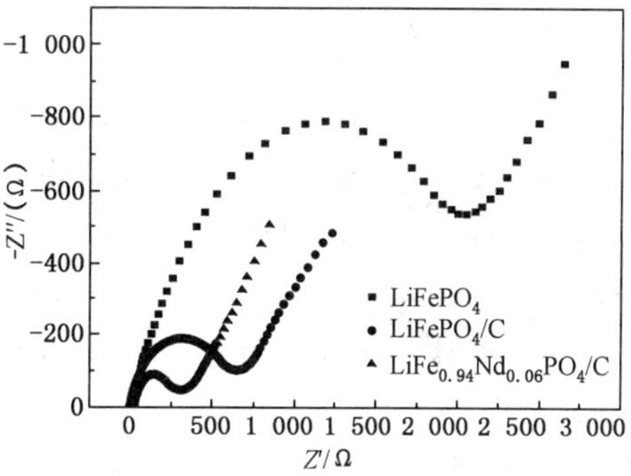

Fig. 11　EIS for $LiFePO_4$, $LiFePO_4$ and $Li_{0.94}Nd_{0.06}PO_4$ after 10 cycles

Table 3 Result of electrochemical impedance and exchange current density.

Sample	R_e/Ω	R_f/Ω	R_{ct}/Ω	I_0/mA g^{-1}
$LiFePO_4$	12.65	924.5	1 039	0.024
$LiFePO_4$/C	8.479	98.73	570.6	0.044
$LiFe_{0.94}Nd_{0.06}PO_4$/C	7.307	67.47	217.3	0.115

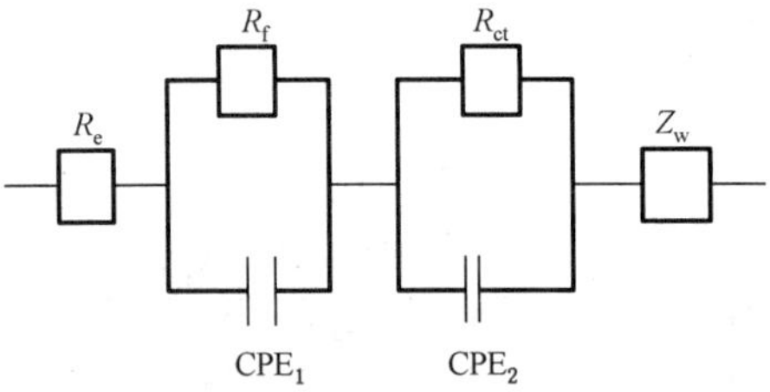

Fig. 12 Equivalent circuit for fitting experimental EIS data.

For $LiFe_{0.94}Nd_{0.06}PO_4$/C electrode, I_0 is 0.115 mA g^{-1}. This value is much larger than 0.044 mA g^{-1} and 0.024 mA g^{-1}, which correspond to $LiFePO_4$/C electrode and $LiFePO_4$ electrode, respectively. This result implies that the catalytic activity of the $LiFe_{0.94}Nd_{0.06}PO_4$/C electrode is the highest of the three kinds of electrodes, which is why $LiFe_{0.94}Nd_{0.06}PO_4$/C has the best electro-chemical performance.

4 Conclusions

1. The synthesis conditions were optimized through the thermal analysis of the precursor by TG-DSC and magnetic measure-ments of $LiFePO_4$/C using SQUID. A 6% (mole fraction) of Nd^{3+} ion-dopant, and a precursor calcined at 400 ℃ for 6 h and at 700 ℃ for 16 h is preferable.

2. The XRD analysis and FE-SEM images showed that the doping a small amount of Nd^{3+} ions does not affect the crystal structure of $LiFePO_4$/C, butsignificantly refines the particle size of $LiFePO_4$/C.

3. $LiFe_{0.94}Nd_{0.06}PO_4$/C delivers a discharge capacity of 165.2 mAh g^{-1} at a rate of 0.2 C. The capacity retention rate is 92.8% after 100 cycles. It delivers discharge capacities of 146.8 mAh g^{-1}, 125.7 mAh g^{-1}, and 114.8 mAh g^{-1} at rates of 1, 2, and 5 C, respectively.

References

[1] P. P. Prosini, D. Zane, M. Pasquali, Electrochem. Acta 46 (23) (2001) 3517.

[2] N. Ravet, Y. Chouinard, J. F. Magnan, S. Besner, M. Gauthier, M. Armand, J. Power Sources 97-98 (2001) 503.

[3] A. K. Padhi, K. S. Nanjundaswamy, J. B. Goodenough, J. Electrochem. Soc. 144 (1997) 1188.

[4] S. J. Kwon, C. W. Kim, T. J. Woon, K. S. Lee, J. Power Sources 137 (1) (2004) 93.

[5] A. Yamada, S. C. Chung, K. Hinokuma, J. Electrechem. Soc. 148 (3) (2001) A224.

[6] C. H. Zhao, J. R. Dahn, J. Electrochem. Soc. 149 (9) (2002) A1184.

[7] Z. Y. Tang, Y. L. Ruan, Acta Chim. Sin. 63 (16) (2005) 1500.

[8] S. Y. Chung, T. B. Jason, Y. M. Chiang, Nat. Mater. 1 (2) (2002) 123.

[9] S. H. Wu, M. S. Chen, C. J. Chien, Y. P. Fu, J. Power Sources 189 (2009) 440.

[10] J. Z. Hu, J. Xie, X. B. Zhao, H. M. Yu, X. Zhou, G. S. Cao, J. Mater. Sci. Technol. 25 (3) (2009) 405.

[11] J. Liu, J. Wang, X. D. Yan, X. F. Zhang, G. L. Yang, A. F. Jalbout, R. S. Wang, Electrochim. Acta 54 (2009) 5656.

[12] X. D. Yan, G. L. Yang, J. Liu, Y. C. Ge, H. M. Xie, X. M. Pan, R. S. Wang, Electro-

chim. Acta 54 (2009) 5770.

[13] H. W. Liu, H. M. Yang, J. L. Li, Electrochim. Acta 55 (2010) 1626.

[14] B. Kang, G. Ceder, Nature 458 (2009) 190.

[15] K. Zaghib, J. B. Goodenough, A. Mauger, C. Julieb, J. Power Sources 194 (2009) 1021.

[16] G. Ceder, B. Kang, J. Power Sources 194 (2009) 1024.

[17] D. Jugovic, D. Uskokovic, J. Power Sources 190 (2009) 538.

[18] M. S. Islam, D. J. Driscoll, C. A. J. Fisher, P. R. Slater, Chem. Mater. 17 (2005) 5085.

[19] B. L. Yu, J. D. Jiang, Applied Thermal Analysis, Textile Industry Press, Beijing, 1990, p. 114.

[20] A. A. Salah, A. Mauger, C. M. Julien, F. Gendron, Mater. Sci. Eng. B 129 (2006) 232.

[21] K. Zaghib, N. Ravet, M. Gauthier, F. Gendron, A. Mauger, J. B. Goodenough, C. M. Julien, J. Power Sources 163 (2006) 560.

[22] A. S. Andersson, J. O. Thomas, J. Power Sources 97 - 98 (2001) 498.

[23] J. Fu, Ph. D. Dissertation, Shanghai Jiao Tong University, March 2009, p. 149.

[24] G. X. Wang, L. Yang, Y. Chen, J. Z. Wang, S. Bewlay, H. K. Liu, Electrochim. Acta 50 (2005) 4649.

[25] S. T. Yang, Y. X. Liu, Y. H. Yin, H. Wang, T. Wang, Chin. J. Inorg. Chem. 23 (2007) 1165.

[26] A. J. Bard, L. R. Faulker, Electrochemical Methods—Fundamental and Applications, John Wiley & Sons, Inc., 1980;
L. Y. Gu, M. X. Lu, S. Z. Song, Chinese Version, Chemical Industry Publishing Company, 1986, p. 121.

Effect of Mn-doping on Performance of $Li_3V_2(PO_4)_3$/C Cathode Material for Lithium Ion Batteries①

Zhai Jing[a], Zhao Minshou[a,b], Wang Dandan[a]
(a College of Environmental and Chemical Engineering, Yanshan University, Qinhuangdao 066004, China)
(b State Key Laboratory of Metastable Material Science and Technology, Yanshan University, Qinhuangdao 066004, China)

Abstract: $Li_3V_{(2-2/3x)}Mn_x(PO_4)_3$ ($0 \leqslant x \leqslant 0.12$) powders were synthesized by sol-gel method. The effect of Mn^{2+}-doping on the structure and electrochemical performances of $Li_3V_2(PO_4)_3$/C was characterized by XRD, SEM, XPS, galvanostatic charge/discharge and electrochemical impedance spectroscopy(EIS). The XRD study shows that a small amount of Mn^{2+}-doped does not alter the structure of $Li_3V_2(PO_4)_3$/C materials, and all Mn^{2+}-doped samples are of pure single phase with a monoclinic structure (space group $P2_1/n$). The XPS analysis indicates that valences state of V and Mn are +3 and +2 in $Li_3V_{1.94}Mn_{0.09}(PO_4)_3$/C, respectively, and the citric acid in raw materials was decomposed into carbon during calcination, and residual carbon exists in $Li_3V_{1.94}Mn_{0.09}(PO_4)$/C. The results of electrochemical measurements show that Mn_{2+}-doping can improve the cyclic stability and rate performance of these cathode materials. The $Li_3V_{1.94}Mn_{0.09}(PO_4)_3$/C cathode material shows the best cyclic stability and rate performance. For example, at the discharge current density of 40 mA/g, after 100 cycles, the discharge capacity of $Li_3V_{1.94}Mn_{0.09}(PO_4)_3$/C declines from initial 158.8 mA · h/g to 120.5 mA · h/g with a capacity retention of 75.9%; however, that of the Mn-undoed sample declines from 164.2 mA · h/g to 72.6 mA · h/g with a capacity retention of 44.2%. When the discharge current is increased up to 1C, the intial discharge capacity of $Li_3V_{1.94}Mn_{0.09}(PO_4)_3$/C still reaches 146.4 mA · h/g, and the discharge capacity maintains at 107.5 mA · h/g after 100 cycles. The EIS measurement indicates that Mn^{2+}-doping with a appropriate amount of Mn^{2+} decreases the charge transfer resistance, which is favorable for the insertion/extraction of Li^+.

Key words: Lithium ion batteries; Cathode materials; $Li_3V_2(PO_4)_3$; Sol-Gel; Doping

1 Introduction

Since lithium iron phosphate, one kind of lithiated transition metal polyanion material based on PO_4^{3-}, was first reported as a cathode material for lithium-ion batteries by PADHI et al 1997 [1], the framework materials based on the

① Trans. Nonferrous Met. Soc. China, 2011(21): 523-528.

phosphate polyanion have been identified as potential electroactive materials for lithium-ion batteries, and $Li_3V_2(PO_4)_3$ is one of them. By comparing with the commercially used $LiCoO_2$, $LiNiO_2$, $LiMn_2O_4$ and their derivatives, $Li_3V_2(PO_4)_3$ cathode material has the outstanding advantages, such as stable framework, relatively high voltage, excellent heat stability, satisfactory safety and large theoretic capacity.

However, the main drawbacks of pristine $Li_3V_2(PO_4)_3$ are its very low intrinsic electronic conductivity and slow transport of Li ion, which results in poor cycling stability and rate performance. This makes it difficult to utilize $Li_3V_2(PO_4)_3$ cathode material fully in lithium ion batteries [2-3]. To solve this problem, many efforts have been made to improve the performance of $Li_3V_2(PO_4)_3$ cathode material, including preparation of small radius and homogeneous particles [4-5], carbon coating [6-11] and metal cation doping [12-15]. The modification researches have improved the comprehensive electrochemical performance of $Li_3V_2(PO_4)_3$ to different extents. However, Mn-doping in $Li_3V_2(PO_4)_3/C$ has not been concerned in published papers yet. In this work, the effect of Mn-doping on the structure and electrochemical performance of $Li_3V_2(PO_4)_3/C$ was investigated.

2 Experimental

2.1 Preparation of $Li_3V_{2-2/3x}Mn_x(PO_4)_3$ ($0 \leqslant x \leqslant 0.12$)

$Li_3V_{2-2/3x}Mn_x(PO_4)_3/C$ ($x=0.03$, 0.06, 0.09, 0.12) cathode materials were synthesized by sol-gel method. $V_2O_5 \cdot nH_2O$ hydro-gel was firstly prepared as follows: 10% (volume fraction) H_2O_2 solution was slowly added to V_2O_5 with vigorously stirring in ice-water until a clear orange solution formed, and then brownish homogeneous V_2O_5 gels were obtained after 4 h at 35 ℃. Aqueous solution of the stoichiometric $NH_4H_2PO_4$, $CH_3COOLi \cdot 2H_2O$, $(CH_3COO)_2Mn \cdot 4H_2O$ and citric acid were added to the $V_2O_5 \cdot nH_2O$ hydro-gels, respectively. The mixture was heated with continuous stirring at 80 ℃ until the blue precursor was obtained. The obtained gel was dried in a vacuum oven at 80 ℃, and then the powder sample was ground, pelletized and heated at 300 ℃ in a furnace with flowing nitrogen gas for 4 h; then temperature rose to 800 ℃ at a rate of 15 ℃/min and kept for 5.5 h with a stream of nitrogen gas. The sample was taken out when the temperature was cooled down to room temperature, and then ground. The undoped $Li_3V_2(PO_4)_3/C$ sample was also prepared through the same method for comparison except without addition of $(CH_3COO)_2Mn \cdot 4H_2O$.

2.2 Sample characterization

X-ray diffraction pattern of the sample was carried out with 2θ between 10° and 60° by using a D/Max Ⅲ diffractometer with Cu K_α radiation, at the scan speed of 2 (°)/min and voltage of 40 kV. The X-ray photoelectron spectroscopy (XPS) was obtained for the $Li_3V_{1.94}Mn_{0.09}(PO_4)_3/C$ sample by using Kratos Axis Ultra DLD spectrometer with monochromatic Al K_α radiation. The morphology of the sample was observed using the Hitachi S-4800 scanning electron microscope instrument (SEM).

2.3 Electrochemical tests

Electrochemical performances of the samples were evaluated in columned Li test cell. The cathode material was prepared by mixing the products with acetylene black and polyvinylidine fluoride (PVDF) binder at a mass ratio of 80 : 15 : 5 in *N*-methyl-2-pyrrolidone (NMP). The obtained slurry was coated on Al foil, dried under the infrared light and foursquare strips with dimensions of 8 mm×8 mm were cut into with active material of about 2 mg. After the strips were dried at 120 ℃ for 12 h in a vacuum, two-electrode electrochemical cell was assembled in a Mikrouna glove box filled with high-pure argon where the lithium metal foil was used as anode, Celgard ®2320 as separator and 1 mol/L $LiPF_6$ in EC : DMC (1 : 1, volume fraction) as electrolyte, then charge/discharge test was carried out using a Neware battery tester. The electrochemical measurements were performed in the voltage range of 3.0—4.8 V at room temperature. EIS measurements were carried out in three-electrode cell by using CHI 660A electrochemical analyzer (Chenhua, Shanghai, China) with ±5 mV ac signal and a frequency range of 10^5—10^{-2} Hz and 4.8 V.

3 Results and discussion

3.1 Sample characterization

XRD patterns of $Li_3V_{2-2/3x}Mn_x(PO_4)_3/C$ ($0 \leqslant x \leqslant 0.12$) are shown in Fig. 1. It is obvious that all samples are of pure single phase with a monoclinic structure (space group $P2_1/n$), and the result is consistent with the published result [16]. No other phases are detected in the XRD patterns, indicating that Mn^{2+} ions are completely substituted into the crystal lattice of $Li_3V_2(PO_4)_3$, and a low dose of Mn^{2+}-doping does not alter the basic $Li_3V_2(PO_4)_3$ crystal structure. The amount of carbon in $Li_3V_2(PO_4)_3/C$ is about 4.4% in mass fraction measured by thermogravimetric analysis.

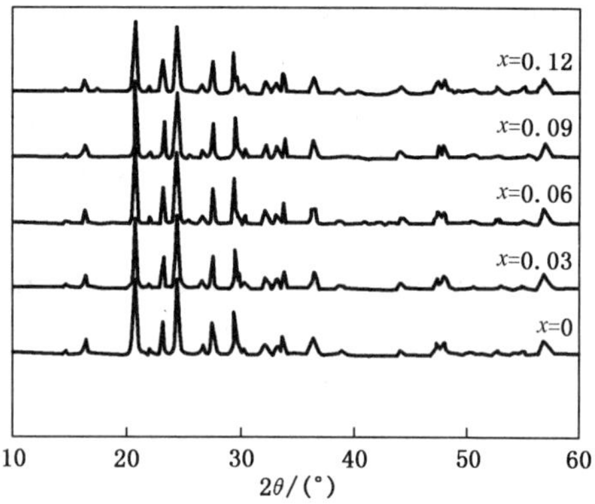

Fig. 1 XRD patterns of $Li_3V_{2-2/3x}Mn_x(PO_4)_3/C$ ($0 \leqslant x \leqslant 0.12$)

The XPS spectra of V 2p, Mn 2p and C 1s in the $Li_3V_{1.94}Mn_{0.09}(PO_4)_3/C$ sample are illustrated in Fig. 2. Fig. 2 shows that the V 2p core level fits to a single peak with a binding energy of 517.2 eV, matching well with the reported result [15], so the oxidation state of V in $Li_3V_{1.94}Mn_{0.09}(PO_4)_3/C$ is +3. The Mn 2p XPS also shows a single peak with a binding energy of 640.9 eV, similar to that observed in MnO (640.6 eV) [17], so the oxidation state of Mn in $Li_3V_{1.94}Mn_{0.09}(PO_4)_3$/C is +2. The C 1s XPS shows that the peak OC—O with a binding energy of 288.4 eV is absent, while the peak C—C with a binding energy of 284.6 eV occurs in the spectra of the $Li_3V_{1.94}Mn_{0.09}(PO_4)_3$/C. This indicates that citrate was decomposed into carbon during calcination, and residual carbon exists in $Li_3V_{1.94}Mn_{0.09}(PO_4)_3$/C. This is beneficial to enhance the electronic conductivity for $Li_3V_{1.94}Mn_{0.09}(PO_4)_3$/C.

The SEM images of the $Li_3V_{1.94}Mn_{0.09}(PO_4)_3$/C and $Li_3V_2(PO_4)_3$/C are presented in Fig. 3. The particles of them show good crystallinity. The particles of the $Li_3V_2(PO_4)_3$/C sample presents piece shape and are agglomerated with each other. The grains of $Li_3V_{1.94}Mn_{0.09}(PO_4)_3$/C sample are like ball shape, and the particles are smaller and more homogeneous than $Li_3V_2(PO_4)_3$/C sample.

3.2 Galvanostatic electrochemical measurements

The second charge/discharge curves are shown in Fig. 4 for the Li/$Li_3V_{1.94}Mn_{0.09}(PO_4)_3$ and Li/$Li_3V_2(PO_4)_3$ test cells at 40 mA/g current density in the range of 3.0—4.8 V at room temperature. For $Li_3V_2(PO_4)_3$/C sample, Fig. 4(a) shows clearly four plateaus in the charge process and three plateaus in the discharge process, which have definite boundary. For $Li_3V_{1.94}Mn_{0.09}(PO4)_3$/C sample, there are four plateaus in the charge process and two plateaus in the discharge process. Compared with the $Li_3V_2(PO_4)_3$/C sample, the first two discharge plateaus of $Li_3V_{1.94}Mn_{0.09}(PO_4)_3$/C sample are merged into one. The result agrees with that of Ti-doped one [14]. Electrochemical reaction leading to multiphase reaction mechanism around plateaus usually presents new interphases, which decreases Li^+ transport and accordingly affects the electrochemical performance. The more complicated the phase transition is, the more difficult the transports of Li^+ is [18]. The conclusion may be drawn that there is a tendency from multiphase reaction to single-phase reaction in the charge-discharge processes by doping Mn to $Li_3V_2(PO_4)_3$/C. This change is beneficial to Li^+ insertion/extraction and reduces the variation of cell volume during cycling, which significantly improves the cycle stability, as confirmed in Fig. 5.

Fig. 5 shows cycling performance of $Li_3V_{2-2/3x}Mn_x(PO_4)_3$ (x=0, 0.03, 0.06, 0.09, 0.12) in the voltage range of 3.0—4.8 V at current density of 40 mA/g. It can be seen that the highest discharge capacity of Mn-doped samples is lower than that of undoped one; however, the cyclic stability is apparently improved except for the sample with Mn-doped 0.03 after 40 cycles, especially the cyclic stability of $Li_3V_{1.94}Mn_{0.09}(PO_4)3$/C is significantly improved. For example, after 100 cycles, the discharge capacity of $Li_3V_{1.94}Mn_{0.09}(PO_4)_3$/C declines from initial 158.8 mA·h/g to 120.5 mA·h/g with a capacity retention of 75.9%; however, the discharge capacity of undoped one declines from initial 164.2mA·h/g to 72.6 mA·h/g with a capacity retention of 44.2%.

Rate performance of the $Li_3V_{1.94}Mn_{0.09}(PO_4)_3/C$ is shown in Fig. 6. The discharge capacity decreases with increasing the cycle number at different current densities, but the change is not sharp. At different current densities of 0.2C, 0.5C and 1C, the initial discharge capacities reach 158.8, 150.8 and 146.4 mA · h/g, respectively, and the discharge capacities maintain 120.4, 110.6 and 107.5 mA · h/g after 100 cycles, respectively. From above data, we believe that the Mn-doping greatly improves the rate performance.

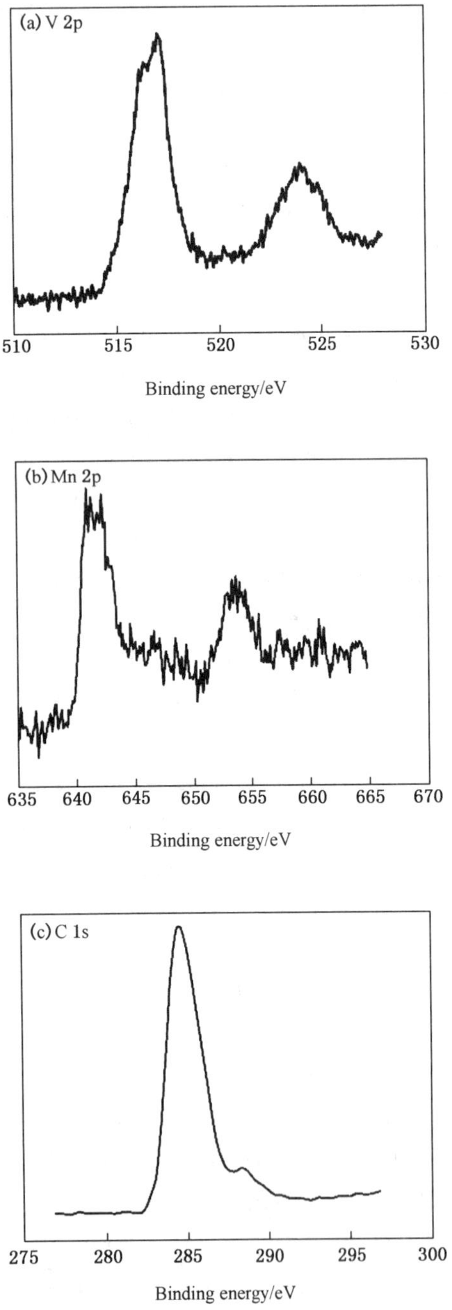

Fig. 2　XPS spectra of V 2p (a), Mn 2p (b) and C 1s (c) in $Li_3V_{1.94}Mn_{0.09}(PO_4)_3/C$

Fig. 3　SEM images of $Li_3V_2(PO_4)_3/C$ (a) and $Li_3V_{1.94}Mn_{0.09}(PO_4)_3/C$ (b)

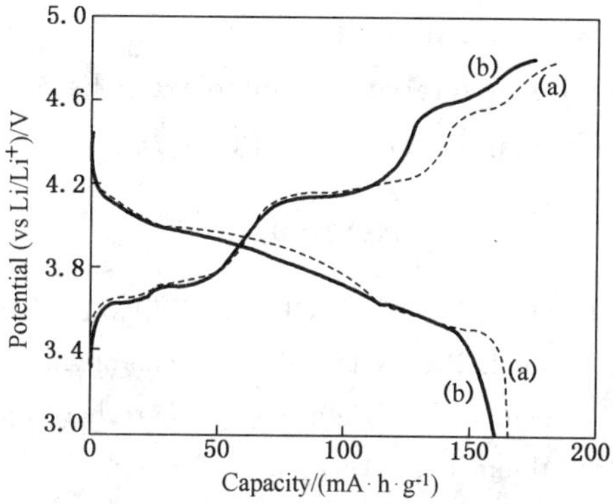

Fig. 4 Second cycle charge/discharge curves of $Li_3V_2(PO_4)_3/C$ (a) and $Li_3V_{1.94}Mn_{0.09}(PO_4)_3/C$ (b)

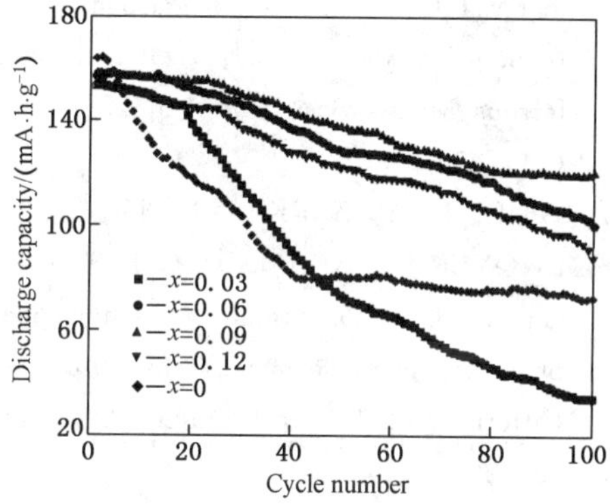

Fig. 5 Cycling performance of $Li_3V_{2-2/3x}Mn_x(PO_4)_3/C$ (x=0, 0.03, 0.06, 0.09, 0.12)

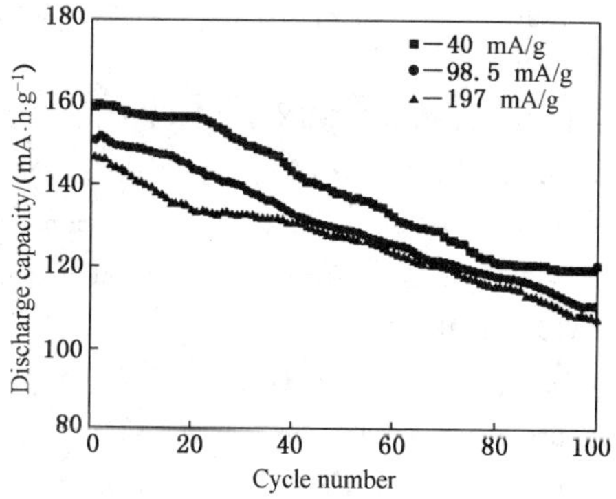

Fig. 6 Discharge capacity vs cycle number for $Li_3V_{1.94}Mn_{0.09}(PO_4)_3/C$ at different current densities

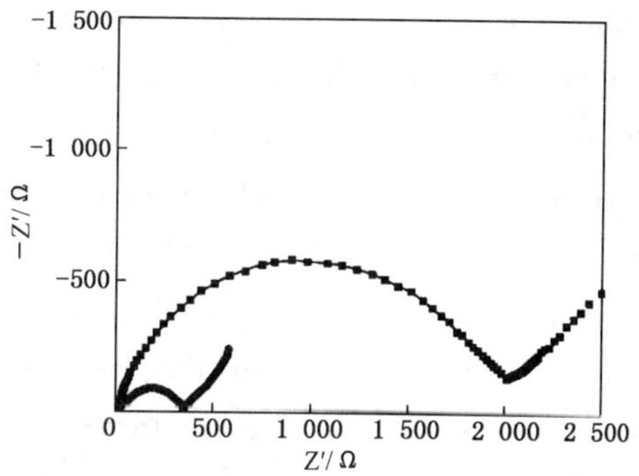

Fig. 7 EIS of $Li_3V_2(PO_4)_3/C$ and $Li_3V_{1.94}Mn_{0.09}(PO_4)_3/C$

3.3 EIS analysis

Fig. 7 shows typical Nyquist plots of the $Li_3V_2(PO_4)_3/C$ and $Li_3V_{1.94}Mn_{0.09}(PO_4)_3/C$ samples. Prior to the EIS measurement, the electrodes are cycled galvanostatically for 20 cycles between 3.0 and 4.8 V to ensure the stable formation of the SEI films on the surface of the electroactive particles. The EIS was then measured in the fully discharged state. As shown in Fig. 7, the Nyquist plots are composed of a small intercept at high frequency, a semi-circle at high to medium frequency and a straight line at low frequency. The small intercept is almost the same (14—16 Ω) for two samples, which represents the solution resistance. The semi-circle corresponds to the charge transfer resistance and double-layer capacitance. The sloping line corresponds to the diffusion of Li^+ ions in the electrode bulk, namely the Warburg impedance. It can be seen that the charge-transfer resistance on $Li_3V_{1.94}Mn_{0.09}(PO_4)_3/C$ electrode is much less than that on the undoped $Li_3V_2(PO_4)_3/C$. This result is similar to those previous reports [19]. The decrease of charge transfer resistance indicates that the Mn-doping significantly can facilitate the kinetic process of electrochemical reaction on $Li_3V_{1.94}Mn_{0.09}(PO_4)_3/C$ electrode. This is favorable to overcome kinetic limit in the course of charge/discharge, enhance the depth of extraction/insertion of Li^+ in active particles, reduce the difference of concentration of Li^+ which lies on surface and inner of active particles, and avoid the fade of capacity because the distortion of inner crystal structure of active particles happens [20].

4 Conclusions

1. The various Mn^{2+}-doped $Li_3V_{2-2/3x}Mn_x(PO_4)_3/C$ ($x=0, 0.03, 0.06, 0.09, 0.12$) cathode materials were synthesized by sol-gel method.

2. XRD diffraction results show that a monoclinic phase is obtained, and according to XPS analysis, the valences of V and Mn in $Li_3V_{1.94}Mn_{0.09}(PO_4)_3/C$ are $+3$, $+2$, respectively. Citrate is decomposed into carbon during calcination, and residual carbon exists in $Li_3V_{1.94}Mn_{0.09}(PO_4)_3/C$.

3. Electrochemical tests indicate that the Mn-doping into $Li_3V_2(PO_4)_3/C$ not only presents a tendency from multiphase reaction to single-phase reaction in the charge-discharge processes, but also reduces the charge transfer resistance. As a result, the cyclic stability and rate performance of $Li_3V_{2-2/3x}Mn_x(PO_4)_3/C$ cathode material can be effectively improved. Mn-doping is very effective for the improvement of the electrochemical performances of $Li_3V_2(PO_4)_3/C$.

References

[1] PADHI A K, NAJUNDASWAMY K S, GOODENOUGH J B. Phospho-olivnes as positive electrode materials for rechargeable lithium batteries [J]. J Electrochem Soc, 1997, 144(4): 1188-1194.

[2] ZHONG Sheng-kui, YIN Zhou-lan, WANG Zhi-xing, GUO Hua-jun, LI Xin-hai. Synthesis and characterization of novel cathode material $Li_3V_2(PO_4)_3$ by carbon-thermal reduction method [J]. Transactions of Nonferrous Metals Society of China, 2006, 16 (S1): S708-S710.

[3] SAIDI M Y, BARKER J, HUANG H, SWOYER J L. ADAMSON G. Performance characteristics of lithium vanadium phosphate as a cathode material for lithium-ion batteries [J]. J Power Sources, 2003, 119-121: 266-272.

[4] LI Y Z, ZHOU Z, REN M M, GAO X P, YAN J. Improved electrochemical Li insertion performances of $Li_3V_2(PO_4)_3$/carbon composite materials prepared by a sol-gel route [J]. Materials Letters, 2007, 61: 4562-4564.

[5] TANG A P, WANG X Y, LIU Z M. Electrochemical behavior of $Li_3V_2(PO_4)_3/C$ composite cathode material for lithium-ion batteries [J]. Materials Letters, 2008, 62: 1646-1648.

[6] LI Y Z, ZHOU Z, GAO X P, YAN J. A promising sol-gel route based on citric acid to synthesize $Li_3V_2(PO_4)_3$/carbon composite material for lithium ion batteries [J]. Electrochim Acta, 2007, 52: 4922-4926.

[7] LI Y Z, ZHOU Z, REN M M, GAO X P, YAN J. Electrochemical performance of

nano-crystalline $Li_3V_2(PO_4)_3$/carbon composite material synthesized by a novel solgel method [J]. Electrochim Acta, 2006, 51: 6498-6502.

[8] CHEN Q Q, WANG J W, TANG Z, HE W C, SHAO H B, ZHANG J Q. Electrochemical performance of the carbon coated $Li_3V_2(PO_4)_3$ cathode material synthesized by a solgel method [J]. Electrochim Acta, 2007, 52: 5251-5257.

[9] CHANG C X, XIANG J F, SHI X X, HAN X X, YUAN L J, SUN J T. Rheological phase reaction synthesis and electrochemical performance of $Li_3V_2(PO_4)_3$/carbon cathode for lithium ion batteries [J]. Electrochim Acta, 2008, 53: 2232-2237.

[10] FU P, ZHAO Y M, DONG Y Z, AN X N, SHEN G P. Synthesis of $Li_3V_2(PO_4)_3$ with high performance by optimized solid-state synthesis routine [J]. J Power Source, 2006, 162: 651-657.

[11] FU P, ZHAO Y M, AN X N, DONG Y Z, HOU X M. Structure and electrochemical properties of nanocarbon-coated $Li_3V_2(PO_4)_3$ prepared by solgel method [J]. Electrochim Acta, 2007, 52: 5281-5285.

[12] SATO M, OHKAWA H, YOSHIDA K, SAITO M, UEMATSU K, TODA K. Enhancement of discharge capacity of $Li_3V_2(PO_4)_3$ by stabilizing the orthorhombic phase at room temperature [J]. Solid-State Ionics, 2000, 135: 137-142.

[13] ZHONG Sheng-kui, LIU Le-tong, JIANG Ji-qiong, LI Yan-wei, WANG Jian, LIU Jie-qun, LI Yan-hong. Preparation and electrochemical properties of Y-doped $Li_3V_2(PO_4)_3$ cathode materials for lithium batteries [J]. Journal of Rare Earths, 2009, 27 (1): 134-137.

[14] LIU Su-qin, LI Shi-cai, HUANG Ke-long, CHEN Zhao-hui. Effect of doping Ti^{4+} on the structure and performances of $Li_3V_2(PO_4)_3$ [J]. Acta Phys Chim Sinca China, 2007, 23: 537-542.

[15] REN M M, ZHOU Z, LI Y Z, GAO X P, YAN J. Preparation and electrochemical studies of Fe-doped $Li_3V_2(PO_4)_3$ cathode materials for lithium-ion batteries [J]. J Power Sources, 2006, 162: 1357-1362.

[16] SAIDI M Y, BARKER J, HUANG H, SWOYER J L, ADAMSON G. Electrochemical properties of lithium vanadium phosphate as a cathode material for lithium-ion batteries [J]. Electrochem Solid State Lett A, 2002, 5: 149-151.

[17] OKU M, HIROKAWA K, IKEDA S. X-ray photoelectron spectroscopy of manganese-oxygen systems [J]. Electron Spectroscopy and Related Phenomena, 1975, 7: 465-473.

[18] PISTOIA G, ANTONINI A, ROSATI R, BELLITTO C. Effect of partial Ga^{3+} substitution for Mn^{3+} in $LiMn_2O_4$ on its behaviour as a cathode for Li cells [J]. Electroanalytical Chemistry, 1996, 410: 115-118.

[19] MI C H, ZHANG X G, ZHAO X B, LI H L. synthesis and performance of $LiMn_{0.6}Fe_{0.4}PO_4$/nano-carbon webs composite cathode [J]. Materials Science and Engineering B, 2006, 129: 8-13.

[20] YANG S T, LIU Y X, YIN Y H, WANG H, WANG T. Effects of Ta ion doping on the physical and electrochemical performance of $LiFePO_4$/C [J]. Chinese Journal of Inorganic Chemistry, 2007, 23: 1165-1168.

Effect of MgO Nanolayer Coated on $Li_3V_2(PO_4)_3$/C Cathode Material for Lithium-ion Battery①

Jing Zhai[a], Minshou Zhao[a,b], Dandan Wang[a], Yuqing Qiao[a]

([a] Provincial Key Laboratory of Applied Chemistry, College of Environmental and Chemical Engineering, Yanshan University, Qinhuangdao 066004, PR China)

([b] State Key Laboratory of Metastable Material Science and Technology, Yanshan, University, Qinhuangdao 066004, PR China)

Abstract: MgO nanolayer coated on $Li_3V_2(PO_4)_3$/C particles was successfully prepared by a sol-gel method. The X-ray diffraction (XRD) shows that the crystal structure of the $Li_3V_2(PO_4)_3$/C cores does not been affected by the coating. Nanolayer-structured MgO on the surface of $Li_3V_2(PO_4)_3$/C particles is demonstrated by high resolution transmission electron microscopy (HRTEM). Galvanostatic charge/discharge, EIS and cyclic voltammetry measurements clearly show that MgO nanocoating stabilizes the structure of the cathode material, decreases the interface charge transfer resistance and enhances the reversibility of electrode reaction. Electrochemical properties of the coated samples were investigated, showing enhancements of the initial discharge capacity, the cyclability and the rate performance. For MgO of 4.5 mol% coated sample, the initial discharge capacity is 194.4 mAh g^{-1} at 40 mA g^{-1} current density, which is close to the theoretical discharge capacity of 197 mAh g^{-1}, and the discharge capacity remains 137.5 mAh g^{-1} after 100 cycles, and its capacity retention of 70.73% is higher than that of pristine $Li_3V_2(PO_4)_3$/C, 43.7%. The initial discharge capacity still reaches 157.81 mAh g^{-1}, 157.29 mAh g^{-1} and 144.64 mAh g^{-1} at 1C, 1.5C, 2C rates, respectively.

Key words: Sol-gel; Magnesium oxide; Nanocoating; Electrochemical performance; Cathode material; Lithium-ion battery

1 Introduction

Rechargeable lithium-ion batteries are considered as one of the most advanced energy storage systems. Currently, $LiCoO_2$ is widely used as cathode material in commercial lithium-ion batteries [1], but its high cost, safety and toxicity inhibit its use in large-scale and biomedical application, so more efforts have been made to explore novel cathode material. In recent years, as part of efforts for identifying new cathode material for rechargeable lithium batteries, lithiated transition metal phosphates such as

① Journal of Alloys and Compounds, 2010(502): 401-406.

$LiFePO_4$ [2,3], $LiCoPO_4$ [4], $LiMnPO_4$ [5,6]and $Li_3V_2(PO_4)_3$ [7-9]have attracted significant interests due to their good lithium ion mobility, high reversible capacity, operative redox potentials and high safety. Among all the phosphates, monoclinic lithium vanadium phosphate ($Li_3V_2(PO_4)_3$, LVP) is a highly promising cathode material proposed for lithium ion batteries, which shows an average intercalation voltage up to 4.0 V and a theoretical capacity of 197 mAh g^{-1}.

However, it is well known that low electronic conductivity of LVP affects its electrochemical properties greatly [10], especially the fast rate performance. In most of the early reports, many efforts including metal doping [11-14], coating with carbon [15,16] and mixing the precursor with some conductive metal powders [17] have been made to improve the performances of $Li_3V_2(PO_4)_3$ cathode material. In addition to, it has been reported that ZrO_2 coated $LiFePO_4$ remarkably enhanced the electrochemical performances of $LiFePO_4$ cathode material [18]. However, up to now, there has been no report yet on metal oxide coated on $Li_3V_2(PO_4)_3$ particle surface. In this work, MgO nanolayer coated on $Li_3V_2(PO_4)_3$/C cathode material by sol-gel method was performed and the resultant electrochemical performances are reported.

2 Experimental

The pristine $Li_3V_2(PO_4)_3$/C was synthesized by a sol-gel method. $V_2O_5 \cdot nH_2O$ hydro-gel was prepared as follows: 10% (v/v) H_2O_2 solution was slowly added to V_2O_5, while vigorously stirred in ice-water until a clear orange solution formed, and then brownish homogeneous V_2O_5 gels were obtained after 4 h at 35 ℃. Aqueous solution of the stoichiometric $NH_4H_2PO_4$, $CH_3COOLi \cdot 2H_2O$ and citric acid were added to the above $V_2O_5 \cdot nH_2O$ hydro-gels, respectively. The mixtures were heated gently with continuous stirring to remove the excess water at 80 ℃ until the blue precursor was obtained, which was dried in a vacuum oven at 80 ℃ for 12 h to get resultant powder, and then the powder sample was ground in an agate mortar, pelletized and heated at 300 ℃ in a furnace with flowing nitrogen gas for 4 h to allow the formation and release of NH_3 and H_2O. Thereafter temperature was risen to 800 ℃ at a rate of 15 ℃ min^{-1} and kept for 5.5 h with a stream of nitrogen gas. The sample was taken out and ground in an agate mortar when the temperature was fallen down to room temperature, getting particle size span from 0.5 to 4 μm, which was used as pristine material, and $Mg(CH_3COO)_2 \cdot 4H_2O$ was used as coating reagent. $Li_3V_2(PO_4)_3$/C powder was initially dispersed into ethanol containing the desired amount of $Mg(CH_3COO)_2 \cdot 4H_2O$ by a blender and followed by an ultrasonic stirring for 10 min, then dried with a rotary evaporator under reflux condition. The residue as-obtained was slightly ground, pressed into pellets, and then sintered at 650 ℃ for 4 h in flowing N_2 atmosphere to decompose the organic radicle and create a MgO coating layer on the particle surface of $Li_3V_2(PO_4)_3/C$. The coated amount of MgO on $Li_3V_2(PO_4)_3/C$ powders was 3.5, 4.0, 4.5 and 5.0 mol%, respectively.

X-ray diffraction (XRD) was performed on $Li_3V_2(PO_4)_3/C$ powders before and after coated using a D/Max-2500/PC X-ray diffractometer (Cu K_α radiation). The surface morphology of powder $Li_3V_2(PO_4)_3/C$ coated and uncoated with MgO was observed by a Hitachi S-4800 scanning electron microscopy instrument (SEM), respectively. The microstructures of the coated particles were examined by a JEM-2010 transmission electron microscope.

Electrochemical performances of the samples were evaluated in columned test cells. To prepare the electrodes used for the electrochemical performances measurement, the powders of pristine $Li_3V_2(PO_4)_3/C$ and MgO coated $Li_3V_2(PO_4)_3/C$ were mixed with acetylene black and polyvinylidine fluoride (PVDF) binder in a weight ratio of 80 : 15 : 5 in *N*-methyl-2-pyrrolidone (NMP) to ensure the homogeneity, respectively. The obtained slurry was coated on Al foil, dried under the infrared light and cut into foursquare strips of 8 mm × 8 mm in size, and the calculation to mass of active materials is carried out by the difference between the mass of active material coated Al foil and the mass of pristine Al foil to multiple 80%. After the strips were dried at 120 ℃ for 12 h in a vacuum, two-electrode electrochemical cells were assembled in a Mikrouna glove box filled with high-purity argon where the lithium metal foil was used as anode, Celgard® 2320 as separator, and 1 M $LiPF_6$ in EC : DMC (1 : 1 vol. %) was used as electrolyte, and then charge/discharge test was carried out using a Neware Battery Tester. The electrochemical measurements were performed in the voltage range of 3.0—4.8 V at room temperature. EIS measurements were carried out in three-electrode cells by using CHI 660A electrochemical analyzer (Chenhua, Shanghai, China) with a ±5 mV ac signal and a frequency range from 10^5 to 10^{-2} Hz. Cyclic voltammograms were obtained on a ZF-9 potentiostat by scanning electrode potential at the rate of 5 mV min^{-1} between 3.0 and 4.8 V.

3 Results and discussion

The XRD patterns of pristine $Li_3V_2(PO_4)_3/C$ and MgO coated $Li_3V_2(PO_4)_3/C$ are presented in Fig. 1, in which All diffraction lines can be indexed to the monoclinic structure with space group 14 ($P2_1/n$) and are consistent with the published results [19]. Additionally, peak shift is not observed before and after the surface modification by MgO within the detectable limit of XRD, and no peaks related to MgO are observed in the XRD patterns of the MgO-modified samples, which is consistent with the result reported in literature [20]. However, the lattice parameter decreases slightly from the value of the uncoated material ($a=8.569$ Å, $b=8.636$ Å) to the value of 4.5 mol% MgO coated $Li_3V_2(PO_4)_3/C$ ($a=8.569$ Å, $b=8.636$ Å). Taking into account the ionic radius of Mg^{2+} (0.72 Å) smaller than that of V^{3+} (0.74 Å), such an decrease suggests that a small amount of Mg^{2+} ions can be incorporated into the monoclinic structure by soft re-heating, which is similar to previously reported results [20,21]. Because of the controlled reaction time, we believe that only a thin layer of solid solution $Li_3Mg_xV_{2-x}(PO_4)_3$ was formed on the surface of the $Li_3V_2(PO_4)_3/C$ particles. Therefore, no traces of solid solution were detected with XRD.

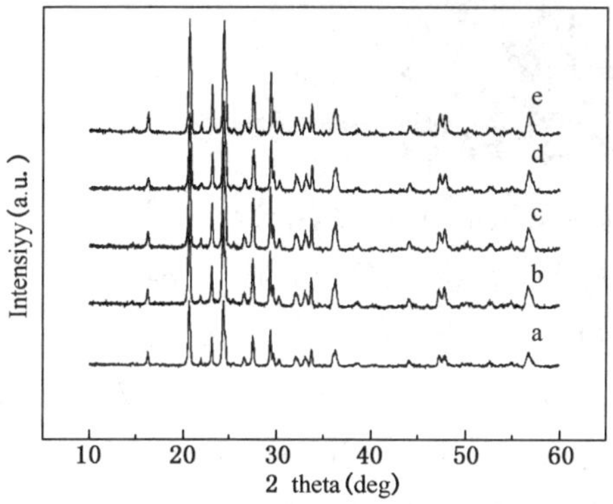

Fig. 1 XRD patterns of $Li_3V_2(PO_4)_3/C$ (a) and MgO coated $Li_3V_2(PO_4)_3/C$ 3.5 mol% (b), 4.0 mol% (c), 4.5 mol% (d) and 5.0 mol% (e)

The morphology of pristine $Li_3V_2(PO_4)_3/C$ and MgO coated $Li_3V_2(PO_4)_3/C$ were observed by SEM. Fig. 2 shows that the size of the particles of uncoated $Li_3V_2(PO_4)_3/C$ is un-uniform. After coated with MgO of 4.5 mol%, the particles do not show obvious change in morphology except for being more homogeneous in particle size distribution.

Fig. 2 Morphology of $Li_3V_2(PO_4)_3/C$ (a) and 4.5mol% MgO coated $Li_3V_2(PO_4)_3/C$(b)

The microstructure of MgO coated $Li_3V_2(PO_4)_3/C$ particle was analyzed by high resolution TEM(Fig. 3), which confirms that MgO is coated on the surface of $Li_3V_2(PO_4)_3/C$. This HRTEM image clearly illustrates that the thickness of MgO coating layer is about 2.0—2.5 nm and the lattice fringe spacing of $Li_3V_2(PO_4)_3/C$ is 0.36 nm. We performed EDS spot analysis at the coating layer, detecting the presence of Mg and O. The figure of EDS and the results of EDS analysis in atom % are shown in Fig. 4 and Table 1, respectively. This confirms that the coating consists of MgO film.

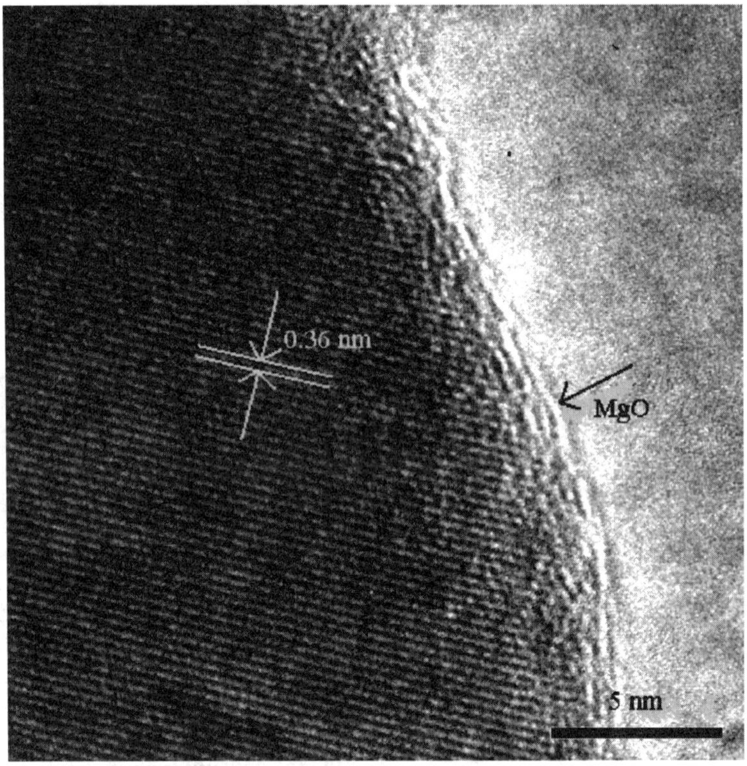

Fig. 3　TEMimage of 4.5mol% MgO-coated $Li_3V_2(PO_4)_3/C$

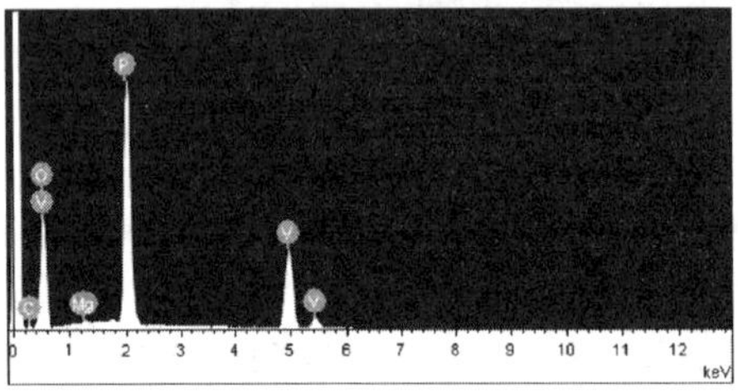

Fig. 4　EDS image of 4.5mol% MgO-coated $Li_3V_2(PO_4)_3/C$

Table 1　Results of EDS analysis

Element	Weight/%	Atom/%
C	4.34	7.98
O	45.89	63.45
Mg	0.32	0.30
P	24.32	17.36
V	25.13	10.91

The second charge/discharge curves are shown in Fig. 5 for pristine $Li_3V_2(PO_4)_3/C$ and MgO of 4.5 mol% coated $Li_3V_2(PO_4)_3/C$ test cells at 40 mA g^{-1} current density in the range of 3.0—4.8 V at room temperature. It can be seen that the profiles of the charge/discharge curves for the two samples are almost the same. Four plateaus appear in the charge process and three plateaus in the discharge process, which consistent with the results [22], but the charge/discharge plateaus are longer for MgO coated $Li_3V_2(PO_4)_3/C$. From the second charge/discharge curves, the effects of modification with MgO are not so apparent, but the significant effects can be observed from the long-term charge/discharge cycle in the following tests, such as the twentieth charge/dischargen curves of pristine $Li_3V_2(PO_4)_3/C$ and the thirtieth charge/discharge curves of MgO of 4.5mol% coated $Li_3V_2(PO_4)_3/C$ (Fig. 6). It is obvious that the profile of discharge curve was changed for pristine $Li_3V_2(PO_4)_3/C$, the first two discharge plateaus of pristine $Li_3V_2(PO_4)_3/C$ were merged into one, and two discharge plateaus appear in the discharge process only. However, the discharge curve profile of MgO coated $Li_3V_2(PO_4)_3/C$ is not altered and there are still three discharge plateaus in the discharge process. This demonstrates that the MgO coating suppresses the microstructure change of $Li_3V_2(PO_4)_3/C$ caused by repetition of lithium-ion insertion-extraction reaction, and thus improves structural stability of the cathode material.

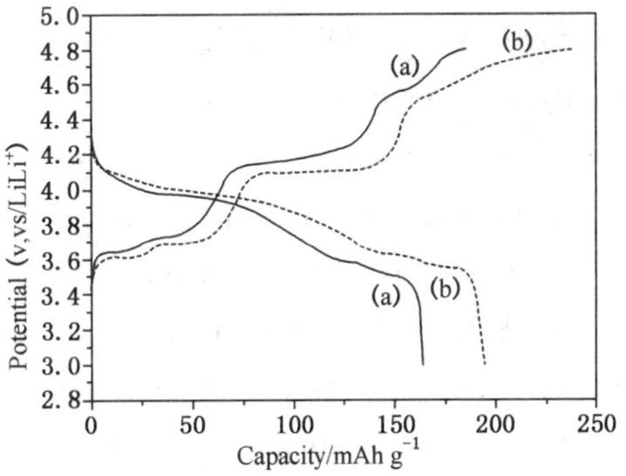

Fig. 5 Second charge/discharge curves of $Li_3V_2(PO_4)_3/C$ (a) and 4.5mol% MgO coated $Li_3V_2(PO_4)_3/C$ (b)

EIS measurements were performed on pristine $Li_3V_2(PO_4)_3/C$ and MgO of 4.5 mol% coated $Li_3V_2(PO_4)_3/C$ electrodes, respectively. The electrodes were galvanostatically charged/discharged for 10 cycles to ensure the stable formation of the SEI layers on the surface of the electroactive particles. The EIS was then measured in the fully discharged state. EIS and an equivalent circuit [23] are shown in Figs. 7 and 8, respectively. EIS data were fitted using Zview-Impedance 2.80 software. Fig. 7 shows typical Nyquist plots of pristine $Li_3V_2(PO_4)_3/C$ and MgO coated $Li_3V_2(PO_4)_3/C$ composite electrodes. The plots show an intercept at high frequency, followed by a depressed semicircle in the high-middle frequency region and a straight line in the low frequency region. The intercept impedance on the Z' axis represents the resistance of solvent, and R_s is used to denote it in equivalent circuit. The semicircle is attributed to the chargetransfer resistance of electrochemical reaction and the line to the diffusion controlled Warburg, and the Rct and W_0 are used to denote them in the equivalent circuit, respectively. A constant phase element CPE is placed to represent the double layer capaci-tance and passivation film capacitance [15,23], and the capacitance resistance is so small to be negligible. The fitting results are shown in Table 2. It can be understood that the resistance of the solvent (R_s) has no large change for pristine $Li_3V_2(PO_4)_3/C$ and MgO coated $Li_3V_2(PO_4)_3/C$ electrodes. This is because the same electrolyte is used when the test cells are assembled. The charge-transfer resis-tance at MgO coated $Li_3V_2(PO_4)_3/C$ electrode is much less than that at pristine $Li_3V_2(PO_4)_3/C$, indicating that the coating is more favorable for the insertion and de-insertion of lithium ions during the charge and discharge process. This result is similar to that of ZrO_2 coated $LiFePO_4$ [18].

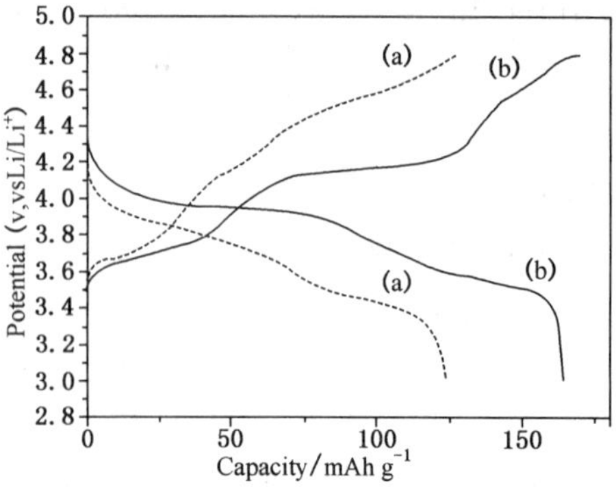

Fig. 6　Charge/discharge curves of $Li_3V_2(PO_4)_3/C$ (twentieth) (a) and 4.5mol% MgO coated $Li_3V_2(PO_4)_3/C$ (thirtieth) (b)

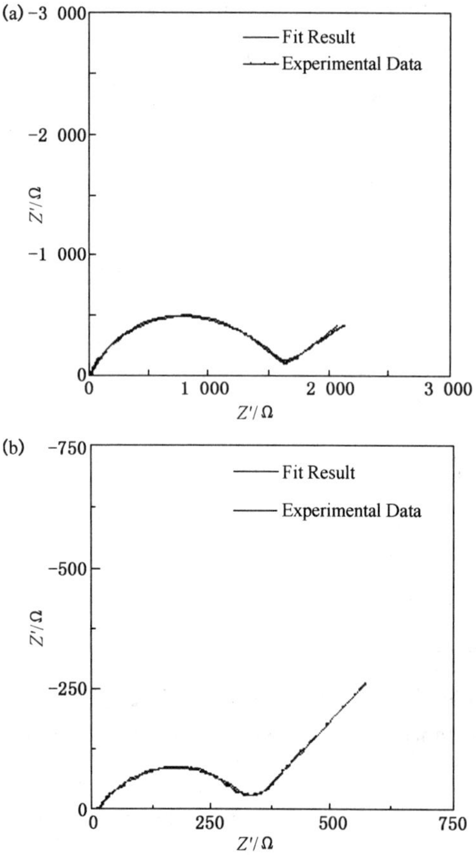

Fig. 7　EIS of $Li_3V_2(PO_4)_3/C$ (a) and 4.5mol% MgO coated $Li_3V_2(PO_4)_3/C$ (b) Fitting lines show fitted results from equivalent circuit.

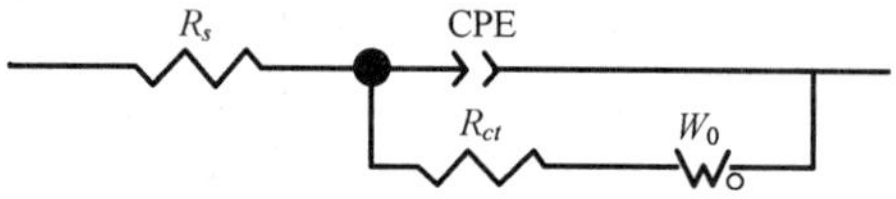

Fig. 8　Equivalent circuit

Table 2　Results of electrochemical impedance

Material	R_s/Ω	R_{ct}/Ω
$Li_3V_2(PO_4)_3/C$	12.18	1 649
MgO coated $Li_3V_2(PO_4)_3/C$	12.56	302.7

The initial CV curves for pristine $Li_3V_2(PO_4)_3/C$ and MgO of 4.5mol% coated $Li_3V_2(PO_4)_3/C$ are shown in Fig. 9. Both curves show a similar profile, and there are four oxidation peaks and three reduction peaks in CV curves, which indicate that the reaction behavior does not change during the lithium extraction/insertion process for the coated electrode. As shown in Fig. 9, the four oxidation peaks of pristine $Li_3V_2(PO_4)_3/C$ are located at about 3.68, 3.74, 4.14 and 4.59 V, respectively, and three reduction peaks are located around 3.51, 3.58 and 3.88 V, respectively. The extraction and intercalation potentials are similar to those reported by Saidi et al. [24]. However, in the case of MgO coated $Li_3V_2(PO_4)_3/C$ electrode, the oxidation peaks shift down to 3.66, 3.73, 4.13, and 4.57 V, respectively, while the reduction peaks shift up to 3.53, 3.61 and 3.92 V, respectively. Namely, all the anodic peaks shift to the higher potentials and cathodic peaks shift to lower potentials, and then the potential differences between anodic peaks and cathodic peaks become smaller. The well-defined peaks and smaller value of potential interval show the enhancement of electrode reaction reversibility.

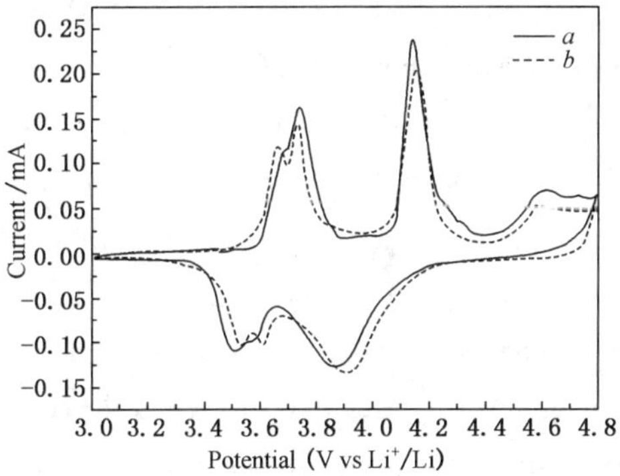

Fig. 9 CV curves of $Li_3V_2(PO_4)_3/C$ (a) and 4.5mol% MgO coated $Li_3V_2(PO_4)_3/C$ (b)

The cycling performances are presented in Fig. 10 for pristine $Li_3V_2(PO_4)_3/C$ and the MgO coated $Li_3V_2(PO_4)_3/C$ samples with various MgO amount. From Fig. 10, it can be seen that all the MgO coated $Li_3V_2(PO_4)_3/C$ samples exhibit higher initial discharge capacity than pristine sample, which may be due to the formation of a surface solid solution $Li_3Mg_xV_{2-x}(PO_4)_3$. In the case of MgO coated samples, low content MgO does not evidently improve the cycling performance. For example, the discharge capacity of MgO of 3.5mol% coated $Li_3V_2(PO_4)_3/C$ is similar to that of pristine $Li_3V_2(PO_4)_3/C$ after 100 cycles, and it is probable that the small amount MgO coated on $Li_3V_2(PO_4)_3/C$ is dissolved with increasing the cycle number. With increasing the amount of MgO, the samples exhibit excellent cycling performances. Especially for MgO of 4.5 mol% coated sample, the initial discharge capacity is 194.4 mAh g^{-1}, which is close to the theoretical discharge capacity of 197 mAh g^{-1}. Upon cycling, the discharge capacity degrades slowly and remains 137.5 mAh g^{-1} after 100 cycles, and the capacity retention is 70.73%, which is higher than that of pristine $Li_3V_2(PO_4)_3/C$, 43.7%. The phenomenon may be related to the following factors: (1) MgO acts as a protective layer to prevent the electro-active material core from direct contact with the electrolytes, and thus improves structural stability; (2) MgO coated suppresses the increase in resistances caused by repeated insertion-extraction of lithium ions during charge/discharge processes; (3) MgO coated enhances the reversibility of electrode reaction. However, when the amount of MgO is increased to 5.0 mol%, the initial discharge capacity and cycling stability are descended, which may be due to excessive amount of MgO. MgO of 4.5mol% coated on $Li_3V_2(PO_4)_3/C$ is reasonable to improve cycling performance.

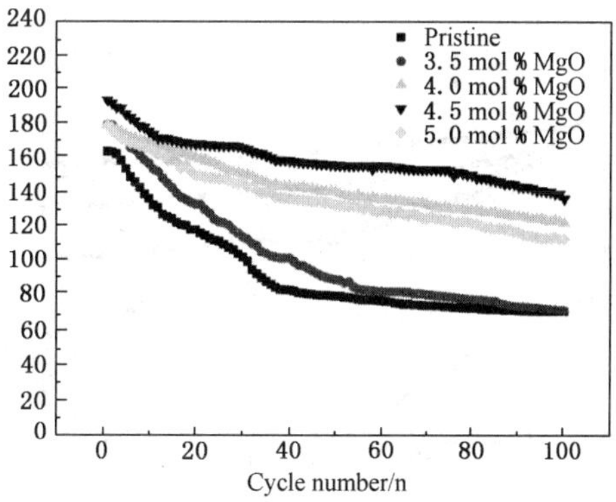

Fig. 10 Discharge capacity *vs.* cycles for $Li_3V_2(PO_4)_3/C$ and different amount of MgO coated $Li_3V_2(PO_4)_3/C$ at 40 mAg^{-1}

Rate performances of pristine $Li_3V_2(PO_4)_3/C$ and MgO of 4.5 mol% coated $Li_3V_2(PO_4)_3/C$ are given in Fig. 11. At 1C current density, it is obvious that the cyclability of MgO coated sample is better than that of pristine $Li_3V_2(PO_4)_3/C$, the initial discharge capacity is 157.81 mAh g^{-1} and the discharge capacity remains 137.02 mAh g^{-1} after 100 cycles, but the discharge capacity of pristine $Li_3V_2(PO_4)_3/C$ degrades sharply and falls from the initial 150.33 mAh g^{-1} to 64.39 mAh g^{-1} after 100 cycles. In addition, the cyclability of MgO of 4.5 mol% coated sample at 1.5 C and 2 C rates was tested, respectively. As shown in Fig. 10, MgO coated sample exhibits good rate performance. When current density is increased to 1.5 C and 2 C, the initial discharge capacity still reaches 157.29 mAh g^{-1} and 144.64 mAh g^{-1}, respectively, and the discharge capacity falls to 119.27 mAh g^{-1} and 97.79 mAh g^{-1} after 100 cycles, respectively.

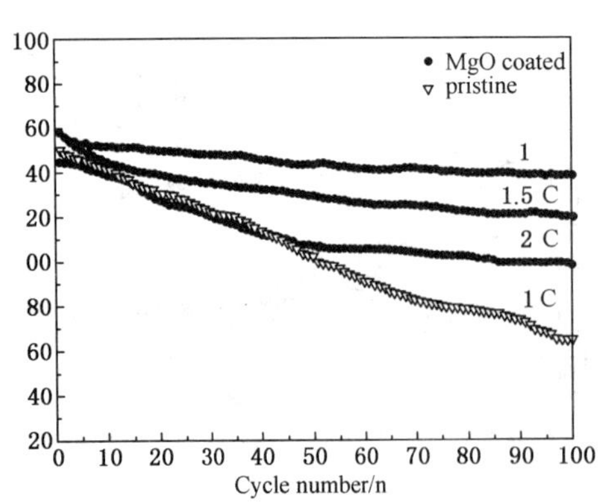

Fig. 11 Discharge capacity *vs*. cycles for $Li_3V_2(PO_4)_3/C$ and 4.5mol% MgO coated $Li_3V_2(PO_4)_3/C$ at different current density

4 Conclusions

MgO coating was performed on the surface of $Li_3V_2(PO_4)_3/C$. HRTEM image confirms that a MgO layer of 2.0—2.5 nm is coated on the surface of $Li_3V_2(PO_4)_3/C$ particles. The MgO nanocoating improves the structural stability of the cathode material, decreases the interface charge transfer resistance and enhances the reversibility of electrode reaction, and thus, remarkably improves the electrochemical performance of the cathode material. Both the initial discharge capacity and the cyclability of $Li_3V_2(PO_4)_3/C$ can be notably improved, particularly the rate performance. The nanocoating method could be a promising approach to improve the electrochemical properties of $Li_3V_2(PO_4)_3/C$ cathode material.

Acknowledgment

This work was financially supported by the National Natural Science Foundation of China (Grant No. 20771100).

References

[1] T. Kerr, J. Gaubicher, L. F. Nazar, Electrochem. Solid State Lett. 3 (2000) 460.

[2] X. F. Ouyang, M. Lei, S. Q. Shi, C. L. Luo, D. S. Liu, D. Y. Jiang, Z. Q. Ye, M. S. Lei, J. Alloys Compd. 476 (2009) 462.

[3] C. S. Sun, Z. Zhou, Z. G. Xu, D. G. Wang, J. P. Wei, X. K. Bian, J. Yan, J. Power Sources 193 (2009) 841.

[4] N. N. Bramnik, K. Nikolowski, D. M. Trots, H. Ehrenberg, Electrochem. Solid State

Lett. 11 (6) (2008) A89.

[5] S.-W. Kim, J. Kim, H. Gwon, K. Kang, J. Electrochem. Soc. 156 (8) (2009) A635.

[6] T. Shiratsuchi, S. Okada, T. Doi, J.-I. Yamaki, Electrochim. Acta 54 (2009) 3145.

[7] X. J. Zhu, Y. X. Liu, L. M. Geng, L. B. Chen, H. X. Liu, M. H. Cao, Solid State Ionics 179 (2008) 1679.

[8] Q. Q. Chen, J. M. Wang, Z. Tang, W. C. He, H. B. Shao, J. Q. Zhang, Electrochim. Acta 52 (2007) 5251.

[9] H. Huang, T. Faulkner, J. Barker, M. Y. Saidi, J. Power Sources 189 (2009) 748.

[10] A. K. Padhi, K. S. Nanjundaswamy, J. B. Goodenough, J. Electrochem. Soc. 144 (1997) 1188.

[11] S. Q. Liu, S. C. Li, K. L. Huang, Z. H. Chen, Acta Phys. Chim. Sin. 23 (4) (2007) 537.

[12] M. M. Ren, Z. Zhou, Y. Z. Li, X. P. Gao, J. Yan, J. Power Sources 162 (2006) 1357.

[13] Q. Kuang, Y. M. Zhao, X. N. An, J. M. Liu, Y. Z. Dong, L. Chen, Electrochim. Acta 55 (2010) 1575.

[14] S. Q. Liu, S. C. Li, K. L. Huang, B. L. Gong, G. Zhang, J. Alloys Compd. 450 (2008) 499.

[15] C. X. Chang, J. F. Xiang, X. X. Shi, X. Y. Han, L. J. Yuan, J. T. Sun, Electrochim. Acta 53 (2008) 2232.

[16] L. J. Wang, X. C. Zhou, Y. L. Guo, J. Power Sources 195 (2010) 2844.

[17] T. Jiang, Y. J. Wei, W. C. Pan, Z. Li, X. Ming, G. Chen, C. Z. Wang, J. Alloys Compd. 488 (2009) L26.

[18] H. Liu, G. X. Wang, D. Wexler, J. Z. Wang, H. K. Liu, Electrochem. Commun. 10 (2008) 165.

[19] M. Y. Saidi, J. Barker, H. Huang, J. L. Swoyer, G. Adamson, Electrochem. Solid State Lett. 5 (2002) A149.

[20] M. Mladenov, R. Stoyanova, E. Zhecheva, S. Vassilev, Electrochem. Commun. 3 (2001) 410.

[21] R. Alcantara, M. Jaraba, P. Lavela, J. L. Tirado, J. Electroanal. Chem. 566 (2004) 187.

[22] Y. Z. Li, Z. Zhou, X. P. Gao, J. Yan, Electrochim. Acta 52 (2007) 4922.

[23] G. X. Wang, L. Yang, Y. Chen, Electrochim. Acta 50 (2005) 4649.

[24] M. Y. Saidi, J. Barker, H. Huang, J. L. Swoyer, G. Adamson, J. Power Sources 119-121 (2003) 266.

Effect of Al_2O_3-coating on the Electrochemical Performances of $Li_3V_2(PO_4)_3$/C Cathode Material①

Zhai Jing[a], Zhao Minshou[b], Wang Yanzhi

([a] Key Laboratory of Applied Chemistry, Hebei Province, College of Environmental and Chemical Engineering, Yanshan University, Qinhuangdao 066004, China)

([b] State Key Laboratory of Metastable Material Science and Technology, Yanshan University, Qinhuangdao 066004, China)

Abstract: The effect of Al_2O_3-coating on $Li_3V_2(PO_4)_3$/C cathode material for lithium-ion batteries has been investigated. The crystalline structure and morphology of the synthesized powders have been characterized by XRD, SEM, and HRTEM, and their electrochemical performances are evaluated by CV, EIS, and galvanostatic charge/discharge tests. It is found that Al_2O_3-coating modification stabilizes the structure of the cathode material, decreases the polarization of electrode and suppresses the rise of the surface film resistance. Electrochemical tests indicate that cycling performance and rate capability of Al_2O_3-coated $Li_3V_2(PO_4)_3$/C are enhanced, especially at high rates. The Al_2O_3-coated material delivers discharge capacity of 123.03 mAh g^{-1} at 4C rate, and the capacity retention of 94.15 % is obtained after 5 cycles. The results indicate that Al_2O_3-coating should be an effective way to improve the comprehensive properties of the cathode materials for lithium-ion batteries.

Key words: Cathodematerial; Al_2O_3-coating; $Li_3V_2(PO_4)_3$; Electrochemical performance

Introduction

Lithium-ion batteries have widely been successfully utilized in various portable electronic devices and are considered as an ideal candidate for power sources in future electric vehicles [1]. Unfortunately, the conventional cathode material cannot be applied in large scale due to various drawbacks, such as cost and safety. Recently, phosphate-based materials such as $LiMPO_4$ (M = Fe, Co, Ni, Mn) [2-5] and $Li_3M_2(PO_4)_3$ (M=Fe, V) [6-8] have been discovered as potential cathode candidates for lithium-ion batteries. Among these materials, monoclinic $Li_3V_2(PO_4)_3$ (LVP) is the most appealing because of its high ionic diffusion coefficient, capacity and remarkable thermal stability. However, the intrinsic low electronic conductivity limits the practical implementation of the LVP material. In order to solve the problem, doping with alien atoms [9-11], coating conductive carbon

① J. Solid State Electrochem, 2014(18): 2857-2862.

[12-14], and reducing the particle size [6,15] have been proposed. Recent reports indicated that coating cathode material with metal oxides, such as ZrO_2 [16], CeO_2 [17], and CuO [18], was an effective way to overcome its drawbacks and improved the electrochemical properties. However, there have been no reports to describe Al_2O_3-coating effect on the $Li_3V_2(PO_4)_3$ cathode material. In this work, Al_2O_3 was coated on the surface of $Li_3V2(PO_4)_3$/C particles. The effect of coating on the structure and the electrochemical performances of $Li_3V_2(PO_4)_3$/C cathode material was studied in detail.

Experimental

$Li_3V_2(PO_4)_3$/C used as the original material was first prepared as described in our previous work [19]. For preparation of Al_2O_3-coating $Li_3V_2(PO_4)$/C sample, $Li_3V_2(PO_4)_3$/C (1.50 g) powder was dispersed in 99.90 mL $NaHCO_3$ solution (0.01 mol L^{-1}) by ultrasonic agitation for 1 h and continuously stirring at room temperature. Then, the suspension was stirred violently while 16.65 mL $Al_2(SO_4)_3$ solution (0.01 mol L^{-1}) was slowly dropped into it, and after 20 min, the final powder was filtered under suction and washed several times with deionized water, and subsequently dried in a vacuum box at 80 ℃ for 12 h. The dried powder was slightly ground, pressed into pellets, and then sintered at 600 ℃ for 2 h in N_2 atmosphere, so the Al_2O_3-coated $Li_3V_2(PO_4)_3$/C material was obtained. The nominal Al_2O_3 amount was $Li_3V_2(PO_4)_3$/C powder of 4.5 mol%.

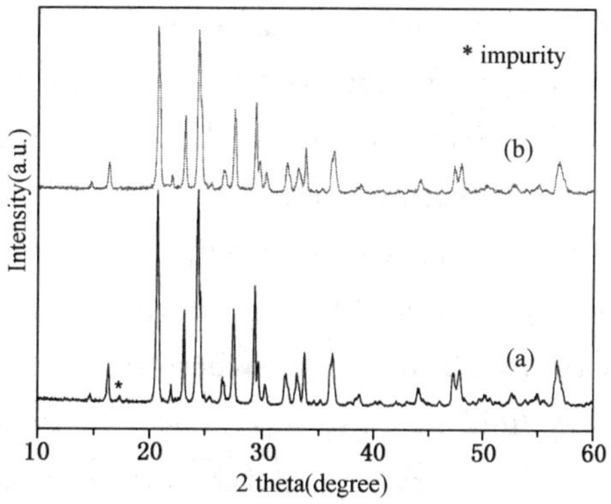

Fig. 1 XRD patterns of bare (a) and Al_2O_3-coated $Li_3V_2(PO_4)_3$/C (b)

The phase identification of the bare and Al_2O_3-coated $Li_3V_2(PO_4)_3$/C powders was conducted with a D/Max-2500/PC X-ray diffractometer (Cu Kα radiation). The surface morphology of the samples was observed by a Hitachi S-4800 scanning electron microscopy instrument (SEM), respectively. The microstructures of the coated particles were examined by a JEM-2010 transmission electron microscope. The content of element in the coated sample was measured with ICAP 6300 Radial.

Electrochemical performances of the samples were evaluated in columned test cells. To prepare the electrodes used for the electrochemical performance measurement, the powders of the bare and Al_2O_3-coated $Li_3V_2(PO_4)_3$/C were mixed with acetylene black and polyvinylidine fluoride (PVDF) binder in a weight ratio of 80 : 15 : 5 in *N*-methyl-2-pyrrolidone (NMP) to ensure the homogeneity, respectively. The obtained slurry was coated on Al foil, dried under the infrared light and cut into four square strips of 8 mm × 8 mm in size, and the mass of active material is about 2.0 mg on the electrode. After the strips were dried in a vacuum box at 120 ℃ for 12 h, two electrode electrochemical cells were assembled in a Mikrouna glove box filled with high-purity argon where the lithium metal foil was used as anode, Celgard® 2320 as separator, and 1 M LiPF6 in EC : DMC (1 : 1 vol. %) was used as electrolyte, and then, charge/discharge test was carried out using a Neware Battery Tester. The electrochemical measurements were performed in the voltage range of 3.0—4.8 V at room temperature. Electrochemical impedance spectroscopy (EIS) measurements were carried out by using CHI 660A electrochemical analyzer (Chenhua, Shanghai, China) with a ±5 mV ac signal and a frequency range from 10^{-2} to 10^{5} Hz. Cyclic voltammograms were obtained on a ZF-9 potentiostat by scanning electrode potential at the rate of 5 $mVmin^{-1}$ between 3.0 and 4.8 V.

Results and discussion

Structure characteristic

Powder X-ray diffraction patterns of the bare and Al_2O_3-coated $Li_3V_2(PO_4)_3$/C composite synthesized are shown in Fig. 1. Except for the impure peak of the bare sample at about 17°, diffraction peaks of both samples can be indexed as monoclinic structure with space group 14 ($P2_1/n$) and are consistent with the published result [20]. The disappearance of impurity peak in Al_2O_3-coated $Li_3V_2(PO_4)_3$/C may be attributed to the second calcination. Additionally, no peaks related to carbon and Al_2O_3 are observed in the X-ray diffraction (XRD) patterns for Al_2O_3-coated $Li_3V_2(PO_4)_3$/C due to their amorphous or low content, which is similar to the result reported in literature [21]. The SEM images of the bare and Al_2O_3-coated $Li_3V_2(PO_4)_3$/C materials are presented in Fig. 2(a) and (b), respectively. It can be seen that the particle size and distribution of $Li_3V_2(PO_4)_3$/C material have no obvious changes after coating modification. The particle size is about hundreds nanometers. To further investigate the microstructure of the as-prepared particles, TEM and high-resolution transmission electron microscopy (HRTEM) are carried out. Fig. 3 shows TEM images of (a) $Li_3V_2(PO_4)_3$/C, (b) a single Al_2O_3-coated $Li_3V_2(PO_4)_3$/C particle, and (c) the HRTEM image of selected area for a single Al_2O_3-coated $Li_3V_2(PO_4)_3$/C particle. HRTEM in Fig. 3c presents clear lattice fringe with dspace of 0.36 nm corresponding to (121) plane of monoclinic LVP and an amorphous layer with 1.5—2.0 nm in thickness on the surface of Al_2O_3-coated $Li_3V_2(PO_4)_3$/C particle. The coating layer should be the mixture of carbon and Al_2O_3, as supported by EDS spot and inductively coupled plasma-atomic emission spectrometry (ICP-AES) analysis shown in Fig. 4 and Table 1. According to element analysis results from ICP-AES, we can see that the content of Li, V, Al, and P are basically consistent with theoretical value. The results give unequivocal evidence to the presence of Al_2O_3 coating on the surface of $Li_3V_2(PO_4)_3/C$.

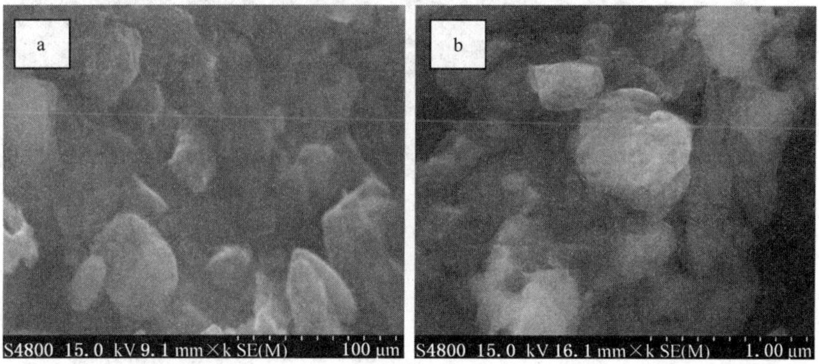

Fig. 2 SEM images of bare (a) and Al_2O_3-coated $Li_3V_2(PO_4)_3/C$ (b)

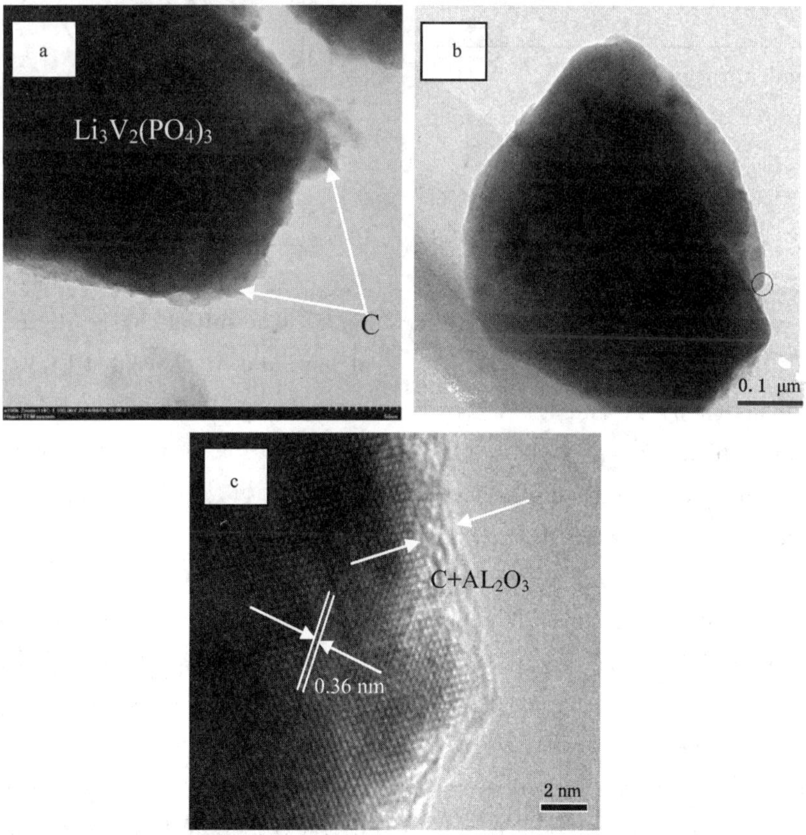

Fig. 3 TEM images of (a) $Li_3V_2(PO_4)_3/C$ and (b) Al_2O_3-coated $Li_3V_2(PO_4)_3/C$ single particle and (c) HRTEM image of Al_2O_3-coated $Li_3V_2(PO_4)_3/C$

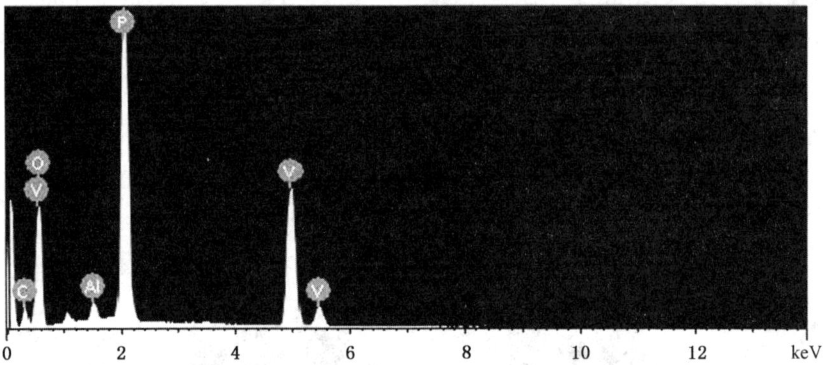

Fig. 4　EDS image of Al_2O_3-coated $Li_3V_2(PO_4)_3/C$

Table 1　Results of ICPAES analysis

Element	Ion concentration/(vg/mL)
Li	4.89
P	21.82
V	23.94
Al	0.57

Electrochemical property

Fig. 5 depicts the initial charge and discharge curves of the bare and Al_2O_3-coated $Li_3V_2(PO_4)_3/C$ electrode at 0.2 C (1 C=197 mA g^{-1}) rate in the range of 3.0—4.8 V. It can be seen that the two electrodes exhibit four charge plateaus (3.6, 3.7, 4.1 and 4.6 V) and three discharge plateaus (3.5, 3.6 and 3.9 V), respectively, which are in agreement with the results of the cyclic voltammetry (CV) curves (Fig. 8). Compared with the bare one, Al_2O_3-coated $Li_3V_2(PO_4)_3/C$ has smaller potential differences between the charge plateau and discharge plateau. It indicates that Al_2O_3-coated $Li_3V_2(PO_4)_3/C$ electrode has lower polarization in charge and discharge processes. The lower electrochemical polarization leads to better electrochemical property. The evidence demonstrates that the cycling performance and rate performance of Al_2O_3-coated $Li_3V_2(PO_4)_3/C$ are superior to that of the bare one.

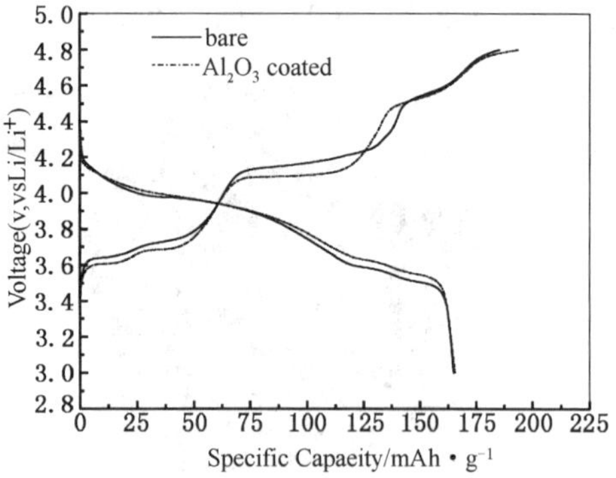

Fig. 5　The initial charge/discharge curves of bare and Al_2O_3-coated $Li_3V_2(PO_4)_3/C$

To further understand the role of Al_2O_3 coating on the electrochemical performance of $Li_3V_2(PO_4)_3/C$ material, electrochemical impedance spectroscopy measurements were used to study the electrode reaction kinetics of two different samples, and they were carried out at the state of fully discharged in the tenth cycles. As shown in Fig. 6, there are three regions of both curves, which include an intercept at high frequency due to the resistance of the electrolyte and electrode, a depressed semi-circle in the high-to-middle frequency range related to the resistance of the film that covers the surface of the cathode material and the charge-transfer resistance, and an inclined line in the low frequency range attributed to Warburg impedance. Their spectra of Nyquist plots were analyzed by fitting to an equivalent electrical circuit shown in Fig. 7 [22]. Here, R_s is the resistance of the electrolyte and electrode; $R_{(sf+ct)}$ is the resistance of surface film (sf) and charge transfer (ct), W_0 is Warburg impedance, and constant phase element CPE represents the double-layer capacitance. The values of R_s and $R_{(sf+ct)}$ are listed in Table 2, respectively. It can be seen that R_s is similar for both electrodes. This is because the same electrolyte is used when the test cells are assembled. The $R_{(sf+ct)}$ at Al_2O_3-coated $Li_3V_2(PO_4)_3/C$ electrode is much less than that at the bare one after 10 cycles, which may be due to the following two reasons: one is that Al_2O_3 coating improves the structural stability of Al_2O_3-coated $Li_3V_2(PO_4)_3/C$ after 10 cycles, and the other one is that Al_2O_3 coating suppresses the rise of the surface film resistance. The impedance of CPE is so small that it can be negligible.

The initial CV curves for the bare and Al_2O_3-coated $Li_3V_2(PO_4)_3/C$ are shown in Fig. 8. It can be found that both curves show a similar profile, and there are four oxidation peaks and three reduction peaks in the CV curves, which are consistent with the charge/discharge plateaus presented in Fig. 5 and previous publication [21]. In Fig. 8, there are some apparent differences between the two curves though the shape does not change greatly. First, the current of the oxidation peaks for the Al_2O_3-coated $Li_3V_2(PO_4)_3/C$ electrode is bigger than that of the bare electrode, indicating enhancement of electrocatalyzing activity. Second, the potential differences between anodic peaks and cathodic peaks become smaller, showing the decrease of electrode polarization and the improvement of electrode reaction reversibility.

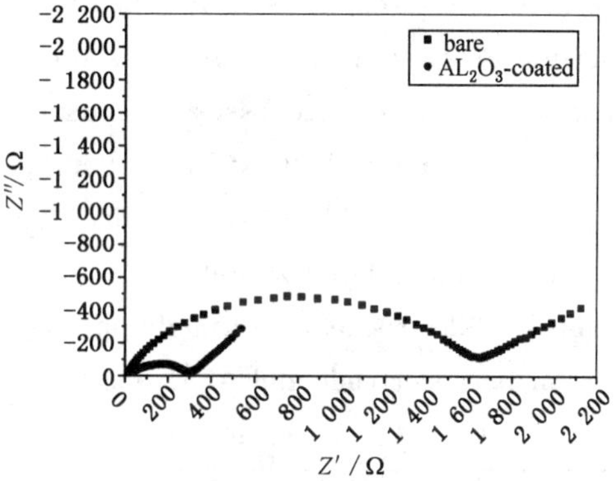

Fig. 6 EIS of bare and Al_2O_3-coated $Li_3V_2(PO_4)_3/C$

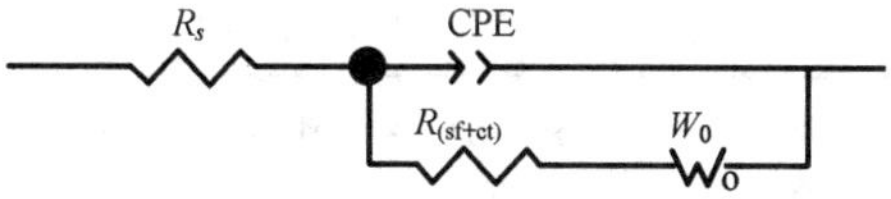

Fig. 7 Equivalent circuit

The cycling performance profile of the bare and Al_2O_3-coated $Li_3V_2(PO_4)_3/C$ at 0.2 C rate are shown in Fig. 9. It is apparent that Al_2O_3-coated electrode exhibits better cycling performance than the bare. For the coated electrode, the discharge capacity decreases from initial 165.1 to 124 mAh g^{-1} after 100 cycles and the capacity retention is 75.1 %, but for the bare one, the discharge capacity decreases from initial 164.2 to 72.7 mAh g^{-1} after 100 cycles and the capacity retention is only 44.3 %. The phenomenon may be related to the following factors: Firstly, the Al_2O_3 and carbon form an integrated and continuous coating on the surface of the $Li_3V_2(PO_4)_3$ particles. This coating acts as a protective layer to prevent the electroactive material core from direct contact with the electrolyte and thus improves structural stability; secondly, Al_2O_3 coated decreases charge transfer resistance caused by repeated insertion-extraction of lithium ions during charge/discharge processes because of the improvement of the structural stability; and finally, Al_2O_3 coated decreases electrochemical polarization.

Table 2　Electrochemical kinetic parameter of bare electrode and Al_2O_3-coated $Li_3V_2(PO_4)_3$/C electrode

Material	R_s/Ω	$R_{(sf+ct)}/\Omega$
$Li_3V_2(PO_4)_3$/C	12.18	1 649
Al_2O_3-coated $Li_3V_2(PO_4)_3$/C	16.63	290.4

Rate performances of the bare and Al_2O_3-coated $Li_3V_2(PO_4)_3$/C at different rates are shown in Fig. 10. It can be seen that the discharge capacity of Al_2O_3-coated $Li_3V_2(PO_4)_3$/C is slightly higher than that of the bare one at low rate. The discharge capacity of the bare one declines rapidly with increasing the discharge rates, whereas Al_2O_3-coated $Li_3V_2(PO_4)_3$/C exhibits a steady cycle performance. For example, when the charge-discharge rate reaches to 4 C, the initial discharge capacity of the coated sample is 123.03 mAh g^{-1} and the capacity retention is 94.15% after 5 cycles, while that of the bare one is only 97.11 mAh g^{-1} and 82.33%, respectively. The result indicates that Al_2O_3 surface modification can greatly improve the high rate performance of $Li_3V_2(PO_4)_3$/C cathode.

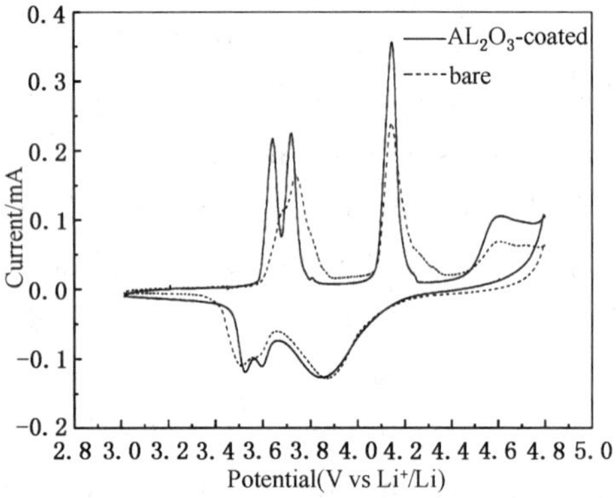

Fig. 8　CV curves of bare and Al_2O_3-coated $Li_3V_2(PO_4)_3$/C

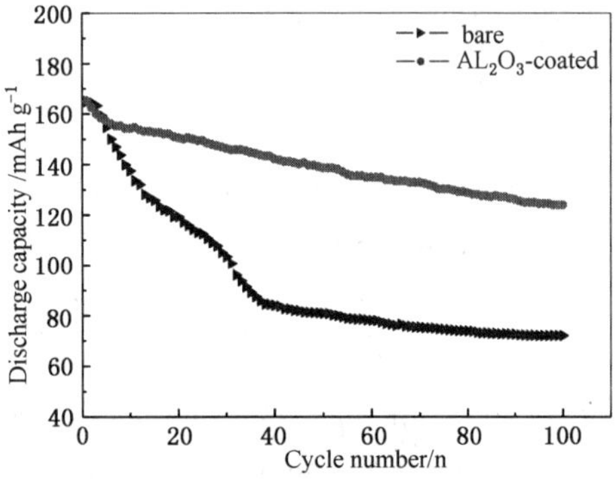

Fig. 9　Cycling performance of bare and Al_2O_3-coated $Li_3V_2(PO_4)_3$/C at 0.2-C current density

Conclusion

Al_2O_3-coated $Li_3V_2(PO_4)_3$/C powder has been synthesized. HRTEM results corroborate that Al_2O_3 thin layer is formed on the surface of the $Li_3V_2(PO_4)_3/C$ particles. After coating, significantly improved cycle stability and rate performance are achieved. The result is likely attributed to the decrease of electrode polarization, improving of the structural stability, and suppression of rise for the surface film resistance. It suggests that Al_2O_3-coating method could be a promising approach to improve electrochemical properties of $Li_3V_2(PO_4)_3/C$ cathode material.

Acknowledgments

This work was financially supported by the Natural Science Foundation of Hebei Province (Contact No. B2011203074).

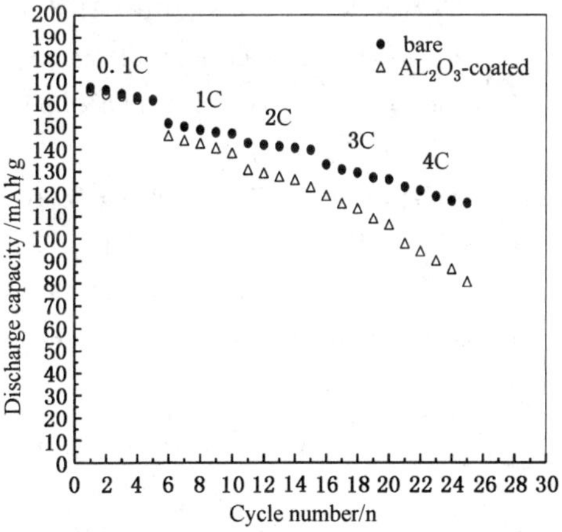

Fig. 10 Rate performances of bare and Al_2O_3-coated $Li_3V_2(PO_4)_3/C$ at different rates

References

[1] Scrosati B, Garche J (2010) Lithium batteries: status, prospects and future. J Power Sources 195:2419-2430.

[2] Padhi AK, Nanjundaswamy KS, Goodenough JB (1997) Phosphoolivines as positive-electrode materials for rechargeable lithium batteries. J Electrochem Soc 144:1188-1194.

[3] Wolfenstine J, Allen J (2005) Ni^{3+}/Ni^{2+} redox potential in $LiNiPO_4$. J Power Sources 142:389-390.

[4] Yang J, Xu JJ (2006) Synthesis and characterization of carbon-coated lithium transition metal phosphates $LiMPO_4$ (M=Fe, Mn, Co, Ni) prepared via a nonaqueous sol-gel route. J Electrochem Soc 153:A716-A723.

[5] Li HH, Jin J, Wei JP, Zhou Z, Yan J (2009) Fast synthesis of coreshell $LiCoPO_4/C$ nanocomposite via microwave heating and its electrochemical Li intercalation performances. Electrochem Commun 11:95-98.

[6] HuangH, Yin SC, Kerr T, Taylor N, Nazar LF (2002) Nanostructured composites: a high capacity, fast rate $Li_3V_2(PO_4)_3$/carbon cathode for rechargeable lithium batteries. Adv Mater 14:1525-1528.

[7] Yin SC, Strobel PS, Grondey H, Nazar LF (2004) $Li_{2.5}V_2(PO_4)_3$: a room-temperature analogue to the fast-ion conducting hightemperature γ-phase of $Li_3V_2(PO_4)_3$. Chem Mater 16:1456-1465.

[8] Wang LN, Li ZC, Xu HJ, Zhang KL (2008) Studies of $Li_3V_2(PO_4)_3$ additives for the $LiFePO_4$-based Li-ion batteries. J Phys Chem C 112:308-312.

[9] Dong YZ, Zhao YM, Duan H (2011) The effect of doping Mg^{2+} on the structure and electrochemical properties of $Li_3V_2(PO_4)_3$ cathode materials for lithium-ion batteries. J Electroanal Chem 660:14-21.

[10] Yuan W, Yan J, Tang ZY, Sha O, Wang JM, Mao WF, Ma L (2012) Mo-doped $Li_3V_2(PO_4)_3/C$ cathode material with high rate capability and long term cyclic stability. Electrochim Acta 72:138-142.

[11] Huang JS, Yang L, Liu KY, Tang YF

(2010) Synthesis and characterization of $Li_3V_{(2-2x/3)}Mg_x(PO_4)_3/C$ cathode material for lithiumion batteries. J Power Sources 195:5013-5018.

[12] Rui XH, Ding N, Liu J, Li C, Chen CH (2010) Analysis of the chemical diffusion coefficient of lithium ions in $Li_3V_2(PO_4)_3$ cathode material. Electrochim Acta 55: 2384-2390.

[13] Qiao YQ, Wang XL, Zhou Y, Xiang JY, Zhang D, Shi SJ, Tu JP (2010) Electrochemical performance of carbon-coated $Li_3V_2(PO_4)_3$ cathode materials derived from polystyrene-based carbon-thermal reduction synthesis. Electrochim Acta 56:510-516.

[14] Jiang T, PanWC, Wang J, Bie XF, Du F, Wei YL, Wang CZ, Chen G (2010) Carbon coated $Li_3V_2(PO_4)_3$ cathode material prepared by a PVA assisted sol-gel method. Electrochim Acta 55:3864-3869.

[15] Pan AQ, Liu J, Zhang JG, XuW, Gao GZ, Nie ZM, Arey BW, Liang SQ (2010) Nanostructured $Li_3V_2(PO_4)_3$/carbon composite for highrate lithium-ion batteries. Electrochem Commun 12:1674-1677.

[16] Amaresh S, Karthikeyan K, Kima KJ, Kima MC, Chung KY, Cho BW, Lee YS (2013) Facile synthesis of ZrO_2 coated Li_2CoPO_4F cathode materials for lithium secondary batteries with improved electrochemical properties. J Power Sources 244:395-402.

[17] Yao JW, Wu F, Qiu XP, Li N, Su YF (2011) Effect of CeO_2-coating on the electrochemical performances of $LiFePO_4/C$ cathode material. Electrochim Acta 56: 5587-5592.

[18] Cui Y, Zhao X, Guo RS (2010) Enhanced electrochemical properties of $LiFePO_4$ cathode material by CuO and carbon co-coating. J Alloys Compd 490:236-240.

[19] Zhai J, Zhao MS, Wang DD, Qiao YQ (2010) Effect of MgO nanolayer coated on $Li_3V_2(PO_4)_3/C$ cathode material for lithium ion battery. J Alloys Compd 502:401-406.

[20] Saidi MY, Barker J, Huang H, Swoyer JL, Adamson G (2002) Electrochemical properties of lithium vanadium phosphate as a cathode material for lithium-ion batteries. Electrochem Solid-State Lett 5:A149-A151.

[21] Cui Y, Zhao XL, Guo RS (2010) High rate electrochemical performances of nanosized ZnO and carbon co-coated $LiFePO_4$ cathode. Mater Res Bull 45:844-849.

[22] Wang GX, Yang L, Chen Y, Wang JZ, Bewlay S, Liu HK (2005) An investigation of polypyrrole-$LiFePO_4$ composite cathode materials for lithium-ion batteries. Electrochim Acta 50:4649-4654.

A Novel Hydrothermal Synthesis and Characterisation of Porous Mn_3O_4 for Supercapacitors with High Rate Capability①

Yang Fengyu[a], Zhao Minshou[a,b], Sun Qujiang[a], Qiao Yuqing[a]
([a] College of Environmental and Chemical Engineering, Yanshan University, Qinhuangdao 066004, China.)
([b] State Key Laboratory of Metastable Material Science and Technology, Yanshan University, Qinhuangdao 066004, China)

Abstract: Porous nanostructured Mn_3O_4 particles were successfully synthesized by a novel hydrothermal method *via* adding the surfactant hexadecyltrimethylammonium bromide (CTAB). They were characterized by the techniques of thermogravimetric and differential thermal analysis (TG/DTA), X-ray difiraction (XRD), field emission scanning electron microscopy (SEM), transmission electron microscopy (TEM), and N_2-adsorption. The electrochemical performance of the sample was studied by galvanostatic charge-discharge, cyclic voltammetry and electrochemical impedance spectroscopy in 1 M Na_2SO_4 aqueous solution electrolyte. It exhibits a high specific capacitance (232.5 F g^{-1} at 0.5 A g^{-1}) and good rate capability (190 F g^{-1} at 5 A g^{-1}), which can be attributed to its porous structure, the defects and vacancies on the surface. The capacitance retention reaches 78% after 5 000 cycles at a current density of 5 A g^{-1}. The results show that Mn_3O_4 has the potential to be used as the electrode material for a supercapacitor with high performance.

Introduction

In the 21st century, the rapid development of the economy and great social progress require many kinds of energy storage and conversion devices, and more research on alternative energy storage and conversion devices is critical. Supercapacitors have attracted much attention for their high power density, excellent reversibility and long cycling life. [1] On the basis of the energy storage mechanism, supercapacitors can be divided into two kinds, namely, electrochemical double-layer capacitors (EDLCS) which store energy between the electrode and electrolyte interfaces simply *via* ion adsorption and desorption, and pseudo-capacitor which undergo a fast and reversible Faradaic reaction. [2,3] Always, the transition metal oxides present high specific capacitance from both double-layer capacitances and pseudo-capacitances, and have a bright prospect in the future. Thus, it is

① RSC A dv., 2015(5): 9843-9847.

of great significance to carry out research on transition metal oxides used as the supercapacitor electrode material.

Among the various transition metal oxides, manganese oxides (MnO_x) have been investigated as the most promising electrode material,[4-6] because they are low-cost and environmentally kindly while still provide a large theoretical capacitance. Pang *et al.* [7] have synthesized a Cu-MnO_2 composite which has a high specific capacity of 1024 F g^{-1} at 1.5 A g^{-1}. As far as we know, only a few reports [8-11] were related to the electrochemical capacitive properties of Mn_3O_4.

It has been noted that the electrochemical capacitive behavior of nanomaterial strongly depends on the size, shape, and the porosity of internal structure.[12,13] Herein, we employ a novel solvent for the hydrothermal method and a surfactant-assistant strategy, a cooperative self-assembly of inorganic species and surfactants to synthesize the mesoporous Mn_3O_4. When the as-obtained Mn_3O_4 is used as supercapacitor electrode material, it exhibits a high specie capacitance (232.5 F g^{-1} at 0.5 A g^{-1}), a good rate capability (190 F g^{-1} at 5 A g^{-1}), and the capacitance retention reaches to 78% after 5 000 cycles at a current density of 5 A g^{-1}.

Experimental

Sample preparation

In a typical synthesis of Mn_3O_4, 0.2 g hexadecyltrimethyl-ammonium bromide (CTAB) dissolved in *N*, *N*-dimethyl-formamide (DMF) with stirring for 1 h to form a stable solution. Then 0.01 mol of $Mn(CH_3COO)_2 \cdot 4H_2O$ was added into the above solution. Followed by stirring for 1 h, 0.6 g urea was introduced into the solution. Until the reactant dissolved completely, the mixed solution was transferred to a Teflon-lined stainless steel autoclave (100 mL) and heated in an electric oven at 140 ℃ for 4 h. The resultant was separated by vacuum filtration, washed with DI water and ethanol, and dried at 60 ℃ under vacuum for 8 h. Mn_3O_4 obtained was heated at 300 ℃ for 5 h in air atmosphere. For comparison, samples without the surfactant of CTAB (WS-Mn_3O_4) were also prepared using the similar route.

Material characterization

X-ray diffraction (XRD) pattern of the sample was recorded by RIGAKU D/max-2500 using Cu Kα radiation (λ = 0.15406 nm) at 40 kV and 100 mA. The patterns were obtained in 2θ ranges between 10° and 90° at a scanning rate of 4° min^{-1} · SEM was performed on a field emission Hitachi S-4800 instrument operating at an accelerating voltage of 10 kV. TEM was performed using Hitachi HT7700 instrument with a field emission gun operating at 200 kV to examine the morphologies. Nitrogen adsorption measurements were performed on a Micromeritics ASAP 2020 adsorption analyzer. Specific surface areas were calculated by the Brunaure-Emmert-Teller (BET) method. Pore volumes and sizes were estimated from the pore size distribution curves from the adsorption isotherms using the Barrett-Joyner-Halenda (BJH) method. TG/DTA was performed at a heating rate of 4 ℃ in flowing air by the Japanese Matsu Atsu analysis workstation TA-60WS.

Preparation of electrode

The working electrodes of Mn_3O_4 were prepared as follow. Primarily, Mn_3O_4 (70 wt%), polyvinylidenefluoride (a binder, 10 wt%) and acetylene black (20 wt%) was mixed in *N*-methyl pyrrolidinone, grinded for half an hour in a mortar, thus the slurry was obtained and then was coated on a foam nickel plate about 1 cm^2, and the plate was dried at 120 ℃ under vacuum, the coating weight was fixed about 1 mg.

Electrochemical characterization

The electrochemical performance of Mn_3O_4 was examined by CV, galvanostatic charge and discharge measurement. Cyclic voltammetry measurements were performed on a CHI660E electrochemical workstation. Galvanostatic charge and discharge measurements were carried on a Neware BTS-5V10mA multichannel battery testing system. The electrochemical cell was a three electrode configuration, the above plate attached to a nickel wire as working electrode, a platinum plate as a counter electrode and a saturated calomel electrode (SCE) as the reference electrode. All the electrochemical measurements were carried out in 1 M Na_2SO_4 electrolyte. CV measurement was performed over the potential range of 0 V to 1.0 V at the scan rate of 1, 5, 10, 50 and 100 mV s^{-1}, respectively. Galvanostatic charge-discharge curves were measured at diffrent current densities from 0.5 A g^{-1} to 5 A g^{-1}. Electro-chemical impedance spectroscopy was also performed on a CHI660E electrochemical workstation over a frequency range from 10^5 Hz to 0.1 Hz.

Results and discussion

Structures characterization

The porous Mn_3O_4 nanoparticles were prepared by a hydro-thermal reaction, followed by a thermal annealing, and the annealing temperature is critical for controlling the phase, morphology and crystallinity of the final resultant of reaction,[14] which will have much influence on the capacitive properties.

Therefore, we have studied the thermal-annealing behavior of the precursor under air atmosphere. The thermogravimetric and differential thermal analysis curves are shown in Fig. 1. The weight loss below 100 ℃ corresponds to the loss of remaining ethanol and adsorbed water in the precursor, and the weight loss in the temperature region of 200—245 ℃ is related to the formation of Mn_3O_4, while the weight gain in the temperature region of 460—510 ℃ corresponds to the phase conversion. The DTA curve shows a small exothermic peak at 160.02 ℃, which is related to the decomposition of trace surfactant CTAB. The obvious peak, located at 236.98 ℃, is also related to the formation of Mn_3O_4, and another smaller peak is located at 472.28 ℃, where a solid-state reaction occurs with the phase transformation. While further increasing temperature, the TG curve almost keeps a constant value until 800 ℃. Referred to the related paper,[15] finally we determined the annealing temperature is 300 ℃.

The structure and phase of the sample was characterized by X-ray diffraction, as shown in Fig. 2. All peaks could be indexed to a tetragonal Hausmannite Mn_3O_4 with space group $I4_1/amd$ (PDF #01-1127). No other crystalline phases were observed. Hausmannite Mn_3O_4 crystal structure has been observed from the XRD pattern, and the peak positions agree well with the PDF card no. 01-1127 with 18.02°, 29.02°, 32.53°, 36.00°, 44.04°, 50.46°, 53.78°, 56.30°, 60.08°, 64.64°, 70.06°, 74.01°, 80.70° and 86.95° at 2θ, which correspond to the (101), (112), (103), (211), (220), (105), (312), (303), (224), (314), (305), (413), (316), and (415) planes of body centered tetragonal manganese oxide for the Mn_3O_4 nanoparticles, respectively. From the width of diffraction peaks and using the Scherrer equation, we estimate a nanoparticle size of around 10 nm.

Morphology characterization

The morphology of the Mn_3O_4 nanoparticles was investigated by FESEM and TEM. Fig. 3a and b shows the SEM images of the Mn_3O_4 nanoparticles. These images present a partially attached particle structure and almost uniform spherical shape nanoparticles. Because the size of the particle' is so small, about 10 nm, that it is liable to aggregate to spherical particles, which look to be larger in the Fig. 3b. Also, there are some vacancies and defects on the surface of the sphere, thus, it seems to be unsmooth. It is probably due to the effect of the CTAB surfactant micelle, which provides the soft template and can decompose to result in porous structure. The vacancies and defects are beneficial to the electron transport and redox reaction, which can improve the electrochemical performance of the Mn_3O_4 as the supercapacitor electrode material to some extent. Fig. 3c shows the TEM images of the Mn_3O_4 nanoparticles. From the images, we could observe the size of a particle is about 9 nm, which is in accord with the result come from the Scherrer equation. The formation of uniform nanoparticles can also be noted in the images, and the uniform structure helps in efficient electron transport at the interface of the electrode/electrolyte. Fig. 3d is a high-resolution transmission electron microscopy (HR-TEM) image of the nanoparticles, from which the lattice fringes of Mn_3O_4 can be identified in [211], [103] and [112] planes with matching d-spacing of 0.247, 0.276 and 0.308 nm, respectively.[16] WS-Mn_3O_4 samples are characterized for comparison also, whose shape and size are in random, Also the aggregation terribly occured among the particles (ESI Fig. S1 †).

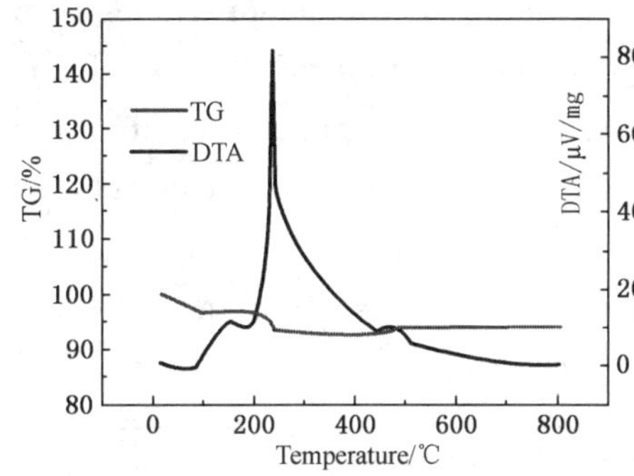

Fig. 1 Thermogravimetric and differential thermal analysis

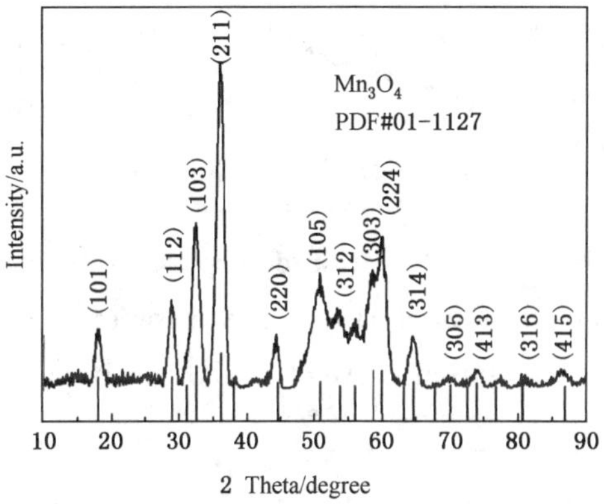

Fig. 2 XRD pattern of Mn_3O_4 nanoparticles

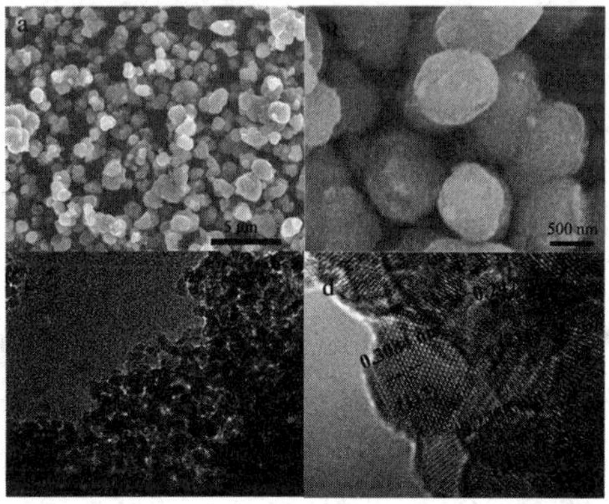

Fig. 3 (a) SEM of low magnification (b) SEM of high magnification (c) TEM and (d) HRTEM images of Mn_3O_4 nanoparticles

The pore size distribution and surface area of Mn_3O_4 samples are examined by nitrogen adsorption-desorption method. The isotherm profiles are shown in Fig. 4. It shows that Mn_3O_4 nanoparticles have a type IV adsorption-desorption curve with hysteresis loop which is characteristic of mesoporous materials. The BET surface area of the Mn_3O_4 sample is measured to be 86.172 $m^2\ g^{-1}$ and a total pore volume of 0.150 $cm^3\ g^{-1}$. The pore-size distribution curve (the inset in Fig. 4) shows a size distribution centered at 5 nm, which is more suitable for the supercapacitors with aqueous neutral electrolytes. [17] The narrow pore size distribution and relative bigger volume contribute to the effective electron transport at the interface of electrode/electrolyte.

Meanwhile, The BET surface area of WS-Mn_3O_4 is 33.97 $m^2\ g^{-1}$ and the total pore volume is 0.096 $cm^3\ g^{-1}$ (ESI Fig. S2).

Electrochemical properties of porous Mn_3O_4

The potential of the porous Mn_3O_4 sample as the super-capacitor electrode material was evaluated by galvanostatic charge-discharge technique and cyclic voltammetry. The WS-Mn_3O_4 samples are also examined for comparison. For the galvanostatic charge-discharge measurements, the potential window was set at 0.0—1.0 V *vs.* SCE, with 1 M Na_2SO_4 solution serving as the electrolyte, and the results are shown in Fig. 5. The charge-discharge curves demonstrate the intrinsic nature of pseudocapacitance for the porous Mn_3O_4 and WS-Mn_3O_4, *i. e.* the longer discharging time and the higher specific capacitance. The specific capacitances of the electrode can be estimated from the discharge curves according to the following equation: $C = I\Delta t/m\Delta V$ where C (F g^{-1}) is the specific capacitance, I(A g^{-1}) is the discharging constant density, Δt (s) is the discharging time, m (g) is the mass of the active material in the working electrode, ΔV (V) is the potential window taken in the test. [18,19]

In the Fig. 5a, at the current density of 0.5, 1, 2, 5 A g^{-1}, the obtained reversible specific capacitance of the porous Mn_3O_4 has reached to 232.5, 228, 222 and 190 F g^{-1}, respectively, matching with those of the composite of the Mn_3O_4 with carbon or graphene, [20-22] overwhelming those of the Mn_3O_4 synthesized by other methods. [10,16] In the Fig. 5b, the corresponding values of WS-Mn_3O_4 are merely 123.5, 119, 112 and 90 F g^{-1}. Fig. 5c makes a comparison of the specific capacitance between the porous Mn_3O_4 and WS-Mn_3O_4, it is evident that the porous Mn_3O_4 has crushing advantages over WS-Mn_3O_4. Also, the results indicate the porous Mn_3O_4 nanoparticles serving as the electrode material have high rate capacitance, which is one of the most important electrochemical parameters for the application of supercapacitor, especially for the electric vehicle. [23,24] The high rate performance of capacitance of Mn_3O_4 is probably ascribed to the small size, porous structure and the vacancies and defects on the surface of the spherical nanoparticles. Due to Mn_3O_4 particles are in nano-size with the diameter of 9 nm as well as the relatively high surface area of the nanoparticles, [25] considerable amount of Mn_3O_4/electrolyte contact areas could be created. Furthermore, the vacancies and defects acting as the active site can facilitate the redox reaction, thus increasing the specific capacitance.

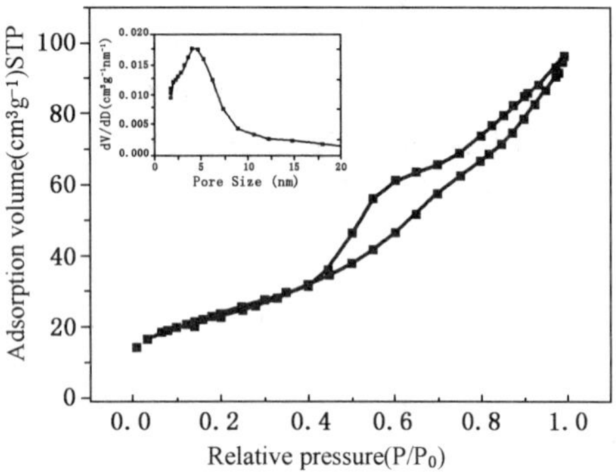

Fig. 4　N_2 adsorption-desorption isotherms of synthesized Mn_3O_4 and mesopore size distribution curve of Mn_3O_4 (in inset)

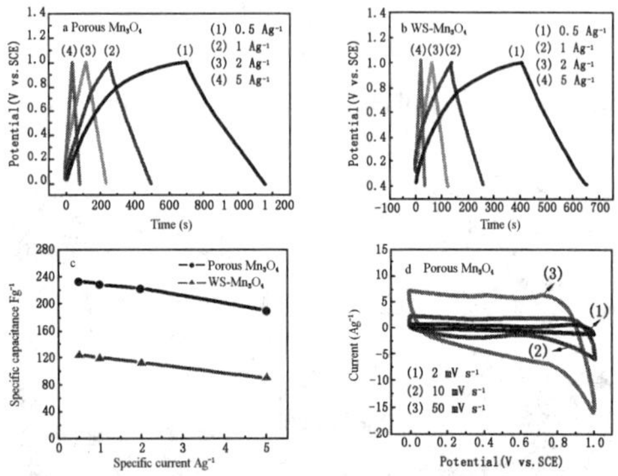

Fig. 5　(a) Charge and discharge curve of porous Mn_3O_4 at different current densities (b) charge and discharge curve of WS-Mn_3O_4 at different current densities (c) current density versus specific capacitance curve (d) cyclic voltammograms of porous Mn_3O_4 electrode at different scan rates

Fig. 5d shows the cyclic voltammograms. The applied potential of the system varied in the range of 0.0 V to 1.0 V *vs.* SCE at a scan rate of 1, 2, 5, 10 and 50 mV s^{-1}. The tests were conducted in 1 M Na_2SO_4 solution. As shown in Fig. 5d, the curve profiles have an approximate rectangular shape and symmetric current-potential characteristics between 0 V to 1.0 V, indicating capacitive behaviour through the 1.0 V voltage window in the Na_2SO_4 solution. [26] At the scan rates of 1, 2, 5, 10 and 50 mV s^{-1}, the corresponding specific capacitances were 236.86, 219.60, 196.77, 173.29 and 115.6 F g^{-1}, respectively. With increasing the scan rate, a decrease in the capacitance occurs, which may due to the ion transport. Usually at the higher scan rate, the ions do not have enough time to diffuse into the interface of electrode/electrolyte.

To investigate the features of the ions and electron transport within the capacitive electrode, electrochemical impedance spectra (EIS) was performed at open circuit potential over the frequency range 0.1—100 000 Hz with the amplitude of 5 mV. Fig. 6a shows the Nyquist plots. The EIS data can be fitted by Zview software according to an equivalent circuit mainly consisting of a bulk solution resistance R_s, charge-transfer R_{ct}, constant phase element (CPE) and Warburg resistance (W_s), as shown in Fig. 6b. At high frequency region, the intercept at real axis (R_s) corresponds to the electrolyte resistance, the values for the two samples are almost the same around 0.58 Ω. A semi-circle near high frequency region can be observed, and the diameter of the semicircle corresponds to the charge transfer resistance (R_{ct}) at the interface of electrode/electrolyte. The charge-transfer resistance R_{ct} was calculated to be 0.91 and 4.87 Ω, for the porous Mn_3O_4 and WS-Mn_3O_4 electrode, respectively. It is obvious that charge-transfer resistance at the porous Mn_3O_4 electrode dramatically reduces compared with the WS-Mn_3O_4 electrode. Another semicircle in the middle-frequency region can be seen in the Nyquist plot of the porous Mn_3O_4 electrode, which perhaps implies a more complicated electrochemical process occurs, but we can't give satisfactory explanation up to now. The resistance resulted from the ions diffusion is known as Warburg resistance (W_s). The slope of the straight line at low frequency region gives a semi-qualitative result of Warburg resistance. It can be seen that the slope of the straight line for WS-Mn_3O_4 electrode is much larger than that for the porous Mn_3O_4 electrode, indicating a lower diffusive resistance at the interface of electrolyte/the porous Mn_3O_4 electrode.

The stability of the electrode with cycling is of great significance for the practical applications of the supercapacitors. [27]

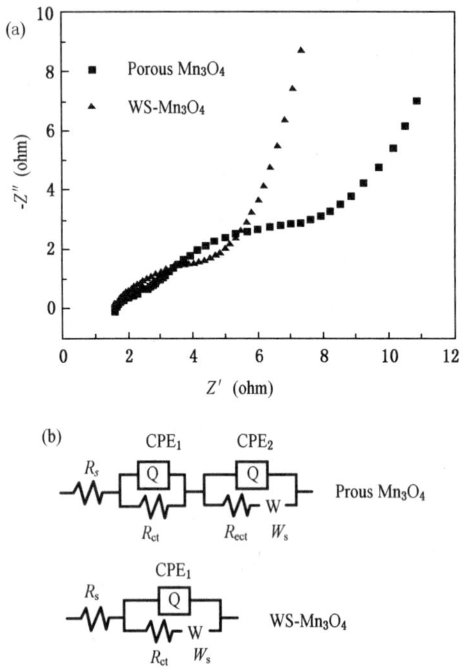

Fig. 6　(a) Nyquist plots for porous Mn_3O_4 and WS-Mn_3O_4 electrode (b) equivalent circuit

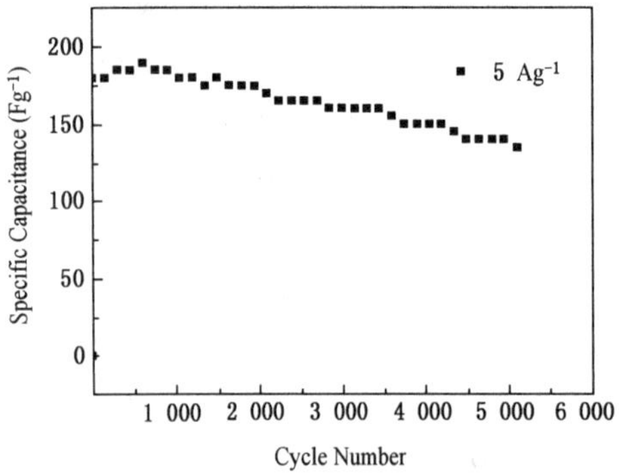

Fig. 7　Cycling stability profile for porous Mn_3O_4 electrode at a current density of 5 A g^{-1}.

The cyclic stability test has been carried out by the galvanostatic charge-discharge technique at a constant density of 5 A g^{-1} in the potential range of 0.0 V to 1.0 V for 5 000 cycles. The specific capacitance as a function of cycle numbers is presented in Fig. 7. During the first 600 cycles, the specific capacitance increases continuously, because the electrochemical activation commonly occurs in front electrochemical process, [28,29] and then, the degradation in specific capacitance slowly occurs, capacitance retention of 78% is kept until 5000 cycles. This indicates that the porous Mn_3O_4 nanoparticles taken as the electrode material are activated at the initial stage and keep relatively stable state in the following cycles.

Conclusions

Porous nanostructured Mn_3O_4 particles were successfully synthesized by a novel hydrothermal method *via* adding the surfactant CTAB. The porous Mn_3O_4 material exhibits a high specific capacitance of 232.5 F g^{-1} at 0.5 A g^{-1} and good rate capability of 190 F g^{-1} at 5 A g^{-1}, which can be attributed to its porous structure and the defects and vacancies on the surface. The capacitance retention reaches to 78% after 5 000 cycles at a current density of 5 A g^{-1}. These results show that the porous Mn_3O_4 is a promising candidate as an electrode material of supercapacitor.

References

[1] C. Wei, H. Pang, B. Zhang, Q. Lu, S. Liang and F. Gao, *Sci. Rep.*, 2013, 3, 2193.

[2] G. Yu, X. Xie, L. Pan, Z. Bao and Y. Cui, *Nano Energy*, 2013, 2, 213.

[3] A. Davies, P. Audette, B. Farrow, F. Hassan, Z. Chen, J.-Y. Choi and A. Yu, *J. Phys. Chem. C*, 2011, 115, 17612.

[4] L. Li, Z. Hu, Y. Yang, P. Liang, A. Lu, H. Xu, Y. Hu and H. Wu, *Chin. J. Chem.*,

2013,31,1290.

[5] W.-Y. Ko, L.-J. Chen, Y.-H. Chen, W.-H. Chen, K.-M. Lu, J.-R. Yang, Y.-C. Yen and K.-J. Lin, *J. Phys. Chem. C*, 2013, 117, 16290.

[6] W. Yan, T. Ayvazian, J. Kim, Y. Liu, K. C. Donavan, W. Xing, Y. Yang, J. C. Hemminger and R. M. Penner, *ACS Nano*, 2011, 5, 8275.

[7] H. Pang, S. Wang, G. Li, Y. Ma, J. Li, X. Li, L. Zhang, J. Zhang and H. Zheng, *J. Mater. Chem. A*, 2013, 1, 5053.

[8] H. Jiang, T. Zhao, C. Yan, J. Ma and C. Li, *Nanoscale*, 2010, 2, 2195.

[9] D. Li, F. Meng, X. Yan, L. Yang, H. Heng and Y. Zhu, *Nanoscale Res. Lett.*, 2013, 8, 1.

[10] D. Yan, Y. Li, Y. Liu, R. Zhuo, Z. Wu, B. Geng, J. Wang, P. Ren, P. Yan and Z. Geng, *Mater. Lett.*, 2014, 117, 62.

[11] H. Pang, J. Deng, J. Du, S. Li, J. Li, Y. Ma, J. Zhang and J. Chen, *Dalton Trans.*, 2012, 41, 10175.

[12] C. Yuan, H. B. Wu, Y. Xie and X. W. D. Lou, *Angew. Chem., Int. Ed.*, 2014, 53, 1488.

[13] F. Wang, H. Dai, J. Deng, G. Bai, K. Ji and Y. Liu, *Environ. Sci. Technol.*, 2012, 46, 4034.

[14] G. An, P. Yu, M. Xiao, Z. Liu, Z. Miao, K. Ding and L. Mao, *Nanotechnology*, 2008, 19, 275709.

[15] J. Gao, M. A. Lowe and H. D. Abruna, *Chem. Mater.*, 2011, 23, 3223.

[16] M. Fang, X. Tan, M. Liu, S. Kang, X. Hu and L. Zhang, *CrystEngComm*, 2011, 13, 4915.

[17] S. Nagamuthu, S. Vijayakumar and G. Muralidharan, *Energy Fuels*, 2013, 27, 3508.

[18] K.-S. Kim and S.-J. Park, *Bull. Korean Chem. Soc.*, 2013, 34, 2343.

[19] G. S. Gund, D. P. Dubal, B. H. Patil, S. S. Shinde and C. D. Lokhande, *Electrochim. Acta*, 2013, 92, 205.

[20] Y. Zhao, W. Ran, D.-B. Xiong, L. Zhang, J. Xu and F. Gao, *Mater. Lett.*, 2014, 118, 80.

[21] Y. Fan, X. Zhang, Y. Liu, Q. Cai and J. Zhang, *Mater. Lett.*, 2013, 95, 153.

[22] J. W. Lee, A. S. Hall, J.-D. Kim and T. E. Mallouk, *Chem. Mater.*, 2012, 24, 1158.

[23] R. Quintero, D. Y. Kim, K. Hasegawa, Y. Yamada, A. Yamada and S. Noda, *RSC Adv.*, 2014, 4, 8230.

[24] H. Xia, B. Li and L. Lu, *RSC Adv.*, 2014, 4, 11111.

[25] B. Wang, J. Park, C. Wang, H. Ahn and G. Wang, *Electrochim. Acta*, 2010, 55, 6812.

[26] S. Bao, W. Jia and M. Xu, *Rare Met.*, 2011, 30, 81.

[27] L. Zhu, S. Zhang, Y. Cui, H. Song and X. Chen, *Electrochim. Acta*, 2013, 89, 18.

[28] Y. H. Lin, T. Y. Wei, H. C. Chien and S. Y. Lu, *Adv. Energy Mater.*, 2011, 1, 901.

[29] Y. Wu, S. Liu, H. Wang, X. Wang, X. Zhang and G. Jin, *Electrochim. Acta*, 2013, 90, 210.

Doping Supervalent Rare Earth Ion in $LiFePO_4$/C Through Hydrothermal Method①

Xu Yan[a,b,c], Zhao Minshou[a,b], Sun Bin[a]

([a] Hebei Key Laboratory of Applied Chemistry, College of Environmental and Chemical Engineering, Yanshan University, Qinhuangdao 066004, China)

([b] State Key Laboratory of Metastable Material Science and Technology, Yanshan University, Qinhuangdao 066004, China)

([c] China University of Geosciences Great Wall College, Baoding 071000, China)

Abstract: Hydrothermal synthesized $LiFePO_4$/C and $LiFe_{0.95}M_{0.05}PO_4$/C (M=Sm, Eu, Yb) are studied in this paper. The samples are characterized by X-ray diffraction (XRD), scanning electron microscope (SEM), energy dispersive spectroscopy (EDS), thermogravimetric analysis and Brunauer-Emmett-Teller (BET). The electrochemical performance is evaluated via galvanostatic charge-discharge, electrochemical impedance spectroscopy (EIS) and cyclic voltammetry (CV). The hydrothermal synthesized particles are nano scale level. The results showthat the first discharge capacity of the as-prepared $LiFePO_4$/C and $LiFe_{0.95}M_{0.05}PO_4$/C (M=Sm, Eu, Yb) is 109.4 mAh/g, 153.6 mAh/g, 144.0 mAh/g and 160.7 mAh/g at 0.2 C, respectively, and reduces to 65.1 mAh/g, 147.7 mAh/g, 141.3 mAh/g and 152.6 mAh/g after 20 cycles, respectively. The specific surface area of $LiFePO_4$/C and $LiFe_{0.95}M_{0.05}PO_4$/C (M=Sm, Eu, Yb) is 18.3m^2/g, 25.2 m^2/g, 21.5m^2/g and 25.4 m^2/g, respectively. The exchange current density for $LiFe_{0.95}M_{0.05}PO_4$/C (M=Sm, Eu, Yb) composite is 121 mA · g^{-1}, 89.8 mA · g^{-1}, 138.8mA · g^{-1}, respectively, which ismuch larger than that for LiFePO4/C, 12.5mA · g^{-1}. The result of cyclic voltammetry indicates that the difference between anode peak potential and cathode peak potential reduces and the reversibility of electrochemical reaction is enhanced at doped electrode materials. The electrochemical performances are apparently improved due to doping supervalent rare earth ion in $LiFePO_4$/C.

Key words: Hydrothermal method; Lithium-ion battery; Rare earth ion-doped

1 Introduction

Lithium battery plays a very important role in power system, especially in electric vehicle (EV) and hybrid electric vehicle (HEV) application [1,2]. The olivine structure $LiFePO_4$ is considered to be one of the most promising battery cathode materials [3,4]. It is expected that $LiFePO_4$ could replace the commercial $LiCoO_2$ as it has many advantages, such as low cost, low toxicity, high speci-

① Soil State Ionics, 2016(291): 14-19.

fic capacity and environmentally friendly [5,6]. Sylvain Franger investigated the in. uences of different synthesis routes on physico-chemical properties of $LiFePO_4$ [6]. Jaewon Lee synthesized LiFePO4 micro and nanoparticles in supercritical water and found that temperature and pH of the solution affected the size and morphology of $LiFePO_4$ particles [7]. One of the most effective strategies to improve the electrochemical performance for Li-ion batteries is to control the dimensions in the nanometer scale of olivine-type $LiFePO_4$ [8].

Since the pioneering work of Padhi and co-workers in 1997 [9], many researchers have studied the synthesis methods of $LiFePO_4$. The preparation method which controls the particle size and morphology of the cathode material is very critical to the material performances [10]. It is well known that solid-phase reaction is the traditional method for synthesizing $LiFePO_4$ while hydrothermal rout is attracting more attention [10,11]. Hydrothermal synthesis as a soft chemical approach expends short processing time and low energy, adopts simple instrument and makes the particle of target sample fine [3,9]. Jiajun Chen stated that the metal disorder increased at lower synthesis temperature, but decreased to nearly zero above 175 ℃[10].

Though $LiFePO_4$ is famous for its safety, stable voltage platform, low toxicity and long cycle life, the intrinsic disadvantages of poor electronic conductivity and slow diffusion coefficient of lithium ion limit its application [12]. Carbon coating and doping some ion are primary approaches to solve the problems [13, 14]. Especially, the addition of graphene to $LiFePO_4$ signifi cantly improves the capacity and capacity retention of $LiFePO_4$ as a cathode material for Li-ion batteries [15]. The carbon coating can not only enhance its electronic conductivity, but meanwhile, the carbon can also protect Fe^{2+} from oxidizing to Fe^{3+} during the synthesis process. $LiFePO_4/C$ composite has been a popular issue for many researchers [16].

Doping ion, especially doping supervalent ion, can improve the chemical activity obviously, and the effect of doping on electrochemical performances is very signi ficant, and Sharma N has proved the existence state of doped ion within $LiFePO_4$ [17]. Jiezi Hu, Xian Zhao and Guorong synthesized $Li(M,Fe)PO_4$ (M=La, Ce, Nd, Mn, Co, Ti) and $Li_{1-4x}Ti_xFePO_4/C$ through solid-phase reaction, respectively [12,18,19]. However, few people investigated the effect of doping rare earth element Sm, Eu, Yb via solid-phase reaction on the $LiFePO_4$ exception of the papers published by our research group [20,21]. Recently Hüseyin G. ktepe synthesized Yb-doped LiFePO4/C composite by solution method, but the specific discharge capacity of 146 mAh/g at 0.1 C is too low [22]. In this paper, we have synthesized $LiFe_{0.95}M_{0.05}PO_4/C$ (M = Sm, Eu, Yb) by hydrothermal rout, and their structure and electrochemical performance have been characterized in detail.

2 Experimental

$LiFe_{0.95}M_{0.05}PO_4/C$ (M = Sm, Eu, Yb) were synthesized from LiOH, H_3PO_4, $Fe(C_2H_3O_2)_2$, $M(C_2H_3O_2)_3$ (M = Sm, Eu, Yb) with the molar ratio of 3 : 1 : 0.95 : 0.05 through hydrothermal route at 190 ℃ for 6 h. In order to avoid Fe^{2+} oxidizing to Fe^{3+}, ascorbic acid was added into the reacting solution during the hydrothermal process. The resultant precipitate was washed with deionized water and filtered, and dried in the vacuum oven at 80 ℃ for 10 h. Then the hydrothermal product with the addition of 10 wt% glucose was calcined at 600 ℃ for 3 h under N_2 gas atmosphere. Finally, the $LiFePO_4/C$ and $LiFe_{0.95}M_{0.05}PO_4/C$ (M=Sm, Eu, Yb) samples were synthesized.

The thermochemical behavior of sample was analyzed using Themogravimetric apparatus (Pyris Diamond, PerkinElmer Thermal Analysis) under nitrogen gas flow. The sample was heated from ambient temperature to 800 ℃ at the rate of 10 ℃ min^{-1}. The crystallographic structure of the sample was characterized by powder X-ray diffractometer on a Rigaku D/max-2500/pc. The morphology of the sample was observed with a field-emission scanning electron microscope (FE-SEM) on S-4800 FE-SEM. The specific surface area of the sample was analyzed by Brunauer-Emmett-Teller (BET) (Micrometeritics ASAP2010 specific surface area) instrument.

The charge-discharge tests of as-synthesized samples were carried on in a half cell in which lithium metal piece was used as the anode. The cathode was composed of 80 wt% active material, 15 wt% acetylene black and 5 wt% polyvinylidene fiuoride (PVDF) binder in N-methylpyrrolidone (NMP) solvent to form a uniform slurry. The slurry was coated on Al foil and cut into square shape (8 × 8 mm). The mass of active material was about 1.5 mg/cm^2. The foil dried in a vacuum oven at 120 ℃ for 12 h. The cell was assembled in the glove box filled up with argon gas of high purity. The electrolyte was 1 M LiPF6/ EC + DEC (1 : 1, v/v). The cell was tested on the charge-discharge equipment over the voltage range 2.5—4.3 V at room temperature. Electrochemical impedance was tested on electrochemical workstation CHI660A. The sinusoidal excitation voltage applied to the cells was 0.5 mV and frequency range was between 0.01 Hz and 100 kHz. Cyclic Voltammetry (CV) was conducted by electrochemical workstation LK2005A at a scanning rate of 0.5 mVs. 1 and the potential span from 2.3 V to 4.2V.

3 Result and discussion

Fig. 1 shows the TG-DTA (Thermogravimetric Analysis and Differential Thermal Analysis) curves of $LiFePO_4$/glucose before heat treatment. The weight loss under 100 ℃ corresponds to water absorbed in the sample. The weight loss during 100—250 ℃ results from the decomposition of the remaining organics, corresponding to the exothermic peaks at 154 and 214 ℃. The weight loss above 250 ℃ is related to volatilization of glucose. The DTA curve shows a small endothermic peak at 521.5 ℃, which is related to transformation of crystalline material [23]. The TG curve almost keeps a constant value above 600 ℃ till 800 ℃. Therefore, the calcined temperature should be higher than 520 ℃.

Fig. 2 shows the XRD patterns of the $LiFePO_4$/C and $LiFe_{0.95}M_{0.05}PO_4$/C (M=Sm, Eu, Yb) compounds. As shown in the Fig. 2, the dominant diffraction peaks can be indexed as the orthorhombic $LiFePO_4$ phase with space group Pmnb (62). The XRD result suggests that $LiFePO_4$/C and $LiFe_{0.95}M_{0.05}PO_4$/C(M=Sm, Eu, Yb) composites are well-crystallized and agree well with the olivine structure. There is no impurity phase to be detected in the as-prepared samples. It has implied that doping rare earth ion in $LiFePO_4$ does not change the lattice structure of $LiFePO_4$ synthesized via hydrothermal rout. Moreover, there is no obvious diffraction response of carbon because of its low content and amorphous state.

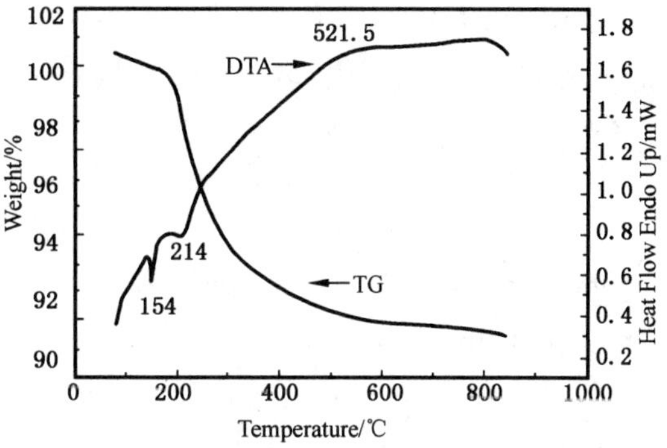

Fig. 1　TG-DTA curves of $LiFePO_4$/glucose before heat treatment

However, doping rare earth ion affects the intensity ratio of $I(200)/I(020)$. The doped composites particles prepared via hydrothermal route have a random crystal orientation. The intensity of (020) plane seemly becomes weaker and the intensity ratio of $I(200)/I(020)$ becomes larger with doping rare earth ion. The phenomenon mentioned above may be related to the fact that a part of rare earth ions occupies Fe site(M_2) into $LiFePO_4$/C, the rest would form solid solution with $LiFePO_4$[17].

SEM images of $LiFePO_4$/C and $LiFe_{0.95}M_{0.05}PO_4$/C (M = Sm, Eu, Yb) composites are shown in Fig. 3. The stick-shaped particles with about dimension 490 nm × 150 nm are smaller than particles with μm level scale produced by conventional solid-phase method. The doping rare earth ion into the $LiFePO_4$/C doesn't make its particle fine further. Actually, doping supervalent rare earth ion would create some defect, leading to the improvement of the electrochemical performance of $LiFePO_4$/C [24]. Another important feature of the SEM is that some particles of 10—30 nano scale level adhere to the surface of doped particles.

EDS image showed in the Fig. 4 indicates that the rare earth element has been doped in $LiFePO_4/C$. Wagemaker [24] reported that low levels of dopants were indeed soluble in the olivine lattice up to the extent of 3 mol%. According to the EDS we have reason to infer that the supervalent ions have occupied Fe^{2+} site in the LiFePO4/C or have been dissolved into $LiFePO_4/C$ to form solid solution [17].

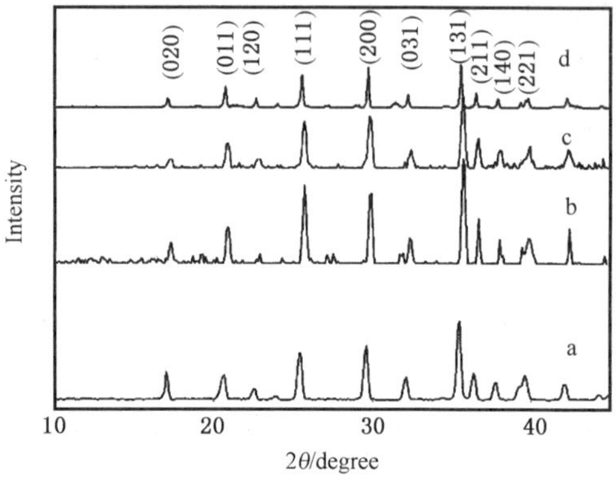

Fig. 2　XRDpatternforLiFePO$_4$/CandLiFe$_{0.95}$M$_{0.05}$PO$_4$/C(M=Sm, Eu, Yb)composite. aLiFePO$_4$/CbLiFe$_{0.95}$Sm$_{0.05}$PO$_4$/CcLiFe$_{0.95}$Eu$_{0.05}$PO$_4$/CdLiFe$_{0.95}$Yb$_{0.05}$PO$_4$/C

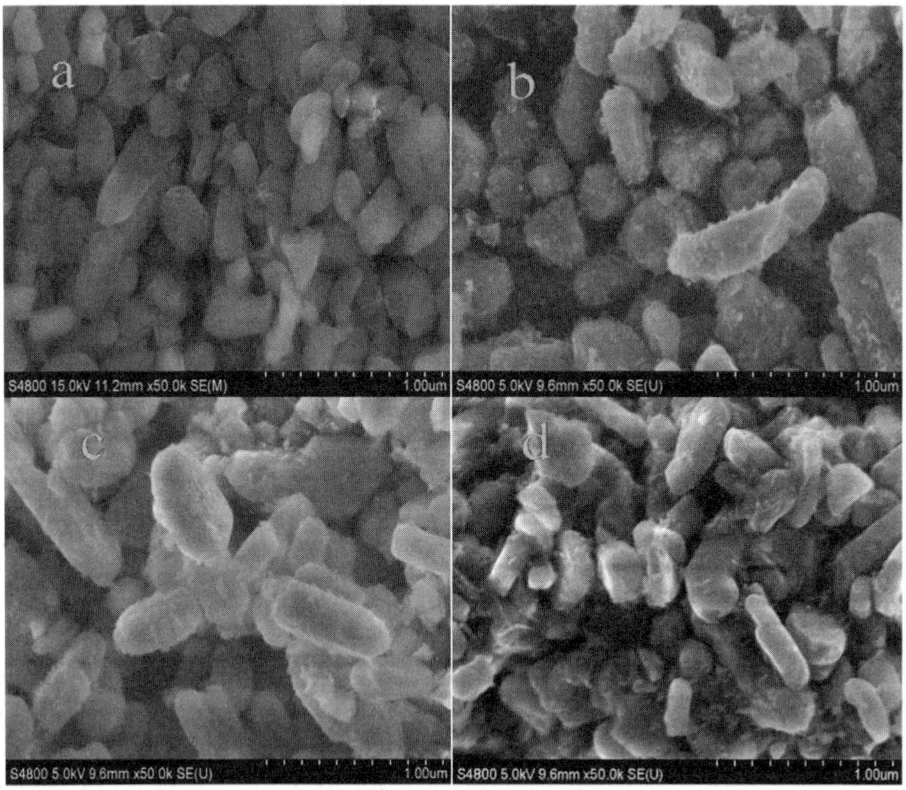

Fig. 3　SEM of as-prepared $LiFePO_4/C$ and $LiFe_{0.95}M_{0.05}PO_4/C$(M=Sm, Eu, Yb) a $LiFePO_4/C$ b $LiFe_{0.95}Sm_{0.05}PO_4/C$ c $LiFe_{0.95}Eu_{0.05}PO_4/C$ d $LiFe_{0.95}Yb_{0.05}PO_4/C$

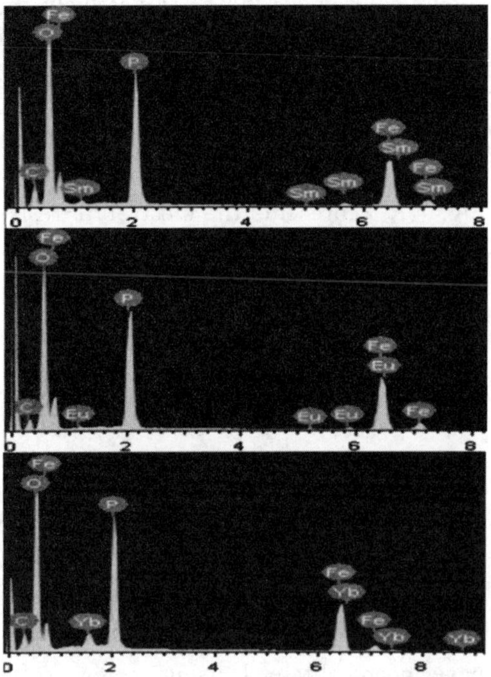

Fig. 4　EDS image of $LiFe_{0.95}M_{0.05}PO_4/C$ (M=Sm, Eu, Yb) a $LiFe_{0.95}Sm_{0.05}PO_4/C$ b $LiFe_{0.95}Eu_{0.05}PO_4/C$ c $LiFe_{0.95}Yb_{0.05}PO_4/C$

Table 1 shows the specific surface area of $LiFePO_4/C$ and $LiFe_{0.95}M_{0.05}PO_4/C$(M=Sm, Eu, Yb). Compared with $LiFePO_4/C$, the rare earth ion-doped samples have lager specific area, indicating that $LiFe_{0.95}M_{0.05}PO_4/C$(M=Sm, Eu, Yb) composite can providemore activesites than $LiFePO_4/C$. This means that $LiFe_{0.95}M_{0.05}PO_4/C$(M=Sm, Eu, Yb) composite with lager specific surface area is more active.

The cycle curves of $LiFePO_4/C$ and $LiFe_{0.95}M_{0.05}PO_4/C$(M=Sm, Eu, Yb) are shown in the Fig. 5. Fig. 5 suggests that the first cycle discharge capacity for $LiFePO_4/C$ and $LiFe_{0.95}M_{0.05}PO_4/C$(M=Sm, Eu, Yb) is 109.4 mAh/g, 153.6 mAh/g, 144.0 mAh/g and 160.7 mAh/g at 0.2 C, respectively, and reduce to 65.1 mAh/g, 147.7 mAh/g, 141.3 mAh/g and 152.6 mAh/g after 20 cycles, respectively. The discharge capacity of $LiFePO_4/C$ and $LiFe_{0.95}M_{0.05}PO_4/C$ (M= Sm, Eu, Yb) is listed in Table 2. The capacity retention remains 59.5%, 96.2%, 98.1% and 94.9%, respectively. The results clearly indicate that doping rare earth ions have improved cycle performance obviously.

Fig. 6 shows the rate discharge curves of uncoped sample and doped samples. It is concluded that doping supervalent rare earth ion can improve rate discharge ability. The discharge capacity of $LiFe_{0.95}Yb_{0.05}PO_4/C$(M=Sm, Eu, Yb) at different rate is listed in Table 3.

Table 1　Specific surface area of $LiFePO_4/C$ and $LiFe_{0.95}M_{0.05}PO_4/C$(M=Sm, Eu, Yb)

	Sample			
	a	b	c	d
Speci. c surface area/(m^2/g)	18.3	25.2	21.5	25.4

a $LiFePO_4/C$

b $LiFe_{0.95}Sm_{0.05}PO_4/C$

c $LiFe_{0.95}Sm_{0.05}PO_4/C$

d $LiFe_{0.95}Sm_{0.05}PO_4/C$

Table 2　Discharge capacity of $LiFePO_4/C$ and $LiFe_{0.95}M_{0.05}PO_4/C$ (M = Sm, Eu, Yb) at 0.2 C

	Sample			
	a	b	c	d
Capacity of first cycle/(mAh · g^{-1})	109.4	153.6	144.0	160.7
Capacity after 20 cycles/(mAh · g^{-1})	65.1	147.7	141.3	152.6
Capacity retention rate/%	59.5%	96.2%	98.1%	94.9%

a $LiFePO_4/C$

b $LiFe_{0.95}Sm_{0.05}PO_4/C$

c $LiFe_{0.95}Sm_{0.05}PO_4/C$

d $LiFe_{0.95}Sm_{0.05}PO_4/C$

Table 3　Discharge capacity of $LiFe_{0.95}Yb_{0.05}PO_4/C$ at different rate

	Discharge rate				
	0.2C	0.5C	1C	2C	5C
Capacity/ (mAh · g^{-1})	160.7	143.2	131.0	108.8	99.7

The vacancy caused by supervalent ions would lead to lattice defect which can sign. canty improve the electrochemical activity.

As well known, there is capacity fade especially during the charge-discharge process at high rate, which may be because the all polarizations, including ohm polarization, concentration polarization and active polarization, become much serious, and structure of electrode material has been destroyed.

Fig. 7 shows the charge-discharge curves of first cycle for $LiFePO_4/C$ and $LiFe_{0.95}M_{0.05}PO_4/C$ (M=Sm, Eu, Yb) at a rate of 0.2 C. It manifests that the doped samples own wider charge/discharge plateau and narrower gap between charge-discharge plateaus, meaning smaller polarization than $LiFePO_4/C$ in the electrochemical process. The results agree with those mentioned above.

The results mentioned above demonstrate that higher intensity ratio of $I(200)/I(020)$ is beneficial to improving electrochemical performance, which is consistent with result by Kaoru Dokko [25].

EIS and equivalent circuit for $LiFePO_4/C$ and $LiFe_{0.95}M_{0.05}PO_4/C$ (M=Sm, Eu, Yb) composite electrode are shown in Figs. 8 and 9, respectively. In Fig. 8, EIS is composed of two parts including overlapped circles at high frequency region and a straight line at low frequency region. In the equivalent circuit Fig. 9, R_s represents the electrolyte resistance, R_{ct} represents the charge-transfer resistance responding to the overlapped circles in the Fig. 8, Z_w represents the diffusion impedance of Li^+ in positive electrode materials. In Fig. 9, a constant phase element (CPE) represents the double layer capacitance and passivation film capacitance [26], which is so small that it is neglectable.

The electrochemical impedances have been obtained using Zview software. The ohmic resistance R_s of all the samples, whether doped or not, does not almost change because the electrolyte is the same during the experiment. Doping supervalent ions Sm^{3+}, Eu^{3+}, Yb^{3+} reduces.

Table 4　Charge-transfer resistance and exchange current density for $LiFePO_4/C$ electrode and $LiFe_{0.95}M_{0.05}PO_4/C$ (M = Sm, Eu, Yb) composite electrode

	Sample			
	a	b	c	d
R_{ct}/Ω	1327.8	137.3	185.1	119.7
j_0/mA · g^{-1}	12.5	121.0	89.8	138.8

a $LiFePO_4/C$

b $LiFe_{0.95}Sm_{0.05}PO_4/C$

c $LiFe_{0.95}Sm_{0.05}PO_4/C$

d $LiFe_{0.95}Sm_{0.05}PO_4/C$

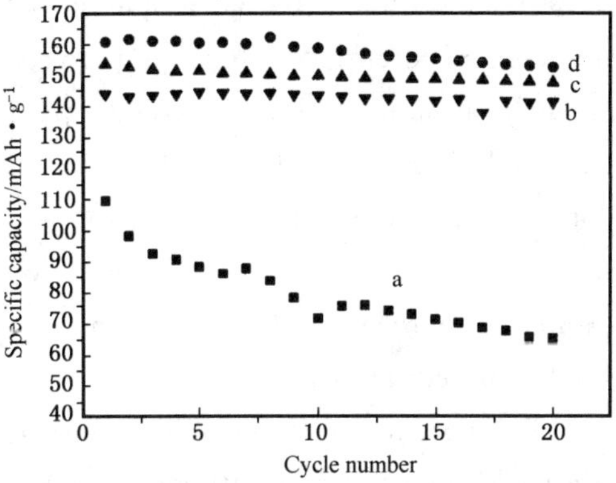

Fig. 5 Cycle performance of $LiFePO_4/C$ and $LiFe_{0.95}M_{0.05}PO_4/C$(M=Sm, Eu, Yb) a $LiFePO_4/C$ b $LiFe_{0.95}Eu_{0.05}PO_4/C$ c $LiFe_{0.95}Sm_{0.05}PO_4/C$ d $LiFe_{0.95}Yb_{0.05}PO_4/C$

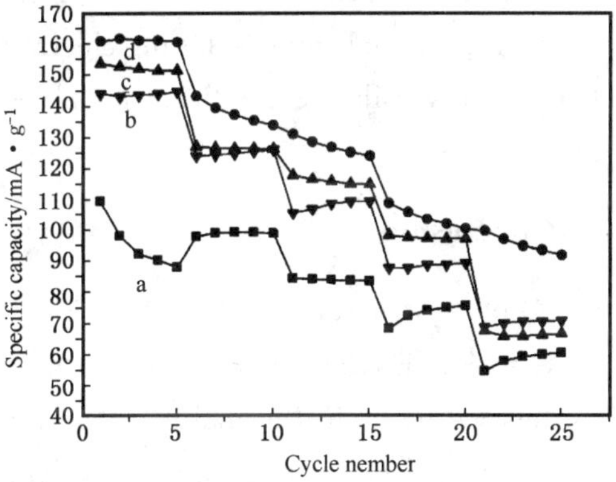

Fig. 6 Rate discharge ability of $LiFePO_4/C$ and $LiFe_{0.95}M_{0.05}PO_4/C$(M=Sm, Eu, Yb) at 0.2 C, 0.5 C, 1 C, 2 C, 5 C a $LiFePO_4/C$ b $LiFe_{0.95}Eu_{0.05}PO_4/C$ c $LiFe_{0.95}Sm_{0.05}PO_4/C$ d $LiFe_{0.95}Yb_{0.05}PO_4/C$

R_{ct} obviously, indicating that the doping rare earth ions is helpful to improvethe electrochemical performance. The charge-transfer resistancefor $LiFePO_4/C$ and $LiFe_{0.95}M_{0.05}PO_4/C$ (M = Sm, Eu, Yb) electrode reactionis 1327.8 Ω, 137.3 Ω, 185.1 Ω and 119.7 Ω, respectively. When over potential is very small and trends to zero, the exchange currentdensity (j_0) can be calculated according to the following Formula [27].

$$j_0 = RT/m\,n\,R_{ct}\,F \tag{1}$$

where m is mass of active material, n is charge-transfer number, R_{ct} is charge-transfer resistance, F is Faraday constant, T is absolute temperature and R is gas constant.

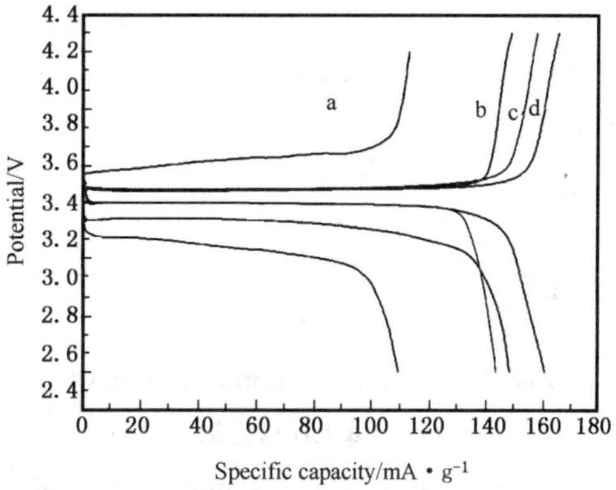

Fig. 7 Charge and discharge curves of first cycle for $LiFePO_4/C$ and $LiFe_{0.95}M_{0.05}PO_4/C$ (M=Sm, Eu, Yb) a $LiFePO_4/C$ b $LiFe_{0.95}Eu_{0.05}PO_4/C$ c $LiFe_{0.95}Sm_{0.05}PO_4/C$ d $LiFe_{0.95}Yb_{0.05}PO_4/C$

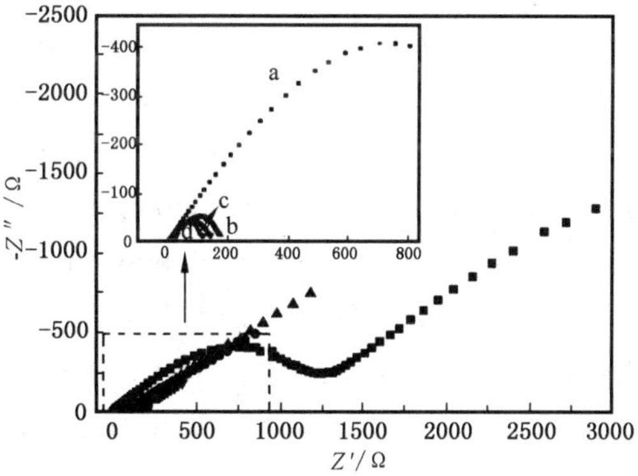

Fig. 8 EIS for $LiFePO_4/C$ electrode and $LiFe_{0.95}M_{0.05}PO_4/C$(M=Sm, Eu, Yb) composite electrode after 5 cycles. a $LiFePO_4/C$ b $LiFe_{0.95}Eu_{0.05}PO_4/C$ c $LiFe_{0.95}Sm_{0.05}PO_4/C$ d $LiFe_{0.95}Yb_{0.05}PO_4/C$

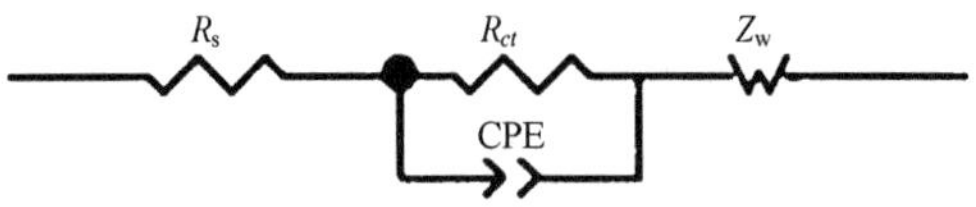

Fig. 9 Equivalent circuit

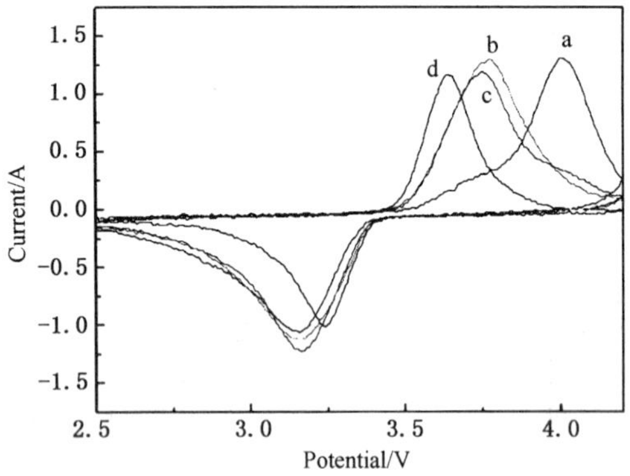

Fig. 10 Cyclic voltammograms of $LiFePO_4/C$ and $LiFe_{0.95}M_{0.05}PO_4/C$ (M=Sm, Eu, Yb) at a scanning rate of 0.5 mVs. 1 and the potential span rom 2.3 V to 4.2 V. a $LiFePO_4/C$ b $LiFe_{0.95}Eu_{0.05}PO_4/C$ c $LiFe_{0.95}Sm_{0.05}PO_4/C$ d $LiFe_{0.95}Yb_{0.05}PO_4/C$

The charge-transfer resistance R_{ct} and calculated results of exchange current density are listed in the Table 4. It is clear that the exchange current density markedly increases after doping rare earth ions, which imply that doping these supervalent ions Sm^{3+}, Eu^{3+}, Yb^{3+} is beneficial to improving the electrochemical catalyst activity of $LiFePO_4/C$. Larger exchange current density indicates better electrochemical reaction activity.

Cyclic Voltammetry (CV) curves of $LiFePO_4/C$ and $LiFe_{0.95}M_{0.05}PO_4/C$ (M = Sm, Eu, Yb) are shown in Fig. 10. It shows the effect of the dopant on the electrochemical reversibility of the electrode reaction. $LiFePO_4/C$ sample shows the bigger potential difference between anode peak potential and cathode peak potential. However, the anode peak of doped sample moves to left direction and the cathode peak moves to right direction compared with $LiFePO_4/C$, leading the smaller potential difference.

The potential difference between anode peak potential and cathode peak potential for $LiFePO_4/C$ and $LiFe_{0.95}M_{0.05}PO_4/C$ (M = Sm, Eu, Yb) is 0.844 V, 0.590 V, 0.602 V, 0.396 V, respectively. In fact, the smaller potential difference between anode peak potential and cathode peak potential implies better electrochemical reversibility of electrode reaction.

4 Conclusion

Olivine-structured $LiFe_{0.95}M_{0.05}PO_4/C$ (M = Sm, Eu, Yb) composite has been synthesized by hydrothermal method . rst time. The effect of doping supervalent rare earth ions on the characteristics is signi. cant and obvious. The discharge capacity of doped sample, $LiFe_{0.95}M_{0.05}PO_4/C$ (M = Sm, Eu, Yb) composite, can deliver 153.6 mAh · g^{-1}, 144.0 mAh · g^{-1} and 160.7 mAh · g^{-1} at 0.2 C, respectively. The rate discharge capacity of $LiFe_{0.95}Yb_{0.05}PO_4/C$ is 143.2 mAh · g^{-1}, 131.0 mAh · g^{-1}, 108.8 mAh · g^{-1} and 99.7 mAh · g^{-1} at rate of 0.5C, 1C, 2C, 5C, respectively. The specific surface area of $LiFe_{0.95}M_{0.05}PO_4/C$ (M = Sm, Eu, Yb) increases to 25.2 m^2/g, 21.5 m^2/g and

25.4 m^2/g, respectively, while specific surface area of $LiFePO_4/C$ is 18.3 m^2/g. The exchange current density for $LiFe_{0.95}M_{0.05}PO_4/C$(M=Sm, Eu, Yb) composite is 121 mA·g^{-1}, 89.8 mA·g^{-1}, 138.8 mA·g^{-1} respectively, which is much larger than that for $LiFePO_4/C$, 12.5 mA·g^{-1}, and the reversibility of electrochemical reaction at doped sample is enhanced, compared with $LiFePO_4/C$.

The doping supervalent rare earth ion in $LiFePO_4/C$ by hydrothermal approach is greatly sinificant to open the facile door for improving the electrochemical performance of cathode material in Lithium ion battery.

References

[1] I. B. Weinstock, J. Power Sources 110 (2002) 471-474.

[2] A. Goodman, A. Hakala, G. Bromhal, D. Deel, T. Rodosta, S. Frailey, M. Small, D. Allen, V. Romanov, J. Fazio, N. Huerta, D. McIntyre, B. Kutchko, G. George, Int. J. Greenh. GasControl 5 (2011) 952-965.

[3] J. Chen, M. J. Vacchio, S. Wang, N. Chernova, P. Y. Zavalij, M. S. Whittingham, Solid-State Ionics 178 (2008) 1676-1693.

[4] W.-J. Zhang, J. Power Sources 196 (2011) 2962-2970. [5] B. Pei, Q. Wang, W. Zhang, Z. Yang, M. Chen, Electrochim. Acta 56 (2011)5667-5672.

[6] S. Franger, F. Le Cras, C. Bourbon, H. Rouault, J. Power Sources 119-121 (2003) 252-257.

[7] J. Lee, A. S. Teja, Mater. Lett. 60 (2006) 2105-2109.

[8] Z. Yu, L. Peng, B. Liu, G. H. Yu, Am. Chem. Soc. 14 (2014) 2849-2853.

[9] A. K. Padhi, K. S. Nanjundaswamy, J. B. Goodenough, J. Electrochem. Soc. 144 (1997)1188-1194.

[10] J. Chen, S. Wang, M. S. Whittingham, J. Power Sources 174 (2007) 442-448.

[11] J. Chen, M. S. Whittingham, Electrochem. Commun. 8 (2006) 855-858.

[12] H. Jiezi, X. Jian, Z. Xinbing, Y. Hongming, Z. Xin, C. Gaoshao, T. Jiangping, J. Mater. Sci. 25 (2009) 5.

[13] Y.-D. Cho, G. T.-K. Fey, H.-M. Kao, J. Power Sources 189 (2009) 256-262.

[14] H. C. Shin, W. I. Cho, H. Jang, Electrochim. Acta 52 (2006) 1472-1476.

[15] K. S. Dhindsa, B. P. Mandal, K. Bazzi, M. W. Lin, M. Nazri, G. A. Nazri, V. M. Naik, V. K. Garg, A. C. Oliveira, P. Vaishnava, R. Naik, Z. X. Zhou, Solid State Ionics, 253 (2013)94-100.

[16] X. Ou, G. Liang, L. Wang, S. Xu, X. Zhao, J. Power Sources 184 (2008) 543-547.

[17] N. Sharma, X. Guo, G. Du, Z. Guo, J. Wang, Z. Wang, V. K. Peterson, J. Am. Chem. Soc. 134 (2012) 7867-873.

[18] Z. Xian, T. Xiaozhen, Z. Li, Z. Minshou, Z. Jing, Electrochim. Acta 55 (2010) 5899-904.

[19] G.-R. Hu, X.-G. Gao, Z.-D. Peng, K. Du, X.-Y. Tan, J.-J. Liu, Trans. Nonferrous Metals Soc. China 17 (2007) 296-00.

[20] Q. Zhang, Y. Qiao, M. Zhao, L. Wang, J. Rare Earths 30 (2012) 78-5.

[21] Q. Zhang, Y. Qiao, M. Zhao, L. Wang, Chinese J. Inorg. Chem. 28 (2012) 67-3.

[22] H. Götepe, Res. Chem. Intermed. 39 (2013) 2979-987.

[23] L. Pang, M. Zhao, X. Zhao, Y. Chai, J. Power Sources 201 (2012) 253-58.

[24] M. Wagemaker, B. L. Ellis, D. Lözenkirchen-Hecht, F. M. Mulder, L. F. Nazar, Chem. Mater. 20 (2008) 6313-315.

[25] K. Dokko, S. Koizumi, H. Nakano, K. Kanamura, J. Mater. Chem. 17 (2007) 4803-810.

[26] G. X. Wang, L. Yanga, Y. Chena, J. Z. Wanga, B. Steve, H. K. Liua, Electrochim. Acta 50(2005) 4649-654.

[27] A. J. Bard, L. R. Faulker, in: L. Y. Gu, M. X. Lu, S. Z. Song (Eds.), Electrochemical Methods-Fundamental and Applications, Chemical Industry Publishing Company, 1986(Chinese Version).

Study on $LiFe_{1-x}Sm_xPO_4$/C Used as Cathode Materials for Iithium-ion Batteries with Low Sm Component①

Wang Wen[a], Qiao Yuqing[a,b,c], He Li[b], Dumée Ludovic[b], Kong Lingxue[b], Zhao Minshou[a], Gao Weimin[b]

([a] College of Environmental and Chemical Engineering, Yanshan University, Qinhuangdao, Hebei 066004, China)

([b] Institute for Frontier Materials, Deakin University, Geelong, VIC 3217, Australia)

([c] State Key Laboratory of Metastable Material Science and Technology, Yanshan University, Qinhuangdao 066004, People's Republic of China)

Abstract: $LiFe_{1-x}Sm_xPO_4$/C cathode materials were synthesized though a facile hydrothermal method. Compared with high-temperature solid-phase sintering, the method can allow for the fabrication of low Sm content (2 %), a scarce and expensive rare earth element, while the presence of an optimized carbon coating with large amount of sp2-type carbon sharply increases the material's electrochemical performance. The high-rate dischargeability at 5 C, as well as the exchange current density, can be increased by 21 and 86 %, respectively, which were attributed to the fine size and the large cell parameter a/c as much. It should be pointed out that the *a/c* value will be increased for the $LiFePO_4$ Sm-doped papered by both of the two methods, while the mechanism is different: The value c is increased for the front and the value a is decreased for the latter, respectively.

Key words: Li-ion batteries; Doping; Electrochemical characterizations; Cathodes

Introduction

For cathode materials of Li-ion battery, improving electrochemical properties and decreasing cost of original materials are of immense technological and practical significance. As compared with other cathode materials including $LiCoO_2$ [1], $Li_4Ti_5O_{12}$-$LiMn_2O_4$ [2], $Li_3V_2(PO_4)_3$/C [3, 4], $Cu_{0.95}V_2O_5$ [5], FeF_3 [6], V_2O_5 [7], and $LiFePO_4$, cathode materials have been extensively studied due to its inexpensive cost, friendliness to the environment, and nontoxicity along with good cycling stability and a good security [8-11]. However, its low electronic conductivity [12] and low diffusion coefficient of Li^+ [13] hinder its commercial applications. At present, various approaches, such as carbon-coating [14, 15], metal-doping [16-20], and particle-size minimizing [21-24], have been tried to

① Ionics, 2015(21): 2119-2125.

tackle these problems. So far, a number of literatures [25-29]have been reported that metal-doping (Co^{2+} , Cr^{3+} , Ti^{4+} , V^{5+} , Al^{3+} , Na^{+} , Ni^{+} , Mg^{2+} , Nd^{3+}) can improve the electrochemical performance of $LiFePO_4$ significantly. Wang et al. [25] reported that the LiFePO4 cathode materials with the Ti^{4+}-doping has a good cycle life with 92% initial capacity after 120 cycles. Zheng et al. [29] thought Ni^{+}-doping can decrease the particle size of $LiFePO_4$. Hüeyin Götepe [30]prepared $LiFePO_4$/CYb-doped with the specific capacity of 146 mAh g^{-1} at 0.1 C.

In our previous work, Zhang [31] prepared that Smdoped LiFePO4/C cathode material has the specific capacity of 152 mAh g^{-1} at 0.2 C. Pang [32] thought Gd doping can refine particle size and get a better temperature performance of LiFePO4/C with the discharge capacity of 163 mAh g^{-1} at 40 ℃. However, high rare element component and the tedious preparation procedures using high-temperature solid-phase reaction forthe $LiFePO_4$/C doped with Sm, Gd, or Nd prevent its practical applications as electrode alloy for lithium-ion battery. In the present work, a lower Sm-doped $LiFePO_4$/C cathode material with good electrochemical performances was prepared using a facile hydrothermal method.

Experimental

$LiFePO_4$ cathode material was prepared by a hydrothermal method using $LiOH \cdot H_2O$ (90 %), $FeSO_4 \cdot 7H_2O$ (99 %), H_3PO_4 (85 %), $(CH_3COO)_3Sm \cdot 6H_2O$, and ascorbic acid ($C_6H_8O_6$) as the precursor materials. The experimental procedures are as follows: (1) $LiOH \cdot H_2O$(0.06 mol) was dissolved in 30 ml distilled water, then H_3PO_4 (0.02 mol) solution was added to $LiOH \cdot H_2O$slowly. (2) $FeSO_4 \cdot 7H_2O$ (0.02 mol) was dissolved in 30 ml distilled water at argon atmosphere, followed by adding 5 wt% $C_6H_{12}O_6$. (3)The two solutions were stirred for 10 min, followed by pouring into a 100-ml Teflon-lined stainless container, and heated at 190 ℃ for 6 h, followed by heating at 700 ℃ for 6 h at nitrogen atmosphere in order to get a better crystal shape.

The structure of $LiFe_{1-x}Sm_xPO_4$/C (x=0.00, 0.01, 0.02, 0.04, 0.06) was characterized by a Rigaku D/max 2500pc X-ray diffractometer (XRD), utilizing a Cu Kαradiation source (λ= 0.15406 nm) operated at 40 kV and 100 mA, a S-4800 field-emission microscope operated at an acceleration voltage of 15 kV and a HT7700 transmission electron microscopy. Raman spectra were performed on a Renishaw Gloucestershire at a laser wavelength of 514 nm. The exposure time, power, accumulation, and spectral resolution used for the spectral data collection were 30 s, 10 %, 1, and 4cm. 1, respectively.

The cathode of $LiFePO_4$ was prepared

as follow. Primarily, $LiFePO_4$ (80 wt%), polyvinylidene fluoride (PVDF, 5 wt%), and acetylene black (15 wt%) were mixed in *N*-methyl pyrrolidinone, grinded for half an hour in a mortar, andthus the slurry was obtained andthen was coated on an aluminum foil and the cathode was dried at 120 ℃ under vacuum; the coating weight was about 16 mg cm^{-2}.

Electrochemical performances were carried out on a BTS-5 V10 mA system in the voltage range of 2.5～4.3 Vat 0.2 C to 5 C current densities. Electrochemical impedance spectroscopy (EIS) was made at a CHI 660A electrochemical workstation with the oscillation voltage of 5 mV and the applied frequency ranging from 100 KHz to 0.01 Hz. The cyclic voltammeter (CV) was conducted by a CHI 660A electrochemical workstation with the scanning voltage range from 2.2 to 4.3 V and at the scanning rate of 0.4 mV/s.

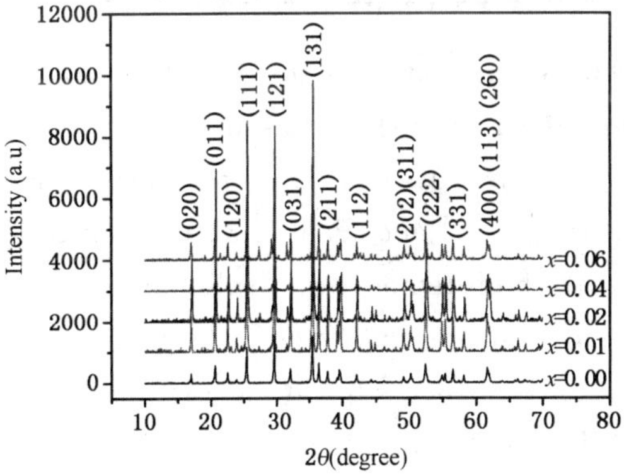

Fig. 1　XRD patterns of $LiFe_{1-x}Sm_xPO_4/C$ ($x=0, 0.01, 0.02, 0.04, 0.06$

Results and discussion

Structures characterization

Figure 1 shows XRD patterns of $LiFe_{1-x}Sm_xPO_4/C$ ($x = 0, 0.01, 0.02, 0.04, 0.06$). It is learnt from Fig. 1 that an appropriate amount of doping Sm decreases the unit cell parameters *a*. At $x=0.02$, the lattice parameter *a* is 1.032 4 nm, which is smaller than that of the un-doped sample (1.0352 nm), as shown in Table 1. Smaller value a results in a larger value of c/a, which is beneficial for Li^+ diffusion in the bulk of the material and the improvement on the electrochemical performance of $LiFePO_4$. Zhang et al. [31] believed that the larger value of c/a comes from the larger value *c* in the Sm-doped sample. So, it can be thought that Sm-doping can increase the a/c value for the $LiFePO_4$ prepared by high-temperature solidphase reaction and hydrothermal method, but their mechanisms are different: The value *c* is increased for the front, and the value *a* is decreased for the latter, respectively.

Lattice parameters, cell volume, and some parameters of$LiFe_{1-x}Sm_xPO_4/C$ ($x=0, 0.01, 0.02, 0.04, 0.06$) are listed in Table 1. It is learnt that the values of $I111/I131$ for the four Smdoped samples are larger than that of the un-doped sample, which are coincided well with the sample papered by hight emperature solid-phase reaction. The large $I111/I131$ value indicates that Sm doping can enhance the discharge capacity.

Table 1　Lattice parameters, cell volume, and some parameters of $LiFe_{1-x}Sm_xPO_4/C$ ($x=0, 0.01, 0.02, 0.04, 0.06$)

Samples	a/nm	b/nm	c/nm	V/nm^3	c/a	I_{111}/I_{131}
$x=0.00$	1.035 2	0.601 3	0.470 1	0.292 6	0.454 1	0.752 2
$x=0.01$	1.034 4	0.601 5	0.470 0	0.292 4	0.454 4	0.762 2
$x=0.02$	1.032 4	0.600 3	0.469 1	0.290 8	0.454 4	0.853 2
$x=0.04$	1.033 2	0.600 6	0.469 5	0.291 3	0.454 4	0.869 6
$x=0.06$	1.034 5	0.601 6	0.470 2	0.292 7	0.454 5	0.768 5

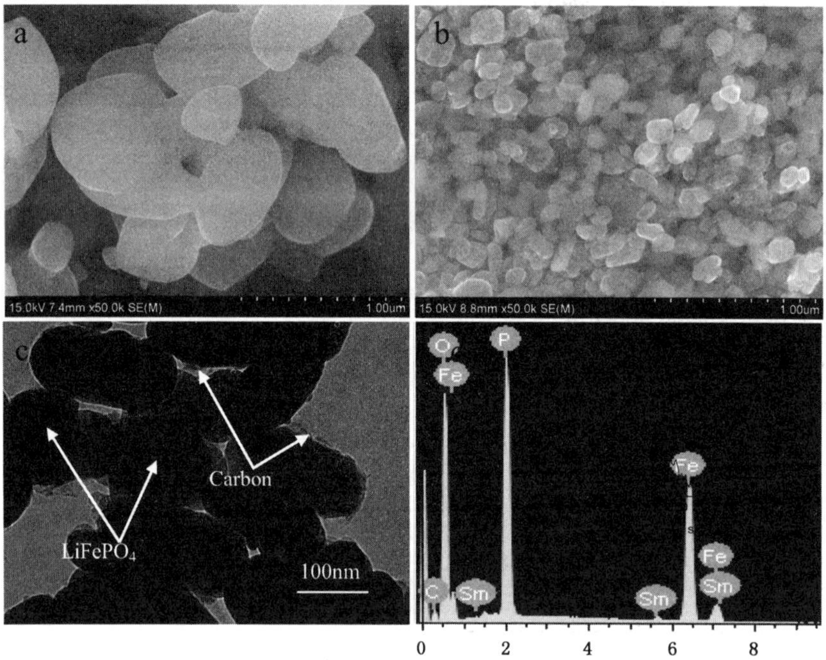

Fig. 2　SEM images of $LiFe_{1-x}Sm_xPO_4/C$ $x=0.00$ (a) and $x=0.02$ (b), TEM (c), and EDS with an inset of Roman result for $LiFe_{1-x}Sm_xPO_4/C$ ($x=0.02$) (d)

Figure 2a—d shows the SEM images of $LiFe_{1-x}Sm_xPO_4/C$ ($x=0.00$), $LiFe_{1-x}Sm_xPO_4/C$ ($x=0.02$), TEM image, and EDS pattern with an inset of Roman result for $LiFe_{1-x}Sm_xPO_4/C$ ($x=0.02$), respectively. It shows that Sm doping can effectively reduce the particle size of $LiFePO_4/C$. The particle size of the $LiFe_{1-x}Sm_xPO_4/C$ with $x=0.02$ is about 100 nm (Fig. 2b,c), which is much smaller than that of the $LiFe_{1-x}Sm_xPO_4/C$ ($x=0$) (1 μm, Fig. 2a). This is in good agreement with the result reported by Zhang [31] and Pang [32]. Compared with high-temperature solidphase reaction, hydrothermal method is more suitable for the fabrication of Sm-doped $LiFePO_4/C$ cathode materials EDS result shows that the atomic ratio of Fe/P/O is 0.984 ∶ 1 ∶ 4.524, which is in good accordance with the designed atomic percentage of $LiFe_{0.98}Sm_{0.02}PO_4/C$ (Fe/P/O is 0.98 ∶ 1 ∶ 4), as shown in Table 2, Fig. 2d. The content of Sm/Fe is 0.018, which also coincided well with the designed composition of the $LiFe_{0.98}Sm_{0.02}PO_4/C$ (Sm/Fe0. 020). It indicates that Sm atoms dissolve in the olivine lattice of $LiFePO_4/C$. However, it cannot be inferred whether Sm^{3+} ions occupy Fe^{2+} ion sites in $LiFePO_4/C$, as the ionic radius of Sm^{3+} ion (0. 096 nm) is much larger than that of Fe^{2+} ion (0. 074 nm).

Table 2 Composition of elements in $LiFe_{1-x}Sm_xPO_4/C$ (x=0. 02)

Elements	CK	OK	PK	FeK	SmL	Total
W%	8. 80	41. 01	17. 55	31. 15	1. 48	100
A%	16. 53	57. 86	12. 79	12. 59	0. 22	100

As seen from Fig. 2c, a carbon layer forms on the surface of the LiFePO4 particles, which coincides well with the result of Roman analysis (see the inset figure in Fig. 2d). The two broad peaks in the range of 1200—1700 cm. 1 can be respectively attributed to the D-band (disordered graphite, sp3-type carbon) and G-band (crystalline graphite, sp2-type carbon). The peak intensity ratio (I_D/I_G) is inversely proportional to the graphitization degree of carbon, the lower I_D/I_G, and the higher degree of graphitization. The peak intensity ratio (I_D/I_G= 0. 61) indicated that an optimized coating with large amount of sp2-type carbon has been achieved, which is beneficial for the improvement on the electronic conductivity.

Discharge capacity

Figure 3a-d shows discharge capacity, effect of temperature on the discharge capacity, initial charge/discharge profiles of $LiFe_{1-x}Sm_xPO_4/C$ (x = 0. 00, 0. 01, 0. 02, 0. 04, 0. 06), and initial charge/discharge profiles of $LiFe_{1-x}Sm_xPO_4/C$ with x=0. 02 at different temperatures. Obviously, Sm doping improves the discharge capacity and cycle stability of $LiFePO_4$. The four Sm-doped samples have a discharge capacity of 120, 154, 151, and 148 mAh g^{-1} at 0. 2 C, respectively, while the sample without Sm has a discharge capacity of 101 mAh g^{-1} (see Fig. 3a). At x =0. 02, $LiFe_{1-x}Sm_xPO_4/C$ cathode material has the maximum discharge capacity of 154 mAh g^{-1}, which is 1. 5 times larger than that of the un-doped sample.

The cycle stability of $LiFe_{1-x}Sm_xPO_4/C$ (x=0. 02) prepared by hydrothermal method is also better than the $LiFe_{1-x}Sm_xPO_4/C$ (x =0. 08) prepared by high-temperature solid-phase reaction. The discharge capacity of $LiFe_{1-x}Sm_xPO_4/C$ (x = 0. 02) prepared by hydrothermal method is 143 mAh g^{-1} after 30 cycles with capacity retention of 92. 5 %, while the discharge capacity of $LiFe_{1-x}Sm_xPO_4/C$ (x=0. 02) prepared by hightemperature solid-phase reaction is 126 mAh g^{-1} with capacity retention of 84 %.

At 40 ℃, $LiFe_{1-x}Sm_xPO_4/C$ (x = 0. 02) cathode material has a discharge capacity of 164 mAh g^{-1}, which is slightly higher than that papered by high-temperature solid-phase reaction (159 mAh g^{-1}) [31]. It is well known that temperature is an important factor for the electronic conductivity of $LiFePO_4$. Figure 3b shows the discharge capacity of five samples at different temperatures ranging from 40 to 60 ℃. The results show that the Sm-doped samples present a better discharge capacity than the undoped sample. However, the discharge capacities are quite low at −20 and −40 ℃. This may be attributed to the electrolyte ($LiPF_6$-EC/EDC). As the freezing point of EC is only 36.4 ℃, it may result in the lower conductivity of electrolyte and the lower diffusion coefficient of Li^+ in $LiPF_6$.

$LiFePO_4$ Sm-doped have a longer voltage plateau and a narrower gap in the initial charge-discharge curves, which illustrates that Sm doping decreases the polarization the charge-discharge and improves efficiency and the reversibility. It can be seen from Fig. 3c that the charge and discharge voltage plateau of $LiFe_{1-x}Sm_xPO_4/C$ ($x=0.02$) are 3.47 and 3.38V, respectively. Their voltage difference (ΔV) is only 90 mV, and Fig. 3d shows initial charge/discharge profiles of $LiFe_{1-x}Sm_xPO_4/C$ ($x=0.02$) at different temperatures. It shows that the $LiFe_{1-x}Sm_xPO_4/C$ ($x=0.02$) cathode material exhibits a lower capacity at lower temperatures from −2 to −40 ℃ with short voltage plateau and wide gap between the charge and discharge curves, especially at −40 ℃. Those results illustrate an unsatisfactory charge-discharge efficiency and reversibility at low temperatures.

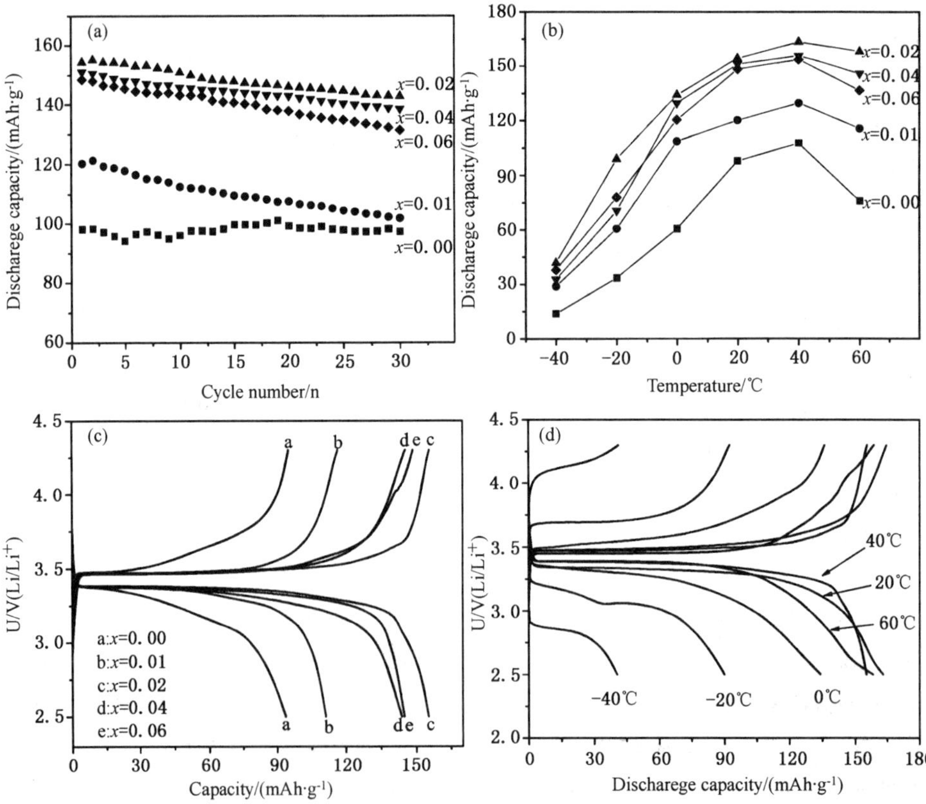

Fig. 3 Discharge capacity (a), effect of temperature on the discharge capacity (b) and initial charge/discharge profiles (c) of $LiFe_{1-x}Sm_xPO_4/C$ ($x=0.00, 0.01, 0.02, 0.04, 0.06$), and initial charge/discharge profiles of $LiFe_{1-x}Sm_xPO_4/C$ with $x=0.02$ (d)

High-rate dischargeability

Figure 4a-c shows high-rate dischargeability (HRD) of $LiFe_{1-x}Sm_xPO_4$/C (x=0. 00,0. 01,0. 02,0. 04,0. 06),cycle stability, and initial charge/discharge profiles of $LiFe_{1-x}Sm_xPO_4$/C with x = 0. 02 at different current densities. The discharge capacity of Sm-doped cathode materials is larger than that of un-doped sample at 0. 2, 0. 5, 1, 2, and 5 C. The $LiFe_{1-x}Sm_xPO_4$/C (x = 0. 02) cathode material has the best rate discharge performance, which are 154, 137, 122, 107, and 81 mAh g^{-1} at 0. 2, 0. 5, 1, 2, and 5 C, respectively. In addition, the discharge capacity is larger than that of sample prepared by high-temperature solid-phase reaction, which are 152, 127, 102, 82, and 67 mAh g^{-1} at 0. 2, 0. 5, 1, 2, and 5 C.

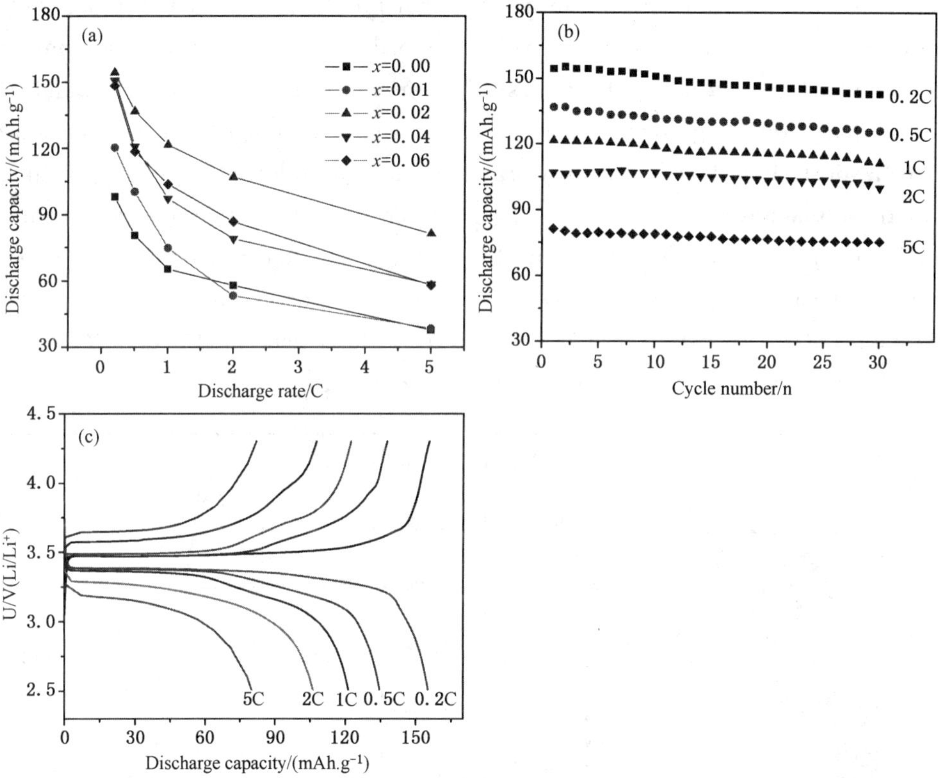

Fig. 4 HRD of $LiFe_{1-x}Sm_xPO_4$/C(x=0. 00,0. 01,0. 02,0. 04,0. 06)(a),cycle stability (b),and initial charge/discharge profiles (c) of $LiFe_{1-x}Sm_xPO_4$/C with x=0. 02

$LiFe_{1-x}Sm_xPO_4$/C (x=0. 02) prepared by hydrothermal method has excellent capacity retention at different current densities. It can be seen from Fig. 4b that the discharge capacity retention of $LiFe_{1-x}Sm_xPO_4$/C (x = 0. 02) after 30 cycles is 92. 5, 92. 1, 91. 5, 93. 5, and 92. 2% at 0. 2, 0. 5, 1, 2, and 5 C, respectively, whereas the discharge capacity retention of the sample prepared by high-temperature solid method is 84, 83. 5, 82. 3, 88. 4, and 81. 3 %, respectively.

The charge-discharge voltage plateau is narrowing, and thecurve gap is widening along with increase of the dischargecurrent density (see Fig. 4c). The probable reason is that the$FePO_4$ interface decreases with increase of the discharge rate, and consequently, Li^+ ion across this interface is not sufficient to maintain adequate current, which leads to the loss of discharge capacity. Furthermore, the de-intercalation of Li^+ in the $LiFePO_4$ may cause defection of the cell structure, which may decrease the reversibility of charge-discharge reaction.

Electrochemical impedance spectroscopy and cyclic voltammeter

Figure 5a-b shows electrochemical impedance spectroscopy (EIS) and cyclic voltammeter (CV) of $LiFe_{1-x}Sm_xPO_4/C$ (x=0.00, 0.01, 0.02, 0.04, 0.06). Evidently, Sm doping decreases the charge transfer resistances (R_{ct}), which implies that electrochemical reaction kinetic of the electrode is improved. The radii of the semicircle in the AC impedance spectra for $LiFePO_4/C$ cathode material doped with Sm is much smaller than that for sample without Sm, which suggests that charge transfer resistance for the sample doped with Sm is smaller than that for the sample without Sm. The AC impedance spectra of five samples were tested at 0.2 C after 3 cycles, and it can be seen that the EIS curve consists of a semicircle followed by a straight line. Diameter of the semicircle represents the charge transfer resistance in the electrochemical reaction at the surface of the electrode, which is defined as R_{ct}.

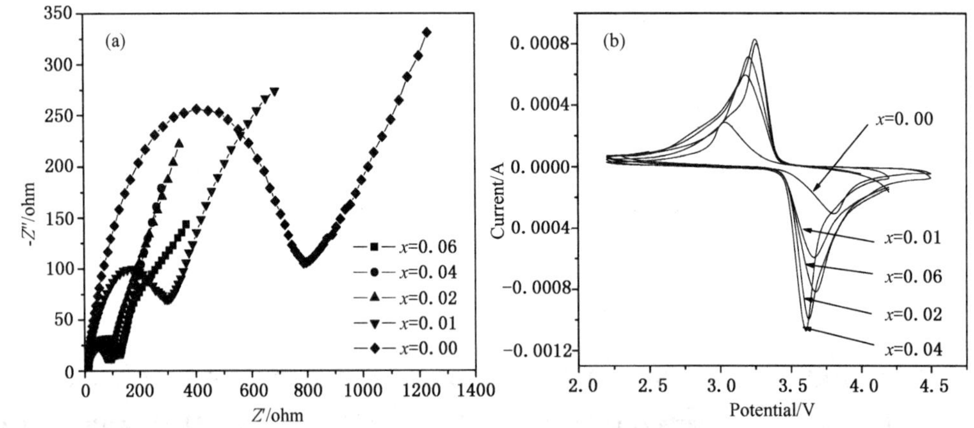

Fig. 5　EIS (a) and CV (b) of $LiFe_{1-x}Sm_xPO_4/C$ (x=0.00, 0.01, 0.02, 0.04, 0.06)

Table 3　Electrochemical parameters of $LiFe_{1-x}Sm_xPO_4/C$ in CV and EIS

Samples	C/(mAh g^{-1})	R_{ct}/Ω	I_0/(mA g^{-1})	ΔE_P/V
x=0.00	101	815.2	22.78	0.766
x=0.02	154	110.1	168.67	0.372

Sm doping decreases the charge transfer resistances (R_{ct}). Especially at x=0.02, the R_{ct} is 110.1 Ω, which is much smaller than that of the un-doped sample (815.2 Ω), as shown in Table 3. The AC impedance spectra are fitted using least-square method with ZVIEW electrochemical impedance software, and the exchange current density I_0 is calculated from $I_0 = RT/FR_{ct}$, where R is the gas constant, T is the temperature, F is the Faraday constant, and R_{ct} represents the charge transfer resistance. The result shows that the exchange current density for the sample with Sm is 168.67 mA g^{-1}, which is about eight times higher than that sample without Sm(22.78 mA g^{-1}).

The charge transfer resistance R_{ct} and exchange current density I_0 are 110.1 Ω and 168.67 mA g^{-1}, respectively. They are much better than that of the sample prepared by hight emperature solid-phase reaction (R_{ct}=217 Ω, I_0=90.62 mA g^{-1}), respectively [31]. The better HRD may be attributed to the better electrochemical reaction kinetic of the electrode.

Cyclic voltammeter (CV) indicates that Sm doping decreases the difference (ΔE_P) between the oxidation peak and the reduction peak and increases the peak intensity, which suggests that samples doped with Sm have better electrochemical reversibility. The ΔE_P between the oxidation peak and the reduction peak for $LiFe_{1-x}Sm_xPO_4/C$ (x = 0.02) prepared by hydrothermal method is 0.372 (Fig. 5b), which is less than that of 0.475 for the sample prepared by high-temperature solid-phase reaction.

Conclusions

Doping Sm decreases the particle size obviously. The $LiFe_{1-x}Sm_xPO_4/C$ (x = 0.02) cathode material has the particle size of less than 100 nm, which is about ten times less than that of the un-doped sample (approximately 1 μm). The lattice parameters of a, c, and the cell volume of the $LiFe_{1-x}Sm_xPO_4/C$ (x=0.02) cathode material are 1.0324 nm, 0.4691 nm, and 0.290 8 nm^3, which is much smaller than that of the undoped sample (1.035 2 nm, 0.470 1 nm, and 0.292 6 nm^3), respectively. Sm doping can improve the maximum discharge capacity and high-rate dischargeability. The maximum discharge capacity of the $LiFe_{1-x}Sm_xPO_4/C$ (x=0.02) cathode material is 154 mAh g^{-1} at 0.2 C, which is about 1.5 times higher than that of the undoped sample.

Acknowledgments This work was supported by the Foundation of State Key Laboratory of Rare Earth Resources Utilization (RERU2013021).

Conflict of interest The authors declare that they have no conflict of interests.

References

[1] Scrosati B (2000) Recent advances in lithium ion battery materials. Electrochim Acta 45: 2461-2466.

[2] Pasquier AD, Huang CC, Spitler T (2009) Nano $Li_4Ti_5O_{12}$-$LiMn_2O_4$ batteries with high power capability and improved cycle-life. J Power Sources 186:508-514.

[3] Wang JW, Liu J, Yang GL et al (2009) Electrochemical performance of $Li_3V_2(PO_4)_3/C$ cathode material using a novel carbon

source. Electrochim Acta 54:6451-6454.

[4] Zhai J, Zhao MS, Wang DD et al (2010) Effect of MgO nanolayer coated on $Li_3V_2(PO_4)_3$/C cathode material for lithium-ion battery. J Alloys Compd 502:401-406.

[5] Hu W, Zhang XB, Cheng YL et al (2011) Low-cost and facile onepot synthesis of pure single-crystallinee-$Cu_{0.95}V_2O_5$ anoribbons: high capacity cathode material for rechargeable Li-ion batteriesw. Chem Commun 47:5250-5252.

[6] Ma DL, Cao ZY, Wang HG et al (2012) Three-dimensionally ordered macroporous FeF_3 and its in situ homogenous polymerization coating for high energy and power density lithium ion batteries. Energy Environ Sci 5:8538-8542.

[7] Wang GG, Ma DL, Huang Y et al (2012) Electrospun V_2O_5 nanostructures with controllable morphology as high-performance cathode materials for lithium-Ion batteries. Chem Eur J 18:8987-8993.

[8] Zhai J, Zhao MS, Wang YZ (2014) Effect of A_2O_3-coating on the electrochemical performances of $Li_3V_2(PO_4)_3$/C cathode material. J Solid State Electrochem 18:2857-2862.

[9] Padhi AK, Nanjundaswamy KS, Masquelier C et al (1997) Effect of structure on the Fe^{3+}/Fe^{2+} redox couple in iron phosphates. Electrochem Soc 144(5):1609-1613.

[10] Padhi AK, Nanjundaswamy KS, Goodenough JB (1997) Phosphoolivines as positive-electrode materials for rechargeable lithium batteries. Electrochem Soc 144(4):1188-1194.

[11] Qin X, Wang J, Xie J et al (2012) Hydrothermally synthesized $LiFePO_4$ crystals with enhanced electrochemical properties simultaneous suppression of crystal growth along [010] and antisite defect formation. Phys Chem Chem Phys 14(8):2669-2677.

[12] Wang Q, Deng S, Wang H et al (2013) Hydrothermal synthesis of hierarchical $LiFePO_4$ microspheres for lithium ion battery. Alloys Compd 553:69-74.

[13] Andersson AS, Thomas JO (2001) The source of first-cycle capacity loss in $LiFePO_4$. Power Sources 97.98:498-502.

[14] Myung ST, Komaba S, Hirosaki N, Yashiro H (2004) Emulsion drying synthesis of olivine $LiFePO_4$/C composite and its electrochemical properties as lithium intercalation material. Electrochim Acta 49(24):4213-4222.

[15] Wu XL, Jiang LY, Cao FF et al (2009) $LiFePO_4$ nanoparticles embedded in a nanoporous carbon matrix: superior cathode material for electrochemical energy-storage devices. Adv Mater 21(25-26):2710-2714.

[16] Cho YD, Fey GTK, Kao HM (2008) Physical and electrochemical properties of La-doped $LiFePO_4$/C composites as cathode materials for lithium-ion batteries. Solid State Electrochemistry 12(7-8):815-823.

[17] Chung SY, Bloking JT, Chiang YM (2002) Electronically conductive phospho-olivines as lithium storage electrodes. NatMater 1(2):123-128.

[18] Ni J, Morishita M, Kawabe Yet al (2010) Hydrothermal preparation of $LiFePO_4$ nanocrystals mediated by organic acid. Power Sources 195(9):2877-2882.

[19] Zhao RR, Hung IM, Li YT et al (2012) Synthesis and properties of Co-doped $LiFePO_4$ as cathode material via a hydrothermal route for lithium-ion batteries. Alloys Compd 513(5):282-288.

[20] Chen YC, Chen JM, Hsu CH et al (2010) Electrochemical and structural studies of $LiCo_{1/3}Mn_1/3Fe_{1/3}PO_4$ as a cathode mate-

rial for lithium ion batteries. Power Sources 195(19):6867-6872.

[21] Bauer EM, Bellitto C, Righini G et al (2005) A versatile method of preparation of carbon-rich $LiFePO_4$: a promising cathodematerial for Li-ion batteries. Power Sources 146(1):544-549.

[22] Bruce PG, Scrosati B, Tarascon JM (2008) Nanomaterials for rechargeable lithium batteries. Angew Chem Int Ed 47(16): 2930-2946.

[23] Saravanan K, ReddyMV, Balaya P et al (2009) Storage performance of $LiFePO_4$ nanoplates. J Mater Chem 19(5):605-610.

[24] Gao B, Fan H, Zhang X (2012) Hydrothermal synthesis of single crystal MoO_3 nanobelts and their electrochemical properties as cathode electrode materials for rechargeable lithium batteries. Phys Chem Solids 73(3):423-429.

[25] Wang G, ChengY, YanMet al (2007) $Li_{0.99}Ti_{0.01}FePO_4/C$ composite as cathode material for lithium ion battery. Solid State Electrochem 11(4):457-462.

[26] Yin XG, Huang K, Liu SQ et al (2010) Preparation and characterization of Na-doped $LiFePO_4/C$ composites as cathode materials for lithium-ion batteries. Power Sources 195(13):4308-4312.

[27] Bard AJ, Faulker LR (1986) Electrochemical methods-fundamental and applications. In: Gu LY, Lu M X, Song S Z, Translate. Beijing: Chemical Industry Publishing Company, 121.

[28] Zhao X, Tang X, Zhang L et al (2010) Effects of neodymium aliovalent substitution on the structure and electrochemical performance of $LiFePO_4$. Electrochim Acta 55(20):5899-5904.

[29] Zheng S, Wang X, Huang X et al (2012) Hydrothermal synthesis of Ni-doped carom-like $LiFe_{0.95}Ni_{0.05}PO_4$ powders. Ceram Int 38(5):4391-4394.

[30] Goktepe H (2013) Electrochemical performance of Yb-doped $LiFePO_4/C$ composites as cathode materials for lithium-ion batteries. Res Chem Intermed 39(7):2979-2987.

[31] Zhang QM, Qiao YQ, Zhao MS et al (2012) Structure and electrochemical performance of Sm-doped lithium Iron phosphate cathode Materials. Chin J Inorg Chem 28(1): 67-73.

[32] Pang LJ, Zhao MS, Zhao X et al (2012) Preparation and electrochemical performance of Gd-doped $LiFePO_4/C$ composites. Power Source 201(1):253-258.

Synthesis of Single-crystalline $LiFePO_4$ with Rhombus-like Morphology①

Yuqing Qiao[a,b,c], Lixia Pan[a], Li He[b], Ludovic Dumée[b],
Lingxue Kong[b], Minshou Zhao[a], Limin Wang[c], Weimin Gao[b]
([a] College of Environmental and Chemical Engineering,
Yanshan University, Qinhuangdao 066004, People's Republic of China)
([b] Institute for Frontier Materials,
Deakin University, Geelong, VIC 3217, Australia)
([c] State Key Laboratory of Rare Earth Resources Utilization,
Changchun Institute of Applied Chemistry,
Chinese Academy of Sciences, Changchun 130022, People's Republic of China)

Abstract: In this investigation, carbon-coated $LiFePO_4$ cathode materials were synthesized with a facile hydrothermal method. The structure and electrochemical properties of the materials were investigated by X-ray diffraction (XRD), Roman, transmission electron microscopy-energy dispersive spectroscopy (TEM-EDS), and electrochemical impedance spectroscopy (EIS). By adjusting the mixing concentration of starting materials, a single-crystalline $LiFePO_4$ with an anisotropic rhombus morphology (Space Group: Pmnb No. 62) were successfully synthesized. In addition, the carbon coated on the surface of $LiFePO_4$ material prepared has a lower I_D/I_G (0.80), which indicates an optimized carbon structure with an increased amount of sp^2-type carbon. Electrochemical performance test shows that the carbon-coated $LiFePO_4$ cathode materials have an initial discharge capacity of 146 mAh g^{-1} at 0.2C.

Key words: Li-ion batteries; Electrochemical characterizations; Electrodes; Cathodes

Introduction

Due to its non-toxicity and low cost, the ordered olivine lithium iron phosphate $LiFePO_4$ has been extensively studied as a promising cathode material for lithium-ion battery. However, it suffers from the slow Li-ion diffusion across the $LiFePO_4/FePO_4$ two-phase boundary and the low electronic conductivity during the charge-discharge process [1-4]. As the Li-ion diffusion distance predominantly controls the diffusion time, it is believed that nanocrystallization [5-11] is an effective approach to enhance the diffusion coefficient of lithium-ion insertion/extraction. So far, a number of synthesized methods, such as ball-milling method

① Ionics, 2015(21): 295-299.

[5], polyacrylatespyrolysis route [6], single-step polyol process at low temperatures [7], template-free sol-gel approach [8], microwave method [9], solvothermal method [10, 11], etc., have been developed to prepare nano-sized $LiFePO_4$ particles. The composites synthesized by most of these methods have good electrochemical performances. Peng et al. [10] synthesized a nanoarchitectures $LiFePO_4$ composed of self-assembled single-crystalline nanowires by solvothermal process, which utilized a homogeneous reaction atmosphere in tetra-ethylene glycol, and the novel one-dimensional (1D) single-crystalline $LiFePO_4$ nanowire exhibits good rate capability with a reversible capacity of 110 mAh g^{-1} at a current rate of 30C. Zhao et al. [11] synthesized a two-dimensional (2D), single crystalline, {010}-oriented $LiFePO_4$ nanosheets with a thickness of 30-60 nm using solvothermal synthesis in diethylene glycol solvent, and the $LiFePO_4$ nanosheets can provide the highest pore density for lithium-ion insertion/ extraction.

Though the down-sizing strategy is an effective way to improve the performance of the cathode electrode, it adversely affects the tap density, volumetric energy density, and cycling performance. To tackle this problem, Sun et al. [12] prepared large-scale $LiFePO_4$ microspheres with three-dimensional (3D) porous microstructure. These micro/nanostructured $LiFePO_4$ microspheres have a high tap density and, as electrodes, show excellent rate capability and cycle stability. Several literatures have been reported on single-crystalline $LiFePO_4$ particles with micro/nanostructured and highly anisotropic morphologies [13-17]. Lu et al. [14] prepared a single-crystalline $LiFePO_4$ with drum-like particles, and they believed that the egg-like $LiFePO_4$ particles form firstly, then progressively evolve into the cubic-and rhombic-like LiFePO4 particles, and finally grow into drum-like particles.

During the preparation process of $LiFePO_4$ composites synthesized by solvothermal process, the mixing procedure of starting materials obviously affects the microstructure and electrochemical performance [10, 18]. By changing the addition sequences of the solutions, 1D $LiFePO_4$ nanostructures with different stacking degrees can be readily obtained by Peng et al. [10]. Olivine $LiFePO_4$ nanoplates [18] can be easily prepared, and the largest crystallographic facet of the $LiFePO_4$ nanoplates can be regulated by the addition sequences of the solutions. The carbon structure has a great effect on the microstructure and electrochemical performances of $LiFePO_4$, whereas few literatures have been reported on the carbon structure by changing the mixing procedure of starting materials so far. In this investigation, carbon-coated $LiFePO_4$ cathode materials were synthesized with a facile hydrothermal method by adjusting the mixing concentration of starting materials, and the microstructure, the carbon coat, and the electrochemical performance of $LiFePO_4$ used as the cathode materials were studied.

Experimental

The precursor of $LiFePO_4$ was synthesized by mixing the solution of $LiOH \cdot H_2O$ (90 %), H_3PO_4 (85 %), and $FeSO_4 \cdot 7H_2O$ (99 %) under magnetic stirring, followed by adding 5 wt% $C_6H_{12}O_6$ as the carbon source. The experimental procedures are as follows: (1) H_3PO_4 (0.02 mol) and $LiOH \cdot H_2O$ (0.06 mol) were, respectively, dissolved in 5 and 20 ml distilled water, then H_3PO_4 solution was added to $LiOH \cdot H_2O$ slowly. (2) $FeSO_4 \cdot 7H_2O$ (0.02 mol) was dissolved in 30 ml distilled water with existence of magnet at argon atmosphere, followed by adding 5 wt% $C_6H_{12}O_6$. (3) The two solutions were stirred for 10 min, followed by pouring into a 100 ml PTFE-lined stainless container, and were subsequently heated at 190 ℃ for 6 h in a vacuum drying oven. Finally, the precursor was sintered at 700 ℃ for 6 h in a pipe-type evenven under nitrogen atmosphere.

The phase constituents were determined on a Rigaku D/max 2500pc X-ray diffractometer equipped with the JAD5 software. The microstructure and composition of the sample mounted on a Cu grid was characterized by a JEM-2100 equipped with energy disperse spectroscopy at 200 kV. Raman spectra were performed on a Renishaw Gloucestershire at a laser wavelength of 514 nm. The exposure time, power, accumulation, and spectral resolution used for the spectral data collection are 30 s, 10 %, and 1 and 4 cm^{-1}, respectively.

The electrochemical performances of the samples were tested on a BTS-5V 10mA system in the range of 2.5—4.3 V at 0.2 to 5C current densities. The electrochemical impedance spectroscopy was conducted on a CHI6660A electrochemical workstation with an oscilla-tion voltage of 5 mV and the applied frequency ranging from 100 kHz to 0.01 Hz.

Results and discussion

Figure 1 is the XRD pattern of $LiFePO_4$ cathode materials. Obviously, the crystallization occurs for the synthesized $LiFePO_4$. The diffraction peaks are in good agreement with the standardcard (JCPDS# 40-1499; Space Group: Pmnb No. 62). Hence, it can be determined that the $LiFePO_4$ particles prepared presents an orthorhombic olivine-type structure with the lattice parameters $a = 0.6019$ nm, $b = 1.0347$ nm, and $c = 0.4704$ nm.

Figure 2 shows TEM images and energy dispersive spectrum (EDS) result of $LiFePO_4$ cathode materials. As seen from Fig. 2a, b, the $LiFePO_4$ presents a rhombic shape with a mean edge length of 1.2 μm, a thickness of 0.25 μm, and a length of 2 μm, and the composition of the $LiFePO_4$ cathode materials were analyzed by energy dispersive spectrum (see Fig. 2c). By changing the concentration of the solutions, $LiFePO_4$ with rhombus-like morphologies can be readily obtained. This finding coincides well with that reported by Pengetal. [10].

From the selected area of electron diffraction patterns shown in Fig. 2d, it can be determined that the $LiFePO_4$ particles present a single crystal structure. The tested R_1 and R_2 are 0.278 (1/nm) and 0.250 (1/nm), which belong to the family of (031) crystal plane 031 with interplanar spacing $d_1 = 0.278$ nm and family of the crystal plane (131) with an interplanar spacing $d_2 = 0.250$ nm, respectively. The calculated R_3 belongs to the family of crystal planes (102). $\angle R_1R_2 = 106°$, and the zone axis of this diffraction pattern is [613].

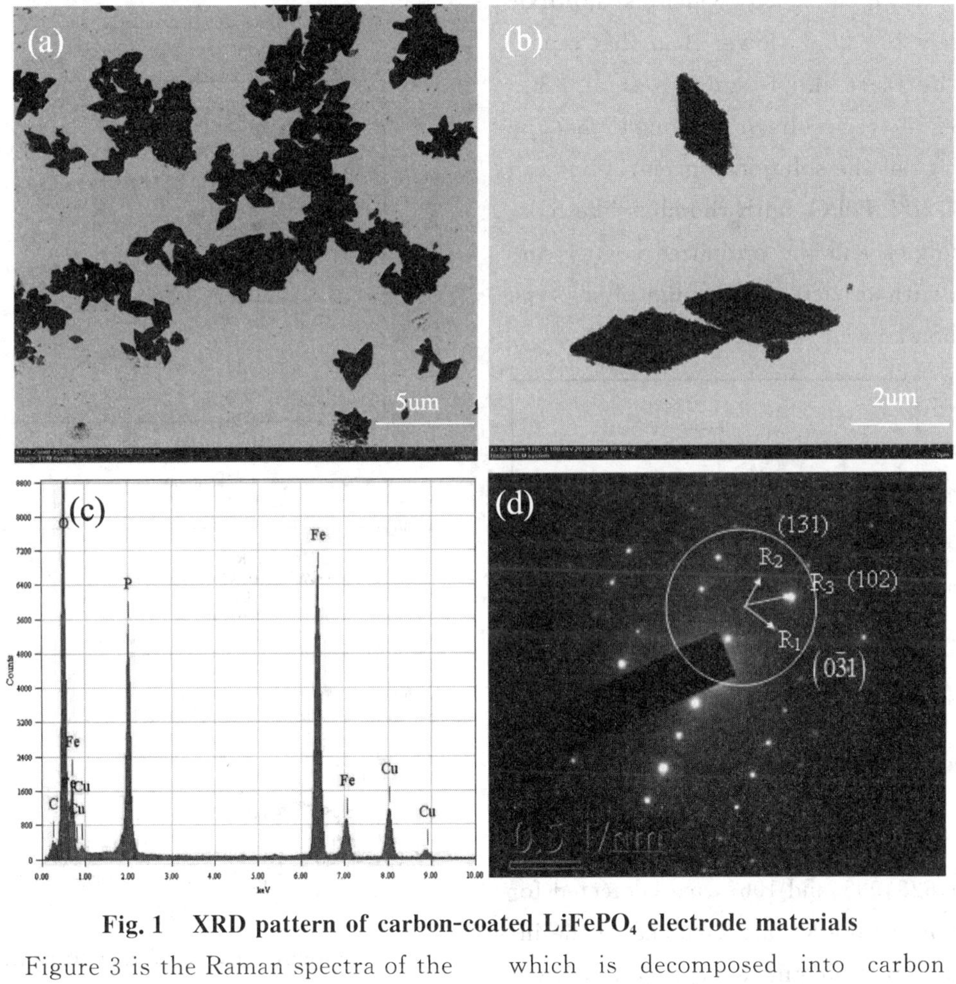

Fig. 1 XRD pattern of carbon-coated $LiFePO_4$ electrode materials

Figure 3 is the Raman spectra of the $LiFePO_4$ cathode materials prepared. As seen from Fig. 3, acarbon layer forms on the surface of the $LiFePO_4$ particles. The carbon layer is derived from $C_6H_{12}O_6$, which is decomposed into carbon at 700 ℃ during the hydrothermal process. The two broad peaks in the range of 1 350—1 580 cm^{-1} can be, respectively, attributed to the disordered graphite (D-band) and crystalline graphite (G-band, sp^2-type carbon). The peak intensity ratio of D-band and G-band (I_D/I_G) is inversely proportional to the graphitization degree of carbon, i. e., lower I_D/I_G, higher the degree of graphitization, so the higher electronic conduc-tivity of the residual carbon can give rise to a better electrode performance. The peak intensity ratio I_D/I_G is 0.80, which is approximately 13—25 % lower than that reported by Bi et al. [4] and Wu et al. [8]. From above results, it is thought that the change of the solution concentrations can achieve $LiFePO_4$ with rhombus-like morphologies and the optimized coated carbon with an increased amount of sp^2-type carbon as well.

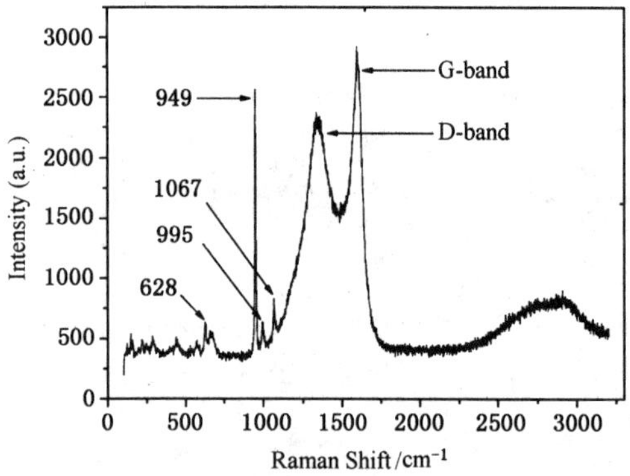

Fig. 3　Raman spectra of carbon-coated $LiFePO_4$ electrode materials

The strong Raman peaks around 949, 628, 995, and 1067 cm^{-1} detected for the pure $LiFePO_4$ are assigned to the internal stretching mode (v_1, v_4, v_3, and v_3) of the PO_4^{3+} anions [8], respectively, while the weak peaks at 100—400 cm^{-1} are ascribed to the external stretching mode of Fe^{2+} cations.

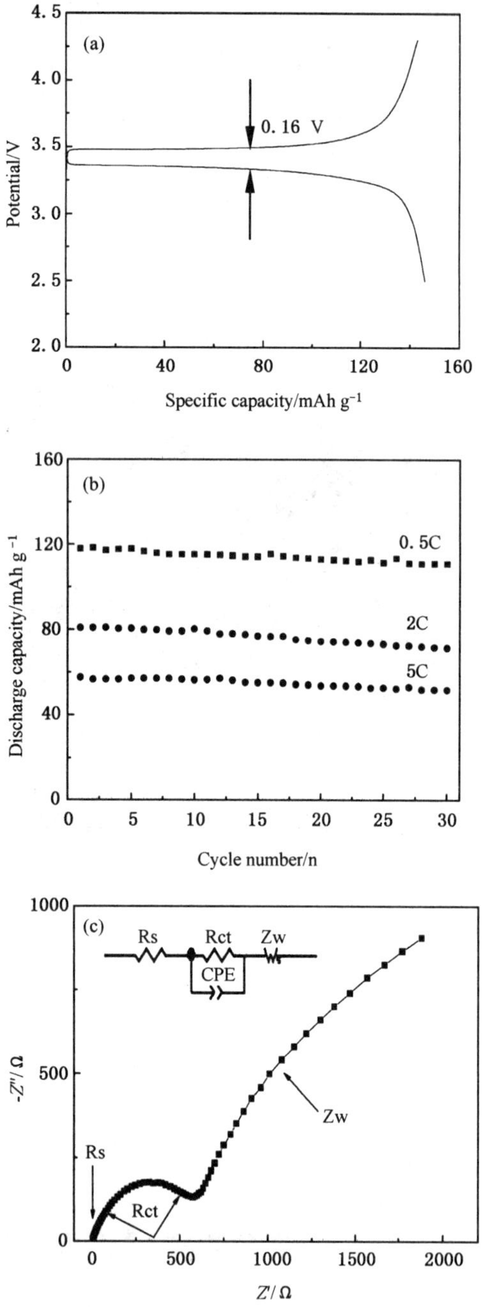

Fig. 4　Raman spectra of carbon-coated $LiFePO_4$ electrode materials

The electrochemical performance of carbon-coated $LiFePO_4$ used as the cathode material was tested. Fig. 4a is the initial charge-discharge curve of the LiFe-

PO_4 cathode material. As seen from Fig. 4a, the $LiFePO_4$ prepared has a specific discharge capacity of 146 mAh g^{-1} at 0. 2C. It is noticed that the discharge capacity of the $LiFePO_4$ prepared by the facile hydro-thermal method by adjusting the mixing concentration is larger than that of the $LiFePO_4$ synthesized by high-temperature solid-phase reaction (115 mAh g^{-1}) [3], solvothermal synthesis (122 mAh g^{-1}) [13], hydrother-malmethod (117mAh g^{-1})[19], and sol-gel method (65 mAh g^{-1})[20]. In addition, it can also be seen from Fig. 4a that the gap between the charge-discharge curves is only about 0. 16 mV, which indicates that the carbon-coated $LiFePO_4$ cathode materials synthesized by the facile hydrothermal method has a reasonable charge-discharge efficiency and reversibility.

The relationship between the discharge capacity and the discharge current density of carbon-coated $LiFePO_4$ cathode materials at 0. 5, 2, and 5C are shown in Fig. 4b. It is learnt from Fig. 4b that the high-rate discharge capacity (HRD) of the carbon-coated $LiFePO_4$ cathode materials at 0. 5, 2, and 5C are 118, 80, and 57 mAh g^{-1}, respectively. The discharge capacity at 0. 5, 2, and 5C after 30 times charge-discharge cycles are 111, 71, and 52 mAh g^{-1}, and the capacity retention are about 94, 89, and 91 %, respectively.

To clarify the electron transfer process of carbon-coated $LiFePO_4$ electrodes, electrochemical impedance spectroscopy (EIS) measurement was performed at the charge state of 4. 3 V after initial cycle at 0. 2C, and the result is shown in Fig. 4c. The inset is an equivalent circuit model which was used to analyze the impedance spectra [21]. In Fig. 4c, the semicircle in the high-frequency region represents the charge-transfer re-sis-tance, which corresponds to Rct in the equivalent circuit. The fitting result indicates that the value of Rct is 596 Ω for the carbon-coated $LiFePO_4$ electrode. With the same equivalent circuit model, it is about 14 and 51 % lower in comparison with that of the $LiFePO_4$ cathode materials reported by Pang et al. [3] and Zhang et al. [22].

Conclusions

Single-crystalline $LiFePO_4$ with an optimized carbon layer was successfully prepared utilizing the hydrothermal synthesis method by adjusting the mixing concentration of starting materials. The $LiFePO_4$ electrode materials has the discharge capacity of 146 mAh g^{-1} at 0. 2C and a charge-transfer resistance of 596 Ω. The occurrences of two broad peaks in the range of 1 350—1 580 cm^{-1} can be attributed to the disordered graphite (D-band) and crystalline graphite (G-band), and the peak intensity ratio I_D/I_G of the carbon-coated $LiFePO_4$ is about 0. 80.

Acknowledgments This work was supported by the Foundation of State Key Laboratory of Rare Earth Resources Utilization(RERU2013021).

References

[1] Nguyen TTD, Dimesso L, Cherkashinin G, Jaud JC, Lauterbach S, Hausbrand R, Jaegermann W (2013) Solid State Ionics 19:1229.

[2] Wu M, Wang ZH, Yuan LX, Zhang WX, Hu XL, Huang YH (2012) Chin Sci Bull 57:4170.

[3] Pang LJ, Zhao MS, Zhao XA, Chai YJ (2012) J Power Sources 201:253.

[4] Bi H, Huang FQ, Tang YF, Liu ZQ, Lin TQ, Chen J, Zhao W (2013) Electrochim Acta 88:414.

[5] Fey GTK, Chen YG, Kao HM (2009) J Power Sources 189:169.

[6] Cao YL, Yu LH, Li T, Ai XP, Yang HX (2007) J Power Sources 172:913.

[7] Wu G, Zhou YK, Shao ZP (2013) Appl Surf Sci 283:999.

[8] Yang JL, Wang JJ, Wang DN, Li XF, Geng DS, Liang GX (2012) J Power Sources 208:340.

[9] Zhang Y, Feng H, Wu XB, Wang LH, Zhang AQ, Xia TC (2009) Electrochim Acta 54:3206

[10] Peng LL, Zhao Y, Ding Y, Yu GH (2014) Chem Commun 50:9569.

[11] Zhao Y, Peng LL, Liu BR, Yu GH (2014) Nano Lett 14:2849.

[12] Sun CW, Rajasekhara S, Googenough JB, Zhou F (2011) J Am Chem Soc 133:2132.

[13] Song JJ, Shao GJ, Shi MW, Ma ZP, Song W, Wang CX (2013) Solid State Ionics 253:39.

[14] Lu ZG, Chen HL, Robert R, Zhu BYX, Deng JQ, Wu LJ (2011) Chem Mater 23:2848.

[15] Ma ZP, Shao GJ, Wang GL, Du JP, Zhang Y (2013) Solid State Ionics 19:437.

[16] Qin X, Wang XH, Xiang HM, Xie J, Li JJ, Zhou YC (2010) J Phys Chem C 114:16806.

[17] Lv YJ, Long YF, Lv XY, Wen YX (2014) Solid State Ionics 20:471.

[18] Wang L, He XM, Sun WT, Wang JL, Li YD, Fan SS (2012) Nano Lett 12:5632.

[19] Talebi-Esfandarani M, Savadogo O (2014) Solid State Ionics 261:81.

[20] Dhindsa KS, Mandal BP, Bazzi K, Lin NW, Nazri M, Nazri GA, Naik VM, Garg VK, Oliveira AC, Vaishnava P, Naik R, Zhou ZX (2013) Solid State Ionics 253:94.

[21] Chen C, Liu GB, Wang Y, Li JL, Liu H (2013) Electrochim Acta 113:46.

[22] Zhang QM, Qiao YQ, Zhao MS, Wang LM (2012) Chin J Inorg Chem 28(1):67.

（二）镍-金属氢化物电池（Ni-MH）负极材料

Structures and Electrochemical Characteristics of Several Kinds of Alloys①

Minshou Zhao, Xinbo Zhang, Yujun Chai' Changying Sun
(Key Laboratory of Rare Earth Chemistry and Physics
Changchun Institute of Applied Chemistry, Chinese Academy
of Sciences, Changchun 130022, P. R. China)

Abstract: The structures and the electrochemical characteristics of $La_{0.7-x}Ce_xMg_{0.3}Ni_{2.8}Co_{0.5}$ ($x=0.1-0.5$) alloy, $Ti_{0.25-x}Zr_xV_{0.35}Cr_{0.1}Ni_{0.3}$ ($x=0.05-0.15$) alloy and $AB_{3<x<5}$-type alloy, which are the representative examples of AB_3-type alloy, solid solution alloy and non-AB_5-type alloy, respectively, have been investigated, and the performances of MH-Ni battery in which $AB_{3<x<5}$ type alloy is used as the negative electrode material are examined at relatively low temperature.

Key words: $La_{0.7-x}Ce_xMg_{0.3}Ni_{2.8}Co_{0.5}$ alloy; $Ti_{0.25-x}Zr_xV_{0.35}Cr_{0.1}Ni_{0.3}$ alloy; $AB_{3<x<5}$-type alloy; Structure; Characteristics.

INTRODUCTION

Hydrogen is expected to be a promising new energy source to replace conventional fossil fuels for solving the shortage of fossil energy sources and global warming in the near future. In order for hydrogen to become to a viable solution for the energy crisis and the environmental problem, hydrogen storage is one of many important processes. Among different ways to store hydrogen, absorption in solid to form hydride is very attractive, since it allows safe storage at pressure and temperature close to ambient conditions [1]. It is the most successful for the metal hydrides that are used as a negative electrode material in many application fields of metal hydrides. The Ni-MH secondary battery has been widely adopted in various portable electronic devices, electric hand tools and hybrid electric vehicles [2, 3]. To date, almost all commercial Ni-MH batteries are employing AB_5-type alloy as the negative electrode material. However, as the electrochemical capacity of the AB_5-type alloy is limited to about 372 mAh/g, the energy density of the Ni-MH battery is not competing favorably with lithium ion battery. Therefore, it is necessary to search for a new type alloy with much higher energy density, better rate dischargeability and lower cost, which perhaps may be an

① Res. Chem. Intermed, 2006, 32(5-6): 403-417.

alternative for the conventional rare-earthbased AB_5-type alloy or another choice.

The structures and electrochemical characteristics of several type alloys have been investigated in our group to ascertain for possibility to be used as the novel negative electrode materials in Ni-MH battery or hydrogen storage alloys. The experimental details are the same as described in our previous papers [4-6].

$La_{0.7-x}Ce_xMg_{0.3}Ni_{2.8}Co_{0.5}$ (x=0.1—0.5) Alloy

Recently, Kadir *et al*. [7] have reported the discovery of a new type of ternary alloy with the general formula RMg_2Ni_9 (R= rare earth, Ca, Y) with a $PuNi_3$-type structure. Some of the R-Mg-Ni based ternary alloys can absorb/desorb 1.8—1.87 mass% H and are, thus, regarded as promising candidates for hydrogen storage [8]. Chen *et al*. [9] have studied the structure and the electrochemical characteristics of $LaCaMg(Ni,M)_9$ (M= Al, Mn) alloy, and almost at the same time, Kohno *et al*. [10] have reported that the discharge capacity of $La_{0.7}Mg_{0.3}Ni_{2.8}Co_{0.5}$ alloy reached 410 mAh/g. Adzic *et al*. [11] pointed out that the degradation rate of electrochemical capacity due to electrode alloy corrosion was significantly decreased by the presence of Ce. Sakai *et al*. [12] reported that the replacement of lanthanum by large amounts of cerium can improve the cycle stability of the alloy even in the low content range of cobalt.

On the basis of our previous studies and the belief that the Ce addition may result in some noticeable modifications, the structure and electrochemical characteristics of the $La_{0.7-x}Ce_xMg_{0.3}Ni_{2.8}Co_{0.5}$ (x=0.1—0.5) alloy have been investigated systematically as a representative example of AB_3-type alloys.

Structure characteristics

Figure 1 shows the Rietveld analysis pattern of the $La_{0.6}Ce_{0.1}Mg_{0.3}Ni_{2.8}Co_{0.5}$ alloy as a representative example of $La_{0.7-x}Ce_xMg_{0.3}Ni_{2.8}Co_{0.5}$ (x=0.1—0.5) alloy. It can be found that, except for small amounts of impurity phases, LaNi and $LaNi_2$, the alloy mainly consisted of a La_2MgNi_9 phase with a $PuNi_3$-type rhombohedral structure and a $LaNi_5$ phase with a $CaCu_5$-type hexagonal structure. The lattice parameter, cell volume and phase abundance of $La_{0.7-x}Ce_xMg_{0.3}Ni_{2.8}Co_{0.5}$ (x=0.1—0.5) alloy are presented in Table 1. The results indicate that the cell volume of the $La(La,Mg)_2Ni_9$ phase and the $LaNi_5$ phase in the alloy decrease monotonically with the increase of x, respectively, which can be attributed to the fact that the atomic radius of Ce (1.824 Å) is smaller than that of La (1.877 Å). The plots of unit cell volume of the $La(La,Mg)_2Ni_9$ and $LaNi_5$ as a function of x are linear, as shown in Fig. 2. Figure 3 shows the abundance of the $La(La,Mg)_2Ni_9$ phase and the $LaNi_5$ phase as a function of x. As can be seen in Fig. 3 and Table 1, the $La(La,Mg)_2Ni_9$ phase abundance decreases from 76.54% to 53.65% but the $LaNi_5$ phase abundance increases from 21.2% to 43.23% with increasing x. These results may influence the hydrogen storage and electrochemical characteristics of the alloy studied.

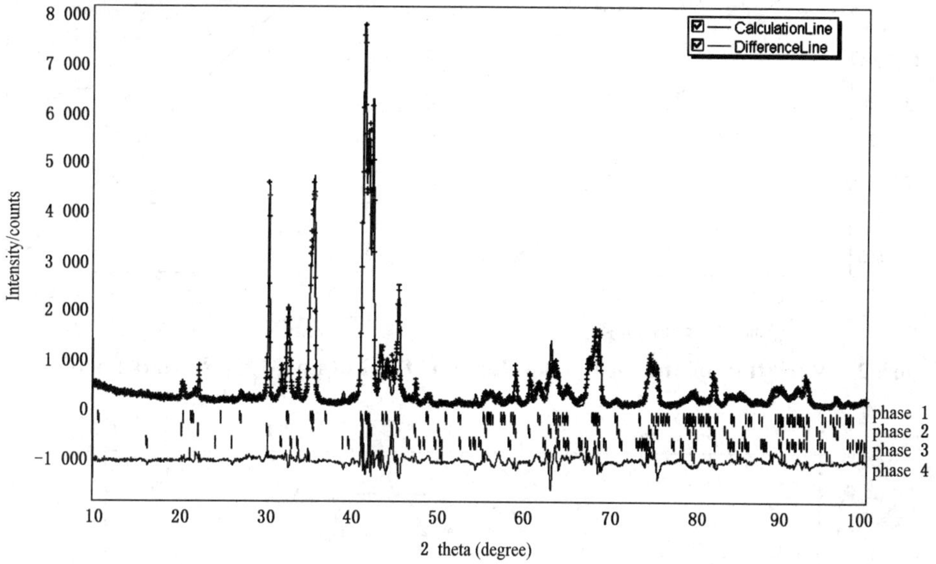

Figure 1 Rietveld profile refinement of XRD pattern of $La_{0.6}Ce_{0.1}Mg_{0.3}Ni_{2.8}Co_{0.5}$ alloy. Phase 1, La (La, Mg)$_2$Ni$_9$; phase 2, LaNi5; phase 3, LaNi; phase 4, $LaNi_2$

Table 1 Characteristics of alloy phase in $La_{0.7-x}Ce_xMg_{0.3}Ni_{2.8}Co_{0.5}$ ($x=0.1-0.5$) alloy

Sample	Phase	Phase abundance (wt%)	Lattice parameter (Å)			Cell volume (Å^3)
			a	b	c	
$x=0.1$	$La(La,Mg)_2Ni_9$	76.54	5.067 2	5.067 2	24.385 1	542.24
	$LaNi_5$	21.21	5.046 0	5.046 0	3.992 0	88.03
	LaNi	1.34	3.876 1	10.759 4	4.323 4	180.31
	$LaNi_2$	0.91	7.212 3	7.212 3	7.212 3	375.16
$x=0.2$	$La(La,Mg)_2Ni_9$	69.78	5.042 5	5.042 5	24.324 7	535.64
	$LaNi_5$	27.68	5.023 3	5.023 3	4.000 7	87.43
	LaNi	2.54	3.834 3	10.746 5	4.322 9	178.13
$x=0.3$	$La(La,Mg)_2Ni_9$	61.56	5.003 5	5.003 5	24.247 8	525.72
	$LaNi_5$	37.23	5.000 4	5.000 4	4.002 8	86.68
	LaNi	1.21	3.824 0	10.732 1	4.298 1	176.39
$x=0.4$	$La(La,Mg)_2Ni_9$	58.68	4.969 1	4.969 1	24.113 8	515.65
	$LaNi_5$	39.35	4.972 8	4.972 8	4.006 4	85.8
	LaNi	1.97	3.786 0	10.725 8	4.269 6	173.38
$x=0.5$	$La(La,Mg)_2Ni_9$	53.65	4.937 2	4.937 2	23.998 5	506.61
	$LaNi_5$	43.23	4.951 2	4.951 2	4.009 7	85.13
	LaNi	3.12	3.676 2	10.702 3	4.250 6	167.23

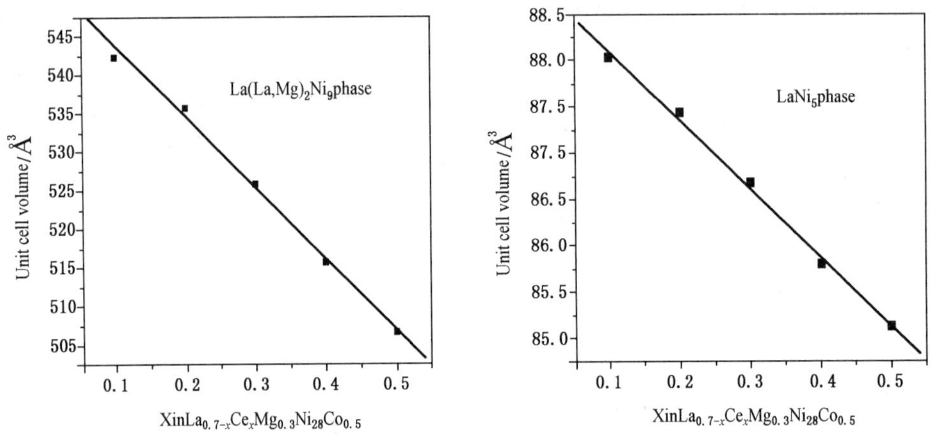

Figure 2　Variation of the unit cell volume of the $La(La,Mg)_2Ni_9$ and $LaNi_5$ with x

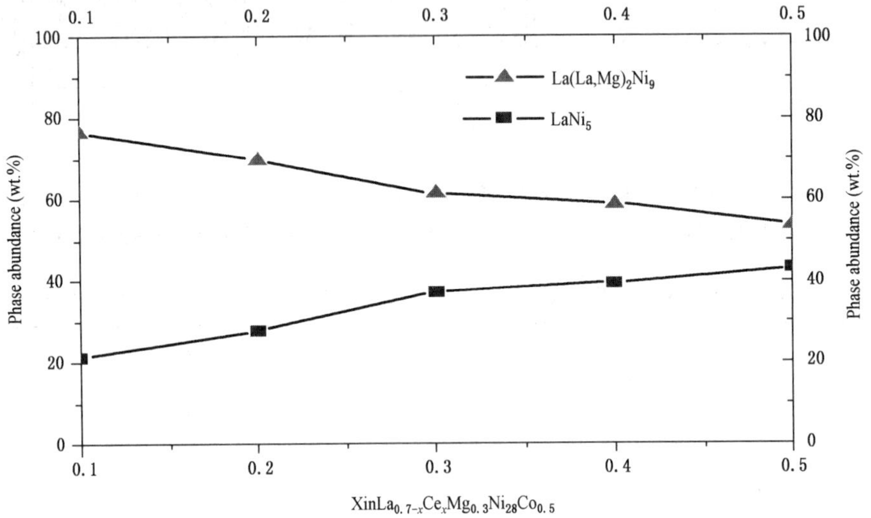

Figure 3　Phase abundance of the $La(La,Mg)_2Ni_9$ phase and the $LaNi_5$ phase in $La_{0.7-x}Ce_xMg_{0.3}Ni_{2.8}Co_{0.5}$ (x=0.1—0.5) alloys

***P-C* isotherms**

The electrochemically measured *P-C-T* curves for hydrogen desorption in the $La_{0.7-x}Ce_xMg_{0.3}Ni_{2.8}Co_{0.5}$ alloy at 298 K are presented in Fig. 4. With increasing x, the plateau pressure of the alloy increases monotonically and the plateau region becomes narrower and steeper, which leads to the decrease of the hydrogen storage capacity (H/M) from 0.952 to 0.177, which is in good agreement with that reported by Liu *et al.* [13]. The change of the *P-C-T* curve profile can be mainly attributed to the reduction of the unit cell volume and the relative change of phase abundance of $La(La,Mg)_2Ni_9$ phase and $LaNi_5$ phase. The increase of the plateau pressure of the $La_{0.7-x}Ce_xMg_{0.3}Ni_{2.8}Co_{0.5}$ alloy can be mainly ascribed to two factors. On the one hand, a unit cell of the AB_3 compound contains 1/3 AB_5 and 2/3 AB_2 structure [7] and, thus, the plateau pressure of the La(La, Mg)$_2$Ni$_9$ phase is essentially similar to that of LaNi$_5$ phase. In fact, the plateau pressure of the La(La, Mg)$_2$Ni$_9$ phase is slightly lower than that of the LaNi$_5$ phase. With increasing Ce content, as mentioned above, the abundance of La(La, Mg)$_2$Ni$_9$ phase decreases, whereas the phase abundance of the LaNi$_5$ phase increases, which thereby slightly increases the plateau pressure of the La$_{0.7-x}$Ce$_x$Mg$_{0.3}$Ni$_{2.8}$Co$_{0.5}$ alloy. On the other hand, the cell volumes of both the La(La, Mg)$_2$Ni$_9$ phase and the LaNi$_5$ phase decrease with increasing Ce content, as shown in Table 1 and Fig. 2, which will also inevitably increase the plateau pressure of the alloy. Precheron-Guegan *et al.* [14] pointed out that the hydrogen absorbed in an alloy enters and stays in the interstitial cavities of crystal lattice of the alloy. The alloy with bigger cell volumes and hence bigger interstitial cavities generally has larger hydrogen storage capacity. The cell volumes of both La(La, Mg)$_2$Ni$_9$ phase and LaNi$_5$ phase decrease with the increasing Ce content, which inevitably lowers the hydrogen storage capacity. These results indicate that the change of hydrogen storage capacity for the alloy results from the relative variation of the phase abundance of the La(La, Mg)$_2$Ni$_9$ phase and LaNi$_5$ phase.

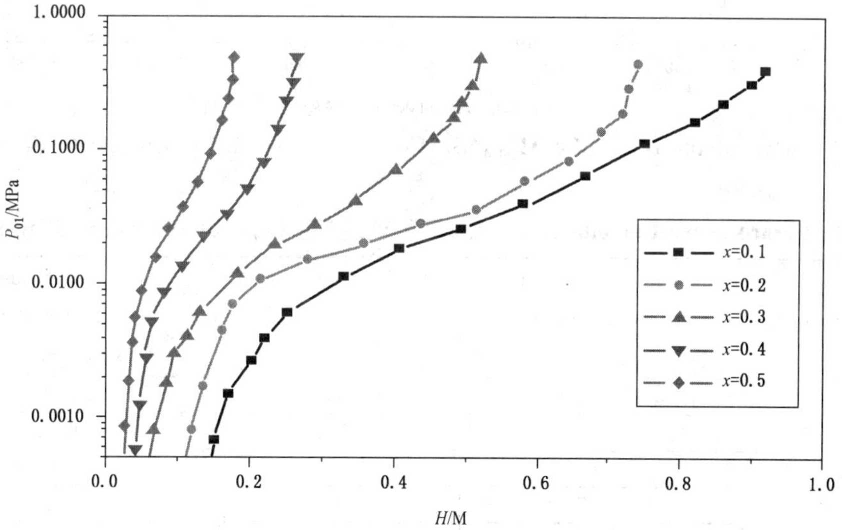

Figure 4 Electrochemical desorption *P-C-T* curve for La$_{0.7-x}$Ce$_x$Mg$_{0.3}$Ni$_{2.8}$Co$_{0.5}$ (x=0.1—0.5) alloy electrodes at 298 K

Maximum discharge capacity and cycle stability

The maximum discharge capacity of La$_{0.7-x}$Ce$_x$Mg$_{0.3}$Ni$_{2.8}$Co$_{0.5}$ (x=0.1—0.5) alloy decreases from 367.5 mAh/g (x=0.1) to 68.3 mAh/g (x=0.5) with increasing Ce content, as shown in Table 2, which is in good agreement with the results of *P-C-T* curves. The capacity retention rate is also listed in Table 2. The capacity retention rate (S_{70}) can be gradually improved with increasing Ce content.

Table 2 Performance of $La_{0.7-x}Ce_xMg_{0.3}Ni_{2.8}Co_{0.5}$ (x=0.1—0.5) alloy electrode

Sample	H/M	C_{max}/(mAh/g)	HRD_{1200}(%)	S_{70}(%)
x=0.1	0.952	367.5	55.4	56.4
x=0.2	0.740	285.7	60.3	63.9
x=0.3	0.519	200.4	67.5	72.5
x=0.4	0.263	101.3	58.1	79.3
x=0.5	0.177	68.3	52.1	87.3

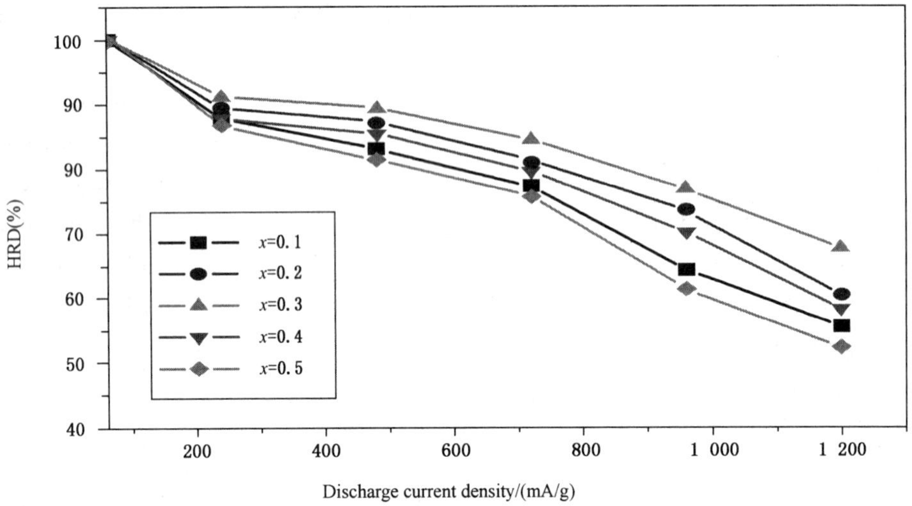

Figure 5 HRD of the $La_{0.7-x}Ce_xMg_{0.3}Ni_{2.8}Co_{0.5}$ (x=0.1—0.5) alloy electrode at 298 K

Table 3 Electrochemical parameter of $La_{0.7-x}Ce_xMg_{0.3}Ni_{2.8}Co_{0.5}$ (x=0.1—0.5) alloy electrode

Sample	Polarization resistance R_p/mΩ	Exchange current density I_0 (mA/g)	Hydrogen diffusion coefficient D/ ($\times 10^{-10}$ cm^2/s)
x=0.1	94.8	270.9	15.17
x=0.2	90.1	285.1	14.32
x=0.3	85.1	301.7	13.14
x=0.4	77.8	330.1	9.34
x=0.5	68.7	373.6	7.32

High-rate dischargeability (HRD)

Figure 5 shows the effect of the discharge current density on the discharge capacity of the $La_{0.7-x}Ce_xMg_{0.3}Ni_{2.8}Co_{0.5}$ (x=0.1—0.5) alloy electrode. The HRD of the alloy electrode increases first and then decreases as x increases. Taking a discharge current density of 1200 mA/g as an example, the HRD of the alloy electrode increases from 55.4% (x=0.1) to 67.5% (x=0.3) and then decreases to 52.1% (x=0.5), as shown in Table 2. Figure 6 shows the linear polarization curves of the alloy electrode at 50% DOD and at 298 K. The polarization resistance R_p of the alloy electrode decreases from 94.8 mΩ ($x=0.1$) to 68.7 mΩ ($x=0.5$); accordingly the exchange current density I_0 of the alloy electrode increases from 270.9 to 373.6 mA/g when x increases from 0.1 to 0.5, as shown in Table 3. Pan [15] pointed out that for La-Mg-Ni-Co system alloys, the $LaNi_5$ phase works not only as an hydrogen reservoir, but also as a catalyst to activate the La(La,Mg)$_2$Ni$_9$ phase to absorb/desorb hydrogen reversibly in the alkaline electrolyte [14]. The $LaNi_5$ phase abundance increases with increasing Ce content, as mentioned above and, hence, increases the I_0 of the alloy electrode. The hydrogen diffusion coefficient D in the alloy bulk is also listed in Table 3 and decreases from 15.17×10^{-10} cm^2/s ($x=0.1$) to 7.32×10^{-10} cm^2/s ($x=0.5$), which can be attributed to the reduction of cell volume of the alloy with increasing Ce content. The I_0 monotonically increases with increasing x, whereas D decreases linearly. Overall, the combined effect of the two factors will result in an optimal value of x for HRD. The optimal value of Ce content for the alloy is 0.3 from our work.

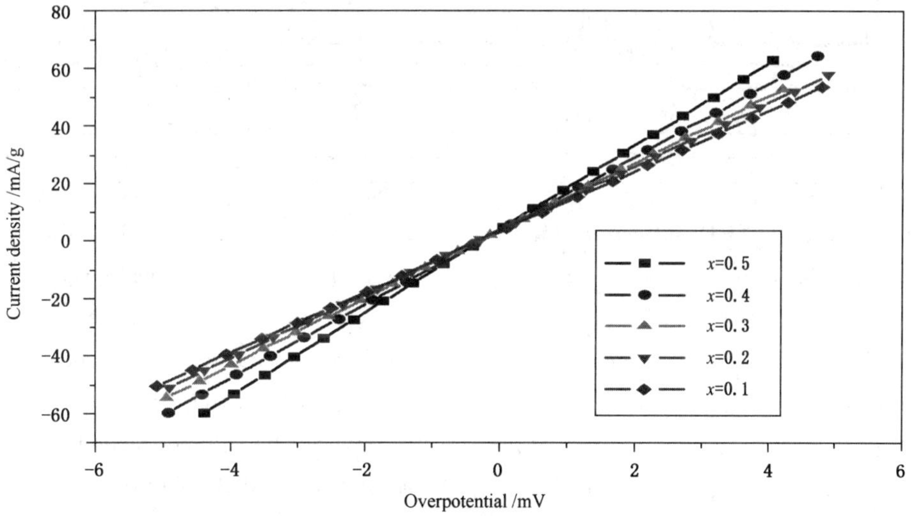

Figure 6 Linear polarization curve for $La_{0.7-x}Ce_xMg_{0.3}Ni_{2.8}Co_{0.5}$ ($x=0.1-0.5$) alloy electrodes at 298 K

$Ti_{0.25-x}Zr_xV_{0.35}Cr_{0.1}Ni_{0.3}$ ($x=0.05-0.15$) Alloy

Vanadium and vanadium-based solid solution alloy have attracted considerable interest due to their higher hydrogen storage capacity. Takahashi *et al.* [16] reported that $V_3TiNi_{0.56}$ and $V_3TiNi_{0.56}Hf_{0.24}$ alloy electrode had higher discharge capacity than other hydrogen storage alloys, and Lei *et al.* further studied the effect of Mn and Cr on the performance of $V_3TiNi_{0.56}Hf_{0.24}$ alloy electrode [17]. Iwakura *et al.* [18] studied the properties of $TiV_{2.1}Ni_{0.3}$ alloy and found that the discharge capacity of the alloy electrode reached 540 mAh/g. Furthermore, Lei *et al*. [19] discussed the effect of Ni on the properties of $TiV_{2.1}$ and pointed out that $TiV_{2.1}Ni_{0.5}$ had high discharge capacity and HRD capability. Ti-V-Cr and Ti-V-Mn are demonstrated to absorb/desorb an appreciable amount of hydrogen, and the effective hydrogen storage capacity is about 2.2 mass%, as reported by Akiba and Iba [20]. However, there are only a few papers on the electrochemical characteristics of Ti-V-Cr alloy. $Ti_{0.25}V_{0.35}Cr_{0.1}Ni_{0.3}$ alloy only delivered an electrochemical capacity of 240 mAh/g at 313 K.

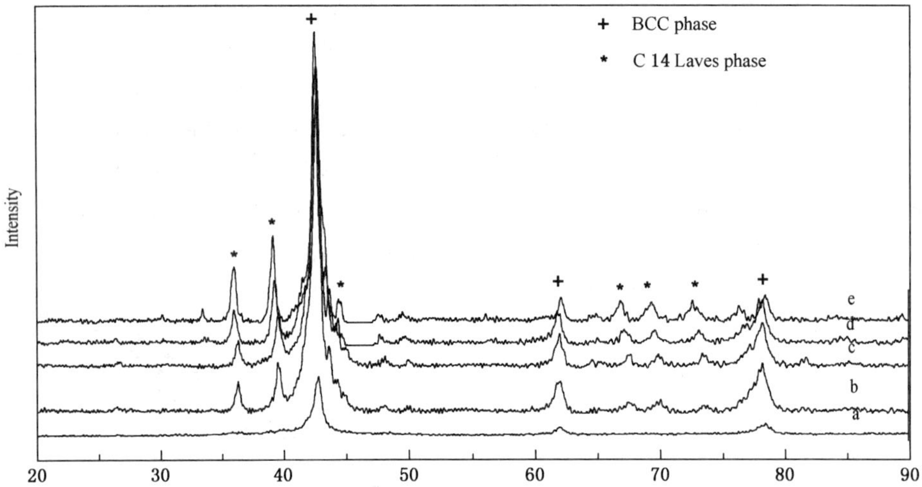

Figure 7　XRD pattern of $Ti_{0.25-x}Zr_xV_{0.35}Cr_{0.1}Ni_{0.3}$ (x=0.05—0.15) alloy

Zirconium is used to substitute partial titanium to improve the property of the Ti-V-Cr-Ni alloy electrode, and the structures and electrochemical characteristics of $Ti_{0.25-x}Zr_xV_{0.35}Cr_{0.1}Ni_{0.3}$ (x = 0.05—0.15) alloy are discussed as a representative example of solid solution alloy.

Alloy structure

When titanium is partially substituted by zirconium, the C14 Laves phase appears. The XRD patterns of $Ti_{0.25-x}Zr_xV_{0.35}Cr_{0.1}Ni_{0.3}$ (x=0.05—0.15) alloy are shown in Fig. 7. The alloy is mainly composed of V-based solid solution phase with a bodycentered cubic (BCC) structure and a C14 Laves phase with hexagonal structure. When x=0.05, the peaks of the Laves phase are not discernible. The peaks of the C14 Laves phase appear and shift to the lower angle evidently, and the volume fraction and the lattice parameter of C14 Laves phase increase with increasing x, as shown in Table 4. Moreover, the lattice parameter of V-based solid solution changes slightly when x increases from 0.05 to 0.10 and decreases as x increases further. It is probable that some zirconium solutes enter the solid solution and cause the lattice swelling due to the partial substitution of zirconium for titanium, while the majority of zirconium forms a C14 Laves phase with other elements. When the content of zirconium is greater than 0. 15, more elements dissolve in the C14 Laves phase and, thus, change the element species in the solid solution alloy.

Table 4 Composition and lattice parameters of $Ti_{0.25-x}Zr_xV_{0.35}Cr_{0.1}Ni_{0.3}$ (x=0. 05—0. 15) alloy

Sample	Phase	Lattice parameter		Unit cell volume ($\times 10^{-3}$ nm^3)	Mol fraction
		a	c		
x=0. 05	BCC	0. 298 5	26. 60		
x=0. 07	BCC	0. 299 1	26. 76	0. 74	
	C14 phase	0. 294 0	0. 803 8	60. 18	0. 26
x=0. 08	BCC	0. 299 4	26. 84	0. 71	
	C14 phase	0. 294 5	0. 803 8	60. 39	0. 29
x=0. 10	BCC	0. 299 5		26. 87	0. 67
	C14 phase	0. 297 7	0. 806 4	61. 91	0. 33
x=0. 15	BCC	0. 298 1		26. 49	0. 51
	C14 phase	0. 298 0	0. 810 5	62. 35	0. 49

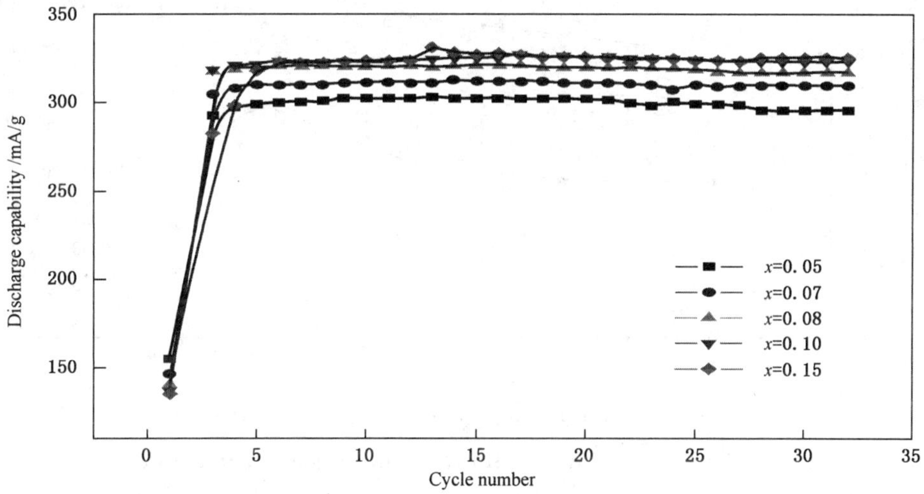

Figure 8 Discharge capacity *vs.* cycle number for $Ti_{0.25-x}Zr_xV_{0.35}Cr_{0.1}Ni_{0.3}$ (x=0. 05—0. 15) alloy at 313 K

Electrochemical property

Figure 8 shows the dependence of discharge capacity on cycle number for $Ti_{0.25-x}Zr_xV_{0.35}Cr_{0.1}Ni_{0.3}$ (x = 0. 05 — 0. 15) alloy at 313 K. It can be seen that the discharge capacity increases with changing x from 0. 05 to 0. 15 after the electrode is activated, and the cyclic stability of the alloy electrode is good. In KOH electrolyte solution, the single solid solution phase has no electrochemical discharge capability because it does not have electrochemical catalytic activity. However, C14 Laves phase can act as the electrochemical catalyst and micro-current collector and make the solid solution alloy reversibly absorb/desorb hydrogen. There is a C14 Laves phase in $Ti_{0.25-x}Zr_xV_{0.35}Cr_{0.1}Ni_{0.3}$ (x = 0. 05 — 0. 15) alloy, as mentioned above, and the content of C14 Laves phase increases as x increases. The contents of solid solution and C14 Laves phase in the alloys are evaluated semi-quantitatively from the peak intensity in XRD patterns. When the mol ratio of the solid solution and C14 Laves phase is less than 3 and greater than 1, the discharge capacity only changes a little, which implies a correlation between the discharge capacity and the fraction of the phase in the alloy. In the meantime the presence of chromium also limits the corrosion of vanadium and leads to cyclic stability to be improved [21]. All the measurements of the discharge capacity are conducted by charging at ambient temperature and discharging at various temperatures. The discharge capacity changes less at 303—323 K and evidently increases up to 333 K, when the maximum discharge capacity of 350 mAh/g is obtained, as shown in Fig. 9. However, the discharge capacity decreases when temperature is above 333 K.

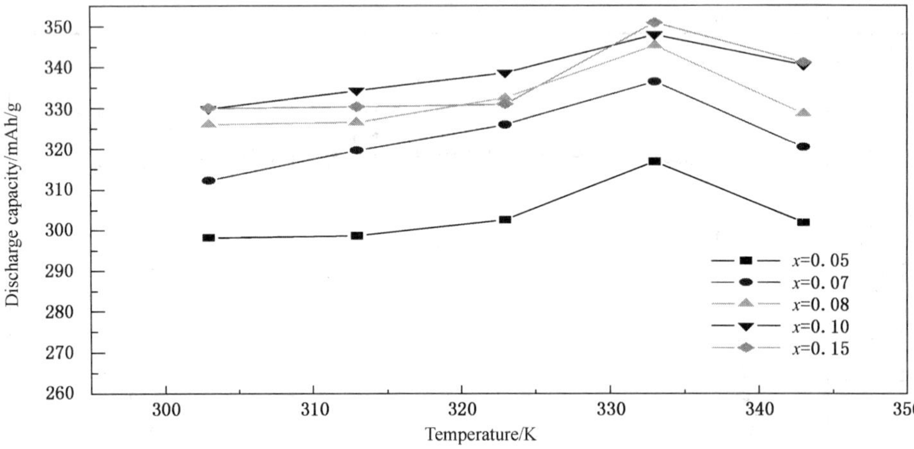

Figure 9　Discharge capacity of $Ti_{0.25-x}Zr_xV_{0.35}Cr_{0.1}Ni_{0.3}$ (x=0.05—0.15) alloy as a function of discharge current density

Figure 10 gives the relation between the discharge capacity and the discharge current density. The discharge capacity increases with increasing x, which is perhaps related to the content of C14 Laves phase. The Laves phase accelerates the cracking of the alloy and creates more fresh surface area, which will affect the rate capability [22].

The electrochemical impedance spectra of the alloy electrode at a DOD of 50% are shown in Fig. 11. It is demonstrated that the spectra of all metal hydrides consist of two semicircles at high frequency and a straight line at low frequency. The first semicircle looks like a straight line, which may be related to the porosity effect of the alloy electrode [23]. The radius of the second semicircle decreases as x changes from 0.05 to 0.08, and then changes slightly. The fitted results by least square method are shown in Fig. 12. It is evident that the electrolyte resistance R1, the contact resistance R2 and R3 are almost independent of x. However, the charge-transfer resistance R4 decreases markedly as x changes from 0. 05 to 0. 08 and then decreases slightly, which corresponds to the result mentioned above. These results indicate that the electrochemical activity is close to the charge-transfer resistance on the alloy surface. From the above results, it can be understood that the partial substitution of zirconium for titanium changes the charge-transfer resistance, decreases the electrochemical reaction resistance and enhances the discharge capacity and rate capability.

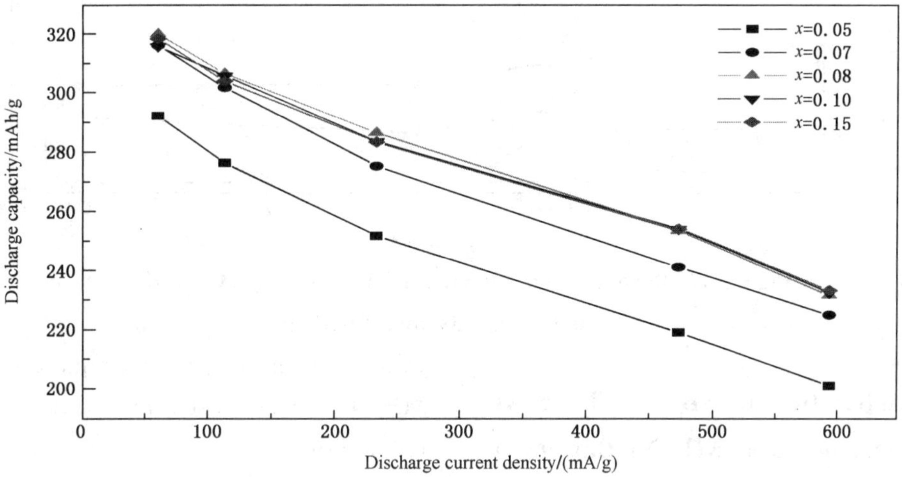

Figure 10　Dependence of discharge capacity of $Ti_{0.25-x}Zr_xV_{0.35}Cr_{0.1}Ni_{0.3}$ (x=0. 05—0. 15) alloy on temperature

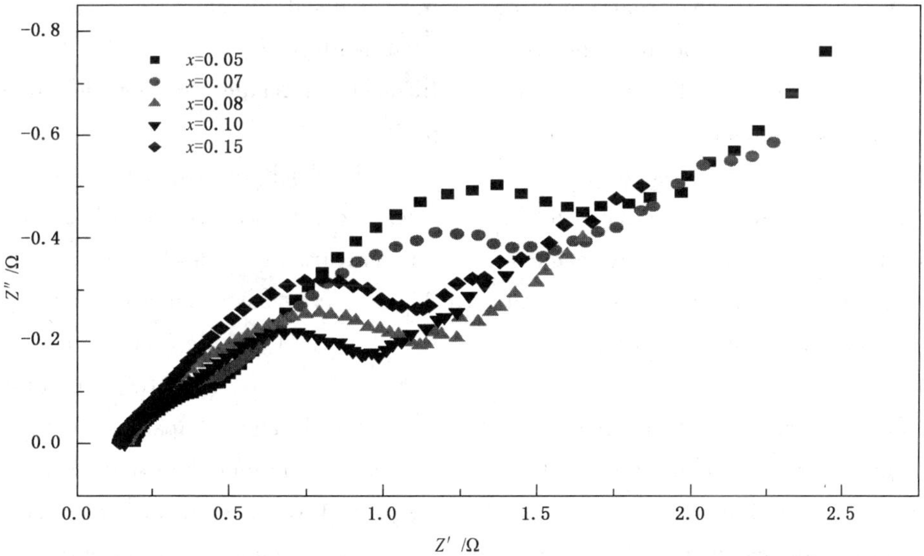

Figure 11　Electrochemical impedance spectra of $Ti_{0.25-x}Zr_xV_{0.35}Cr_{0.1}Ni_{0.3}$ (x=0. 05—0. 15) alloy electrode

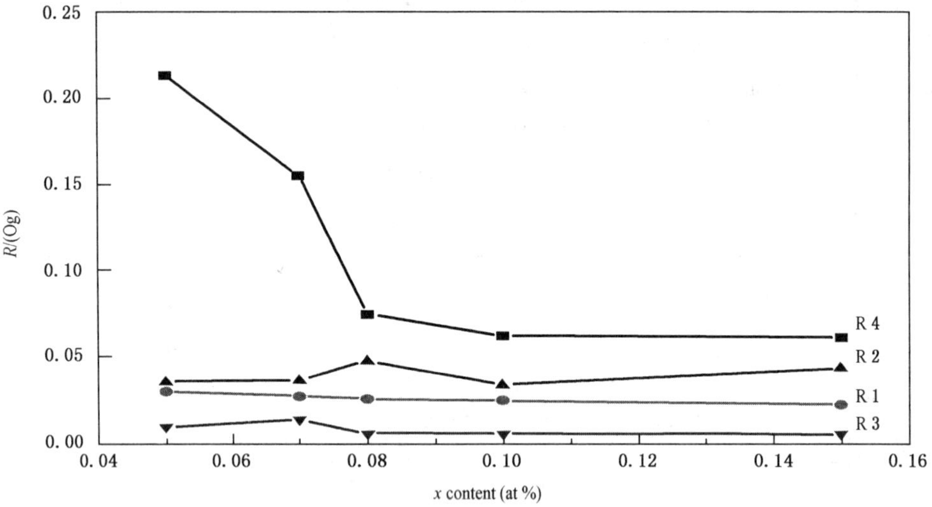

Figure 12. Resistive component for $Ti_{0.25-x}Zr_xV_{0.35}Cr_{0.1}Ni_{0.3}$ ($x=0.05-0.15$) metal hydride

Characteristics of $AB_{3<x<5}$-Type Alloy Electrode and MH-Ni Battery at Relatively Low Temperature

The commercial MH-Ni battery with AB_5-type alloy electrode is required to be used at the span of temperature between −18 and 40 ℃ because discharge capacity of the battery decreases dramatically below −20 ℃, and is almost zero at −40 ℃. The experimental results have indicated that the influence of the negative electrode material on performances of the MH-Ni battery is the most critical at low temperatures.

The performance of the battery at low temperature should be improved, especially when used in places, which include more than the third of land area over the world where the temperature could decrease down to −40 ℃ in winter. It is urgent and significant to find a valuable negative electrode material for MH-Ni battery used at relatively low temperature.

The electrochemical characteristics of hydrogen storage alloy have been investigated at low temperatures [24-26], but the discharge characteristics have not been dealt yet at −40 ℃.

Influence of temperature on discharge capacity

The discharge capacity of any alloy electrode would decrease with decreasing temperature. The discharge capacity of $AB_{3<x<5}$-type as a function of temperature is listed in Table 5 and that of commercial AB_5 type is listed for comparison. The discharge capacity of $AB_{3<x<5}$-type alloy is higher than that of AB_5-type alloy at low temperature, especially at −40 ℃, although the situation is inverse at ambient temperature. The former belongs to the $CaCu_5$ structure and is made of single phase, and the latter is constituted of multiphase and is non-stoichiometric, as mentioned above. The influences of the structure and the non-stoichiometry of the alloy on electrochemical characteristics are two critical factors at low temperature.

Table 5　Discharge capacity as a function of temperature

	Temperature/℃			
	20	−26	−33	−40
Discharge capacity for $AB_{3<x<5}$ type alloy (mAh/g)	300	264	246	214
Discharge capacity for commercial AB_5-type alloy (mAh/g)	320	35	149	14.4

I_d = 65 mA/g.

Table 6　Measured discharge capacity of *D*-type battery sample (in Ah/g)

Measured	0.2 CsA capacity at ambient temperature			0.4 CsA capacity at −40 ℃	
	Battery 1	Battery 2	Battery 3	Battery 1	Battery 2
1	7.54	7.67	7.67	5.40	5.77
2	8.56	8.75	8.55	7.42	7.35
3	8.56	8.50	8.58	7.13	7.35
4	7.69	7.80	7.80	5.45	5.64
Average	8.01	8.09	8.06	6.06	6.28

Manufacture of a D-type battery sample

A D-type battery sample is fabricated, in which $AB_{3<x<5}$-type alloy is used as electrode material. The measured capacity is listed in Table 6. It is evaluated that the discharge capacity of the D-type battery sample at −40 ℃ is about 75% of that at ambient temperature. The results indicated that the uniformity of the battery sample is fairly good, but not desirable enough.

Essential consideration for synthesis of low-temperature electrode alloy

In general, the position of a plateau in the *P-C-T* plot for hydrogen storage alloy would move down with decreasing temperature, and desorbing hydrogen is an endothermic reaction. Therefore, desorbing hydrogen and the diffusion of hydrogen in alloy bulk will be very difficult at very low temperatures and equilibrium hydrogen pressure is very low. Besides, the information in the literature and our results indicated that non-stoichiometeic compound is appropriate for improving performances of metal hydride electrode at low temperature. All situations mentioned above should be essentially considered for the synthesis of alloys. The following hypotheses have been proposed preliminarily.

(1) Hydrogen desorption is the rate-limiting step, although charge transfer on the alloy electrode surface and diffusion of hydrogen in the hydride bulk are two important factors for discharge process.

(2) Composition and structure of the alloy should be chosen to be beneficial to hydrogen diffusion in the alloy and enhancing the plateau pressure of hydrogen desorption.

(3) Effect of the alloy electrode corrosion in alkali solution on electrochemical performances of the alloy electrode is an important factor, but not a very key factor yet.

Of course, these hypotheses should be examined in the future.

Acknowledgements

This work was financially supported by the National Natural Science Foundation of China (Grant No. 20171042).

References

[1] M. Latroche and A. Percheron-Guegan, J. *Alloys Compd*. 356, 461 (2003).

[2] J. J. G. Willems and K. H. J. Buschow, J. *Less-Common Met*. 129, 13 (1987).

[3] T. Sakai, H. Miyamura, N. Kuriyama, A. Kato, K. Oguro and H. Ishikawa, *J. Electrochem. Soc*. 137, 795 (1990).

[4] X. Zhang, Y. Chai, W. Yin and M. Zhao, *J. Solid State Chem*. 177, 2373 (2004).

[5] Y. Chai and M. Zhao, *Int. J. Hydrogen Energ*. 30, 279 (2005).

[6] M. Zhao and C. Sun, *NATO Sci. Ser. II* 82, 29 (2002).

[7] K. Kadir, T. Sakai and I. Uahara, *J. Alloys Compd*. 287, 264 (1999).

[8] K. Kadir, T. Sakai and I. Uahara, *J. Alloys Compd*. 302, 112 (2000).

[9] J. Chen, N. Kuriyama, H. T. Takeshita, H. Tanaka, T. Sakai and M. Haruta, *Electrochem. Solid-State Lett*. 3, 249 (2000).

[10] T. Kohno, H. Yoshida, F. Kawashima, T. Inaba, I. Sakai, M. Yamamoto and M. Kanda, *J. Alloys Compd*. 311, L5 (2000).

[11] G. Adzic, J. R. Johnson, J. J. Reilly, J. McBreen, S. Mukerjee, M. P. S. Kumar, W. Zhang and S. Srinivasan, *J. Electrochem. Soc*. 142, 3429 (1995).

[12] T. Sakai, T. Hazama, H. Miyamura, N. Kuriyama, A. Kato and H. Ishikawa, *J. Less-Common Met*. 172, 1175 (1991).

[13] H. G. Pan, Q. W. Jin, M. X. Gao, Y. F. Liu, R. Li and Y. Q. Lei, J. *Alloys Compd*. 373, 237(2004).

[14] A. Precheron-Guegan, C. Lartigue and J. C. Achard, J. *Less-Common Met*. 161, 193 (1990).

[15] H. G. Pan, Y. F. Liu, M. X. Gao, Y. Q. Lei and Q. D. Wang, *J. Electrochem. Soc*. 150, A565(2003).

[16] M. Tsukahara, K. Takahashi, T. Mishima, A. Isomura and T. Sakai, *J. Alloys Compd*. 243, 133(1996).

[17] Q. A. Zhang, Y. Q. Lei, X. G. Yang, Y. L. Du and Q. D. Wang, *Int. J. Hydrogen Energ*. 25, 977(2000).

[18] C. Iwakura, W. Kyung, R. Miyauchi and H. Inoue, J. *Electrochem. Soc*. 147, 2503 (2000).

[19] R. Guo, L. X. Chen, Y. Q. Lei, B. Liao, T. Ying and Q. D. Wang, *Int. J. Hydrogen Energ*. 28, 803(2003).

[20] E. Akiba and H. Iba, Intermetallics 6, 461 (1998).

[21] S. R. Ovshinsky, M. A. Fetcenko and J. Poss, *Nature* 260, 176 (1993).

[22] D. M. Kim, K. J. Jang and J. Y. Lee, *J. Alloys Compd*. 293-295, 583 (1999).

[23] N. Kuriyanma, T. Sakai, H. Miyamura, I. Uehara, H. Ishikawa and T. Iwasaki, *J. Alloys Compd*. 202, 183 (1993).

[24] M. Zhao and C. Sun, Hydrogen Energy Pro-

gress, in: *XIII Proceedings of the 13th World Hydrogen Energy Conference*, Beijing, June 12-15, p. 1106 (2000).
[25] H. Ye and H. Zhang, J. *Electrochem. Soc.* 149, A122 (2002).
[26] H. Senoh, Y. Hara, H. Inoue and C. Iwakura, *Electrochim. Acta* 46, 967 (2001).

A Novel Negative Electrode Material for MH-Ni Battery at Low Temperature

Minshou Zhao, Changying Sun
(Key Laboratory of Rare Earth Chemistry and Physics Changchun Institute of Applied Chemistry, 159 Ren Min Street 130022 China)

Abstract: A novel non-AB_5-type alloy $(RENiAlMnCoA)_x$; RE=La or La-rich mischmetal; $2 \leqslant x < 5$; A=a trace element= has been synthesized by arc melting of constituent elements, and characterized by XRD and electrochemical properties first time. The results showed the alloy has multi-phase structures, and has discharge capacity more 10 times than that of commercial AB_5-type alloy as negative electrode material for MH-Ni battery at low temperature, even at −40 ℃. The effect of discharge current and temperature on the electrochemical properties has been studied. Some hypotheses have been preliminarily proposed for synthesis of negative electrode material used at low temperature.

1 Introduction

MH-Ni battery with AB_5-type alloy as negative electrode material has been commercially produced and applied in many field as power source, for example, portable phone, cellar phone, video camera, personal computer of note book type, electric bicycle, motor bike, pure electric vehicle, hybrid electric vehicle and so on. However; the battery is required to be used at the span of temperature from 40 ℃ to −18 ℃. The discharge capacity of the battery would dramatically decrease below −20 ℃.

The performance of the battery to be improved at low temperature is necessary at North-East and North-West in China, North America, Europe and Russia, which include more than the third of land area over the world. The temperature at the places mentioned above in winter would decrease down to −40 ℃.

The electrochemical characteristics of hydrogen storage alloy was investigated at low temperatures [1-4], and a few researchers dealt with the performance of MH-Ni battery at various low temperatures [5-6], but the electrochemical properties of hydrogen storage alloys as negative electrode materials and the performance of MH-Ni battery haven't been dealt yet at −40 ℃.

In this paper the electrochemical properties of the novel negative electrode material have been performed at room temperature and −40 ℃, respectively.

① Hydrogen Materials Science and Chemistry of Metal Hydrides, 2002: 29-34.

2 Experimental Detail

The sample alloy was synthesized by arc melting of constituent elements of RE (RE= La, mischmetal, rich-La mischmetal), Ni, Al, Mn, Co and trace other elements on a water-cooled copper crucible under argon atmosphere. The Ar gas was purified by sieve and silicon gel. The sample alloy was turned over and remelted three times at least in order to improve the alloy homogeneity. The alloy ingot was mechanically pulverized to be 300 meshes for XRD analysis, and The pulverized powder of 200—250 meshes was used for the preparation of metal hydride electrode. The metal hydride electrodes were prepared by pressing the mixtures of alloy powder with nickel powder in the weight ratio of 1 : 5 to form electrode pellets of diameter of 10 mm at the compacting pressure of 200 MPa. The electrochemical tests were carried out in an open cell using 6 M KOH electrolyte solution and sintered $Ni(OH)_2$/NiOOH plat is used as counter electrode with sufficiently large discharge capacity at room temperature (20 ℃) and low temperature. The cut-off voltages for discharge were 1. 0 V at room temperature and 0. 9 V at −40 ℃, respectively. The charge/discharge test was conducted on DC-5 Battery Testing instrument controlled by a computer.

3 Results and Discussion

3. 1 Xrd Analysis

The X-ray diffraction pattern of the sample alloy indicated that the sample alloy has multiphase structure. The second phase in the muttiphase structure may be beneficial to enhance the discharge capacity, as shown in non-stoichiometric AB_5-type alloy [7].

3. 2 Discharge Capacity Varied With Cycle Number

The discharge capacity of the sample alloy electrode *vs.* cycles was shown in Fig. 1 at room temperature. With cycle numbers, the discharge capacity of the sample alloy electrode was almost not changed for 45 cycles and attained about 300 mAh/g.

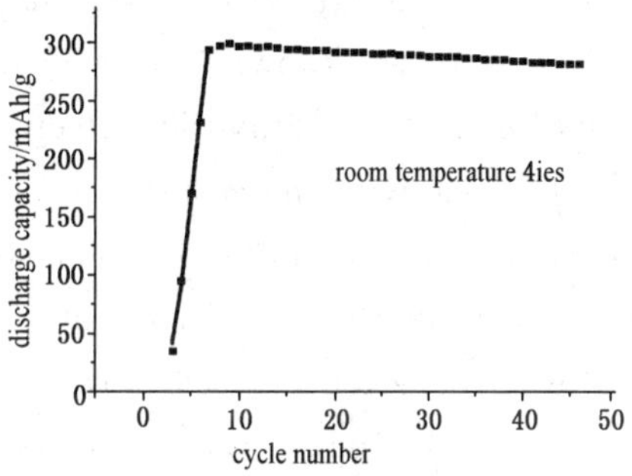

Fig. 1 Discharge capacity of sample alloy electrode as function of cycle number at room temperature

3. 3 The Effect of Temperature on Discharge Capacity of The Metal Hydride Electrode

The discharge capacities of the sample alloy and commercial AB_5-type alloy at low temperatures were listed in table 1 to compare with each other. It was found that the discharge capacities of the sample alloy would decrease with decreasing temperature and extending cycle numbers, but very slow and keep large enough capacity, as shown in Table 1. However, the discharge capacities of the commercial AB_5-type alloy very sharply decrease with decreasing temperature.

Table 1 Discharge capacity at −26 ℃ and −33 ℃, mAh/g($I_c=I_d$=65 mA/g)

Cycle number	3	6	10	25	45
Sample at −26 ℃	264	263	261	254	244
Sample at −33 ℃	246	240	219	220	193
AB_5-type alloy at −33 ℃	149	74	45	32	31

3.4 The Effect of Discharge Current on Discharge Capacity of The Metal Hydride Electrode

At −40 ℃ the discharge capacity as function of discharge current was listed in Table 2. As we known, the discharge capacity of any metal hydride electrode would decrease with increasing discharge current, the sample alloy so behaved. However, the discharge capacity of sample alloy electrode decreased slowly and kept considerable large value to be used, even at discharge current of 145 mA/g. On contrast, the discharge capacity of commercial AB_5-type alloy electrode decreased dramatically and can't been used at all.

Table 2 Discharge capacity as function of I_d at −40 ℃, mAh/g

Discharge current/mA/g	65	100	145
Alloy sample	214	193	158
Commercial AB_5-type alloy	14.4	16.2	8.8
Discharge capacity ratio	14.4	16.2	17.9

3.5 Discharge Characteris of Metal Hydride Electrode

Typical galvanostatic discharge curves of the metal hydride electrodes were shown in Fig. 2. The middle voltage of the sample alloy electrode would been determined from Curve 1 to be 1.089 V, but that of commercial AB_5-type alloy electrode couldnot be determined from Curve 2.

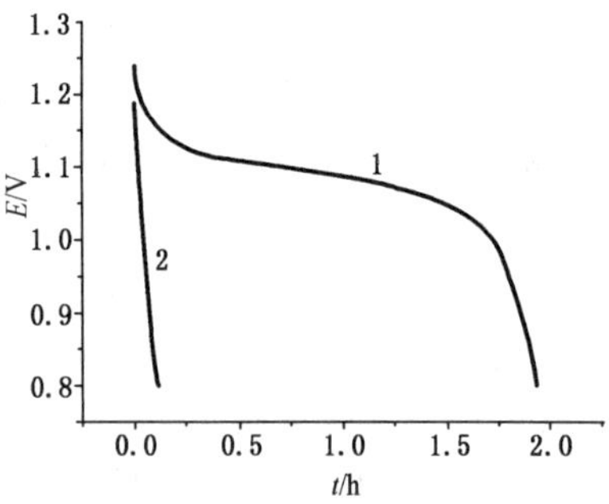

Fig. 2 Discharge characteristics of metal hydride electrodes at −40 ℃ Curve 1 sample alloy; Curve 2 AB_5-type alloy

4 Hypotheses For Synthesis Of Negative Electrode Alloy Used At Low Temperature

In general the position of a plateau in P-C-T plot for hydrogen storage alloy would move down with decreasing temperature, and desorbing hydrogen is an endothermic reaction. So desorbing hydrogen and the diffusion of hydrogen in the alloy will be very difficult at deeply low temperature circumstance. So the structure and composition of the metal hydride alloy used in MH-Ni battery at low temperature should be essentially considered. Based on our experimental results, the following hypotheses have been proposed preliminarily.

(1) Desorbing hydrogen is a limiting step during discharge process.

(2) Compositions and structure of the alloy should be chosen to be beneficial for hydrogen diffusion in the alloy.

(3) Effect of the alloy corrosion in alkali solution on electrochemical characteristics of negative electrode is a factor, but not a very key factor yet.

Of course, the hypotheses should be corrected, explained and demonstrated by more many experiment results in future.

Acknowledgments

This work was supported by the National Natural Science Foundation of China (No. 20171042) and National Defend Foundation of Chinese Academy of Sciences.

References

[1] Zhao, M. S and Sun, C. Y. (2000) Electrochemical properties of rare earth AB_3-type alloy as negative electrode material in MH-Ni battery. Hydrogen Energy Progress Ⅹ Ⅲ Proceedings of the 13th World Hydrogen Energy Conference; Beijing, China, June 12-15; P. 1106-1110.

[2] Sakai, T. and Ishikawa, H. (1990) Metal hydride anodes for nickel-hydrogen secondary battery. J. Electrochem. Soc.; 137 (3): 795-799.

[3] Zhao, M. S and Sun, C. Y. (2001) Negative electrode material in MH-Ni battery at low temperature. Proceedings of the 3rd China National Hydrogen Energy Conference, 13-15 April; Hangzhou China; P. 220-223.

[4] Yie, H. and Zhang, H. (2001) Study of the low temperature electrochemical performance of hydrogen storage alloy. ibd.; P. 127-134.

[6] Guo H. and Pan C. (2000) Discharge performance of MH-Ni battery at low temperature. Chinese Journal of Power Sources; 24 (4): 189-191.

[7] Furukawa, N. and Nogami, M. (1995) Development of high capacity hydrogen absorbing alloys for high performance, nickel-metal hydride batteries. 46th ISE Annual Meeting, Xiamen, China, K-8-2.

Microstructure and High-temperature Electrochemical Characteristics of $Zr_{0.9}Ti_{0.1}Ni_{1.0}Mn_{0.7}V_{0.3}Si_x$ (x=0.05, 0.10, 0.15, 0.20) Alloy①

Shu-Min Han[a,b], Min-Shou Zhao[a,b], Bao-Zhong Liu[a]

([a] Department of Environmental and Chemical Engineering, Yanshan University, Qinhuangdao 066004, PR China)

([b] Key Laboratory of Rare Earth Chemistry and Physics, Changchun Institute of Applied Chemistry, Chinese Academy of Sciences, Changchun 130022, PR China)

Abstract: The crystal structure, the phase composition and electrochemical characteristics of non-stoichiometric $Zr_{0.9}Ti_{0.1}Ni_{1.0}Mn_{0.7}V_{0.3}Si_x$ (x=0.05, 0.10, 0.15, 0.20) alloys under high temperature were investigated by means of XRD, SEM, EDS and electrochemical measurements. It was shown that Si addition greatly improved high-temperature electrochemical characteristics of the AB_2 Laves phase alloys. At 338 K, the discharge capacity of $Zr_{0.9}Ti_{0.1}Ni_{1.0}Mn_{0.7}V_{0.3}Si_{0.10}$ alloy reached 249 mAh g^{-1}, and the charge retention was 94.20% for 24 h, and the capacity retention for 300 charge/discharge cycles was 45.17%. The improvement in the high-temperature electrochemical characteristics of the alloy was attributed to the formation of the Zr-rich second phase in the matrix and the increasing stability of AB_2-type Laves phase alloy hydride due to Si addition in alloy. They seem to be also related with the formation of a compact silicon oxide film on the alloy surface, which increases the corrosion resistance performance of the alloy in KOH solution. At high temperature, the main cause of further decreasing of alloy cycle stability may be due to the corrosion and the oxidizing deteriorate on alloy surface, and the expansion ratio of crystal cell volume probably is not a critical effect on the cycle stability of alloy.

Key words: Metal hydride electrode; High-temperature electrochemical characteristics; Hydrogen storage alloy

1 Introduction

Environment protection and energy saving are the two main subjects in the world. The electric vehicle (EV) sprang up in recent years is one of the effective

① Materials Chemistry and Physics, 2005(89): 221-227.

ways to solve the environment and energy problems [1]. Estimated by world electric power research institute (EPRI), effluent of city proper waste gas could be decreased by 160,000 tons every year and 60,000 barrels of petrol should be saved every day if average 2,000,000 eV were used. In order to make EV to be widely used, it is critical to develop a kind of battery which have high rate energy, high rate power, long cycle life and low cost. In recent years, with further research and development of EV, Ni-MH battery is considered as one of the most promising secondary power batteries for EV [2]. However, due to influence of work conditions, such as high current and electric-motor heat radiation etc., working temperature of the battery can reach to above 313—333 K, which leads to rapidly decrease in discharge capacity of Ni-MH battery [3]. Meanwhile, after some charge/discharge cycles for Ni-MH battery, its inherent resistance will increase gradually, especially at higher temperature, and the increasing rate will accelerate, which not only leads to reduction of kinetics, but also makes the cycle life shorten sharply. All of these are related to the poor endurance of negative electrode materials under high temperature.

The researches [4-6] showed that the adsorption and storage of hydrogen in electrode active material—hydrogen storage alloy are difficult and the corrosion and destruction of electrode by the boiling alkaline solution are more serious. Therefore, improving the electrochemical performance of negative electrode material at high temperature is very useful for Ni-MH battery used in EV. In this paper, the effects of Si addition on the microstructure and electrochemical characteristics of non-stoichiometric AB_2-type $Zr_{0.9}Ti_{0.1}Ni_{1.0}Mn_{0.7}V_{0.3}Si_x$ ($x=0.05, 0.10, 0.15, 0.20$) alloy were investigated, especially the electrochemical characteristics of the alloy at 313—333 K.

2 Experimental details

$Zr_{0.9}Ti_{0.1}Ni_{1.0}Mn_{0.7}V_{0.4}Si_x$ ($x = 0.05, 0.10, 0.15, 0.20$) alloys were prepared by arc-melting the constituent elements (the purity of the metals was 99.5 mass%) with the stoichiometries under argon atmosphere in the water-cold copper mold. To assure the homogeneity of the alloys, the ingots were turned over and remelted three times. Then, the alloys were mechanically crushed and grounded to powder with the particle size below 200 meshes. The electrodes were prepared by cold pressing the alloy powder and electrolytic Ni powder (300 meshes) in the mass ration of 1 : 4 into pellets of 10mm in diameter, under a pressure of 15 MPa.

The electrochemical measurement was determined on a two-electrodes testing system. The positive electrode is a commercial sintered $Ni(OH)_2/NiOOH$ plate with more discharge capacity than MH electrode. The electrolyte in the cell is 6 mol L^{-1} KOH solution. A charge/discharge test of experimental cell was conducted on DC-5 Battery Testing Equipment made in China by computer control.

The parameters for electrochemical testing were as following: (1) for activation characteristics and discharge capacity tests, the electrodes were fully charged (the over-charged ratio approximately 20%) at current density of 60 mA g^{-1}, then, the electrodes discharged at the same current to cut-off voltage of 0.800 V. When the discharge capacity of alloy electrode reached the maximum, the alloys was considered to be fully activated, and the value is the maximum discharge capacity (represented as C_{max} hereafter). (2) For self-discharge tests (24 h), the self-discharge characteristics were represented by the charge retention (CR, %). It was calculated by CR $= (C_b/C_a) \times 100$, where C_a is the discharge capacity at discharge current of 60 mA g^{-1} and C_b is the addition discharge capacity at discharge current of 60 mA g^{-1} measured after open circuit for 24 h and following the full charge of 60 mA g^{-1}. (3) For the high rate discharge capacity, the high-rate dischargeability (HRD, %) was calculated by HRD$=(C_i/C_{max}) \times 100$, where C_{is} the discharge capacity at discharge current of imA g^{-1} after a full charge of 60 mA g^{-1}. (4) For cycle life tests, the electrodes were charged at current density of 300 mA g^{-1} and discharged at the same current, the discharge capacity of alloys were measured after every 50 cycles at discharge current of 60 mA g^{-1}. The capacity retention (%) of the electrodes for the *N* cycle is ratio of the discharge capacity of the *N* cycle to the maximum discharge capacity. (5) For the effect of temperature, high-temperature electrochemical characteristics of the electrodes were measured after constant temperature for 30 min using a auto constant temperature equipment (±1 K). (6) The cut-off voltage is 0.800 V, the interval between charge and discharge is 10 min.

The crystal structures of hydrogen storage alloys were characterised by XRD analysis utilising Cu Kα radiation on D/Max-ⅡB X-ray diffractometer. The SEM images were observed on a KYKY-2800 Scanning Electron Microscope. At the same time, the alloy components were analysed by energy dispersive spectroscopy (EDS).

3 Results

3.1 XRD of $Zr_{0.9}Ti_{0.1}Ni_{1.0}Mn_{0.7}V_{0.4}Si_x$ ($x= 0.05, 0.10, 0.15, 0.20$)

The XRD patterns of the five alloys are shown in Fig. 1. It is found that all the alloys consist of a large amount of the hexagonal C14-type Laves phases as main phase crystal structure, along with a small level of the cubic C15-type Laves phases and some second phases. Si addition does not change the basic C14-type Laves phase crystal structure of AB_2-type alloys. However, as amount of Si addition increases, the second phases increasc gradually and the diffraction peaks are gradually broadened.

The lattice parameters of the Laves phase, calculated with the 2θ value for the highest peak, are listed in Table 1. It can be seen that the lattice parameters and cell volumes gradually decrease as x increases from 0 to 0.20. The change of lattice parameters of the Laves phase in the alloy is mainly explained that the atom radius of Si (0.146 nm) is less than that of Ni (0.162 nm), Mn (0.162 nm) and V (0.162 nm). Consequently, the Si element content increasing leads to lattice parameters of C14-type and C15-type Laves phase shrinking.

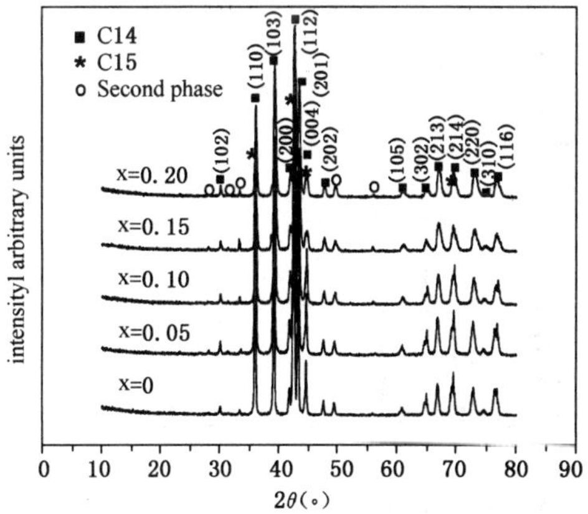

Fig. 1　XRD patterns of $Zr_{0.9}Ti_{0.1}Ni_{1.0}Mn_{0.7}V_{0.3}Si_x$ (x=0, 0.05, 0.10, 0.15, 0.20) alloys

Table 1　Crystalline parameters of $Zr_{0.9}Ti_{0.1}Ni_{1.0}Mn_{0.7}V_{0.3}Si_x$ (x=0, 0.05, 0.10, 0.15, 0.20)

x	C14 Laves phase			C15 Laves phase	
	a/nm	c/nm	V/nm^3	a/nm	V/nm^3
0	0.498 4	0.814 0	0.175 1	0.704 6	0.349 8
0.05	0.497 9	0.813 2	0.174 6	0.704 2	0.349 2
0.10	0.497 7	0.811 8	0.174 1	0.703 6	0.348 3
0.15	0.496 8	0.811 7	0.173 5	0.703 5	0.348 2
0.20	0.493 3	0.811 2	0.171 0	0.702 4	0.346 5

3.2　SEM and EDS of $Zr_{0.9}Ti_{0.1}Ni_{1.0}Mn_{0.7}V_{0.4}Si_x$ (x=0.05, 0.10, 0.15, 0.20)

The SEM images and EDS analysis of $Zr_{0.9}Ti_{0.1}Ni_{1.0}Mn_{0.7}V_{0.4}Si_x$ (x=0.05, 0.10, 0.15, 0.20) are showed in Fig. 2. It can be seen that Si addition alloy has a uniform segregated phase (the second phase) with a round shape in the matrix. The results of EDS analysis show that the main component in the matrix is Ni, and the main component in the segregated phase is Zr, the segregated phase is a Zr-rich particle. The Zr-rich particles, approximately 2—3 μm in diameter, are found to be dispersed throughout the surface.

Fig. 3 shows elements distribution images on surface of $Zr_{0.9}Ti_{0.1}Ni_{1.0}Mn_{0.7}V_{0.3}Si_{0.20}$ alloy. It is easily observed that, compared with the matrix phase, the segregated phases have more Zr and less Ni, Mn, V, Ti, and Si element is well distributed on the surface of alloy. This result is the same as the XRD, SEM and EDS analysis.

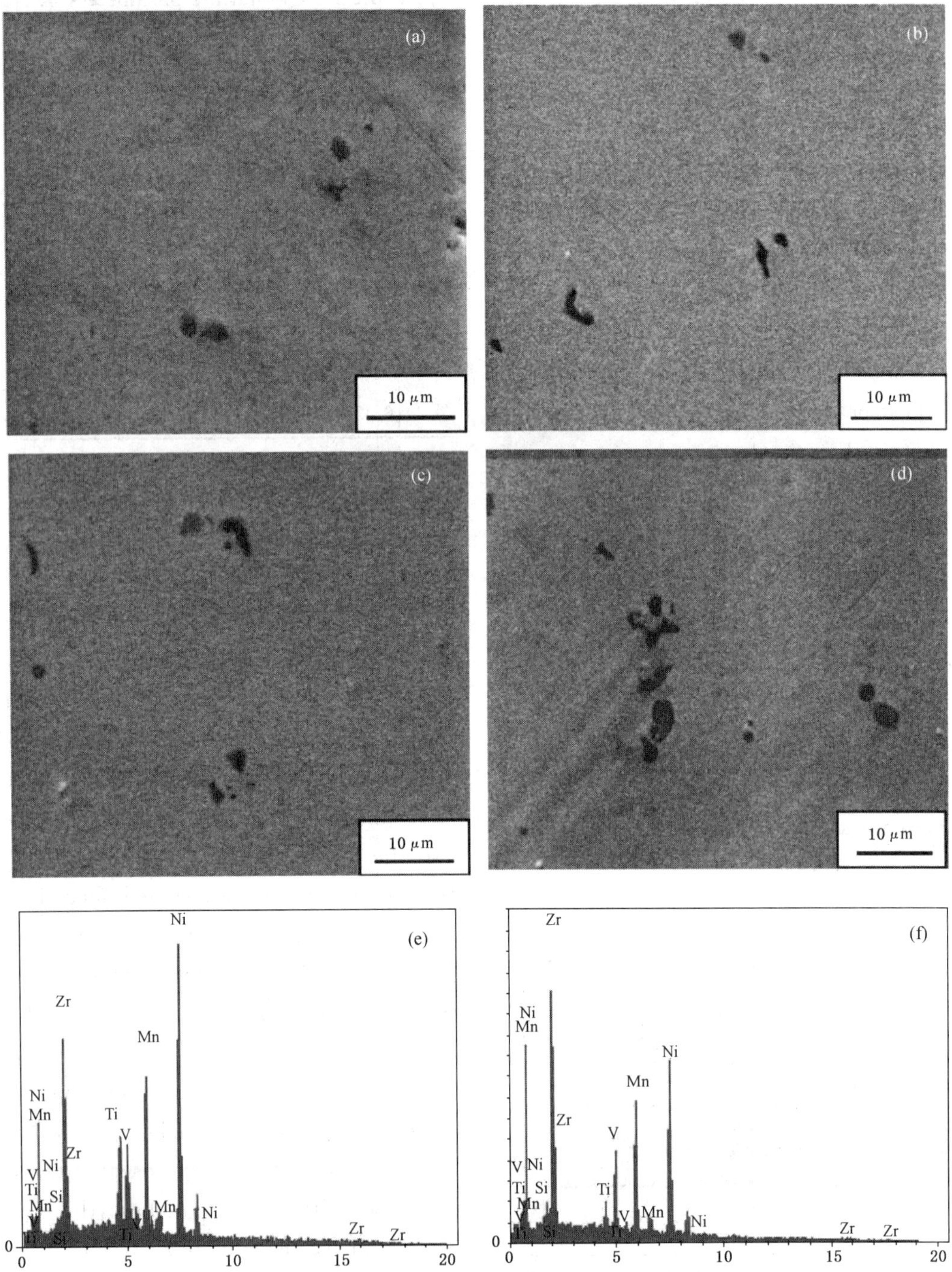

Fig. 2　SEM images of $Zr_{0.9}Ti_{0.1}Ni_{1.0}Mn_{0.7}V_{0.3}Si_x$ alloys and EDS analysis: (a) $x=0.05$; (b) $x=0.10$; (c) $x=0.15$; (d) $x=0.20$; (e) matrix phase; (f) black phase

Fig. 3　Elements distribution images on surface of $Zr_{0.9}Ti_{0.1}Ni_{1.0}Mn_{0.7}V_{0.3}Si_{0.20}$ alloy by EDS

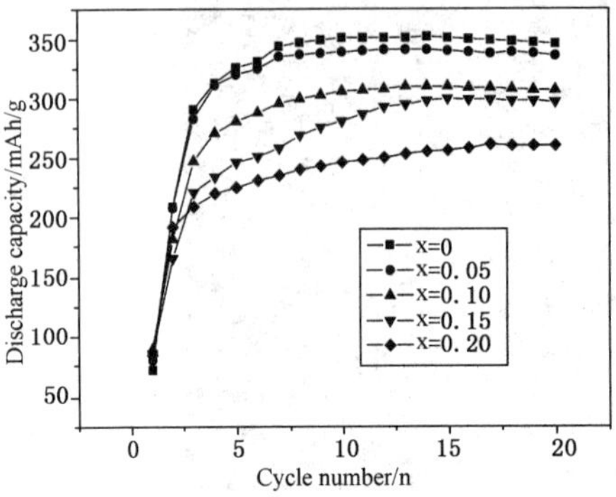

Fig. 4　Activation profiles of $Zr_{0.9}Ti_{0.1}Ni_{1.0}Mn_{07}V_{0.3}Si_x$ alloy electrodes

3.3　Electrochemical characteristics of the alloys at room temperature

At 298 K, the relationship between the discharge capacity and activation cycles of $Zr_{0.9}Ti_{0.1}Ni_{1.0}Mn_{0.7}V_{0.4}Si_x$ ($x=0.05, 0.10, 0.15, 0.20$) alloy electrodes is shown in Fig. 4. Table 2 shows the cycle number for activation and the maximum discharge capacity of the five alloys electrodes. It is seen that the activation cycles of alloy electrodes increased with increasing Si content. The cycle number of the alloy for $x=0$ is 10, and that of the alloy for $x=0.20$ is 17. It is not difficult to understand that Si forms fine oxide film on alloys surface easily, and the activation reduces [7]. Meanwhile, it is noted that the maximum discharge capacity of $Zr_{0.9}Ti_{0.1}Ni_{1.0}Mn_{0.7}V_{0.4}Si_x$ ($x=0.05$, $0.10, 0.15, 0.20$) alloys gradually decrease from 351 mAh g^{-1} for $x=0$ to 258 mAh g^{-1} for $x=0.20$. As it was mentioned before, the unit cell volume of the alloy decreases with increasing Si content. So, the discharge capacity of $Zr_{0.9}Ti_{0.1}Ni_{1.0}Mn_{0.7}V_{0.4}Si_x$ ($x=0.05, 0.10$, $0.15, 0.20$) also decreases with increasing Si content.

Table 2　Activation performance and max discharge capacity of $Zr_{0.9}Ti_{0.1}Ni_{1.0}Mn_{0.7}V_{0.3}Si_x$ alloy electrodes

Alloy(x)	Activation cycles (N)	Max capacity (mAh g^{-1})
0	10	351
0.02	12	341
0.05	13	310
0.10	15	300
0.20	17	258

3.4　Effect of high-temperature on electrochemical characteristics of the alloys

3.4.1　Effect of temperature on discharge capacity of the alloys

The ratio of discharge capacity C_T of the five $Zr_{0.9}Ti_{0.1}Ni_{1.0}Mn_{0.7}V_{0.4}Si_x$ ($x=0.05, 0.10, 0.15, 0.20$) alloys at 298—338 K to that C_{298} at 298 K as a function of temperature is shown in Fig. 5. It is seen that the discharge capacities of all the five alloys decrease at different extents with increasing temperature. For $x=0$, the discharge capacity ratio of $Zr_{0.9}Ti_{0.1}Ni_{1.0}Mn_{0.7}V_{0.4}$ alloy at 338 and 298 K is 33.01%. For $x=0.05$, the discharge capacity ratio of $Zr_{0.9}Ti_{0.1}Ni_{1.0}Mn_{0.7}V_{0.4}Si_{0.05}$ alloy at 338 and 298K is 78.81%. For $x=0.10$, the discharge capacity ratio of 338K and at 298K is 81.60%. The results indicate that Si addition apparently improve the discharge capacity of $Zr_{0.9}Ti_{0.1}Ni_{1.0}Mn_{0.7}V_{0.4}Si_x$ ($x=0.05, 0.10$, $0.15, 0.20$) at high-temperature. The discharge capacity of $Zr_{0.9}Ti_{0.1}Ni_{1.0}Mn_{0.7}V_{0.4}Si_{0.10}$ alloy reaches 249 mAh g^{-1} at 338 K.

3.4.2 Effect of temperature on self-discharge characteristics of the alloys

Fig. 6 shows the self-discharge characteristics of $Zr_{0.9}Ti_{0.1}Ni_{1.0}Mn_{0.7}V_{0.4}Si_x$ (x=0.05, 0.10, 0.15, 0.20) alloys electrodes. It can be seen that the charge retention of the alloy without Si decrease sharply with increasing temperature, but the alloy for x=0.15—0.20, the charge retention of the alloy decreases somewhat with increasing temperature, the charge retention of $Zr_{0.9}Ti_{0.1}Ni_{1.0}Mn_{0.7}V_{0.4}Si_{0.1}$ alloy is 94.20% for 24 h. It indicates that Si addition greatly improve the charge retention of $Zr_{0.9}Ti_{0.1}Ni_{1.0}Mn_{0.7}V_{0.4}Si_x$ (x=0.05, 0.10, 0.15, 0.20) alloys at high temperature, and is beneficial to improve the self-discharge characteristics of the alloy.

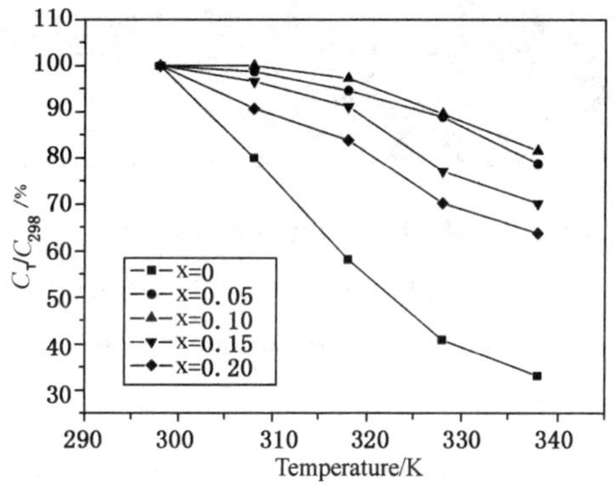

Fig. 5 Capacity retention (%) of $Zr_{0.9}Ti_{0.1}Ni_{1.0}Mn_{0.7}V_{0.3}Si_x$ alloy electrodes at 298-338 K

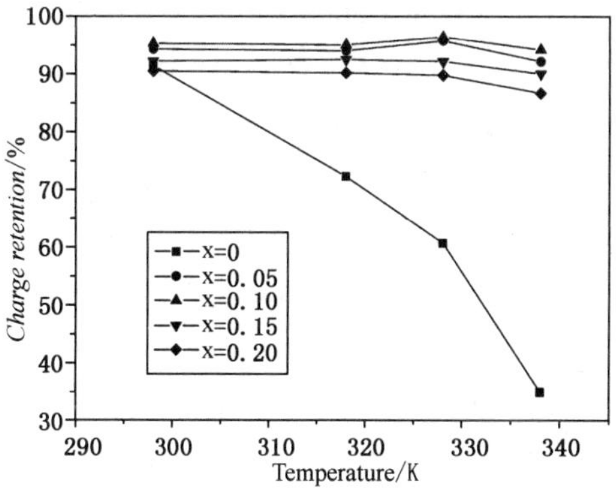

Fig. 6 Charge retention (%) of $Zr_{0.9}Ti_{0.1}Ni_{1.0}Mn_{0.7}V_{0.3}Si_x$ alloy electrodes at 298—338 K for 24 h

3.4.3 Effect of temperature on the cycle stability of the alloys

Fig. 7 shows the discharge capacity retention of the five $Zr_{0.9}Ti_{0.1}Ni_{1.0}Mn_{0.7}V_{0.4}Si_x$ (x=0.05, 0.10, 0.15, 0.20) alloys at 298—338 K after 300 cycles. It can be seen that the discharge capacity retention of all the five alloys decrease with increasing temperature, but the decreasing extent is different apparently. The discharge capacity of the alloy with Si addition is obviously higher than that of the alloy without Si addition. The capacity retention of all alloys increases with increasing the Si content at 298—338 K. The capacity retention of $Zr_{0.9}Ti_{0.1}Ni_{1.0}Mn_{0.7}V_{0.4}Si_{0.1}$ alloy can reach 45.71% at 338K after 300 cycles. The results

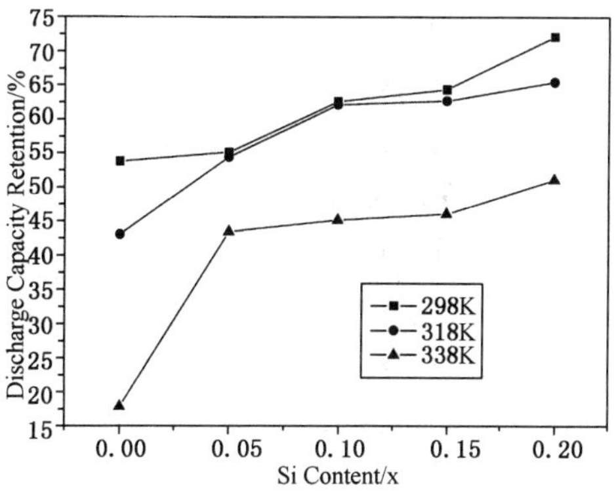

Fig. 7. Discharge capacity retention (%) of $Zr_{0.9}Ti_{0.1}Ni_{1.0}Mn_{0.7}V_{0.3}Si_x$ alloy electrodes after 300 cycles at 298—338 K

indicate that Si addition apparently improve the cycle stability of AB_2-type Laves phase alloy at high temperature.

The discharge capacity decay of $Zr_{0.9}Ti_{0.1}Ni_{1.0}Mn_{0.7}V_{0.4}Si_x$ (x = 0.05, 0.10, 0.15, 0.20) alloys are mainly due to the surface oxidation and pulverisation of the alloy [8]. It is usually thought that, with increasing the temperature, the corrosion and oxidation process of alloy surface is accelerated, and the cycle stability of alloy further decreasing. Moreover, the expansion and contraction of crystal lattice during hydriding/dehydriding process of the alloy would lead to the pulverisation of alloy, which is another important factor for further decreasing cycle stability of alloy. The results indicate that the discharge capacity of the alloy decrease at larger extent when temperature changes from 298 to 338 K, so the expansion and contraction ratio of the crystal lattice during hydriding/dehydriding process surely decreases at larger extent. However, the capacity retention of alloy still decreased further. It seems to imply that the expansion and contraction ratio of the crystal lattice of the alloy during hydriding/dehydriding process is not a key factor for the further capacity decay of the alloy at higher temperature, the main cause of decreasing of alloy cycle stability may be due to the corrosion and the oxidation on alloy surface.

Fig. 8 shows the surface morphology of $Zr_{0.9}Ti_{0.1}Ni_{1.0}Mn_{0.7}V_{0.3}Si_{0.1}$ hydride electrode after 100 cycles under 338 K. It is found that the corrosion on the surface of the alloy particles is distinctly shown, but the cracks do not appeared. This is just as the above results.

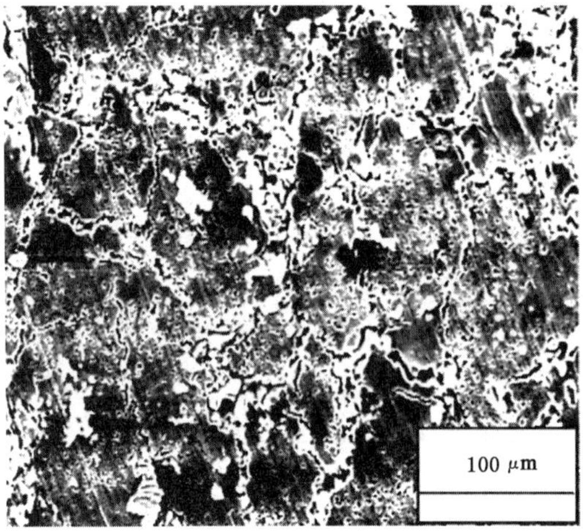

Fig. 8 SEM morphology of $Zr_{0.9}Ti_{0.1}Ni_{1.0}Mn_{0.7}V_{0.3}Si_{0.1}$ hydride electrode after 100 cycles under 338 K

Temperature is of an importance factor to influence electrochemical characteristics of hydrogen storage alloy. It was found [9,10] that the hydrogen diffusion in the hydrogen storage alloys is accelerated, and hydrogen adsorbed on alloy surface tends to escape easier at high-temperature. At the same time, the corrosion of strong alkaline solution on alloy increases. As a result, the self-discharge ability of hydrogen storage alloy electrodes increases, and the discharge capacity and cycle life decay rapidly. Consequently, increasing the discharge capacity and cycle stability of hydrogen storage alloy and decreasing self-discharge are the three critical problems for improving high-temperature electrochemical characteristics of hydrogen storage alloy, and it is also a subject widely concerned.

From above the results, it can be seen that Si addition greatly improved the high-temperature electrochemical characteristics (the discharge capacity, the charge retention, the cycle stability) of the AB_2-Laves phase alloys. The improvement of the alloys investigated was attributed to the formation of the Zr-rich second phase in the matrix and the increasing stability of AB_2-type Laves phase alloy hydride due to Si addition in alloy.

Degradation behaviour of AB_2-type alloy be caused by the reaction that the component atoms to occupy some certain lattice sites are selectively dissolved into the alkaline solution and oxidation during the anodic polarisation [5]. Because of Zr oxide film formed in the alkaline solution, the Zr-rich particles precipitated along boundaries of the second phase are considered as protective coating and decreased the dissolution and oxidation of the alloy component elements.

The discharge capacity of alloy is related to the stability of the hydride. According to equation $\ln p_{eq} = \Delta H^\circ / RT - \Delta S^\circ / R$, the equilibrium pressure of hydrogen in the alloy, p_{eq}, increases with increasing the temperature, and as a result the stability of alloy hydride decreases, the hydrogen stored in the alloy easily escapes from the alloy, which lead the actual hydrogen storage amount of alloy to reduce, and the discharge capacity of the alloy to decrease sharply. As seen from Fig. 5, suitable Si addition can apparently improve the stability of AB_2-type Laves phase alloy hydride and decrease the capacity loss. At the same time, there is a compact silicon oxide film on the alloy surface, which improves the corrosion resistance performance of the alloy and also decreases the capacity loss.

4 Conclusion

In this paper, the microstructure and higher-temperature electrochemical characteristics of non-stoichiometric AB_2-type Laves phase $Zr_{0.9}Ti_{0.1}Ni_{1.0}Mn_{0.7}V_{0.4}Si_x$ (x=0.05, 0.10, 0.15, 0.20) alloys have been studied, the conclusions are as follows:

(1) Si content does not change the matrix crystal structure of AB_2 alloy. However, with increasing the Si content, the non-Laves phase of the alloy increases and the discharge capacity decreases.

(2) The particle size of second phase with a round shape formed in the matrix is approximately 2—3 μm. Compared with the main phase, there are more Zr, and less Ni, Mn, V and Ti in the second phase. But Si element distributes on the alloy surface.

(3) Si addition greatly improved electrochemical characteristics of $Zr_{0.9}Ti_{0.1}Ni_{1.0}Mn_{0.7}V_{0.3}Si_x$ (x=0.05, 0.10, 0.15, 0.20) alloys at high temperature. At 338 K, the discharge capacity of $Zr_{0.9}Ti_{0.1}Ni_{1.0}Mn_{0.7}V_{0.3}Si_{0.10}$ alloy reached 249

mAh g^{-1}, and the charge retention was 94.20% for 24 h, and the capacity retention for 300 charge/discharge cycles was 45.17%.

(4) The improvement in the high-temperature electrochemical characteristics of the alloy investigated was attributed to the formation of the Zr-rich second phase in the matrix and the increasing stability of AB_2-type Laves phase alloy hydride due to Si addition in alloy.

(5) At high temperature, the main cause for decreasing of cycle stability may be due to the corrosion and the oxidising deterioration on alloy surface.

Acknowledgements

This work was financial supported by Chinese National Science Foundation (20171042) and Key Laboratory of Rare Earth Chemistry and Physics, Chinese Academy of Sciences.

References

[1] G. Paul, A. John, C. Dennis, V. Srinivasan, Development of advanced nickel/metal hydride batteries for electric and hybrid vehicles, J. Power Sources 80 (1999) 157.

[2] R. F. Nelson, Power requirements for batteries in hydride electric vehicles, J. Power Sources 91 (2000) 2.

[3] H. Senoh, M. Ueda, N. Furukawa, H. Inoue, C. Iwakura, Theoretical evaluation for thermodynamic stability of constituents of Mm-based hydrogen storage alloy in 6M KOH solution at relatively high temperatures, J. Alloys Compd. 280 (1998) 114.

[4] M. E. Fiorino, R. L. Opila, K. Konstadinidas, W. C. Fang, Electrochemical and X-ray photoelectron spectroscopy characterization of surface films on $MmNi_{3.5}Al_{0.8}Co_{0.7}$, J. Electrochem. Soc. 143 (1996) 2422.

[5] H. H. Lee, K. Y. Lee, J. Y. Lee, Degradation mechanism of Ti-Zr-V-Mn-Ni metal hydride electrodes, J. Alloys Compd. 260 (1997) 201.

[6] J. H. Jung, H. H. Lee, D. M. Kim, K. J. Jang, J. Y. Lee, Degradation behavior of Cu-coated Ti-Zr-V-Mn-Ni metal hydride electrodes, J. Alloys Compd. 266 (1998) 266.

[7] T. Sakai, K. Oruro, H. Miyamura, Some factors affecting the cycle lives of $LaNi_5$-based alloy electrodes of hydrogen batteries, J. Less-Common Met. 161 (1990) 193.

[8] X. P. Gao, Y. M. Sun, E. Toyoda, E. Higuchi, T. Nakagima, S. Suda, The effect of the particle pulverization on electrochemical properties of Laves phase alloys, Electrochim. Acta 45 (2000) 3099.

[9] Y. H. Xu, C. P. Chen, Q. D. Wang, The influence of small amounts of added elements on the electrode performance characteristics for Ti_3Ni_2 hydrogen storage alloy, Mater. Chem. Phys. 71 (2001) 190.

[10] C. Jeong, W. Chung, C. Iwakura, I. Kim, Effect of temperature on the discharge capacity of the Laves alloy used in nickel/metal-hydride batteries, J. Power Sources 79 (1999) 19.

Electrochemical Characteristics and Microstructure of $Zr_{0.9}Ti_{0.1}Ni_{1.1}Mn_{0.6}V_{0.3}$-$LaNi_5$ Composite Hydrogen Storage Alloys①

Shu-Min Han[a,b], Zhong Zhang[a], Min-Shou Zhao[a,b], Yang-Zeng Zheng[a]
([a] Department of Environmental and Chemical Engineering,
Yanshan University, Qinhuangdao 066004, PR China)
([b] Key Laboratory of Rare Earth Chemistry and Physics,
Changchun Institute of Applied Chemistry,
Chinese Academy of Sciences, Changchun 130022, PR China
Available online 22 July 2005)

Abstract: AB_2-x%$LaNi_5$ ($x=0$, 1, 5, 10) composite alloys were prepared by melting $Zr_{0.9}Ti_{0.1}Ni_{1.1}Mn_{0.6}V_{0.3}$ with a small amount of $LaNi_5$ alloy as addition. The microstructure and electrochemical characteristics of the composite alloys were investigated by means of XRD, SEM, EDS and electrochemical measurements. It was shown that $LaNi_5$ addition does not change the basic hexagonal C_{14} Laves phase of AB_2 alloys, but some second phases have segregated. It was found that the addition of $LaNi_5$ greatly improves the activation property, high-rate dischargeability (HRD) and charge-discharge cycling stability of AB_2 Laves phase alloy. At current density of 1 200 mA/g, HRD of the alloy increases from 38.92% ($x=0$) to 60.09% ($x=10$). The capacity retention of the alloy after 200 charge/discharge cycles increases from 57.10% ($x=0$) to 83.86% ($x=5$) and 67.31% ($x=10$). The improvement of the electrochemical characteristics caused by $LaNi_5$ addition seems to be related to formation of the second phases.

Key words: Composite hydrogen storage alloys; Metal hydride electrode; Second phase; Electrochemical characteristics

1 Introduction

Zr-based AB_2-type Laves phase hydrogen storage alloys are promising materials for use as negative electrode material in Ni-MH batteries due to their higher discharge capacity compared with commercially used AB_5-type rare earth based alloys [1]. However, Zr-based Laves phase alloy electrodes exhibit in general very slow activation behavior, poor high-rate dischargeability and cycling stability. For improving electrode characteristics of Zr-based Laves phase alloy electrodes, many investigations have been carried out to improve the activation per-

① International Journal of Hydrogen Energy, 2006(31): 563-567.

formance and kinetic properties of Zr-based AB_2 Laves phase alloys by adding new alloying elements and synthesizing composite alloys [2-4].

Chen [5] has greatly improved the activation performance and discharge capacity of $ZrNi_{1.1}Mn_{0.5}V_{0.3}Cr_{0.1}$ by adding Ce or Ce-rich rare earth (Mm) to it. It is considered that this is caused by formation of the second phases, Ce-Ni phase and Mm-Ni phase. Bououdina et al. [6] synthesized composite alloys consisting of $Zr_{0.5}Ti_{0.5}Cr_{1.5}$ and 5—20 wt% $LaNi_5$, and investigated its hydrogen storage properties in solid state. The absorbing, desorbing hydrogen kinetic properties were improved due to the segregation of pure Cr phase and existence of a small amount of $LaNi_5$ phase, but electrochemical properties were not reported yet. Chen et al. [7] reported that the electrochemical activity of the composite alloy prepared by ball-milling $Zr_{0.5}Ti_{0.5}V_{0.75}Ni_{1.25}$ alloy and a small a 2 wt% of nanocrystalline $LaNi_5$ was improved. Lee et al. [8] applied a ball-milling process to the Ti-based AB_2 alloy using the Ni flake powder as a surface modifier and the electrochemical durability of the Ti-based hydrogen storage alloy electrode was greatly increased.

In our earlier studies, the AB_2-AB_5 composite alloys were prepared using a ball-milling process [9]. The activation performance and high rate dischargeability of AB_2 Laves phase alloy $Zr_{0.9}Ti_{0.1}Ni_{1.1}Mn_{0.7}V_{0.3}$ were improved by adding a commercial AB_5 alloy. It was shown that the AB_5 alloy could work not only as a hydrogen reservoir but also as a catalyst for hydriding and dehydriding. The hydrogen storage alloy $LaNi_5$ is not only easy to prepare, but it also has very fast hydrogen sorption kinetics. Therefore, we choose $LaNi_5$ alloy as addition for improving the electrochemical properties of AB_2 Laves phase hydrogen storage alloy in this paper, the AB_2-$LaNi_5$ composite alloys are prepared by melting AB_2 Laves phase $Zr_{0.9}Ti_{0.1}Ni_{1.1}Mn_{0.6}V_{0.3}$ and $LaNi_5$ alloy. SEM and EDS were used to characterize the microstructure of the composite alloy, and the electrode properties of AB_2 alloy with $LaNi_5$ addition were investigated by galvanostatic cycling tests.

2 Experiment

$LaNi_5$ alloy and AB_2-type Laves phase alloy $Zr_{0.9}Ti_{0.1}Ni_{1.1}Mn_{0.6}V_{0.3}$ (represented as AB_2 hereafter) were prepared by arc-melting the constituent elements (the purity of the metals was no less than 99.5%) according to stoichiometric ratio under argon atmosphere in the water-cooled copper mold. To assure the homogeneity of the alloys, the ingots were turned over and re-melted 3 times.

The powder of AB_2 alloy and $LaNi_5$ alloy was mixed homogenously in the mass ratio of 9.9 : 0.1, 9.5 : 0.5, 9.0 :

1.0, respectively, and pressed into pellets, then arc-melted 2 times under 0.06 Mpa Ar atmosphere. Then, the composite alloys AB_2-x%$LaNi_5$ (x=1,5,10) (represented as AB_2-$LaNi_5$ hereafter) had been prepared.

The preparation of metal hydride alloy electrode and the half-cell, and the methods and conditions to measure the electrochemical characteristics were the same as shown in our previous paper [9].

The crystal structure of hydrogen storage alloy was characterized by XRD analysis utilizing Cu Kα radiation on D/Max-rB X-ray diffractometer. The morphologies of the alloys were observed using KYKY2800-type scanning electron microscopy (SEM). The distribution of the alloy components was analyzed by a Kevex-sigma Level 4 energy-dispersive spectrometer (EDS). The alloy ingots were burnished using sand paper and the impurity (including some oxidation) on the surface was removed using a chemical method before analyzing.

3 Results and discussion

3.1 Microstructure of AB_2-$LaNi_5$ composite alloys

Fig. 1 shows the XRD patterns of $LaNi_5$ and AB_2-x%$LaNi_5$ (x=0,1,5,10) alloy. It can be seen that

$LaNi_5$ addition does not change the basic hexagonal C14 Laves phase structure of AB_2 alloys, but some second phase is exhibited as small additional peaks in XRD patterns of AB_2-$LaNi_5$ alloys. As the amount of $LaNi_5$ addition increases, the second phases increase and the diffraction peaks move towards the right gradually, but a $LaNi_5$ phase is not detected.

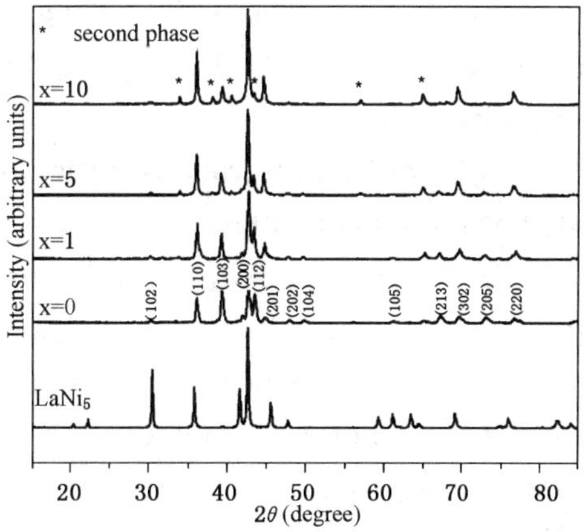

Fig. 1 XRD patterns of $LaNi_5$ and AB_2-x%$LaNi_5$ (x=0,1,5,10) alloys

Fig. 2 shows SEM morphologies of AB_2-x%$LaNi_5$ (x=1,5,10) composite alloys. It can be seen that uniform second phases (black phase and white phase) segregate from the matrix phase, and the second phases increase with increasing $LaNi_5$ addition, this is consistent with the results from XRD. The white phase is dispersed between the black phase and the matrix phase, and shapes and sizes of the segregated particles change with increasing x. For x = 1, the particles are round, about 10 μm in size; for x=5, they are like strips, about 10—20 μm and for x=10, like petals, about 10—30 μm.

EDS analyses of different phases are shown in Fig. 3. It indicates that the matrix phase has a composition close to (Zr, Ti)(Ni, Mn, V)$_2$ Laves phase, the black phase contains more Zr, that is to say, the black phase is Zr-rich, and the white phase contains more La and Ni, as La-Ni phase. Thus, it can be believed that $LaNi_5$ has been broken down, some La and Ni segregate as La-Ni phase, and the rest of the La replaces Zr, making Zr segregate as Zr-rich phase in AB_2-$LaNi_5$ composite alloys.

3.2 Electrochemical characteristics of AB_2-$LaNi_5$ composite alloys

Fig. 4 shows discharge capacity vs. cycle number of the AB_2-$x\%$ $LaNi_5$ ($x=0,1,5,10$) alloy electrodes. It can be seen that the activation cycle number decreases with increasing $LaNi_5$ content. It is 12 cycles for $x=0$, and 6 for $x=10$. It is generally considered that, it is easier for hydrogen to diffuse through grain boundaries, which have a more open structure than in the grains. Therefore, it is easy to understand that La-Ni phase segregating out between Zr-rich phase and the matrix phase due to $LaNi_5$ addition may become the active sites and pathways for hy-drogen diffusion [10].

Thus, the activation performance is improved. It can also be seen that, the maximum capacity of AB_2-$x\%$ $LaNi_5$ ($x=0, 1, 5, 10$) alloy electrodes decreases from 328 mAh/g ($x=0$) to 275 mAh/g ($x=10$). The second phases increase with increasing x, and the Laves phase decreases with increasing x. As a result, the discharge capacity of AB_2-$x\%$ $LaNi_5$ ($x=0,1,5,10$) alloy decreases with increasing x.

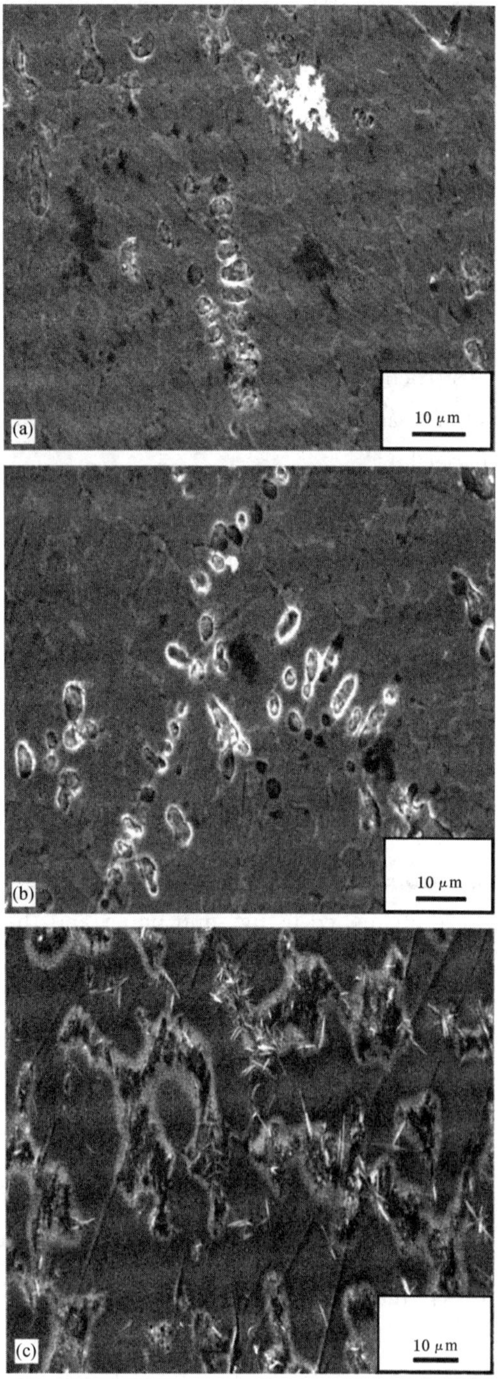

Fig. 2 SEM morphologies of AB_2-$x\%$ $LaNi_5$ alloys: (a) $x=1$; (b) $x=5$; (c) $x=10$

Fig. 5 shows discharge capacity of AB_2-x% $LaNi_5$ (x=0,1,5,10) alloys at different current densities (120—1 200 mA/g). It can be seen that the discharge capacity of the alloy decreases remarkably as discharge current density increases. But the amplitudes of decrease are different with different x value of the alloy. The amplitude decreases with increasing x, especially when the current density is more than 720 mA/g.

In order to find the effect of $LaNi_5$ addition content on high-rate dischargeability (HRD), HRD of AB_2-x% $LaNi_5$ (x =0, 1, 5, 10) alloys at various current density is shown in Fig. 6. It can be seen that the HRD of $Zr_{0.9}Ti_{0.1}Ni_{1.1}Mn_{0.6}V_{0.3}$ is the lowest of all, and it increases with increasing x. For example, the HRD increases from 38.92% (x=0) to 60.09% (x=10) at current density of 1 200 mA/g. The result shows that the HRD of the AB_2 alloy is improved due to $LaNi_5$ addition.

Charge-discharge cycle curves of AB_2-x% $LaNi_5$ (x= 0,1,5,10) alloy electrodes are shown in Fig. 7. It can be seen that the capacity retention of the alloy increases when x value changes from 1 to 5, i. e. the cycling stability of the alloys increase with increasing x. The capacity retention of AB_2 alloy after 200 cycles increases from 57.10% (x=0) to 83.86% (x = 5), and then decreases to 67.31% (x=10). It can be concluded that addition of $LaNi_5$ in small amount is helpful in improving charge-discharge cycling stability of AB_2 Laves phase, but an extra addition of $LaNi_5$ deteriorates the stability.

The degradation process of AB_2 Laves phase alloy electrodes can be properly described with pulverization-oxidation [11]. Pulverization rate is an important factor affecting cycling stability of the alloy electrodes. It has been reported [12] that segregation of Zr-rich phase can restrain the lattice expansion of metal hydride and decrease the micro-rigidity of the alloy, which has greatly decreased the pulverization rate, and as a result, charge-discharge cycling stability of AB_2 type Laves phase alloy has been greatly improved. But segregation of La-Ni phase accelerates the pulverization and deteriorates the charge-discharge cycling stability of AB_2 Laves phase alloy [5]. When a small amount (1—5%) of $LaNi_5$ is added, La-Ni phase segregate less, and Zr-rich phase can effectively restrain the lattice expansion. So the cycling stability of the AB_2-(1—5)% $LaNi_5$ composite alloy can be enhanced. But when more $LaNi_5$ (>5%) is added, more La-Ni phase will segregate. Therefore, pulverization of the alloy will be accelerated, and the cycling stability will be deteriorated.

4 Conclusions

In order to improve the electrochemical characteristics of AB_2 Laves phase alloy, AB_2-x% $LaNi_5$ (x=0,1,5,10) composite alloys were prepared by melting $Zr_{0.9}Ti_{0.1}Ni_{1.1}Mn_{0.6}V_{0.3}$ with small amounts of $LaNi_5$ alloy as addition. These composite alloys have special multiphase microstructure and meaningful electrochemical properties.

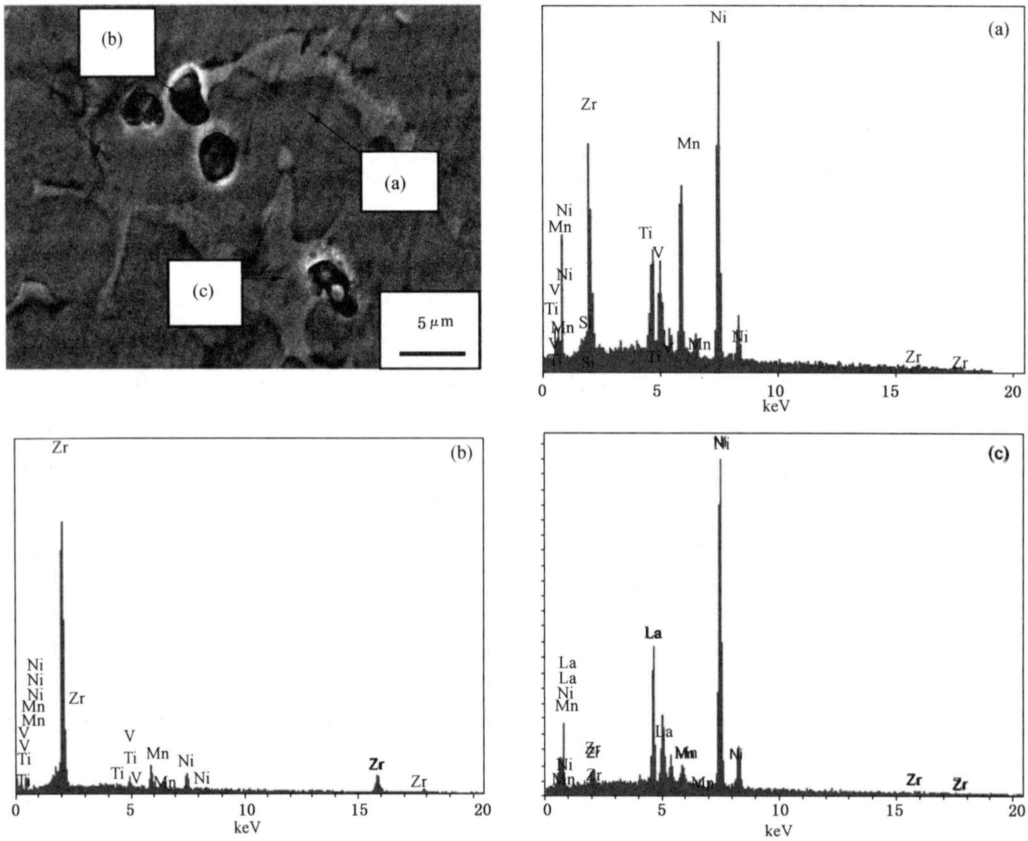

Fig. 3　EDS analysis of AB_2-x%$LaNi_5$ composite alloys: (a) matrix phase; (b) black phase; (c) white phase

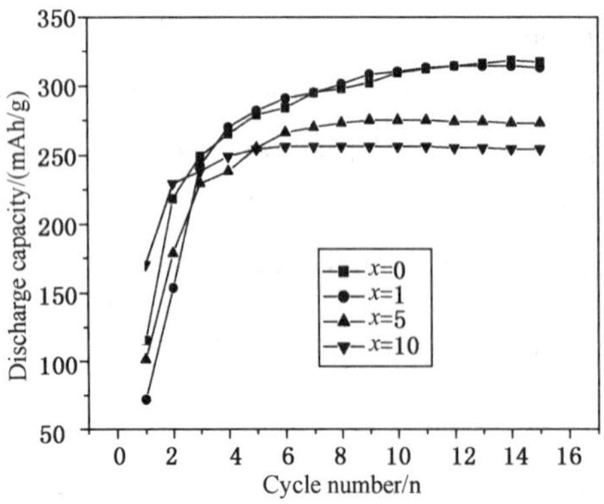

Fig. 4　Activation profiles of AB_2-x% $LaNi_5$ (x=0, 1, 5, 10) alloy electrodes

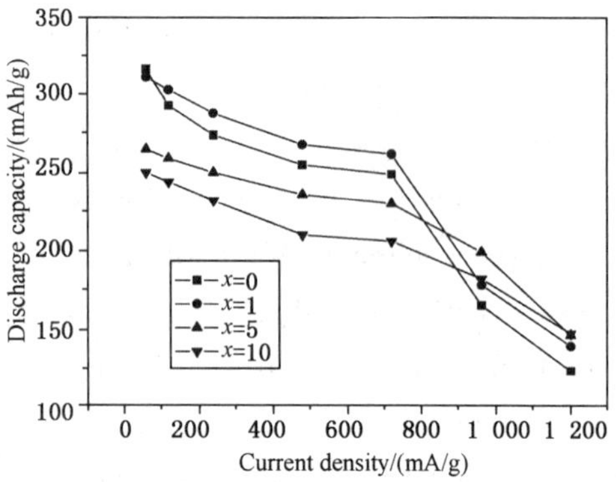

Fig. 5　Dependence of discharge capacity of AB_2-x%$LaNi_5$ (x=0, 1, 5, 10) alloys vs. current density

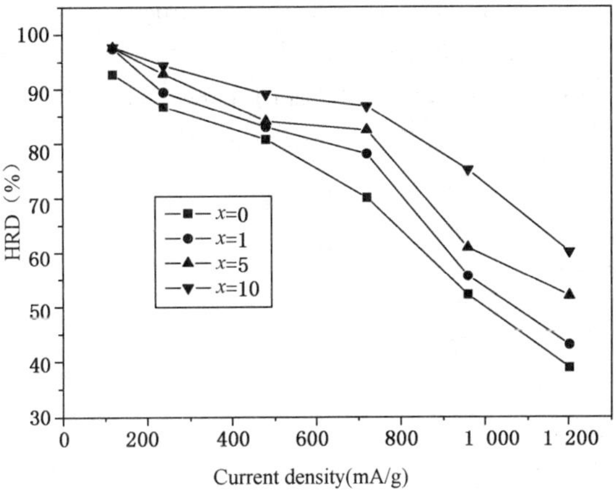

Fig. 6　HRD (%) of AB_2-x% $LaNi_5$ (x=0,1,5,10) alloys

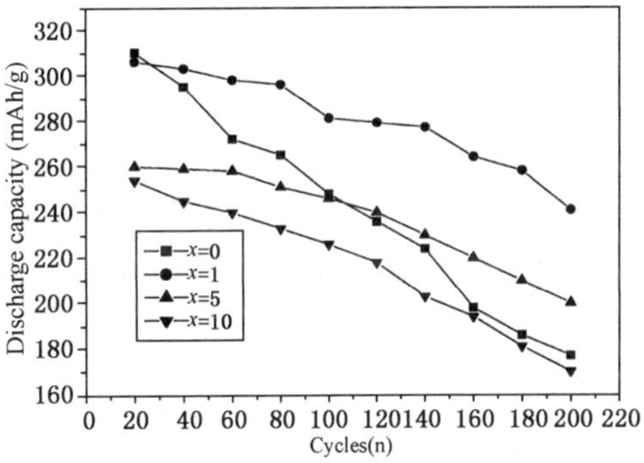

Fig. 7　Charge-discharge cycle curves of AB_2-x%$LaNi_5$ (x=0,1,5,10) alloys electrodes

(1) $LaNi_5$ addition does not change the basic hexagonal C14 Laves phase of AB_2 alloy, but some second phase segregated with $LaNi_5$ addition. In the segregated second phases, the black phase is Zr-rich and the white phase is a La-Ni phase. The white phase is dispersed between the black phase and the matrix phase, and shapes and sizes of the segregated particles change with increasing x.

(2) Compared with AB_2 Laves phase alloy, the activation performance and high rate dischargeability of AB_2-x%$LaNi_5$ (x=0,1,5,10) composite alloy are both improved. It may be caused by the segregated La-Ni phase, which becomes active sites and pathways for hydrogen diffusion.

(3) The capacity retention of the alloy after 200 charge-discharge cycles increases from 57.10% (x=0) to 83.86% (x=5) and then decreases to 67.31% (x=10). The charge-discharge cycling stability will be enhanced by a small amount of $LaNi_5$ addition, but deteriorated by a large amount of $LaNi_5$ addition.

Acknowledgements

This research was financially supported by the National Natural Science Foundation of China (20171042), the Natural Science Foundation of Hebei Province (B2004000188) and Natural Science Foundation of Hebei Education Department, PR China (2004466).

References

[1] Hong K. J Alloys Compd 2001;321:307.
[2] Shu KY, Yang XG, Zhang SK, Lu GL, Lei YQ, Wang QD. J Alloys Compd 2000;306:122.
[3] Kim JS, Paik CH, Cho WI, Cho BW, Yun KS, Kim SJ. J Power Sources 1998;75:1.
[4] Percheron-Guégan A, Joubert JM, Latroche M, Bouet J. J Alloys Compd 1996;240:219.
[5] Chen WX. J Alloy Compd 2001;319:119.
[6] Bououdina M, Sun DL, Enoki H, Akiba E. J Alloys Compd 1999;288:229.
[7] Chen ZH, Chen ZH, Huang KL, Huang PY. J Alloys Compd 1999;293-295:712.
[8] Lee SM, Yu JS, Lee PS, Lee JY. Mater Sci

Eng 2002;A329-331:339.

[9] Han SM, Zhao MS, Wu YM, Zheng YZ. Chinese J Inorg Chem 2003;19(3):262.

[10] Park HY, Cho WI, Cho BW, Lee SR, Yun KS. J Power Sources 2001;92:149.

[11] Gao XP, Sun YM, Toyoda E, Higuchi E, Nakagima T, Suda S. Electrochim Acta 2000;45:3099.

[12] Seo CY, Choi SJ, Choi J, Park CN, Lee PS, Lee JY. Int J Hydrogen Energy 2003;28:317.

Effect of AB_2 Alloy Addition on the Phase Structures and Electrochemical Characteristics of $LaNi_5$ Hydride Electrode①

Shu-Min Han[a,b,c], Min-Shou Zhao[a,b,c], Zhong Zhang[c], Yang-Zeng Zheng[c], Tan-fu Jing[c]

([a] Department of Environmental and Chemical Engineering, Yanshan University, Qinhuangdao 066004, PR China)

([b] Key Laboratory of Rare Earth Chemistry and Physics, Chinese Academy of Sciences, Changchun 130022, PR China)

([c] Key Laboratory of Metastable Materials Science and Technology, Qinhuangdao 066004, PR China)

Abstract: Hypo-stoichiometric $AB_{5-\alpha}$ ($\alpha>0$) type alloy $LaNi_5$-$x\%$ AB_2 ($x=1,5,10,20$) composite alloys were successfully prepared by sintering the powder mixtures of $LaNi_5$ and AB_2-type Laves phase alloy $Zr_{0.9}Ti_{0.1}(Mn_{0.35}Ni_{0.55}V_{0.15})_2$ as addition. The phase structure and electrochemical characteristics of the composite alloys were investigated by means of XRD, EDS and electrochemical measurements. It was shown that $LaNi_5$-$x\%$ AB_2 ($x=1,5,10,20$) composite alloys have multi-phase structure, the matrix phase is $CaCu_5$ structure of $LaNi_5$ alloy, the second phase is rich-Zr phase which dispersed in the matrix phase as strips. The discharge capacity and rate-discharge capacity of $LaNi_5$ alloy electrodes were greatly improved after composite treated by adding AB_2 alloy. The maximum discharge capacity of the composite alloy electrodes increased from 188 mAh/g for $x=0$ to 305 mAh/g for $x=10$, and the rate-discharge capacity of the composite alloy for $x=5$ at the current density of 300 mA/g and 2 040 mA/g was 97% and 55% of that of the alloy at 60 mA/g, respectively. The electrochemical characteristics of $LaNi_5$ alloy at low temperature were also significantly improved by adding AB_2 alloy. The discharge capacity of LaNi-5% AB_2 composite alloy electrode at 233 K was up to 215 mAh/g.

Key words: Composite hydrogen storage alloy; Hypo-stoichiometric AB_5-type alloy; Metal hydride electrode; Low-temperature electrochemical characteristics

1 Introduction

AB_5-type rare earth-based alloy, a kind of hydrogen storage alloy used as negative electrode materials of the nickel/metal hydride (Ni/MH) secondary battery, has easy initial activation, long cycle life and low cost [1], but still a

① Journal of Alloys and Compounds, 2005(392): 268-273.

small discharge capacity and poor properties at low temperature. Therefore, many studies have been done in order to increase the discharge capacity and improve the overall properties of AB_5-based alloys until now [2-4].

Recently, studies showed that the discharge capacity of bcc solid solution alloy based on hydride forming elements such as V and Ti, a novel higher energy density hydrogen storage alloy, has reached to 420 mAh/g [5], which was 40% higher than that of commercial rare-earth based AB_5-type alloy. Zr belongs to a strong hydrogen-absorbing element and come to be bcc metal at the temperature over 1 136 K. Moreover, Zr is also one of the most efficient elements for reducing the hysteresis effect of AB_5 alloy [6]. Therefore, it would be a meaningful study to improve the electrochemical characteristics of AB_5-type alloy by adding Zr, V and Ti into it [7, 8]. On the other hand, it was shown that non-stoichiometric mixed RE-based AB_5-type alloys with multi-phase, especially hypo-stoichiometric $AB_{5-\alpha}$ ($\alpha>0$) type alloys usually have better electrochemical characteristics [9]. For improving the electrochemical characteristics of hydrogen storage alloys, it is an effective method to prepare the composite hydrogen storage alloys using addition [10]. In this paper, a kind of hypo-stoichiometric $AB_{5-\alpha}$ ($\alpha>0$) type composite alloy with multi-phase was prepared by sintering the powder mixtures of $LaNi_5$ alloy and AB_2 alloy which contained Zr, V, Ti elements and worked as addition, the phase structure and electrochemical characteristics of the composite hydrogen storage alloys are also studied.

2 Experimental

$LaNi_5$ alloy and AB_2-type Laves phase alloy $Zr_{0.9}Ti_{0.1}(Mn_{0.35}Ni_{0.55}V_{0.15})_2$ (represented as AB_2 hereafter) were prepared by arc-melting the constituent elements (the purity of the metals was no less than 99.9 mass%) with stoichiometries under argon atmosphere in the water-cold copper mold. To assure the homogeneity of the alloys, the ingots were turned over and remelted three times.

The power of $LaNi_5$ alloy and AB_2 alloy was mixed homogenous in the mass ratio of 9.9 : 0.1, 9.5 : 0.5, 9.0 : 1.0, 8.0 : 2.0, respectively, and pressed into pellets, then sintering for 8 h under 600-1 050 ℃ and 0.06 MPa Ar atmosphere. Then, the composite alloys $LaNi_5$-x% AB_2 ($x=1,5,10,20$) (represented as $LaNi_5$-AB_2 hereafter) were prepared.

The electrochemical characteristics under lower temperature were measured after constant temperature for 4 h using a low-temperature equipment (WGD701). The preparation of metal hydride alloy electrode and half cell, and the methods and conditions to measure the electrochemical characteristics were same as [11].

The crystal structure of hydrogen storage alloy was characterized by XRD analysis utilizing Cu Kα radiation on D/Max-rB X-ray diffractometer. The alloy components were analyzed by a Kevex-Sigma Level 4 energy dispersive spectroscopy (EDS) which was coupled with scanning electron microscope (SEM).

3 Results and discussion

3.1 XRD and EDS of $LaNi_5$-AB_2 composite alloys

The XRD patterns of $LaNi_5$-$x\%$ AB_2 ($x=1,5,10,20$) composite alloys are shown in Fig. 1. It is found that the matrix phase $CaCu_5$ structure of $LaNi_5$ is not changed after adding AB_2 for composite treating in the experiment conditions, however, the amount of second phase increased with the amount of AB_2 increasing in the composite alloys.

The EDS analysis of $LaNi_5$-$x\%$ AB_2 ($x = 1, 5, 10, 20$) composite alloys is shown in Fig. 2. It is easily seen that it has more Zr and less La in the second phase compared than the matrix phase. That is, the second phase is Zr-rich. Element Ni is well distributed on the surface of the alloys, but the Zr-rich phase is dispersed in the matrix phase as strips. Moreover, the amount of the second phase is increasing gradually with the amount of adding AB_2 increasing, as indicated by XRD analysis. It usually considers that it is difficult to make La metal and AB_2 alloy dissolving and alloying together [12]. So, the Zr-rich particles of the second phase in the composite alloys were easily segregated and dispersed in the matrix phase.

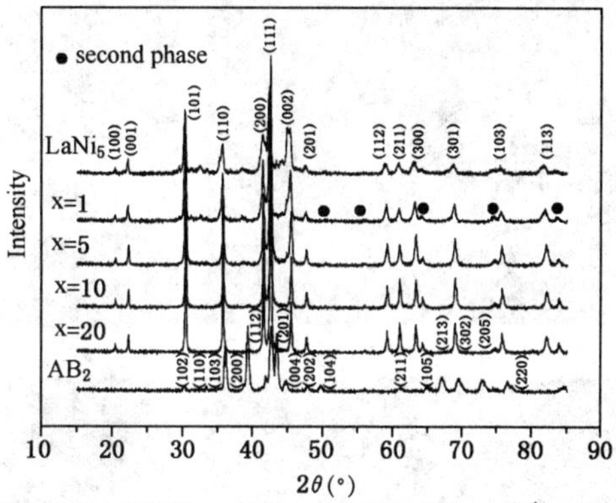

Fig. 1 XRD patterns of $LaNi_5$-$x\%$ AB_2 and AB_2 alloy powders

3.2 Activation and maximum capacity of $LaNi_5$-AB_2 composite alloys

The relationships between the discharge capacity and activation cycles of $LaNi_5$-$x\%$ AB_2 ($x=1,5,10,20$) composite alloys at room temperature are shown in Fig. 3. It can be seen that the activation cycles of $LaNi_5$-AB_2 composite alloy for $x=1$-20 is more than $LaNi_5$ alloy for x is zero. So, the activation performance of composite alloy is decreased.

Fig. 4 shows the relationship between the maximum discharge capacity of $LaNi_5$-$x\%$ AB_2 ($x=1,5,10,20$) and the amount of adding AB_2. It is also easily observed that the discharge capacity of $LaNi_5$ alloy electrode are improved with the AB_2 alloy addition for $x=1-20$. The maximum discharge capacity of the composite alloy electrodes increased from 188 mAh/g for $x=0$ to 305 mAh/g for $x=10$, whereas when $x>10$, it is decreased gradually.

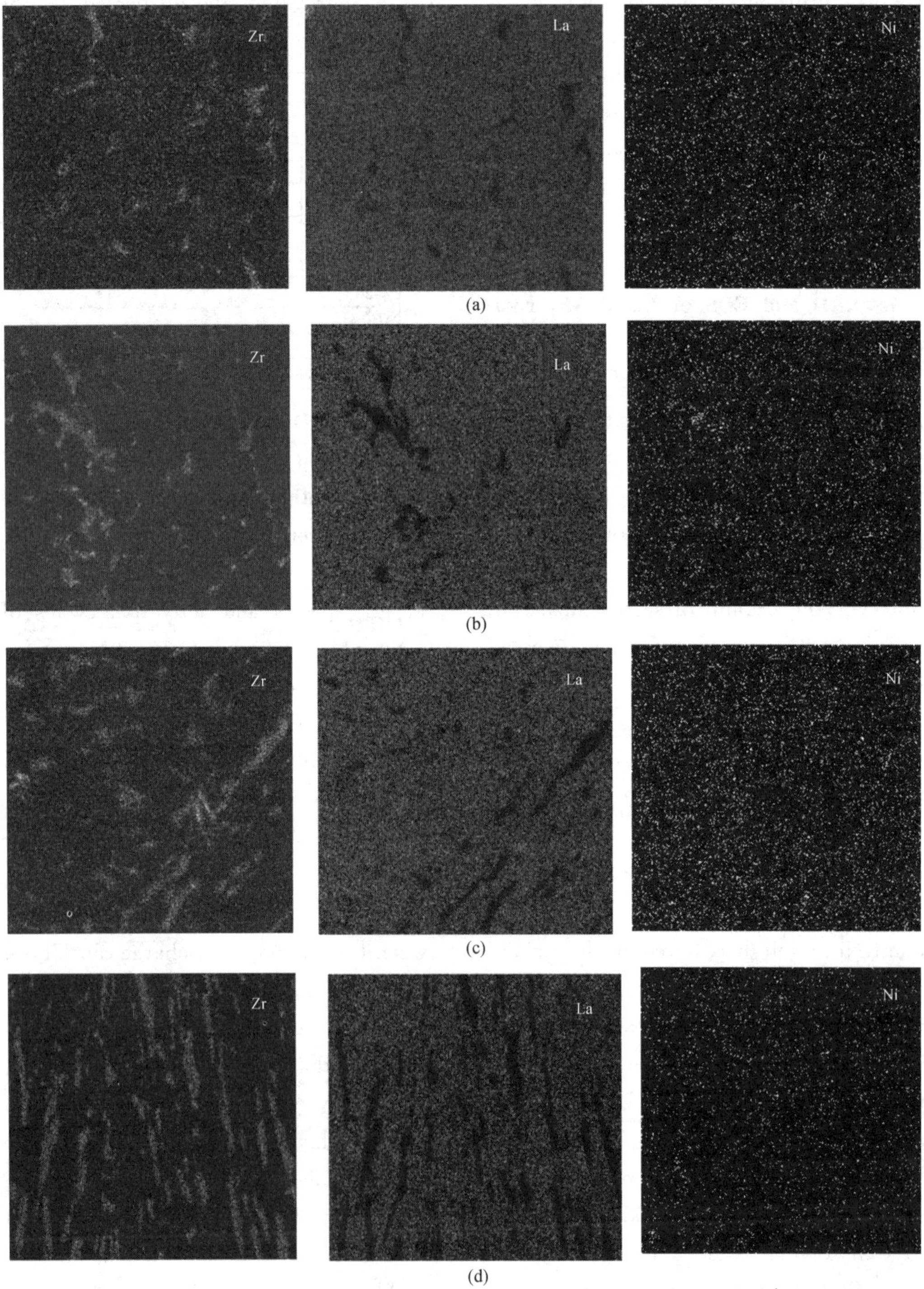

Fig. 2　Elements distribution images on surface of $LaNi_5$-x% AB_2 alloys by EDS:(a) $x=1$,(b) $x=5$,(c) $x=10$,(d) $x=20$

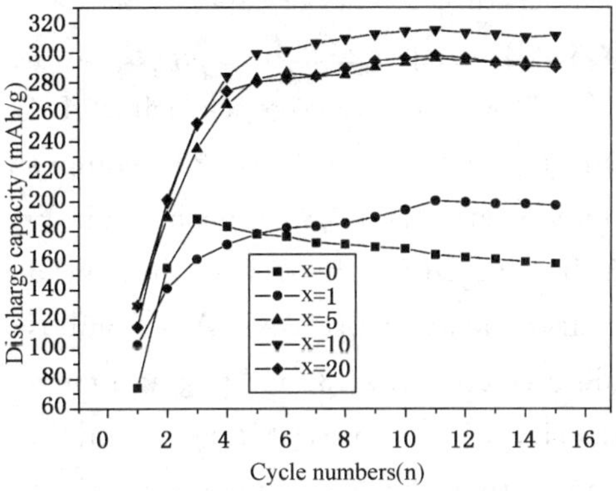

Fig. 3 Activation profiles of $LaNi_5$-$x\%$ AB_2 alloy electrodes

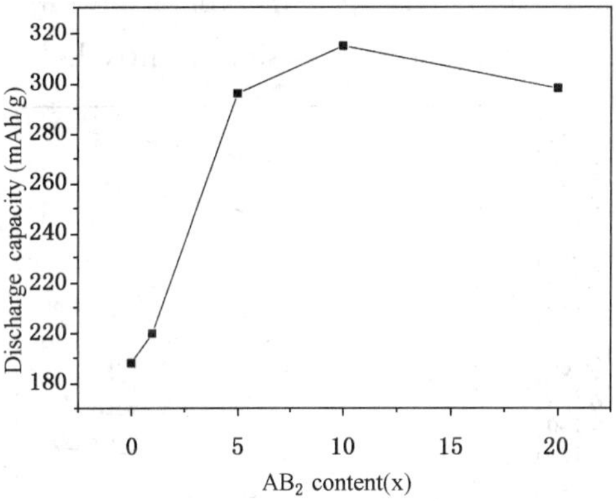

Fig. 4 Discharge capacities of $LaNi_5$-$x\%$ AB_2 alloy electrodes vs. AB_2 content

Zr, Ti and V belong to hydrogen-absorbing elements, and can be easily formed into stable hydrides. So, adding a small amount of AB_2 alloy containing Zr, Ti and V elements into La-based alloy can improve the discharge capacity of metal hydride [7]. However, the discharge capacity decreased when the amount of AB_2 is too much in the $LaNi_5$-AB_2 composite alloy, it is due to the increasing of the amount of second phase and the decreasing of the active matters.

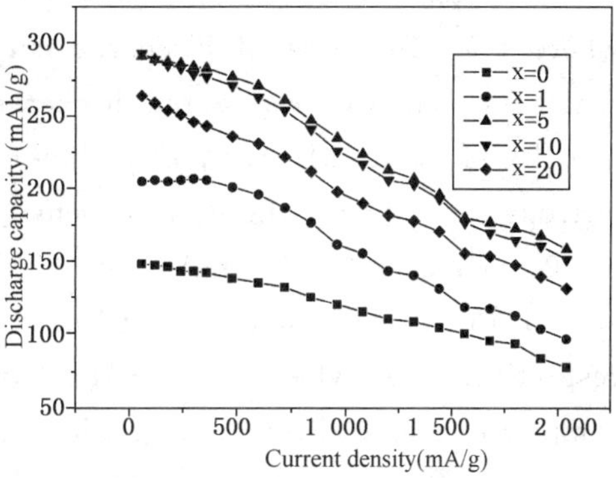

Fig. 5 Discharge capacities of $LaNi_5$-$x\%$ AB_2 alloy electrodes vs. current densities

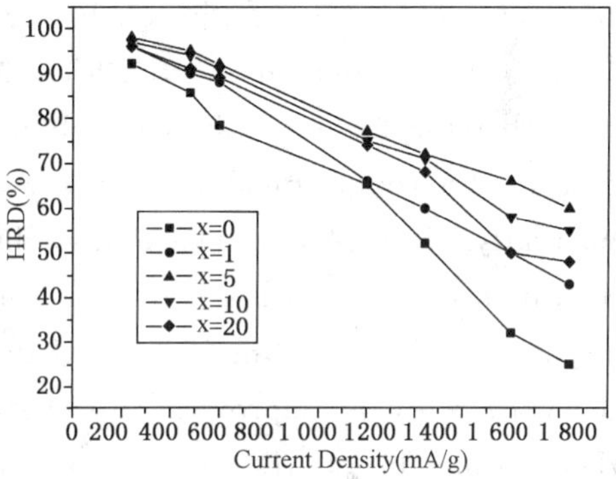

Fig. 6 HRD (%) of $LaNi_5$-$x\%$ AB_2 alloy electrodes

3.3 High-rate dischargeability (HRD) of $LaNi_5$-AB_2 composite alloys

The discharge capacity of $LaNi_5$-$x\%$ AB_2 ($x=1, 5, 10, 20$) alloy electrodes as a function of discharge current density is shown in Fig. 5. It is shown that the rate-discharge capacity of the $LaNi_5$ alloy electrode is improved significantly after adding AB_2 alloy. Fig. 6 shows the high-rate dischargeability (HRD) of the composite alloys, where HRD is expressed by the ratio of the discharge capacity at high current versus the discharge capacity at 60 mA/g ($C_{ymA/g}/C_{60mA/g} \times 100\%$, where y is the value of discharge current). As seen from Fig. 6, the discharge capacity of $LaNi_5$-AB_2 composite alloy electrode for $x=5$ at the current density of 300 mA/g and 2 040 mA/g are 97% and 55% of that of the alloy at 60 mA/g respectively, but when $x>10$, HRD of composite alloys decreased gradually. Comparing with $LaNi_5$ alloy, the high-rate dischargeability of composite alloys improved apparently, which indicates that the kinetics of composite alloys is better.

It may be related to the rich-Zr phase that the high-rate dischargeability of $LaNi_5$-AB_2 composite alloy is improved apparently. The rich-Zr phase may be worked as active sites for hydriding and dehydriding, therefore, the kinetics of the composite alloy is improved. However, when the amount of AB_2 was too large in the $LaNi_5$-AB_2 composite alloy, the active matters are decreased, the discharge capacity is decreased.

3. 4 Electrochemical characteristics of $LaNi_5$-AB_2 composite alloys at low temperature

The discharge capacity of $LaNi_5$-$x\%$ AB_2 ($x=1,5,10,20$) composite alloy electrodes from 253K to 233K is shown in Fig. 7. It can be seen that the discharge capacity of $LaNi_5$ alloy at low temperature is improved apparently after adding AB_2 alloy. The low-temperature discharge capacity of $LaNi_5$-AB_2 composite alloy electrode for $x=5$ is 215 mAh/g at 233 K, this result shows that the low-temperature discharge capacity of $LaNi_5$-5% AB_2 composite alloy is excellent.

The rate-discharge capacity of $LaNi_5$-$x\%$ AB_2 ($x=1,5,10,20$) composite alloy electrodes at 233 K is shown in Fig. 8. It is not difficult to seen that the discharge capacity of $LaNi_5$-AB_2 composite alloy electrode is 132 mAh/g at a current density of 240 mA/g for $x=5$. This shows that the low-temperature kinetics of $LaNi_5$-5% AB_2 composite alloy is also excellent. The electrochemical characteristics of $LaNi_5$-5% AB_2 composite alloy at low temperature is significantly better

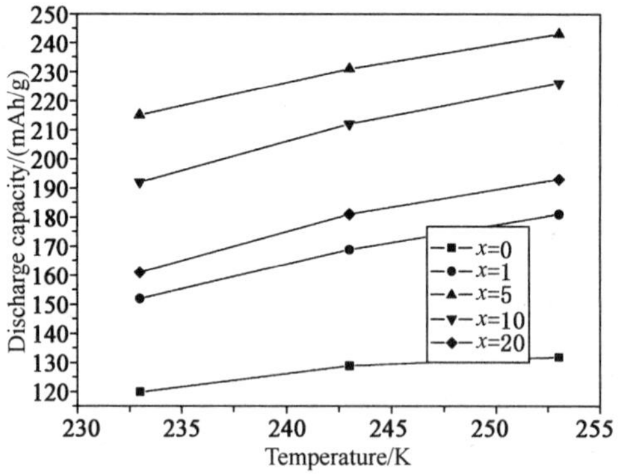

Fig. 7 Effect of low temperature on discharge capacity of $LaNi_5$-$x\%$ AB_2 alloy electrodes

than that of commercial RE-based AB_5-type alloys. The good electrochemical characteristics of $LaNi_5$-AB_2 composite alloys at low temperature may be also due to the rich-Zr phase in composite alloy worked as catalytic sites. It is commonly considered that the dispersing speed of hydrogen in alloy is the key-step which impacting on the discharge capacity of hydrogen storage alloy, and only the hydrogen storage alloy with good catalytic active structure which is beneficial to hydrogen dispersing can show good electrochemical characteristics at low temperature.

3.5 Self-discharge characteristics of $LaNi_5$-AB_2 composite alloys

The charge retentions (%) of $LaNi_5$-x% AB_2(x=1,5,10,20) alloy electrodes after 24 h, which represents the selfdischarge characteristics of the alloy electrodes, is shown in Fig. 9. It is clearly observed that the charge retention of $LaNi_5$ alloy electrode is apparently improved after adding 1—20% AB_2 alloy, especially, the charge retention of $LaNi_5$-5% AB_2 composite alloy is the better, namely its self-discharge ratio is the lower.

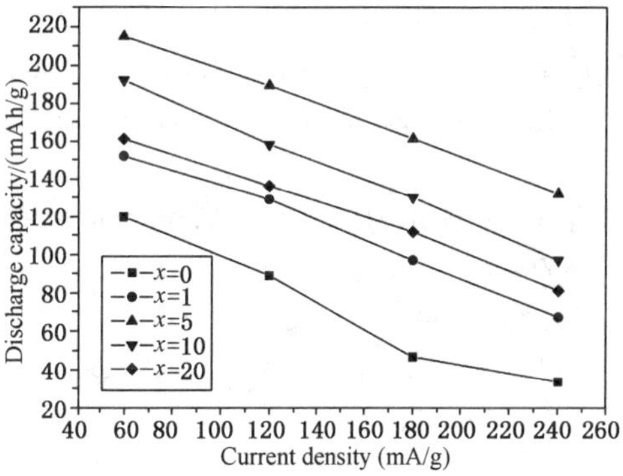

Fig. 8 Discharge capacities of $LaNi_{5-x}$% AB_2 alloy electrodes vs. current densities under 233 K

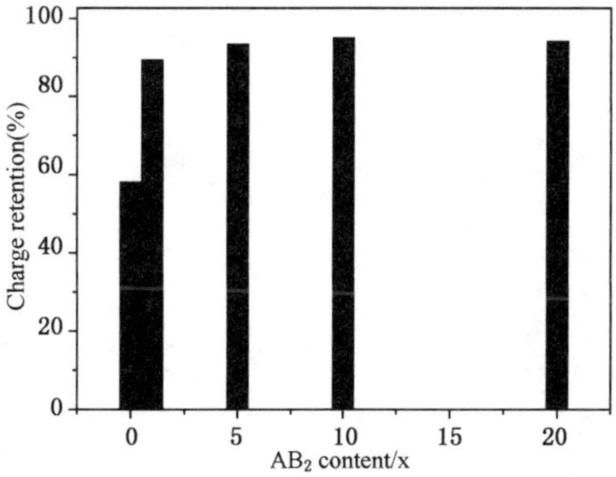

Fig. 9 Charge retention of $LaNi_{5-x}$%AB_2 alloy electrodes after 24 h

4 Conclusions

In order to improve the electrochemical characteristics of AB_5-type alloys, hypo-stoichiometric $AB_{5-\alpha}$ ($\alpha > 0$) type alloy $LaNi_5$-x% AB_2 (x = 1, 5, 10, 20) composite alloys were successfully prepared by sintering the powder mixtures of $LaNi_5$ and AB_2-type Laves phase alloy $Zr_{0.9}Ti_{0.1}(Mn_{0.35}Ni_{0.55}V_{0.15})_2$ as addition. The phase microstructure and electrochemical characteristics of the composite hydrogen storage alloys were studied. The conclusions are as follows:

(1) $LaNi_5$-x% AB_2(x=1,5,10,20) composite alloys have multi-phase structure, the matrix phase $CaCu_5$ structure of $LaNi_5$ alloy is not changed after adding AB_2 alloy, however, the amount of the second phase increases with increasing of adding AB_2 alloy. Compared with the matrix phase, Zr is richer and La is poorer in the second phase. The rich-Zr phase dispersed in the matrix phase as strips.

(2) The discharge capacity of $LaNi_5$ alloy electrodes was apparently improved by adding 1—20% AB_2 alloy. The maximum discharge capacity of composite alloy electrodes increased from 188 mAh/g for x=0 to 305 mAh/g for x=10.

(3) Comparing with $LaNi_5$ alloy, the rate-discharge capacity of $LaNi_5$-x% AB_2 (x = 1, 5, 10, 20) composite alloy electrodes were greatly improved. The discharge capacity of the composite alloy for

$x=5$ at the current density of 300 mA/g and 2040 mA/g was 97% and 55% of that of the alloy at 60 mA/g, respectively.

(4) The electrochemical characteristics of $LaNi_5$ alloy at low temperature were significantly improved after composite treated by adding AB_2 alloy. The discharge capacity of LaNi-5% AB_2 composite alloy electrode at 233 K was up to 215 mAh/g, it noticed that the performances of composite alloy electrodes were excellent at low temperatures.

Acknowledgements

Financial supported by the Chinese National Science Foundation (20171042) and the Natural Science Foundation of Hebei Province (B2004000188), PR China.

References

[1] C. Y. Seo, S. J. Choi, J. Choi, C. N. Park, J. Y. Lee, Int. J. Hydrogen Energy 28 (2003) 317.

[2] H. Ye, Y. X. Huang, J. X. Chen, H. Zhang, J. Power Sources 103 (2002) 293.

[3] C. J. Li, F. R. Wang, W. H. Cheng, W. Li, W. T. Zhao, J. Alloys Compd. 315 (2001) 218.

[4] Q. Arnaud, P. Barbic, P. Bernard, A. BouVier, B. Knosp, B. M. Riegel, J. Alloys Compd. 330-332 (2002) 262.

[5] M. Tsukahara, K. Takahashi, T. Mishima, A. Isomura, T. Sakai, J. Alloys Compd. 245 (1996) 59.

[6] Y. Osumi, H. Suzuki, A. Kato, K. Oguro, J. Less-Common Met. 89 (1983) 287.

[7] C. Y. Seo, S. J. Choi, J. Choi, C. N. Park, J. Y. Lee, J. Alloys Compd. 351 (2003) 255.

[8] C. Y. Seo, S. J. Choi, J. Choi, C. N. Park, P. S. Lee, J. Y. Lee, J. Alloys Compd. 350 (2003) 324.

[9] P. H. L. Notten, R. E. F. Einerhand, J. L. C. Daams, J. Alloys Compd. 210 (1994) 221.

[10] Y. F. Zhu, H. G. Pen, M. X. Gao, Y. F. Liu, Q. D. Wang, Int. J. Hydrogen Energy 28 (2003) 395.

[11] S.-M. Han, M.-S. Zhao, Y. M. Wu, Y.-Z. Zheng, Chin. J. Inorg. Chem. 19 (3) (2003) 262.

[12] W. X. Chen, J. Alloys Compd. 319 (2001) 119.

Crystallographic and Electrochemical Characteristics of $La_{0.7}Mg_{0.3}Ni_{5.0-x}(Al_{0.5}Mo_{0.5})_x$ Hydrogen-Storage Alloys①

Xin Bo Zhang[a], Dan Zi Sun[b], Wen Ya Yin[a], Yu Jun Chai[a], and Min Shou Zhao[a]
([a] Kcy Laboratory of Rare Earth Chemistry and Physics,
Changchun Institute of Applied Chemistry, Chinese Academy of Sciences,
5625 Remin Street, Changchun 130022, P. R. China)
([b] State Key Laboratory of Electroanalytical Chemistry Changchun Institute
of Applied Chemistry, Chinese Academy of Sciences 5625 Remin Street,
Changchun 130022, P. R. China)

Abstract: The structure, hydrogen-storage property and electrochemical characteristics of $La_{0.7}Mg_{0.3}Ni_{5.0-x}(Al_{0.5}Mo_{0.5})x$ ($x=0-0.8$) hydrogen-storage alloys have been studied systematically. X-ray diffraction Rietveld analysis shows that all the alloys consist of an La (La, $Mg)_2Ni_9$ phase and an $LaNi_5$ phase. The pressure-composition isotherms indicate that the hydrogen-storage capacity first increases and then decreases with increasing x, and the equilibrium pressure decreases with increasing x. Electrochemical measurements show that the maximum discharge capacity and the exchange-current density of the alloy electrodes increase as x increases from 0 to 0.6 and then decrease when x increases further from 0.6 to 0.8. Moreover, the low-temperature dischargeability of the alloy electrodes increases monotonically with increasing x in the alloys.

Key words: Diffusion; Electrochemistry; Energy transfer; Materials science; X-ray diffraction

1 Introduction

Hydrogen-storage alloys have been successfully used as negative electrode materials in the nickel-metal hydride battery (Ni-MH). [1-3] Besides the merits of higher energy density, higher charge and discharge ability, and longer charge/discharge cyclic life, the Ni-MH battery also has a smaller memory effect and causes less environmental pollution compared with the rechargeable nickel-cadmium battery. [4-6]

To date, almost all commercial Ni-MH batteries employ AB_5-type alloys as negative electrode materials because of their good overall electrode properties. [7] However, they are not yet satisfactory due to their limited discharge capacity. [8] A search for new types of hydrogen-storage-electrode alloys with higher energy density, rapid activation, high-

① ChemphysChem, 2005(6): 520-525.

rate dischargeability, long cyclic life and low cost to replace the conventional hydrogen-storage alloys, especially the rare earth-based AB_5-type alloys, is underway. [9]

Kadir et al. [10-12] reported that RMg_2Ni_9 (R: rare earth, Ca, Y) alloys with $PuNi_3$-type structures can absorb/desorb 1.8—1.87 wt% H_2 and are thus promising candidates for reversible gaseous-hydrogen storage. [13,14] The electrochemical properties and structures of $LaCaMg(Ni,M)_9$ (M = Al, Mn) alloys were studied by Chen et al. [6] Almost at the same time, Kohno et al. [3] reported that the discharge capacity of the $La_{0.7}Mg_{0.3}Ni_{2.8}Co_{0.5}$ alloy reached 410 $mAhg^{-1}$. However, up to now, the La-Mg-Ni-Co hydrogen-storage alloys cannot be used as negative electrode material for Ni-MH secondary batteries due to their serious corrosion in KOH electrolyte; [15] hence their cyclic stability must be upgraded for practical applications. In commercial AB_5-type alloys, the presence of 10 wt% of Co has indeed improved the cyclic life of Ni-MH batteries. However, it deteriorates the discharge capacity, as well as the initial activation, and also constitutes about 40% of the material cost. [15] Numerous studies have been directed to find a more cost-effective substitute element, with a high reliability, to improve the cyclic life of Ni-MH batteries. It is believed that Al is one of the best candidates for cobalt substitution. [17] However, Al addition is detrimental to hydrogen diffusion from the electrode surface to the alloy bulk and thus inevitably decreases the high-rate discharge of the alloy electrodes. [2] It is reported that Mo addition can remarkably increase the kinetic property [18] as well as the electrochemical capacity of alloy electrodes. [19] Therefore, it can be expected that the overall electrochemical properties of the La-Mg-Ni-Co-type hydrogen-storage alloys could be improved by substitution of Al and Mo for Ni in the alloys.

Here, on the basis of our previous studies and the belief that the Al and Mo addition may result in some noticeable modification, the structure and electrochemical characteristics of the $La_{0.7}Mg_{0.3}Ni_{5.0-x}(Al_{0.5}Mo_{0.5-x}$ ($x=0-0.8$) hydrogen-storage alloys have been systematically investigated.

Experimental Section

Alloy Preparation and Structure Analyses: All alloy samples were prepared by arc-melting constituent metals with purities above 99% under argon atmosphere on a water-cooled copper hearth. To ensure good homogeneity of the alloys, ingots were turned over and remelted five times. A slight excess of Mg was needed to compensate for evaporative loss of Mg under preparation conditions. Thereafter, these alloy samples were mechanically crushed into fine powders of 200—300 mesh in a mortar. The final alloys were carefully checked by inductively coupled plasma-atomic emission spectrometry (ICP-AES) using a TJA Poems-type instrument.

The crystal structure was determined by X-ray diffraction on a Rigaku D/Max 2500PC X-ray diffractometer (Cu K_α radiation, Bragg-Brentano geometry, 2θ range 10—100°, step size 0.02°, 4 s per step, backscattered rear graphite monochromator) using the JADE5 software.[20] The phase abundance and the lattice parameter were calculated by means of the RIETICA program.

Electrochemical Measurements: Electrodes of different alloys were prepared by mixing 0.15 g alloy powder with 0.75 g nickel carbonyl powder to uniformity and then cold-pressing the material into a pellet, which had a diameter of 13 mm and a thickness of 1.5 mm. Electrochemical measurements were performed in a standard open three-electrode cell that consisted of a working electrode (metal hydride electrode), a counter electrode ($NiOOH/Ni(OH)_2$ electrode), and a reference electrode (Hg/HgO electrode). The electrolyte in the cell was a 6 M KOH aqueous solution. Charge and discharge tests were carried out on an automatic galvanostatic system (DC-5). Each electrode was charged at 60 mA g^{-1} for 7 h followed by a 30 min rest and then discharged at the same discharge current density to the cutoff voltage of -0.60 V versus Hg/HgO. For investigation of the high-rate dischargeability, the discharge capacities at various discharge-current densities were measured.

Pressure-composition isotherms (P-C-T) were electrochemically obtained by converting the equilibrium potential of the metal-hydride electrode to the equilibrium pressure of hydrogen on the basis of the Nernst equation using electrochemical data [21] as reported in ref. [22].

The linear polarisation curves of the alloy electrodes were measured by scanning the electrode potential at the rate of 0.1 mV s^{-1} from -5 to 5 mV (versus open circuit potential) at 50% depth of discharge at 298 K and 233 K, respectively. The polarisation resistance R_p was obtained from the slope of the linear polarisation curves. Then, the exchange-current density I_0 was calculated from the value of R_p from Equation (1).[16]

$$I_0 = \frac{RT}{FR_p} \tag{1}$$

where R is the gas constant; T is the absolute temperature; F is the Faraday constant. For the potentiostatic discharge, the test electrodes in the fully charged state were discharged following a +500 mV potential step for 500 s. Both the linear polarisation curves and the potentiostatic discharge were measured on an EG&G PARC Model 273 Potentiostat/Galvanostat.

2 Results and Discussion

2.1 Alloy Composition and Structure Characteristics

Low-melting Mg metal is known to be inevitably lost during the sample preparation by arc-melting. Numerous studies have been made to overcome this problem, such as using a Mg-Ni master alloy as a Mg additive, decreasing the melting current, adding a slight excess of Mg over sample composition, and so on. Among all these methods, we find that the third is the most effective way to compensate evaporative loss of Mg. Several attempts were made until the optimum preparative conditions were found. Herein, the lost weight during sample preparation is almost the same as the excess Mg added. The results of ICP-AES analysis for all compounds are given in Table1. It can be seen that the final composition of all the alloys is identical to the target composition.

Table 1　Chemical composition of the $La_{0.7}Mg_{0.3}Ni_{5.0-x}(Al_{0.5}Mo_{0.5})_x$ (x=0—0.8) alloys

Sample	La [mg g^{-1}]	Mg [mg g^{-1}]	Ni [mg g^{-1}]	Al [mg g^{-1}]	Mo [mg g^{-1}]	La:Mg:Ni:Al:Mo[a]
x=0.0	244.30	18.32	737.38	0.00	0.00	1.76:0.75:12.56:0:0
x=0.2	243.96	18.30	706.91	6.77	24.07	1.76:0.75:12.04:0.25 :0.25
x=0.4	243.62	18.27	676.51	13.52	48.07	1.75:0.75:11.52:0.50:0.50
x=0.6	243.28	18.25	646.21	20.25	72.01	1.75:0.75:11.01:0.75:0.75
x=0.8	242.95	18.22	615.98	26.96	95.88	1.75:0.75:10.49:1.00:1.00

[a] Atomic ratio.

The XRD and Rietveld analysis patterns for the $La_{0.7}Mg_{0.3}Ni_{4.8}$-($Al_{0.5}Mo_{0.5})_{0.2}$ hydrogen-storage alloy, given as an example of the $La_{0.7}Mg_{0.3}Ni_{5.0-x}(Al_{0.5}Mo_{0.5})_x$ (x = 0 — 0.8) hydrogen-storage alloys, are shown in Figure 1. It can be seen that the alloy mainly consists of an La_2MgNi_9 phase with a $PuNi_3$-type rhombohedral structure and an $LaNi_5$ phase with a $CaCu_5$-type hexagonal structure. The final Rietveld structure

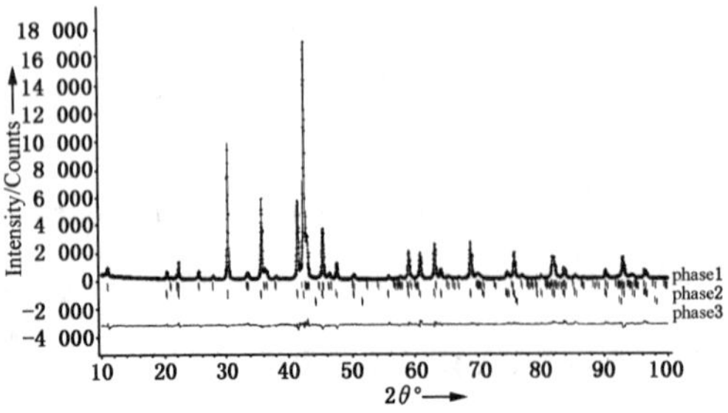

Fig. 1　Rietveld refinement of the XRD profiles for the $La_{0.7}Mg_{0.3}Ni_{4.8}(Al_{0.5}Mo_{0.5})_{0.2}$ hydrogen-storage alloy (Phase1: $La(La,Mg)_2Ni_9$; phase$_2$: $LaNi_5$; phase3: Ni)

Table 2　Crystallographic parameters for La_2MgNi_9 using X-ray diffraction Cu $K\alpha_1$ (λ=1.540 598 1) at 298 K in a space group R-3m and Z=3[a]

Atom	Site	Meal atom position			Occupancy
		x	y	z	
La1	3a	0	0	0	1
La2	6c	0	0	0.142 8(2)	0.478
mg1	6c	0	0	0.142 8(2)	0.522
Ni1	6c	0	0	0.331 0(3)	1
Ni2	3b	0	0	0.5	1
Ni3	18h	0.499 5(1)	0.500 5(1)	0.085 5(2)	1

[a] Structure was refined using the Rietveld refinement program Rietica. The pattern factor R_p=5.6, the weighted pattern factor R_{wp}=7.5 and the goodness-of-fit S=1.8.

parameter of the La_2MgNi_9 phase is tabulated in Table 2. It should be noted that La atoms in La_2MgNi_9 are located not only at the 3*a* site (the Pu1 atom position of the $PuNi_3$ structure), but also at the 6c sites (the Pu2 atom position of the $PuNi_3$ structure), while Mg atoms in the alloy exhibit a strong preference for the 6c sites. The final structure of La_2MgNi_9 phase can thus be designated as $La(La,Mg)_2Ni_9$. The phase abundance and lattice parameter of various phases of the $La_{0.7}Mg_{0.3}Ni_{5.0-x}(Al_{0.5}Mo_{0.5})_x$ ($x=0-0.8$) hydrogen-storage alloys are listed in Table 3. It can be found that all the alloys consisted of an impurity Ni phase and two main crystallographic phases, namely the $La(La,Mg)_2Ni_9$ phase and the $LaNi_5$ phase. Figure 2 shows the lattice parameter and unit-cell volume of the two main phases as a function of x in the alloys. It can be seen that a, c and the cell volumes of both the $La(La,Mg)_2Ni_9$ phase and the $LaNi_5$ phase increase monotonically with increasing x in the alloys. This is mainly ascribed to the fact that the atomic radii of Al (1.432Å) and Mo (1.363Å) are larger than that of Ni (1.246Å). The relationship between the phase abundance of the $La(La,Mg)_2Ni_9$ phase and the $LaNi_5$ phase and x in the alloys is shown in Figure 3. It can be seen that, with the increase of x in the alloys, the $La(La,Mg)_2Ni_9$ phase abundance decreases from 29.13% to 22.13%; on the contrary, the $LaNi_5$ phase abundance increases from 70.17% to 77.58%. These results influence the hydrogen-storage and electrochemical characteristics of the alloys studied.

Table 3 Characteristics of alloy phases in $La_{0.7}Mg_{0.3}Ni_{5.0-x}(Al_{0.5}Mo_{0.5})_x$ ($x=0-0.8$) alloys

Sample	Phase	Phase Abundance [wt%]	Lattice Parameter[Å] α	cell Volume [Å] c	
$x=0.0$	$La(La,Mg)_2Ni_9$	29.13	4.968	23.991	512.79
	$LaNi_5$	70.17	5.042	4.008	88.24
	Ni	0.70	3.520	3.520	43.61
$x=0.2$	$La(La,Mg)_2Ni_9$	27.38	4.992	24.266	523.7
	$LaNi_5$	72.18	5.051	4.025	88.93
	Ni	0.43	3.531	3.531	44.02
$x=0.4$	$La(La,Mg)_2Ni_9$	24.95	5.022	24.308	530.93
	$LaNi_5$	74.69	5.056	4.028	89.17
	Ni	0.36	3.534	3.534	44.14
$x=0.6$	$La(La,Mg)_2Ni_9$	24.33	5.055	24.519	542.6
	$LaNi_5$	75.39	5.069	4.053	90.19
	Ni	0.28	3.547	3.547	44.63
$x=0.8$	$La(La,Mg)_2Ni_9$	22.13	5.103	24.609	554.98
	$LaNi_5$	77.58	5.075	4.061	90.58
	Ni	0.28	3.559	3.559	45.08

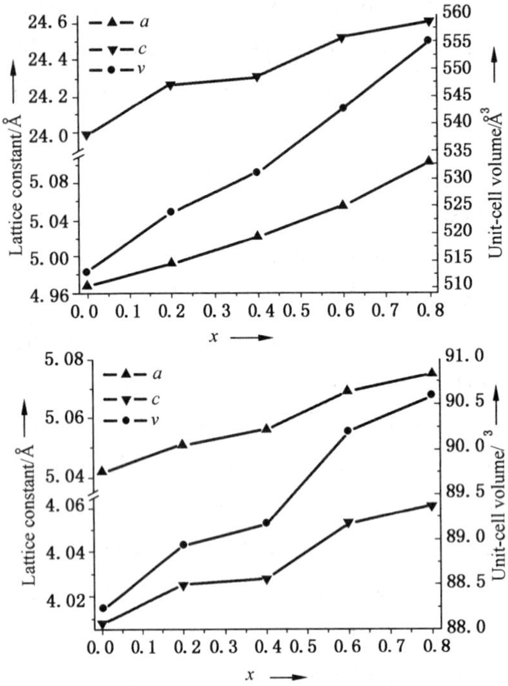

Fig. 2 Cell parameter and volume as a function of x in $La_{0.7}Mg_{0.3}Ni_{5.0-x}(Al_{0.5}Mo_{0.5})_x$ alloys($x=0-0.8$):(top)La(La,Mg)$_2$Ni$_9$ phase;(bottom) LaNi$_5$ phase.

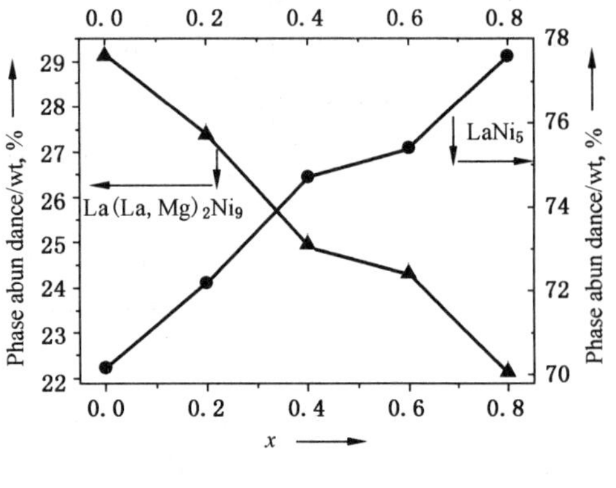

Fig. 3 Variation of phase abundance of the La(La,Mg)$_2$Ni$_9$ and LaNi$_5$ phases in the $La_{0.7}Mg_{0.3}Ni_{5.0-x}(Al_{0.5}Mo_{0.5})_x$ ($x=0-0.8$) alloys

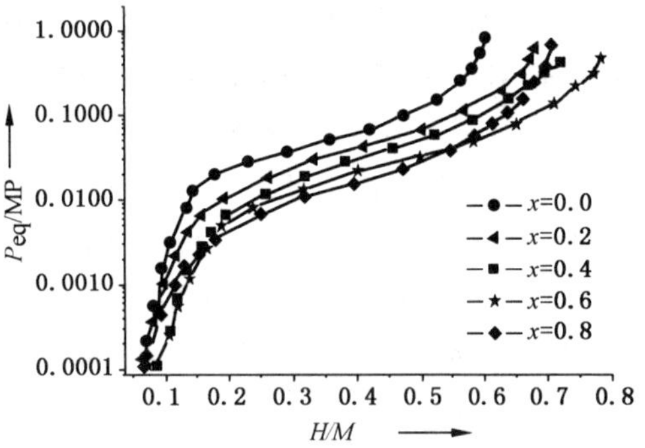

Fig. 4 Electrochemical P-C-T curves for $La_{0.7}Mg_{0.3}Ni_{5.0-x}(Al_{0.5}Mo_{0.5})_x$ alloy electrodes at 298 K

2.2 P-C Isotherms

Figure 4 shows the electrochemical P-C-T curves for the $La_{0.7}Mg_{0.3}Ni_{5.0-x}(Al_{0.5}Mo_{0.5})_x$ ($x=0-0.8$) alloy electrodes at 298 K. It can be seen that the desorption pressure reduces continually as the Al and Mo additions increase. This means that the stability of the hydrides of alloys increases with increasing Al and Mo content due to the larger unit-cell volume of the alloy. This phenomenon is consistent with those reported previously for AB$_3$ alloys [14] and most AB$_5$ alloys. [23] Moreover, it can be seen that there is only one quasiplateau region in each P-C-T curve, as shown in Figure 4. The unit cells of the AB$_3$ compounds contain one-third AB$_5$ structure and two-thirds AB$_2$ structure,[6] so it is possible that the plateau pressure of the La(La,Mg)$_2$Ni$_9$ phase is similar to that of the LaNi$_5$ phase, or that the difference between the plateau pressures of the AB$_3$ and AB$_5$ compounds is too small to be observed.

With the increase of Al and Mo contents in the alloys, the hydrogen-storage capacity first increases from 0.603 to 0.782, and then decreases to 0.706. This may be due to two reasons: As mentioned above, the plateau pressure decreases with increase of Al and Mo addition to the alloys, which enhances the intrinsic hydrogen-storage capacity of the alloys. On the other hand, it is known that the hydrogen-storage capacity of the $La(La,Mg)_2Ni_9$ phase is larger than that of the $LaNi_5$ system alloy;[24] however, the $La(La,Mg)_2Ni_9$ phase abundance decreases with increasing x. Therefore, it is believed that there is an optimum Al and Mo content for improving the overall properties of the La-Mg-Ni-Al-Mo-type hydrogen-storage alloys. The recommended amount of Al and Mo addition is 0.6 from this work.

2.3 Discharge Capacity and Discharge Potential

The number of cycles needed to activate the electrodes, and the maximum discharge capacity of the $La_{0.7}Mg_{0.3}Ni_{5.0-x}(Al_{0.5}Mo_{0.5})_x$ ($x=0-0.8$) alloy

Table 4 Electrode performance of $La_{0.7}Mg_{0.3}Ni_{5.0-x}(Al_{0.5}Mo_{0.5})_x$ ($x=0-0.8$) alloys

Sample	H/M	C_{max} [mAh g^{-1}]	N_a [a]	HRD_{1200} [b] [%]	S_{70} [%]
$x=0.0$	0.603	243.8	3	58.6	49.0
$x=0.2$	0.678	273.7	3	61.4	53.2
$x=0.4$	0.719	289.7	2	66.7	57.8
$x=0.6$	0.782	314.6	2	74.2	63.0
$x=0.8$	0.706	287.6	2	77.6	66.6

[a] The number of cycles needed to activate the electrodes.

[b] The high-rate dischargeability at the discharge-current density of 1 200 mAg^{-1}.

electrodes are listed in Table 4. It can be seen that all these alloys can be easily activated to reach the maximum capacity within three cycles. In addition, the maximum discharge capacity of the alloy electrodes increases first and then decreases as x increases from 0 to 0.8. The maximum discharge capacity of the alloy electrodes reaches a maximum of 314.6 mAh g^{-1} when $x=0.6$ and then decreases to 287.6 mAh g^{-1} when $x=0.8$. The variation of maximum discharge capacity of the alloys is basically consistent with the variation of the H/M with the Al and Mo content in the alloys.

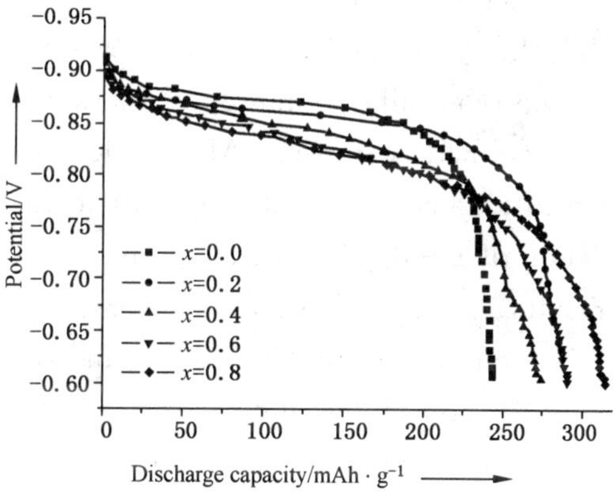

Figure 5 Discharge curves of $La_{0.7}Mg_{0.3}Ni_{5.0-x}(Al_{0.5}Mo_{0.5})_x$ ($x=0-0.8$) alloy electrodes at a discharge current density of 60 mA g^{-1} and 298 K

Figure5 shows the discharge curves (fifth cycle) of the alloy electrodes at 60 mA g^{-1} and 298 K. Obviously each curve has a wide discharge-potential plateau based on the oxidation of desorbed hydrogen from the hydride. Moreover, the discharge plateau shifts to the negative side as Al and Mo addition increases in the alloys. As shown in Figure 5, the mid-discharge (potential at 50% depth of discharge) potential decreases from −0.8721 to −0.8189V when x increases from 0 to 0.8, which is in agreement with the reduction of the desorption plateau pressure with the increase of Al and Mo content in the alloys.

2.4 Cyclic Stability

The cycling capacity retention rate, expressed as S_{70} (%) = C_{70}/C_{max} × 100 (where C_{max} is the maximum discharge capacity, C_{70} is the discharge capacity after 70 cycles), S_{70} at 60 mA g^{-1} is also listed in Table 4. It can be seen that S_{70} increases noticeably from 49.0 to 66.6% as x increases from 0 to 0.8, indicating that the cyclic stability of the La-Mg-Ni-Al-Mo-type alloys improves markedly with an increase in their Al and Mo content. It is known that the capacity degradation of La-Mg-Ni-type alloy electrodes results primarily from two factors: the corrosion of Mg and La elements and the pulverisation of the alloy particles. [23] Here, the improved cyclic stability may be due to the formation of a dense Al oxide (hydroxide) layer on the alloy surface, which subsequently provides the alloy with strong protection from further corrosion of La and Mg. Further investigations in this aspect are on-going.

2.5 High-Rate Dischargeability (HRD) and Electrochemical Kinetics

For hydride electrodes in batteries, it is very important to inhibit the decrease of the discharge capacity even at the high

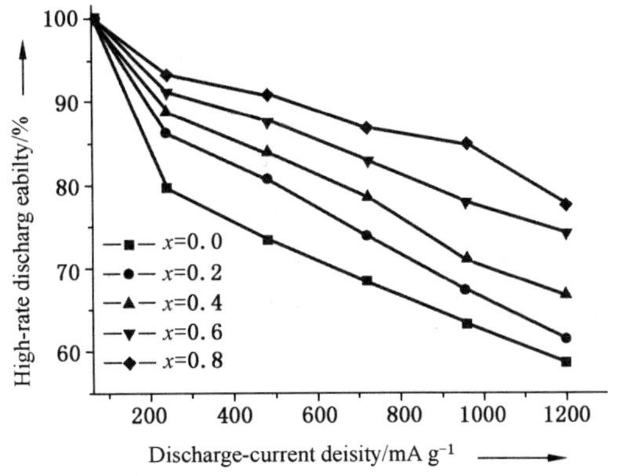

Figure 6 High-rate dischargeability of $La_{0.7}Mg_{0.3}Ni_{5.0-x}(Al_{0.5}Mo_{0.5})_x$ alloy electrodes at 298 K

charge/discharge current density. Figure 6 shows the relationship between the high-rate dischargeability and the discharge current density of the $La_{0.7}Mg_{0.3}Ni_{5.0-x}(Al_{0.5}Mo_{0.5})_x$ ($x=0-0.8$) alloy electrodes. It can be seen that HRD of

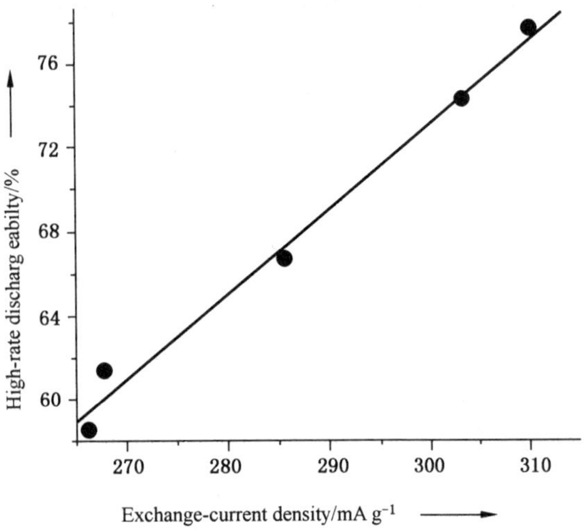

Figure 7 High-rate dischargeability as a function of exchange-current density for the hydrogen-evolution reaction at $La_{0.7}Mg_{0.3}Ni_{5.0-x}(Al_{0.5}Mo_{0.5})_x$ alloy electrodes

Table 5　Electrochemical kinetic parameters of $La_{0.7}Mg_{0.3}NI_{5.0-x}(Al_{0.5}Mo_{0.5})_x$ (x=0—0.8) alloy electrodes

Sample	Polarization resistance, R_p [mΩ]		Exchange-current density, I_0[mA g^{-1}]		Hydrogen-diffusion coefficient D[$\times 10^{-10} cm^2 s^{-1}$]	
	298K	233K	298K	233K	298K	233K
x=0.0	86.32	240.99	266.23	83.21	13.4	1.7
x=0.2	85.81	239.72	267.8	83.65	13.5	3.2
x=0.4	80.5	238.81	285.5	83.97	13.8	3.9
x=0.6	75.81	238.32	303.15	84.14	13.9	5.1
x=0.8	74.14	237.62	310	84.39	13.9	6.5

the alloy electrodes increases monotonously with increasing x. The HRD of the alloy electrodes for the discharge current density of 1200 mA g^{-1} is also listed in Table 4. It can be seen that as x increases, the HRD of the alloy electrodes increases from 58.6% (x=0) to 77.6%(x=0.8). It is well-known that the HRD values of metal-hydride electrodes are influenced mainly by the electrochemical reaction kinetics on the alloy powder surface and the diffusion rate of hydrogen in the bulk of the alloy. [25] The exchange-current density I_0 of the hydrogen-storage alloy electrodes is commonly used to characterise the catalytic activity for charge-transfer at the alloy electrode surface. When the overpotential is changed within a small range, the polarisation resistance R_p can be estimated from the slope of the linear polarisation curve. Then the I_0 is calculated from the value of R_p according to Equation (1). The obtained values of I_0 and R_p are summarisedin Table5. Figure 7 shows high-rate dischargeability as a function of I_0 for the hydrogen-evolution reaction at the alloy electrodes. It can be seen that the HRD is a linear function of I_0. Moreover, we find that the hydrogen diffusion coefficient D is almost unchanged (13.4—13.9 $\times 10^{-10}$ cm^2 s^{-1}). Iwakura et al. [26] have shown that, if the electrochemical reaction on the surface is the rate-determining factor, a linear dependence of the high-rate dischargeability on the exchange-current density should be observed. In contrast, if the diffusion of hydrogen in the bulk is the rate-determining factor, the high-rate dischargeability should be constant, irrespective of exchange density. Therefore, herein, the HRD is essentially controlled by the charge-transfer reaction of hydrogen on the surface at a discharge-current density of 1200 mA g^{-1}.

2.6　Low-Temperature Dischargeability

It has been reported that the conventional nickel-metal battery exhibits a poor low-temperature dischargeability (LTD). [27] Sakai et al. [2] pointed out that the dischargeability of the negative electrodes at relatively low temperatures depended on hydrogen diffusion and/or charge-transfer process occurring at the metal/electrolyte interface. The D of hydrogen in the bulk is evaluated using the method described by lwakura et al. [18] The LTD, expressed as LTD_{233} (%) = $C_{233}/C_{298} \times 100$ (where C_{233} and C_{298} are the discharge capacity at 233 K and 298 K, respectively). The D and the I_0 of the $La_{0.7}Mg_{0.3}Ni_{5.0-x}(Al_{0.5}Mo_{0.5})_x$ ($x=0-0.8$) alloy electrodes at 233 K are also listed in Table 5. It can be found that both the I_0 and the D are smaller than that at 298 K. However, the D is much larger than that of other alloys [28] even at low temperature, indicating the $La_{0.7}Mg_{0.3}Ni_{5.0-x}(Al_{0.5}Mo_{0.5})_x$ alloys aid hydrogen diffusion. Meanwhile, we can find that the I_0 remains almost unchanged (83.21—84.39 mA g^{-1}); whereas the D increases remarkably with increasing x, which implies that the hydrogen diffusion in the alloy probably becomes the rate-determining factor for low-temperature dischargeability at 233 K. Figure 8 shows the LTD as a function of D in the alloy electrodes. It can be easily found that the D increases with the increases of x, which can be attributed to the cell-volume expansion, as shown in Table 3. The increasing D accordingly increases the LTD of the alloy electrodes.

3 Conclusions

The structure, hydrogen-storage characteristics and electrochemical properties of the $La_{0.7}Mg_{0.3}Ni_{5.0-x}(Al_{0.5}Mo_{0.5})_x$ ($x=0-0.8$) hydrogen-storage alloys were investigated systematically. The X-ray powder diffraction and Rietveld analysis reveal that all the alloys consist of an impurity Ni phase and two main crystallographic phases, namely $La(La, Mg)_2Ni_9$ and $LaNi_5$, and that the lattice parameters and cell volumes of both the $La(La,Mg)_2Ni_9$ and $LaNi_5$ phases increase with increasing Al and Mo content.

The P-C-T curves indicate that the hydrogen-storage capacity first increases and then decreases, and that the plateau pressure decreases with increasing x. The electrochemical measurements show that the maximum discharge capacity increases from 243.8 ($x=0$) to 314.6 mAh g^{-1} ($x=0.6$) and then decreases to 256.4 mAh g^{-1} ($x=0.8$). For the discharge current density of 1200 mA g^{-1}, the high-rate dischargeability of the alloy electrodes increases progressively from 58.6% ($x=0$) to 77.6% ($x=0.8$). The hydrogen-diffusion coefficient increases with increasingAl and Mo content, and thus increases the low-temperature dischargeability of the alloy electrodes.

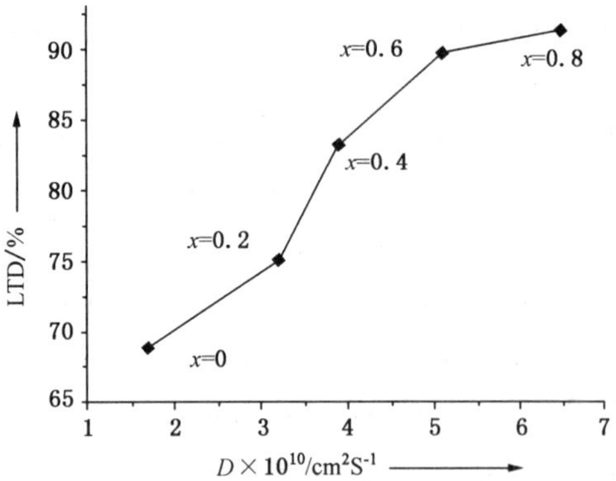

Figure 8 Low-temperature dischargeability (LTD) as a function of the hydrogen diffusion coefficient for $La_{0.7}Mg_{0.3}Ni_{5.0-x}(Al_{0.5}Mo_{0.5})_x$ alloy electrodes at 233 K

Acknowledgements

This work was financially supported by the National Natural Science Foundation of China (20171042).

References

[1] H. G. Pan, Y. F. Zhu, M. X. Gao, Q. D. Wang, J. Electrochem. Soc. 2002, 149, A829-A833.

[2] T. Sakai, H. Miyamura, N. Kuriyama, A. Kato, K. Oguro, H. Ishikawa, J. Electrochem. Soc. 1990, 137, 795-799.

[3] T. Kohno, H. Yoshida, F. Kawashima, T. Inaba, I. Sakai, M. Yamamoto, M. Kanda, J. Alloys Compd. 2000, 311, L5-L7.

[4] J. J. G. Willems, Philips J. Res. 1984, 39 (Suppl. 1), 1-94.

[5] J. J. G. Willems, K. H. J. Buschow, J. Less-Common Met. 1987, 129, 13-30.

[6] J. Chen, N. Kuriyama, H. T. Takeshita, H. Tanaka, T. Sakai, M. Haruta, Electrochem. Solid-State Lett. 2000, 3, 249-252.

[7] T. Sakai, I. Uehara, H. Iwakura, J. Alloys Compd. 1999, 293-295, 762-769.

[8] J. J. Reilly, G. D. Adzic, J. R. Johnson, T. Vogt, S. Mukerjee, J. McBreen, J. Alloys Compd. 1999, 293-295, 569-582.

[9] Y. FLiu, H. G. Pan, Y. F. Zhu, R. Li, Y. Q. Lei, Mater. Sci. Eng., A 2004, 372, 163-172.

[10] K. Kadir, T. Sakai, I. Uahara, J. Alloys Compd. 1997, 257, 115-121.

[11] K. Kadir, N. Nuriyama, T. Sakai, I. Uehara, L. Eriksson, J. Alloys Compd. 1999, 284, 145-154.

[12] K. Kadir, T. Sakai, I. Uahara, J. Alloys Compd. 1999, 287, 264-270.

[13] K. Kadir, T. Sakai, I. Uahara, J. Alloys Compd. 2000, 302, 112-117.

[14] J. Chen, H. T. Takeshita, H. Tanaka, N. Kuriyama, T. Sakai, J. Alloys Compd. 2000, 302, 304-313.

[15] B. Liao, Y. Q. Lei, L. X. Chen, G. L. Lu, H. G. Pan, Q. D. Wang, J. Power Sources 2004, 129, 358-367.

[16] P. H. Notton, P. Hokkeling, J. Electrochem. Soc. 1991, 138, 1877-1885.

[17] T. Sakai, H. Miyamura, N. Kuriyama, A. Kato, K. Oguro, H. Ishikawa, J. Less-Common Met. , 1990, 159, 127-139.

[18] C. Iwakura, H. Senoh, K. Morimoto, Y. Hara, H. Inoue, Electrochem. 2002, 70, 2-7.

[19] M. T. Yeh, V. M. Beibutian, S. E. Hsu, J. Alloys Compd. 1999, 293-295, 721-723.

[20] Materials Data JADE Realease 5, XRD pattern processing, Materials Data Inc. (MDI), 1997.

[21] T. Sakai, K. Oguro, H. Miyamura, N. Kuriyama, A. Kato, H. Ishikawa, C. Iwakura, J. Less-Common Met. 1990, 161, 193-202.

[22] H. G. Pan, Q. W. Jin, M. X. Gao, Y. F. Liu, R. Li, Y. Q. Lei, J. Alloys Compd. 2004, 373, 237-245.

[23] J. J. Reilly in Handbook of Battery Materials (Ed. :J. O. Bessenhard), Wiley, New-York, 2000.

[24] H. G. Pan, Y. F. Liu, M. X. Gao, Y. Q. Lei, Q. D. Wang, J. Electrochem. Soc. 2003, 150, A565-A570.

[25] T. Sakai, H. Miyamura, N. Kuriyama, A. Kato, K. Oguro, H. Ishikawa, J. Less-Common Met. 1990, 159, 127-139.

[26] C. Iwakura, T. Oura, H. Inoue, M. Matsuoka, Electrochim. Acta 1996, 41, 117-121.

[27] H. Senoh, Y. Hara, H. Inoue, C. Iwakura, Electrochim. Acta 2001, 46, 967-971.

[28] Y. F. Liu, H. G. Pan, Y. F. Zhu, R. Li, Y. Q. Lei, Mater. Sci. Eng., A 2004, 372, 163-172.

Crystallographic and Electrochemical Characteristics of $La_{0.7}Mg_{0.3}Ni_{3.5-x}(Al_{0.5}Mo_{0.5})_x$ ($x=0-0.8$) Hydrogen-Storage Alloys①

Xin Bo Zhang[a], Dan Zi Sun[b], Wen Ya Yin[a], Yu Jun Chai[a], Min Shou Zhao[a]

([a] Graduate School of Chinese Academy of Sciences,
Key Laboratory of Rare Earth Chemistry and Physics,
Changchun Institute of Applied Chemistry,
Chinese Academy of Sciences, Changchun 130022, PR China)

([b] Graduate School of Chinese Academy of Sciences, State Key Laboratory of Electro-analytical Chemistry, Changchun Institute of Applied Chemistry,
Chinese Academy of Sciences, Changchun 130022, PR China)

Abstract: The crystal structure, hydrogen storage property and electrochemical characteristics of the $La_{0.7}Mg_{0.3}Ni_{3.5-x}(Al_{0.5}Mo_{0.5-x}$ ($x=0-0.8$) alloys have been investigated systematically. It can be found that with X-ray powder diffraction and Rietveld analysis the alloys are of multiphase alloy and consisted of impurity LaNi phase and two main crystallographic phases, namely the $La(La, Mg)_2Ni_9$ phase and the $LaNi_5$ phase, and the lattice parameter and the cell volume of both the $La(La, Mg)_2Ni_9$ phase and the $LaNi_5$ phase increases with increasing Al and Mo content in the alloys. The P-C isotherms curves indicate that the hydrogen storage capacity of the alloy first increases and then decreases with increasing x, and the equilibrium pressure decreases with increasing x. The electrochemical measurements show that the maximum discharge capacity first increases from 354.2 ($x=0$) to 397.6 mAh g^{-1} ($x=0.6$) and then decreases to 370.4 mAh g^{-1} ($x=0.8$). The high-rate dischargeability of the alloy electrode increases lineally from 55.7% ($x=0$) to 73.8% ($x=0.8$) at the discharge current density of 1200 mA g^{-1}. Moreover, the exchange current density of the alloy electrodes also increases monotonously with increasing x. The hydrogen diffusion coefficient in the alloy bulk increases with increasing Al and Mo content and thus enhances the low-temperature dischargeability of the alloy electrode.

Key words: Structure characteristics; High-rate dischargeability; Low-temperature dischargeability; Exchange current density; Hydrogen diffusion coefficient

① Journal of Power Sources, 2006(154): 290-297.

1 Introduction

Hydrogen storage alloy has attracted considerable attention in view of its potential as a new energy storage material. Recently, nickel-metal hydride battery (Ni-MH) in which a hydrogen storage alloy is employed as a negative electrode material has become a focus of interest as a candidate consumer-use battery by virtue of its several advantages: high reversible energy storage density, high resistance to overcharging and overdischarging, good charge-discharge kinetics, environmental compatibility and interchangeable with nickel-cadmium battery [1-6]. To date, almost all commercial Ni-MH batteries are employing AB_5-type alloys as negative electrode materials because of their good overall electrode properties [7]. However, the electrochemical capacity of the AB_5-type alloys is limited by the single $CaCu_5$-type hexagonal structure [8], the energy densities of the Ni-MH batteries are not competing favorably with some other advanced secondary batteries. Therefore, new type alloys with higher energy density, faster activation, better rate dischargeability and lower cost are urgently needed to replace the conventional rare earth-based AB_5-type alloys [9].

Fortunately, a new type of ternary alloys with the general formula of RMg_2Ni_9 (R: rare earth, Ca, Y) with $PuNi_3$ type structure have been found by Kadir et al. [10-12]. It is found that some of the R-Mg-Ni based ternary alloys can absorb-desorb 1.8—1.87 wt% H_2 and are thus regarded as promising candidates for reversible gaseous hydrogen storage [13, 14]. Whereafter, Chen et al. [6] have studied the structure and electrochemical characteristics of $LaCaMg(Ni, M)_9$ (M = Al, Mn) alloys, and almost at the same time, Kohno et al. [15] have reported that the discharge capacity of $La_{0.7}Mg_{0.3}Ni_{2.8}Co_{0.5}$ alloy reached 410 mAh g^{-1}. Unfortunately, the La-Mg-Ni-Co system hydrogen storage electrode alloys have some disadvantages, such as a high absorption-desorption plateau pressure, poor cyclic stability and so on [16]. In commercial AB_5-type alloys the presence of 10 wt% of Co has indeed improved the cycling life of Ni-MH batteries. However, it influences negatively the discharge capacity as well as initial activation, and it constitutes about 40% of the material cost [17]. Much effort has been devoted to search for a more cost-effective substitute element with high reliability to improve the cycling life of Ni-MH batteries. It is believed that Al is one of the best candidates for cobalt substitution [18]. However, Al addition is detrimental to hydrogen diffusion from the alloy bulk to the surface and thus inevitably decreases the high-rate dischargeability of alloy electrode [2]. It is reported that Mo addition can remarkably improve the kinetic property [19]. Therefore, it can be expected that the overall electrochemical characteristics of the La-Mg-Ni-Co-type hydrogen storage alloys could be improved by substitution of Al and Mo for Ni in the alloys.

In this work, on the basis of our previous studies and the belief that the Al and Mo addition may result in some noticeable modification of the alloys, the structure and electrochemical characteristics of the $La_{0.7}Mg_{0.3}Ni_{3.5-x}(Al_{0.5}Mo_{0.5})_x$ (x=0,0.2,0.4,0.6,0.8) hydrogen storage alloys have been investigated systematically.

2 Experimental details

2.1 Alloy preparation and X-ray diffraction analysis

All alloy samples were prepared by arc-melting carefully the constituent metals on a water-cooled copper hearth under argon atmosphere followed by annealing in vacuum for 100 h at 770 ℃. The purity of the metals, i. e., La, Mg, Ni, Al and Mo is higher than 99.9 mass%. The samples were all inverted and remelted five times to ensure good homogeneity. A slight excess of Mg over composition was needed in order to compensate for evaporative loss of Mg under preparation conditions. Several attempts were done until the optimum preparative conditions were found. The final compounds were carefully checked by inductively coupled plasma-atomic emission spectrometry (ICP-AES) method using TJA Poems-type instrument. Thereafter, these alloy samples were mechanically crushed into fine powders of −300 mesh in mortar.

Crystallographic characteristics of the hydrogen storage alloys were investigated by X-ray diffraction on Rigaku D/Max 2500PC X-ray diffractometer (Cu Kα radiation, Bragg-Brentano geometry, 2θ range 10—100°, step size 0.02°, back-scattered rear graphite monochromator) using JADE5 software [20]. The lattice constants and cell volume were calculated by RIETICA program after internal theta calibration using silicon as standard reference materials.

2.2 Electrochemical measurement

The preparation of the disk-type electrodes, the setup of the electrochemical cell and the test of electrochemical properties were similar as described in our previous paper [21].

Pressure-composition isotherms (P-C-T) curves were electrochemically obtained by converting the equilibrium potential of the metal hydride electrode to the equilibrium pressure of hydrogen on the basis of Nernst equation using electrochemical data [22] as reported in Ref. [23]. The equilibrium potential curves were obtained by alternating the following two processes: (1) a pulse discharge of (25 mA $g^{-1}\times$0.25 h) and (2) a rest period until the potential became almost constant.

Linear polarization curves were performed on a EG&G PARC's Model 273 Potentiostat/Galvanostat station by scanning the electrode potential at the rate of 0.1 mV s^{-1} from −5 to 5 mV (versus open circuit potential) at 50% depth of discharge at 298 and 233 K, respectively. The exchange current density I_0 was calculated from the slopes of polarization curves by the following equation [18]:

$$I_0=\frac{RT}{FR_p}$$

where R, T and F have their general meanings. The potential step experiments were performed on the same instrument (using the M352 CorrWare electrochemical/corrosion software) at 100% charge state. A +500 mV potential was applied and the discharge time was 500 s.

3 Results and discussion

3.1 Alloy composition and structure characteristic

It is well known that the low melting Mg metal will be inevitably lost during the sample preparation by arc melting. We have tried many ways to overcome this problem, such as using Mg-Ni master alloy as an Mg additive, decreasing the melting current, adding a slight excess of Mg over sample composition and so on. Among all these methods, we found that the third one is the most effective ways to compensate evaporative loss of Mg. Several attempts had been done until the optimum preparative conditions were found. In this paper, the lost weight during sample preparation is almost the same as excess Mg added. The results of ICP-AES analysis for all compounds are given in Table 1. It can be seen that the final composition of all the alloys is identical with the original composition.

The crystal structures of the $La_{0.7}Mg_{0.3}Ni_{3.5-}(Al_{0.5}Mo_{0.5})_x$ (x=0−0.8) alloy have been identified and refined by means of X-ray powder diffraction data. Fig. 1 shows the Rietveld refinement pattern of the XRD profiles for $La_{0.7}Mg_{0.3}Ni_{3.3}(Al_{0.5}Mo_{0.5})_{0.2}$ alloy as a representative example of $La_{0.7}Mg_{0.3}Ni_{3.5-x}(Al_{0.5}Mo_{0.5})_x$ (x=0−0.8) hydrogen storage alloys. The final crystallographic parameter of the pseudo-La_2MgNi_9 phase (Ni is partially substituted by Al and Mo) and pseudo-$LaNi_5$ phase (Ni is partially substituted by Al and Mo) is tabulated in Tables 2 and 3, respectively. It

Table 1 Composition of the $La_{0.7}Mg_{0.3}Ni_{3.5-x}(Al_{0.5}Mo_{0.5})_x$ (x=0−0.8) alloys

Sample	La (mg g^{-1})	Mg(mg g^{-1})	Ni (mg g^{-1})	Al(mg g^{-1})	Co(mg g^{-1})	La : Mg : Ni : Al : Mo[a]
x=0.0	313.69	23.53	662.78	0	0	2.26 : 0.97 : 11.29:0:0
x=0.2	313.13	23.49	623.80	8.69	30.90	2.25 : 0.97 : 10.63 : 0.32 : 0.32
x=0.4	312.57	23.44	584.95	17.35	61.68	2.25 : 0.96 : 9.97 : 0.64 : 0.64
x=0.6	312.02	23.40	546.25	25.97	92.36	2.25 : 0.96 : 9.31 : 0.96 : 0.96
x=0.8	311.47	23.36	507.67	34.57	122.93	2.24 : 0.96 : 8.65 : 1.28 : 1.28

[a] Atomic ratio.

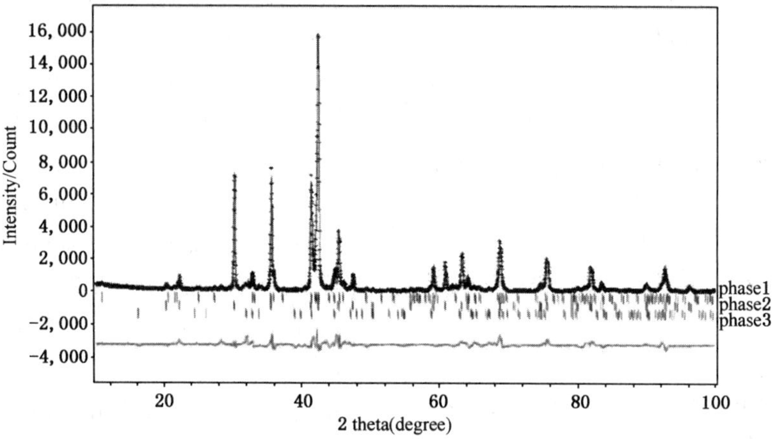

Fig. 1 Rietveld refinement pattern of the XRD profiles for the $La_{0.7}Mg_{0.3}Ni_{3.3}(Al_{0.5}Mo_{0.5})_{0.2}$ hydrogen storage alloy (phase 1, $La(La, Mg)_2Ni_9$; phase 2, $LaNi_5$; phase 3, LaNi)

Table 2 Crystallographic parameter for pseudo-La_2MgNi_9 by using X-ray diffraction Cu Kα(λ=1.540 598 1 Å) at 298 K in a space group *R*-3m and Z=3[a]

Atom	Site	Metal atom position			Occupancy
		x	*y*	*z*	
La1	3a	0	0	0	1
La2	6c	0	0	0.144 8(1)	0.463
Mg1	6c	0	0	0.144 8(1)	0.537
Ni1	6c	0.328 8(2)	0	0.328 8(2)	0.891
Ni2	3b	0.5	0	0.5	0.912
Ni3	18h	0.084 3(3)	0.502 8(1)	0.084 3(3)	0.934
Al1	6c	0.328 8(2)	0	0.328 8(2)	0.036
Al2	3b	0.5	0	0.5	0.045
Al3	18h	0.084 3(3)	0.502 8(1)	0.084 3(3)	0.054
Mo1	6c	0.328 8(2)	0	0.328 8(2)	0.073
Mo2	3b	0.5	0	0.5	0.043
Mo3	18h	0.084 3(3)	0.502 8(1)	0.084 3(3)	0.012

[a] Structure was refined by using the Rietveld refinement program Rietica. The pattern factor R_p=6.7, the weighted pattern factor R_{wp}=9.0 and the goodness of fit GoF=2.5.

can be seen that the substitution of Al and Mo for Ni still retain the rhombohedral $PuNi_3$-type structure and the hexagonal $CaCu_5$-type structure, respectively. This phenomenon is consistent with the result in Liao et al.'s paper [16]. For convenience of discussing, in this work $La(La, Mg)_2Ni_9$ phase and $LaNi_5$ phase are employed to represent the pseudo-La_2MgNi_9 phase and pseudo-$LaNi_5$, respectively. The lattice parameter, cell volume, and phase abundance of the $La_{0.7}Mg_{0.3}Ni_{3.5-x}(Al_{0.5}Mo_{0.5})_x$ (x=0—0.8) alloys are presented in Table 4. We can find that all the alloys consist of impurity LaNi phase and two main crystallographic phases, namely the $La(La, Mg)_2Ni_9$ phase and the $LaNi_5$ phase. Fig. 2 shows the lattice parameters and unit cell volume of the alloys as a function of x. It can be seen that a and c parameters of both the $La(La, Mg)_2Ni_9$ phase and the $LaNi_5$ phase in the alloys all increase linearly with the increase of x, which is mainly attributed to the fact that the atomic radius of Al (1. 432 Å) and Mo (1. 363 Å) is larger than that of Ni (1. 246 Å), respectively.

Table 3 Crystallographic parameter for pseudo-$LaNi_5$ by using X-ray diffraction Cu Kα(λ=1. 5405981 Å) at 298 K in a space group *P6/mmm* and *Z*=1[a]

Atom	Site	Metal atom position			Occupancy
		x	*y*	*z*	
La1	1a	0	0	0	1
Ni1	2c	0. 333 3	0. 666 7	0	0. 673
Ni2	3g	0. 5	0	0. 5	0. 684
Al1	2c	0. 333 3	0. 666 7	0	0. 152
Al2	3g	0. 5	0	0. 5	0. 192
Mo1	2c	0. 333 3	0. 666 7	0	0. 175
Mo2	3g	0. 5	0	0. 5	0. 124

[a] Structure was refined by using the Rietveld refinement program Rietica. The pattern factor R_p=6. 3, the weighted pattern factor R_{wp}=8. 2 and the goodness of fit GoF=2. 1.

Fig. 3 shows the abundances of the La (La, Mg)$_2$Ni$_9$ phase and the $LaNi_5$ phase as a function of *x* in the alloys. As can be seen in Fig. 3 and Table 4, the La (La,Mg)$_2$Ni$_9$ phase abundance decreases from 80. 23% to 60. 96% with increasing of *x*, however, the $LaNi_5$ phase abundance increases from 19. 53% to 38.72%. These results may influence the electrochemical characteristics of the alloy studied.

Table 4 Characteristics of alloy phases in $La_{0.7}Mg_{0.3}Ni_{3.5-x}$(Al$_{0.5}$Mo0. 5)*x*(*x*=0−0. 8) alloys

Sample	Phase	Phase abundance (wt%)	Lattice parameter(Å)			Cell volume(Å)
			a	*b*	*c*	
x=0. 0	La(La,Mg)$_2$Ni$_9$	80. 23	5. 040		24. 339	535. 42
	$LaNi_5$	19. 53	5. 115		4. 066	92. 13
	LaNi	0. 24	3. 909	10. 945	4. 542	194. 32
x=0. 2	La(La,Mg)$_2$Ni$_9$	75. 41	5. 064		24. 618	546. 73
	$LaNi_5$	24. 33	5. 125		4. 083	92. 87
	LaNi	0. 26	3. 910	10. 951	4. 543	194. 52
x=0. 4	La(La,Mg)$_2$Ni$_9$	68. 73	5. 095		24. 660	554. 39
	$LaNi_5$	31. 06	5. 130		4. 086	93. 12
	LaNi	0. 21	3. 911	10. 956	4. 544	194. 71
x=0. 6	La(La,Mg)$_2$Ni$_9$	67. 01	5. 129		24. 874	566. 69
	$LaNi_5$	32. 97	5. 143		4. 112	94. 19
	LaNi	0. 02	3. 912	10. 963	4. 541	194. 75
x=0. 8	La(La,Mg)$_2$Ni$_9$	60. 96	5. 177		24. 966	579. 48
	$LaNi_5$	38. 72	5. 149		4. 120	94. 6
	LaNi	0. 32	3. 913	10. 964	4. 543	194. 9

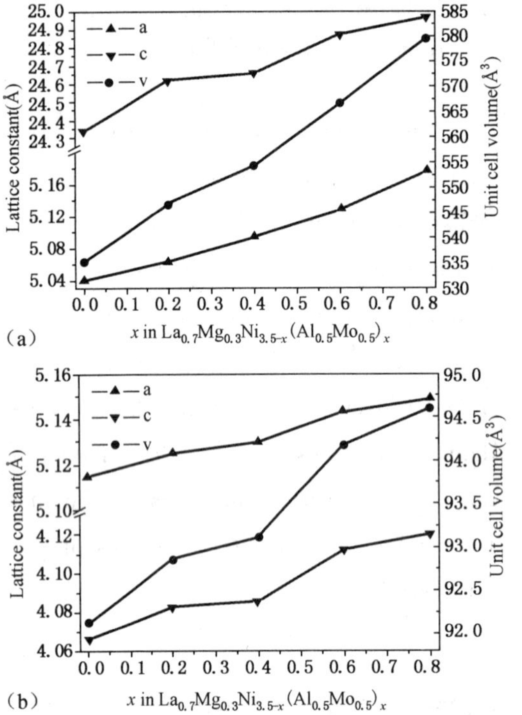

Fig. 2　Variations of the cell parameters and volumes as the function of xin $La_{0.7}Mg_{0.3}Ni_{3.5-x}(Al_{0.5}Mo_{0.5})_x$ alloys (x=0—0.8): (a) $La(La,Mg)_2Ni_9$ phase; (b) $LaNi_5$ phase

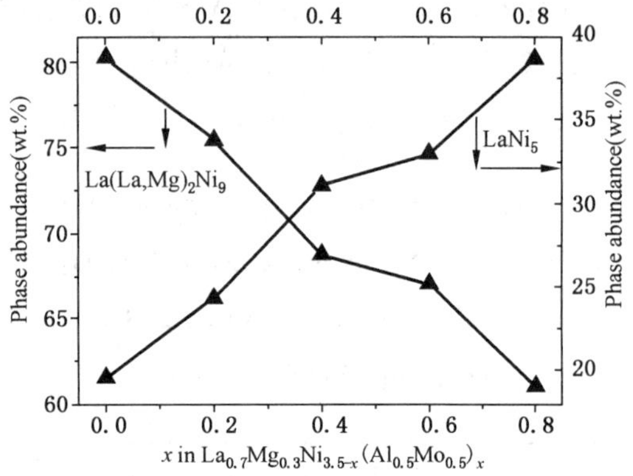

Fig. 3　Phase abundance of the $La(La,Mg)_2Ni_9$ phase and the $LaNi_5$ phase existing in the $La_{0.7}Mg_{0.3-x}(Al_{0.5}Mo_{0.5})_x$

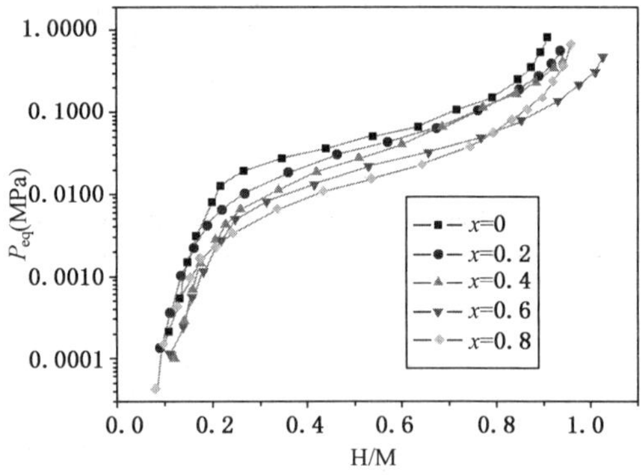

Fig. 4　The electrochemical desorption *P-C-T* curves for $La_{0.7}Mg_{0.3}Ni_{3.5-x}(Al_{0.5}Mo_{0.5})$ (x=0, 0.2, 0.4, 0.6, 0.8) alloys at 298 K

3.2　P-C isotherms

The electrochemical pressure-composition isotherms method is very useful for examining the charging and discharging levels of hydrogen in an anode, although the calculated pressures pertain to a quasi-equilibrium state [18]. Fig. 4 shows the electrochemical *P-C* isotherms for $La_{0.7}Mg_{0.3}Ni_{3.5-x}(Al_{0.5}Mo_{0.5})_x$ (x = 0, 0.2, 0.4, 0.6, 0.8) alloy electrodes at 298 K. It can be seen that the desorption pressure reduces continually as the Al and Mo additions increase. This means that the stability of the hydrides of alloys increases with increasing Al and Mo content because of the larger unit cell volume of the alloy. The phenomenon observed here is consistent with those reported previously for AB_3 alloys [14] and most AB_5 alloys [24]. Moreover, it can be seen that there is only one plateau in each *P-C-T* curve as shown in Fig. 4. Since the unit cell of the AB_3 compounds contains one-third AB_5 structure and two-thirds AB_2 structure [6], it is possible that the plateau pressure of the $La(La,Mg)_2Ni_9$ phase is similar to that of the $LaNi_5$ phase or the difference between their plateau pressures is too small to be observed.

With the increase of Al and Mo contents in the alloys, the hydrogen storage capacity first increases from 0.910 to 1.027, and then decreases to 0.959. This may be due to causes described as follows: As mentioned above, the plateau pressure decreases with increase of Al and Mo addition in the alloys, which enhances the intrinsic hydrogen storage capacity of the alloys. However, Sakai et al. [2,18] pointed out that the formation of passive layer of $Al(OH)_3$ inevitably decreases the hydrogen storage capacity, because such a layer not only weakens the surface electrocatalytic activity and prevents the diffusion of hydrogen into or from the alloy bulk, but also decreases the content of hydrogen absorption elements La and Mg in the alloys and thus reduces hydrogen storage capacity of the alloy. On the other hand, it is reported that the addition of Mo to the alloy leads to the improvement of the electrocatalytic activity on the alloy surface [19]. Therefore, it is reasonable to assume that, with Al and Mo content addition of lower than a certain amount, the positive effect is dominant and will cause an increase in the hydrogen storage capacity. However, when Al and Mo content exceed the critical content, the negative effect will become dominant and give rise to a decrease in the specific capacity. Overall, the combined effect of the above factors will inevitably result in an optimal value for the hydrogen storage capacity. The recommended amount of Al and Mo addition is $x=0.6$ from our work.

3.3 Discharge performance

The cyclic numbers needed to activate the electrodes and the maximum discharge capacity of the $La_{0.7}Mg_{0.3}Ni_{3.5-x}(Al_{0.5}Mo_{0.5})_x$ ($x=0-0.8$) alloy electrodes are listed in Table 5. It can be seen that all these alloys can be easily activated to reach the maximum capacity within two cycles. For the alloys with composition range of $x=0-0.8$, the maximum discharge capacity C_{max} improves significantly with the increase in x and reaches a maximum at $x=0.6$, and then decreases as x increases further. The variation of maximum discharge capacity of the alloys is essentially consistent with the variation of the H/M in the alloys. The maximum discharge capacity of the $La_{0.7}Mg_{0.3}Ni_{2.9}(Al_{0.5}Mo_{0.5})_{0.6}$ alloy electrodes is 397.6 mAh g^{-1}, which is noticeably higher than that of the commercial AB_5-type alloys.

Table 5 Electrode performance of $La_{0.7}Mg_{0.3}Ni_{3.5-x}(Al_{0.5}Mo_{0.5})_x$ (x=0—0.8) alloy electrodes

Sample	H/M	C_{max} ($mAh\ g^{-1}$)	N_a [a]	HRD_{1200} [b] (%)	S_{70} (%)
x=0.0	0.910	354.2	2	55.7	54.2
x=0.2	0.939	364.6	2	58.8	61.3
x=0.4	0.979	379.7	1	63.5	66.6
x=0.6	1.027	397.6	1	70.5	70.8
x=0.8	0.959	370.4	1	73.8	75.7

a The cycle numbers needed to activate the electrodes.

b The high-rate dischargeability at the discharge current density of 1200 mA g^{-1}.

Fig. 5 shows the discharge curves (the fifth cycle) of the alloy electrodes. Obviously, each curve has a wide discharge potential plateau based on the oxidation of desorbed hydrogen from the hydride. Besides, the discharge plateau shifts towards a more positive potential as Al and Mo addition increases in the alloys. As shown in Fig. 5, the middle-discharge potential (potential at 50% depth of discharge) decreases from −0.870 7 to −0.818 V in agreement with the reduction of desorption plateau pressure when x increases from 0 to 0.8 in the alloys.

3.4 Cyclic stability

The cycling capacity retention rate, expressed as S_{70} (%) = $C_{70}/C_{max} \times 100$ (where C_{max} is the maximum discharge capacity, C_{70} is the discharge capacity at the 70th cycles), is also listed in Table 5 after 70 cycles at discharge current of 60 mA g^{-1}. As seen in Table 5, the capacity retention rate (S_{70}) increases noticeably from 54.2% to 75.7% with x increasing from 0 to 0.8, indicating that the cyclic stability of the La-Mg-Ni-Al-Mo system alloys is improved markedly

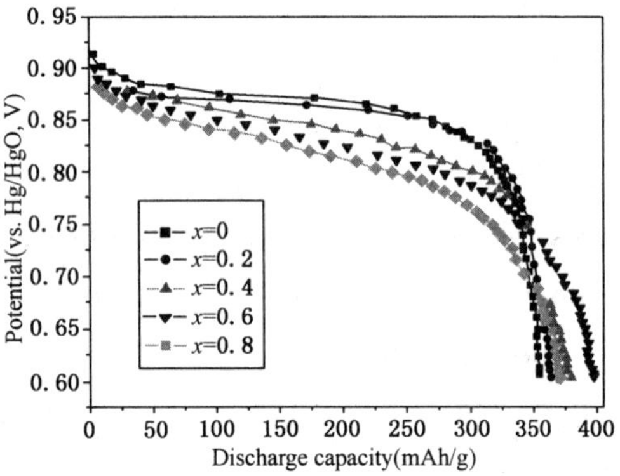

Fig. 5 The discharge curves of $La_{0.7}Mg_{0.3}Ni_{3.5-x}(Al_{0.5}Mo_{0.5})_x$ (x=0−0.08) alloy electrodes at the discharge current density of 60 mA g^{-1} and 298 K

with the increase of Al and Mo content in the alloys. It is known that the capacity degradation of La-Mg-Ni-type alloy electrode results primarily from two factors, the corrosion of Mg and La elements and the pulverization of the alloy particles [24]. The Al substitution results in the formation of the protective oxide (hydroxide) of Al on the alloy surface and a subsequent strong protection to the alloy from further corrosion of La and Mg.

3.5 High-rate dischargeability (HRD) and electrochemical kinetics

As an important kinetics property of

the hydride electrode in battery, it is very important to hold back the decrease of the discharge capacity even at the high charge-discharge current density. Fig. 6 shows the relationship between the high-rate dischargeability and the discharge current density of the $La_{0.7}Mg_{0.3}Ni_{3.5-x}(Al_{0.5}Mo_{0.5})_x$ ($x=0-0.8$) alloy electrodes. The HRD of the alloy electrodes

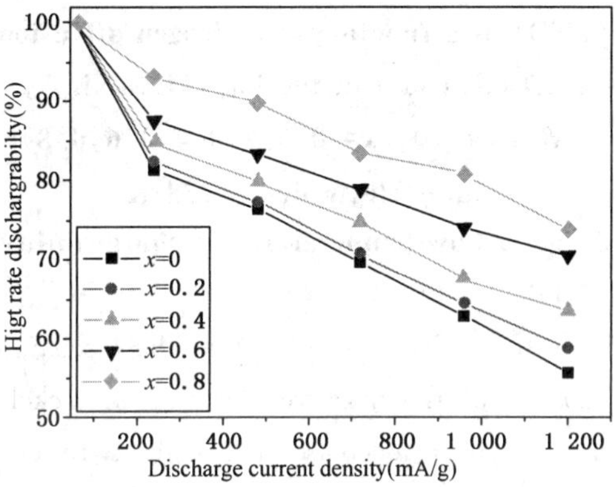

Fig. 6 The high-rate dischargeability (HRD) of the $La_{0.7}Mg_{0.3}Ni_{3.5-x}(Al_{0.5}Mo_{0.5})_x$ ($x=0,0.2,0.4,0.6,0.8$) alloy electrodes at 298 K

Table 6 Electrochemical kinetic parameters of $La_{0.7}Mg_{0.3}Ni_{3.5-x}(Al_{0.5}Mo_{0.5})x$ ($x=0-0.8$) alloy electrodes

Sample	Exchange current density, I_0 (mA g^{-1})		Hydrogen diffusion coefficient, D ($\times 10^{-10} cm^2\ s^{-1}$)	
	298 K	233 K	298 K	233 K
$x=0.0$	205.42	53.42	11.6	1.4
$x=0.2$	208.26	53.56	11.7	2.6
$x=0.4$	226.33	53.98	11.7	3.2
$x=0.6$	237.14	54.12	12.1	4.2
$x=0.8$	240.12	54.63	12.3	5.4

for the discharge current density of 1200 mA g^{-1} are also listed in Table 5. It can be seen that as x increases, the HRD of the alloy electrodes increases from 55.7% ($x=0$) to 73.8% ($x=0.8$). It is well known that the HRD of metal hydride electrode are mainly influenced by the electrochemical reaction kinetics on the alloy powder surface and the diffusion rate of hydrogen in the bulk of the alloy [25]. To examine the effect of the partial substitution of Al and Mo for Ni on the discharge kinetics, linear polarization was preformed on these alloy electrodes. Based on the measured linear polarization curves, values of exchange current density I_0 were evaluated for the alloy electrodes and are summarized in Table 6. It can be seen that the I_0 increases monotonically with increasing Al and Mo content in the alloys. This may be attributed to the reasons as follows; Iwakura et al. [19] pointed out that the addition of Mo to the alloy leads to the improvement of the electrocatalytic activity on the alloy surface. Moreover, perhaps there is a metallic Ni/Mo work with higher activity on the alloy surface [26]. Overall, due to increase of Mo content in the alloy, the concentration of the Mo on the alloy surface increases and thus increases the I_0 of the alloy electrodes. Further investigations in this aspect are going on in our group. Fig. 7 shows high-rate dischargeability as a function of the I_0 for the hydrogen evolution reaction at the alloy electrodes. It is found that the HRD is a linear function of I_0, while the hydrogen diffusion coefficient maintains almost unchanged (11.6−12.3×10^{-10} cm^2 s^{-1}). Iwakura et al. [19] have pointed out that if the electrochemical reaction on the surface is a rate-determining factor, a linear dependence of the high-rate dischargeability on the exchange current density should be observed. In contrast if the diffusion of hydrogen in the alloy bulk is a rate-determining factor, the high-rate dischargeability should be constant, irrespective of exchange current density. Therefore, in the present study, the HRD is essentially controlled by the charge-transfer reaction of hydrogen on the surface at a discharge current density of 1200 mAh g^{-1}.

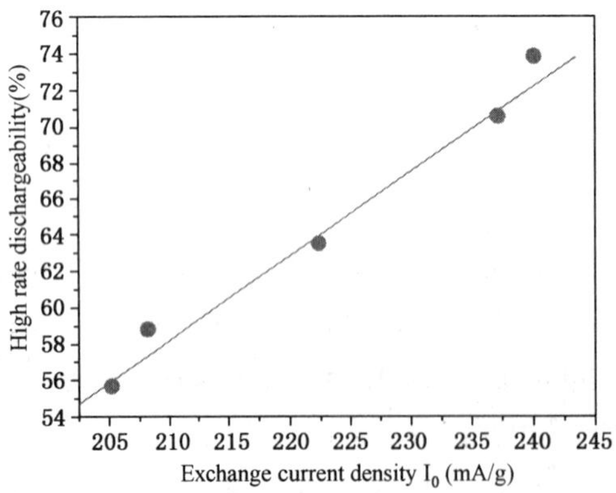

Fig. 7　High-rate dischargeability as a function of exchange current density for hydrogen evolution of $La_{0.7}Mg_{0.3}Ni_{3.5-x}(Al_{0.5}Mo_{0.5})_x$ (x=0—0.8) alloy electrodes

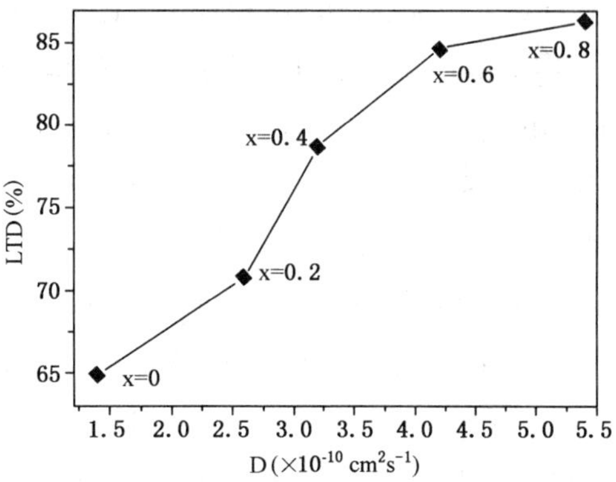

Fig. 8　The low-temperature dischargeability (LTD) as a function of hydrogen diffusion coefficient (D) of the $La_{0.7}Mg_{0.3}Ni_{3.5-x}(Al_{0.5}Mo_{0.5})_x$ (x=0, 0.2, 0.4, 0.6, 0.8) alloy electrodes at 233 K

3.6　Low-temperature dischargeability (LTD)

It has been reported that the discharge capacity of the negative electrode in nickel-metal hydride decrease drastically with decreasing temperature [27-29]. Sakai et al. [2] pointed out that the dischargeability of the negative electrodes at relatively low temperature depended on the hydrogen diffusion and/or charge-transfer process occurring at the metal electrolyte interface. The hydrogen diffusion coefficient D of hydrogen in the alloy bulk is evaluated using the method described by Iwakura et al. [19]. The low-temperature dischargeability, expressed as $LTD_{233}(\%)=C_{233}/C_{298}\times 100$ (where C_{233} and C_{298} are the discharge capacity at 233 and 298 K, respectively). Fig. 8 shows the LTD as a function of D in the alloy electrodes. It can be that the LTD increases with increasing D. The D of the $La_{0.7}Mg_{0.3}Ni_{3.5-x}(Al_{0.5}Mo_{0.5})_x$ (x=0, 0.2, 0.4, 0.6, 0.8) alloy electrodes at 233 K are also listed in Table 6, respectively.

It can be found that the I_0 maintain almost unchanged (53.42—54.63 mA g^{-1}); however, the D increases remarkably with increasing x, which implies that the hydrogen diffusion in alloy bulk probably becomes the rate-determining factor for low-temperature dischargeability at 233 K. In general, the cell volume expansion results in the stability of hydride (decrease of ΔH), leading to the decrease of D value [27]. However, the D value increases with increasing of x (increasing of the unit cell volume) in present work, which can be attributed to the change in the relative amounts of $La(La, Mg)_2Ni_9$ phase and $LaNi_5$ phase owing to Al and Mo substitution. As mentioned above, the $La(La, Mg)_2Ni_9$ phase abundance decreases from 80.23% to 60.96% with increasing of x, however, the $LaNi_5$ phase abundance increases from 19.53% to 38.72%. These results may result more phase boundary, which will provide path for hydrogen diffusion and thus increase the D. Zhao and Sun thought [29] that desorption of hydrogen in metal hydride is an endothermal reaction and may be a rate-limiting step during the discharge process of metal hydride at relatively low temperature (for example, at 233 K).

4 Conclusion

The effect of Al and Mo substitution for Ni on the structure, hydrogen storage characteristics and electrochemical properties of the $La_{0.7}Mg_{0.3}Ni_{3.5-x}(Al_{0.5}Mo_{0.5})_x$ ($x=0-0.8$) hydrogen storage alloys have been investigated systematically. The results of X-ray powder diffraction and Rietveld analysis show that the alloys are all consisted of the $La(La, Mg)_2Ni_9$ phase and the $LaNi_5$ phase, and the lattice parameter and cell volume of both the $La(La, Mg)_2Ni_9$ phase and the $LaNi_5$ phase increase with increasing Al and Mo content. The *P-C* isotherms reveal that the hydrogen storage capacity increases to a maximum and then decreases with increasing x, but the plateau pressure decreases continuously with increasing x. The electrochemical measurements show that the maximum discharge capacity increases first when x increases from 0.0 (354.2 mAh g^{-1}) to 0.6 (397.6 mAh g^{-1}) and then decreases when x reaches 0.8 (370.4 mAh g^{-1}). For the discharge current density of 1200 mA g^{-1}, the high-rate dischargeability of the alloy electrodes increases lineally from 54.2% ($x=0$) to 75.7% ($x=0.8$) due to the increase of the exchange current density at 298 K. The hydrogen diffusion coefficient D increases with increasing Al and Mo content, and thus increases the low-temperature dischargeability LTD of the alloy electrodes.

Acknowledgement

This work was financially supported by the National Natural Science Foundation of China (Grant No. 20171042).

References

[1] J. J. G. Willems, K. H. J. Buschow, J. Less-Common Met. 129 (1987) 13.

[2] T. Sakai, H. Miyamura, N. Kuriyama, A. Kato, K. Oguro, H. Ishikawa, J. Electrochem.

Soc. 137(1990)795.

[3] T. Kohno, H. Yoshida, F. Kawashima, T. Inaba, I. Sakai, M. Yamamoto, M. Kanda, J. Alloys Compd. 311(2000)5.

[4] J. J. G. Willems, Philips J. Res. 39(Suppl. 1)(1984)1.

[5] H. G. Pan, Y. F. Zhu, M. X. Gao, Q. D. Wang, J. Electrochem. Soc. 149(2002)829.

[6] J. Chen, N. Kuriyama, H. T. Takeshita, H. Tanaka, T. Sakai, M. Haruta, Electrochem. Solid—State Lett. 3 (6) (2000) 249.

[7] T. Sakai, I. Uehara, H. Ishikawa, J. Alloys Compd. 293-295 (1999)762.

[8] J. J. Reilly, G. D. Adzic, J. R. Johnson, T. Vogt, S. Mukerjee, J. McBreen, J. Alloys Compd. 293-295 (1999) 569.

[9] Y. F. Liu, H. G. pan, Y. F. Zhu, R. Li, Y. Q. Lei, Mater. Sci. Eng. A. 372 (2004) 163.

[10] K. Kadir, T. Sakai, I. Uahara, J. Alloys Compd. 257 (1997) 115.

[11] K. Kadir, N. Kuriyama, T. Sakai, I. Uehara, L. Eriksson, J. Alloys Compd. 284 (1999) 145.

[12] K. Kadir, T. Sakai, I. Uahara, J. Alloys Compd. 287 (1999) 264.

[13] K. Kadir, T. Sakai, I. Uahara, J. Alloys Compd. 302 (2000) 112.

[14] J. Chen, H. T. Takeshita, H. Tanaka, N. Kuriyama, T. Sakai, J. Alloys Compd. 302 (2000) 304.

[15] T. Kohno, H. Yoshida, F. Kawashima, T. Inaba, I. Sakai, M. Yamamoto, M. Kanda, J. Alloys Compd. 311(2000) 5.

[16] B. Liao, Y. Q. Lei, L. X. Chen, G. L. Lu, H. G. Pan, Q. D. Wang, J. Power Sources 129 (2004) 358.

[17] P. H. Notton, P. Hokkeling, J. Electrochem. Soc. 138 (1991) 1877.

[18] T. Sakai, H. Miyamura, N. Kuriyama, A. Kato, K. Oguro, H. Ishikawa, J. Less-Common Met. 159 (1990) 127.

[19] C. Iwakura, H. Senoh, K. Morimoto, Y. Hara, H. Inoue, Electrochem. 70 (1) (2002) 2.

[20] Materials Data JADE Release 5, XRD Pattern Processing, Materials Data Inc. (MDI), 1997.

[21] X. B. Zhang, Y. J. Chai, W. Y. Yin, M. S. Zhao, J. Solid State Chem. 177 (2004) 2373.

[22] J. Balej, Int. J. Hydrogen Energy 10 (1985) 365.

[23] C. Iwakura, T. Asaoka, H. Yoneyama, T. Sakai, K. Oguro, H. Ishikawa, Nippon Kagaku Kaishi (1988) 1482.

[24] H. G. Pan, Q. W. Jin, M. X. Gao, Y. F. Liu, R. Li, Y. Q. Lei, J. Alloys Compd. 373 (2004) 237.

[25] H. G. Pan, Y. F. Liu, M. X. Gao, Y. Q. Lei, Q. D. Wang, J. Electrochem. Soc. 150 (5) (2003) 565.

[26] M. T. Yeh, V. M. Beibutian, S. E. Hsu, J. Alloys Compd. 293-295(1999) 721.

[27] C. Iwakura, T. Oura, H. Inoue, M. Matsuoka, Electrochim. Acta 41(1996) 117.

[28] H. Senoh, Y. Hara, H. Inoue, C. Iwakura, Electrochim. Acta 46 (2001) 967.

[29] M. Zhao, C. Sun, Hydrogen materials science and chemistry of metal hydrides, in: T. Nejet Vezirogle, et al. (Eds.), II Materials, Physics and Chemistry, vol. 82, Kluwer Academic Publisher, 2002, pp. 29-34.

Effect of Mn Content on the Structure and Electrochemical Characteristics of $La_{0.7}Mg_{0.3}Ni_{2.975-x}Co_{0.525}Mn_x$ ($x=0-0.4$) Hydrogen Storage Alloys①

X. B. Zhang[a], D. Z. Sun[b], W. Y. Yin[a], Y. J. Chai[a], M. S. Zhao[a]
([a] Key Laboratory of Rare Earth Chemistry and Physics, Changchun Institute of Applied Chemistry, Graduate School of Chinese Academy of Sciences, Chinese Academy of Sciences, Changchun 130022, PR China)
([b] State Key Laboratory of Electro-analytical Chemistry, Changchun Institute of Applied Chemistry, Graduate School of Chinese Academy of Sciences, Chinese Academy of Sciences, Changchun 130022, PR China)

Abstract: The effect of Mn content on the crystal structure and electrochemical characteristics of $La_{0.7}Mg_{0.3}Ni_{2.975-x}Co_{0.525}Mn_x$ ($x=0, 0.1, 0.2, 0.3, 0.4$) alloys has been studied systematically. The results of the Rietveld analyses show that all these alloys mainly consist of two phases: the $La(La,Mg)_2Ni_9$ phase with the rhombohedral $PuNi_3$-type structure and the $LaNi_5$ phase with the hexagonal $CaCu_5$-type structure. The pressure-composition isotherms shows that the partial substitution of Mn for Ni results in lower desorption plateau pressure and steeper pressure plateau of the alloy electrodes. For a Mn content of $x=0.3$, the electrochemical performances, including specific discharge capacity, high rate chargeability (HRC) and high rate dischargeability (HRD), of the alloy are preferable. Moreover, the data of the polarization resistance R_p and the exchange current density I_0 of the alloy electrodes is consistent with the results of HRC and HRD. The hydrogen diffusion coefficient D increases with increasing Mn content, and thereafter increases the low temperature dischargeability (LTD) of the alloy electrodes.

Key words: Structure characteristics; High rate chargeability; High rate dischargeability; Low temperature dischargeability; Exchange current density; Hydrogen diffusion coefficient

1 Introduction

Owing to the shortage of fossil energy and global warming, hydrogen is expected to be a promising energy carrier in near future. In order for hydrogen to become a viable solution to the energy crisis and the environmental problems, storage processes must be improved in terms of specific capacity and security. Among different ways to store hydrogen, absorption in solid is very attractive since it allows

① Electrochimica Acta, 2005(50): 2911-2918.

safe storage at pressure and temperature close to ambient conditions [1]. There are many kinds of metals and alloys which are able to absorb large quantity of hydrogen, and they are used in many fields, such as heat pump, thermal storage system, as catalysts, fuel cells, nickel-metal hydride (Ni-MH) rechargeable batteries and so on.

In recent years, Ni-MH secondary battery, in which hydrogen storage alloy is employed as negative electrode material, has been widely adopted in various portable electronic devices, electric hand tools and electric vehicles because of its high reversible energy storage density, fast electro-chemical activation, long cyclic life, good charge/discharge kinetics and environmental compatibility [2-7]. Nowadays, two kinds of metal-hydride alloys, namely the rare earth-based AB_5 type and the Zr-based AB_2 type alloys, espe-cially the former, have been widely commercialized in the nickel metal-hydride (Ni-MH) battery industry. However, AB_5 alloys are now not very satisfactory due to their limited discharge capacity (about 372 mAh g^{-1}) [8]. Moreover, although the Zr-based AB_2-type alloys have a higher specific energy than that of the AB_5 alloys [9], they have the demerits of slow activation, higher cost and poor high rate dischargeability [10]. Therefore, alloys with higher energy density, faster activation and lower cost are urgently to be found to replace the conventional rare earth-based AB_5-type alloys. Oesterreicher et al. [11, 12] pointed out that the hydrogen storage capacity of $LaNi_3$ and $CaNi_3$ alloys exceeds that of the well-known $LaNi_5$ alloy. They also indicated that the $LaNi_3$ and $CaNi_3$ could react rapidly with hydrogen under ambient conditions to form $LaNi_3H_5$ and $CaNi_3H_{4.6}$, respectively. Recently, Kadir et al. [13-15] have discovered a new type of ternary alloys with the general formula of RMg_2Ni_9 (R: rare earth, Ca, Y) with $PuNi_3$ type structure. It is found that some of the R-Mg-Ni based ternary alloys can absorb-desorb 1.8—1.87 mass% H_2 and are thus regarded as promising candidates for reversible gaseous hydrogen storage [16, 17]. As to their electrochemical hy-drogen storage, Pan et al. [18] have reported that the dis-charge capacity of $La_{0.7}Mg_{0.3}Ni_{2.975}Co_{0.525}$ alloy reaches 398.4 mAh g^{-1}, which is very attractive for practical application. However, the La-Mg-Ni-Co system hydrogen storage electrode alloys have some disadvantages, such as a high absorption/desorption plateau pressure, poor cyclic stability and so on. It is well known that elemental substitution is one of the most effective methods for improving the overall properties of the hydrogen storage alloys and obtaining the desired overall properties, e.g. proper capacity at a favorable hydrogen pressure, favorable HRD and good cyclic stability [19-22]. For rare earth-based hydrogen storage alloys, partial substitution of Ni by elements such as Al [19], Mn [20], Cu [21], Sn [22] and Fe [23] has been widely studied. Several metals have turned out to be good candidates for lowering the plateau pressure [19,20]. It has been found that the Mn element is beneficial to many aspects for rare earth-based hydrogen storage alloys [24-27]. Sakai et al. [26] pointed out that the maximum discharge capacity of the $LaNi_{4.5}Mn_{0.5}$ alloy electrode reaches 318 mAh g^{-1}. Ogawa and Ikoma [27] have studied the hydrogen storage property and electrochemical characteristics of the $MnNi_{3.95-x}Mn_xAl_{0.3}Co_{0.75}$ electrode alloys and indicated that the equilibrium pressure decreased from 0.24 to 0.083 MPa with increasing x from 0.2 to 0.4, and the activity, discharge capacity and high rate dischargeability of the alloy electrodes can be improved. In addition, previous researches indicated that the partial substitution of Mn for Ni can increase the lattice parameters and the cell volume, decrease the plateau equilibrium pressure and improve electrochemical catalytic activity of alloys [28]. Therefore, it is believed that partial substitution of Mn for Ni will be a very effective way to improve the overall properties of the La-Mg-Ni-Co system hydrogen storage alloys.

In this paper, we focus on the detailed influence of partial substitution for Ni with Mn on the structural and electrochemical characteristics of the $La_{0.7}Mg_{0.3}Ni_{2.975-x}Co_{0.525}Mn_x$ ($x=0-0.4$) hydrogen storage alloys.

2 Experimental details

2.1 Alloy preparation and X-ray diffraction analysis

All alloy samples were prepared by arc-melting carefully the constituent elements or master alloy on a water-cooled copper hearth under the protection of argon atmosphere. The purity of the metals, i.e., La, Mg, Ni, Co and Mn is higher than 99.9 mass%, respectively. The samples were all turned over and remelted five times to ensure good homogeneity. A slight excess of Mg over composition was needed in order to compensate for evaporative loss of Mg under preparation conditions. Several attempts were done until the optimum preparative conditions were found. The final compounds were carefully checked by Inductively Coupled Plasma—Atomic Emission Spectrometry (ICP-AES) method using TJA Poems-type instrument. Thereafter, these alloy samples were mechanically crushed to particle with an average diameter of 26.24 μm(300 mesh).

Crystallographic characteristics of the hydrogen storage alloys were investigated by X-ray diffraction on Rigaku D/Max 2500PC X-ray diffractometer (Cu Karadiation, Bragg-Brentano geometry, 2θ range 10—100°, step size 0.02°, backscattered rear graphite monochromator). The lattice constants and cell volume were calculated by Rietica program [29] after internal theta calibration using silicon as standard reference materials.

2.2 Electrochemical measurement

The preparation of the disk-type electrodes, the setup of the electrochemical cell and the measurement of electrochemical properties were similar as described in our previous paper [30].

Pressure-composition isotherms(P-C-T) curves were electrochemically obtained by converting the equilibrium potential of the metal hydride electrode to the equilibrium pressure of hydrogen on the basis of Nernst equation using electrochemical data [31] as reported in reference [32]. The equilibrium potential curves were obtained by alternating the following two processes: (1) a pulse discharge of (25 mA $g^{-1}\times 0.25$ h) and (2) a rest period until the potential became almost constant. The equilibrium potential change of approximately 30 mV corresponds to the equilibrium pressure change by one order of magnitude. Since the measured potentials have an error of 1—2 mV, the calculated pressure values are accurate to be within 10% [31].

To evaluate the HRD (in the range of 60—1 200 mA g^{-1}), the charging current density was kept constant at 60 mA g^{-1} and the obtained discharge capacity was denoted as C_i. On the other hand, when the HRC (60—1 200 mA g^{-1}) was investigated, the discharging current density was held at 60 mA g^{-1} and thus we got the discharge capacity (C_j). HRD (or HRC) are generally defined as the ratio of the discharge capacity C_i (or C_j) at the cut off voltage of -0.6 V to the maximum capacity C_{max}, namely: HRD $= C_i/C_{max}\times 100\%$, HRC $= C_j/C_{max}\times 100\%$, respectively.

For investigating the electrocatalytic activity of the hydrogen electrode reaction, the linear polarization curves of the electrode were plotted on a EG&G PARC's Model 273 Potentiostat/Galvanostat station by scanning the electrode potential at the rate of 0.1 mV s^{-1} from -5 to 5 mV (versus open circuit potential) at 50% depth of discharge (DOD) at 298 and 233 K, respectively. The polarization resistance, R_p, can be obtained from the slope of the linear polarization curves. Moreover, the exchange current density, I_0, which is a measure of the catalytic activity of electrode, was calculated from the slopes of polarization curves by the following equation [33], $I_0=\frac{RT}{FR_p}$ where R, T and F have their general meanings and R_p is the polarization resistance. The potentiostatic discharge technique was used to evaluate the coefficient of diffusion within the bulk of the alloy electrodes. After being fully charged followed by a 30 min open-circuit lay-aside, the electrodes were discharged with +500 mV potentialstep for 500 s on a EG&G PARC's Model 273 Potentiostat/Galvanostat station, using the M352 CorrWare electrochemical/corrosion software.

3 Results and discussion

3.1 Alloy composition and structure characteristic

It is well known that the low melting Mg metal will be inevitably lost during the sample preparation. We have tried many ways to overcome this problem, such as using Mg-Ni master alloy as Mg additive, decreasing the melting current, adding a slight excess of Mg over sample composition and so on. The third way is the most effective way to compensate for evaporative loss of Mg among all these methods mentioned above. The loss of Mg should be seriously paid in the alloy preparation process, whereas no compensation on Mg loss is described in Pan et al.'s paper [33]. In present paper, the lost weight during sample preparation is about 0.5 mass%, which is almost the same as excess Mg added. The results of ICP-AES analysis for all compounds are summarized in Table 1. It can be seen that the final composition of all the alloys is identical with the original composition.

Fig. 1 shows the result of Rietveld refinement of XRD profiles for $La_{0.7}Mg_{0.3}Ni_{2.875}Co_{0.525}Mn_{0.1}$ hydrogen storage alloy as a representative example of $La_{0.7}Mg_{0.3}Ni_{2.975-x}Co_{0.525}Mn_x$ (x=0, 0.1, 0.2, 0.3, 0.4) hydrogen storage alloys. The result shows that the $La_{0.7}Mg_{0.3}Ni_{2.875}Co_{0.525}Mn_{0.1}$ alloy consists of two phases: a La_2MgNi_9 phase with a $PuNi_3$-type rhombohedral structure and a $LaNi_5$ phase with a $CaCu_5$-type hexagonal structure. The final Rietveld structure parameters are tabulated in Table 2. The crystallographic results reveal that the Mg atoms only occupy the 6c sites whereas the La atoms can occupy both the 3a and the 6c sites in the phase with rhombohedral (Space group: $R\text{-}3m$ 166) $PuNi_3$-type structure by Rietveld refinement. So the final formula of La_2MgNi_9 phase can be designated as $La(La,Mg)_2Ni_9$. The lattice parameters and cell volumes of the phases of the hydrogen storage alloys are listed in Table 3. We can find that all the alloys mainly consisted of two crystallographic phases, namely the $La(La,Mg)_2Ni_9$ phase and the $LaNi_5$ phase. Fig. 2 shows the lattice parameters and unit cell volumes of the alloys as a function of x. It can be seen that a and c parameters of both the $La(La,Mg)_2Ni_9$ phase and the $LaNi_5$ phase in the alloys all increase linearly with increasing Mn content, which is mainly ascribed to the larger atomic radius of Mn(1.79 Å) than that of Ni(1.62 Å The Fig. 3 shows the abundances of the $La(La,Mg)_2Ni_9$ phase and the $LaNi_5$ phase as a function of Mn content in the alloys. It can be seen that the $La(La,Mg)_2Ni_9$ phase abundance decrease from 71.32 to 60.35% with increasing x, on the contrary, the $LaNi_5$ phase abundance increases from 28.68 to 39.65%. The above results are somewhat different to those obtained by Pan et al. For instance, there are no existences of MnO_2 phase in our experiment, and the phase abundances of $LaNi_5$ phase and $La(La,Mg)_2Ni_9$ phase are different to their results. It is well known that all La-Mg-Ni-Co-Mn system hydrogen storage alloys are of multiphase and different preparation conditions will result in different phase abun-dance. Magnetic levitation melting and arc-melting method are used in Pan et al.'s and our experiments, respectively. Those two preparation methods would be responsible for the above different results, which will inevitably influence the hydrogen storage and electrochemical characteristics of the alloys studied.

Table 1 Composition of the $La_{0.7}Mg_{0.3}Ni_{2.975-x}Co_{0.525}Mn_x$ (x=0,0.1,0.2,0.3,0.4) alloys

Samples	La/ (mg g^{-1})	Mg/ (mg g^{-1})	Ni/ (mg g^{-1})	Co/ (mg g^{-1})	Mn/ (mg g^{-1})	La : Mg : Ni : Co : Mn[a]
$La_{0.7}Mg_{0.3}Ni_{2.975}Co_{0.525}$	313.57	23.52	563.14	99.77	0.00	2.26 : 0.97 : 9.59 : 1.69
$La_{0.7}Mg_{0.3}Ni_{2.875}Co_{0.525}Mn_{0.1}$	313.95	23.55	544.87	99.89	17.74	2.26 : 0.97 : 9.28 : 1.70 : 0.32
$La_{0.7}Mg_{0.3}Ni_{2.775}Co_{0.525}Mn_{0.2}$	314.33	23.58	526.56	100.01	35.52	2.26 : 0.97 : 8.97 : 1.70 : 0.65
$La_{0.7}Mg_{0.3}Ni_{2.675}Co_{0.525}Mn_{0.3}$	314.71	23.60	508.22	100.13	53.34	2.27 : 0.97 : 8.66 : 1.70 : 0.97
$La_{0.7}Mg_{0.3}Ni_{2.575}Co_{0.525}Mn_{0.4}$	315.09	23.63	489.82	100.25	71.21	2.27 : 0.97 : 8.34 : 1.70 : 1.30

[a] Atomic ratio.

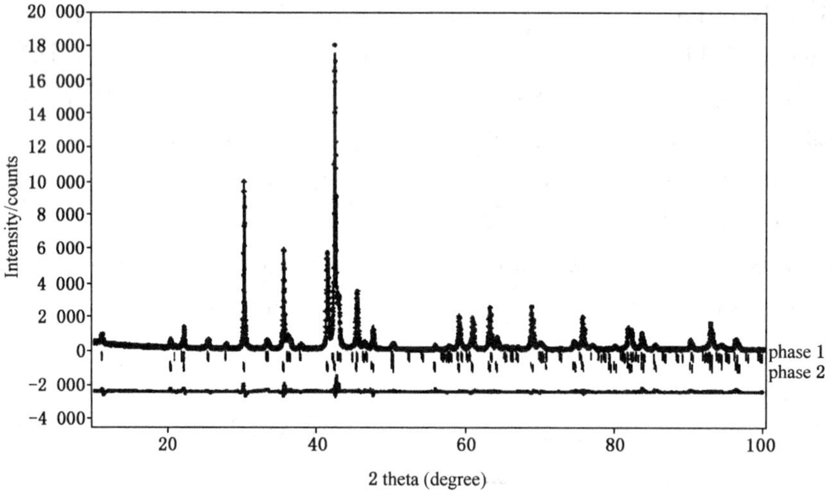

Fig. 1 Rietveld profiles refinement of XRD patterns $La_{0.7}Mg_{0.3}Ni_{2.875}Co_{0.525}Mn_{0.1}$ alloy (phase 1: $La(La,Mg)_2Ni_9$; phase 2: $LaNi_5$)

Table 2 Crystallographic parameters for La_2MgNi_9 by using X-ray diffraction Cu Kα(λ=1.540 598 1 Å) at 298 K in a space group *R*-3*m* and *Z*=3[a]

Atom	Site	Metal atom position			Occupancy
		x	*y*	*z*	
La1	3a	0	0	0	1
La2	6c	0	0	0.147 49(17)	0.484
Mg1	6c	0	0	0.147 49(17)	0.516
Ni1	6c	0	0	0.325 63(11)	1
Ni2	3b	0	0	0.5	1
Ni3	18h	0.494 7(2)	0.505 4(8)	0.083 33(12)	1

[a] Structure was refined by using the Rietveld refinement program Rietica. The pattern factor R_p = 5.6, the weighted pattern factor R_{wp} = 7.5 and the goodness of fit S = 1.8.

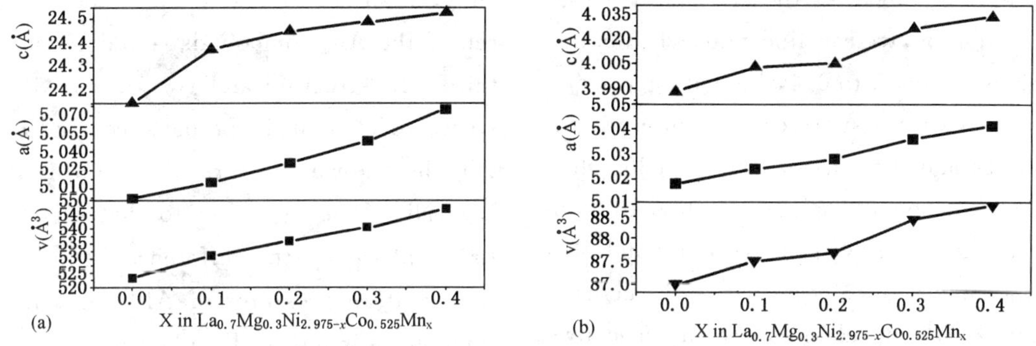

Fig. 2　The lattice parameters and cell volume of the $La_{0.7}Mg_{0.3}Ni_{2.975-x}Co_{0.525}Mn_x$ (x=0−0.4) alloys (a) $La(La,Mg)_2Ni_9$ phase and (b) $LaNi_5$ phase

Table 3　The characteristics of alloy phases in $La_{0.7}Mg_{0.3}Ni_{2.975-x}Co_{0.525}Mn_x$ (x=0−0.4) alloys[a]

Samples	Phases	Phase abundance (wt%)	Parameters of fit[b]	Lattice parameter (Å)		Cell volume (Å³)
				a	c	
x=0.0	$La(La,Mg)_2Ni_9$	71.32	R_p=8.7	5.002	24.153	523.35
	$LaNi_5$	28.68	R_{wp}=11.4	5.018	3.988	86.97
x=0.1	$La(La,Mg)_2Ni_9$	69.21	R_p=9.7	5.015	24.375	530.91
	$LaNi_5$	30.79	R_{wp}=13.1	5.024	4.003	87.5
x=0.2	$La(La,Mg)_2Ni_9$	67.53	R_p=8.6	5.031	24.450	535.94
	$LaNi_5$	32.47	R_{wp}=11.3	5.028	4.005	87.68
x=0.3	$La(La,Mg)_2Ni_9$	64.16	R_p=6.3	5.049	24.488	540.62
	$LaNi_5$	35.84	R_{wp}=8.5	5.036	4.026	88.43
x=0.4	$La(La,Mg)_2Ni_9$	60.35	R_p=8.6	5.075	24.526	547.05
	$LaNi_5$	39.65	R_{wp}=11.3	5.041	4.033	88.75

[a] The Rietveld refinement program RIETICA was used.

[b] R_p: the pattern factor; R_{wp}: the weighted pattern factor.

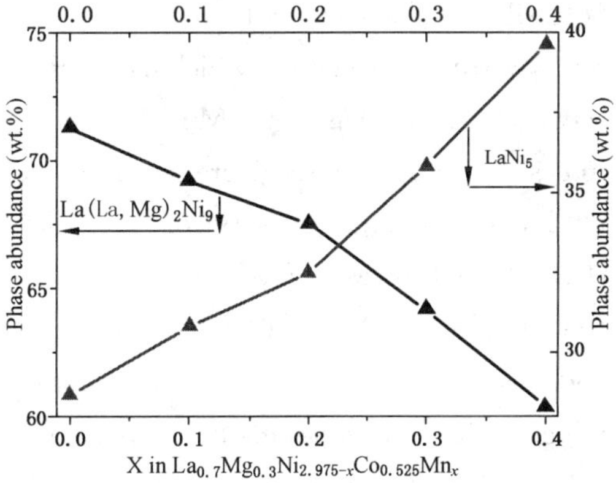

Fig. 3　Phase abundance of the $La(La,Mg)_2Ni_9$ phase and the $LaNi_5$ phase existing in the $La_{0.7}Mg_{0.3}Ni_{2.975-x}Co_{0.525}Mn_x$ (x=0−0.4) alloys

3.2　P-C isotherms

The electrochemical method is very useful for examining the charging and discharging levels of hydrogen in an anode, although the calculated pressures pertain to a quasiequilibrium state. The *P-C* isotherms (PCT) of hydrogen desorption for hydrogenated $La_{0.7}Mg_{0.3}Ni_{2.975-x}Co_{0.525}Mn_x$ (x=0, 0.1, 0.2, 0.3, 0.4) compounds at 298 K are presented in Fig. 4. It should be noted that the partial substitution of Mn for Ni results in lower desorption pressure plateau and steeper pressure plateau of the alloy electrodes. In addition, we can find that, when x increases from 0 to 0.4, the hydrogen storage capacity first increases from 0.868 to 0.912 and then decreases to 0.836. This phenomenon is mainly ascribed to two reasons as follows: On the one hand, the plateau pressure decreases with increasing x, which enhances the intrinsic hydrogen storage capacity of alloys. On the other hand, as Oesterreicher et al. [11] has pointed out that the hydrogen storage capacity of the $LaNi_3$ phase is larger than that of the $LaNi_5$ phase. Moreover, as shown in Fig. 3 and Table 3, the $La(La, Mg)_2Ni_9$ phase abundance decreases while the $LaNi_5$ phase abundance increases with increasing x in alloys. The above contrary effects result in an optimum Mn content for the hydrogen storage capacity of the La-Mg-Ni-Co-Mn-type hydrogen storage alloys. The recommended amount of Mn addition is 0.3 from our work. Moreover, it is observed that there is only one plateau in each *P-C-T* curve of the

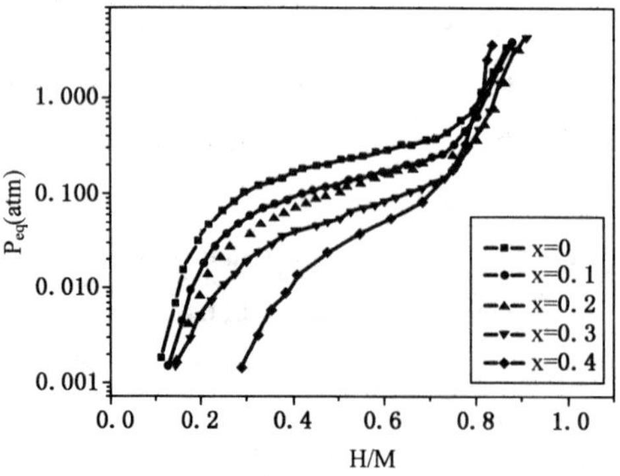

Fig. 4　The electrochemical *P-C-T* curves for $La_{0.7}Mg_{0.3}Ni_{2.975-x}Co_{0.525}Mn_x$ (x=0−0.4) alloy electrodes at 298 K

alloy, as shown in Fig. 4. Since the unit cell of the AB_3 compounds contains one-third AB_5 structure and two-thirds AB_2 structure [7], it is perhaps concluded that the plateau pressure of the $La(La, Mg)_2Ni_9$ phase is similar to that of the $LaNi_5$ phase or the difference between their plateau pressures of AB_3 and AB_5 compounds is too small to be observed.

3.3　Activation and maximum discharge capacity

When hydrogen storage alloy electrode is first charged, the stored hydrogen in the alloy is released sparingly after absorption. The process that the freshly formed hydride electrodes are continuously charged and discharged in order to obtain the maximum electrochemical capacity is called activation. This is important for practical use of Ni-MH battery. Fig. 5 shows the activation profiles of the $La_{0.7}Mg_{0.3}Ni_{2.975-x}Co_{0.525}Mn_x$ (x=0−0.4) alloy electrodes, and the electrochemical characteristics are summarized in Table 4. It can be seen that all the alloys can be easily activated to reach their maximum capacity within two cycles, which means that activation of La-Mg-Ni-Co-Mn alloy electrodes is easy. With the increase of x, the maximum discharge capacity of the alloy electrode first increases from 337.6 mAh g^{-1} (x=0) to 356 mAh g^{-1} (x=0.3) and then decreases to 326.6 mAh g^{-1} (x=0.4), which is in good agreement with the results of *P-C-T* curves measurement mentioned above. The cycling capacity retention rate, expressed as $S_{70}(\%)=C_{70}/C_{max}\times 100$ (where C_{max} is the maximum discharge capacity, C_{70} is the discharge capacity at the 70th cycles) is also listed in Table 4. It is found that S_{70} is not changed obviously (S_{70} = 50.2—49.6%) with increasing Mn content. In fact, the cycle stability of the alloy electrodes is decreased slightly with increasing x. Although the existence of Co would effectively prevent the corrosion of Mn in La-Mg-Ni-Co-Mn system alloys electrodes, their cycling stability is rather poor and hence has to be upgraded for practical applications.

Table 4　Summary of the electrode performance of $La_{0.7}Mg_{0.3}Ni_{2.975-x}Co_{0.525}Mn_x$ (x=0—0.4) alloy electrodes

Alloys	H/M	C_{max}/(mAh g^{-1})	N_a[a]	HRC_{1200}[b] (%)	HRD_{1200}[c] (%)	S_{70} (%)
x=0.0	0.868	337.6	2	79	64.4	50.2
x=0.1	0.879	342.2	1	81.2	68.5	50.1
x=0.2	0.894	348.7	1	85.3	74.3	49.9
x=0.3	0.912	356.0	1	89.7	81.5	49.7
x=0.4	0.836	326.6	1	82.5	70.7	49.6

[a] The cycle numbers needed to activate the electrodes.

[b] The high rate chargeability at the discharge current density of 1 200 mA g^{-1}.

[c] The high rate dischargeability at the discharge current density of 1 200 mA g^{-1}.

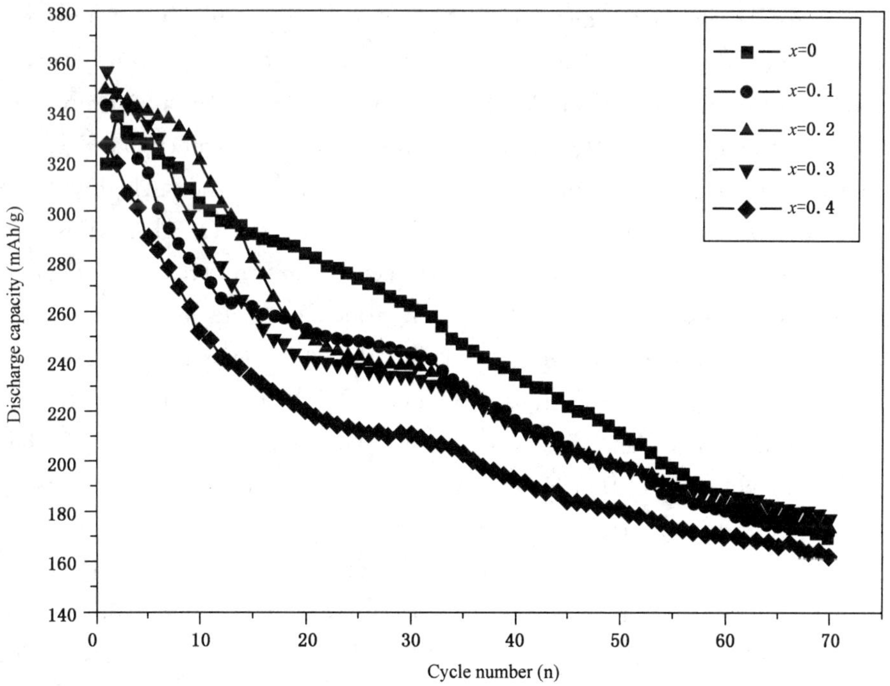

Fig. 5　The cycle life curves of the $La_{0.7}Mg_{0.3}Ni_{2.975-x}Co_{0.525}Mn_x$ (x=0—0.4) alloy electrodes at 298 K

3.4 High rate chargeability and dischargeability

It is very important to restrain the decrease of the discharge capacity even at the high charge/discharge current density for practical application of hydride electrode in Ni-MH battery. The dependence of discharge capacity of the $La_{0.7}Mg_{0.3}Ni_{2.975-x}Co_{0.525}Mn_x$ ($x=0-0.4$) alloy electrodes on current density is shown in Fig. 6. The HRC and HRD of the alloy electrodes at 1 200 mA g^{-1} current density are also listed in Table 4. As expected, the HRC and HRD (taking the discharge capacity at charging/discharging rate of 60 mAg^{-1} as unity) of all the alloy electrodes decays with increasing current density. Nevertheless, the $La_{0.7}Mg_{0.3}Ni_{2.675}Co_{0.525}Mn_{0.3}$ alloy electrode shows the most satisfactory HRC and HRD than that of the other alloy electrodes. Taking the current density being 1 200 mA g^{-1} as an example, the HRC of the alloy electrodes increases from 79% ($x=0$) to 89.7% ($x=0.3$) and then decreases to 82.5% ($x=0.4$), and the HRD of the alloy electrodes increases from 64.4% ($x=0$) to 81.5% ($x=0.3$) and then decreases to 70.7% ($x=0.4$). Those characteristic are quite different to Pan et al.'s results [33]. They pointed out that HRD of the alloy elec-trodes first increases from 66.7% ($x=0.0$) to 70.2% ($x=0.1$) and then decreases to 50.0% with further increase of x. The HRD of the alloy electrodes in their paper are worse than that in our paper. The better HRD can be attributed to two reasons: on the one hand, the $LaNi_5$ phase works not only as a hydrogen reservoir but also as a catalyst to activate the $La(La,Mg)_2Ni_9$ phase to absorb/desorb reversibly hydrogen in the alkaline electrolyte [34]; on the other hand, as Meli et al. [36] has pointed out that when Ni is partially substituted by Mn in rare earth-based hydrogen storage alloys, the dissolution of Mn into electrolyte leads to the increase of Ni content on the alloy surface, which has good electrochemical catalytic property to improve the reaction rate of hydrogen. With increase of Mn content in the alloys, the $LaNi_5$ phase abundance increases, this is bene fi cial to the HRD. However, the total Ni content decreases, which are detrimental to the HRD. Those two contrary factors will result in an optimum Mn content in the alloys. Moreover, we can find that the $LaNi_5$ phase abundance in present paper is much perfect than that in Pan et al.'s study, which will reasonably lead to higher HRD. It is generally accepted that the HRC and HRD of metal hydride electrode are influenced mainly by the electrochemical reaction kinetics on the alloy surface and the diffusion rate of hydrogen in the bulk of the alloy [34]. To examine the effect of the partial substitution of Mn for Ni on the charge and discharge kinetics, linear polarization is preformed on these alloy electrodes. Based on the measured linear polarization curves, values of exchange current density I_0 and polarization resistance R_p was evaluated for the alloy electrodes and are summarized in Table 5. Fig. 7 shows the HRC and HRD as a function of the exchange current density, I_0, for hydrogen evolution reaction of the alloy electrodes. The HRC and HRD show a linear relationship with the exchange density for the electrodes. Moreover, we can find that the hydrogen diffusion coefficient almost unchanged (14.4 − 15.0 × 10^{-10} $cm^2 s^{-1}$). Iwakura et al. [37] have shown that if the electrochemical reaction on the surface is the rate-determining factor, a linear dependence of the high rate dischargeability on the exchange current density should be observed. In contrast, if the diffusion of hydrogen in the bulk is the rate-determining factor, the high rate chargeability/dischargeability should be constant, irrespective of exchange density. Therefore, in the present study, the HRC and HRD are essentially controlled by the charge-transfer reaction of hydrogen on the surface at a discharge current density of 1 200 mAh g^{-1}.

Table 5 The electrochemical kinetic parameters of $La_{0.7}Mg_{0.3}Ni_{2.975-x}Co_{0.525}Mn_x$ (x=0−0.4) alloy electrodes

Samples	Polarization resistance, R_p (mΩ)		Exchange current density, I_0 (mA g^{-1})		Hydrogen diffusion coefficient, D($\times 10^{-10}$ cm^2 s^{-1})	
	298 K	233 K	298 K	233 K	298 K	233 K
x=0	130.6	466.3	198.7	43.0	14.4	0.9
x=0.1	124.1	461.5	209.1	43.6	14.5	1.7
x=0.2	107.2	459.4	242.1	43.8	14.6	2.1
x=0.3	94.6	455.6	274.0	44.1	14.8	2.7
x=0.4	117.3	454.0	221.2	44.1	15.0	3.5

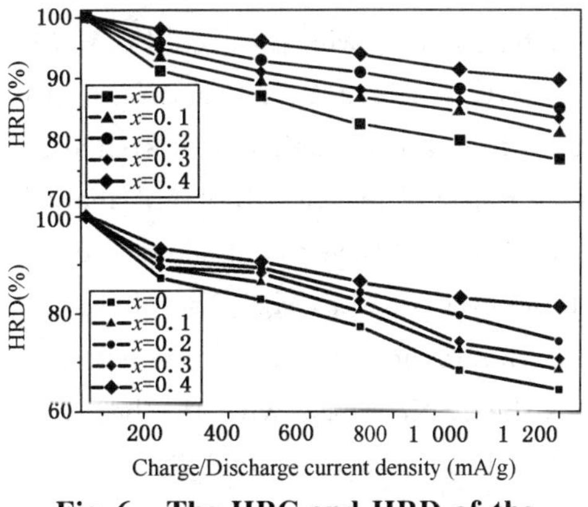

Fig. 6　The HRC and HRD of the $La_{0.7}Mg_{0.3}Ni_{2.975-x}Co_{0.525}Mn_x$ (x=0−0.4) alloy electrodes

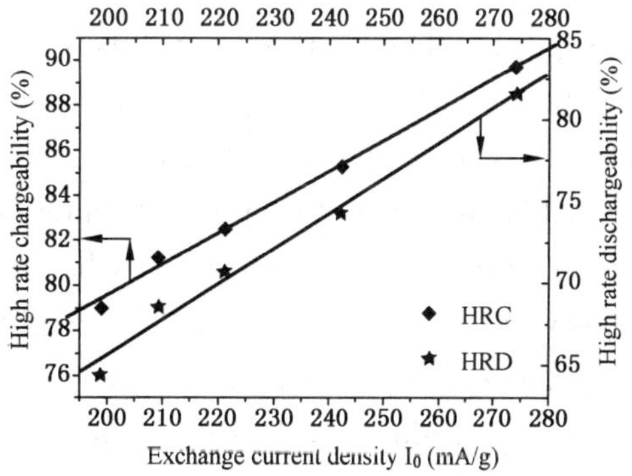

Fig. 7　HRC and HRD at 1 200 mA g^{-1} of $La_{0.7}Mg_{0.3}Ni_{2.975-x}Co_{0.525}Mn_x$ (x=0−0.4) alloy electrodes as a function of exchange current density

3.5 Low-temperature dischargeability (LTD)

It has been reported that the discharge capacity of the negative electrode in nickel-metal hydride decrease drastically with decreasing temperature [38]. Sakai et al. has [2] pointed out that the dischargeability of the negative electrodes at relative low temperature depended on the hydrogen diffusion and/or charge-transfer process occurring at the metal electrolyte interface. The hydrogen diffusion coefficient (D) of hydrogen in the bulk is evaluated using the method described by Iwakura et al. [39]. The LTD, expressed as $LTD_{233}(\%) = C_{233}/C_{298} \times 100$ (where C_{233} and C_{298} are the discharge capacity at 233 and 298 K, respectively). The D and I_0 of the $La_{0.7}Mg_{0.3}Ni_{2.975-x}Co_{0.525}Mn_x$ ($x=0, 0.1, 0.2, 0.3, 0.4$) alloy electrodes at 233 K are also listed in Table 5, respectively. It can found that both the I_0 and the D are smaller than that at 298 K. Moreover, we can find that the I_0 maintain almost unchanged (43.0—44.1 mA g^{-1}), whereas the D increases remarkably with increasing x, which implies that the hydrogen diffusion in alloy probably becomes the rate-determining factor for low-temperature dischargeability at 233 K. Zhao et al. [40] thought that desorption of hydrogen in metal hydride is an endothermal reaction and may be a rate-limiting step during the discharge process of metal hydride at relatively low temperature (for example, at 233 K). Fig. 8 shows the LTD as a function of D in the alloy electrodes. It can be easily found that the D increases with the increase of x, which can be attributed to the cell volume expansion with increasing x as shown in Table 3. The larger D, the larger LTD of the alloy electrodes.

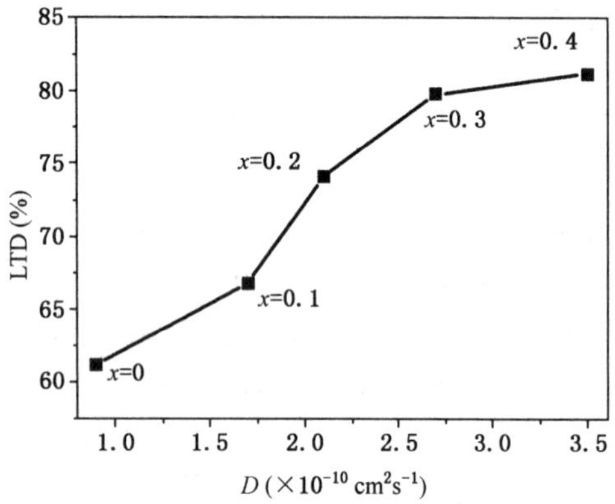

Fig. 8 The low-temperature dischargeability (LTD) as a function of hydrogen diffusion coefficient (D) of the $La_{0.7}Mg_{0.3}Ni_{2.975-x}Co_{0.525}Mn_x$ ($x=0, 0.1, 0.2, 0.3, 0.4$) alloy electrodes at 233 K

4 Conclusion

The effects of Mn content on the structure and the electrochemical characteristics of $La_{0.7}Mg_{0.3}Ni_{2.975-x}Co_{0.525}Mn_x$ ($x=0, 0.1, 0.2, 0.3, 0.4$) hydrogen storage alloys are investigated systematically. It is found by XRD Rietveld analy-sis that all these alloys mainly consist of two phases: the $La(La, Mg)_2Ni_9$ phase with the rhombohedral $PuNi_3$-type structure and the $LaNi_5$ phase with the hexagonal $CaCu_5$-type structure. *P-C-T* curves reveal that the plateau pressure decreases progressively and the hydrogen storage capacity increases first and thendecreases with increasing Mn content in the alloys. The electrochemical measurements show that the maximum discharge capacity of the alloy electrode increases first from 337. 6 mAh g^{-1} (x=0) to 356 mAh g^{-1} (x=0. 3) and then decreases to 326. 6 mAh g^{-1} (x = 0. 4). For a discharge current density of 1 200 mA g^{-1}, the HRC of the alloy electrodes increases from 79% (x=0) to 89. 7% (x=0. 3) and then decreases to 82. 5% (x=0. 4), and the HRD of the alloy electrodes increases from 64. 4% (x=0) to 81. 5% (x=0. 3) and then decreases to 70. 7% (x=0. 4). Linear polarization shows that the exchange current density I_0 first increases from 198. 7 mA g^{-1} (x=0) to 274. 0 mA g^{-1} (x=0. 3) and then decreases to 221. 2 mA g^{-1} (x=0. 4) with increasing Mn content, which suggests that the electrochemical kinetics of the alloy electrodes first increase and then decrease when Ni is partially substituted by Mn in the alloys. The D increases with increasing Mn content and thus increases the low temperature dischargeability LTD of the alloy electrodes.

Acknowledgement

This work was financially supported by the National Natural Science Foundation of China (Grant No. 20171042).

References

[1] M. Latroche, A. Percheron-Guegan, J. Alloys Compd. 356-357(2003)461.

[2] J. J. G. Willems, K. H. J. Buschow, J. Less-Common Met. 129(1987)13.

[3] T. Sakai, H. Miyamura, N. Kuriyama, A. Kato, K. Oguro, H. Ishikawa, J. Electrochem. Soc. 137(1990)795.

[4] T. Kohno, H. Yoshida, F. Kawashima, T. Inaba, I. Sakai, M. Ya-mamoto, M. Kanda, J. Alloys Compd. 311(2000)L5.

[5] J. J. G. Willems, Philips J. Res. 39(Suppl. 1)(1984)1.

[6] H. G. Pan, Y. F. Zhu, M. X. Gao, Q. D. Wang, J. Electrochem. Soc. 149(2002)A829.

[7] J. Chen, N. Kuriyama, H. T. Takeshita, H. Tanaka, T. Sakai, M. Haruta, Electrochem. Solid-State Lett. 3(6)(2000)249.

[8] H. Ogawa, M. Ikoma, H. Kawano, I. Matsumoto, J. Power Sources 12(1988)393.

[9] S. R. Ovshinsky, M. A. Fetcenko, J. Ross. Sci. 260(1993)176.

[10] J. J. Reilly, in: J. O. Besenhard(Ed.), Handbook of Battery Materials, Wiley, New York, 2000.

[11] H. Oesterreicher, J. Clinton, H. Bittner, Mater. Res. Bull. 11(1976)1241.

[12] H. Oesterreicher, K. Ensslen, A. Kerlin, E. Bucher, Mater. Res. Bull. 15(1980)275.

[13] K. Kadir, T. Sakai, I. Uahara, J. Alloys Compd. 257(1997)115.

[14] K. Kadir, N. Nuriyama, T. Sakai, I. Uehara, L. Eriksson, J. Alloys Compd. 284(1999)145.

[15] K. Kadir, T. Sakai, I. Uahara, J. Alloys Compd. 287(1999)264.

[16] K. Kadir, T. Sakai, I. Uahara, J. Alloys Compd. 302(2000)112.

[17] J. Chen, H. T. Takeshita, H. Tanaka, N. Kuriyama, T. Sakai, J. Alloys Compd. 302(2000)304.

[18] H. G. Pan, Y. F. Liu, M. X. Gao, Y. F. Zhu, Y. Q. Lei, Q. D. Wang, J. Alloys Compd. 351(2003)228.

[19] J. M. Wu, J. Li, W. P. Zhang, F. J. Muo, L. C. Tai, R. G. Xu, J. Alloys Compd. 248(1997)180.

[20] P. H. L. Notten, M. Latroche, A. Percheron-Guegan, J. Electrochem. Soc. 146 (9) (1999) 3181.

[21] W. E. Wallace, F. Pourarlan, J. Phys. Chem. 86 (1982) 4958.

[22] J. X. Ma, H. G. Pan, C. P. Chen, Q. D. Wang, J. Alloys Compd. 343 (2002) 164.

[23] A. Apostolov, N. Stanev, P. Tcholakov, J. Less-Common Met. 110 (1985) 127.

[24] C. Lartigue, A. Percheron-Gu′egan, J. C. Achard, J. Less-Common Met. 75 (1980) 23.

[25] J. J. Reilly, G. D. Adzic, J. R. Johnson, T. Vogt, S. Mukerjee, J. McBreen, J. Alloys Compd. 293-295 (1999) 569.

[26] T. Sakai, K. Oguro, H. Miyamura, A. Kato, H. Ishikawa, J. Less-Common Met. 161 (1990) 193.

[27] H. Ogawa, M. Ikoma, J. Power Sources 12 (1998) 393.

[28] A. Percheron-Gu′egan, C. Lartigue, J. C. Achard, J. Less-Common Met. 109 (1985) 287.

[29] C. J. Howard, J. Appl. Cryst. 15 (1982) 615.

[30] X. B. Zhang, Y. J. Chai, W. Y. Yin, M. S. Zhao, J. Solid State Chem. 177 (2004) 2373.

[31] D. N. Gruen, M. H. Mendelsohn, A. E. Dwight, J. Less-Common Met. 161 (1977) 193.

[32] H. G. Pan, Q. W. Jin, M. X. Gao, Y. F. Liu, R. Li, Y. Q. Lei, J. Alloys Compd. 373 (2004) 237.

[33] H. G. Pan, Y. F. Liu, M. X. Gao, Y. F. Zhu, Y. Lei, Q. Wang, J. Elec-trochem. Soc. 151 (2004) A374.

[34] H. G. Pan, Y. F. Liu, M. X. Gao, Y. Q. Lei, Q. D. Wang, J. Electrochem. Soc. 150 (5) (2003) A565.

[35] Y. F. Liu, H. G. Pan, M. X. Gao, Y. F. Zhu, Y. Q. Lei, Q. D. Wang, Int. J. Hydrogen Energy 29 (2004) 297.

[36] F. Meli, A. Zuttel, L. Schlabach, J. Alloys Compd. 202 (1993) 81.

[37] C. Iwakura, T. Oura, H. Inoue, M. Matsuoka, Electrochim. Acta 41 (1996) 117.

[38] H. Senoh, Y. Hara, H. Inoue, C. Iwakura, Electrochim. Acta 46 (2001) 967.

[39] C. Iwakura, H. Senoh, K. Morimoto, Y. Hara, H. Inoue, Electro-chemistry 70 (1) (2002) 2.

[40] M. Zhao, C. Sun, in: T. Nejet Vezirogle, et al. (Eds.), II. Materials, Physics and Chemistry, vol. 82, Kluwer Academic Publisher, 2002, p. 29.

Crystallographic and Electrochemical Characteristics of $La_{0.7}Mg_{0.3}Ni_{3-x}(Al_{0.5}Mo_{0.5})_x$ (x=0—0.4) Hydrogen Storage Alloys①

X. B. Zhang[a], D. Z. Sun[b], W. Y. Yina, Y. J. Chai[a], M. S. Zhao[a]

([a] Key Laboratory of Rare Earth Chemistry and Physics, Changchun Institute of Applied Chemistry, Chinese Academy of Sciences, Graduate School of Chinese Academy of Sciences, Changchun 130022, PR China)

([b] State Key Laboratory of Electro-analytical Chemistry, Changchun Institute of Applied Chemistry, Chinese Academy of Sciences, Graduate School of Chinese Academy of Sciences, Changchun 130022, PR China)

Abstract: The effect of partial substitution of Al and Mo for Ni on the structure and electrochemical properties of the $La_{0.7}Mg_{0.3}Ni_{3-x}(Al_{0.5}Mo_{0.5})_x$ (x=0—0.4) hydrogen storage alloys have been investigated systematically. The result of X-ray powder diffraction (XRD) and Rietveld analysis show that all the alloys consist of the $La(La,Mg)_2Ni_9$ phase and the $LaNi_5$ phase. Meanwhile, the lattice parameter and the cell volume of both the $La(La,Mg)_2Ni_9$ phase and the $LaNi_5$ phase increase with increasing Al and Mo contents in the alloys. The pressure composition isotherms curves indicate that the hydrogen storage capacity first increases and then decreases with increasing x. The electrochemical measurements show that the maximum discharge capacity of the alloy electrodes first increases from 343.3 (x=0) to 377.6 mAh/g (x=0.3) and then decreases to 350.4 mAh/g (x=0.4). Moreover, the high rate dischargeability (HRD) and the exchange current density of the alloy electrodes decrease first and then increases with the increase of x in the alloys. The hydrogen diffusion coefficient increases with increasing Al and Mo content and thus increases the low temperature dischargeability (LTD) of the alloy electrodes.

Key words: Hydrogen storage alloy; Metal hydride electrode; Crystal structure; Electrochemical properties

1 Introduction

Hydrogen is expected to be a promising new energy source to replace conventional fossil for solving shortage of fossil energy resources and global warming in near future. In order for hydrogen to become a viable solution to the energy crisis and the environmental problem the hydrogen storage is one of many important processes. Among different ways to store hydrogen, absorption in solid to form hydride is very attractive

① Electrochimica Acta, 2005(50): 3407-3413.

since it allows safe storage at pressure and temper-ature close to ambient conditions [1]. It is the most successful for the metal hydrides to be applied as a negative electrode material in many application fields of metal hydrides. Nickel metal hydride (Ni-MH) secondary battery has been widely adopted in various portable electronic devices, electric hand tools and hybrid electric vehicles [2-6]. To date, almost all commercial Ni-MH batteries are employing AB_5-type alloys as the negative electrode materials [7]. However, the electrochemical capacity of the AB_5-type alloys is limited by the single CaCu5-type hexagonal structure [8], the energy densities of the Ni-MH batteries are not competing favorably with some other advanced secondary batteries. Therefore, it is necessary to search for new type alloys with much high energy density, better rate dischargeability and lower cost, which perhaps may be alternative for the conventional rare earth-based AB_5-type alloys or another choice [9].

Recently, R-Mg-Ni (R = rare earth element, Ca or Y) system hydrogen storage electrode for Ni-MH batteries have attracted considerable attention because of their higher hydrogen storage capacities (absorb-desorb 1.8—1.87 wt% H2) than of the $LaNi_5$ alloy (absorb-desorb 1.4 wt% H_2) [10-14]. As to their electrochemical hydrogen storage, Chen et al. [6] found that the maximum discharge capacity of $LaCaMgNi_9$ alloy reached 356 mAh/g. Kohno et al. [15] have studied the structure and electrochemical characteristics of La-Mg-(NiCo)x (x = 3—3.5) system alloys and found that $La_{0.7}Mg_{0.3}Ni_{2.8}Co_{0.5}$ alloy reached 410 mAh/g. Although the La-Mg-Ni-Co alloy has high hydrogen storage capacity, the cyclic stability is too low to be used as negative material of the Ni-MH secondary batteries [16], and hence their cycling stability has to be upgraded for practical applications. In commercial AB_5-type alloys the presence of 10 wt% of Co has indeed improved the cycling life of Ni-MH batteries. However, it influences negatively the discharge capacity as well as initial activation and it constitutes about 40% of the material cost [17]. Much effort has been devoted to search for cheaper substitute element with high reliability to improve the cycling life of Ni-MH batteries. It is believed that Al is one of the best candidates for cobalt substitution [18]. However, Al addition is detrimental to hydrogen diffusion from electrode surface to alloy bulk and thus inevitably decrease the high rate dischargeability (HRD) of alloy electrode [19]. It is reported that Mo addition can remarkably increase the kinetic property [20] as well as the electrochemical capacity of alloy electrode [21]. Therefore, it can be expected that the overall electrochemical properties of the La-Mg-Ni type hydrogen storage alloys could be improved by substitution of Al and Mo for Ni in the alloys.

In present study, the structure and electrochemical characteristics of the $La_{0.7}Mg_{0.3}Ni_{3-x}(Al_{0.5}Mo_{0.5})_x$ (x = 0 —

0.4) hydrogen storage alloys has been investigated systematically.

2 Experimental details

2.1 Alloy preparation and X-ray diffraction analysis

All alloys were prepared by arc-melting carefully the constituent elements with the purity all above 99.9% on a water-cooled copper hearth under argon atmosphere. A slight excess of Mg over composition was needed to compensate for evaporative loss of Mg under preparation conditions. The alloys were turned over and remelted five times to ensure the good homogeneity. The weight loss of the alloys is less than 1 mass% during melting. Therefore, no chemical analyses were carried out. Thereafter, the alloy samples were crushed in mortar intofine powders of -300 meshes powder.

Crystallographic characteristics of the hydrogen storage alloys were investigated by X-ray diffraction on Rigaku D/Max 2500PC X-ray diffractometer (Cu Kα radiation, Bragg-Brentano geometry, 2θ range 10—100°, step size 0.02°, 4 s per step, backscattered rear graphite monochromator). The lattice constants and cell volume were calculated by Rietica program [22]. Silicon is used as standard reference material to calibrate the instrument before we obtain the XRD data.

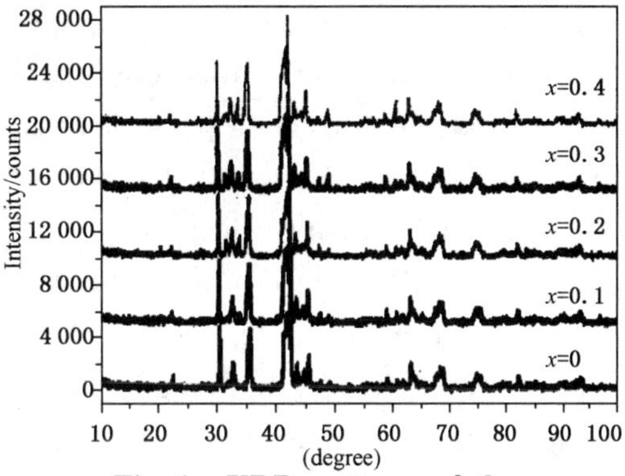

Fig. 1 XRD patterns of the $La_{0.7}Mg_{0.3}Ni_{3-x}(Al_{0.5}Mo_{0.5})_x$ hydrogen storage alloy

2.2 Electrochemical measurement

The preparation of the disk-type electrodes, the set-up of the electrochemical cell and the measurement of electrochemical properties were similar as described in our previous paper [23]. Pressure-composition isotherms (P-C-T) curves, HRD, linear polarization curves and coefficient of diffusion of the alloy electrodes were measured according to our previous paper [24].

3 Results and discussion

3.1 Crystal structure

The X-ray diffraction patterns of the $La_{0.7}Mg_{0.3}Ni_{3-x}(Al_{0.5}Mo_{0.5})_x$ ($x=0-0.4$) hydrogen storage alloys are shown in Fig. 1. It can be seen that all alloys have similar diffraction patterns, which indicates that the structure of the alloys almost unchanged with increasing Al and

Mo content in the alloys. Moreover, careful examination of the diffraction angle reveals that the diffraction peaks shift to lower angles as a function of the increase of Al and Mo content in the alloys. Fig. 2 shows the XRD pattern and Rietveld analysis pattern of the $La_{0.7}Mg_{0.3}Ni_{2.9}(Al_{0.5}Mo_{0.5})_{0.1}$ hydrogen storage alloy as a representative example of $La_{0.7}Mg_{0.3}Ni_{3-x}(Al_{0.5}Mo_{0.5})_x$ ($x=0-0.4$) hydrogen storage alloys. It can be seen that the calculated pattern by Rietveld method is in good agreement with the observed patterns. Besides small amount of LaNi phase, all alloys consist of a La_2MgNi_9 phase with a $PuNi_3$-type rhombohedral structure and a $LaNi_5$ phase with a $CaCu_5$-type hexagonal structure. The final Rietveld structure parameter of the La_2MgNi_9 phase is tabulated in Table 1. The crystallographic results reveal that La atoms in La_2MgNi_9 can locate both at the $3a$ site and at the $6c$ site, while Mg atoms can only locate the $6c$ site, indicating that the alloy is a ordered compound with the same structure as the previously reported RMg_2Ni_9 (R=La, Ca, Y) alloys. So the final forum of La_2MgNi_9 phase can be designated as $La(La,Mg)_2Ni_9$. The lattice parameter, cell volume, and phase abundance of various phases of the hydrogen storage alloys are listed in Table 2. Variations of the cell parameters and volumes as a function of x in the alloys are shown in Fig. 3. It can be seen that a and c parameters of both the $La(La,Mg)_2Ni_9$ phase and the $LaNi_5$ phase in the alloys increase linearly with the increase of x, which is mainly ascribed to the fact that the atomic radius of Al(1.432 Å) and

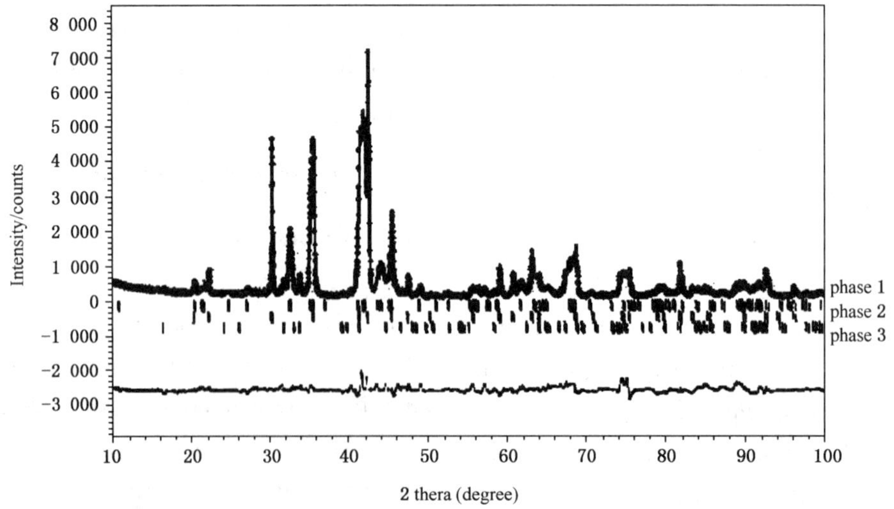

Fig. 2　Rietveld refinement pattern of the XRD profiles for the $La_{0.7}Mg_{0.3}Ni_{2.9}(Al_{0.5}Mo_{0.5})_{0.1}$ hydrogen storage alloy (phase 1: $La(La,Mg)_2Ni_9$; phase 2: LaNi5; phase 3: LaNi)

Mo (1.363 Å) is larger than that of Ni (1.246 Å). The Fig. 4 shows the abundances of the $La(La,Mg)_2Ni_9$ phase and the $LaNi_5$ phase as a function of x in the alloys. It can be seen that the La(La, Mg)$_2$Ni$_9$ phase abundance decrease from 79.56% to 60.16% with increasing of x, however the LaNi$_5$ phase abundance increases from 16.64% to 30.64%. These results will influence the hydrogen storage and electrochemical characteristics of the alloys studied.

Table 1 Crystallographic parameters for La$_2$MgNi$_9$ by using X-ray diffraction Cu Kα. 1 (λ=1.540 598 1 Å) at 298 K in a space group *R*-3*m* and *Z*=3[a]

Atom	Site	Metal atom position			Occupancy
		x	y	z	
La1	3a	0	0	0	1
La2	6c	0	0	0.146 69(11)	0.487
Mg1	6c	0	0	0.146 69(11)	0.513
Ni1	6c	0	0	0.328 1(7)	1
Ni2	3b	0	0	0.5	1
Ni3	18h	0.498 7(3)	0.498 8(6)	0.083 27(16)	1

[a] Structure was refined by using the Rietveld refinement program Rietica. The pattern factor R_p = 6.7, the weighted pattern factor R_{wp} = 9.0 and the goodness of fit S=2.5.

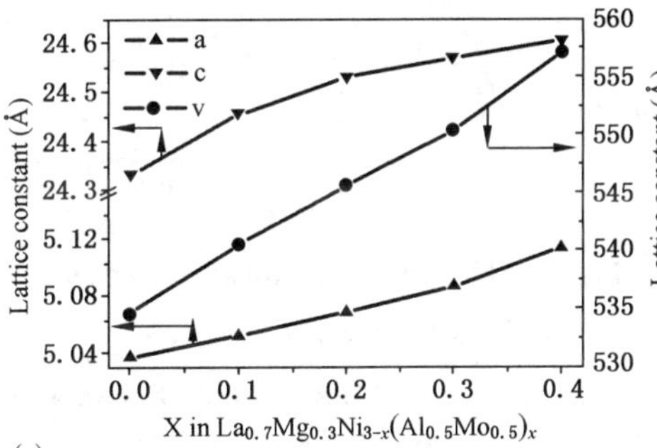

(a)

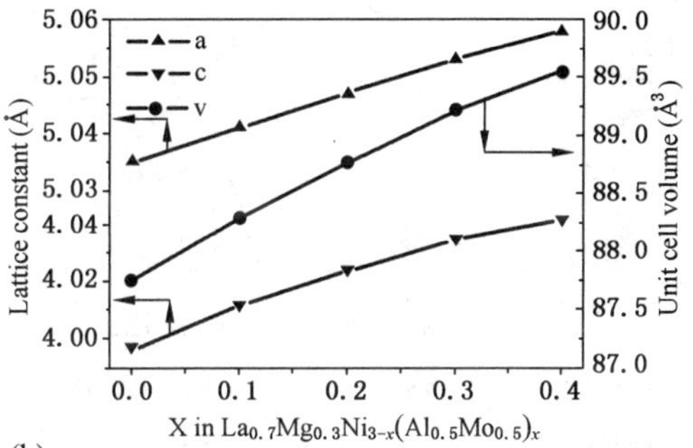

(b)

Fig. 3 Variations of the cell parameters and volumes as the function of x in La$_{0.7}$Mg$_{0.3}$Ni$_{3-x}$(Al$_{0.5}$Mo$_{0.5}$)$_x$ hydrogen storage alloys (x=0−0.4)

Table 2 Characteristics of alloy phases in La$_{0.7}$Mg$_{0.3}$Ni$_{3-x}$(Al$_{0.5}$Mo$_{0.5}$)$_x$ (x=0−0.4) alloys[a]

Sample	Phase	Phase abundance (wt%)	Lattice parameter (Å)			Cell volume (Å)
			a	b	c	
x=0.0	La(La,Mg)$_2$Ni$_9$	79.56	5.037	5.037	24.331	534.61
	LaNi$_5$	16.64	5.035	5.035	3.997	87.75
	LaNi	3.8	3.821	11.002	4.454	187.24
x=0.1	La(La,Mg)$_2$Ni$_9$	74.82	5.052	5.052	24.455	540.54
	LaNi$_5$	20.68	5.041	5.041	4.012	88.29
	LaNi	4.5	3.823	11.004	4.457	187.5
x=0.2	La(La,Mg)$_2$Ni$_9$	69.98	5.068	5.068	24.530	545.63
	LaNi$_5$	23.62	5.047	5.047	4.024	88.77
	LaNi	6.4	3.827	11.009	4.459	187.86

Continued

Sample	Phase	Phase abundance (wt%)	Lattice parameter (Å)			Cell volume (Å)
			a	b	c	
x=0.3	La(La,Mg)$_2$Ni$_9$	66.77	5.086	5.086	24.568	550.37
	LaNi$_5$	25.43	5.053	5.053	4.035	89.22
	LaNi	7.8	3.831	11.013	4.461	188.21
x=0.4	La(La,Mg)$_2$Ni$_9$	60.16	5.113	5.113	24.606	557.09
	LaNi$_5$	30.64	5.058	5.058	4.042	89.55
	LaNi	9.2	3.836	11.021	4.464	188.72

[a] The Rietveld refinement program RIETICA was used.

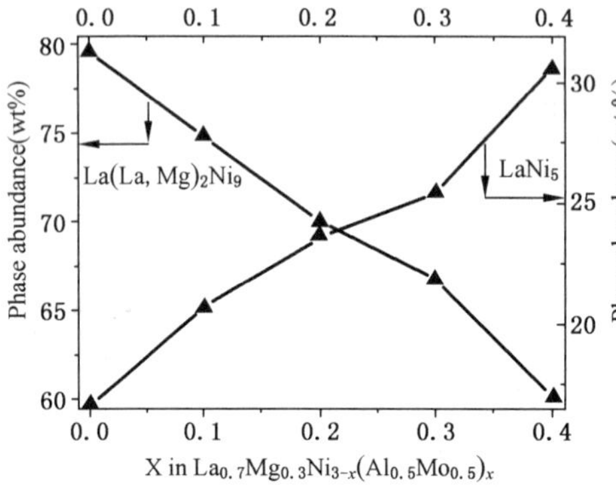

Fig. 4　Phase abundance of the La(La,Mg)$_2$Ni$_9$ phase and the LaNi$_5$ phase existing in the La$_{0.7}$Mg$_{0.3}$Ni$_{3-x}$(Al$_{0.5}$Mo$_{0.5}$)$_x$(x=0−0.4) alloys

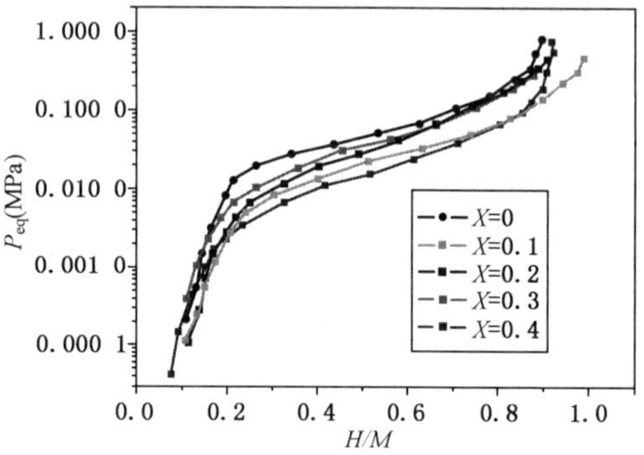

Fig. 5　The electrochemical desorption P-C-T curves for La$_{0.7}$Mg$_{0.3}$Ni$_{3-x}$(Al$_{0.5}$Mo$_{0.5}$)$_x$(x=0,0.1,0.2,0.3,0.4) alloys at 298 K

3.2　P-C isotherms

Fig. 5 shows the hydrogen desorption electrochemical pressure-composition isotherms (P-C-T) of the La$_{0.7}$Mg$_{0.3}$Ni$_{3-x}$(Al$_{0.5}$Mo$_{0.5}$)$_x$(x=0,0.1,0.2,0.3,0.4) alloy electrodes at 298 K. It can be seen that the desorption pressure reduces continually as the Al and Mo additions increase. This means that the stability of the hydrides of alloys increases with the increasing Al and Mo content in the alloys. This is because of the unit cell volume of the alloys increases with increasing Al and Mo additions in the alloys. Moreover, Oesterreicher et al. pointed out that the unit cell of the AB$_3$ compounds contains one-third AB$_5$ structure and two-thirds AB$_2$ structure [10]. Therefore, we can assume that the plateau pressure of the La(La, Mg)$_2$Ni$_9$ phase is similar to that of the LaNi$_5$ phase or the difference between their plateau pressures of AB$_3$ and AB$_5$ compounds is too small to be observed. The plateau characteristic of the P-C-T curve shown in Fig. 5 gives evidence of our supposition. With the increase of Al and Mo content in the alloy, the hydrogen storage capacity increases from 0.899 to 0.991. This is mainly attributed to the decrease in plateau pressure which enhances the intrinsic hydrogen storage capacity of alloys. However, when x further increase to 0.4, the hydrogen storage capacity decreases to 0.921, which can be attributed to the change in the relative amounts of $La(La,Mg)_2Ni_9$ phase and $LaNi_5$ phase owing to Al and Mo substitution. According to the work of Oesterreicher et al. [25], the hydrogen storage capacity of the $LaNi_3$ phase is larger than that of the $LaNi_5$ phase. Therefore, with the decrease of the $La(La,Mg)_2Ni_9$ phase in the alloys, the hydrogen storage capacity would decrease accordingly.

Table 3　Summary of the electrode performance of $La_{0.7}Mg_{0.3}Ni_{3-x}(Al_{0.5}Mo_{0.5})_x$ (x=0−0.4) alloy electrodes

Samples	H/M	C_{max}(mAh/g)	N_a^a	HRD_{1200}^b(%)	S_{70}(%)
x=0.0	0.899	343.3	2	61.3	49.3
x=0.1	0.926	353.5	3	59.2	55.7
x=0.2	0.944	359.8	3	69.8	60.5
x=0.3	0.991	377.6	2	77.6	64.4
x=0.4	0.921	350.4	2	81.2	68.8

[a] The cycle numbers needed to activate the electrodes.

[b] The high rate dischargeability at the discharge current density of 1 200 mA/g.

3.3　Discharge capacity and discharge potential

The cycle numbers needed for activation and maximum discharge capacity of the $La_{0.7}Mg_{0.3}Ni_{3-x}(Al_{0.5}Mo_{0.5})_x$ (x=0, 0.1, 0.2, 0.3, 0.4) alloy electrodes are listed in Table 3. It can be seen that all these alloys can be easily activated to reach the maximum capacity within three cycles, which means that activation of La-Mg-Ni-Al-Mo alloy electrodes is easy. The maximum discharge capacities of the alloy electrodes first increases from 343.3 mAh/g (x=0) to 377.6 mAh/g (x=0.3) and then decreases to 350.4 mAh/g (x=0.4) when Al and Mo content increases from 0 to 0.4, which is basically consistent with the results of the P-C-T measurement mentioned above. Fig. 6 shows the discharge curves of the 4th cycle for the alloy electrodes at 60 mA/g and 298 K. It can be easily seen that each curve has a wide discharge potential plateau based on the oxidation of desorbed hydrogen from the hydride. It should be noted that the discharge plateau shifts towards a more positive potential as Al and Mo additions increase in the alloys, indicating that the partial substitution of Al and Mo leads to an increase in discharge overpotential of the alloy electrode at different extent.

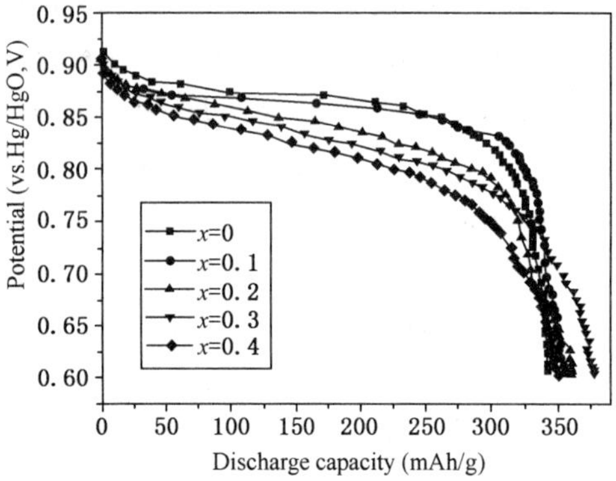

Fig. 6　The discharge curves of $La_{0.7}Mg_{0.3}Ni_{3-x}(Al_{0.5}Mo_{0.5})x(x=0-0.4)$ alloy electrodes at the discharge current density of 60 mA/g and 298 K

3.4　Cyclic stability

The cyclic capacity retention rate after 70 cycles at 60 mA/g, expressed as $S_{70}(\%)=C_{70}/C_{max}\times 100$ (where C_{max} is the maximum discharge capacity, C_{70} is the discharge capacity at the 70 th cycles), is also listed in Table 3. It can be seen that the S_{70} of the alloy electrodes increases noticeably from 49.3% to 68.8% with x increasing from 0 to 0.4, indicating that the cyclic stability of the La-Mg-Ni system alloys is improved markedly along with the increase of Al and Mo content in the alloys. As reported previously [2,5], the formation of passive layer of $La(OH)_3$ and $Mg(OH)_2$ on the alloy surface is ascribed as the main cause of cycling capacity degradation, because such a layer decreases the content of hydrogen absorption elements La and Mg in the alloys and thus reduces hydrogen storage capacity of the alloy. It is known that Al substitution results in the formation of protective oxide (hydroxide) of Al on the alloy surface and a subsequent strong protection to the alloy from further corrosion of La and Mg [26,27]; therefore results in an obviously increase of cycling capacity retention rate of the alloy electrodes. Further investigations in this aspect are going on in our research group.

3.5　High rate dischargeability and electrochemical kinetics

It is very important to restrain the decrease of the discharge capacity even at the high charge/discharge current density. Fig. 7 shows the relationship between the high rate dischargeability and discharge current density of the $La_{0.7}Mg_{0.3}Ni_{3-x}(Al_{0.5}Mo_{0.5})_x$ $(x=0-0.4)$ alloy electrodes. To make the comparison more exact, the HRD of the alloy electrodes for the discharge current density of 1 200 mA/g are also listed in Table 3. It can be seen that as the x increases, the HRD of the alloy electrodes decreases first from

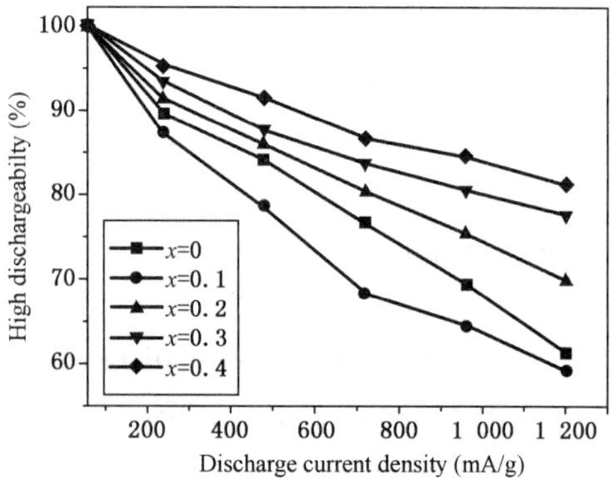

Fig. 7　High rate dischargeability of the $La_{0.7}Mg_{0.3}Ni_{3-x}(Al_{0.5}Mo_{0.5})_x$ $(x=0,0.1,0.2,0.3,0.4)$ alloy electrodes at 298 K

61.3% ($x=0$) to 59.2% ($x=0.1$), and then increases to 81.2% ($x=0.4$). As mentioned above, Al substitution is prone to form a passive layer on the electrode surface in KOH electrolyte, which inevitably weakens the surface electrochemical catalytic activity and prevents the diffusion of hydrogen into or from the alloy bulk. Fortunately, it is reported that the addition of Mo to the alloy leads to the improvement of the electrocatalytic activity on the alloy surface [20]. Therefore, it is reasonable to assume that, with Al and Mo content addition of lower than a certain amount, the negative effect of Al is dominant and will cause a decrease in the HRD. However, when Al and Mo content exceed the critical content, the positive effect of Mo will become dominant and will give rise to increase of HRD. It present study, the critical content amount of Al and Mo addition is $x=0.2$ from our work.

It is generally accepted that the HRD of metal hydride electrode is determined jointly by the exchange current density and the diffusion coefficient of hydrogen [28]. To e xamine the effect of the partial substitution of Al and Mo for Ni on the discharge kinetics, linear polarization is preformed on these alloy electrodes. Based on the measured linear polarization curves, values of exchange current density I_0 and polarization resistance R_p were calculated for the alloy electrodes and summarized in Table 4. Fig. 8 shows HRD and R_p as a function of I_0 for the hydrogen evolution reaction at the alloy electrodes. The HRD shows a linear relationship with the exchange density for the alloy electrodes. Moreover, we can find that the hydrogen diffusion coefficient D maintains almost unchanged (12.3−13.1×10.10 cm^2/s). Therefore, in the present study, the HRD is essentially controlled by the charge-transfer reaction of hydrogen on the surface at a discharge current density of 1 200 mAh/g. In addition, it can be seen that the R_P decreases with increasing I_0 while the high rate dischargeability increases reversely, implying that the R_P value is closed related to the HRD.

Table 4　Electrochemical kinetic parameter of $La_{0.7}Mg_{0.3}Ni_{3-x}(Al_{0.5}Mo_{0.5})_x$ ($x=0-0.4$) alloy electrodes

Sample	Polarization resistance, R_p (mΩ)		Exchange current density, I_0 (mA/g)		Hydrogen diffusion coefficient, D (×10^{-10} cm^2/s)	
	298K	233K	298K	233K	298K	233K
$x=0$	102.42	363.60	224.38	55.15	12.3	1.3
$x=0.1$	103.83	359.04	221.33	55.85	12.3	2.4
$x=0.2$	94.24	353.54	243.85	56.72	12.7	2.9
$x=0.3$	89.95	352.54	255.5	56.88	12.8	3.8
$x=0.4$	88.83	349.65	258.71	57.35	13.1	4.9

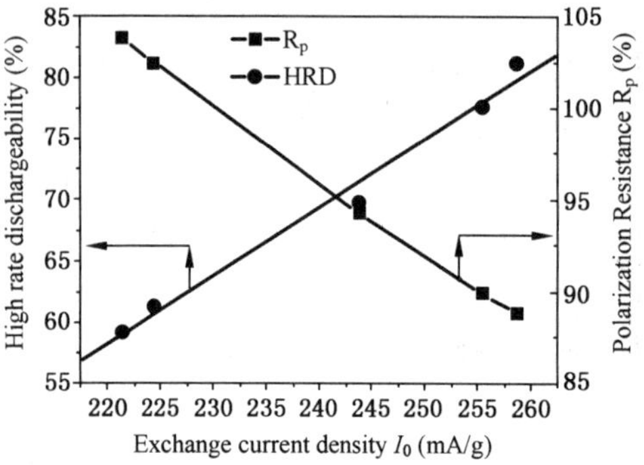

Fig. 8 High rate dischargeability and polarization resistance as a func-tion of exchange current density for hydrogen evolution reaction at $La_{0.7}Mg_{0.3}Ni_{3-x}(Al_{0.5}Mo_{0.5})_x$ (x=0—0.4) alloy electrodes

3.6 Low temperature dischargeability (LTD)

Ni-MH battery is expected to be capable of working at temperature down to 233 K in some civil applications at very cold areas [29]. However, the discharge capacity of the negative electrode in nickel-metal hydride decreases drastically with decreasing temperature [30]. Sakai et al. [19] pointed out that the dischargeability of the negative electrodes at relative low temperature is mainly influenced by the hydrogen diffusion and charge-transfer process occurring at the metal electrolyte interface. The hydrogen D of hydrogen in the bulk is measured using the method described by Iwakura et al. [20]. The LTD, expressed as LTD_{233} (%) $=C_{233}/C_{298}\times 100$ (where C_{233} and C_{298} are the discharge capacity at 233 and 298 K, respectively). The D and the I_0 of the $La_{0.7}Mg_{0.3}Ni_{3-x}(Al_{0.5}Mo_{0.5})_x$ (x=0, 0.1, 0.2, 0.3, 0.4) alloy electrodes at 233 K are also tabulated in Table 4. It can found that both the I_0 and the D are smaller than that at 298 K. Moreover, we canfind that the I_0 maintain almost unchanged (55.15—57.35 mA/g); whereas the D increases remarkably with increasing x, which implies that the hydrogen diffusion in alloy probably becomes the rate-determining factor for Low-temperature dischargeability at 233 K. Fig. 9 shows the LTD as a function of D in the alloy electrodes. It can be easily found that the D increases monotonically with increasing x in the alloys, and thus increases the LTD of the alloy electrodes.

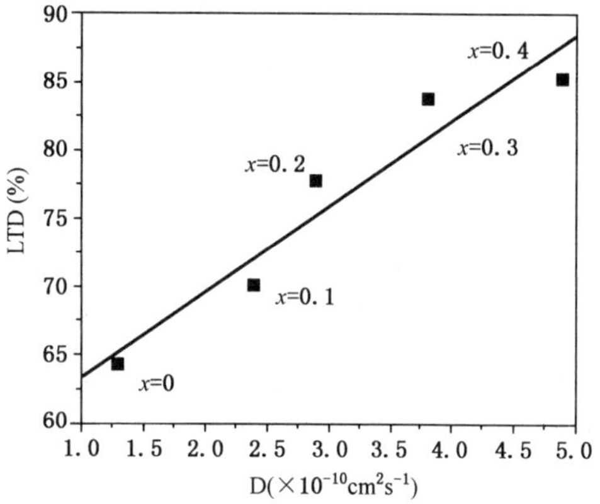

Fig. 9 The LTD as a function of D of the $La_{0.7}Mg_{0.3}Ni_{3-x}(Al_{0.5}Mo_{0.5})_x$ (x=0, 0.1, 0.2, 0.3, 0.4) alloy electrodes at 233 K

4 Conclusion

The structure and electrochemical properties of the $La_{0.7}Mg_{0.3}Ni_{3-x}(Al_{0.5}Mo_{0.5})_x$ (x = 0 — 0.4) hydrogen storage alloys have been investigated systematically. The Rietveld analysis results show that all these alloys consist mainly of a $La(La,Mg)_2Ni_9$ phase and a $LaNi_5$

phase. The P-C-T curves indicate that the hydrogen storage capacity first increases and then decreases with increasing x. The electrochemical measurements show that the maximum discharge capacity of the alloy electrode increases first from 343.3 ($x=0$) to 377.6 mAh/g ($x=0.3$) and then decreases to 350.4 mAh/g ($x=0.4$). For the discharge current density of 1200 mA/g, the high rate HRD first decreases from 61.3% to 59.2% and then increases to 81.2%, which is consistent with the results of the exchange current density of the alloy electrodes. The hydrogen diffusion coefficient increases with increasing Al and Mo content, and thus increases the low temperature dischargeability of the alloy electrodes.

Acknowledgement

This work was financially supported by the National Natural Science Foundation of China (grant No. 20171042).

References

[1] M. Latroche, A. Percheron-Guegan, J. Alloys Compd. 356 (2003) 461.

[2] J. J. G. Willems, K. H. J. Buschow, J. Less-Common Met. 13 (1987) 129.

[3] H. G. Pan, Y. F. Zhu, M. X. Gao, Q. D. Wang, J. Electrochem. Soc. 149 (2002) 829.

[4] T. Kohno, H. Yoshida, F. Kawashima, T. Inaba, I. Sakai, M. Ya-mamoto, M. Kanda, J. Alloys Compd. 311 (2000) 5.

[5] J. J. G. Willems, Philips J. Res. 39 (Suppl. 1) (1984) 1.

[6] J. Chen, N. Kuriyama, H. T. Takeshita, H. Tanaka, T. Sakai, M. Haruta, Electrochem. Solid-State Lett. 3 (6) (2000) 249.

[7] T. Sakai, I. Uehara, H. Iwakura, J. Alloys Compd. 293-295 (1999) 762.

[8] J. J. Reilly, G. D. Adzic, J. R. Johnson, T. Vogt, S. Mukerjee, J. McBreen, J. Alloys Compd. 293-295 (1999) 569.

[9] Y. F. Liu, H. G. pan, Y. F. Zhu, R. Li, Y. Q. Lei, Mater. Sci. Eng. A A372 (2004) 163.

[10] H. Oesterreicher, H. Bittner, J. Less-Common Met. 73 (1980) 339.

[11] K. Kadir, N. Nuriyama, T. Sakai, I. Uehara, L. Eriksson, J. Alloys Compd. 284 (1999) 145.

[12] K. Kadir, T. Sakai, I. Uahara, J. Alloys Compd. 287 (1999) 264.

[13] K. Kadir, T. Sakai, I. Uahara, J. Alloys Compd. 302 (2000) 112.

[14] J. Chen, H. T. Takeshita, H. Tanaka, N. Kuriyama, T. Sakai, J. Alloys Compd. 302 (2000) 304.

[15] T. Kohno, H. Yoshida, F. Kawashima, T. Inaba, I. Sakai, M. Ya-mamoto, M. Kanda, J. Alloys Compd. 311 (2000) L5.

[16] B. Liao, Y. Q. Lei, L. X. Chen, G. L. Lu, H. G. Pan, Q. D. Wang, J. Power Sources 129 (2004) 358.

[17] P. H. Notton, P. Hokkeling, J. Electrochem. Soc. 138 (1991) 1877.

[18] T. Sakai, H. Miyamura, N. Kuriyama, A. Kato, K. Oguro, H. Ishikawa, J. Less-Common Met. 159 (1990) 127.

[19] T. Sakai, H. Miyamura, N. Kuriyama, A. Kato, K. Oguro, H. Ishikawa, J. Electrochem. Soc. 137 (1990) 795.

[20] C. Iwakura, H. Senoh, K. Morimoto, Y. Hara, H. Inoue, Electrochemistry 70 (1) (2002) 2.

[21] M. T. Yeh, V. M. Beibutian, S. E. Hsu, J. Alloys Compd. 293-295 (1999) 721.

[22] C. J. Howard, J. Appl. Cryst. 15 (1982) 615.

[23] X. B. Zhang, Y. J. Chai, W. Y. Yin, M. S.

Zhao, J. Solid State Chem. 177 (2004) 2373.

[24] X. B. Zhang, D. Z. Sun, W. Y. Yin, Y. J. Chai, M. S. Zhao, Electrochim. Acta, 50 (2005) 2911-2918.

[25] H. Oesterreicher, J. Clinton, H. Bittner, Mater. Res. Bull. 11 (1976) 1241.

[26] D. L. Sun, Y. Q. Lei, W. H. Liu, J. J. Jiang, J. Wu, Q. D. Wang, J. Alloys Compd. 231 (1995) 621.

[27] H. G. Pan, Y. F. Liu, M. X. Gao, Y. Q. Lei, Q. D. Wang, J. Electrochem. Soc. 150 (5) (2003) 565.

[28] T. Sakai, H. Miyamura, N. Kuriyama, A. Kato, K. Oguro, H. Ishikawa, J. Less-Common Met. 159 (1 990) 127.

[29] T. B. Atwater, P. J. Cygan, F. C. Leung, J. Power Sources 91 (2000) 27.

[30] H. Senoh, Y. Hara, H. Inoue, C. Iwakura, Electrochim. Acta 46 (2001) 967.

Effect of La/Ce Ratio on the Structure and Electrochemical Characteristics of $La_{0.7-x}Ce_xMg_{0.3}Ni_{2.8}Co_{0.5}$ ($x=0.1-0.5$) Hydrogen Storage Alloys①

X. B. Zhang[a], D. Z. Sun[b], W. Y. Yin[a], Y. J. Chai[a], M. S. Zhao[a]

([a] Key Laboratory of Rare Earth Chemistry and Physics, Changchun Institute of Applied Chemistry, Graduate School of Chinese Academy of Sciences, Chinese Academy of Sciences, No. 5625, Changchun 130022, PR China)

([b] State Key Laboratory of Electro-analytical Chemistry, Changchun Institute of Applied Chemistry, Graduate School of Chinese Academy of Sciences, Chinese Academy of Sciences, Changchun 130022, PR China)

Abstract: The effect of La/Ce ratio on the structure and electrochemical characteristics of the $La_{0.7-x}Ce_xMg_{0.3}Ni_{2.8}Co_{0.5}$ ($x=0.1, 0.2, 0.3, 0.4, 0.5$) alloys has been studied systematically. The result of the Rietveld analyses shows that except for small amount of impurity phases including LaNi and $LaNi_2$, all these alloys mainly consist of two phases: the $La(La,Mg)_2Ni_9$ phase with the rhombohedral $PuNi_3$-type structure and the $LaNi_5$ phase with the hexagonal $CaCu_5$-type structure. The abundance of the $La(La,Mg)_2Ni_9$ phase decreases with increasing cerium content whereas the $LaNi_5$ phase increases with increasing Ce content, moreover, both the *a* and cell volumes of the two phases decrease with the increase of Ce content. The maximum discharge capacity decreases from 367.5 mAh g^{-1} ($x=0.1$) to 68.3 mAh g^{-1} ($x=0.5$) but the cycling life gradually improve. As the discharge current density is 1 200 mA g^{-1}, the HRD increases from 55.4% ($x=0.1$) to 67.5% ($x=0.3$) and then decreases to 52.1% ($x=0.5$). The cell volume reduction with increasing x is detrimental to hydrogen diffusion *D* and accordingly decreases the low temperature dischargeability of the $La_{0.7-x}Ce_xMg_{0.3}Ni_{2.8}Co_{0.5}$ ($x=0.1-0.5$) alloy electrodes.

Key words: Structure characteristics; High rate dischargeability; Low temperature dischargeability; Exchange current density; Hydrogen diffusion coefficient

1 Introduction

According to the problem induced by the shortage of fossil energy and global warming, hydrogen is expected to be a promising energy vector for near future. In order for hydrogen to become a viable solution to the energy crisis and the environmental problems, storage processes must be improved in terms of specific ca-

① Electrochimica Acta, 22005(50): 1957-1964.

pacity and security. Among different ways to store hydrogen, absorption in solid is very attractive since it allows safe storage at pressure and temperature close to ambient conditions [1]. There are many kinds of metals and alloys which are able to absorb large amount of hydrogen and they are used in many fields, such as heat pump, thermal storage system, as catalysts, fuel cells, nickel-metal hydride (Ni-MH) rechargeable batteries and so on.

In recent years, Ni-MH secondary batteries, in which hydrogen storage alloy is employed as negative electrode, have been widely adopted in various portable electronic devices, electric hand tools and electric vehicles because of their high reversible energy storage density, fast electrochemical activation, long cyclic stability, good charge/discharge kinetics and environmental compatibility [2-7]. To date, almost all commercial Ni-MH batteries are employing AB_5-type alloys as negative electrode materials because of their good overall electrode properties [8]. However, the electrochemical capacity of the AB_5-type alloys is limited by the single $CaCu_5$-type hexagonal structure [9], the energy densities of the Ni-MH batteries are not competing favorably with some other advanced secondary batteries. Therefore, new type alloys with higher energy density, faster activation, better rate dischargeability and lower cost are urgently needed to replace the conventional rare earth-based AB_5-type alloys [10].

Recently, Kadir et al. [11-13] have reported the discovery of a new type of ternary alloys with the general formula of RMg_2Ni_9 (R: rare earth, Ca, Y) with $PuNi_3$ type structure. It is found that some of the R-Mg-Ni-based ternary alloys can absorb/desorb 1.8—1.87 wt% H_2 and are thus regarded as promising candidates for reversible gaseous hydrogen storage [14,15]. As to their electrochemical hydrogen storage, Chen et al. [7] have studied the structure and electrochemical characteristics of $LaCaMg(Ni,M)_9$ (M=Al, Mn) alloys, and almost at the same time, Kohno et al. [16] have reported that the discharge capacity of $La_{0.7}Mg_{0.3}Ni_{2.8}Co_{0.5}$ alloy reached 410 mAh g^{-1}. However, up to now, the La-Mg-Ni-Co system hydrogen storage electrode alloys can not used as negative material of the Ni-MH secondary batteries due to theirs serious corrosion in KOH electrolyte [17]. Adzic et al. [18] pointed out that the rate of loss of electrochemical capacity per charge/discharge cycle due to electrode corrosion was significantly decreased due to the presence of Ce. Sakai et al. [19] reported that the replacement of lanthanum by large amounts of cerium gave the alloy a satisfactory cycle lifetime even in the low content range of cobalt.

In this work, on the basis of our previous studies and the belief that the Ce addition may result in some noticeable modification, the structure and electrochemical characteristics of the $La_{0.7-x}Ce_xMg_{0.3}Ni_{2.8}Co_{0.5}$ (x=0.1—0.5) alloys has been investigated systematically.

2 Experimental details

2.1 Alloy preparation and X-ray diffraction analysis

All alloy samples were prepared by arc-melting carefully the constituent elements or master alloy on a water-cooled copper hearth under argon atmosphere. The purity of the metals, i. e., La, Ce, Mg, Ni and Co is higher than 99.9 mass%. The samples were all inverted and remelted 5 times to ensure good homogeneity. Thereafter, these alloy samples were mechanically crushed intofine powders of 300 mesh in mortar.

Crystallographic characteristics of the hydrogen storage alloys were investigated by X-ray diffraction on Rigaku D/Max 2500PC X-ray diffractometer (Cu Kα, monochromator) using JADE5 software [20].

2.2 Electrochemical measurement

The well-mixed alloy powder and carbonyl nickel powder in weight ratio of 1∶5 were pressed into the tablets as metal hydride electrode, which had the diameter of 13 mm and thickness of 1.5 mm, and the weight of each electrode was about 0.9 g.

The electrochemical properties were then measured in a standard three electrode cell consisting of a working electrode (metal-hydride electrode), a counter electrode ($NiOOH/Ni(OH)_2$ electrode) and a reference electrode (Hg/HgO electrode). The electrolyte in the cell was 6 M KOH aqueous solution. Charge and discharge tests were carried out on an automatic galvanostatic system (DC-5). The emphasis of these charge/discharge tests was on the electrochemical capacity and stability of the negative electrode, thus the capacity of the positive electrode plate was designed to be much higher than that of the negative electrode. At 298 K, these experimental cells were firstly charged at current of 60 mA g^{-1} for 7 h followed a rest for 30 min and were discharged at the same discharge current density to the cut-off voltage of −0.60 V versus Hg/HgO.

Pressure-composition isotherms (P-C-T) curves were electrochemically obtained by converting the equilibrium potential of the metal hydride electrode to the equilibrium pressure of hydrogen on the basis of Nernst equation using electrochemical data [21] as reported in reference [22]. The equilibrium potential curves were obtained by alternating the following two processes: (1) a pulse discharge of (25 mA g^{-1} × 0.25 h); (2) a rest period until the potential became almost constant. The equilibrium potential change of approximately 30 mV corresponds to the equilibrium pressure change by one order of magnitude. Since the measured potentials have an error of 1−2 mV, the calculated pressure values are accurate to be within 10% [22].

To evaluate the high rate dischargeability (HRD) (in the range of 60−1 200 mA g^{-1}), discharge capacities of the alloy electrode at different discharge current densities were measured. The high rate dischargeability (%) defined as $C_n \times 100/(C_n + C_{60})$, was determined from the ratio of the discharge capacity C_n (with $n = 60, 240, 480, 720, 960, 1\,200$ mA g^{-1}, respectively) to the total discharge capacity defined as the sum of C_n and C_{60} which was the additional capacity measured subsequently at 60 mA g^{-1} after C_n was measured.

For investigating the electrocatalytic activity of the hydrogen electrode reaction, the linear polarization curves of the electrode were plotted on an EG&G PARC's Model 273 Potentiostat/Galvanostat station by scanning the electrode potential at the rate of 0.1 mV^{-s} from −5 to 5 mV (versus open circuit potential) at 50% depth of discharge (DOD) at 298 K. The polarization resistance R_p can be obtained from the slope of the linear polarization curves. Moreover, the exchange current density (I_0), which is a measure of the catalytic activity of electrode, was calculated from the slopes of polarization curves by the following equation[23], $I_0 = \frac{RT}{FR_p}$, where R is the gas constant, T the absolute temperature, F the Faraday constant, and R_p the polarization resistance. The potentiostatic discharge technique was used to evaluate the coefficient of diffusion within the bulk of the alloy electrodes. After being fully charged followed by a 30 min open-circuit lay-aside, the test electrodes were discharged with +500 mV potential-step for 500 s on a EG&G PARC's Model 273 Potentiostat/Galvanostat station, using the M352 CorrWare electrochemical/corrosion software.

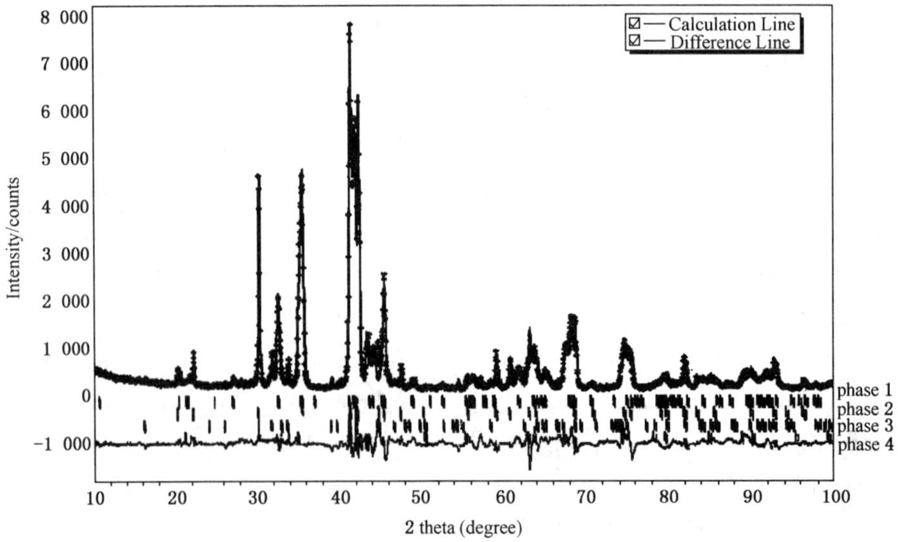

Fig. 1　Rietveld profiles refinement of XRD patterns $La_{0.6}Ce_{0.1}Mg_{0.3}Ni_{2.8}Co_{0.5}$ alloy (Phase 1: $La(La,Mg)_2Ni_9$; Phase 2: $LaNi_5$; Phase 3: LaNi; Phase 4: $LaNi_2$)

3 Results and discussion

3.1 Structure characteristic

Fig. 1 shows the Rietveld analysis pattern of the $La_{0.6}Ce_{0.1}Mg_{0.3}Ni_{2.8}Co_{0.5}$ hydrogen storage alloy as an example of $La_{0.7-x}Ce_xMg_{0.3}Ni_{2.8}Co_{0.5}$ ($x=0.1-0.5$) alloys. It can be found that, except for small amounts of impurity phase including LaNi and $LaNi_2$, the $La_{0.6}Ce_{0.1}Mg_{0.3}Ni_{2.8}Co_{0.5}$ alloy mainly consisted of a La_2MgNi_9 phase with a $PuNi_3$-type rhombohedral structure and a $LaNi_5$ phase with a $CaCu_5$-type hexagonal structure. Furthermore, it can be derived that the Mg atoms only occupy the 6c sites and the La atoms can occupy both the 3a and the 6c sites in the phase with rhombohedral (Space group: $R\text{-}3m$ 166) $PuNi_3$-type structure by Rietveld refinement. So the final structure of La_2MgNi_9 phase can be designated as $La(La,Mg)_2Ni_9$. The lattice parameters, cell volume and phase abundance of $La_{0.7-x}Ce_xMg_{0.3}Ni_{2.8}Co_{0.5}$ ($x=0.1-0.5$) alloys are all presented in Table 1. It can be seen that all the $La_{0.7-x}Ce_xMg_{0.3}Ni_{2.8}Co_{0.5}$ ($x=0.1-0.5$) alloys are composed of the $La(La,Mg)_2Ni_9$ phase and $LaNi_5$ phase besides some minor impurity phases, $LaNi_2$ or LaNi. Moreover, we can find that cell volume of the $La(La,Mg)_2Ni_9$ phase and the $LaNi_5$ phase in the alloys all decrease monotonically with the increase of x, which can be attributed to the fact that the atomic radius of Ce

Table 1 Characteristics of alloy phases in $La_{0.7-x}Ce_xMg_{0.3}Ni_{2.8}Co_{0.5}$ ($x=0.1-0.5$) alloys

Samples	Phases	Phase abundance (wt%)	Parameters of fit[a]	Lattice parameter (Å)			Cell volume (Å)
				a	b	c	
$x=0.1$	$La(La,Mg)_2Ni_9$	76.54	$R_p=10.1$, $R_{wp}=13.8$	5.0672	5.0672	24.3851	542.24
	$LaNi_5$	21.21		5.0460	5.0460	3.9920	88.03
	LaNi	1.34		3.8761	10.7594	4.3234	180.31
	$LaNi_2$	0.91		7.2123	7.2123	7.2123	375.16
$x=0.2$	$La(La,Mg)_2Ni_9$	69.78	$R_p=8.7$, $R_{wp}=11.4$	5.0425	5.0425	24.3247	535.64
	$LaNi_5$	27.68		5.0233	5.0233	4.0007	87.43
	LaNi	2.54		3.8343	10.7465	4.3229	178.13
$x=0.3$	$La(La,Mg)_2Ni_9$	61.56	$R_p=10$, $R_{wp}=13.7$	5.0035	5.0035	24.2478	525.72
	$LaNi_5$	37.23		5.0004	5.0004	4.0028	86.68
	LaNi	1.21		3.8240	10.7321	4.2981	176.39
$x=0.4$	$La(La,Mg)_2Ni_9$	58.68	$R_p=5.7$, $R_{wp}=7.8$	4.9691	4.9691	24.1138	515.65
	$LaNi_5$	39.35		4.9728	4.9728	4.0064	85.8
	LaNi	1.97		3.7860	10.7258	4.2696	173.38
$x=0.5$	$La(La,Mg)_2Ni_9$	53.65	$R_p=8.6$, $R_{wp}=11.2$	4.9372	4.9372	23.9985	506.61
	$LaNi_5$	43.23		4.9512	4.9512	4.0097	85.13
	LaNi	3.12		3.6762	10.7023	4.2506	167.23

The Rietveld refinement program RIETICA was used.

[a] R_p: the pattern factor; R_{wp}: the weighted pattern factor.

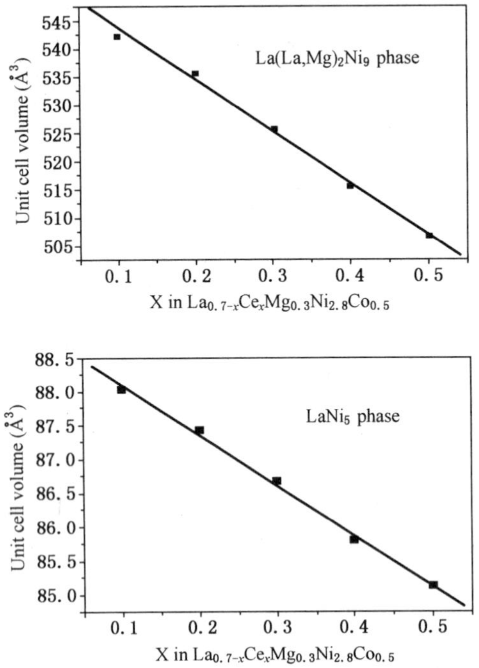

Fig. 2　Variation of the unit cell volume of the La(La,Mg)$_2$Ni$_9$ and LaNi$_5$ with *x*

(1.824Å) is smaller than that of La (1.877Å). The unit cell volume of the La(La,Mg)$_2$Ni$_9$ and LaNi$_5$ as a function of x in La$_{0.7-x}$Ce$_x$Mg$_{0.3}$Ni$_{2.8}$Co$_0$.5 (x=0.1−0.5) alloys is shown in Fig. 2. The cell volume is of interest because it can be correlated with the stability of the hydride phase in any homologous alloys series [21]. The cell volume is also a linear function of the Ce content and a useful check on the intermetallic composition [22]. The equation for the cell volume of La(La, Mg)$_2$Ni$_9$ phase as a function of x is:

$$\text{cell volume} = (553.959 - 92.39x)\,\text{Å}^3 \quad (1)$$

and the relationship between the cell volume of LaNi$_5$ phase and x can be expressed as:

$$\text{cell volume} = (88.843 - 7.43x)\,\text{Å}^3 \quad (2)$$

The Fig. 3 shows the abundances of the La(La, Mg)$_2$Ni$_9$ phase and the LaNi$_5$ phase as a function of x in the La$_{0.7-x}$Ce$_x$Mg$_{0.3}$Ni$_{2.8}$Co$_{0.5}$ (x = 0.1 − 0.5) alloys. As can be seen in Fig. 3 and Table 1, the La(La, Mg)$_2$Ni$_9$ phase abundance decreases from 76.54% to 53.65% with increasing x, however, the LaNi$_5$ phase abundance increases from 21.2% to 43.23%. These results may infiuence the hydrogen storage and electrochemical characteristics of the alloys studied.

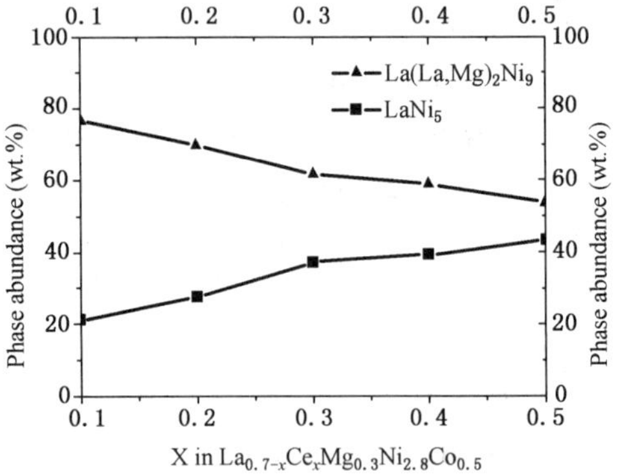

Fig. 3　Phase abundance of the La(La, Mg)$_2$Ni$_9$ phase and the LaNi$_5$ phase existing in the La$_{0.7-x}$Ce$_x$Mg$_{0.3}$Ni$_{2.8}$Co$_{0.5}$ (x=0.1−0.5) alloys

3.2　P-C isotherms

The electrochemical pressure-composition isotherms method is very useful for examining the charging and discharging levels of hydrogen in an anode, although the calculated pressures pertain to a quasi-equilibrium state [23]. The P-C-T curves for hydrogen desorption in the La$_{0.7-x}$Ce$_x$Mg$_{0.3}$Ni$_{2.8}$Co$_{0.5}$-H system at 298 K are presented in Fig. 4.

With the increase of x, the plateau pressure of the La$_{0.7-x}$Ce$_x$Mg$_{0.3}$Ni$_{2.8}$Co$_{0.5}$

(x=0. 1—0. 5) alloys increases monotonously and the plateau region becomes narrower and steeper, which leads to the decrease of the hydrogen storage capacity (H/M) from 0. 952 to 0. 177. This result is in good agreement with that reported by Liu et al. [22]. The change of the P-C-T characteristics can be mainly attributed to the reduction of the unit cell volume and the relative change of phase abundance of La(La, Mg)$_2$Ni$_9$ phase and LaNi$_5$ phase. The increase of the plateau pressure of the La$_{0.7-x}$Ce$_x$Mg$_{0.3}$Ni$_{2.8}$Co$_{0.5}$ hydrogen storage alloy can be mainly ascribed to two reasons. On the one hand, it is well known that unit cell of the AB$_3$ compounds contains onethird AB$_5$ and two-third AB$_2$ structure [7, 10] and thus the plateau pressure of the La (La, Mg)$_2$Ni$_9$ phase is similar to that of LaNi$_5$ phase. In fact, the plateau of the La(La, Mg)$_2$Ni$_9$ phase is slightly lower than that of the LaNi$_5$ phase. With the increase of Ce content, as mentioned above, the abundance of La(La, Mg)$_2$Ni$_9$ phase decreases whereas the phase abundance of the LaNi$_5$ phase increases, which thereby slightly increases the plateau pressure of the La$_{0.7-x}$Ce$_x$Mg$_{0.3}$Ni$_{2.8}$Co$_{0.5}$ hydrogen storage alloy. On the other hand, the cell volume of both the La (La, Mg)$_2$Ni$_9$ phase and the LaNi$_5$ phase decreases with increasing Ce content, as shown in Table 1 and Fig. 2, which will also inevitably increases the plateau pressure of the La$_{0.7-x}$Ce$_x$Mg$_{0.3}$Ni$_{2.8}$Co$_{0.5}$ hydrogen storage alloy. Precheron-Guegan et al. [24] pointed out that the hydrogen absorbed in a hydrogen storage alloy enters and stays in the atomic state in the interstitial cavities of crystal lattice of the alloy. So the crystal structure of the alloy plays an important role on the hydrogen storage performance, especially the hydrogen storage capacity. Alloys with bigger cell volumes and hence bigger interstitial cavities generally have larger hydrogen storage capacity. The cell volumes of both La(La, Mg)$_2$Ni$_9$ phase and LaNi$_5$ phase decrease with the increase of the Ce content, which inevitably lowers the hydrogen storage capacity. Those lends credence to our assumption that the change of hydrogen storage capacity for La$_{0.7-x}$Ce$_x$Mg$_{0.3}$Ni$_{2.8}$Co$_{0.5}$ alloys results from the relative variation of the phase abundance of the La(La, Mg)$_2$Ni$_9$ phase and LaNi$_5$ phase.

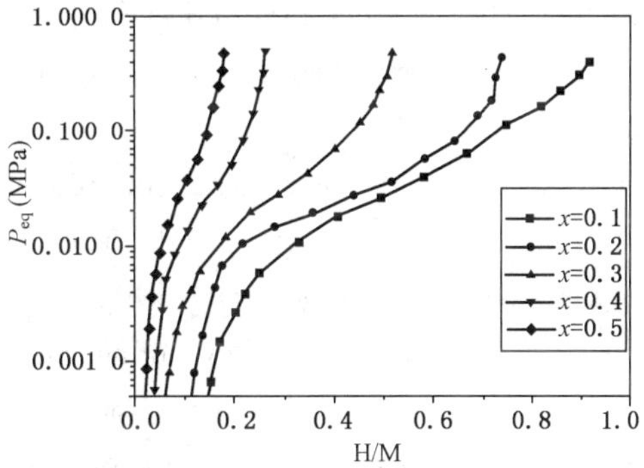

Fig. 4 The electrochemical desorption P-C-T curves for La$_{0.7-x}$Ce$_x$Mg$_{0.3}$Ni$_{2.8}$Co$_{0.5}$ (x=0. 1—0. 5) alloy electrodes at 298 K

3. 3 Activation, maximum discharge capacity and cycle stability

Fig. 5 shows the activation profiles of the La$_{0.7-x}$Ce$_x$Mg$_{0.3}$Ni$_{2.8}$Co$_{0.5}$ (x=0. 1—0. 5) alloy electrodes. Both the first cycle and the maximum discharge capacity decrease with the increases of the Ce content. It can be seen that their activations become slower with an increase of Ce content, which is in good agreement with the results reported by Adzic et al. [25]. The cycles needed to activate the electrodes and the maximum discharge capacities of the alloy electrodes are summarized in Table 2. With the increase of x, the maximum discharge capacity of the alloy electrode decreases from 367.5 mAh g^{-1} ($x=0.1$) to 68.3 mAh g^{-1} ($x=0.5$) a, which is in good agreement with the results of P-C-T curves measurement. The cycling capacity retention rate, expressed as $S_{70}(\%)=C_{70}/C_{max}\times 100$ (where C_{max} is the maximum discharge capacity, C_{70} is the discharge capacity at the 70th cycle), after 70 cycles at 60 mA g^{-1} is also listed in Table 2. As seen in Fig. 5 and Table 2, it is found that the capacity retention rate (S_{70}) improves gradually with increasing Ce content. There are two major effects of La/Ce ratio on the electrochemical cycling stability of $La_{0.7-x}Ce_xMg_{0.3}Ni_{2.8}Co_{0.5}$ ($x=0.1-0.5$) alloy electrodes. First is the effect of the unit-cell volume which decreases with increasing cerium contents. It is generally believed that the volume change of an alloy during hydriding is proportional to the amount of hydrogen absorbed in alloy or to the electrochemical capacity. The increase of the Ce content generally leads to a smaller lattice cavity and lower hydrogen storage capacity and smaller changer of unit cell on hydriding and hence less pulverization and improvement in the cycling life. The second is the formation of a protective surface film. As the Ce^{3+} ions can be oxidized to Ce^{4+} ions in the alkaline electrolyte they form a dense and strong CeO_2 oxide film on the alloy surface. The dense oxide film rather effectively inhibits further oxidation of the alloy and slows down the corrosion rate and thereby, improves the cyclic stability of the alloy.

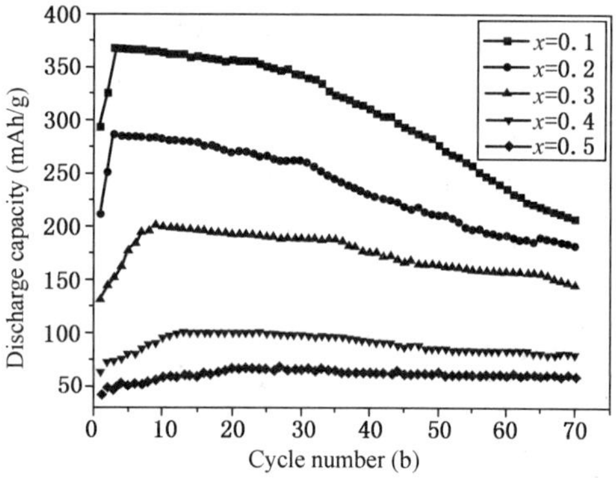

Fig. 5 The cycle life curves of the $La_{0.7-x}Ce_xMg_{0.3}Ni_{2.8}Co_{0.5}$ ($x=0.1, 0.2, 0.3, 0.4, 0.5$) alloy electrodes at 298 K

Table 2 Summary of the electrode performance of $La_{0.7-x}Ce_xMg_{0.3}Ni_{2.8}Co_{0.5}$ ($x=0.1-0.5$) alloy electrodes

Samples	H/M	C_{max} (mAh g^{-1})	Na^{a}	HRD_{1200} (%)[b]	S_{70} (%)
$x=0.1$	0.952	367.5	3	55.4	56.4
$x=0.2$	0.740	285.7	3	60.3	63.9
$x=0.3$	0.519	200.4	9	67.5	72.5
$x=0.4$	0.263	101.3	13	58.1	79.3
$x=0.5$	0.177	68.3	21	52.1	87.3

[a] Cycle numbers needed to activate the electrodes.

[b] High rate dischargeability at a discharge current density of 1 200 mA g^{-1}.

3.4 High rate dischargeability

Fig. 6 shows the effect of the discharge current density (60－1 200 mA g^{-1}) on the discharge capacity of the $La_{0.7-x}Ce_xMg_{0.3}Ni_{2.8}Co_{0.5}$($x$=0.1－0.5) alloy electrodes. The HRD of the alloy electrodes for the discharge current density of 1 200 mA g^{-1} are also listed in Table 2. It can be seen that as x increases, the HRD of the alloy electrodes increases first and then decreases. Taking the discharge current density being 1 200 mA g^{-1} as an example, the HRD of the alloy electrodes increases from 55.4% (x=0.1) to 67.5% (x=0.3) and then decreases to 52.1% (x=0.5). This is an indication of the occurrence of two opposing factors that contribute to the HRD of the alloy electrodes. It is generally accepted that the high rate dischargeability of a metal-hydride electrode is mainly determined by the charge-transfer process occurring at the metal electrolyte interface and the hydrogen diffusion process in the hydride bulk [26,27]. Fig. 7 shows the linear polariza-tion curves of the $La_{0.7-x}Ce_xMg_{0.3}Ni_{2.8}Co_{0}.5$ (x=0.1－0.5) alloy electrodes at 50% DOD and at 298 K. The polarization resistance R_p and exchange current density I_0 of the alloy electrodes are obtained and listed in Table 3. It can be seen that the polarization resistance R_p of the alloy electrodes decreases from 94.8 mΩ(x=0.1) to 68.7 mΩ(x=0.5), accord-ingly the exchange current density I_0 of the alloy electrodes increases from 270.9 to 373.6 mA g^{-1} when x increases from 0.1 to 0.5. Pan [28] pointed that, for La-Mg-Ni-Co system alloys, the $LaNi_5$ phase works not only as a hydrogen reservoir, but also as a catalyst to activate the $La(La,Mg)_2Ni_9$ phase to absorb/desorb hydrogen reversibly in the alkaline electrolyte [24]. The $LaNi_5$ phase abundance increases with increasing Ce content, as mentioned above and hence increases the exchange current density I_0 of the alloy electrodes. The diffusion coefficient of hydrogen in the bulk of the alloys was determined by means of the potential-step method and also listed in Table 3. The hydrogen diffusion coefficient decreases from 15.17×10^{-10} cm^{2-s} (x=0.1) to 7.32×10^{-10} cm^{2-s} (x=0.5), which can be attributed to the reduction of cell volume of the alloys with increasing Ce content. With the increase of x in $La_{0.7-x}Ce_xMg_{0.3}Ni_{2.8}Co_{0.5}$($x$=0.1－0.5) alloy electrodes, the exchange current density I_0 increase monotony, whereas the hydrogen diffusion coefficient D decrease linearly. Overall, the combined effect of the two opposing factors will thereby result in an optimal value of x for HRD. The optimal value of Ce content for $La_{0.7-x}Ce_xMg_{0.3}Ni_{2.8}Co_{0.5}$($x$=0.1－0.5) system hydro-gen alloy is 0.3 from our work.

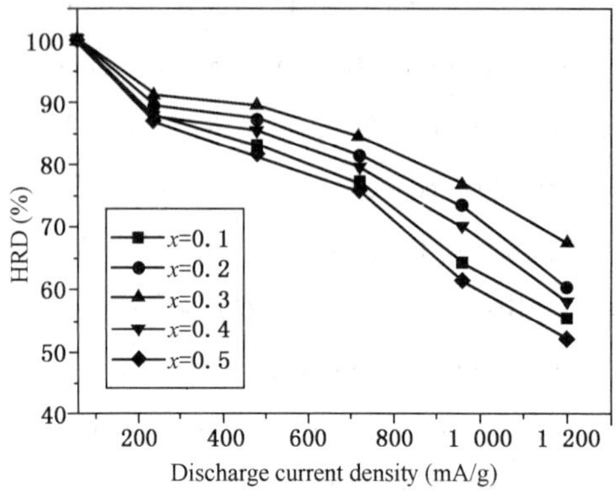

Fig. 6　The high rate dischargeability (HRD) of the $La_{0.7-x}Ce_xMg_{0.3}Ni_{2.8}Co_{0.5}$ (x=0.1, 0.2, 0.3, 0.4, 0.5) alloy electrodes at 298 K

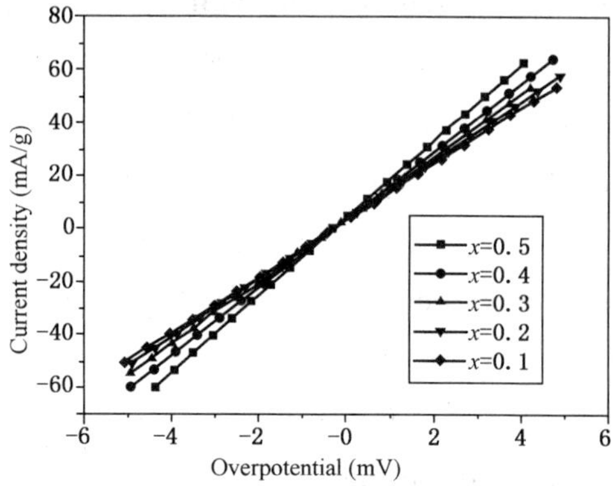

Fig. 7　Linear polarization curves for the $La_{0.7-x}Ce_xMg_{0.3}Ni_{2.8}Co_{0.5}$ (x=0.1−0.5) alloy electrodes at the 50% depth of discharge (DOD) and 298 K

Table 3　Electrochemical kinetic parameters of $La_{0.7-x}Ce_xMg_{0.3}Ni_{2.8}Co_{0.5}$ (x=0.1−0.5) alloy electrodes

Samples	Polarization resistance, R_p (mΩ)		Exchange current density, I_0 (mA g^{-1})		Hydrogen diffusion coefficient (D) ($\times 10^{-10}$ cm^{2-s})	
	298K	233K	298K	233K	298K	233K
x=0.1	94.8	872	270.9	23.0	15.17	3.53
x=0.2	90.1	863	285.1	23.3	14.32	2.78
x=0.3	85.1	859	301.7	23.4	13.14	2.16
x=0.4	77.8	852	330.1	23.6	9.34	1.73
x=0.5	68.7	849	373.6	23.6	7.32	0.97

3.5　Low temperature dischargeability (LTD)

It has been reported that the discharge capacity of the negative electrode in nickel-metal hydride decrease drastically with decreasing temperature [29]. Sakai et al. [30] pointed out that the dischargeability of the negative elec-trodes at relative low temperature depended on the hydrogen diffusion and/or charge-transfer process occurring at the metal electrolyte interface. The hydrogen diffusion coefficient (D) of hydrogen in the bulk is evaluated using the method described by Iwakura et al. [31]. The LTD, expressed as LTD_{233} (%) = $C_{233}/C_{298} \times 100$ (where C_{233} and C_{298} are the discharge capacity at 233 K and 298 K, respectively). The hydrogen diffusion coefficient (D) and the exchange current density (I_0) of the $La_{0.7-x}Ce_xMg_{0.3}Ni_{2.8}Co_{0.5}$ (x=0.1−0.5) alloy electrodes at 233 K are also listed in Table 3. It can be found that both the I_0 and the D are smaller than that at 298 K. Moreover, we can find that the I_0 maintain almost unchanged

(23.0—23.6 mA g^{-1}) and, whereas D decreases remarkably with increasing x, which implies that the hydrogen diffusion in alloy probably becomes the rate-determining factor for low temperature dischargeability at 233 K. Fig. 8 shows LTD as a function of D in $La_{0.7-x}CexMg_{0.3}Ni_{2.8}Co_{0.5}$ ($x=0.1-0.5$) alloy electrodes. It can be easily found that D decreases with the increase of x, which can be attributed to the cell volume reduction with increasing x as shown in Table 1. The decreasing D accordingly decreases the LTD of $La_{0.7-x}Ce_xMg_{0.3}Ni_{2.8}Co_{0.5}$ ($x=0.1-0.5$) alloy electrodes.

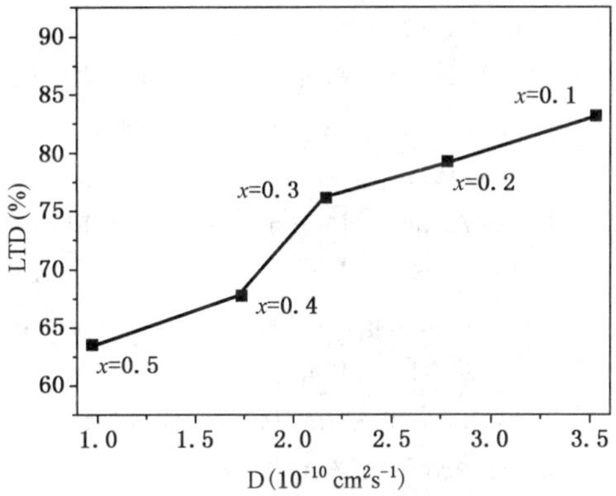

Fig. 8 The low temperature dischargeability (LTD) as a function of hydrogen diffusion coefficient (D) of the $La_{0.7-x}Ce_xMg_{0.3}Ni_{2.8}Co_{0.5}$ ($x=0.1, 0.2, 0.3, 0.4, 0.5$) alloy electrodes at 233 K

4 Conclusion

In this paper, the effect of the cerium content on the structural and electrochemical characteristics of the $La_{0.7-x}Ce_xMg_{0.3}Ni_{2.8}Co_{0.5}$ ($x=0.1-0.5$) hydrogen storage alloys has been studied systematically. It is found by XRD Rietveld analysis that, except for small amount of impurity phases including LaNi and $LaNi_2$, all these alloys mainly consist of two phases: the $La(La, Mg)_2Ni_9$ phase with the rhombohedral $PuNi_3$-type structure and the $LaNi_5$ phase with the hexagonal $CaCu_5$-type structure. The abundance of the $La(La, Mg)_2Ni_9$ phase decreases with increasing cerium content, whereas the $LaNi_5$ phase increases with increasing Ce content. The P-C isotherm curves show that with increasing Ce content in the alloys, the plateau pressure of the hydrogen desorption increases steeply and the plateau region becomes narrower and steeper. It is found that with increasing Ce content the discharge capacity decreases and the cycling life can be gradually improved. The high rate dischargeability (HRD) and the exchange current density I_0 of the alloy electrodes increases from $x=0.1$ to 0.3 and then decreases with further increase of Ce content. The hydrogen diffusion coefficient D decreases with the increases of Ce content and thus decreases the low temperature discharge-ability of $La_{0.7-x}Ce_xMg_{0.3}Ni_{2.8}Co_{0.5}$ ($x=0.1-0.5$) alloy electrodes.

Acknowledgement

This work was nancially supported by the National Natfiural Science Foundation of China (Grant No. 20171042).

References

[1] M. Latroche, A. Percheron-Guegan, J. Alloys Comp. 356-357 (2003) 461.

[2] J. J. G. Willems, K. H. J. Buschow, J. Less-

Common Met. 129 (1987) 13.

[3] T. Sakai, H. Miyamura, N. Kuriyama, A. Kato, K. Oguro, H. Ishikawa, J. Electrochem. Soc. 137 (1990) 795.

[4] T. Kohno, H. Yoshida, F. Kawashima, T. Inaba, I. Sakai, M. Yamamoto, M. Kanda, J. Alloys Comp. 311 (2000) L5.

[5] J. J. G. Willems, Philips J. Res. 39 (Suppl. 1) (1984) 1.

[6] H. G. Pan, Y. F. Zhu, M. X. Gao, Q. D. Wang, J. Electrochem. Soc. 149 (2002) 829.

[7] J. Chen, N. Kuriyama, H. T. Takeshita, H. Tanaka, T. Sakai, M. Haruta, Electrochem. Solid-State Lett. 3 (6) (2000) 249.

[8] T. Sakai, I. Uehara, H. Iwakura, J. Alloys Comp. 293-295 (1999) 762.

[9] J. J. Reilly, G. D. Adzic, J. R. Johnson, T. Vogt, S. Mukerjee, J. McBreen, J. Alloys Comp. 293-295 (1999) 569.

[10] Y. F. Liu, H. G. Pan, Y. F. Zhu, R. Li, Y. Q. Lei, Mater. Sci. Eng. A. A372 (2004) 163.

[11] K. Kadir, T. Sakai, I. Uahara, J. Alloys Comp. 257 (1997) 115.

[12] K. Kadir, N. Nuriyama, T. Sakai, I. Uehara, L. Eriksson, J. Alloys Comp. 284 (1999) 145.

[13] K. Kadir, T. Sakai, I. Uahara, J. Alloys Comp. 287 (1999) 264.

[14] K. Kadir, T. Sakai, I. Uahara, J. Alloys Comp. 302 (2000) 112.

[15] J. Chen, H. T. Takeshita, H. Tanaka, N. Kuriyama, T. Sakai, J. Alloys Comp. 302 (2000) 304.

[16] T. Kohno, H. Yoshida, F. Kawashima, T. Inaba, I. Sakai, M. Yamamoto, M. Kanda, J. Alloys Comp. 311 (2000) 5.

[17] B. Liao, Y. Q. Lei, L. X. Chen, G. L. Lu, H. G. Pan, Q. D. Wang, J. Power Sources 129 (2004) 358.

[18] G. Adzic, J. R. Johnson, J. J. Reilly, J. McBreen, S. Mukerjee, M. P. S. Kumar, W. Zhang, S. Srinivasan, J. Electrochem. Soc. 142 (1995) 3429.

[19] T. Sakai, T. Hazama, H. Miyamura, N. Kuriyama, A. Kato, H. Ishikawa, J. Less-Common Met. 172-174 (1991) 1175.

[20] Materials Data JADE Release 5, XRD pattern processing, Materials Data Inc. (MDI), 1997.

[21] D. N. Gruen, M. H. Mendelsohn, A. E. Dwight, J. Less-Common Met. 161 (1977) 193.

[22] H. G. Pan, Q. W. Jin, M. X. Gao, Y. F. Liu, R. Li, Y. Q. Lei, J. Alloys Comp. 373 (2004) 237.

[23] T. Sakai, H. Miyamura, N. Kuriyama, A. Kato, K. Oguro, H. Ishikawa, J. Less-Common Met. 159 (1990) 127.

[24] A. Precheron-Guegan, C. Lartigue, J. C. Achard, J. Less-Common Met. 161 (1990) 193.

[25] G. D. Adzic, J. R. Johnson, J. J. Reilly, J. McBreen, S. Mukerjee, M. P. Sridhar Kumar, W. Zhang, S. Srinivasan, J. Electrochem. Soc. 142 (1995) 3429.

[26] C. lwakura, T. Oura, H. Inoue, M. Matsuoka, Electrochem. Acta 41(1)(1996)117.

[27] C. lwakura, M. Matsuoka, K. Asai, T. Kohno, J. Power Source 38(1992)335.

[28] H. G. Pan, Y. F. Liu, M. X. Gao, Y. Q. Lei, Q. D. Wang, J. Electrochem. Soc. 150 (5) (2003)565.

[29] H. Senoh, Y. Hara, H, Inoue, C. lwakura, Electrochim. Acta 46(2001)967.

[30] T Sakai, H. Miyamura, N. Kuriyama, A. Karo, K. Ogura, H. Ishikawa, J. Elcctrochem. Soc. 137(1990)795.

[31] C. lwakura, H. Senoh, K. Morimoto, Y. Hara, H. Inoue, Electrochemistry 70(1)(2002)2.

Crystallographic and Electrochemical Characteristics of $La_{0.7}Mg_{0.3}Ni_{4.5-x}(Al_{0.5}Mo_{0.5})_x (x=0-0.8)$ Hydrogen Storage Alloys①

Xin-Bo Zhang[a], Dan-Zi Sun[b], Wen-Ya Yin[a], Yu-Jun Chai[a], and Min-Shou Zhao[a]
([a] Key Laboratory of Rare Earth Chemistry and Physics, Changchun Institute of Applied Chemistry, Chinese Academy of Sciences, Graduate School of Chinese Academy of Sciences, Changchun 130022, P. R. China)
([b] State Key Laboratory of Electro-analytical Chemistry, Changchun Institute of Applied Chemistry, Chinese Academy of Sciences, Graduate School of Chinese Academy of Sciences, Changchun 130022, P. R. China)

Abstract: The structure, hydrogen storage property, and electrochemical characteristics of the $La_{0.7}Mg_{0.3}Ni_{4.5-x}(Al_{0.5}Mo_{0.5})_x (x=0, 0.2, 0.4, 0.6, 0.8)$ hydrogen storage alloys have been investigated systematically. The X-ray powder diffraction and Rietveld analysis results reveal that all the alloys mainly consist of the $La(La,Mg)_2Ni_9$ phase and the $LaNi_5$ phase. The electrochemical measurements show that the maximum discharge capacity increases first from 246.3 ($x=0$) to 345.4 mAh/g ($x=0.6$) and then decreases to 317.6 mAh/g ($x=0.8$), which is consistent with the variation of the hydrogen storage capacity indicated by the P-C isotherms. For the discharge current density of 1 200 mA/g, the high-rate discharge ability of the alloy electrodes increases linearly from 47.2% ($x=0$) to 73.8% ($x=0.8$). Moreover, according to the linear polarization curves, the exchange current density of the alloy electrodes also increases monotonously with increasing x. The hydrogen diffusion coefficient increases with increasing Al and Mo content, and thus increases the low-temperature dischargeability of the alloy electrodes.

Key words: High-rate dischargeability; Low-temperature dischargeability; Exchange current density/Hydrogen diffusion coefficient; Alloys; X-ray diffraction

Introduction

Hydrogen storage alloys have attracted considerable attention in view of their potential as a new energy storage material. Recently, the nickel-metal hydride battery (Ni-MH), in which a hydrogen storage alloy is employed as a negative electrode material, has become the focus of interest as a candidate consumer-used battery by virtue of its several advantages: high reversible energy storage densi-

① Eur. J. Inorg. Chem, 2005: 2235-2241.

ty, high resistance to overcharging and overdischarging, good charge/discharge kinetics, environmental compatibility, and inter-changeability with the nickel-cadmium battery. [1-6] To date, almost all commercial Ni-MH batteries are employing AB_5-type alloys as negative electrode materials because of their good overall electrode properties. [7] However, the electro-chemical capacity of the AB_5-type alloys is limited by the single CaCu5-type hexagonal structure; [8] the energy densities of the Ni-MH batteries cannot compete favorably with some other advanced secondary batteries. Therefore, new types of alloys with higher energy densities, faster activation, better rate dischargeabilities, and lower cost are urgently needed to replace the conventional rare-earth-based AB_5-type alloys. [9]

Recently, Kadir et al. [10-12] have reported the discovery of a new type of ternary alloys with the general formula RMg_2Ni_9 (R: rare earth, Ca, Y) with $PuNi_3$-type structure. It is found that some of the R-Mg-Ni-based ternary alloys can absorb-desorb 1.8—1.87 wt% H_2, which is much more than the $LaNi_5$ alloys (which can only absorb 1.4 wt% H_2), and are thus regarded as promising candidates for reversible gaseous hydrogen storage. [13,14] As for their electrochemical hydrogen storage, Chen et al. [6] have studied the electrochemical characteristics of $LaCaMg(Ni,M)_9$ [M = Al, Mn] alloys, and almost at the same time, Kohno et al. [3] have reported that the discharge capacity of the $La_{0.7}Mg_{0.3}Ni_{2.8}Co_{0.5}$ alloy reached 410 mAh/g. However, up to now, the La-Mg-Ni-Co-system hydrogen storage electrode alloys could not be used as the negative material of the Ni-MH secondary batteries due to their serious corrosion in KOH electrolyte, [15] and hence their cycling stability had to be upgraded for practical applications. In commercial AB_5-type alloys, the presence of 10 wt% Co has indeed improved the cycling life of Ni-MH batteries. However, it negatively influences the discharge capacity as well as initial activation, and it constitutes about 40% of the material cost. [16] Much effort has been devoted to search for a more cost-effective substitute element with high reliability of improving the cycling life of Ni-MH batteries. It is believed that Al is one of the best candidates for cobalt substitution. [17] However, the addition of Al is detrimental to the diffusion of hydrogen from the electrode surface to the alloy bulk, and thus inevitably decreases the high-rate dischargeability of the alloy electrode. [2] It is reported that the addition of Mo can remarkably increase the kinetic property [18] as well as the electrochemical capacity of the alloy electrode. [19] Therefore, it can be expected that the overall electrochemical properties of the La-Mg-Ni-type hydrogen storage alloys could be improved by substitution of Al and Mo for Ni in the alloys.

In this work, on the basis of our previous studies and the belief that the Al and Mo addition may result in some noticeable modifications, the structure and electrochemical characteristics of the $La_{0.7}Mg_{0.3}Ni_{4.5-x}(Al_{0.5}Mo_{0.5})_x$ ($x=0-0.8$) hydrogen storage alloys has been investigated systematically.

Results and Discussion

Alloy Composition and Structure Characteristics

It is well known that the low-melting Mg metal will inevitably be lost during the sample preparation by arc melting. We have tried many ways to overcome this problem, for example, by using an Mg-Ni master alloy as an Mg additive, by decreasing the melting current, by adding a slight excess of Mg over sample composition, and so on. Among all these methods, we found that the latter is the most effective way to compensate evaporative loss of Mg. Several attempts were made until the optimum preparative conditions were found. In this paper, the weight lost during sample preparation is almost the same as excess Mg added. The results of the ICP-AES analysis for all compounds are given in Table 1. It can be seen that the final composition of all the alloys is identical to the original composition.

Table 1　Composition of the $La_{0.7}Mg_{0.3}Ni_{4.0-x}(Al_{0.5}Mo_{0.5})x$ ($x=0-0.8$) alloys

Sample	La [mg/g]	Mg [mg/g]	Ni [mg/g]	Al [mg/g]	Co [mg/g]	La:Mg:Ni:Al:Mo[a]
x=0.0	263.74	19.78	716.47	0	0	1.90:0.81:12.21:0:0
x=0.2	263.35	19.75	683.61	7.31	25.98	1.90:0.81:11.65:0.27:0.27
x=0.4	262.96	19.72	650.84	14.59	51.89	1.89:0.81:11.09:0.54:0.54
x=0.6	262.56	19.69	618.17	21.86	77.72	1.89:0.81:10.53:0.81:0.81
x=0.8	262.17	19.66	585.59	29.10	103.47	1.89:0.81:9.98:1.08:1.08

[a] Atomic ratio.

The crystal structures have been identified and refined by means of X-ray powder diffraction data. Figure 1 shows the Rietveld refinement pattern of the XRD profiles for the $La_{0.7}Mg_{0.3}Ni_{4.3}(Al_{0.5}Mo_{0.5})_{0.2}$ hydrogen storage alloy as a representative example of the $La_{0.7}Mg_{0.3}Ni_{4.5-x}(Al_{0.5}Mo_{0.5})_x$ ($x=0, 0.2, 0.4, 0.6, 0.8$) hydrogen storage alloys. The results show that, besides an impurity Ni phase, the $La_{0.7}Mg_{0.3}Ni_{4.3}(Al_{0.5}Mo_{0.5})_{0.2}$ alloy mainly consists of two phases: a La_2MgNi_9 phase with a $PuNi_3$-type rhombohedral structure and a $LaNi_5$ phase with a $CaCu_5$-type hexagonal structure. The final Rietveld structure parameters of the La_2MgNi_9 phase are tabulated in Table 2. It can be easily found that the La atoms in La_2MgNi_9 are located not only at the 3a site (the Pu1 atom position of the $PuNi_3$ structure), but also at the 6c sites (the Pu2 atom position of the $PuNi_3$ structure), while the Mg atoms in the alloy exhibit a strong preference for the 6c site, which indicates that the alloy is an ordered compound with the same structure as the previously reported RMg_2Ni_9 (R=La, Ca, Y) alloys.

Hence, the final formula of the La_2MgNi_9 phase can be designated as $La(La, Mg)_2Ni_9$. The characteristics of the alloy phases in the $La_{0.7}Mg_{0.3}Ni_{4.5-x}(Al_{0.5}Mo_{0.5})_x$ ($x=0-0.8$) alloys are listed in Table 3. We find that all the alloys consist of an impurity Ni phase and two other main crystallographic phases, namely, the $La(La, Mg)_2Ni_9$ phase and the $LaNi_5$ phase. In addition, variations of the cell parameters and volume of the two main phases as a function of x in $La_{0.7}Mg_{0.3}Ni_{4.5-x}(Al_{0.5}Mo_{0.5})_x$ alloys is shown in Figure 2. It can be seen that the parameters a and c of both the $La(La, Mg)_2Ni_9$ phase and the $LaNi_5$ phase in the alloys increase linearly with an increase in x, which is mainly ascribed to the fact that the atomic radius of Al (1.432Å) and Mo (1.363Å) is larger than that of Ni (1.246Å). Figure 3 shows the abundance of the $La(La, Mg)_2Ni_9$ phase and the $LaNi_5$ phase as a function of x in the alloys. As can be seen in Figure 3 and Table 3, it can be seen that the $La(La, Mg)_2Ni_9$ phase abundance decreases from 39.21% to 29.79% with increasing x, while the $LaNi_5$ phase abundance increases from 60.34% to 70.07%. These results may influence the hydrogen storage and electrochemical characteristics of the alloys studied.

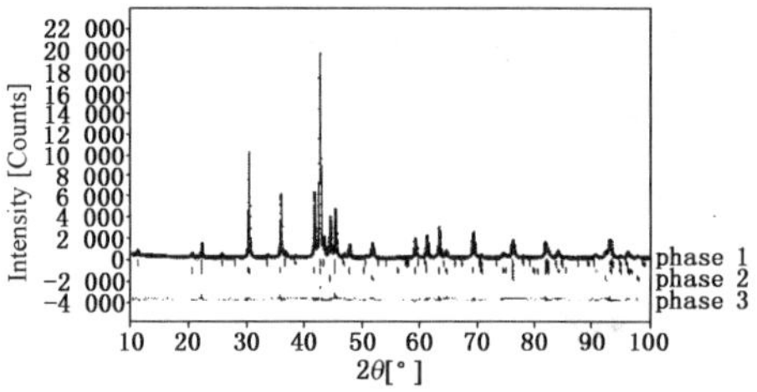

Figure 1　Rietveld refinement pattern of the XRD profiles for the $La_{0.7}Mg_{0.3}Ni_{4.3}(Al_{0.5}Mo_{0.5})_{0.2}$ hydrogen storage alloy (Phase 1: $La(La, Mg)_2Ni_9$; phase 2: LaNi5; phase 3: Ni)

Table 2　Crystallographic parameters for La_2MgNi_9 by using X-ray diffraction Cu-$K_{\alpha 1}$ ($\lambda=1.540\ 598\ 1$) at 298 K with a space group of $R\bar{3}m$ and $Z=3$[a]

Atom	Site	Metal atom position			Occupancy
		x	y	z	
La1	3a	0	0	0	1
La2	6c	0	0	0.142 7(2)	0.476
Mg1	6c	0	0	0.142 7(2)	0.524
Ni1	6c	0	0	0.331 1(2)	1
Ni2	3b	0	0	0.5	1
Ni3	18h	0.499 6(5)	0.500 4(5)	0.085 5(6)	1

[a] Structure was refined by using the Rietveld refinement program Rietica. The pattern factor is 6.2, the weighted pattern factor is 8.1, and the goodness of fit $S=2.0$.

Table 3　Characteristics of alloy phases in $La_{0.7}Mg_{0.3}Ni_{4.5-x}(Al_{0.5}Mo_{0.5})_x$ ($x=0-0.8$) alloys

Samples	Phases	Phase abundance (wt.-%)	Lattice parameter [A]			Cell volume [A]
			A	b	c	
$x=0.0$	$La(La, Mg)_2Ni_9$	39.21	4.989	4.989	24.093	519.34
	$LaNi_5$	60.34	5.064	5.064	4.025	89.39
	Ni	0.45	3.536	3.536	3.536	44.21

Continued

Samples	Phases	Phase abundance (wt. -%)	Lattice parameter [A]			Cell volume [A]
			A	b	c	
$x=0.2$	$La(La,Mg)_2Ni_9$	36.85	5.013	5.013	24.369	530.35
	$LaNi_5$	62.90	5.073	5.073	4.042	90.09
	Ni	0.25	3.545	3.545	3.545	44.55
$x=0.4$	$La(La,Mg)_2Ni_9$	33.59	5.043	5.043	24.410	537.62
	$LaNi_5$	65.83	5.078	5.078	4.045	90.33
	Ni	0.58	3.548	3.548	3.548	44.66
$x=0.6$	$La(La,Mg)_2Ni_9$	32.41	5.077	5.077	24.622	549.63
	$LaNi_5$	67.32	5.091	5.091	4.070	91.35
	Ni	0.27	3.561	3.561	3.561	45.16
$x=0.8$	$La(La,Mg)_2Ni_9$	29.79	5.124	5.124	24.713	561.92
	$LaNi_5$	70.07	5.097	5.097	4.078	91.75
	Ni	0.14	3.572	3.572	3.572	45.58

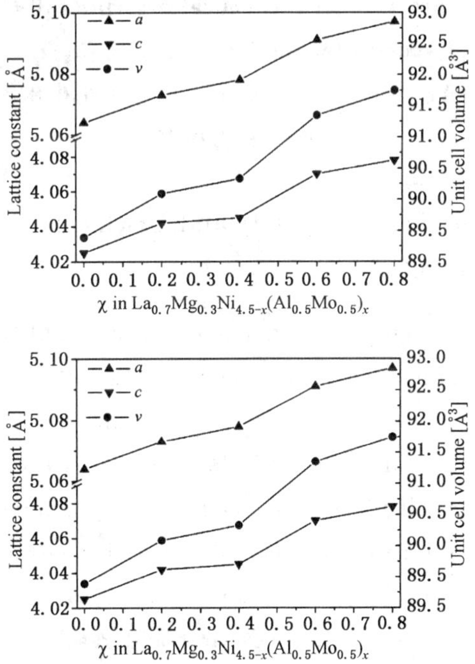

Figure 2 Variations of the cell parameters and volumes as a func-tion of x in $La_{0.7}Mg_{0.3}Ni_{4.5-x}(Al_{0.5}Mo_{0.5})_x$ alloys ($x=0-0.8$) (a) $La(La,Mg)_2Ni_9$ phase; (b) $LaNi_5$ phase.

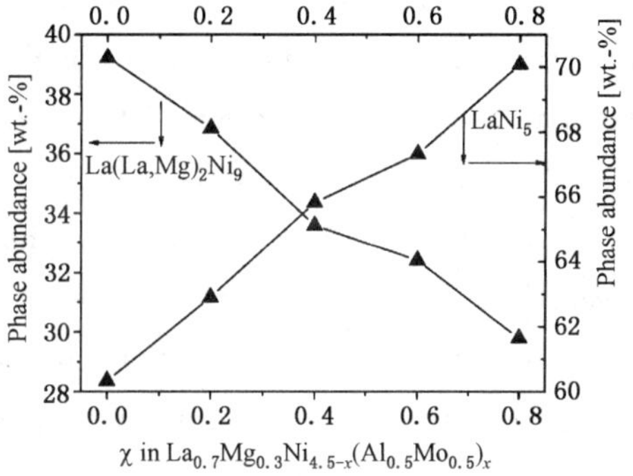

Figure 3 Phase abundance of the $La(La,Mg)_2Ni_9$ phase and the $LaNi_5$ phase existing in the $La_{0.7}Mg_{0.3}Ni_{4.5-x}(Al_{0.5}Mo_{0.5})_x$ ($x=0-0.8$) alloys

P-C Isotherms

The electrochemical pressurecomposition isotherm method is very useful for examining the charging and discharging levels of hydrogen in an anode, although the calculated pressures pertain to a quasi-equilibrium state.[17] Figure 4 shows the electrochemical P-C isotherms for

$La_{0.7}Mg_{0.3}Ni_{4.5-x}(Al_{0.5}Mo_{0.5})_x$ ($x=0-0.8$) alloy electrodes at 298 K. It can be seen that desorption pressure decreases continually as the addition of Al and Mo increases, which indicates that the stability of the hydrides of the alloys increases with the increasing Al and Mo content. The phenomenon observed here is consistent with those reported previously for AB_3 alloys [14] and most AB_5 alloys. [20] Moreover, it can be seen that there is only one plateau in each P-C curve as shown in Figure 4. Since the unit cell of the AB_3 compounds contains one-third of the AB_5 structure and two-thirds of the AB_2 structure, [6] it is perhaps concluded that the plateau pressure of the La(La,Mg)$_2$Ni$_9$ phase is similar to that of the $LaNi_5$ phase or that the difference between their plateau pressures of the AB_3 and AB_5 compounds is too small to be observed. With regard to the hydrogen storage capacity, it increases from 0.616 to 0.868 wt% as x increases from 0 to 0.6. This is mainly attributed to the enhancement of the intrinsic hydrogen storage capacity of the alloy, which results from the decrease in plateau pressure. However, as x increases further, the hydrogen storage capacity decreases to 0.799 wt% when x reaches 0.8. This is mainly attributed to the reasons as follows: it is known that the hydrogen storage capacity of the $LaNi_3$ phase (1.8–1.87 wt.% H_2) is larger than that of the $LaNi_5$ phase (1.4 wt% H_2). [13-14] However, as shown in Figure 3 and Table 3, the La(La,Mg)$_2$Ni$_9$ phase abun-dance decreases while the $LaNi_5$ phase abundance increases with increasing x in the alloys.

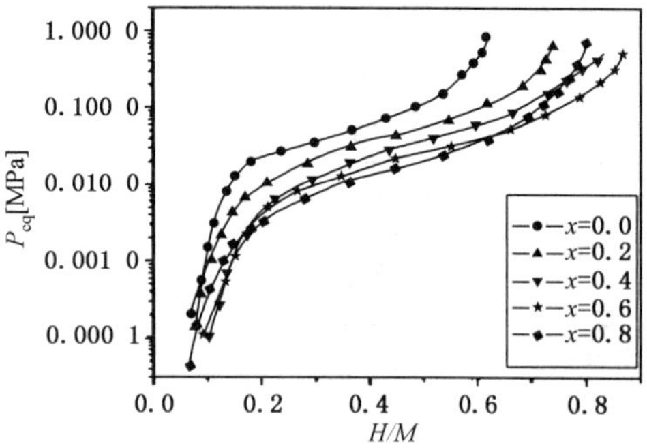

Figure 4　Electrochemical desorption P-C curves for the $La_{0.7}Mg_{0.3}Ni_{4.5-x}(Al_{0.5}Mo_{0.5})_x$ ($x=0,0.2,0.4,0.6,0.8$) alloys at 298 K

Discharge Capacity and Discharge Potential

The activation and maximum discharge capacity of the $La_{0.7}Mg_{0.3}Ni_{4.5-x}(Al_{0.5}Mo_{0.5})_x$ ($x=0-0.8$) alloy electrodes are listed in Table 4. It can be seen that all these alloys can be easily activated to reach the maximum capacity within five cycles. The maximum discharge capacity C_{max} improves first and reaches a maximum at $x=0.6$, and then decreases as x increases further. The variation of the maximum discharge capacity of the alloys is basically consistent with the variation of the H/M with the Al and Mo content in the alloys.

Table 4 Electrode performance of $La_{0.7}Mg_{0.3}Ni_{4.5-x}(Al_{0.5}Mo_{0.5})_x$ (x=0−0.8) alloy electrodes

Sample	H/M	C_{max} [mAh/g]	N_a[a]	HRD_{1200}[b] [%]	S_{70} [%]
x=0.0	0.616	246.3	5	47.2	54.1
x=0.2	0.738	294.8	4	50.6	54.7
x=0.4	0.822	327.6	3	55.8	58.9
x=0.6	0.868	345.4	2	64.7	62.3
x=0.8	0.799	317.6	2	73.8	68.9

[a] The cycle numbers needed to activate the electrodes. [b] The high-rate dischargeability at a discharge current density of 1 200 mA/g.

Figure 5 shows the discharge curves (fifth cycle) of the $La_{0.7}Mg_{0.3}Ni_{4.5-x}(Al_{0.5}Mo_{0.5})_x$ (x = 0 − 0.8) alloy electrodes at 60 mA/g and 298 K.

Obviously, each curve has a wide discharge potential plateau based on the oxidation of desorbed hydrogen from the hydride. Besides, the discharge plateau shifts towards a more positive potential as Al and Mo addition increases in the alloys. As shown in Figure 5, the mid-discharge potential (potential at 50% depth of discharge) decreases from −0.871 0 to −0.8194 V when x increases from 0 to 0.8, which is in good agreement with the reduction of the desorption plateau pressure with increasing Al and Mo content in the alloys.

Cyclic Stability

The cycling capacity retention rate, expressed as S_{70} (%) = $C_{70}/C_{max} \times 100$ (where C_{max} is the maximum discharge capacity, C_{70} is the discharge capacity at the 70th cycle), after 70 cycles at 60 mA/g is also listed in Table 4. It can be seen that the capacity retention rate (S_{70}) increases noticeably from 54.1% to 68.9% as x increases from 0 to 0.8, which indicates that the cyclic stability of the La-Mg-Ni-Al-Mo-system alloys is improved markedly with the increase in Al and Mo content in the alloys. It is known that the capacity degradation of the La-Mg-Ni-type alloy electrode results primarily from two factors: the corrosion of Mg and La and the pulverization of the alloy particles. [20] The Al substitution results in the formation of a protective oxide (hydroxide) of Al on the alloy surface and a subsequent strong protection to the alloy from further corrosion of La and Mg. Moreover, the pulverization of the alloy particles can be improved effectively by substitution of Ni by Mo. In conclusion, the combined effect of the addition of Al and Mo results in the notable increase in the stability of the alloy electrodes. Further investigations in this aspect are going on in our research group.

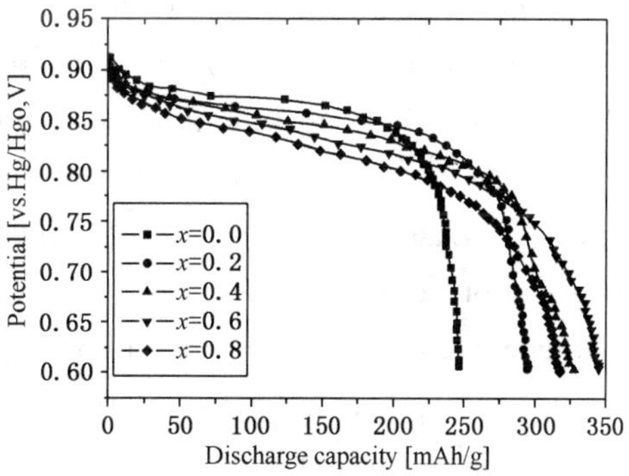

Figure 5 Discharge curves for the $La_{0.7}Mg_{0.3}Ni_{4.5-x}(Al_{0.5}Mo_{0.5})_x$ (x=0−0.8) alloy electrodes at the discharge current density of 60 mA/g and 298 K

High-Rate Dischargeability (HRD) and Electrochemical Kinetics

As an important kinetics property of the hydride electrode in batteries, it is very important to restrain the decrease in the discharge capacity even at high discharge current density. Figure 6 shows the relationship between the HRD and the discharge current density of the $La_{0.7}Mg_{0.3}Ni_{4.5-x}(Al_{0.5}Mo_{0.5})_x$ ($x=0-0.8$) alloy electrodes. It can be seen that HRD of the alloy electrodes increases monotonously with increasing x. The HRD of the alloy electrodes at a discharge current density of 1 200 mA/g are also listed in Table 4. It can be seen that as x increases, the HRD of the alloy electrodes increases from 47.2% ($x=0$) to 73.8% ($x=0.8$). It is well known that the HRD of metal hydride electrodes is influenced mainly by the electrochemical reaction kinetics on the alloy powder surface and the diffusion rate of hydrogen in the bulk of the alloy. [22] To examine the effect of the partial substitution of Ni by Al and Mo on the discharge kinetics, linear polarization was preformed on these alloy electrodes. Based on the measured linear polarization curves, values of the exchange current density I_0 and polarization resistance R_p were evaluated for the alloy electrodes and are summarized in Table 5. Figure 7 shows HRD and R_p as a function of I_0 for the hydrogen evolution reaction at the alloy electrodes. It can be seen that the HRD is a linear function of I_0. Moreover, we can find that the hydrogen diffusion coefficient (D) remains almost unchanged ($13.1-13.6\times10^{-10}$ cm^2/s). Iwakura et al. [23] have pointed out that, if the electrochemical reaction on the surface is the rate-determining factor, a linear dependence of the high-rate dischargeability on the exchange current density should be observed. In contrast, if the diffusion of hydrogen in the bulk is the rate-determining factor, the high-rate dischargeability should be constant, irrespective of exchange density. Therefore, in the present study, the HRD is essentially controlled by the charge-transfer reaction of hydrogen on the surface at a discharge current density of 1 200 mAh/g. As the same time, from Figure 7, it can be seen that R_p decreases with increasing exchange current density, while HRD shows the reverse trend, which implies that the R_p value is closely related to HRD.

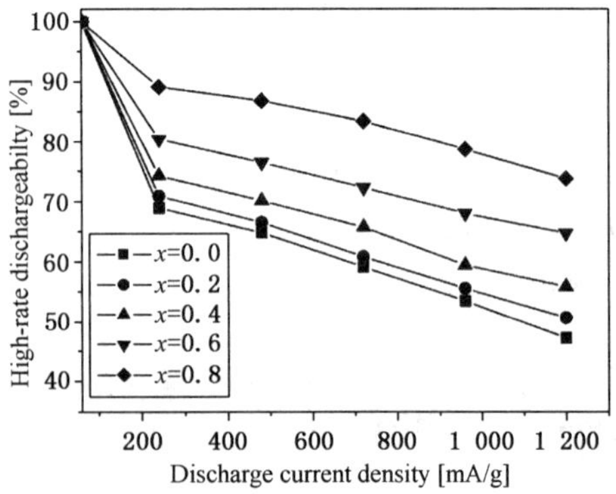

Figure 6　High-rate dischargeability of the $La_{0.7}Mg_{0.3}Ni_{4.5-x}(Al_{0.5}Mo_{0.5})_x$ ($x=0, 0.2, 0.4, 0.6, 0.8$) alloy electrodes at 298 K

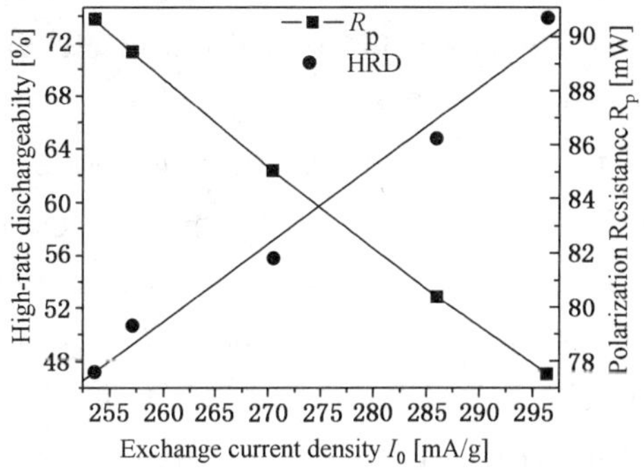

Figure 7　High-rate dischargeability and polarization resistance as a function of exchange current density for hydrogen evolution at $La_{0.7}Mg_{0.3}Ni_{4.5-x}(Al_{0.5}Mo_{0.5})_x$ (x=0—0.8) alloy electrodes

Low-Temperature Dischargeability (LTD)

It has been reported that the discharge capacity of the negative electrode in nickel-metal hydrides decreases drastically with decreasing temperature. [24] Sakai et al. [2] pointed out that the dischargeability of the negative electrodes at relatively low temperatures depended on hydrogen diffusion and/or the charge-transfer process occurring at the metal electrolyte interface. The value of D in the bulk is evaluated using the method described by Iwakura et al. [18] The LTD is expressed as $LTD_{233}(\%)=C_{233}/C_{298}\times 100$ (where C_{233} and C_{298} are the discharge capacities at 233 K and 298 K, respectively). The values of D and I_0 for the $La_{0.7}Mg_{0.3}Ni_{4.5-x}(Al_{0.5}Mo_{0.5})_x$ (x=0—0.8) alloy electrodes at 233 K are also listed in Table 5. It can be found that both I_0 and D are smaller than that at 298 K. Moreover, we find that I_0 remains almost unchanged (80.35—82.17 mA/g), whereas D increases remarkably with increasing x, which implies that hydrogen diffusion in the alloy probably becomes the rate-determining factor for low-temperature dischargeability at 233 K. Figure 8 shows the LTD as a function of D in the alloy electrodes. It can be easily seen that D increases with an increase in x, which can be attributed to cell-volume expansion. The larger the value of D, the greater the LTD of the alloy electrodes.

Table 5　Electrochemical kinetic parameters for the $La_{0.7}Mg_{0.3}Ni_{4.5-x}(Al_{0.5}Mo_{0.5})_x$ (x=0—0.8) alloy electrodes

Sample	Polarization resistance, R_p[mΩ]		Exchange current density, I_0[mA/g]		Hydrogen diffusion coefficient, D[$\times 10^{-10}$ cm^2/s]	
	298 K	233 K	298 K	233 K	298 K	233 K
x=0.0	90.61	249.56	253.62	80.35	13.1	1.6
x=0.2	89.38	248.20	257.12	80.79	13.1	3.0
x=0.4	84.98	246.93	270.43	81.21	13.3	3.7
x=0.6	80.36	245.62	286	81.64	13.5	4.8
x=0.8	77.52	244.04	296.45	82.17	13.6	6.2

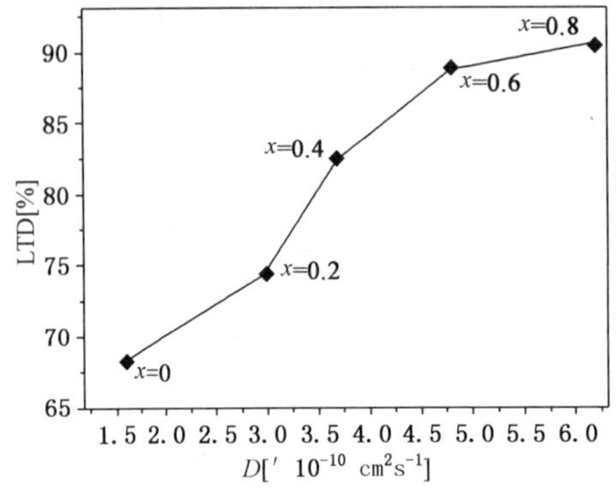

Figure 8　The low-temperautre dischargeability (LTD) as a function of hydrogen diffusion coefficient (*D*) of the $La_{0.7}Mg_{0.3}Ni_{4.5-x}(Al_{0.5}Mo_{0.5})_x$ (x=0, 0.2, 0.4, 0.6, 0.8) alloy electrodes at 233 K

Conclusions

The structure, hydrogen storage characteristics, and electrochemical properties of the $La_{0.7}Mg_{0.3}Ni_{4.5-x}(Al_{0.5}Mo_{0.5})_x$ (x=0, 0.2, 0.4, 0.6, 0.8) hydrogen storage alloys have been investigated systematically. It is found that, by X-ray powder diffraction and Rietveld analysis, all the $La_{0.7}Mg_{0.3}Ni_{4.5-x}(Al_{0.5}Mo_{0.5})_x$ alloys consist of an impurity Ni phase and two main crystallographic phases, namely, the $La(La,Mg)_2Ni_9$ phase and the $LaNi_5$ phase. Moreover, the lattice parameters and cell volumes of both the $La(La,Mg)_2Ni_9$ and the $LaNi_5$ phases increase with increasing Al and Mo content in the alloys. The P-C isotherm curves indicate that the hydrogen storage capacity first increases and then decreases with increasing x, while the desorption pressure always decreases with an increase in x. The electrochemical measurements show that the maximum discharge capacity increases from 246.3 ($x=0$) to 345.4 mAh/g ($x=0.6$), and then decreases to 317.6 mAh/g ($x=0.8$). For a discharge current density of 1 200 mA/g, the HRD of the alloy electrodes increases linearly from 47.2% ($x=0$) to 73.8% ($x=0.4$). Moreover, according to the linear polarization curves, the exchange current density of the alloy electrodes also increases monotonously with increasing x. The value of D increases with increasing Al and Mo content, and thus increases the LTD of the alloy electrodes.

Experimental Section

Alloy Preparation and X-ray Diffraction Analysis: All alloy samples were prepared by carefully arc-melting the constituent elements on a water-cooled copper hearth under argon, followed by annealing in vacuo for 100 h at 770 ℃. The purity of the metals, i. e. La, Mg, Ni, Al, and Mo is higher than 99.9 mass-%, respectively. The samples were all inverted and remelted 5 times to ensure good homogeneity. A slight excess of Mg over sample composition was needed in order to compensate for evaporative loss of Mg under the preparation conditions. Several attempts were performed to find the optimum preparative conditions. The final compounds were carefully checked by Inductively Coupled Plasma-Atomic Emission Spectrometry (ICP-AES) with a TJA Poems-type instrument. There-after, these alloy samples were crushed in a mortar into fine powders of 200—300 mesh.

Crystallographic characteristics of the hydrogen storage alloys were investigated by X-ray diffraction on a Rigaku D/Max 2 500PC X-ray diffractometer (Cu-K_{α} radiation, Bragg-Brentano geometry, 2θ range 10—100°, step size 0.02°, back-scattered rear graphite mono-chromator) by using JADE5 software. [25] The lattice constants and cell volume were calculated by the RIETICA program after internal θ calibration by using silicon as standard reference material.

Electrochemical Measurement: The alloy powder and carbonyl nickel powder were mixed well in a weight ratio of 1 : 5 and pressed into tablets as metal hydride electrodes, which had a diameter of 13 mm and a thickness of 1.5 mm; the weight of each electrode was about 0.9 g.

The electrochemical properties were then measured in a standard three-electrode cell consisting of a working electrode (metal hydride electrode), a counter electrode ($NiOOH/Ni(OH)_2$ electrode), and a reference electrode (Hg/HgO electrode). The electrolyte in the cell was a 6 m KOH aqueous solution. Charge and discharge tests were carried out on an automatic galvanostatic system (DC-5).

The emphasis of these charge/discharge tests was on the electrochemical capacity and stability of the negative electrode, thus the capacity of the positive electrode plate was designed to be much higher than that of the negative electrode. At 298 K, these experimental cells were first charged at current of 60 mA/g for 7 h followed by a rest for 30 min, and were discharged at the same discharge current density to the cut-off voltage of −0.60 V vs. Hg/HgO.

Pressure-composition isotherm (P-C) curves were electrochemically obtained by converting the equilibrium potential of the metal hydride electrode into the equilibrium pressure of hydrogen on the basis of the Nernst equation by using electrochemical data [26] as reported in reference. [27] The equilibrium potential curves were obtained by alternating the following two processes: (1) a pulse discharge of (25 mA/g × 0.25 h), and (2) a rest period until the potential became almost constant. The equilibrium potential change of approximately 30 mV corresponds to the equilibrium pressure change by one order of magnitude. Since the measured potentials have an error of 1—2 mV, the calculated pressure values are accurate to within 10%. [27]

The high-rate dischargeability (HRD) was defined by the following formula:

$$\text{HRD}(\%) = C_n \times 100/(C_n + C_{60})$$

where C_n is the discharge capacities of the alloy electrode at a discharge current of n mA/g (n=60, 240, 480, 720, 960, 1 200); C_{60} is the additional discharge capacity measured subsequently at 60 mA/g after C_n was measured.

For investigating the electrocatalytic

activity of the hydrogen electrode reaction, the linear polarization curves of the electrode were plotted on a EG&G PARC's Model 273 Potentiostat/Galvanostat station by scanning the electrode potential at the rate of 0.1 mV/s from −5 to 5 mV (vs. open circuit potential) at 50% depth of discharge at 298 K and 233 K. The polarization resistance R_p can be obtained from the slope of the linear polarization curves. Moreover, the exchange current density (I_0), which is a measure of the catalytic activity of the electrode, was calculated from the slopes of the polarization curves by the following Equation (1),[17]

$$I_0 = \frac{RT}{FR_p} \tag{1}$$

where R is the gas constant; T is the absolute temperature; F is the Faraday constant; and R_p is the polarization resistance. The potentiostatic discharge technique was used to evaluate the coefficient of diffusion within the bulk of the alloy electrodes. After being fully charged followed by a 30 min open-circuit lay-aside, the test electrodes were discharged with a +500−mV potential-step for 500 s on a EG&G PARC's Model 273 Potentiostat/Galvanostat station, by using the M352 CorrWare electrochemical/corrosion software.

Acknowledgments

This work was financially supported by the National Natural Science Foundation of China (Grant No. 20171042).

References

[1] J. J. G. Willems, K. H. J. Buschow, *J. Less-Common Met.* 1987, *129*, 13-30.

[2] T. Sakai, H. Miyamura, N. Kuriyama, A. Kato, K. Oguro, H. Ishikawa, *J. Electrochem. Soc.* 1990, *137*, 795-799.

[3] T. Kohno, H. Yoshida, F. Kawashima, T. Inaba, I. Sakai, M. Yamamoto, M. Kanda, *J. Alloys Compd.* 2000, *311*, L5-L7.

[4] J. J. G. Willems, *Philips J. Res.* 1984, *39*, 1-94.

[5] H. G. Pan, Y. F. Zhu, M. X. Gao, Q. D. Wang, *J. Electrochem. Soc.* 2002, *149*, A829-A833.

[6] J. Chen, N. Kuriyama, H. T. Takeshita, H. Tanaka, T. Sakai, M. Haruta, *Electrochem. Solid-State Lett.* 2000, *3*, 249-252.

[7] T. Sakai, I. Uehara, H. Iwakura, *J. Alloys Compd.* 1999, *293- 295*, 762-769.

[8] J. J. Reilly, G. D. Adzic, J. R. Johnson, T. Vogt, S. Mukerjee, J. McBreen, *J. Alloys Compd.* 1999, *293-295*, 569-582.

[9] Y. F Liu, H. G. Pan, Y. F. Zhu, R. Li, Y. Q. Lei, *Mater. Sci. Eng. A* 2004, *372*, 163-172.

[10] K. Kadir, T. Sakai, I. Uahara, *J. Alloys Compd.* 1997, *257*, 115-121.

[11] K. Kadir, N. Nuriyama, T. Sakai, I. Uehara, L. Eriksson, *J. Alloys Compd.* 1999, *284*, 145-154.

[12] K. Kadir, T. Sakai, I. Uahara, *J. Alloys Compd.* 1999, *287*, 264-270.

[13] K. Kadir, T. Sakai, I. Uahara, *J. Alloys Compd.* 2000, *302*, 112-117.

[14] J. Chen, H. T. Takeshita, H. Tanaka, N. Kuriyama, T. Sakai, *J. Alloys Compd.* 2000, *302*, 304-313.

[15] B. Liao, Y. Q. Lei, L. X. Chen, G. L. Lu, H. G. Pan, Q. D. Wang, *J. Power Sources* 2004, *129*, 358-367.

[16] P. H. Notton, P. Hokkeling, *J. Electro-*

chem. Soc. 1991,*138*,1877-1885.

[17] T. Sakai, H. Miyamura, N. Kuriyama, A. Kato, K. Oguro, H. Ishikawa, *J. Less-Common Met.* 1990,*159*,127-139.

[18] C. Iwakura, H. Senoh, K. Morimoto, Y. Hara, H. Inoue, *Elec-trochem.* 2002,*70*,2-7.

[19] M. T. Yeh, V. M. Beibutian, S. E. Hsu, *J. Alloys Compd.* 1999,*293-295*,721-723.

[20] J. J. Reilly, "Metal Hydrides Electrodes", in *Handbook of Bat-tery Materials* (Ed.: J. O. Bessenhard), Wiley, New York, 2000, pp. 123-127.

[21] H. G. Pan, Y. F. Liu, M. X. Gao, Y. Q. Lei, Q. D. Wang, *J. Electrochem. Soc.* 2003,*150*, A565-A570.

[22] T. Sakai, H. Miyamura, N. Kuriyama, A. Kato, K. Oguro, H. Ishikawa, *J. Less-Common Met.* 1990,*159*,127-139.

[23] C. Iwakura, T. Oura, H. Inoue, M. Matsuoka, *Electrochim. Acta* 1996,*41*,117-121.

[24] H. Senoh, Y. Hara, H. Inoue, C. Iwakura, *Electrochim. Acta* 2001,*46*,967-971.

[25] *Materials Data JADE Realease* 5, *XRD Pattern Processing*, Materials Data Inc. (MDI), 1997.

[26] T. Sakai, K. Oguro, H. Miyamura, N. Kuriyama, A. Kato, H. Ishikawa, C. Iwakura, *J. Less-Common Met.* 1990,*161*,193-202.

[27] H. G. Pan, Q. W. Jin, M. X. Gao, Y. F. Liu, R. Li, Y. Q. Lei, *J. Alloys Compd.* 2004, *373*,237-245.

Structure and Electrochemical Properties of $Ti_{0.25}V_{0.35}Cr_{0.40-x}Ni_x$ (x =0.05−0.40) Solid Solution Alloys①

Yujun Chai, Minshou Zhao

(Key Laboratory of Rare Earth Chemistry and Physics, Changchun Institute of Applied Chemistry, Chinese Academic of Science, Changchun 130022, China)

Abstract: The structure and electrochemical properties of $Ti_{0.25}V_{0.35}Cr_{0.40-x}Nix$ (x=0.05−0.40) solid solution alloys have been studied in the paper. It is found that these alloys consist of a main solid solution phase with body centered cubic (bcc) structure and a little TiNi-based secondary phase. The solid solution alloys show easier activation behavior at 313 K as a negative electrode material for MH-Ni battery. With changing x from 0.05 to 0.30, the discharge capacity and the high-rate dischargeability increase. The discharge capacity increases with increasing temperature. The maximum discharge capacity is 240 mA h/g at 313 K for x =0.30 and 280 mA h/g at 343 K for x =0.15.

Key words: Solid solution alloy; Electrochemical property; Negative electrode material

1 Introduction

Nickel-metal hydride battery has attracted more attention than Ni-Cd battery due to its high-energy density, long cycle life, high-rate capability and its cleanliness. Among hydrogen storage alloys, solid solution alloy with body-centered cubic (bcc) structure, such as V and V-based alloy, can reversibly absorb/desorb more amount of hydrogen, and some papers are published on this topic[1,2]. The negative electrode materials in nickel-metal hydride battery, which contain solid solution alloy, essentially include $V_3TiNi_{0.56}$, $TiV_{2.1}Ni_{0.3}$ and non-stoichiometric AB_2-type alloys (Ti-based). In general, the solid solution alloy works as a hydrogen storage medium, and C14 Laves phase or TiNibased second phase acts as a micro-current collector or electrocatalyst, and then improves the electrochemical property of alloy electrodes [3-6]. Ti-V-based solid solution alloy, which has a high effective

① Internation Journal of Hydrogen Energy, 2005(30):279-283.

hydrogen storage capacity, has recently been presented by Akiba [7, 8]. It has been pointed out that the alloy of $Ti_{0.25}V_{0.35}Cr_{0.40}$ with bcc structure has a high effective hydrogen storage capacity, and the highest is 2.2 mass% at 313 K. Iba further reported that the addition of Ni from 0.05 to 0.15 could remarkably improve the discharge capacity [9]. However, the effect of Ni on the electrochemical property of the solid solution alloy has not yet been systematically reported. In this paper, the structure and electrochemical properties of $Ti_{0.25}V_{0.35}Cr_{0.40-x}Ni_x$ (x =0.05−0.40) solid solution alloys are relatively discussed in detail.

2 Experimental

Samples of $Ti_{0.25}V_{0.35}Cr_{0.40-x}Ni_x$ (x =0.05−0.40) alloys were melted by arc melting under an argon atmosphere. In order to get a homogeneous alloy, the alloy ingots were turned over and remelted at least four times. Then the as-cast alloys were crushed mechanically in air and further pulverized with a ceramic mortar to the project supported by powder of 200 meshes. The electrodes were prepared by mixing the alloy powder with porous nickel powder in a weight ratio of 1 : 5, and then cold pressing the mixture to form pellets. Prior to electrochemical testing, all alloy electrodes were activated by immersion in 6 M KOH aqueous solution for 2 days. The positive electrode was a sintered $Ni(OH)_2$/NiOOH plate. The charge/discharge tests were carried out by DC-5 battery testing instrument with computer control. The alloy electrodes were charged with a current density of 60 mA/g or discharged with a current density of 60 mA/g to the cut-off voltage of 0.8 V in a water-bath.

In order to evaluate the crystal structure, XRD analysis of $Ti_{0.25}$ VM 0.35$Cr_{0.40-x}$ Nix alloys was carried out on a RIGAKU D/max-II B X-ray diffractometer using Cu $K\alpha$ radiation at 40 kV and 200 mA. The microstructure of the solid solution alloy and composition of each phase were determined by scanning electron microscopy and energy dispersion X-ray spectroscopy.

3 Result and discussion

3.1 Alloy structure

The typical X-ray diffraction patterns are shown in Fig. 1. It can be seen that the alloys are composed of a main phase with a bcc structure and a little Ti-Ni-based secondary phase determined by energy dispersion X-ray spectroscopy. With changing x, from 0.05 to 0.40, the substitution of Ni for Cr makes the main peak position to gradually shift to a higher angle direction, which implies that the increase in x leads to lattice parameter shrinkage. The calculated lattice parameter of solid solution changes from 3.010 to 2.987 Åas shown in Table 1. When x =0.40, more peaks appear and the microstructure of the alloy would change.

Fig. 2 gives the scanning electron micrographs of $Ti_{0.25}V_{0.35}Cr_{0.40-x}Ni_x$

(x=0.05—0.40) solid solution alloys. From the graphs, it can be seen that with increasing Ni the secondary phase increases and further increasing secondary phase aggregates at grain boundary, encircles the solid solution, and finally forms the network structure. The composition of the solid solution and TiNi-based secondary phase is examined semi-quantitatively by energy dispersion X-ray spectroscopy. The results are listed in Table 1. With increasing Ni content, Ti content decreases and V content increases in solid solution phase. However, Cr content decreases and Ni content increases in both solid solution and TiNi-based secondary phase. The results indicate that V mainly exists in the solid solution, and a large amount of Ti precipitates with the element Ni along grain boundary as imaged by SEM, which agrees well with the result presented by Tsukahara [3].

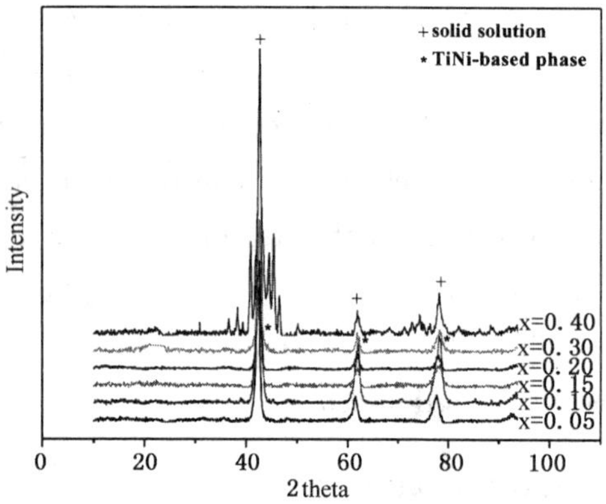

Fig. 1 XRD patterns for $Ti_{0.25}V_{0.35}Cr_{0.40-x}Ni_x$ (x =0.05—0.40) alloys

Table 1 Composition and structure of $Ti_{0.25}V_{0.35}Cr_{0.40-x}Ni_x$ (x =0.05—0.40) alloys

x	Phase	Composition(atom %)				Lattice parameter(Å)	Cell volume(Å)
		Ti	V	Cr	Ni		
0.05	bcc	17.19	42.37	38.16	1.83	3.010	27.27
	Secondary phase	17.69	58.42	22.21	1.68		
0.10	bcc	16.51	44.05	36.84	2.59	2.989	26.70
	Secondary phase	27.42	49.97	20.79	1.83		
0.15	bcc	12.78	48.81	35.46	2.95	2.989	26.70
	Secondary phase	31.11	45.72	20.22	2.95		
0.20	bcc	11.1	58.9	24.22	5.78	2.988	26.68
	Secondary phase	35.34	40.57	7.34	16.75		
0.30	bcc	11.43	62.82	15.19	10.55	2.986	26.62
	Secondary phase	38.5	25.13	3.58	32.79		
0.40	bcc	7.81	67.51	—	24.68	2.987	26.65
	Secondary phase	21.73	38.71	—	39.56		

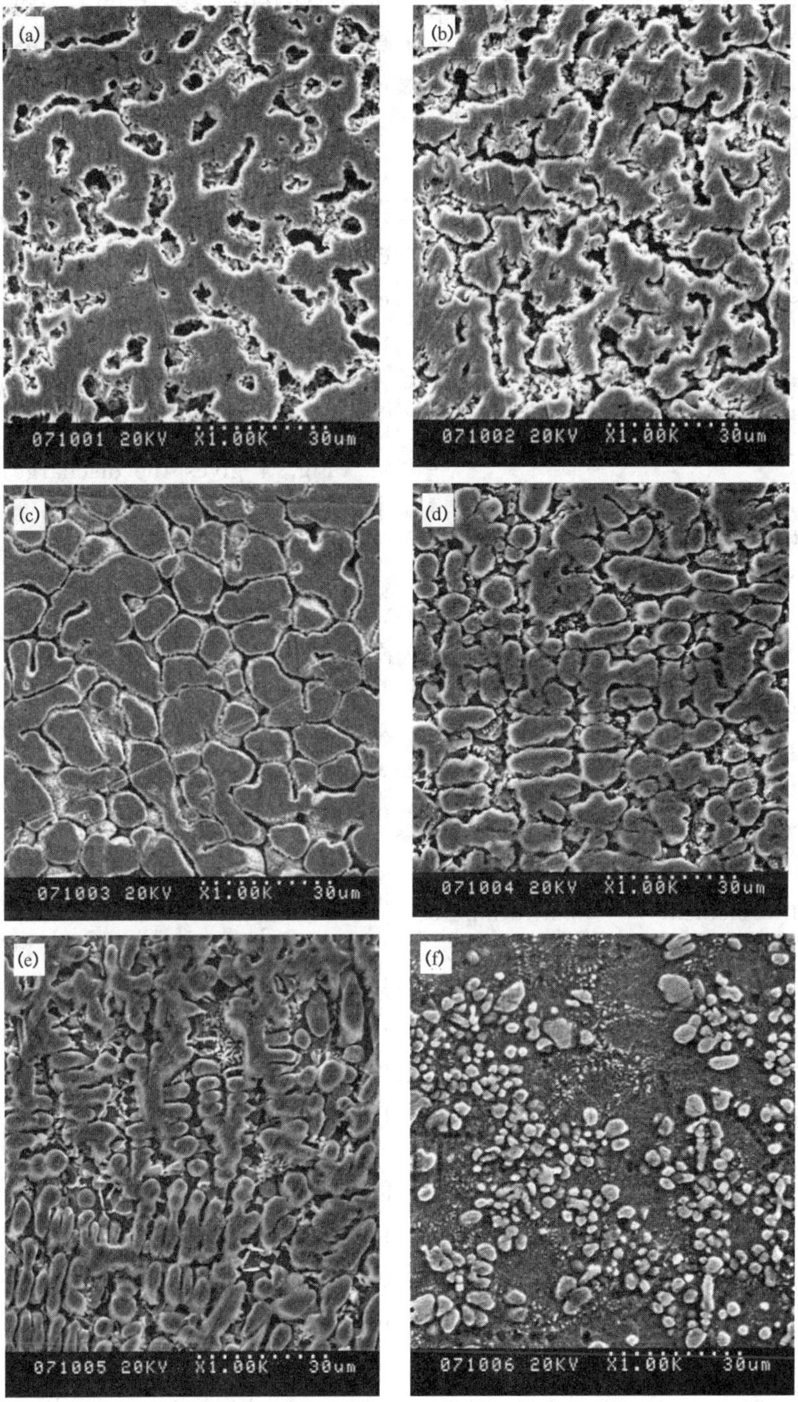

Fig. 2 Scanning electron micrographs of $Ti_{0.25}V_{0.35}Cr_{0.40-x}Ni_x$ alloys (a) $x=0.05$, (b) $x=0.10$, (c) $x=0.15$, (d) $x=0.20$, (e) $x=0.30$, (f) $x=0.40$

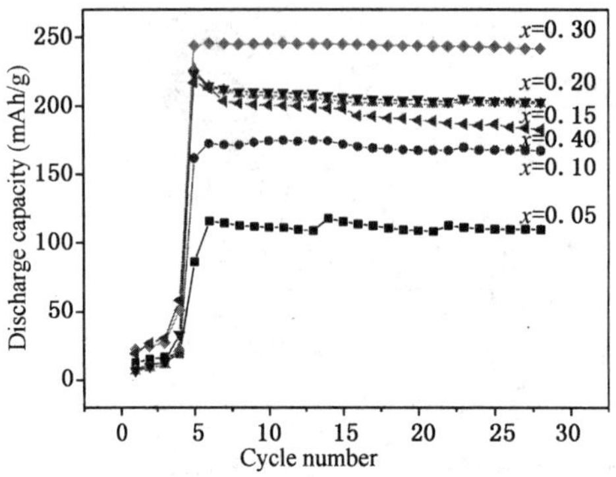

Fig. 3 Relation between discharge capacity and cycle number for $Ti_{0.25}V_{0.35}Cr_{0.40-x}Ni_x$ (x=0.05−0.40) alloys at current density of 60 mA/g at 313 K

3.2 Electrochemical property

$Ti_{0.25}V_{0.35}Cr_{0.40}$ alloy electrode has little electrochemical discharge capacity in KOH electrolyte because it has almost no electrocatalytic action. Its discharge capacity is only 15 mA h/g at 313 K. As we know the element Ni is a good catalyst for the electrochemical reaction concerning hydrogen, and so attention has been focused on the element Ni substitution for Cr. The relation between discharge capacity and cycle number is shown in Fig. 3. It can be found that the alloy electrode is activated for 5−6 charge-discharge cycles, and the discharge capacity increases with changing 0.8 x from 0.05 to 0.30. When x =0.40, the discharge capacity decreases slightly. TiNi-based secondary phase as the electrocatalyst or a current collector improves the electrochemical property of the alloy electrode [1]. At the same time, because the element Cr exists in the alloy, it can form a passive oxide film on the electrode surface, and then improve the alloy electrode corrosion-resistant capability in the alkaline electrolyte, which retards the oxidation and dissolution of other elements [10], so the cyclic durability of the alloy electrode is good. When x = 0.40 the cyclic durability decreases a little. The phenomenon may be explained by the change in the secondary phase and other element's dissolution in the alkaline electrolyte without element Cr, which finally results in decreasing the cyclic durability of the alloy electrode.

Fig. 4 gives the dischargeability for $Ti_{0.25}V_{0.35}Cr_{0.40-x}Ni_x$ (x =0.05−0.40) alloy electrodes. It can be seen that the high-rate dischargeability (HRD) of the alloy electrodes increases with increase in the element Ni. The reason is probably that formed secondary phase accelerates the dehydriding and oxidation of hydrogen on the alloy surface.

The discharge curves of the alloy electrode for x =0.15 at different temperatures are shown in Fig. 5. It can be seen that with increasing temperature, the initial voltage decreases and the platform is even flat. That is to say, the discharge capacity at a higher temperature is higher than that at a lower temperature. The discharge capacity as a function of temperature is shown in Fig. 6. When x =0.05−0.20 the discharge capacity increases dramatically, and when x =0.30−0.40 the discharge capacity increases little or even decreases. We conjecture that very high Ni content may be unfavorable to the discharge capacity at higher temperature. The discharge capacity increases with increasing temperature, but the high-rate dischargeability changes slightly (in Fig. 7). The composition, distribution and content of secondary phase and the influence of the secondary phase on the characteristics for $Ti_{0.25}V_{0.35}Cr_{0.40-x}Ni_x$ alloy electrode at temperature 293 to 343 K are being examined in detail.

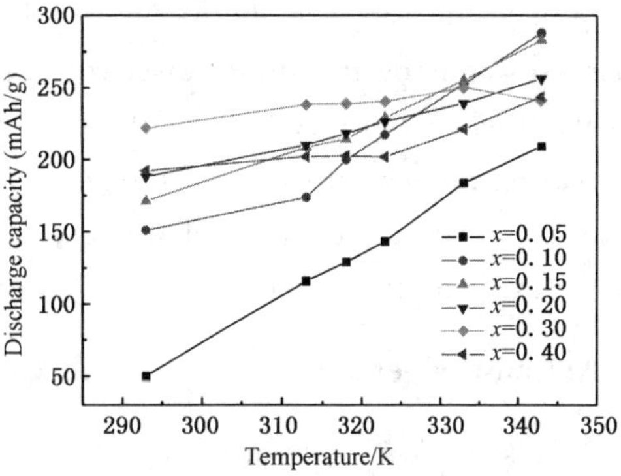

Fig. 6　Relation between discharge capacity and temperature for $Ti_{0.25}V_{0.35}Cr_{0.40-x}Ni_x$ ($x=0.05-0.40$) alloy electrodes

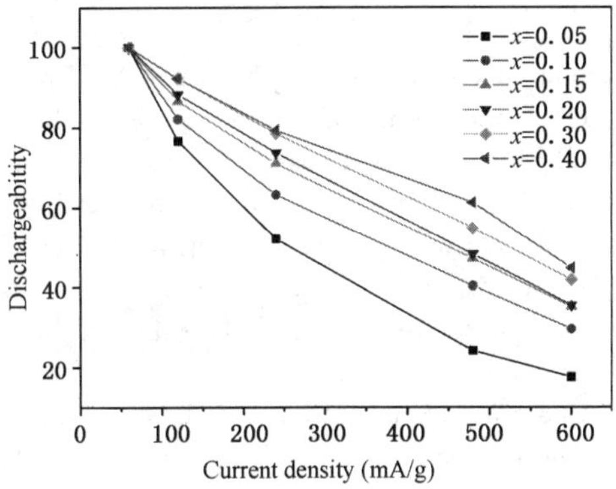

Fig. 4　High-rate dischargeability (HRD) of $Ti_{0.25}V_{0.35}Cr_{0.40-x}Ni_x$ $Ti_{0.25}V_{0.35}Cr_{0.40-x}Ni_x$ ($x=0.05-0.40$) alloys at current density of ($x=0.05-0.40$) alloy electrodes

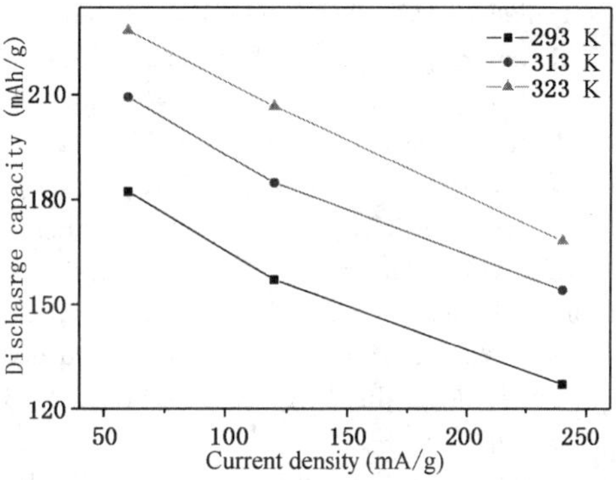

Fig. 7　Dependence of discharge capacity on current density for $Ti_{0.25}V_{0.35}Cr_{0.25}Ni_{0.15}$ alloy electrode at different temperatures

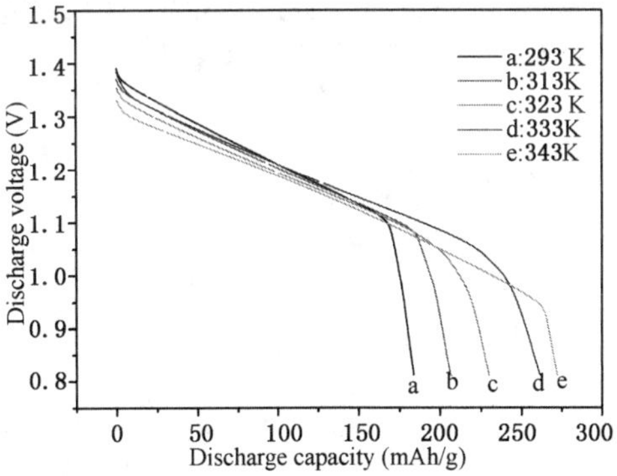

Fig. 5　Discharge curves for $Ti_{0.25}V_{0.35}Cr_{0.40-x}Ni_{0.15}$ ($x=0.05-0.40$) alloy electrodes at different temperatures

4　Conclusion

$Ti_{0.25}V_{0.35}Cr_{0.40-x}$ ($x=0.05-0.30$) alloys are composed of solid solution with bcc structure and TiNi-based secondary phase. TiNi-basded secondary phase aggregates at grain boundary and forms the network stucture, which acts as an eletrocatalyst to accelerate the dehydriding and oxidation of hydrogen on the alloy surface and then improves the electrochemical property of the alloy. With increasing x, from 0.05 to 0.30, the discharge capacity increases and the maximum discharge capacity reaches 240 mA h/g at 313 K. At increasing temperatures, the voltage platform is even flat and the discharge capacity increases to 280 mA h/g at 343 K.

Acknowledgements

This work is supported by the National Natural Science Foundation of China (Grant No. 20171042).

References

[1] Tsukahara M, Takahashi K, Mishima T, Miyamura H, Sakai T, Kuriyama N, Uehara I. The $TiV_3Ni0.56$ hydride electrode: its electrochemical and cycle life characterization. J Alloys Compounds 1995;231:616-20.

[2] Guo R, Chen LX, Lei Y-Q, liao B, Ying T, Wang Q-D. The effect of Ni content on the phase structures and electrochemical properties of V2:1TiNix (x = 0.1 − 0.9) hydrogen storage alloys. Int J Hydrogen Energy 2003; 289: 803-8.

[3] Tsukahara M, Tahashi K, Mishima T, Isomura A, Sakai T. Heat-treatment eBects of V-based solid solution alloy with TiNi-based network structure on hydrogen storage and electrode properties. J Alloys Compounds 1996;243:133-8.

[4] Iwakura C, W-Kyung R, Miyauchi, Inoue H. Electrochemical and structural characterization of Ti-V-Ni hydrogen storage alloys with BCC structure. J Electrochem Soc 2000;147: 2503-6.

[5] Lee H-H, Lee Ki-Y, Lee J-Y. The Ti-based metal hydride electrodes for Ni-MH rechargeable batteries. J Alloys Compounds 1996; 239:63-70.

[6] Zhu YF, Pan HG, Gao MX, Liu YF, Wang QD. Study on the structural and electrochemical properties of Ti-based Discharge capacity (mAh/g) multiphase hydrogen storage alloys. J Alloys Compounds 2002;345:201-9.

[7] Akiba E, Iba H. Hydrogen absorption by laves phase related BCC solid solution. Intermetallics 1998;6:461-70.

[8] Cho SW, Han Ch-S, Park Ch-N, Akiba E. The hydrogen storage Chara-cteristics of Ti-Cr-Valloy.

[9] Iba H, Mori T. Hydrogen-absorbing alloy and hydrogen-absorbing alloy electrode. US 6338764.

[10] Pan HG, Zhu YF, Gao MX, Wang QD. Investigation of the structure and electrochemical properties of superstoichiometric Ti-Zr-V-Mn-Cr-Ni hydrogen storage alloys. J Electrochem Soc 2002;149:A829-33.

Electrochemical Properties of $Ti_{0.17}Zr_{0.08}V_{0.35}Cr_{0.10}Ni_{0.30}$ Alloy Electrode①

Yujun CHai[a], Zhiying Li[b], Wenya Yin[a], Xinbo Zhang[a], Minshou Zhao[a]
([a]Key Laboratory of Rare Earth Chemisitry and Physics, Changchun Institute of Applied Chemisitry, Chinese Academy of Sciences, Changchum, 130022, China)
([b]Sate Key Laboratory of Electroanalytical Chemistry, Changchum Institute of Applied Chemistry, Chinese Academy of Sciences, Changchum, 130022, China)

Abstract: The electrochemical properties of the $Ti_{0.17}Zr_{0.08}V_{0.35}Cr_{0.10}Ni_{0.30}$ alloy electrode were investigated. This alloy has good cycle life at 303 K, 313 K, and even at 323 K, but the discharge capacity decreases gradually at 333 K with increasing cycle number. Both the charge-discharge efficiency and the charge-discharge voltage reduce. The electrochemical impendence spectra indicate that the charge-transfer resistance decreases while the exchange current density increases as temperature increases. The apparent activation energy of the charge-transfer reaction is about 50 kJ mol^{-1}, which is higher than that on the AB_5 type alloy electrode.

Key words: Electrochemical property; Hydrogen storge alloy; Metal hydride electrode; Ni-MH battery

1 Introduction

Recently vanadium and vanadium-based solid solution alloys have attracted considerable interest because of their high theoretical discharge capacity. Takahashi [1, 2] reported that hydrogen storage alloys, $V_3TiNi_{0.56}$ and $V_3TiNi_{0.56}Hf_{0.24}$ had higher discharge capacity than AB_5 type alloy and $Ti_{22}V_{66}Ni_{12}$ had discharge capacity up to 800 mAh g^{-1} at 293 K. Thereafter, the properties of $TiV_{2.1}Ni_x$ alloy electrodes were studied and it was shown that this negative electrode had higher discharge capacity than the above-mentioned alloy [3, 4]. Pan et al. [5, 6] studied $(Ti_{0.8}Zr_{0.2})(V_{0.533}Mn_{0.107}Cr_{0.16}Ni_{0.2})$ (x= 2, 3, 4, 5, 6, 7) multiphase hydrogen storage electrode alloys and pointed out that the alloys had good cycling stability and high rate dischargeability at 303 K. Up to now, the influence of temperature on the discharge capacity of the multiphase alloy has received little attention.

Our results indicated that Ti-Cr-V solid solution alloy itself has no electrochemical activity in KOH solution, and the addition of Ni is essential if the alloy is

① Journal of Applied Electrochemistry, 2006(36):739-743.

used as metal hydride electrode. Therefore we have designed Ti-Zr-V-Cr-Ni alloys and found that they have good electrochemical properties as potential negative electrode materials for Ni-MH batteries. In the present work, the electrochemical properties of $Ti_{0.17}Zr_{0.08}V_{0.35}Cr_{0.10}Ni_{0.30}$ alloy were investigated.

2 Experimental

The sample of $Ti_{0.17}Zr_{0.08}V_{0.35}Cr_{0.1}Ni_{0.3}$ alloy was melted by arc melting under argon. In order to produce homogeneous alloy, the ingot was turned over and remelted at least four times. Thereafter, the as-cast alloy was crushed mechanically in air and further pulverized with a mortar to a powder of 300 mesh. The electrode was prepared by mixing the alloy powder with porous nickel powder in a weight ratio of 1 : 5 and cold-pressing the mixture to form pellets. Prior to electrochemical testing, the alloy electrode was activated by immersion in 6 M KOH aqueous solution for two days. The positive electrode was a sintered $Ni(OH)_2/NiOOH$ plate. The charge and discharge test was carried out using a DC-5 battery testing instrument under computer control. The alloy electrode was charged at a current density of 120 mA g^{-1} for 4 h and discharged at a current density of 60 mA g^{-1} to a cut-off voltage of 0.8 V in a water bath.

The concentration of alloy elements in the KOH solution after 15 charge-discharge cycles was examined by emission spectrochemical analysis with radio frequency inductively coupled plasma (ICP). Electrochem-ical impedance spectroscopy (EIS) measurements were conducted at 50% depth of discharge using a Solartron 1470 Battery Test Unit and a 1255B Frequency Response Analyzer. The EIS spectra were obtained in the frequency range 10^5-10^2 Hz with AC amplitude of 5 mV under open circuit conditions.

3 Results and discussion

Figure 1 gives the relation between the discharge capacity of $Ti_{0.17}Zr_{0.08}V_{0.35}Cr_{0.10}Ni_{0.30}$ alloy electrode and the cycle number at different temperatures. It can be seen that the electrode has good cyclic stability both at 303 and 313 K. The capacity retention after 50th cycles is about 97 and 95%, respectively. When the temperature rises to 323 K the discharge capacity of the electrode remains stable after some cycles. It reaches a maximum at the first cycle at 333 K and then decreases slightly, as shown in Figure 1 b. It can be concluded that this material has potential at medium and high temperatures as the negative electrode material in Ni/MH batteries. The concentration of alloy elements in KOH solution after 15 charging-discharging cycles at various temperatures was examined and the results are shown in Table 1. Vanadium and zirconium were dissolved in the KOH solution. The concentration of vanadium clearly increases with increasing temperature. The dissolution of vanadium mainly existing in solid solution alliy leads to a decrease in the hydrogen storagecapacity, and then reduces the discharge capacity of the alloy. But the concentration of zirconium in the electrolyte changes only slightil with increasing temperature, which indicates that the dissolution of this element is not sensitive to temperature. During the charge-discharge cycles, zirconium, chromium and titanium form a dense oxide film on the electrode surface, which reduces the dissolution of vanadium further [7].

Table 1 Concentration of element dissolved in the KOH electrolyte after 15 charging-discharching cycle

Temperature/K	Concentration/mg/L				
	Ti	Zr	V	Cr	Ni
303	—	13.5	22.3	—	—
313	—	14.5	29.0	—	—
323	—	19.7	68.9	—	—
333	—	12.0	94.1	—	—

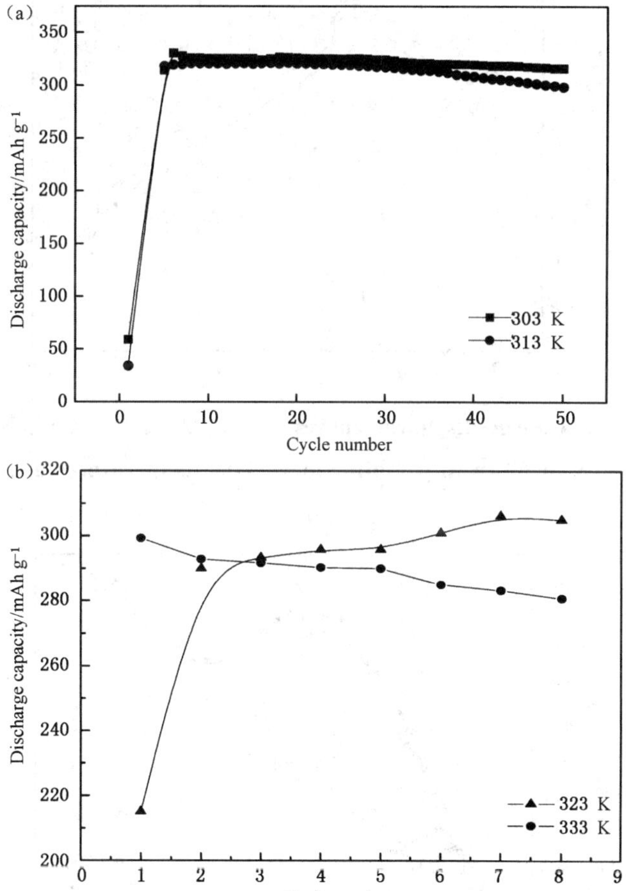

Fig. 1 Relation between discharge capacity and cycie number for $Ti_{0.17}Zr_{0.08}V_{0.35}Cr_{0.10}Ni_{0.30}$ alloy at different temperatures (a: 303 K, 313 K; b 323K, 333 K)

The charge-discharge curve at the 8th cycle at various temperatures is shown in Figure 2. The charge voltage and discharge voltage decrease gradually with increasing temperature. The charge-discharge efficiency at the 8th cycle at different temperatures is 83.7%, 81%, 78.6% and 74.7%, respectively. There are two discharge voltage plateaus in the discharge curve. The first is related to the electrochemical reaction of $(V,M)H_2$ to (V,M) H, and another small plateau appears between A and B. The discharge curve of this alloy electrode is similar to that of $V_3TiNi_{0.56}Hf_{0.24}$. All have two discharge plateaus. Lei et al. [8] believed that the secondary plateau is attributable to the reaction of (Ti,Hf) $(V,Ni)_2H_x$ to (Ti,Hf) $(V,Ni)_2$. We consider the secondary discharge plateau may relate to the discharge process of the secondary phases in the alloy.

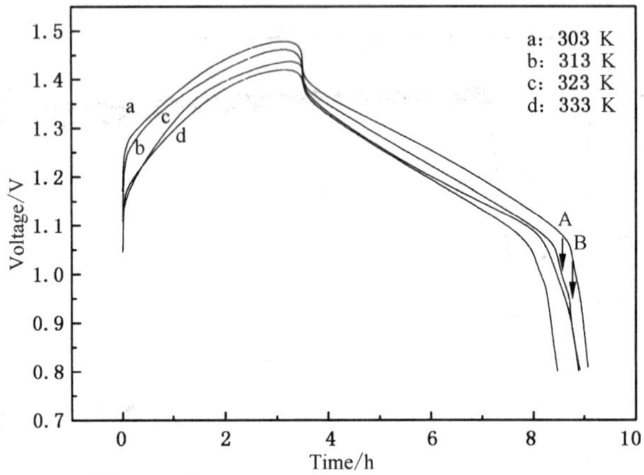

Fig. 2 Charge-discharge curves of $Ti_{0.17}Zr_{0.08}V_{0.35}Cr_{0.10}Ni_{0.30}$ with current density of 60 mAh g^{-1} alloy at various temperatures at 8th cycle number

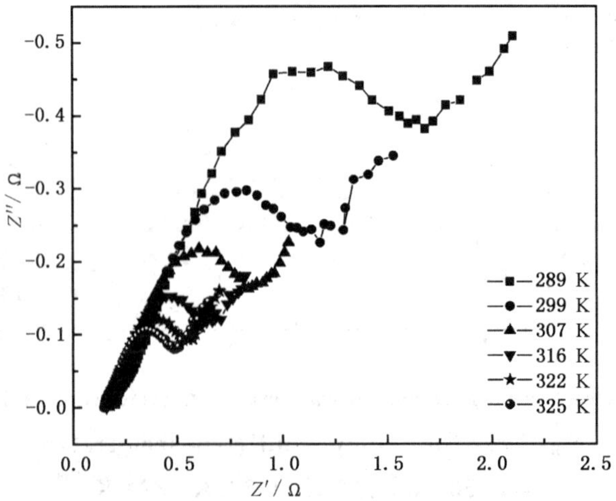

Fig. 3 EIS of $Ti_{0.17}Zr_{0.08}V_{0.35}Cr_{0.10}Ni_{0.30}$ alloy at various temperatres

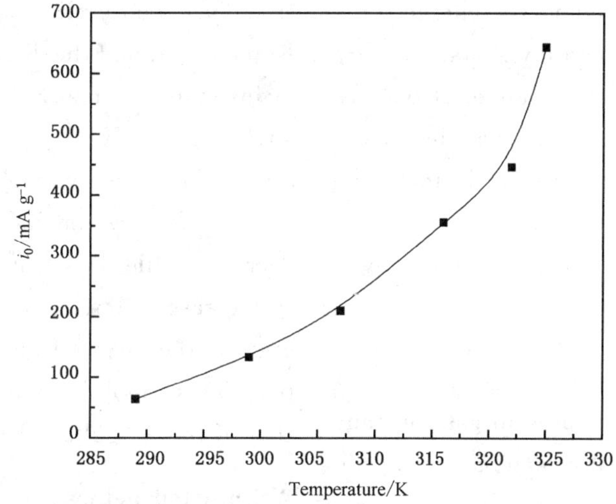

Fig. 4 Exchange current density of $Ti_{0.17}Zr_{0.08}V_{0.35}Cr_{0.10}Ni_{0.30}$ alloy at various temperatures

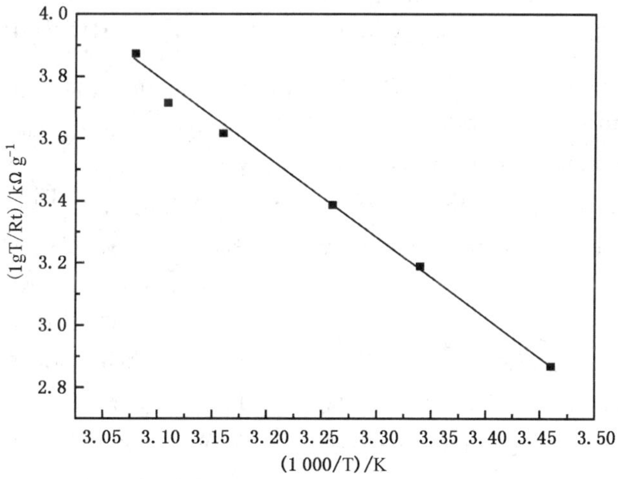

Fig. 5 Relation between lg(T/R_t) and 1 / T at 50% DOD of $Ti_{0.17}Zr_{0.08}Cr_{0.10}Ni_{0.30}$ alloy

The hydrogen in the solid solution alloy is released and initially oxidized during the discharge process; then with increasing depth of discharge the concentration of hydrogen in solid solution is continually reduced and therafter the hydrogen in the secondary phases is released and oxidized, forming the second discharge plateau as described by Xu [9].

The EISs of $Ti_{0.17}Zr_{0.08}V_{0.35}Cr_{0.10}Ni_{0.30}$ alloy at different temperatures are shown in Figure 3. The two semicircles and the straight line are related to the contact resistance between the current collector and the alloy pellet, the charge-transfer resistance on the alloy surface and hydrogen diffusion in the alloy electrode, respectively. It can be seen that the charge-transfer resistance falls with increasing temperature. The exchange current density was calculated using the following equation:

$$I = \frac{RT}{FR_t}$$

where R, T and F represent gas constant, absolute temperature and Faraday constant, respectively. The charge-transfer resistance R_t was calculated according to the model proposed by Kuriyama [10]. The exchange current density increases from 64 mA g^{-1} at 289K to 644 mA g^{-1} at 325 K, as shown in Figure 4, which indicates that the exchange current density is strongly dependent on temperature.

The apparent activation energy, ΔH, of the charge-transfer reaction occurring on the electrode surface is determined by the equation [10]:

$$\lg\left(\frac{T}{R_t}\right) = \frac{\Delta H}{2.3TR} + A$$

where A is a constant and Rt is the charge-transfer resistance. The dependence $\lg(T/R_t)$ on $1/T$ is shown in Figure 5. From the slope of the straight line the apparent activation energy ΔH can be calculated to be about 50 kJ mol^{-1}, which is higher than the activation energy for the AB_5 alloy electrode, about 40 kJ mol^{-1} [11].

4 Conclusion

$Ti_{0.17}Zr_{0.08}V_{0.35}Cr_{0.10}Ni_{0.30}$ alloy electrode has good cyclic stability both at 303 K and 313 K and the discharge capacity remains stable even at 323 K, but decreases slightly at 333 K. With increasing temperature, the charge voltage, the charge-discharge effciency and the discharge voltage decrease while the exchange current density increases. The apparent activation energy of the charge-transfer reaction is about 50 kJ mol^{-1}, which is higher than that of the AB_5 alloy electrode.

Acknowledegement

This project was financially supported by the National Natural Science Foundation of China (Grant No. 20171042).

References

[1] M. Tsukahara, K. Takahashi, T. Mishima, A. Isomura and T. Sakai, *J. Alloys Compd.* 243 (1996) 133.

[2] M. Tsukahara, K. Takahashi, T. Mishima, T. Sakai, H. Miyamura, N. Kuriyama and I. Uehara, *J. Alloys. Compd.* 224 (1995) 162.

[3] C. Iwakura, W. K. Choi, R. Miyauchi and H. Inoue, J. *Electro-chem. Soc.* 147 (2000) 2503.

[4] R. Guo, L. X. Chen, Y. Q. Lei, S. Q. Li, Y. W. Zeng and Q. D. Wang, *J. Alloys. Compd.* 258 (2003) 223.

[5] H. G. Pan, Y. F. Zhu, M. X. Gao and Q.-D. Wang, *J. Electrochem. Soc.* 149 (2002) A829.

[6] H. G. Pan, Y. F. Zhu, M. X. Gao, Y. F. Liu, R. Li, Y. Q. Lei and Q. D. Wang, *J. Alloys. Compd.* 364 (2004) 271.

[7] J. S. Yu, B. H. Liu, K. Cho and J. Y. Lee, *J. Alloys Compd.* 278 (1998) 283.

[8] Q. A. Zhang, Y. Q. Lei, L. X. Chen and Q. D. Wang, *Mater. Chem. Phys.* 71 (2001) 58.

[9] Y. H. Xu, C. P. Chen, X. L. Wang and Q.

D. Wang, *J. Power Sources* 112 (2002) 105.
[10] N. Kuriyanma, T. Sakai, H. Miyamura, I. Uehara, H. Ishikawa and T. Iwasaki, *J. Alloys. Compd*. 202 (1993) 183.
[11] H. Senoh, Y. Hara, H. Inoue and C. Iwakura, *Electrochim. Acta* 46 (2001) 967.

Structure and Electrochemical Characteristics of $Ti_{0.25-x}Zr_xV_{0.35}Cr_{0.1}Ni_{0.3}$ (x=0.05−0.15) Alloys

Yujun Chai[a], Wenya Yin[a], Zhiying Li[b], Xinbo Zhang[a], Minshou Zhao[a]
([a] Key Laboratory of Rare Earth Chemistry and Physics, Changchun Institute of Applied Chemistry, Chinese Academic of Sciences, Changchun 130022, China)
([b] State Key Laboratory of Electroanalytical Chemistry, Changchun Institute of Applied Chemistry, Chinese Academic of Sciences, Changchun 130022, China)

Abstract: The structure and electrochemical properties of the $Ti_{0.25-x}Zr_xV_{0.35}Cr_{0.1}Ni_{0.3}$ (x= 0.05−0.15) alloy electrodes have been investigated. These alloys mainly consist of a V-based solid solution with BCC structure and a C14 Laves phase with hexagonal structure as determined byX-ray diffraction analysis. Scanning electron micrographs show that these alloys form dendritic crystal. The discharge capacities of the alloys increase with increasing temperature from 303 to 333 K, and then decrease while the temperature is above 333 K. The cycle life, the rate capability and the electrochemical impedance spectra are also investigated. The Laves phase as electrocatalyst increases the fresh surface during charging-discharging process, improving the electrochemical performance of these alloy electrodes.

Key words: Multiphase intermetallics; Hydrogen storage

1 Introduction

Vanadium and vanadium-based solid solution alloys have attracted considerable research interest due to higher hydrogen storage capacity. Takahashi and coworkers [1, 2] reported that the electrodes of $V_3TiNi_{0.56}$ and $V_3TiNi_{0.56}Hf_{0.24}$ alloys had higher discharge capacity than other hydrogen storage alloys, and Lei et al. further studied the effect of Mn and Cr on the performance of $V_3TiNi_{0.56}Hf_{0.24}$ hydride electrode [3, 4]. Iwakura et al. [5] studied the properties of $TiV_{2.1}Ni_{0.3}$ hydrogen storage alloy and found that the discharge capacity of the alloy electrode reached 540 mAh/g at a small discharge current density. Further-more, Lei et al. [6] discussed the effect of Ni on the properties of $TiV_{2.1}$ and pointed out that $TiV_{2.1}Ni_{0.5}$ had high discharge capacity and high-rate discharge capability. For other V-based alloys, few investigations have been presented. Recently, the Ti-V-based alloys, such as Ti-V-Cr, Ti-V-Mn reported by Akiba, are demonstrated to absorb/desorb an appreciable amount of hydrogen, and the most effec-

① Intermetallics, 2005(13): 114-1145.

tive hydrogen storage capacity is about 2.2 mass% [7,8]. However, few papers are concerned with the electrochemical characteristics of Ti-V-Cr alloy. The electrochemical performance of the Ti-V-Cr-Ni alloy as metal hydride electrode had been studied and the maximum discharge capacity of 240 mAh/g has been obtained at 313 K for $Ti_{0.25}V_{0.35}Cr_{0.1}Ni_{0.3}$ in our research group.

In order to improve the property of the alloy electrode further, zirconium is used to substitute for titanium. In this paper, the structures and electrochemical characteristics of $Ti_{0.25-x}Zr_xV_{0.35}Cr_{0.1}Ni_{0.3}$ ($x = 0.05 - 0.15$) alloys are discussed.

2 Experimental

The samples of $Ti_{0.25-x}Zr_xV_{0.35}Cr_{0.1}Ni_{0.3}$ ($x=0.05-0.15$) alloys were melted by arc melting under an argon atmosphere. In order to acquire a homogeneous alloy, the alloy ingots were turned over and remelted at least four times. Then the as-cast alloys were crushed mechanically in air and further pulverized with a ceramic mortar to 300 meshes. The electrodes were prepared by mixing the alloy powder with porous nickel powder in a weight ratio of 1 : 5 and cold-pressing the mixture to form pellets. Prior to electrochemical testing, all alloy electrodes were activated by immersion in 6 M KOH aqueous solution for two days. The positive electrode was a sintered $Ni(OH)_2$/NiOOH plate. The charge/discharge tests were carried out with DC-5 battery testing instrument under computer control. The alloy electrodes were charged with a current density of 120 mA/g and discharged with a current density of 60 mA/g to a cut-off voltage of 0.8 V in a water-bath.

The X-ray diffraction (XRD) analysis was used to evaluate the crystal structure of the $Ti_{0.25-x}Zr_xV_{0.35}Cr_{0.1}Ni_{0.3}$ alloys. The experiment was carried out on a RIGAKU D/max-IIB X-ray diffractometer with Cu Kα radiation at 40 kV and 200 mA. Scanning electron microscopy (SEM) was used to study the microstructure of the solid solution alloy. Electrochemical impedance spectroscopy (EIS) measurements were conducted using a Solartron 1 470 battery test unit with a 1255B frequency response analyzer. The EIS spectra were obtained in the frequency range of $10^5 - 10^{-2}$ Hz with ac amplitude perturbation of 5 mV for a depth of discharge of 50% under open circuit condition.

3 Result and discussion

3.1 Structure

It is well known that zirconium has a strong tendency to form Laves phase [9]. When titanium is partially substituted by zirconium, the peaks of the C14 Laves phase appear. The XRD patterns of $Ti_{0.25-x}Zr_xV_{0.35}Cr_{0.1}Ni_{0.3}$ ($x = 0.05 - 0.15$) alloys are shown in Fig. 1. It can be seen that the alloys are mainly composed of a V-based solid solution phase with body-centered cubic (BCC) structure and C14 Laves phase with a hexagonal structure. When $x=0.05$, the peaks of Laves phase are not discernible. With increasing x, the peaks of the Laves phase appear and shift to the low angle. The volume fraction and the lattice parameter of the Laves phase increase as shown in Table 1. Moreover, the lattice parameter of V-based solid solution increases slightly when x increases from 0.05 to 0.10 and decreases as x increases further. It is probable that some zirconium solutes enter the solid solution and cause the lattice swelling due to the partial substitution of zirconium for titanium, while the majority of zirconium forms the C14 Laves phase with other elements. When the content of zirconium is greater than 0.15, more elements dissolve in the Laves phase, and thus make the element in solid solution alloy change.

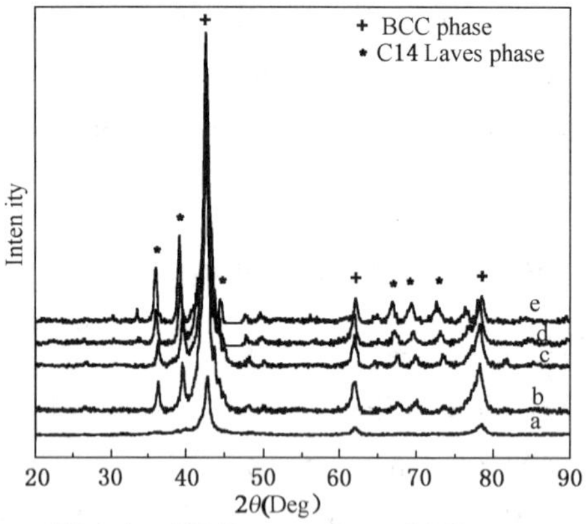

Fig. 1　XRD patterns of $Ti_{0.25-x}Zr_xV_{0.35}Cr_{0.1}Ni_{0.3}$ ($x=0.05-0.15$) alloys (a, 0.05; b, 0.07; c, 0.08; d, 0.10; e, 0.15)

The SEM micrographs of $Ti_{0.25-x}Zr_xV_{0.35}Cr_{0.1}Ni_{0.3}$ ($x=0.05-0.15$) alloys are shown in Fig. 2. The content of zirconium has a pronounced effect on the structure of the alloy. It can be seen from the photographs that the alloys have a dendritic structure when $x=0.05-0.07$, but form columnar crystals when $x=0.08-0.15$, and the grain size decreases when x increases.

Table 1 Compositions and lattice parameters of $Ti_{0.25-x}Zr_xV_{0.35}Cr_{0.1}Ni_{0.3}$ ($x=0.05-0.15$) alloys

X	Phase	Lattice parameter		Unit cell (×10^{-3} nm^3)	Molar fraction
		a	c		
0.05	BCC	0.298 5		26.60	
	BCC	0.2991		26.76	0.74
0.07	$C14_{phase}$	0.294 0	0.803 8	60.18	0.26
	BCC	0.299 4		26.84	0.71
0.08	$C14_{phase}$	0.294 5	0.803 8	60.39	0.29
	BCC	0.299 5		26.87	0.67
0.10	$C14_{phase}$	0.297 7	0.806 4	61.91	0.33
	BCC	0.298 1		26.49	0.51
0.15	$C14_{phase}$	0.298 0	0.810 5	62.35	0.49

3.2　Electrochemical property

Fig. 3 shows the dependence of discharge capacity on cycle number for $Ti_{0.25-x}Zr_xV_{0.35}Cr_{0.1}Ni_{0.3}$ ($x=0.05-0.15$) alloy electrodes at 313 K. It can be seen that the activation property worsens slightly as x increases. The discharge capacity increases with changing x from 0.05 to 0.15 after the electrode is activated, and the cyclic stability of these alloy electrodes is good. In the KOH electrolyte solution, the single solid solution phase has little electrochemical discharge capability because it does not have electrocatalytic activity. However, the C14

Laves phase can act as the electrocatalyst and micro-current collector and make the alloy reversibly absorb/desorb hydrogen [3]. The C14 Laves phase is present in the $Ti_{0.25-x}Zr_xV_{0.35}Cr_{0.1}Ni_{0.3}$ (x=0.05−0.15) alloys as mentioned above, and the content of the C14 Laves phase increases as x increases. The contents of solid solution and C14 Laves phase in the alloys are evaluated semi-quantitatively from the peak intensity in XRD patterns. When the molar ratio of the solid solution and Laves phase is less than 3 and greater than 1, the discharge capacity only changes a little, which implies a correlation between the discharge capacity and the fraction of the phases in the alloys. In the meantime the presence of chromium limits the corrosion of vanadium and also leads to improved cyclic stability [10].

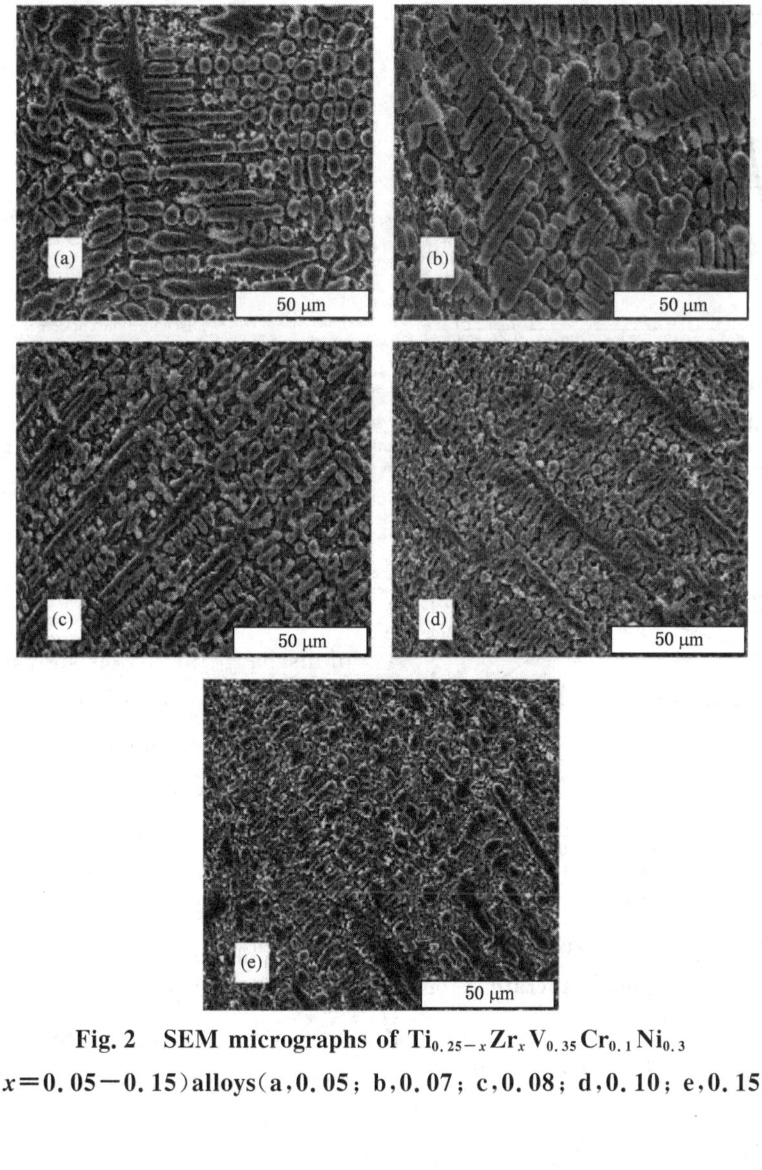

Fig. 2　SEM micrographs of $Ti_{0.25-x}Zr_xV_{0.35}Cr_{0.1}Ni_{0.3}$ (x=0.05−0.15) alloys (a, 0.05; b, 0.07; c, 0.08; d, 0.10; e, 0.15)

All measurements of discharge capacity were conducted by charging at ambient temperature and discharging at various temperatures. The dependence of the discharge capacity of these alloys on temperature is shown in Fig. 4. It can be seen that the discharge capacity changes slightly at 303—323 K, and it evidently increases at 333 K and the maximum discharge capacity of 350 mAh/g is observed. However, the discharge capacity decreases when the temperature is above 333 K.

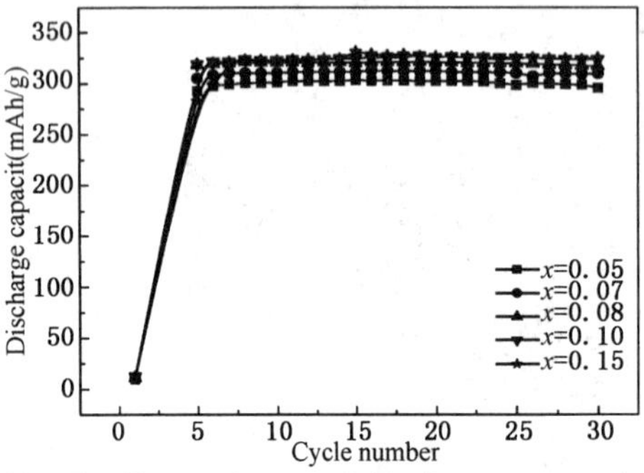

Fig. 3　Dependence of discharge capacity on cycle number for $Ti_{0.25-x}Zr_xV_{0.35}Cr_{0.1}Ni_{0.3}$ (x=0. 05—0. 15) alloy electrodes at 313 K

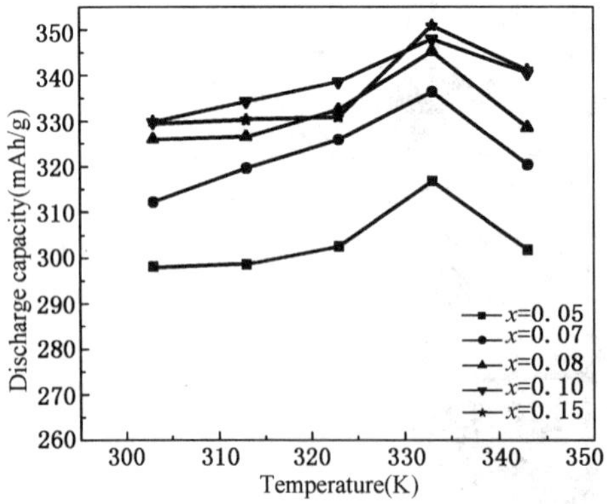

Fig. 4　Dependence of discharge capacity with a discharge current density of 60 mA/g on temperature for $Ti_{0.25-x}Zr_xV_{0.35}Cr_{0.1}Ni_{0.3}$ (x=0. 05—0. 15) alloy electrodes

Fig. 5 gives the relation between the discharge capacity and the discharge current density. The discharge capacity increases with increasing x, which is perhaps related to the content of the Laves phase. The Laves phase accelerates the cracking of the alloys, and creates more fresh surface, which is the specific reaction surface that affects the rate capability [11,12].

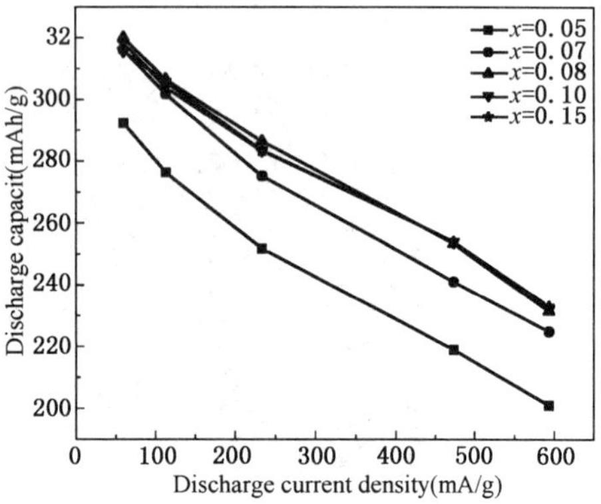

Fig. 5　Relation between the discharge capacity and the discharge current density for $Ti_{0.25-x}Zr_xV_{0.35}Cr_{0.1}Ni_{0.3}$ (x=0. 05—0. 15) alloy electrodes

The electrochemical impedance spectra of $Ti_{0.25-x}Zr_xV_{0.35}Cr_{0.1}Ni_{0.3}$ (x=0. 05—0. 15) alloy electrodes at a DOD (depth of discharge) of 50% is shown in Fig. 6. It is demonstrated that the spectra of all metal hydride consist of two semicircles at high frequency and a straight line at low frequency. The first semicircle looks like a straight line, which may be related to the porosity effect of the alloy electrode. The radius of the second semicircle decreases as x changes from 0. 05 to 0. 08, then changes slightly. The equivalent circuit proposed by Kuriyama and coworkers for the alloy electrode is shown in Fig. 7 [13]. *R*1 is the electrolyte resistance. *R*2 and *Q*2 characterize the contact resistance and the contact capacitance between the current collector and the alloy pellet, respectively, which corresponds to the semicircle in the high frequency region. The contact resistance and the contact capacitance between alloy powders in the electrode pellet are described by *R*3 and *Q*3, respectively. *R*4 and *Q*4 present the charge-transfer resistance and the double-layer capacitance, respectively, which is characterized by the second semicircle. *W* is the Warburg resistance, which is due to the hydrogen diffusion process in the alloy electrode. The fit results by least square method according to this model are shown in Fig. 8. It is evident that the electrolyte resistance *R*1 and the contact resistances *R*2 and *R*3 are almost independent of x. However, the charge-transfer resistance *R*4 decreases markedly as x changes from 0.05 to 0.08 and then decreases slightly, which corresponds to the result mentioned above. These results indicate that the electrochemical activity is close to the charge-transfer resistance on the alloy surface.

From the above result, it can be understood that the substitution of zirconium for titanium changes the charge-transfer resistance, decreases the electrochemical reaction resistance, and enhances the discharge capacity and rate capability.

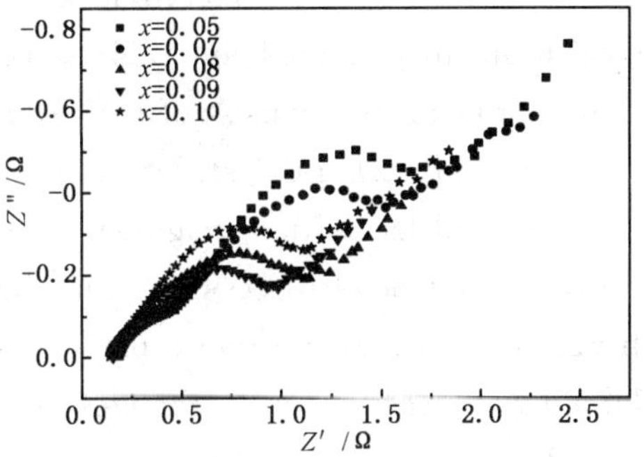

Fig. 6 Electrochemical impedance spectra of $Ti_{0.25-x}Zr_xV_{0.35}Cr_{0.1}Ni_{0.3}$ (x=0.05−0.15) alloy electrodes

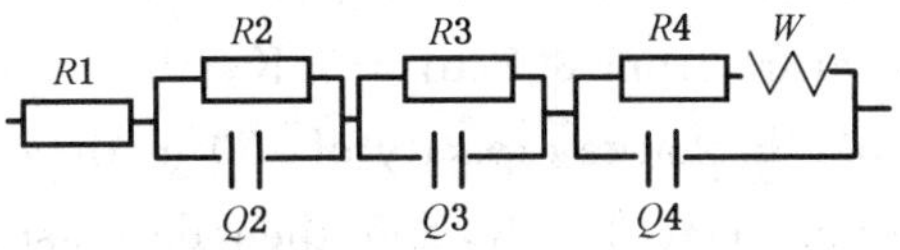

Fig. 7 Equivalent circuit of $Ti_{0.25-x}Zr_xV_{0.35}Cr_{0.1}Ni_{0.3}$ (x=0.05−0.15) alloy electrodes

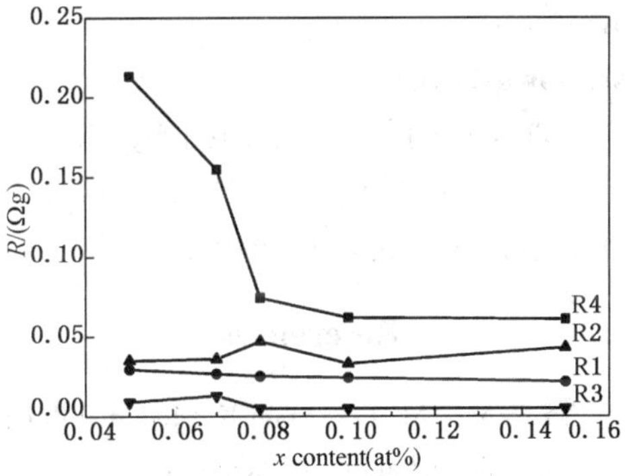

Fig. 8 Resistive component for $Ti_{0.25-x}Zr_xV_{0.35}Cr_{0.1}Ni_{0.3}$ (x=0.05−0.15) metal hydride. (*R*1, the electrolyte resistance; *R*2 *R*3, the contact resistances; *R*4, the charge-transfer resistance)

4 Conclusion

The structures and the electrochemical properties of the $Ti_{0.25-x}Zr_xV_{0.35}Cr_{0.1}$

$Ni_{0.3}$ ($x=0.05-0.15$) electrode alloys have been investigated in this work. These alloys mainly consist of a V-based solid solution with BCC structure and a C14 Laves phase with hexagonal structure, and form dendritic crystal. The discharge capacity and the rate capability of the alloy increase when x changes from 0.05 to 0.15, but the change is small when x varies from 0.8 to 0.15. The discharge capacity is dependent on temperature and is enhanced with increasing temperature from 303 to 333 K; the maximum discharge capacity of 350 mAh/g is obtained at 333 K, and then decreases. The EIS results show that the charge-transfer resistance decreases markedly with increasing x from 0.05 to 0.08 and then decreases slowly.

Acknowledgements

This work is supported by the National Natural Science Foundation of China(Grant No. 20171042).

References

[1] Tsukahara M, Takahashi K, Mishima T, Isomura A, Sakai T. J Alloys Compd 1996; 243:133.

[2] Tsukahara M, Takahashi K, Mishima T, Sakai T, Miyamura H, Kuriyama N, Uehara I. J Alloys Compd 1995;224:162.

[3] Zhang QA, Lei YQ, Yang XG, Du YL, Wang QD. Int J Hydrogen Energy 2000;25:977.

[4] Zhang QA, Lei YQ, Yang XG, Du YL, Wang QD. Int J Hydrogen Energy 2000;25:657.

[5] Iwakura C, Kyung W, Miyauchi R, Inoue H. J Electrochem Soc 2000; 147:2503.

[6] Guo R, Chen LX, Lei YQ, Liao B, Ying T, Wang QD. Int J Hydrogen Energy 2003; 28:803.

[7] Akiba E, Iba H. Intermetallics 1998;6:461.

[8] Cho SW, Han CS, Park CN, Akiba E. J Alloys Compd 1999;288:294.

[9] Ovshinsky SR, Fetcenko MA, Poss J. Nature 1993;260:176.

[10] Park HY, Chang I, Cho WE, Cho BW, Jang H, Lee SR, et al. J Int Hydrogen Energy 2001;26:949.

[11] Tsukahara M, Tsukahara K, Takahash K, Mishima T, Isomura A, Sakai T. J Alloys Compd 1996;236:151.

[12] Kim DM, Jang KJ, Lee JY. J Alloys Compd 1999;293-295:583.

[13] Kuriyanma N, Sakai T, Miyamura H, Uehara I, Ishikawa H, Iwasaki T. J Alloys Compd 1993;202:183.

Structure and Electrochemical Characteristics of $TiV_{1.1}Mn_{0.9}Ni_x$ ($x=0.1-0.7$) Alloys①

Wenya Yin[a,b], Minshou Zhao[a]
([a] Key Laboratory of Rare Earth Chemistry and Physics, Changchun Institute of Applied Chemistry, CAS, 5625 Renmin Street, Changchun 130022, China)
([b] Graduate School of the Chinese Academy of Sciences, 19 Yuquan Road, Beijing 100049, China)

Abstract: The structure and electrochemical properties of $TiV_{1.1}Mn_{0.9}Ni_x$ ($x=0.1-0.7$) solid solution electrode alloys have been investigated. It is found that these alloys mainly consist of a solid solution phase with body centered cubic (bcc) structure and a C14 Laves secondary phase. The solid solution alloys show easy activation behavior, high temperature dischargeability, high discharge capacity and favorable high-rate dischargeability as a negative electrode material in Ni-MH battery. The maximum discharge capacity is 502 mAh g^{-1} at 303Kwhen $x=0.4$. Electrochemical impedance spectroscopy (EIS) test shows that the charge-transfer resistance at the surface of the alloy electrodes decreases obviously with increasing

Key words: Metal hydride electrode; Solid solution alloy; Negative electrode material; Electrochemical property

1 Introduction

Nickel-metal hydride (Ni-MH) secondary batteries have been widely adopted in various portable electronic devices, electric hand tools and hybrid electric vehicles [1-3]. Nowadays, almost all commercial Ni-MH batteries are employing AB_5-type alloys as negative electrode materials. However, AB_5 alloys are not very satisfactory due to their limited discharge capacity (about 372 mAh g^{-1}) [4]. Moreover, although the Zr-based AB_2 type alloys have a higher specific capacity than that of the AB_5 alloys [5], they have the demerits of slow activation and poor rate dischargeability [6].

Vanadium-based solid solution alloys have attracted considerable research interests due to their higher hydrogen storage capacity. Takahashi and coworkers [7] reported that $V_3TiNi_{0.56}$ and $V_3TiNi_{0.56}Hf_{0.24}$ electrode alloys have higher discharge capacity than other hydrogen storage alloys, and Lei and coworkers [8] further studied the effect of Mn and Cr on the performance of $V_3TiNi_{0.56}Hf_{0.24}$ hydride electrode. Re-

① Electrochimica Acta, 2007(52): 2723-27280.

cently, the researches on the application of new V-based alloys as hydrogen storage materials have gained considerable interests. Akiba and coworkers [9-13] found that two kinds of the BCC solid-solution alloys with the compositions Ti-V-Mn and Ti-V-Cr have high hydrogen storage capacity as well as improved activation property and kinetics. The alloys are demonstrated to absorb/desorb an appreciable amount of hydrogen, and the most effective hydrogen storage capacity is about 2.2 mass% at 313 K. However, few works are concerned with the electrochemical characteristics of these Ti-V alloys. The electrochemical performance of the Ti-V-Cr-Ni alloy as a metal hydride electrode had been studied and the maximum discharge capacity of 280 mAh g^{-1} has been obtained at 343 K for $Ti_{0.25}V_{0.35}Cr_{0.25}Ni_{0.15}$ in our research group [14]. Unfortunately, just like Ti-V-Cr alloy, the electrochemical activity of Ti-V-Mn alloy electrode is poor, though it holds higher effective hydrogen storage capacity. Notten and Hokkeling [15] pointed out that additives of Ni in hydrogen storage alloys can significantly improve their high rate discharge ability. In fact nickel has become an indispensable element in hydrogen storage alloy because of its high electrocatalytic activity [16]. Therefore, additive of Ni is expected to be an effective method for improving electrochemical performance of Ti-V-Mn alloy electrode.

In present work, we reported the effect of Ni addition on the structure and electrochemical characteristics of the $TiV_{1.1}Mn_{0.9}Ni_x$ ($x=0.1-0.7$) alloys.

2 Experimental details

2.1 Alloy preparation and X-ray diffraction analysis

All samples were prepared by arc melting the constituent metals or master alloy on a water-cooled cuprum hearth under an argon atmosphere. The purity of all the metals, i.e., Ti, V, Mn and Ni, was higher than 99.9 mass%, respectively. In order to obtain homogeneous alloys, the ingots of alloys were turned over and remelted at least four times. Then the as-cast alloys were crushed mechanically to particles with the average size of 26.24 μm (300 meshs).

The crystal structure of the hydrogen storage alloys was determined by X-ray diffraction (XRD) analysis on a Rigaku D/Max 2500PC X-ray diffractometer with Cu Kα radiation at 40 kV and 200 mA (Bragg-Brentano geometry, 2θ range 20—90°, step size 0.02°, backscattered rear graphite monochromator). Scanning electron microscopy (SEM) was used to study the microstructure of the solid solution alloy.

2.2 Electrochemical measurement

The electrodes were prepared by mixing the alloy powders with carbonylic nickel powders in a weight ratio of 1 : 5 and then cold-pressing the mixture to form pellets of 10 mm in diameter and thickness of 1.5 mm under a pressure of

14 MPa. Prior to electrochemical testing, all alloy electrodes were activated by immersion in 6 M KOH aqueous solution for 48 h. The positive electrode was a sintered $Ni(OH)_2$/NiOOH plate.

The charge/discharge tests were carried out with DC-5 battery testing instrument under a computer control. Each alloy electrode was charged with a current density of 60 mA g^{-1} and discharged with a current density of 60 mA g^{-1} to a cut-off voltage of 0.8 V at different temperatures (303, 318, and 333 K, respectively).

Table 1　Phase composition and lattice parameter of $TiV_{1.1}Mn_{0.9}Ni_x$ (x=0.0−0.7) alloy

x	Phase	Composition (at. %)				Lattice parameter (Å)		Cell volume (Å^3)
		Ti	V	Mn	Ni	a	c	
0.00	BCC	33.33	36.67	30.00		3.0352		27.96
0.10	BCC	32.36	38.28	27.12	2.24	3.0285		27.78
	$C14_{phase}$	34.48	36.07	26.51	2.94	4.9449	8.1152	171.84
0.25	BCC	23.21	45.00	28.27	3.52	3.0110		27.30
	$C14_{phase}$	35.46	23.88	27.76	12.90	4.9133	8.0382	168.05
0.40	BCC	18.88	50.48	26.85	3.79	2.9939		26.84
	$C14_{phase}$	35.49	22.44	27.80	14.27	4.8837	8.0593	166.47
0.55	BCC	17.03	51.35	27.27	4.35	2.9854		26.61
	$C14_{phase}$	35.25	22.10	26.90	15.75	4.8768	7.9926	164.62
0.70	BCC	14.31	53.00	27.35	5.34	2.9601		25.94
	$C14_{phase}$	36.01	18.61	26.18	19.20	4.8638	7.9672	163.22

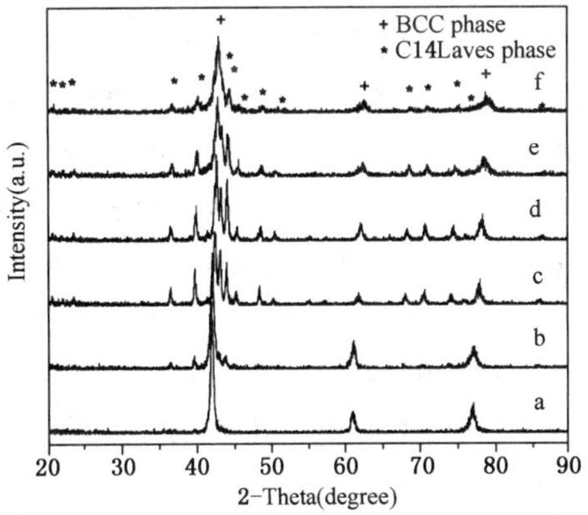

Fig. 1　XRD patterns of $TiV_{1.1}Mn_{0.9}Ni_x$ (x=0.0−0.7) alloys: (a) 0.00; (b) 0.10; (c) 0.25; (d) 0.40; (e) 0.55; (f) 0.70

To evaluate the high-rate discharge (HRD) (in the range of 60-1000 mA g^{-1}), the charging current density was kept a constant of 60 mA g^{-1} and the obtained discharge capacity was denoted as C_n (with n=30, 60, 180, 360, 600, 1 000 mA g^{-1}, respectively). HRD was generally defined as $C_n \times 100/(C_n + C_{30})$.

Electrochemical impedance spectroscopy measurements were conducted using a solartron 1287 battery test unit with a 1255 B frequency response analyzer with Z-POLT software for WINDOWS. The EIS spectra were obtained in the frequency range of 10^5 to 10^{-2} Hz with an ac amplitude perturbation of 5 mV for a depth of discharge (DOD) of 50% under open circuit condition.

3 Results and discussion

3.1 Structure characteristic

The X-ray diffraction patterns of $TiV_{1.1}Mn_{0.9}Ni_x$ ($x=0.0-0.7$) alloys are shown in Fig. 1. Besides the main body-centered cubic (BCC) phase C14 Laves phase appears in the Ni-containing alloy ($x>0$) also. Moreover, the peaks of the C14 Laves phase shift toward higher angle with increasing nickel content in the alloys. The SEM micrographs of $TiV_{1.1}Mn_{0.9}Ni_x$ ($x=0.0-0.7$) alloys are shown in Fig. 2. It can be easily seen that, with increasing nickel content, the secondary phase increases and finally forms a three-dimensional phase structure, which contains two distinct crystal phases: the V-based solid solution phase (identified as α) and the C14 Laves phase (identified as β). The compositions of the solid solution and the Laves phase were examined by energy dispersion X-ray spectroscopy (EDS). The results are listed in Table 1. It can be seen from Table 1 that with increasing nickel content, vanadium content increases from 38.28% ($x=0.1$) to 53% ($x=0.7$) and titanium content decreases from 32.36% ($x=0.1$) to 14.31% ($x=0.7$) in the solid solution phase, and former decreases from 36.07% ($x=0.1$) to 18.61% ($x=0.7$) and latter increases from 34.48% ($x=0.1$) to 36.01% ($x=0.7$) in C14 Laves phase. Therefore, it can be concluded that the addition of nickel has a pronounced effect on the structure of the solid solution alloy.

The lattice parameter and the cell volume of $TiV_{1.1}Mn_{0.9}Ni_x$ ($x=0.0-0.7$) alloys are also listed in Table 1. It is found that the lattice parameter of V-based solid solution and the cell volume decrease monotonically with increasing nickel content. The former decreases from 3.0285 Å ($x=0.1$) to 2.9601 Å ($x=0.7$) and the latter decreases from 27.78 Å^3 ($x=0.1$) to 25.94 Å^3 ($x=0.7$), respectively. The shrinkage of the cell volumes of the two phases mentioned above is due to the dissolving of Ni into the two phases to form a substitution solid solution and C14 Laves phase, respectively, while the atomic radius of Ni (1.24 Å) is smaller than that of V (1.35 Å) and Mn (1.32Å), which finally result in the decrease of the cell volumes.

3.2 Electrochemical property

Fig. 3 shows the dependence of discharge capacity on cycle number for $TiV_{1.1}Mn_{0.9}Ni_x$ ($x=0.0-0.7$) alloy electrodes at 303 K. As can be seen from Fig. 3, electrochemical discharge capability (less than 100 mAh g^{-1}) of the primitive V-based solid solution alloy electrode is very low because of its poor electrochemical activity. Fortunately, additive of Ni obviously improves the activation property of the alloy electrodes. The discharge capacity firstly increases with increasing x from 0.1 to 0.4 and then decreases when x increases further. The maximum discharge capacity is 502 mAh g^{-1} at 303 K when $x=0.4$. The formation of the C14 Laves phase in $TiV_{1.1}Mn_{0.9}Ni_x$ ($x=0.0-0.7$) alloys makes the alloy reversiblely absorb/desorb hydrogen because it could serve as an electrochemical catalyst and micro-current collector [17]. Furthermore, with increasing nickel content, vanadium content increases in solid solution phase and decreases in C14 Laves phase, respectively. Decreasing vanadium content in the secondary phase limits the corrosion of vanadium and also leads to improve cycle stability [7].

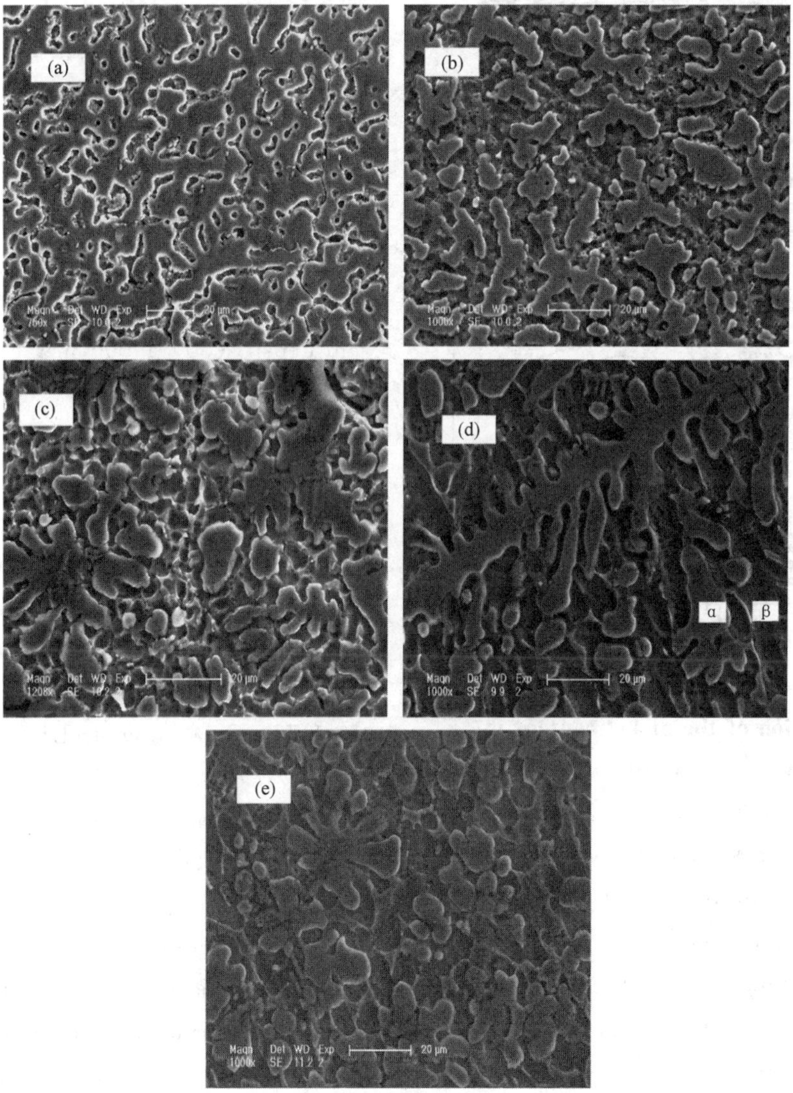

Fig. 2 SEM images of $TiV_{1.1}Mn_{0.9}Ni_x$ ($x=0.0-0.7$) alloys: (a) 0.10; (b) 0.25; (c) 0.40; (d) 0.55; (e) 0.70

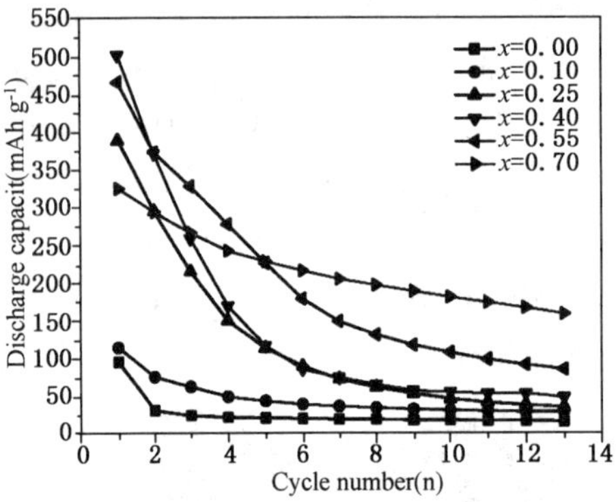

Fig. 3　Relationship of discharge capacity with cycle number for $TiV_{1.1}Mn_{0.9}Ni_x$ (x=0. 0—0. 7) hydrogen storage alloy electrodes at 303 K

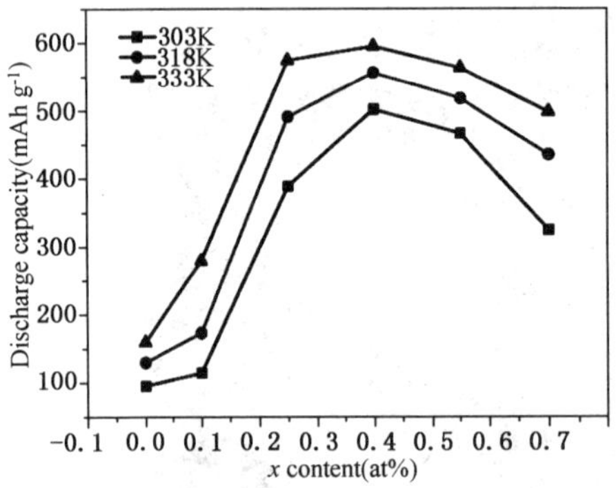

Fig. 4　Discharge capacity as a function of the nickel content in $TiV_{1.1}Mn_{0.9}Ni_x$ (x=0. 0—0. 7) alloy electrodes at 303, 318, 333 K, respectively

In order to investigate the temperature-related properties of the hydrogen storage electrodes, they are fully charged at room temperature and discharged at various temperatures. Discharge capacity as a function of the nickel content in $TiV_{1.1}Mn_{0.9}Ni_x$ (x=0. 0—0. 7) alloy electrodes is shown in Fig. 4 at various temperatures. It can be easily seen that the discharge capacity of $TiV_{1.1}Mn_{0.9}Ni_x$ (x=0. 0—0. 7) alloys increases with increasing nickel content first and then decreasing at different temperatures, and $TiV_{1.1}Mn_{0.9}Ni_{0.4}$ has higher discharge capacity than other one. Moreover, the discharge capacity of each sample alloy increases with increasing temperature. For example, the maximum discharge capacity is increased from 502 mAh g^{-1} at 303 K to 595 mAh g^{-1} at 333 K when x=0. 4.

It is very important to restrain the decrease of the discharge capacity even at the high charge/discharge current density for practical application of metal hydride electrode. The effect of the discharge current density (30—1 000 mA g^{-1}) on the discharge capacity of $TiV_{1.1}Mn_{0.9}Ni_x$ (x=0. 1—0. 7) alloy electrodes is shown in Fig. 5. It can be observed that the HRD of the alloy electrodes increases with increasing content of nickel, which is perhaps related to the content of C14 Laves phase. Taking the discharge current density being 1 000 mA g^{-1} as an example, the HRD of the alloy electrodes increases from 3% (x=0. 1) to 35. 2% (x=0. 7). It is possible that the formed secondary phase accelerates the dehydriding and oxidation of hydrogen on the alloy surface.

The charge-transfer process occurring at the electrode/electrolyte interface is an important factor for the rate dischargeability of a metal-hydride electrode [18].

Fig. 6 shows the electrochemical impedance spectra of $TiV_{1.1}Mn_{0.9}Ni_x$ (x=0. 1—0. 7) alloy electrodes at a DOD (depth of discharge) of 50%. It can be observed that the electrochem ical impedance spectrum consists of two semicircles at high frequency and a straight line at low frequency. On the basis of the equivalent circuit proposed by Kuriyama et al. [19], the R_{ct}, charge-transfer resistance, values are obtained by means of the fitting program Z-View. Table 2 gives the values of R_{ct} and exchange current density I_0 obtained by the following equation [20]: where R is the gas constant, T the absolute temperature, and F is the Faraday constant.

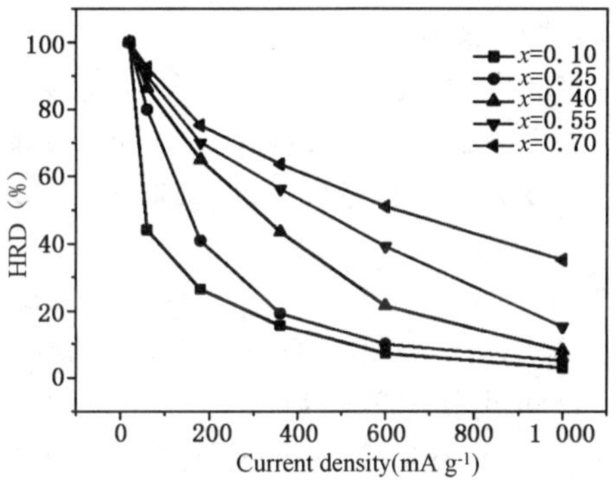

Fig. 5 High-rate dischargeability (HRD) of $TiV_{1.1}Mn_{0.9}Ni_x$ (x=0.1—0.7) hydrogen storage alloy electrodes

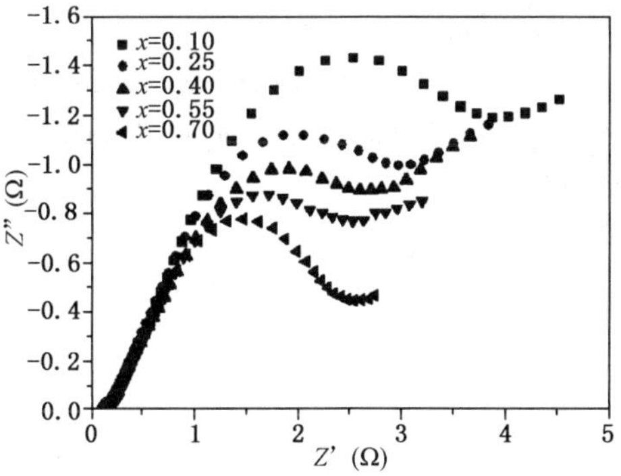

Fig. 6 Electrochemical impedance spectra for $TiV_{1.1}Mn_{0.9}Ni_x$ (x=0.1—0.7) hydrogen storage alloy electrodes at 50% DOD

The calculated results show R_{ct} decreases from 499 mΩ at x=0.1 to 211 mΩ at x = 0.7 and accordingly I_0 increases from 52 mA g^{-1} to 124 mA g^{-1}, respectively. This indicates that the increasing nickel content is beneficial to the charge-transfer reaction at the electrode/electrolyte interface, which in good accordance with the results mentioned above.

Table 2 The charge-transfer resistance R_{ct}, exchange-current density I_0 for $TiV_{1.1}Mn_{0.9}Ni_x$ (x=0.1—0.7) electrodes

Sample	Charge-transfer resistance, R_{ct} (mΩ)	Exchange-current density, I_0 (mA g^{-1})
x=0.10	499	52
x=0.25	407	64
x=0.40	345	76
x=0.55	290	90
x=0.70	211	124

$$I_0 = \left(\frac{RT}{F}\right)\left(\frac{1}{R_{ct}}\right) \quad (1)$$

4 Conclusions

$TiV_{1.1}Mn_{0.9}Ni_x$ (x=0.1—0.7) alloys mainly consist of a V-based solid solution with BCC structure and a C14 Laves secondary phase. C14 Laves phase as electrochemical catalyst improves the electrochemical properties of the alloy electrode during the charging/discharging cycle. The solid solution alloys show easier activation behavior, higher discharge capacity and high-rate dischargeability as a negative electrode material in Ni-MH battery. The discharge capacity of the alloy increases with increasing temperature. The maximum discharge capacity is

502 mAh g^{-1} at 303 K and 595 mAh g^{-1} at 333 K, respectively, when $x=0.4$. The EIS results show that the charge-transfer resistance decreases markedly with increasing x from 0.1 to 0.7.

Acknowledgement

This work was financially supported by the National Natural Science Foundation of China(Grant No. 20171042).

References

[1] H. G. Pan, Y. F. Zhu, M. X. Gao, Q. D. Wang, J. Electrochem. Soc. 149(2002)829.

[2] J. Chen, N. Kuriyama, H. T. Takeshita, H. Tanaka, T. Sakai, M. Haruta, Electrochem. Solid State Lett. 3(6)(2000)249.

[3] X. B. Zhang, D. Z. Sun, W. Y. Yin, Y. J. Chai, M. S. Zhao, Electrochim. Acta 50 (2005)2911.

[4] H. Ogawa, M. Ikoma, H. Kawano, I. Matsumoto, J. Power Sources 12 (1988)393.

[5] S. R. Ovshinsky, M. A. Fetcenko, J. Ross. Sci. 260(1993)176.

[6] J. J. Reilly, in: J. O. Besenhard(Ed.), Handbook of Battery Materials, Wiley, New York, 2000.

[7] M. Tsukahara, K. Takahashi, T. Mishima, A. Isomura, T. Sakai, J. Alloys Compd. 243 (1996)133.

[8] Q. A. Zhang, Y. Q. Lei, X. G. Yang, Y. L. Du, Q. D. Wang, Int. J. Hydr. Energy 25 (2000)977.

[9] H. Iba, E. Akiba, J. Alloys Compd. 231 (1995)508.

[10] E. Akiba, H. Iba, Intermetallics 6 (1998) 461.

[11] E. Akiba, H. Enoki, Materia Jpn. 37(1998) 645(in Japanese).

[12] J. Huot, E. Akiba, H. Iba, J. Alloys Compd. 228(1995)181.

[13] H. Iba, T. Mouri, M. Shionoya, E. Akiba, Materia Jpn. 36(1997)640(in Japanese).

[14] Y. J. Chai, M. S. Zhao, Int. J. Hydr. Energy 30(2005)279.

[15] P. H. Notten, P. Hokkeling, J. Electrochem. Soc. 138(1991)1877.

[16] J. Kleperis, G. Wojcik, A. Czerwinski, J. Skowronski, M. Kopczyk, M. Beltowska-Brzezinska, J. Solid State Electrochem. 5 (2001)229.

[17] H. G. Pan, Y. F. Zhu, M. X. Gao, Y. F. Liu, R. Li, Y. Q. Lei, Q. D. Wang, J. Alloys lompd. 370(2004)254.

[18] T. Sakai, H. Miyamura, N. Kuriyama, A. Kato, K. Oguro, H. Ishikawa, J. Less-Common Met. 159(1990)127.

[19] N. Kuriyama, T. Sakai, H. Miyamura, I. Uehara, H. Ishikawa, T. Iwasaki, J. Electrochem. Soc. 139(1992)172.

[20] N. Kuriyama, T. Sakai, H. Miyamura, I. Uehara, H. Ishikawa, J. Alloys. Compd. 202 (1993)183.

Microstructure and Some Dynamic Performances of $Ti_{0.17}Zr_{0.08}V_{0.34}RE_{0.01}Cr_{0.1}Ni_{0.3}$ (RE=Ce, Dy) Hydrogen Storage Electrode Alloys

Yuqing Qiao[a,b], Minshou Zhao[a,b], Xinjian Zhu[c], Guangyi Cao[c]

([a] State Key Laboratory of Metastable Material Science and Technology, Yanshan University, Qinhuangdao 066004, PR China)

([b] Key Laboratory of Rare Earth Chemistry and Physics, Changchun Institute of Applied Chemistry, Chinese Academy of Science, Changchun 130022, PR China)

([c] Institute of Fuel Cell, Shanghai Jiaotong University, Shanghai 200030, PR China)

Abstract: Microstructure and some dynamic performances of $Ti_{0.17}Zr_{0.08}V_{0.34}RE_{0.01}Cr_{0.1}Ni_{0.3}$ (RE=Ce, Dy) hydrogen storage electrode alloys have been investigated using XRD, FESEM-EDS, ICP-MS and EIS measurements. The alloy is composed of V-based solid solution phase with a dendritic shape and a continuous C14 Laves phase with a network shape surrounding the dendrite. Pressure-composition isotherm curves indicate that the alloy with Dy addition has a lower equilibrium hydrogen pressure and a wider plateau region. The alloy electrode with Dy addition has higher discharge capacity, while the alloy electrode with Ce addition has better activation and higher cycle stability. The alloy electrode with Ce addition has better electrochemical activity with higher exchange current density (127.5 mA g^{-1}), lower charge transfer resistance (1.37 Ω) and lower apparent activation energy (30.5 kJ mol^{-1}). The capacity degradation behavior for the alloy electrode is attributed to two main factors: one is the dissolutions of V and Zr element to KOH solution, and another is the larger charge transfer resistance which increases with increasing cycle number. Hydrogen diffusion coefficient is a rate-limiting factor at higher discharge current, while exchange current density is the rate-limiting factor at lower discharge current, both hydrogen diffusion coefficient and exchange current density are responsible for the poor high-rate dischargeability of the alloy in this case.

Key words: Hydrogen storage electrode alloys; Ni-MH battery; V-based solid solution; Electrochemical impedance spectroscopy

1 Introduction

In recent years, various promising electrode alloys used as the negative electrode materials of Ni-MH secondary batteries have been evaluated and examined, such as AB_5

① International Journal of Hydrogen Energy, 2007(32): 3427-3434.

type alloy, AB_2 type alloy, Mg-based alloy and V-based solid solution alloy [1-5]. In fact, nearly all the commercial Ni-MH batteries are employing the rare earth-based AB_5-type alloy because of their overall electrochemical properties. However, the comparatively low discharge capacity and the poor dynamic performances in higher/lower temperature have made Ni-MH secondary batteries not compete favorably with some other batteries. Therefore, demand for electrode alloy with high performances such as higher discharge capacity and better dynamic performances in a wide temperature region has increased rapidly.

The higher hydrogen storage capacity of V-based solid solution alloy [6-9] makes it a promising hydrogen storage material; however, the poor electrochemical activity of the dehydriding kinetics [10-15] has prevented it from being practically used as an electrode alloy for Ni-MH batteries. It was reported [2] that V-based solid solution phase had no or very low surface electrochemical activity and could obtain hydrogen only from its neighboring C14 Laves phase, although there is not much C14 Laves phase in the alloy. The composition and concentration of the secondary phase have a direct effect on the electrochemical properties, especially on the discharge capacity. The secondary phase may provide an effective pathway for solving the problem of the unfavorable dynamic properties of V-based solid solution alloy.

In our previous work, rare earth Ce has been used as the additional element to Ti-V-Cr-Ni electrode alloy and the result showed that Ce with only 0.5% atom fraction has a great effect on the microstructure and electrochemical properties, especially on the discharge capacity and cycle stability. Electrochemical impedance spectroscopy indicates that the addition of Ce improves the kinetic performance of the alloy electrode for Ti-V-Cr-Ni alloy, such as enhances the exchange current density, which is beneficial to the electrochemical performance of Ti-V-Cr-Ni alloy electrode. To investigate the effect of rare earth on the electrochemical properties of V-based solid solution alloy electrode, La, Ce, Pr, Nd, Sm, Gd, Tb, Dy, Ho, Er and Y (1% atom fraction) have been used as additional elements to Ti-Zr-V-Cr-Ni electrode alloy, and the result indicates that Ce and Dy have higher electrochemical activity than the other elements. In this paper, the microstructure and some dynamic performances of $Ti_{0.17}Zr_{0.08}V_{0.34}RE_{0.01}Cr_{0.1}Ni_{0.3}$ (RE=Ce, Dy) hydrogen storage electrode alloys have been investigated.

2 Experimental details

$Ti_{0.17}Zr_{0.08}V_{0.34}RE_{0.01}Cr_{0.1}Ni_{0.3}$ (RE = Ce, Dy) alloys were prepared by arc-melting the constituent elements on a water cooled copper hearth under argon and then re-melted three times to ensure the homogeneity of the electrode alloys. The purity of the individual starting metal was higher than 99.9 mass%. The microstructure and the phase compositions of alloys were measured by using filed emission scanning electron microscopy-energy dispersive spectroscopy (FESEM-EDS) analysis on XL30 ESEM FEG scanning electron microscope. Crystal structure of $Ti_{0.17}Zr_{0.08}V_{0.34}RE_{0.01}Cr_{0.1}Ni_{0.3}$ (RE = Ce, Dy) alloys, lattice parameter and cell volume of the V-based solid solution phase and C14 Laves phase were investigated by XRD (CuKα, Si internal standard) on Rigaku D/max 2500pc X-ray diffraction meter using JAD5 software.

Electrochemical measurements were performed in a standard three electrode cell system. The metal hydride electrode was used as the working electrode which was prepared by mixing the alloy powder with carbonyl nickel powder in a weight ratio of 1 : 5 and cold pressed under a pressure of 12 MPa into tablet with 10 mm in diameter and 1.5 mm in thickness, a sintered $Ni(OH)_2$/NiOOH electrode with excess capacity was used as the counter electrode, and Hg/HgO electrode was used as the reference electrode in 6 mol/L KOH electrolyte solution. For examining the discharge capacity, cycle stability and effect of temperature on discharge capacity, all metal hydride electrodes were charged and discharged at a current density of 60 mA g^{-1}.

Pressure-composition isotherm curve (p-c-t) is an important description to characterize the electrode alloys. The p-c-t curves of $Ti_{0.17}Zr_{0.08}V_{0.34}RE_{0.01}Cr_{0.1}Ni_{0.3}$ (RE = Ce, Dy) alloys were measured by electrochemical method which converts the equilibrium potential of metal hydride electrode to the equilibrium pressure of hydrogen [16].

Potentiostatic discharge technique [1,17,18] was used to evaluate the hydrogen coefficient of diffusion (D) within the bulk of the alloy electrode. After being fully charged followed by a 30 min open-circuit to reach a stable state, the electrodes were discharged with +500 mV potential-step for 600 s on EG G PARC's Model 273 Potentiostat/Galvanostat station, us-ing the M352 Corr Ware electrochemical/corrosion software. Hydrogen diffusion coefficient D can be obtained from the slope of the linear section at long-time region according to the following:

$$\log I = \log[\pm(C_0 - C_s) \times 6FD/r^2] - t \times \pi^2 D/2.303r^2, \qquad (1)$$

where I is the responding current (A), C_0 is the initial hydrogen concentration in the electrode alloys (mol cm^3), and C_s is hydrogen concentration on the electrode surface after a potential step (mol cm^3), F is Faraday constant (96 485 C mol^{-1}), t is time (s), D is diffusion coefficient ($cm^2 s^{-1}$) and r is the sphere radius of the alloy particle (cm).

Electrochemical impedance spectroscopy (EIS) was used for determining the charge-transfer resistance (R_T) and the exchange current density (I_0) to clarify the kinetic properties of dehydrating action at different temperature and different number of cycles. After the test electrodes were completely activated, EIS measurements were conducted at 50% depth of discharge (DOD) using a Solartron SI1187 Electrochemical Interface with 1255B Frequency Response Analyzer and ZPLOT electrochemical impedance software. The EIS spectra of the electrodes were obtained in the frequency range of 100 kHz to 10^{-2} Hz with alternating current amplitude of 5 mV under open-circuit conditions. According to the analysis model proposed by Kuriyama et al. [19], an equivalent circuit for the metal hydride electrode was used and the parameters in the equivalent circuit were fitted using least-square method with ZVIEW electrochemical impedance software; I_0 is calculated from Eq. (2). According to Arrhenius relationship [20], the logarithm of R_T follows a linear dependence with the reciprocal temperature $(1/T)$, and the apparent activation energy $(\Delta_r H)$ of the electrochemical reaction on the surface of the electrode alloys is calculated from Eq. (3), where R, T and F have their general meanings:

$$I_0 = RT/FR_T, \quad (2)$$

$$\lg(T/R_T) = -\Delta_r H/2.303RT + A. \quad (3)$$

3 Result and discussion

3.1 Microstructure characterization

Fig. 1 shows the XRD pattern of $Ti_{0.17}Zr_{0.08}V_{0.34}RE_{0.01}Cr_{0.1}Ni_{0.3}$ (RE=Ce, Dy) hydrogen storage electrode alloys. The as-cast alloys are mainly composed of V-based solid solution phase with body-centered-cubic (bcc) structure and C14 Laves phase with hexagonal structure. The lattice parameter and cell volume of the bcc phase and C14 Laves phase are calculated with JAD 5 software, respectively, and the results are summarized in Table 1. The lattice parameter and cell volume of the bcc phase and C14 Lave phases in the alloy with Dy addition are both larger than that with Ce addition, as shown in Table 1, and the larger cell volume would be beneficial for a larger hydrogen storage capacity.

Fig. 2 shows the FESEM micrographs of $Ti_{0.17}Zr_{0.08}V_{0.34}RE_{0.01}Cr_{0.1}Ni_{0.3}$ (RE=Ce, Dy) hydrogen storage electrode alloys. It is obvious that the alloy is composed of V-based solid solution phase with a dendritic shape and a continuous C14 Laves phase with a network shape surrounding the dendrite. It can also be seen in Fig. 2 (a2 and b2) that there are some lard with irregular shape embedded in C14 Laves phase. The constituents of the two phases and the lard have been semi-quantitatively analyzed with EDS as summarized in Table 1. It is found that for the alloy with Ce addition rare earth Ce does not exist in bcc phase or in C14 Laves phase, it exists in the lard and as Ce-rich small particles embedded in C14 Laves phase, while for the alloy with Dy addition rare earth Dy exists in all the parts of the alloy, the V-based solution phase, the C14 Laves phase and the white lard.

It is well known that the atomic radius and melting point of the constituent elements must be considered in solid solution alloying process. It is accepted that a large difference in the atomic radii between the matrix element and other constituent elements affects the microstructure and phase composition of the solid solution alloy, and may be a key issue in forming a solid solution alloy. Among all the constituents, Ce has the largest atomic radius, r_{Ce} 0.182 nm, which is far more than that of V, r_V 0.135 nm, and enters in the solid solution alloy difficultly. Moreover, a large difference in the melting point(T_{Ce} 1 071 K < T_V 1 900 K) would result in the segregating of Ce during solidification and forming lard, which is perhaps another reason why Ce exists only in the lard .

The FESEM-EDS line scanning profile shows the distribution of the composition elements in each phase, and the result shows that the distributions of the constituent element in the two phases has a mirror-relationship, as shown in Fig. 3, the bcc phase is mainly composed of V and Cr, while the C14 Laves phase is mainly composed of Ti, Zr and Ni.

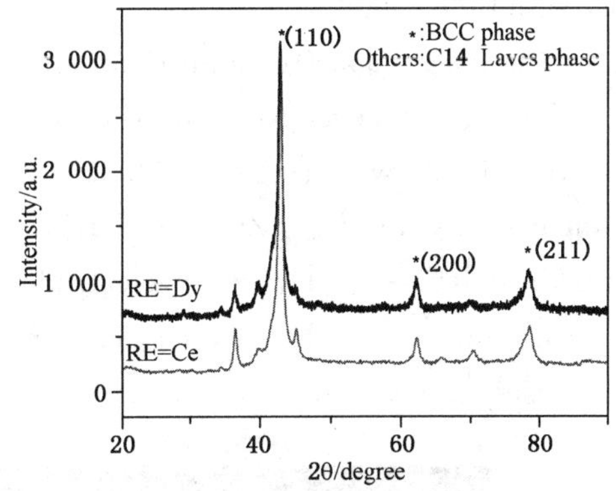

Fig. 1 X-ray diffraction pattern of $Ti_{0.17}Zr_{0.08}V_{0.34}RE_{0.01}Cr_{0.1}Ni_{0.3}$ (RE=Ce, Dy) hydrogen storage electrode alloys

Table 1 Phase composition, lattice parameter and cell volume of $Ti_{0.17}Zr_{0.08}V_{0.34}RE_{0.01}Cr_{0.1}Ni_{0.3}$ (RE=Ce, Dy) alloys: (a) RE=Ce, (b) RE=Dy

Samples phase	Composition(atom%)						Lattice parameter(nm)		Cell Volume (nm^3)
	Ti	V	Cr	Ni	Zr	RE	a	c	
(a) V-based C14 Laves phase lard	4.25	66.00	21.99	7.44	0.40	0.00	0.298		0.0226
	27.87	11.58	2.14	48.19	10.22	0.00	0.492	0.803	0.168
	15.78	19.78	4.34	36.66	12.83	10.60			
(b) V-based C14 Laves phase lard	16.37	35.65	6.97	31.20	8.95	0.87	0.299		0.0268
	23.36	14.21	1.65	43.79	15.47	1.52	0.494	0.808	0.170
	26.86	12.27	1.58	47.62	10.44	1.23			

3.2 Pressure-composition isotherms

The p-c-t curves of $Ti_{0.17}Zr_{0.08}V_{0.34}RE_{0.01}Cr_{0.1}Ni_{0.3}$ (RE = Ce, Dy) hydrogen storage electrode alloys are measured by electrochemical method [16] and the results are shown in Fig. 4. The hydrogen pressure of plateau region for $Ti_{0.17}Zr_{0.08}V_{0.34}RE_{0.01}Cr_{0.1}Ni_{0.3}$ (RE = Dy) alloy is lower than that of $Ti_{0.17}Zr_{0.08}V_{0.34}RE_{0.01}Cr_{0.1}Ni_{0.3}$ (RE = Ce) alloy, and also the plateau region becomes wider and flatter for the alloy with Dy addition, which means that the reversible hydrogen capacity of the alloy with Dy addition has increased, and the results imply the alloy with Dy addition would have a higher discharge capacity than that with Ce addition.

3.3 Discharge capacity and activation

The discharge capacity of the alloy electrode is shown in Fig. 5. The maximum capacity of $Ti_{0.17}Zr_{0.08}V_{0.34}RE_{0.01}Cr_{0.1}Ni_{0.3}$ (RE = Ce, Dy) alloy electrodes are 309 and 321 mAh g^{-1}, respectively, this result is coincided well with that of the p-c-t curves. It is generally thought that V-based solid solution alloy has a higher hydrogen capacity, but the electrochemical activity of dehydriding kinetic is poor that bcc phase can only obtain hydrogen from its neighboring C14 phase [15]. The poor dehydriding kinetics is perhaps related to the higher stabilization of the hydride. The lower plateau pressure of $Ti_{0.17}Zr_{0.08}V_{0.34}Dy_{0.01}Cr_{0.1}Ni_{0.3}$ (RE=Dy) alloy in the p-c-t curve is beneficial for hydrogen to be desorbed from the electrode alloy, which leads to the increase of discharge capacity.

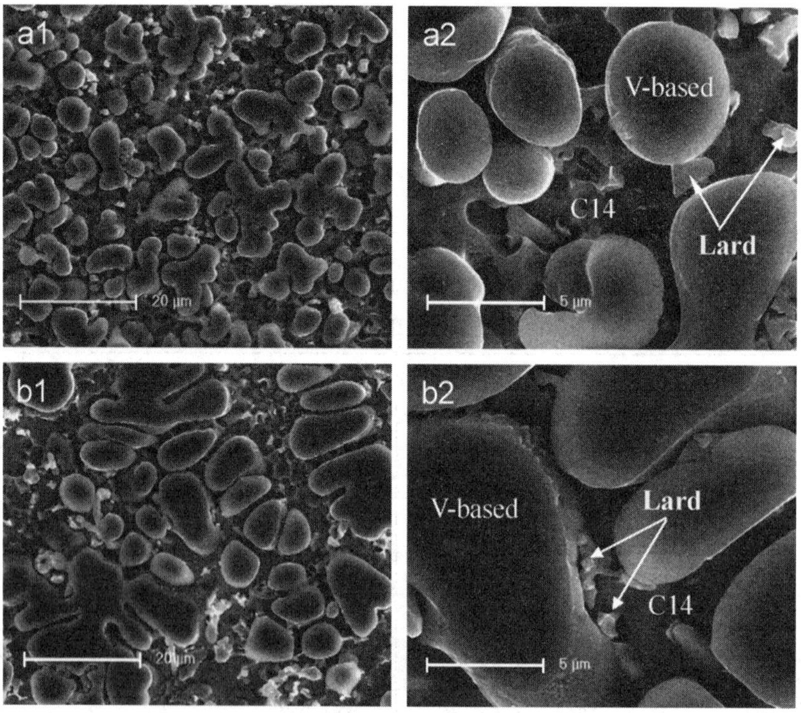

Fig. 2 FESEM of $Ti_{0.17}Zr_{0.08}V_{0.34}RE_{0.01}Cr_{0.1}Ni_{0.3}$ (RE=Ce, Dy) hydrogen storage electrode alloys. (a) RE=Ce; (b) RE=Dy

The activation of $Ti_{0.17}Zr_{0.08}V_{0.34}RE_{0.01}Cr_{0.1}Ni_{0.3}$ (RE=Ce) alloy electrode needs only five cycles, while $Ti_{0.17}Zr_{0.08}V_{0.34}RE_{0.01}Cr_{0.1}Ni_{0.3}$ (RE=Dy) alloy electrode needs eight cycles, as shown in Fig. 5. This result shows that Ce is beneficial for the alloy in improving the electrochemical activity of the V-based solid solution phase. It is reported [21] that the electrochemical properties of electrode alloy are closely related to Ni content for its high electrocatalytic activity. The good activation properties of $Ti_{0.17}Zr_{0.08}V_{0.34}RE_{0.01}Cr_{0.1}Ni_{0.3}$ (RE=Ce) alloy perhaps relate to the higher Ni content (48.19%) in C14 Laves phase and the coexistence of Ce-rich lard with C14 Laves phase which acts as active sites for hydriding/dehydriding.

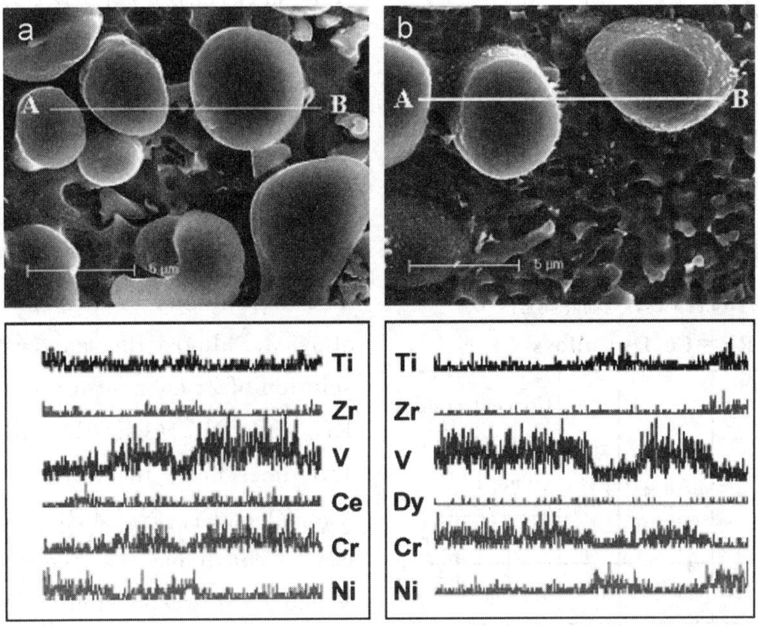

Fig. 3 FESEM-EDS line scanning profile for $Ti_{0.17}Zr_{0.08}V_{0.34}RE_{0.01}Cr_{0.1}Ni_{0.3}$ (RE=Ce, Dy) hydrogen storage electrode alloys. (a) RE=Ce; (b) RE=Dy

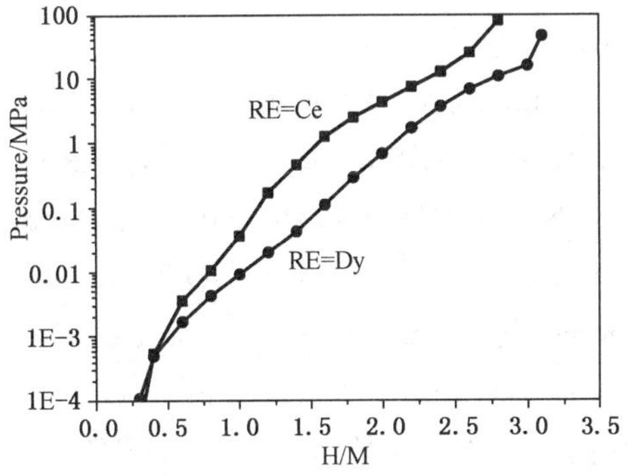

Fig. 4 p-c-Isotherms of the $Ti_{0.17}Zr_{0.08}V_{0.34}RE_{0.01}Cr_{0.1}Ni_{0.3}$ (RE=Ce, Dy) hydrogen storage electrode alloys at 303 K

3.4 Cycle stability

The cycle stability of the alloy electrode is also shown in Fig. 5 and it can be described as [3] $S_{100}(\%) = C_{100}/C_{max} \times 100$, and the calculated results are summarized in Table 2. The result shows that $Ti_{0.17}Zr_{0.08}V_{0.34}RE_{0.01}Cr_{0.1}Ni_{0.3}$ (RE = Ce) alloy electrode has higher cycle stability (86.3%) than that of $Ti_{0.17}Zr_{0.08}V_{0.34}RE_{0.01}Cr_{0.1}Ni_{0.3}$ (RE = Dy) alloy (85.5%), but the difference is not so prominent.

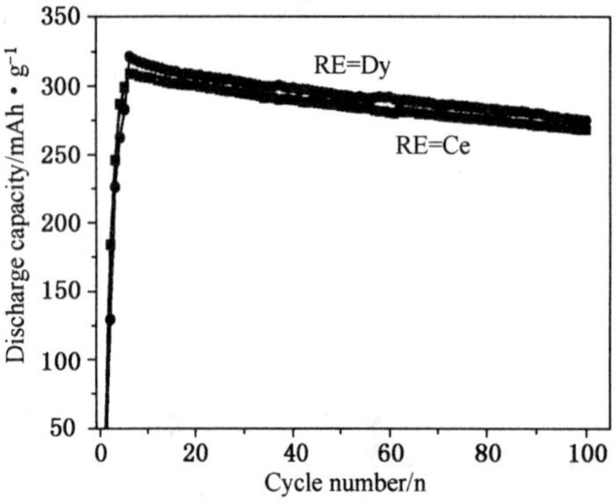

Fig. 5　Discharge capacity as a function of cycle number for $Ti_{0.17}Zr_{0.08}V_{0.34}RE_{0.01}Cr_{0.1}Ni_{0.3}$ (RE=Ce, Dy) hydrogen storage electrode alloys at 303 K

Table 2　Summary of the performance for $Ti_{0.17}Zr_{0.08}V_{0.34}RE_{0.01}Cr_{0.1}Ni_{0.3}$ (RE=Ce, Dy) alloys

Samples	C_{max} mAh g^{-1}	C_{100} mAh g^{-1}	S_{100} (%)	Concentration in KOH (mg L^{-1})		
				Ti	V	Zr
RE=Ce	309.0	266.7	86.3	4.9	59.6	12.4
RE=Dy	321.0	274.9	85.5	4.5	60.5	18.9

C_{max} The maximum discharge capacity; C_{100} The discharge capacity at the 100th cycles; S_{100} The cycle stability.

To elucidate the capacity degradation behavior of the alloy electrode during cycling in alkaline electrolyte, the concentrations of the constituent elements dissolved in KOH electrolyte are analyzed with ICP-MS measurement for 100 cycles, and the results are also summarized in Table 2. The results show that only three elements (V, Ti and Zr) are detected and the amount of other elements may be too lower to be detected. As the main hydrogen absorbing element, the dissolution of V is so important that it is about 12 times more than Ti element and 3 times more than Zr element, respectively, and the dissolved V element is essentially responsible for the capacity degradation of the alloy.

On the other hand, the dissolution of Zr element is rather distinct. As a main element in C14 Laves phase, the dissolution of Zr would result in a decrease of the electro-catalytic activity in the alloy, which would affect the activation of hydriding/dehydriding action in the alloy. The dissolutions of V element for both alloys are almost the same, while the dissolution of Zr element for $Ti_{0.17}Zr_{0.08}V_{0.34}RE_{0.01}Cr_{0.1}Ni_{0.3}$ (RE=Dy) alloy is about 1.5 times more than that of $Ti_{0.17}Zr_{0.08}V_{0.34}RE_{0.01}Cr_{0.1}Ni_{0.3}$ (RE=Ce) alloy. It can be concluded that the dissolution of V and Zr are responsible for the capacity degradation of $Ti_{0.17}Zr_{0.08}V_{0.34}RE_{0.01}Cr_{0.1}Ni_{0.3}$ (RE=Ce, Dy).

3.5 Electrochemical impedance spectroscopy

Fig. 6 (A) shows the effect of temperature on EIS of $Ti_{0.17}Zr_{0.08}V_{0.34}RE_{0.01}Cr_{0.1}Ni_{0.3}$ (RE=Ce, Dy) alloy electrodes in the 50th cycle at 50% DOD. Fig. 6 (B) shows the semi-logarithmic plot of R_T against reciprocal temperature ($1/T$) for $Ti_{0.17}Zr_{0.08}V_{0.34}RE_{0.01}Cr_{0.1}Ni_{0.3}$ (RE=Ce, Dy) alloy electrode. It is obvious that R_T decreases with increasing temperature, and this phenomenon is beneficial for the alloy electrode to discharge at higher temperature. The charge transfer resistance R_T, the exchange current density I_0 at 50th cycle(303 K)and the apparent activation energy $\Delta_r H$ are summarized in Table 3. It should point out that $\Delta_r H$ of the electrochemical reaction on the surface of the electrode alloy with Ce addition is 30.5 kJ mol^{-1}, which is similar with that of $MlNi_{3.75}Co_{0.65}Mn_{0.4}Al_{0.2}$(Ml =La-rich mischmetal)[22] electrode alloy(28.1 kJ mol^{-1}. The result shows that the electrochemical reaction on the alloy surface of the alloy with Ce addition has lower R_T, higher I_0 and lower $\Delta r H$ than that with Dy addition, which indicates that the alloy electrode with Ce addition has higher electrochemical activity than that alloy electrode with Dy addition.

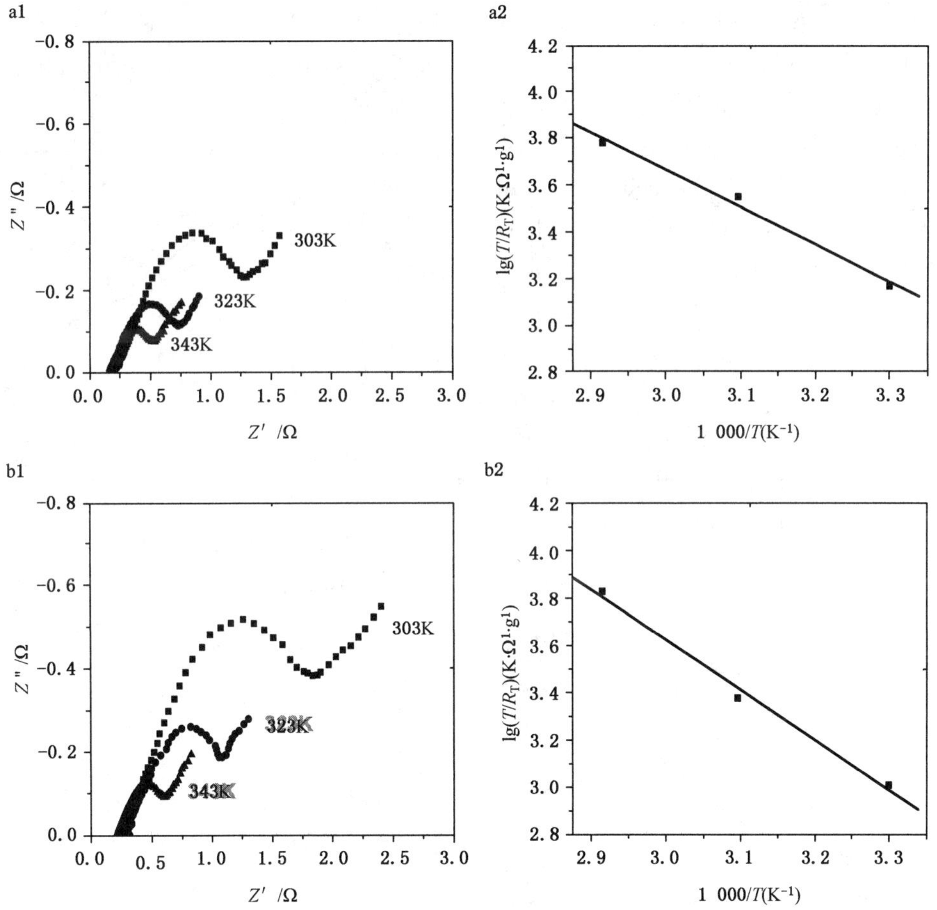

Fig. 6 Effect of temperature on electrochemical impedance spectroscopy and lg(T/R_T) with $1/T$ at the 50th cycle for $Ti_{0.17}Zr_{0.08}V_{0.34}RE_{0.01}Cr_{0.1}Ni_{0.3}$ (RE=Ce, Dy) alloy electrode. (a) RE=Ce; (b) RE=Dy

Table 3　Charge-transfer reaction resistance, exchange current density, hydrogen diffusion coefficient and apparent activation energy of $Ti_{0.17}Zr_{0.08}V_{0.34}RE_{0.01}Cr_{0.1}Ni_{0.3}$ (RE=Ce, Dy) alloy electrodes at the 50th cycle

Samples	R_T (Ω)	I_0 (mA g^{-1})	D ($cm^2 s^{-1}$)	$\Delta_r H$ (kJ mol^{-1})
RE=Ce	1.37	127.5	8.88×10^{-10}	30.5
RE=Dy	1.98	88.1	9.07×10^{-10}	40.7

Fig. 7 shows the EIS of $Ti_{0.17}Zr_{0.08}V_{0.34}RE_{0.01}Cr_{0.1}Ni_{0.3}$ (RE = Ce, Dy) alloy electrodes in the 50th and 100th cycles at 50% DOD and 303 K, respectively. It is obvious that the radii of the semicircles in low-frequency region at the 100th cycle is much larger than that at the 50th cycle, which indicate that the R_T increases with increasing cycle number and this results in the decrease of I_0, which may be responsible for the capacity degradation behavior of $Ti_{0.17}Zr_{0.08}V_{0.34}RE_{0.01}Cr_{0.1}Ni_{0.3}$ (RE=Ce, Dy) with cycle number.

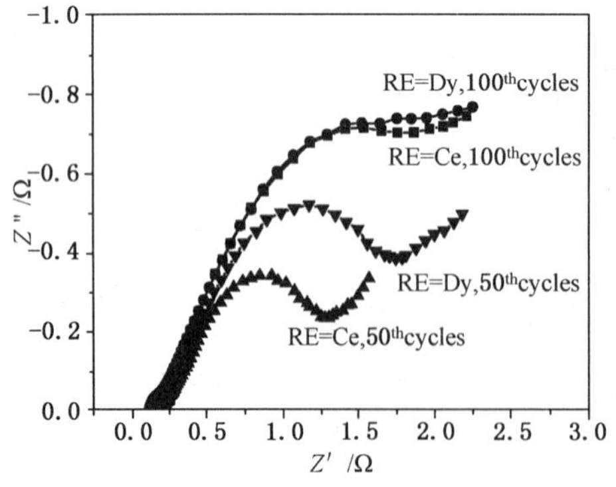

Fig. 7　Electrochemical impedance spectros copy of $Ti_{0.17}Zr_{0.08}V_{0.34}RE_{0.01}Cr_{0.1}Ni_{0.3}$ (RE=Ce, Dy) alloy electrode at the 50th and 100th cycles

3.6　High-rate dischargeability (HRD)

It is noteworthy that V-based solid solution alloy has a poorer HRD than other electrode alloy such as AB_5-type alloy, while HRD is an important property of electrode alloy used as negative electrode material in Ni-MH battery, especially for Ni-MH battery used in electric vehicles. Fig. 8 shows the relationship between the discharge capacity and the discharge current density of $Ti_{0.17}Zr_{0.08}V_{0.34}RE_{0.01}Cr_{0.1}Ni_{0.3}$ (RE = Ce, Dy) alloys. It is obvious that both the HRD values are relatively low.

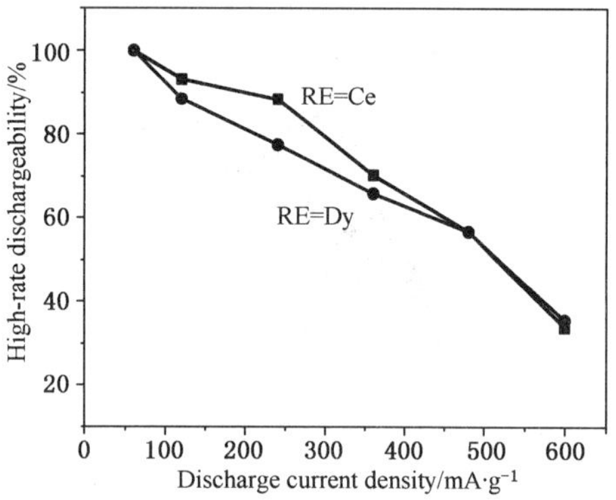

Fig. 8　HRD of $Ti_{0.17}Zr_{0.08}V_{0.34}RE_{0.01}Cr_{0.1}Ni_{0.3}$ (RE=Ce, Dy) alloy electrode at 303 K

The poor kinetic performance of V-based solid solution alloy electrode is usually due to their stronger M-H bond and higher R_T. The issue of how to improve the electrocatalytic activity of the alloy is a crucial one in enhancing the HRD, I_0 and D are often employed to evaluate the kinetic performance of an alloy electrode, and it is generally thought that I_0 and D are crucial issues for the HRD of a electrode alloy [13].

The potentiostatic discharge technique [1,17] and EIS has been employed to determine D and I_0, and the results are summarized in Table 3 also. It is indicated that the D value for the alloy with Dy addition, 9.07×10^{-10} cm^2 s^{-1}, is a little larger than that with Ce addition, 8.88×10^{-10} cm^2 s^{-1}, while the I_0 value for the alloy with Ce addition, 127.5 mA g^{-1}, is larger than that with Dy addition, 88.1 mA g^{-1}. As mentioned above, can be considered that D is a rate-limiting factor at higher discharge current, while I_0 is the rate-limiting factor at lower discharge current, both D and I_0 are responsible for the poor HRD of the alloy in this case.

4 Conclusions

Rare earth Ce and Dy have been used as additional elements and the microstructure and electrochemical properties of $Ti_{0.17}Zr_{0.08}V_{0.34}RE_{0.01}Cr_{0.1}Ni_{0.3}$ (RE=Ce, Dy) hydrogen storage electrode alloys have been investigated.

(1) $Ti_{0.17}Zr_{0.08}V_{0.34}RE_{0.01}Cr_{0.1}Ni_{0.3}$ (RE=Ce, Dy) hydrogen storage electrode alloys is composed of V-based solid solution phase with a dendritic shape and a continuous C14 Laves phase with a network shape surrounding the dendrite. The distribution of the constituents in the two phases has a mirror-relationships, the V-based solid solution phase is mainly composed of V and Cr, while the C14 Laves phase is mainly composed of Ti, Zr and Ni.

(2) The alloy with Dy addition has a lower equilibrium hydrogen pressure and a wider and flatter plateau region. The $Ti_{0.17}Zr_{0.08}V_{0.34}RE_{0.01}Cr_{0.1}Ni_{0.3}$ (RE=Dy) alloy has higher discharge capacity (321 mAh g^{-1}) than that of $Ti_{0.17}Zr_{0.08}V_{0.34}RE_{0.01}Cr_{0.1}Ni_{0.3}$ (RE = Ce) (309 mAh g^{-1}), while the alloy electrode with Ce addition has higher cycle stability.

(3) The result shows that the electrochemical reaction on the alloy surface of the alloy with Ce addition has lower R_T, higher I_0 and lower $\Delta_r H$ than that with Dy addition, which indicates that the alloy electrode with Ce addition has higher electrochemical activity than that alloy electrode with Dy addition.

(4) The capacity degradation behavior for the alloy electrode is attributed to two main factors, one is the dissolutions of V and Zr element to KOH solution, and another is the larger charge transfer resistance which increases with increasing cycle number.

(5) Hydrogen diffusion coefficient is a rate-limiting factor at higher discharge current, while exchange current density is the rate-limiting factor at lower discharge current, both hydrogen diffusion coefficient and exchange current density are responsible for the poor HRD of the alloy in this case.

Acknowledgment

This work was financially supported by the National Natural Science Foundation of China(Grant No. 20171042).

References

[1] Zhang XB, Chai YJ, Yin WY, Zhao MS. J Solid State Chem 2004;177:2373.

[2] Pan HG, Zhu YF, Gao MX, Lui YF, Li R, Lei YQ. et al. J Alloys Compd 2004;364:271.

[3] Qiao YQ, Zhao MS, Li ML, Zhu XJ, Cao GY. Scripta Mater 2005;55:279.

[4] Iba H, Akiba E. J Alloys Compd 1995;231:508.

[5] Tsukahara M, Tskahasha K, Mishima T, Isomuar A, Sakai T. J Alloys Compd 1996;243:133.

[6] Cho SW, Han ChS, Park ChN, Akiba E. J Alloys Compd 1999;289:244.

[7] Cho SW, Enoki H, Akiba E. J Alloys Compd 2000;307:304.

[8] Mouri T, Iba H. Mater Sci Eng A 2002;329-331:346.

[9] Akiba E, Iba H. Intermetallics 1998;6:461.

[10] Chai YJ, Zhao MS. Int J Hydrogen Energy 2005;30:279.

[11] Zhu YF, Pan HG, Gao MX, Ma JX, Li SQ, Wang QD. Int J Hydrogen Energy 2002;27:287.

[12] Cui N, Luan B, Zhao HJ, Liu HK, Dou SX. J Alloys Compd 1996;233:236.

[13] Li R, Pan HG, Gao MX, Zhu YF, Jin QW, Lei YQ. J Alloys Compd 2004;373:223.

[14] Tsukahara M, Tskahasha K, Mishima T, Miyamura H, Sakai T, Kuriyama N. et al. J Alloys Compd 1995;231:616.

[15] Pan HG, Zhu YF, Gao MX, Lui YF, Li R, Lei YQ. et al. J Alloys Compd 2004;370:254.

[16] Iwakura C, Kajiya Y, Yoneyama H, Sakai T, Oguro K, Ishikawa H. J Electrochem Soc 1989;136:1351.

[17] Yuan XX, Xu NX. Trans Nonferrous Met Soc China 2001;11(5):700.

[18] Yuan XX, Xu NX. Electrochemistry 2001;7(4):445 [in Chinese].

[19] Kuriyama N, Sakai T, Miyamura H, Uehara I, Ishikawa H, Iwasaki T. J Alloys Compd 1993;202:183.

[20] Liu YF, Pan HG, Gao MX, Zhu YF, Lei YQ, Wang QD. Electrochim Acta 2004;49:545.

[21] Kleperis J, Wojcic G, Czerwinski A, Skowronski J, Kopczyk M, Beltowska Brzezinska M. J Solid State Electrochem 2001;5:229.

[22] Yuan XX, Xu NX. Acta Chimica Sin 2002;60(1):13.

Microstructure and Electrochemical Performance of $Ti_{0.17}Zr_{0.08}V_{0.34}Pd_{0.01}Cr_{0.1}Ni_{0.3}$ Electrode Alloy①

Yuqing Qiao[a,b], Minshou Zhao[a,b], Meiye Li[b], Xinjian Zhu[c], Guangyi Cao[c]
([a] State Key Laboratory of Metastable Material Science and Technology, Yanshan University, Qinhuangdao 066004, PR China)
([b] Key Laboratory of Rare Earth Chemistry and Physics, Changchun Institute of Applied Chemistry, Chinese Academic of Science, Changchun 130022, PR China)
([c] Institute of Fuel Cell, Shanghai Jiaotong University, Shanghai 200030, PR China)

Abstract: The microstructure and electrochemical performance of $Ti_{0.17}Zr_{0.08}V_{0.34}Pd_{0.01}Cr_{0.1}Ni_{0.3}$ electrode alloy have been investigated using X-ray diffraction, field emission scanning electron microscopy-energy dispersive spectroscopy, inductively coupled plasma and electrochemical impedance spectroscopy. The alloy electrode has a higher discharge capacity than an AB_5 type alloy within a wider temperature span. The increase of the charge-transfer-resistances, and the dissolutions of V and Zr were responsible for the performance degradation of the alloy electrode.

Key words: V-based solid solution; Metal hydride; Electrochemical impedance spectroscopy; Ni-MH battery

V-based hydrogen storage alloy used as the negative electrode materials of Ni-MH secondary batteries has been intensively investigated due to its high hydrogen capacity [1-4]. However, the poor electrochemical activity of the dehydriding kinetics [5-7] has prevented it from being practically used as an electrode alloy for Ni-MH batteries.

In our previous work, elements with different atomic radii, such as Dy, Zr, Nb, Pd, Al and Cu, have been used as the additional element for the $Ti_{0.25}V_{0.34}M_{0.01}Cr_{0.1}Ni_{0.3}$ solid solution alloy. The results showed that the alloy with Pd addition had the highest discharge capacity of 272 mAh g^{-1} at 303 K, the smallest charge transfer resistance ($R_T = 1.35\ \Omega$) on the alloy surface and the largest exchange current density ($I_0 = 130.2$ mA g^{-1}), which suggested that the addition of Pd is beneficial for $Ti_{0.25}V_{0.34}M_{0.01}Cr_{0.1}Ni_{0.3}$ alloy to improve the kinetic performance of the alloy electrode. This result coincides with that reported by Zaluski et al. [8], and may be related to the fact that palladium is an especially good catalyst for the hydrogen dissociation reaction

① Scripta Materialia, 2006(55): 279-282.

and it has almost the same atomic radius (1.37Å) as V (1.35Å). In this paper, the microstructure and electrochemical performance of $Ti_{0.17}Zr_{0.08}V_{0.34}Pd_{0.01}Cr_{0.1}Ni_{0.3}$ electrode alloy have been investigated.

$Ti_{0.17}Zr_{0.08}V_{0.34}Pd_{0.01}Cr_{0.1}Ni_{0.3}$ alloy was prepared by arc-melting the constituent elements on a water cooled copper hearth under argon and then re-melting three times to ensure the homogeneity. The purity of the metal was higher than 99.9 mass%. The crystal structure of the alloy was investigated by X-ray diffraction (CuKα, Si internal standard) on a Rigaku D/max 2500pc X-ray diffraction meter using JAD5 software. The microstructure and the phase compositions of the alloy were measured by using field emission scanning electron microscopy energy dispersive spectroscopy (FESEM-EDS) analysis on a XL30 ESEM FEG scan-ning electron microscope.

The electrochemical measurements were performed in a half-cell system, and the measurement was similar to those described in our previous work [3].

Electrochemical impedance spectroscopy (EIS) was used for determining the charge-transfer resistance (R_T) and the exchange current density (I_0), to clarify the kinetic properties of dehydrating action at different temperatures and different numbers of cycles.

To investigate the capacity degradation behavior of $Ti_{0.17}Zr_{0.08}V_{0.34}Pd_{0.01}Cr_{0.1}Ni_{0.3}$ solid solution alloy, SEM, EIS and inductively coupled plasma (ICP) have been used to analyse the electrode surface, the kinetic performance of the alloy electrode and the concentrations of elements dissolved in alkaline solution at the 50th and 100th cycles, respectively.

Figure 1 shows the XRD pattern of $Ti_{0.17}Zr_{0.08}V_{0.34}Pd_{0.01}Cr_{0.1}Ni_{0.3}$ electrode alloy. It is found that the alloy is mainly composed of V-based solid solution phase with a body-centered cubic (bcc) structure and C14 Laves phase with hexagonal structure. The lattice parameter and cell volume of the bcc phase and C14 Laves phase are calculated with JAD5 software, respectively, and the results are summarized in Table 1. It is accepted that a difference in the atomic radii between the matrix element and the additional element affects the microstructure of the solid solution alloy and may be a predominant factor in forming a solid solution alloy in some cases, and can result in crystal distortion if the difference is too large. The addition of Pd element does not change the major phase of the alloy, which is perhaps because palladium has almost the same atomic radius (1.37Å) as V (1.35Å).

Figure 2 shows the FESEM micrographs of $Ti_{0.17}Zr_{0.08}V_{0.34}Pd_{0.01}Cr_{0.1}Ni_{0.3}$ electrode alloy. It is obvious that the alloy is composed of V-based solid solution phase with a dendritic shape and a continuous C14 Laves phase with a networked shape surrounding the dendrite.

The phase composition of the alloy

has been semi-quantitatively analyzed with EDS, as shown in Figure 3 and the results are also summarized in Table 1. The V-based solid solution phase is mainly composed of V and Cr, while the C14 Laves phase is mainly composed of Ti, Zr and Ni. It should be pointed out that the dis-tribution of Pd element in the two phases is rather different, and the content of Pd element in C14 Laves phase is about four times higher than that in the V-based solid solution phase. This result is beneficial for the alloy in improving the electrochemical activity of the V-based solid solution phase.

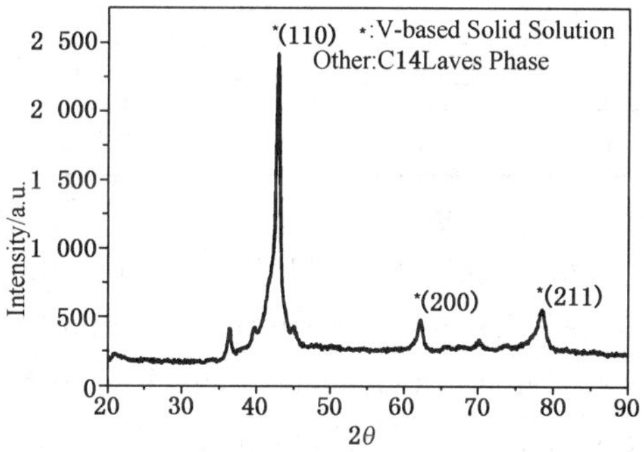

Figure 1　X-ray diffraction pattern of $Ti_{0.17}Zr_{0.08}V_{0.34}Pd_{0.01}Cr_{0.1}Ni_{0.3}$ alloy

The cycle stability of $Ti_{0.17}Zr_{0.08}V_{0.34}Pd_{0.01}Cr_{0.1}Ni_{0.3}$ alloy electrode is shown in Figure 4 and the cycle stability can be described by $S_{100}(\%) = C_{100}/C_{max} \times 100$, where S_{100}, C_{100} and C_{max} denote the cycle stability, the discharge capacity at the 100th cycles and the maximum discharge capacity, respectively. The result shows that the discharge capacity at the 100th cycle is 272 mAh g^{-1}, which is about 86% of the maximum discharge capacity (317 mAh g^{-1}), and implies the cycle stability of the alloy electrode is acceptable. The alloy electrode containing Pd is gradually activated during the charge/discharge cycle process and reached the maximum discharge capacity at the 5th cycle, which proved to have the highest electrochemical activity. It can be considered that palladium is a good catalyst for Ti-V-Cr-Ni solid solution alloy in the hydrogen dissociation reaction, in agreement with the report of Zaluski et al. [8].

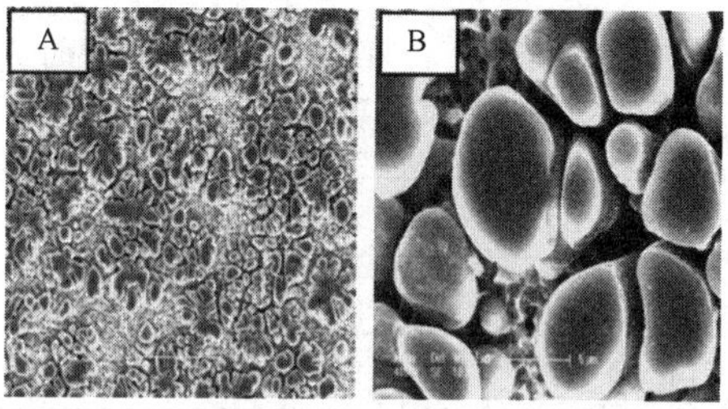

Figure 2　FESEM of $Ti_{0.17}Zr_{0.08}V_{0.34}Pd_{0.01}Cr_{0.1}Ni_{0.3}$ solid solution alloy

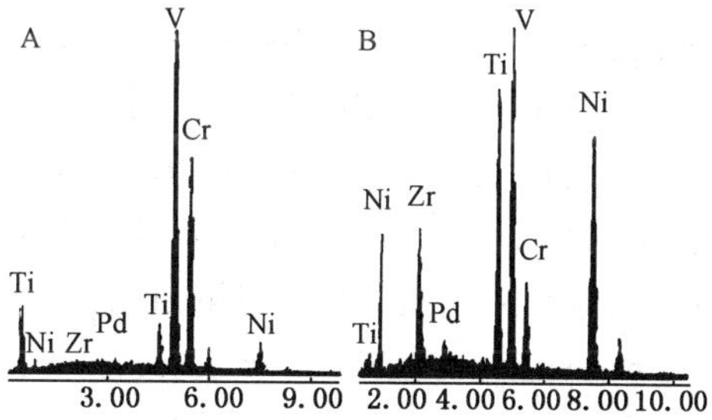

Figure 3　EDS profile for $Ti_{0.17}Zr_{0.08}V_{0.34}Pd_{0.01}Cr_{0.1}Ni_{0.3}$ solid solutionalloy: (A) V-based solid solution; (B) C14 Laves phase

Figure 5(A) shows the dependence of the discharge capacity of $Ti_{0.17}Zr_{0.08}V_{0.34}Pd_{0.01}Cr_{0.1}Ni_{0.3}$ alloy electrode on temperature. For example, the discharge capacity of the alloy electrode is 325 mAh

g^{-1} and 321 mAh g^{-1} at 323K and at 343K, respectively. The alloy electrode has a higher discharge capacity, 317—321 mAh g^{-1}, with in a wide temperature region from 303K to 343 K. It implies that the discharge capacity of the $Ti_{0.17}Zr_{0.08}V_{0.34}Pd_{0.01}Cr_{0.1}Ni_{0.3}$ alloy electrode is not sensitive to temperature within the temperature span. This characteristic of thealloy is crucial if it is to be used as a negative electrode material of Ni-MH batteries.

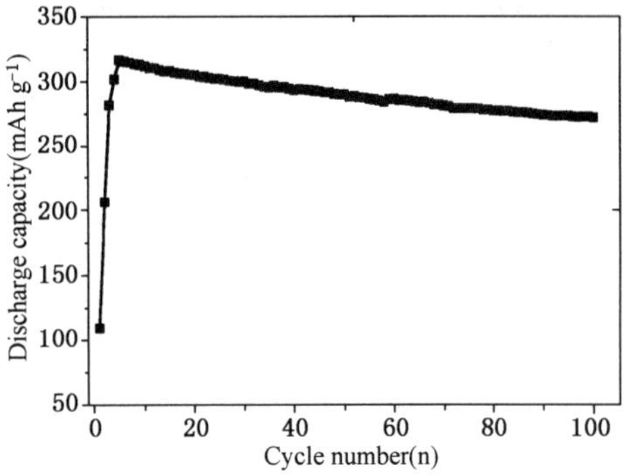

Figure 4　Discharge capacity as a function of cycle number for $Ti_{0.17}Zr_{0.08}V_{0.34}Pd_{0.01}Cr_{0.1}Ni_{0.3}$ alloy electrode at 303 K

Table 1　Phase composition, lattice parameter and cell volume of $Ti_{0.17}Zr_{0.08}V_{0.34}Pd_{0.01}Cr_{0.1}Ni_{0.3}$ solid solution alloy

Phase	Composition(atom%)						Lattice parameter (Å)		Cell volume (Å)
	Ti	Zr	V	Pd	Cr	Ni	*a*	*c*	
bcc	4.2	0.2	68.0	0.4	20.2	7.0	2.98	—	26.6
C14	21.6	9.5	25.0	1.7	4.7	37.5	4.93	8.03	169.2

Figure5(B) shows the effectof temperature on EIS of $Ti_{0.17}Zr_{0.08}V_{0.34}Pd_{0.01}Cr_{0.1}Ni_{0.3}$ alloy electrode in the 50th cycles at 50% DOD. It is obvious that temperature has a great effect on the radii of the semicircles in the low-frequency region, which decreases markedly with increasing temperature. Part of the fitting results of R_T and the calculated I_0 are summarized in Table 2. It is found that R_T decreases with increasing temperature, and is 1.61, 0.70 and 0.22 Ω at 303, 323 and 343 K, respectively. However, I_0 increases with increasing temperature, with values of 108.3, 248.3 and 802.0 mA g^{-1} at 303, 323 and 343 K, respectively.

Figure 5(C) shows the semi-logarithmic plot of the charge transfer resistance against reciprocal temperature ($1/T$) for the $Ti_{0.17}Zr_{0.08}V_{0.34}Pd_{0.01}Cr_{0.1}Ni_{0.3}$ alloy electrode. It can be seen that the plot follows a linear dependence, which is in accordance with the Arrhenius relationship and coincides with that presented by Liu et al. [9]. The activation energy($\Delta_r H$) for the charge-transfer reaction is calculated from: $\lg(T/R_T) = -\Delta_r H/\ 2.303RT + A$. The result shows that the activation energy for the charge-transfer reaction is 46.7 kJ mol^{-1} and larger than that of the $MlNi_{3.75}Co_{0.65}Mn_{0.4}Al_{0.2}$ hydrogen storage alloy (28.1 kJ mol^{-1}) (Ml = La-rich mischmetal) [10]. The electrochemical activity of the alloy seems to be poor compared to AB_5 type alloy.

To elucidate the capacity degradation behavior of the $Ti_{0.17}Zr_{0.08}V_{0.34}Pd_{0.01}$

$Cr_{0.1}Ni_{0.3}$ solid solution alloy electrode during cycling, SEM, EIS and ICP methods have been used to examine the electrode surface, the kineticperformance of the alloy electrode and the concentrations of the elements dissolved in alkaline electrolyte at the 50th and 100th cycles, respectively.

Figure 6 shows the microstructure of the alloy electrode surface at 50th and 100th cycles. It can be easily seen that there are some cracks on the surface, especially on the contact spot between the alloy particle and the carbonyl nickel powder, and the crack widens with increasing cycle numbers, which leads to an increase in contact resistance and a decrease in electrical conductivity between alloy particles [2], and thereby will certainly inffuence the diflusion of hydrogen in the bulk of the alloy.

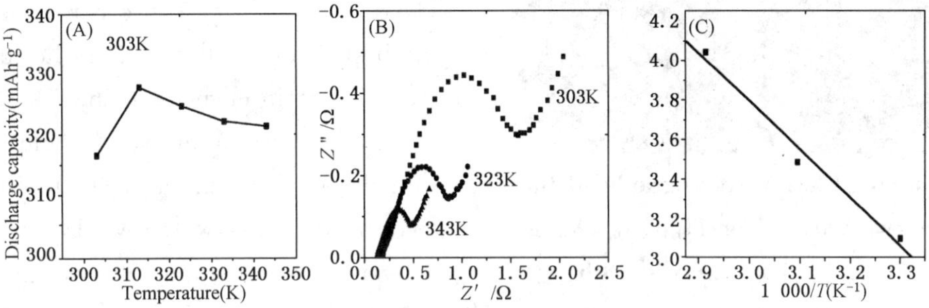

Figure 5　Effect of temperature on discharge capacity (A), electrochemical impedance spectra (B) and lg(T/R_T) with $1/T$ at 50% DOD (C) for $Ti_{0.17}Zr_{0.08}V_{0.34}Pd_{0.01}Cr_{0.1}Ni_{0.3}$ alloy electrode

Table 2　Summary of the performance for $Ti_{0.17}Zr_{0.08}V_{0.34}Pd_{0.01}Cr_{0.1}Ni_{0.3}$ alloy electrodes

Cycles	R_T(Ω)		I_0(mA g^{-1})		Concentration in KOH (mg L^{-1})		
	303K	343K	303K	343K	Ti	V	Zr
50th	1.61	0.22	108.3	802.0	—	26.4	—
100th	3.09	0.59	56.3	297.5	8.4	68.6	14.6

Figure 7 shows the EIS for the $Ti_{0.17}Zr_{0.08}V_{0.34}Pd_{0.01}Cr_{0.1}Ni_{0.3}$ alloy electrode at the 50th and 100th cycles. The EIS curve consists of two semicircles followed by a straight line at the 50th cycle and at 100th cycle, but the semicircle in the high-frequency region is not clearly observed. The radii of the semicircle in the low-frequency region at the 100th cycle is much larger than that at the 50th cycle, which indicates that the R_T of the alloy increases with increasing cycle number at both 303K and 343K, and the results are shown in Table 2 also. It should be pointed out that R_T on the alloy surface is increasing with increasing cycle number and this results in the decrease of I_0, which may be responsible for the capacity degradation behavior of $Ti_{0.17}Zr_{0.08}V_{0.34}Pd_{0.01}Cr_{0.1}Ni_{0.3}$ with increasing cycle number.

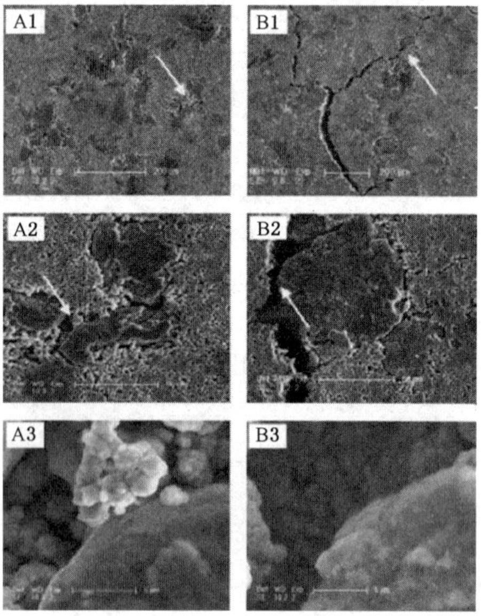

Figure 6　FESEM micrographs of the electrode surface for $Ti_{0.17}Zr_{0.08}V_{0.34}Pd_{0.01}Cr_{0.1}Ni_{0.3}$ alloy at 50th cycle (A) and 100th cycle(B)

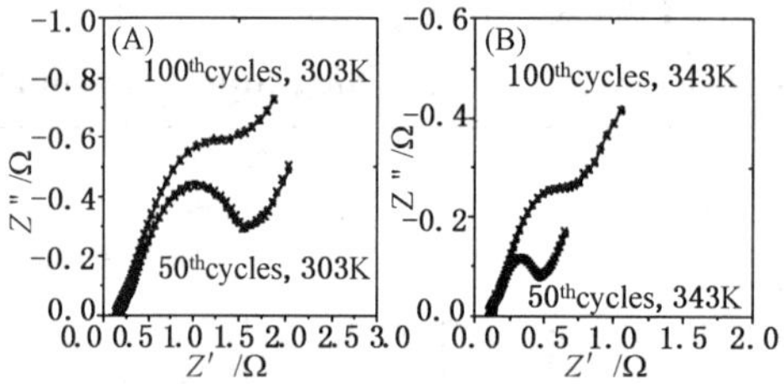

Figure 7　Electrochemical impedance spectra for $Ti_{0.17}Zr_{0.08}V_{0.34}$-$Pd_{0.01}Cr_{0.1}Ni_{0.3}$ alloy electrode at 50% DOD

The dissolution of constituent elements into the KOH electrolyte was analyzed with ICP measurement at the 50th and 100th cycles and the results are also summarized in Table 2. The results show that only V element was detected at the 50th cycle, while three kinds of elements (V, Ti and Zr) were detected at the 100th cycle. As the main hydrogen absorbing element, the dissolution of V is so significant that the concentration of V in the electrolyte is about 8.1 times higher than that of Ti element and 4.7 times higher than that of Zr element, respectively, and the dissolved V element would result in the $Ti_{0.17}Zr_{0.08}V_{0.34}Pd_{0.01}Cr_{0.1}Ni_{0.3}$ alloy electrode losing hydrogen storage capacity, which is perhaps the main factor in the capacity degradation behavior of the electrode alloy. On the other hand, the dissolution of Zr element is rather different. As a main element in the C14 Laves phase, the dissolution of Zr would result in a decrease of the electro-catalytic activity in the alloy, which would affect the activation of hydriding/dehydriding action in the alloy, and is perhaps another reason for the capacity degradation behavior of the electrode alloy.

In summary, $Ti_{0.17}Zr_{0.08}V_{0.34}Pd_{0.01}Cr_{0.1}Ni_{0.3}$ electrode alloy was investigated by XRD, SEM-EDS, ICP, EIS and charge-discharge measurements. It was found that the alloy is composed of a V-based solid solution main phase with bcc structure and C14 Laves phase with hexagonal structure. The distribution of the alloy constituent elements in the two phases have a mirror-relationship, wherein the V-based solid solution phase is mainly composed of V and Cr, while the C14 Laves phase is mainly composed of Ti, Zr and Ni. The alloy electrode has a higher discharge capacity within a wider temperature region from 303K to 343 K. The charge transfer resistance decreases with increasing temperature and the apparent activation energy for the charge-transfer reaction is 46.7 kJ mol^{-1}, larger than that for the $MlNi_{3.75}Co_{0.65}Mn_{0.4}Al_{0.2}$ hydrogen storage alloy (28.1 kJ mol^{-1}), which is perhaps responsible for the poor electrochemical activity of the $Ti_{0.17}Zr_{0.08}V_{0.34}Pd_{0.01}Cr_{0.1}Ni_{0.3}$ solid solution alloy. The increase of the charge transfer resistances and the dissolution of V and Zr elements into the KOH solution with increasing cycle numbers were considered responsible for the degradation in the performance of the alloy electrode.

This work was financially supported by the National Natural Science Foundation of China(Grant No. 20171042).

References

[1] M. Tsukahara, K. Tskahasha, T. Mishima, A. Isomuar, T. Sakai, J. Alloys Compd. 243 (1996)133.

[2] H. G. Pan, Y. F. Zhu, M. X. Gao, Y. F. Lui, R. Li, Y. Q. Lei, Q. D. Wang, J. Alloys Compd. 364(2004)271.

[3] X. B. Zhang, Y. J. Chai, W. Y. Yin, M. S. Zhao, J. Solid State Chem. 177(2004)2373.

[4] E. Akiba, H. Iba, Intermetallics 6(1998)461.

[5] S. W. Cho, C. S. Han, C. N. Park, E. Akiba, J. Alloys Compd. 289(1999)244.

[6] S. W. Cho, H. Enoki, E. Akiba, J. Alloys Compd. 307(2000)304.

[7] N. Cui, B. Luan, H. J. Zhao, H. K. Liu, S. X. Dou, J. Alloys Compd. 233(1996)236.

[8] L. Zaluski, A. Zaluska, P. Tessier, J. O. Strom-Olsen, R. Schulz, J. Alloys Compd. 217(1995)295.

[9] Y. F. Liu, H. G. Pan, M. X. Gao, Y. F. Zhu, Y. Q. Lei, Q. D. Wang, Electrochim. Acta 49 (2004)545.

[10] X. X. Yuan, N. X. Xu, Acta Chim. Sin. 60(1) (2002)13.

Effect of Cerium on Microstructure and Electrochemical Performance of Ti-V-Cr-Ni Electrode Alloy①

Qiao Yuqing (乔玉卿)[a,b], Zhao Minshou (赵敏寿)[a,b],
Zhu Xinjian (朱新坚)[c], Cao Guangyi (曹广义)[c]
([a] State Key Laboratory of Metastable Materials Science and Technology, Yanshan University, Qinhuangdao 066004, China)
([b] Key Laboratory of Rare Earth Chemistry and Physics, Changchun Institute of Applied Chemistry, Chinese Academy of Sciences, Changchun 130022, China)
([c] Institute of Fuel Cell, Shanghai Jiaotong University, Shanghai 200030, China)

Abstract: Effect of cerium on the microstructure and electrochemical performance of the $Ti_{0.25}V_{0.35-x}Ce_xCr_{0.1}Ni_{0.3}$ ($x=0, 0.005$) electrode alloy was investigated by X-ray diffraction (XRD), field emission scanning electron microscopy/energy dispersive X-ray spectrometry (FESEM-EDS), and electrochemical impedance spectroscopy (EIS) measurements. On the basis of XRD and FESEM-EDS analysis, the alloy was mainly composed of V-based solid solution with body-centered-cubic structure and TiNi-based secondary phase. Ce did not exist in two phases, instead, it existed as Ce-rich small white particles, with irregular edges, distributed near the grain boundaries of the V-based solid solution phase. Discharge capacity, cycle stability, and high-rate discharge ability of the alloy electrode were effectively improved with the addition of Ce at 293 K. it was very surprising that the charge retention was abnormal with larger discharge capacity after standing at the open circuit for 24 h. EIS indicated that addition of Ce improved the dynamic performance, which caused the charge transfer resistance (R_T) to decrease and exchange current density (I_0) to increase markedly. The exchange current density of the electrochemical reaction on the alloy surface with Ce addition was about 2.07 and 3.10 times larger than that of the ahoy without Ce at 303 and 343 K, respectively. The diffusion coefficient of hydrogen (D) in the bulk alloy electrode decreased with addition of Ce, but it did not decrease so much, and the apparent activation energy ($\Delta_r H$) was far higher than that of the AB_5 type ahoy.

Key words: Electrode alloy; Solid solution alloy; EIS; Rare earths

In recent years, hydrogen storage alloys used as negative electrode materials in nickel-metal hydride rechargeable batteries with high performance[1-3] were researched intensively because of the energy crisis induced by the shortage of

① Journal of Rare Earths, 2007, 25(3): 341-347.

fossil energy. High capacity was the key issue for various applications of the hydrogen storage alloy. V-based solid solution alloy[4-7] and M g-based alloy[8] were candidates of promising hydrogen storage alloys, on account of their large hydrogen storage capacity. However, both the above-mentioned hydrogen storage alloys had grave problems, for instance, poor cycle stability of the Mg-based alloy and unfavorable dynamic properties of the V-based solid solution alloy.

As reported by Tsukahara et al.[1,7], the V-Ti-Cr solid solution alloy had a much larger hydrogen storage capacity, but almost without electrochemical activity in the KOH electrolyte. The coexistence of the TiNi-based secondary phase was considered to have electrochemical catalytic activity and act as a micro-current collector and electrochemical catalyst[9-11]. In the previous study, Ce has been used as an additive element to the $Ti_{0.25}V_{0.35}Cr_{0.1}Ni_{0.3}$ alloy. The result showed that Ce segregated to the surface of the alloy obviously during arc-melting whereas, little Ce affected the microstructure and electrochemical properties. To resolve the problem of Ce segregation to the alloy surface, the master alloy of $CeNi_3$ was used to substitute Ce during the arc-melting of the alloy. The effect of minor Ce on the microstructure and electrochemical perfonmance of the $Ti_{0.25}V_{0.35-x}Ce_xCr_{0.1}Ni_{0.3}$ ($x=0, 0.005$) electrode alloy was investigated in this article.

1 Experimental

$Ti_{0.25}V_{0.35-x}Ce_xCr_{0.1}Ni_{0.3}$ ($x=0, 0.005$) alloys were prepared by arc-melting the component metals or master alloy under argon in a water-cooled copper hearth and remelted thrice, to ensure homogeneity. The purity of the Ti, V, Cr, Ni, and Ce metals was higher than 99.9 % (mass fraction) respectively. A little of the as-cast alloy was mechanically crushed into particles and then further pulverized with a ceramic mortar to fine powder, of about 75 μm. The powder sample was used for X-ray analyses and electrochemical characterization. Some of the as-cast alloy was used for field emission scanning electron microscope (FESEM) analysis.

The crystal structure and lattice parameters of the alloy were determined by XRD (Cu Kα, Si internal standard) on Rigaku D/max 2500pc X-ray diffractometer using JAD5 software. The microstructure of the $Ti_{0.25}V_{0.35-x}Ce_xCr_{0.1}Ni_{0.3}$ ($x=0, 0.005$) alloys was determined on XL30 ESEM FEG field emission scanning electron microscope and the compositions of the two phases were determined semi-quantitatively with the help of EDS.

All metal hydride electrodes were prepared by pressing the mixture of alloy powder and carbonyl nickel powder, with a mass ratio of 1 : 5, into tablets, with a diameter of about 10 mm and a thickness of about 1.5 mm. The electrochemical properties were performed on a DC-5 battery testing instrument using the half-cell system, which consisted of a metal hydride electrode as the negative electrode and a sintered $Ni(OH)_2/NiOOH$ electrode with excess capacity in 6 mol · L^{-1} KOH electrolyte solution, the cut-off voltage for discharging was 0.8 V.

The ElS was measured for deteminging the charge-transfer resistance and exchange current density, to clarify kinetic properties of the dehydrating action at different temperatures, for the $Ti_{0.25}V_{0.35-x}Ce_xCr_{0.1}Ni_{0.3}$ ($x=0, 0.005$) alloy electrodes. ElS measurements were conducted at 50% depth of discharge (DOD) using solartron SI1187 electrochemical interface with a 1255 B frequency response analyzer and ZPLOT electrochemical impedance software. The EIS spectra of the electrodes were obtained in the frequency range of 100 kHz to 1×10^{-2} Hz with ac amplitude of 5 mV under open-circuit conditions.

According to the analysis model proposed by Kuriyama et al[12], an equivalent circuit for the metal hydride electrode was used, the parameters of charge-transfer resistance R_T in the equivalent circuit were fitted using the least-square method with ZVIEW electrochemical impedance software. The exchange current density I_0, the diffusion coefficient of hydrogert D in the bulk alloy, and the apparent energy $\Delta_r H$ can be calculated from Eqs. (1), (2) and (3)[12,13], respectively, where R is the gas constant, T is the temperature, F is the Faraday constant, δ is the Warburg coefficient in EIS, n is the number of transferred electrons, A is a constant and C_0 is the initial hydrogen concentration in the electrode when EIS is determined.

$$I_0=RT/FR_T \quad (1)$$

$$\delta^2=R^2T^2/2n^4F^4DC_0{}^2 \quad (2)$$

$$\lg(T/R_T)=-\Delta_r H/2.303RT+A \quad (3)$$

2 Results and discussion

2.1 Microstructure characterization

The XRD patterns of $Ti_{0.25}V_{0.35-x}Ce_xCr_{0.1}Ni_{0.3}$ ($x=0, 0.005$) alloys are shown in Fig. 1. As shown in Fig. 1, the main phase in the alloy has a body-centered-cubic structure identified as a V-based solid solution. The lattice parameter and cell volume of the V-based solid solution phase are calculated using the JAD5 software, and the results are summarized in Table 1. It can be seen that the lattice parameter and cell volume of the V-based solid solution phase for alloys with Ce is the same as that without Ce, which indicates that addition of Ce does not change the lattice parameter or cell volume.

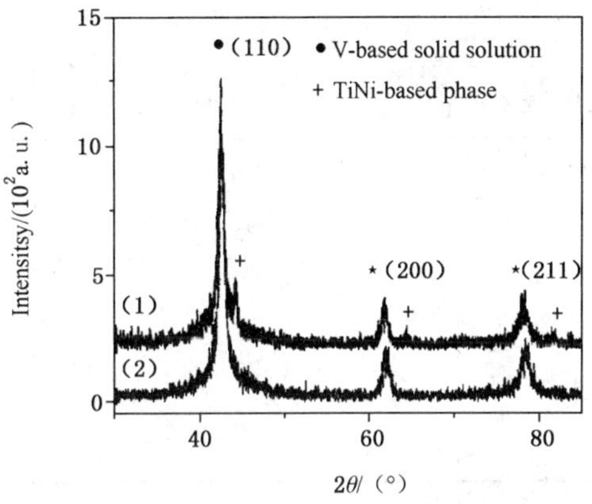

Fig. 1 X-ray diffraction patterns of $Ti_{0.25}V_{0.35-x}Ce_xCr_{0.1}Ni_{0.3}$ ($x=0$, 0.005) alloy (1) $x=0$; (2) $x=0.005$

Fig. 2 shows FESEM image of $Ti_{0.25}V_{0.35-x}Ce_xCr_{0.1}Ni_{0.3}$ ($x=0, 0.005$) alloys. The distribution of constituent elements of each phase is observed with EDS, as shown in Table 1. It can be easily seen that addition of Ce has great effect on the microstructure of the alloy, the structure of the V-based solid solution phase has a dendritic shape, and the grain size of the dendrite is finer than that of the alloy without Ce. The V-based solid solution phase and the secondary phase contain all the constituent elements, but the former is mainly composed of V and Cr, whereas, the latter is mainly composed of Ti and Ni. It should be pointed out that the Ni content in the secondary phase for the alloy with Ce addition is much higher than that of the alloy without Ce, as shown in Table 1. It is known that Ni is an electrocatalytic element for the V-based solid solution electrode alloy, therefore, a higher content of Ni in a TiNi-based secondary phase would be beneficial for the enhancement of the electrochemical activity of the alloy.

It can be seen from Fig. 2 (b) that there are some white particles with irregular edges distributed near the grain boundaries of the V-based solid solution phase, which were proved to be Ce-rich particles, by energy dispersion X-ray spectroscopy. It can be concluded that Ce does not exist in the fnrst two phases, although it exists in the Ce-rich small white particles distributed near the grain boundaries of the V-based solid solution phase.

2.2 Discharge profile

Fig. 3 shows typical discharge capacity-potential curves of the alloy electrodes at 293 K, at the ninth cycle. It can be clearly seen that the alloy electrode with Ce addition has a higher discharge voltage and wider discharge voltage plateau, and the discharge efficiency is effectively improved. Iwakura et al.[14] Have compared the electrochemical data with the pressure-composition isotherms (P-C isotherms) of the La-Ni_4Cu negative electrode. The result shows that the curve of equilibrium potential-discharge capacity and the curve of P-C isotherm are rather coordinate, especially for the tendency in the plateau region. The plateau region of equilibrium potential is identical to the P-C isotherms, so the discharge capacity-potential curves can be used to simulate the P-C isotherms. It can be stated that addition of Ce makes the plateau region broader, which is beneficial for the enhance-ment of the discharge capacity of the alloy.

Table1　Phase compositlon of $Ti_{0.25}V_{0.35-x}Cex Cr_{0.1}Ni_{0.3}$ ($x=0,0.005$) alloy

Samples	Phase	Compositios(%, atom fraction)					Lattice parameter/nm	Cell volumc/nm^3
		Ti	V	Cr	Ni	Cr		
$x=0$	V-based	19.43	53.14	22.69	4.74	/	0.299	0.027
	TiNi-based	47.13	21.29	5.29	26.30	/		
$x=0.005$	V-based	7.10	64.95	19.93	8.02	/	0.299	0.027
	TiNi-based	38.73	11.61	1.54	48.13	/		
	Ce-rich particles	4.81	/	4.58	11.37	79.24		

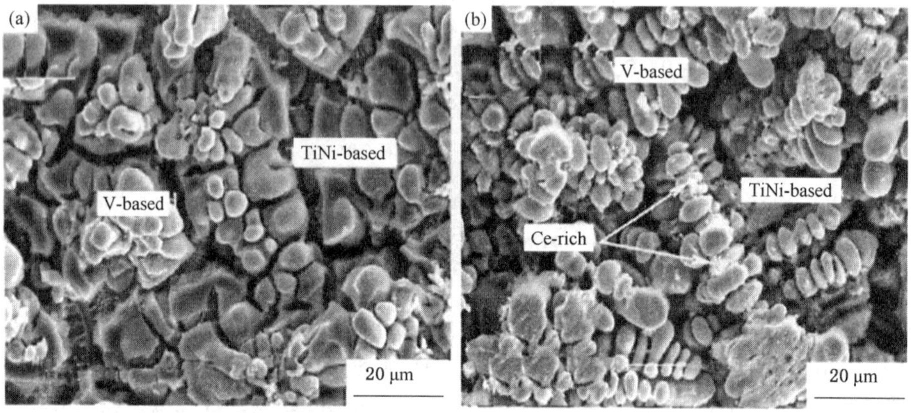

Fig. 2　FESEM of the $Ti_{0.25}V_{0.35-x}Ce_xCr_{0.1}Ni_{0.3}$ ($x=0,0.005$) alloy

(a) $x=0$; (b) $x=0.005$

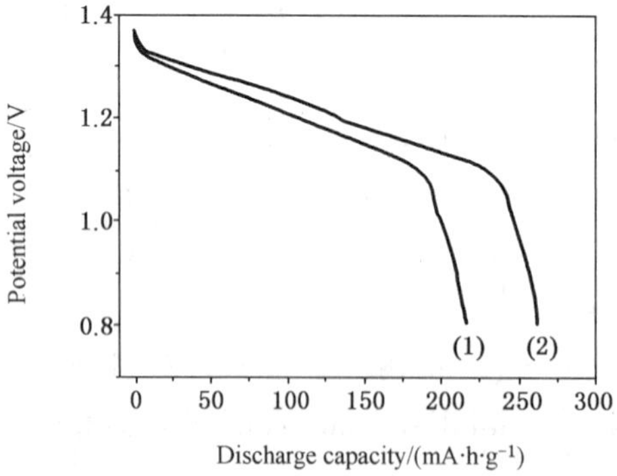

Fig. 3　Discharge capacity as a function of cycle number for $Ti_{0.25}V_{0.35-x}Ce_xCr_{0.1}Ni_{0.3}$ ($x=0,0.005$) lalloy electrode at 293 K

(1) $x=0$; (2) $x=0.005$

2.3　Discharge capacity

The discharge capacity of $Ti_{0.25}V_{0.35-x}Ce_xCr_{0.1}Ni_{0.3}$ ($x=0,0.005$) alloy electrodes at 293 K is shown in Fig. 4. As shown in Fig. 4, the discharge capacity of the alloy electrode with Ce is significantly increased. A discharge capacity of 270.9 mA · h · g^{-1} at a current density of 60 mA · g^{-1} and 293 K has been achieved, which is almost comparable to the capacity of the AB_5-type alloy electrode, whereas, the discharge capacity of the alloy electrode without Ce is 224 mA · h · g^{-1}. The result suggests that the alloy with Ce addition has a higher electrochemical catalyst activity than the alloy without Ce, for hydriding/dehydriding. The increase of discharge capacity may be attributed to the electrocatalytic activity improved by the higher Ni content in the TiNi-based secondary phase, or by the coexistence of the Ce rich particle and TiNi-based secondary phase.

After adding Ce to the alloy, the amount of TiNi based secondary phase decreases. As shown in Fig. 1, the electrocatalytic activity of the alloy decreases, but in fact, the electrocatalytic activity of the alloy is effectively improved. These results also imply that Ce plays an important role in the improvement of the electrocatalytic activity of the alloy.

2.4 Temperature effect

The discharge capacity of the alloy electrodes as a function of temperature is shown in Fig. 5. It can be found that the discharge capacity of the alloy electrodes is sensitive to temperature. With increasing temperature, the discharge capacity of the alloy electrode, with Ce addition, increases at first and then decreases. The alloy electrode with Ce has a higher discharge capacity than that of the alloy electrode without Ce when the temperature is lower than 323 K, and a maximum discharge capacity of 270.9 mA · h · g^{-1} is achieved at 293 K.

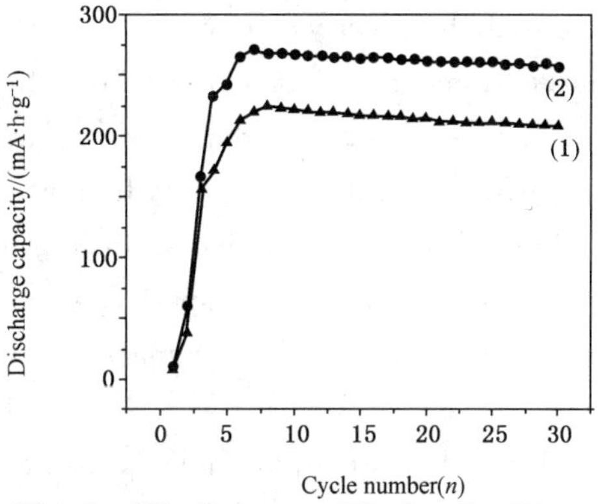

Fig. 4 Discharge profile for the $Ti_{0.25}V_{0.35-x}Ce_xCr_{0.1}Ni_{0.3}$ (x=0, 0.005) alloy electrode at 293 K

(1) x=0; (2) x=0.005

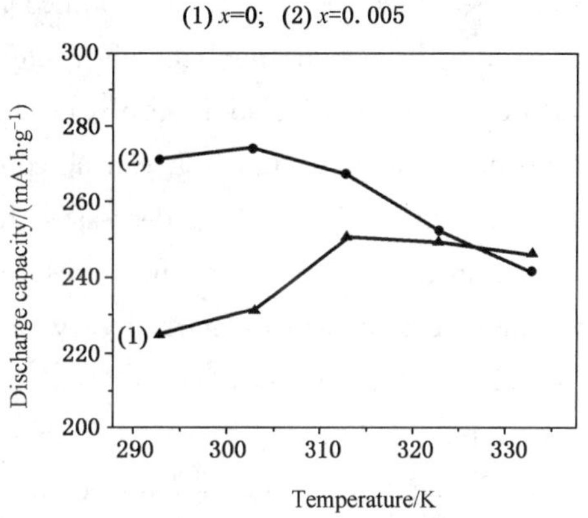

Fig. 5 Effect of temperature on the discharge capacity of $Ti_{0.25}V_{0.35-x}Ce_xCr_{0.1}Ni_{0.3}$ (x=0, 0.005) alloy electrode

(1) x=0; (2) x=0.005

2.5 Electrochemical impedance spectroscopy

Fig. 6 shows the electrochemical impedance spectroscopy (EIS) of $Ti_{0.25}V_{0.35-x}Ce_xCr_{0.1}Ni_{0.3}$ (x=0, 0.005) alloy electrodes at 50% DOD at different temperatures. According to the analysis model proposed by Kuriyama et al[12], the charge transfer resistance has been fitted. The exchange current density and the diffusion coefficient of hydrogen in the bulk alloy are calculated according to equations (1) and (2), respectively, and the results are all summarized in Table 2.

It can be seen from Table 2 that the exchange current density of the electrode reaction on the surface of the alloy electrode with Ce is about 2.07 and 3.10 times larger than that on the alloy without Ce, at 303 and 343 K, respectively. The diffusion coefficient of hydrogen in the bulk alloy electrode decreases with the addition of Ce, but it does not decrease so much. It can be concluded that the addition of Ce decreases the charge transfer resistance and increases the ex-change current density markedly, which is beneficial to the enhancement of the discharge capacity of the hydrogen storage alloy. Unfortunately the decrease in the diffusion coefficient of hydrogen is harmful to the electrochemical performance of the alloy.

Fig. 7 shows that there is straight relationship between lg (T/R_T) and $1/T$, which coincides well with the Arrhenius relationship. The apparent energy can be calculated according to Eq. (3), and the results are also summarized in Table 2. The apparent energies of the electrode reaction for $Ti_{0.25}V_{0.35-x}Ce_xCr_{0.1}Ni_{0.3}$ ($x=0, 0.005$) alloy electrode are 42.30 and 51.18 kJ · mol^{-1}, respectively, which are larger than that of the $MINi_{3.75}Co_{0.65}Mn_{0.4}Al_{0.2}$ hydrogen storage alloy electrode (28.1 kJ · mol^{-1})[13]. The apparent higher energy may be responsible for the poor dynamic properties of the V-based solid solution alloy.

2.6 High rate dischargeability (HRD)

Fig. 8 shows the effect of the discharge current density on the discharge capacity of the $Ti_{025}V_{0.35-x}Ce_xCr_{0.1}Ni_{0.3}$ ($x=0, 0.005$) alloy electrode. The results show that addition of cerium appreciably improves the rate discharge characteristic of the alloy electrode.

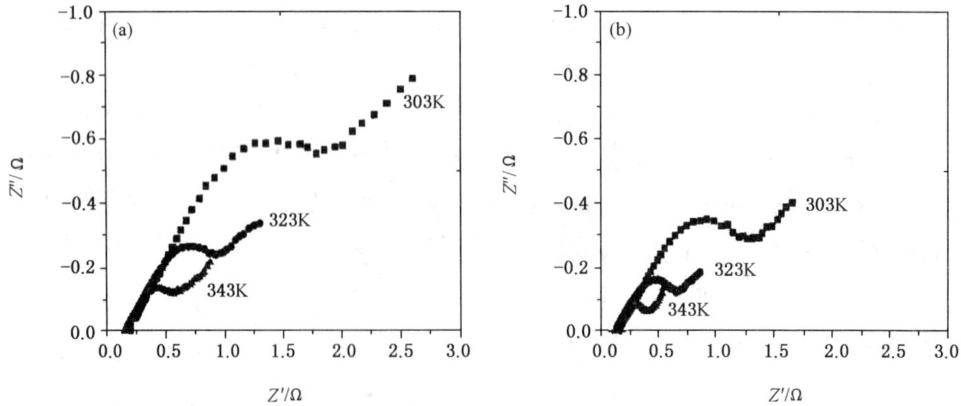

Fig. 6 Electrochemical impedance spectroscopy of $Ti_{0.25}V_{0.35-x}Ce_xCr_{0.1}Ni_{0.3}$ ($x=0, 0.005$) alloy electrode at 50% DOD at different temp eratures
(a) $x=0$; (b) $x=0.005$

Table 2　Charge-transfer reaction resistance (R_T), exchange current density (I_0), and apparent energy($\Delta_r H$) of $Ti_{0.25}V_{0.35-x}Ce_xCr_{0.1}Ni_{0.3}$ ($x=0, 0.005$) alloy electrode

Samples	R_T/Ω	$I_0/(mA \cdot g^{-1})$					$\Delta_r H/$	$D(303\ K)/$
	303K	323K	343K	303K	323K	343K	$(kJ \cdot mol^{-1})$	$(cm^2 \cdot s^{-1})$
$x=0$	2.632	0.957	0.416	66.12	181.85	425.51	42.30	4.809×10^{-11}
$x=0.005$	1.273	0.409	0.134	136.71	425.51	1298.76	51.18	3.435×10^{-11}

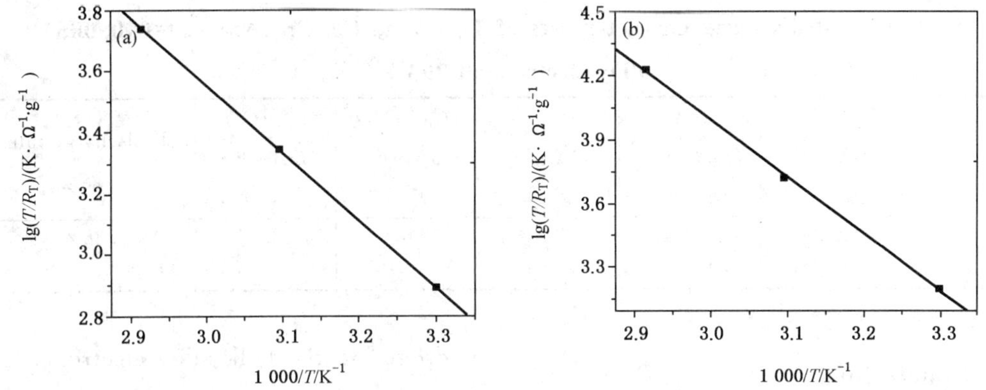

Fig. 7　Plot of lg (T/R_T) vs. $1/T$ for $Ti_{0.25}V_{0.35-x}Ce_xCr_{0.1}Ni_{0.3}$ ($x=0, 0.005$) alloy electrode (a) $x=0$; (b) $x=0.005$

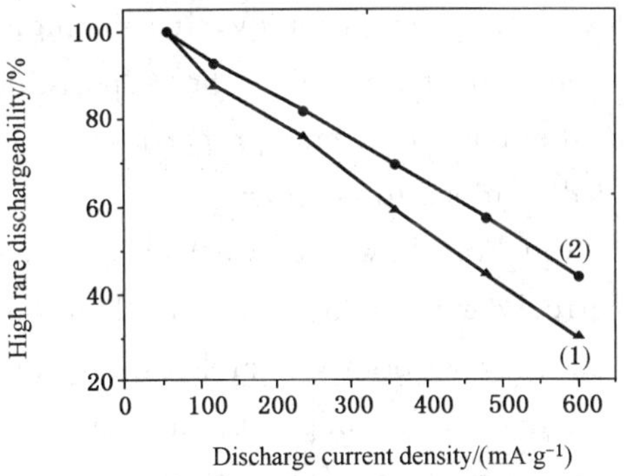

Fig. 8　High rate discharge ability of $Ti_{0.25}V_{0.35-x}Ce_xCr_{0.1}Ni_{0.3}$ ($x=0, 0.005$) alloy electrode at 293 K (1) $x=0$; (2) $x=0.005$

It is known that the HRD of the alloy electrode is affected by two factors, that is, chargetransfer and hydrogen-diffusion. According to the result of the EIS analysis, for the alloy with Ce addition, both charge-transfer resistance and diffusion coefficient of hydrogert decrease, but only the decrease of the former is beneficial to the enhancement of HRD.

2.7 Self-discharge

According to the literature[15], the self-discharge of the hydrogen storage alloy can be divided into two parts, that is, reversible (C_3-C_2) and irreversible (C_1-C_3), respectively, where C_1 is the discharge capacity of the alloy electrode with normal cycles, C_2 is the discharge capacity of the alloy electrode at the open circuit for 24 h after charging, and C_3 is measured with the next cycle immediately after the measurement of C_2.

The self-discharge characteristics of $Ti_{0.25}V_{0.35-x}Ce_xCr_{0.1}Ni_{0.3}$ ($x=0, 0.005$) alloy electrodes are measured at 293 K and the results are shown in Table 3. As shown in Table 3, the self-discharge characteristics are abnormal. Larger discharge capacity (C_3) has been obtained and the irreversible parts of self-discharge (C_1-C_3) are negative.

In the present study, it has been found that the charge transfer resistance after self-discharge measurement is lower than that before self-discharge measurement, detail research study on this abnormal phenomenon will be investigated and published in a later article.

Table 3　Self-discharge characteristics of $Ti_{0.25}V_{0.35-x}Ce_xCr_{0.1}Ni_{0.3}$ (x=0, 0.005) alloy electrode at 293 K*

Samples	C_1/ (mA·h·g^{-1})	C2/ (mA·h·g^{-1})	C_3/ (mA·h·g^{-1})	(C_1-C_3)/ (mA·h·g^{-1})	(C_3-C_2)/ (mA·h·g^{-1})	Self-discharge rate/ %
x=0	221.9	220.4	222.8	−0.9	2.4	0.88%
x=0.005	266.7	270.9	268.0	−1.3	−2.9	−1.33%

* Self-discharge rate={1−2C_2/(C_1+C_3)}×100%

3　Conclusions

(1) The test alloy was mainly composed of a V-based solid solution with a body-centered-cubic structure and a small amount of TiNi-based secondary phase. Rare earth Ce did not exist in these two phases; instead it existed in Ce-rich small white particles with irregular edges distributed near the grain boundaries of the V-based solid solution phase.

(2) Addition of Ce substantially increased the discharge capacity, cycle stability, and high-rate dischargeability of the alloy electrode at 293 K, whereas, the self-discharge characteristic was abnormal with a larger discharge capacity after standing at an open circuit for 24 h.

(3) Addition of Ce improved the dynamic performance of the alloy, causing charge transfer resistance to decrease and exchange current density to increase markedly. The diffusion coefficient of hydrogen in the bulk alloy electrode decreased with the addition of Ce, but it did not decrease significantly. The apparent activation energy was far higher than that for the AB_5 type alloy, and the higher apparent energy might be responsible for the poor dynamic properties of V-based solid solution alloy.

(4) An alloy with Ce had a higher electrochemical catalyst activity than that of an alloy without Ce for hydriding/dehydriding, which might be attributed to the improvement of the electrocatalytic activity, by a higher content of Ni in the TiNi-based secondary phase or the coexistence of the Ce-rich particle with the TiNi-based secondary phase.

References

[1] Tsukahara M, Tskahasha K, M ishima T, Isomura A, Sakai T. Heat-treatment effects of V-based solid solu-tion alloy with TiNi-based network structure on hydrogen storage

and electrode properties [J]. *J. Alloys Comp.*, 1996,243:133

[2] Mouri T, lba H. Hydrogen-absorbing alloys with a large capacity for a new energy carrier [J]. *Materids Science and Engineering A*, 2002, 329-331: 346.

[3] Akiba E, Iba H. Hydrogen absorption by Laves phase related BCC solid solution [J]. *Intermetallics*, 1998, 6:461.

[4] Huot J, Akiba E, Ogura T. Crystal structure, phase a-bundance and electrode performances of Laves phase compounds (Zr, A) $V_{0.5}$ $Ni_{1.1}$ $Mn_{0.2}$ $Fe_{0.2}$ (A≡Ti, Nb or Hf) [J]. *J. Alloys Comp.*, 1995, 218: 101.

[5] Cho S W, Han C S, Park C N, Akiba E. The hydrogen storage characteristics of Ti-Cr-V alloys [J]. *J. Alloys Comp.*, 1999, 288: 294.

[6] Tsukahara M, Tskahasha K, Mishima T, Miyamura H, Sakai T, Kuriyama N, Uehara I. The $TiV_3Ni_{0.56}$ hydride electrode: its electrochemical and cycle life charac-terization [J]. *J. Alloys Comp.*, 1995, 231: 616.

[7] Li Jia, Zhao Minshou, Hou Chtmping, Huang Liang, Zhu Xinjian, Cao Guangyi. Effects of Rare Earth Addition on Microstructure and Electrochemical Properties of Ti-Zr-V-Cr-Ni Alloys [J]. *Journal of Rare Earths Societry* (in Chin.), 2006, 24 (6): 764.

[8] Cui N, Luan B, Zhao H J, Liu H K, Dou S X. Effects of yttrium additions on the electrode performance of magnesium-based hydrogen storage alloys [J]. *J . Alloys Comp.*, 1996, 233: 236.

[9] Pan H G, Zhu Y F, Gao M X, Liu Y F, Li R, Lei Y Q, Wang Q D. XRD study of the hydrogenation and dehydrogenation process of the two different phase com-ponents in a Ti-V-based multiphase hydrogen storage e-lectrode alloy [J]. *J. Alloy s Comp.*, 2004, 370: 254.

[10] Li R, Pan H G, Gao M X, Liu Y F, Jin Q W, Lei Y Q. Structural and electrochemical properties of hydrogen storage alloys $Ti_{0.8}$ $Zr_{0.2}$ $V_{2.7}$ $Mn_{0.5}$ $Cr_{0.8}$ Ni_x ($x=1.50\sim2.25$) [J]. *J. Alltoy s Comp.*, 2004, 373: 223.

[11] Liu Y F, Pan HG, Gao M X, ZhuYF, LeiYQ, Wang Q D. The electrochemical performance of a La-Mg-Ni-Co-Mn metal hy dride electrode alloy in the temperature range of −20 to 30 ℃ [J]. *Electrochimica Acta* 2004, 49: 545.

[12] Kuriyama N, Sakai T, M iyamura H, Uehara J, Ishikawa H. Electrochemical impedance and deterioration behavior of metal hydride electrodes [J]. *J. Alloy s Comp.*, 1993,202: 183.

[13] Yuan X X, Xu N X. Effects of temperature on the kinetic performance of hydrogen storage alloy $MINi_{3.75}$ $Co_{0.65}$ $Mn_{0.4}$ $Al_{0.2}$ [J]. *Acta Chimica Sinica*, 2002,60(1):13.

[14] Iwakura C, Askahiko T, Yoneyama H, Sakai T, Oguro K, Ishikawa H. Electrochemical characteristics of $La\text{-}Ni_5$ system hydrogen-absorbing alloys as negative electrode materials for Nickel-hydrogen batteries [J]. *J. Chem. Soc. of Jap an*, 1988, 8: 1482.

[15] Iwakura C, Kajiya Y, Yoneyama H, Sakai T, Oguro K, lshikawa H. Self-discharge mechanism of Nickel-hydrogen batteries using metal hydride anodes [J]. *J. Electrochem. Soc.*, 1989, 136: 1351.

Distinct Synergistic Effect in $Ti_{0.10}Zr_{0.15}V_{0.35}Cr_{0.10}Ni_{0.30}$ + 1.0 wt% $LaNi_5$ Hydrogen Storage Composite Electrode①

Yanzhi Wang[a,b], Minshou Zhao[a,b]
([a] Hebei Key Laboratory of Applied Chemistry,
Yanshan University, Qinhuangdao 066004, China)
([b] State Key Laboratory of Metastable Materials Science and Technology,
Yanshan University, Qinhuangdao 066004, China)

Abstract: Distinct synergistic effect of $Ti_{0.10}Zr_{0.15}V_{0.35}Cr_{0.10}Ni_{0.30}$ + 1.0 wt% $LaNi_5$ hydrogen storage composite prepared by two-step arc-melting has been analyzed and discussed systematically. X-ray diffractometry (XRD) and scanning electron microscopy-energy dispersive spectroscopy (SEM-EDS) show that the main phase of composite alloy is composed of V-based solid solution phase with a BCC structure and C14 Laves phase with hexagonal structure, while secondary phase also exists in the composite alloy. Electrochemical properties of the composite alloy electrode have significantly been improved. It is suggested that distinct synergistic effect appears in the activation process, in the composite process, in the cyclic process, in the discharge process at low/high temperature and at different current density, and in the charge-transfer resistance and the exchange current density for the hydrogen storage composite electrode, which is probably ascribed to the formation of the secondary phase in the composite alloy.

Key words: Hydrogen storage alloy; Ti-V-based solid solution; Composite; Synergistic effect

1 Introduction

Ti-V-based multiphase hydrogen storage alloys, namely "Laves phase related BCC solid solution" [1], with high discharge capacities mainly consist of a V-based solid solution BCC phase as the main hydrogen absorption phase and a network of TiNi BCC phase or C14 Laves phase as the secondary phase of electro-catalyst and micro-current collector. However, these alloys also have some problems of high cost, poor electro-catalytic activity and high rate of degradation of vanadium [2,3]. Therefore, many researches were carried out for the commercial usage as negative electrode for Ni/MH batteries [4-8].

In order to obtain excellent comprehensive performance, some novel com-

① International Journal of Hydrogen Energy, 2012(37): 3276-3282.

posites are manufactured. Presently, most of composite hydrogen storage materials are obtained by mechanical alloying [9-11]. However, there are two disadvantages such as long mechanical alloying time and short cycle stability. In addition, phases cannot be joined closely with each other together in the mechanical alloying process, particle surface is easy to be oxidized and polluted, as well as some impurity is also easy to be introduced into alloy in the processing. In above references about composite, synergistic effect cannot be found and discussed.

In our previous work [12], $Ti_{0.10}Zr_{0.15}V_{0.35}Cr_{0.10}Ni_{0.30}$-$LaNi_5$ composite hydrogen storage alloy was prepared by two-step arc-melting. There are two advantages for two-step arc-melting method, namely, the phases in the composite alloy can be joined closely with each other together, and the composite alloy cannot be oxidized and polluted, while there are two disadvantages such as the necessity of inert argon atmosphere, longer times of annealing and the high energy consumption of the process. In Ref. [12], infiuence of $LaNi_5$ content on the microstructure and electrochemical characteristics of the composite alloy were investigated systematically. It was found that overall electrochemical properties of the composite alloy were significantly improved. The results showed that synergistic effect possibly appeared in the composite process. Thus, in this paper, distinct synergistic effect in many performances of $Ti_{0.10}Zr_{0.15}V_{0.35}Cr_{0.10}Ni_{0.30}$ +1.0 wt% $LaNi_5$ hydrogen storage composite electrode has been analyzed and discussed systematically.

2 Experimental details

$Ti_{0.10}Zr_{0.15}V_{0.35}Cr_{0.10}Ni_{0.30}$ (represented as TVS hereafter) alloy, $LaNi_5$ alloy and TVS+1.0 wt% $LaNi_5$ composite alloy (represented as COM hereafter) were prepared by arc-melting, respectively. The sample alloys were crushed mechanically in air and ground to powder within an agate mortar. The sample powders with a size of 200—300 meshes for electrochemical measurements, and those with a size of 400 meshes were used for XRD analysis utilizing with Cu Kα radiation on D/Max-rB X-ray diffractometer, respectively. The morphology of COM alloy was observed using KYKY 2800-type scanning electron microscopy (SEM) and composition of the phases was estimated by a Kevex-sigma Level 4 energy dispersive spectrom-eter (EDS), respectively.

Electrochemical properties were measured in a standard three electrode cell system consisting of working electrode (the metal hydride electrode), a counter electrode ($Ni(OH)_2$/NiOOH electrode) with excess capacity and a reference electrode (Hg/HgO). The electrolyte in the cell was 6 mol L^{-1} KOH solution. The metal hydride electrode was prepared by mixing the alloy powder with carbonyl nickel powder in a weight ratio of 1 ∶ 5 and cold-pressing the mixture to form pellets under a pressure of 15 MPa with 10 mm in diameter and about 1.5 mm in thickness. The charge/discharge tests were carried out with DC-5 battery testing instrument under computer control. The low temperature dischargeability (LTD) was measured after being fully charged at constant temperature using a low temperature equipment (WGD701). During the charge/discharge tests, the electrodes were fully charged (the over-charged ratio approximately 30%) at current density of 60 mA g^{-1}, and then discharged to −0.6 V versus Hg/HgO at 60 mA g^{-1}.

After the test electrodes were completely activated, the electrochemical impedance spectroscopy (EIS) measurements were conducted at 50% depth of discharge (DOD) using a Solartron 1287 Potentiostat/Galvanostat and a Solartron 1255 frequency response analyzer with Z-POLT software in the frequency range of 0.1 Hz—1 MHz with an ac amplitude perturbation of 5 mV under open circuit condition. The measurement of electrochemical properties was similar to those described in our previous paper [12].

3 Results and discussion

3.1 Structure characteristics

XRD pattern of COM, TVS and $LaNi_5$ as-cast alloy is shown in Fig. 1. The result indicates that the main phase of COM alloy is composing of V-based solid solution phase with a BCC structure and C14 Laves phase with hexagonal structure, which is as same as that of TVS as-cast alloy. However, the secondary phase is exhibited as small additional peaks and the $CaCu_5$ phase of $LaNi_5$ alloy can not be detected in COM alloy. The lattice parameters of the BCC phase and C14 Laves phase in the composite are calculated using the MDI Jade 5.0 software, which are summarized in Table 1. It can be seen that the lattice parameter and cell volume of the BCC phase in COM alloy is larger than that of TVS alloy, and the larger cell volume of the main phase would be beneficial for a larger hydrogen storage capacity.

Fig. 2 shows the SEM morphology of COM alloy. EDS patterns of different phases in COM alloy are shown in Fig. 3. It is found that COM alloy consists of V-based solid solution phase with a dendritic shape and a continuous C14 Laves phase with a network shape. Comparing to the SEM morphology of TVS alloy [13], it can be seen that the white lard phase embedded in C14 Laves phase with irregular shape is the secondary phase formed during composite process. The EDS analysis indicates that the V-based solid solution phase is mainly composed of V, Zr, Cr and Ni, the C14 Laves phase is mainly composed of Zr, V, Ti and Ni, and the secondary phase is mainly composed of Zr, V, Ti and Ni (namely Zr-rich phase), which shows that the additive $LaNi_5$ alloy is decomposed during composite process, and La can be only detected in the secondary phase of COM alloy.

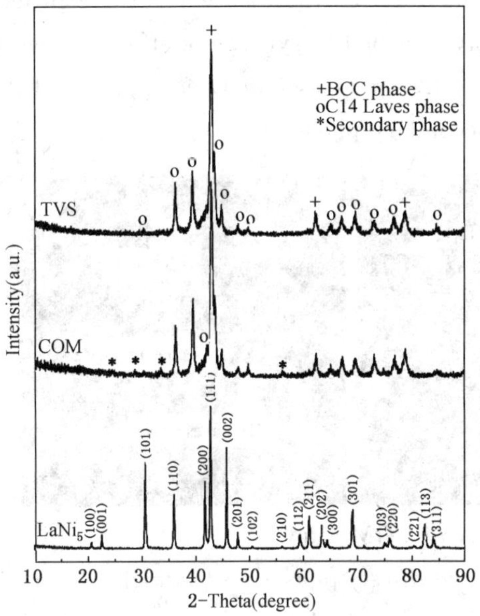

Fig. 1　XRD pattern of COM, TVS and $LaNi_5$ as-cast alloy

Table 1　Lattice parameters of BCC and C14 Laves phas ein TVS and COM alloy

Sample	Phase	Lattice parameter		Cell volume/nm^3
		a/nm	c/nm	
TVS alloy	BCC phase C14 Laves phase	0.2969 0.4948	0.8093	0.02617 0.1716
COM alloy	BCC phase C14 Laves phase	0.2970 0.4948	0.8066	0.02620 0.1710

3.2　Activation performance and synergistic effect

The activation performance of COM, TVS and $LaNi_5$ alloy electrode is shown in Fig. 4, wherein calculated value is obtained according to the value measured and composite ratio of TVS and $LaNi_5$ alloy. First, it can be found that the activation of COM alloy electrode needs 7 cycles, the activation number of COM alloy electrode is 11 cycles fewer than that of TVS alloy electrode, which indicates that additive $LaNi_5$ alloy is beneficial for improving the electrochemical activity of TVS alloy. Second, it is obvious that the curve measured is above that calculated for COM alloy electrode, which means the actual discharge capacity of COM alloy electrode is higher than the sum of all the discharge capacity of TVS and $LaNi_5$ alloy electrode during activation process. This indicates that there is distinct synergistic effect between the TVS alloy and $LaNi_5$ alloy in the composite hydrogen storage alloy electrode during the activation process of COM alloy electrode. Firstly, according to the concept of synergetic systems of composite proposed by O. Savadogo [14], if no electronic effect is observed, it may be concluded that the synergetic effect is due to an increase in the number of active-sites at the electrocatalyst surface. Thus, the secondary phase may become the active sites [15] and pathways for hydrogen diffusion. Secondly, diffusion through grain boundary having an open structure is easier than that in grain having a perfect lattice [16]. As mentioned above, there are three phases, namely BCC phase, C14 Laves phase and the secondary phase in COM alloy, which induce the phase boundaries and vices in composite alloy particles, not only result in enhanced hydrogen atomic diffusivities in the composite alloy, but also promote the dissociation and recombination of hydrogen in COM alloy. Thirdly, it is reported [17] that the bulk hydrogen transport property of the alloys is dominated by synergetic effects between major and minor phases. Therefore, the distinct synergistic effect and improved activation performance for COM alloy electrode are probably ascribed to synergetic effects between the BCC phase, C14 Laves phase and the secondary phase.

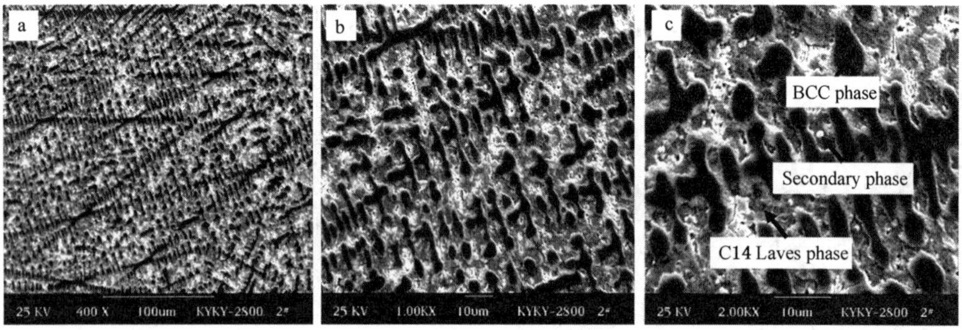

Fig. 2　SEM morphology of COM alloy

3. 3　Maximum discharge capacity and synergistic effect

The maximum discharge capacity of COM, TVS and $LaNi_5$ alloy electrode is also shown in Fig. 4. First, it can be found that the real maximum discharge capacity of COM alloy electrode is 18. 0 mAh g^{-1} bigger than that of TVS alloy electrode. Second, it shows that the real maximum discharge capacity of COM alloy electrode is 342. 9 mAh g^{-1}, the real value is 19. 8 mAh g^{-1} higher than that calculated, which illuminates that the real maximum discharge capacity of COM alloy electrode is bigger than the sum of all the discharge capacity of the constituent alloys. It is suggested that distinct syner-gistic effect occurs in the composite process. As mentioned above, COM alloy have three phases, of which the BCC phase and C14 Laves phase are the hydrogen storage phase, and the C14 Laves phase and the secondary phase may work as active sites, the catalyst or the micro-current collector. In a way, the distinct synergistic effect between TVS and $LaNi_5$ alloy in the composite process is similar to the results with $MgNi_{1+x}$-CNT composite [18], which is believed to be caused by an increase in the number of active sites for hydrogen storage.

3. 4　Cyclic stability and synergistic effect

Fig. 5 shows the dependence of discharge capacity on cycle number for COM, TVS and $LaNi_5$ alloy electrode. The capacity retention (S_n) used to represent the cyclic stability can be calculated in the following equation:

$$S_n(\%)=(C_n/C_{max})\times 100\% \quad (1)$$

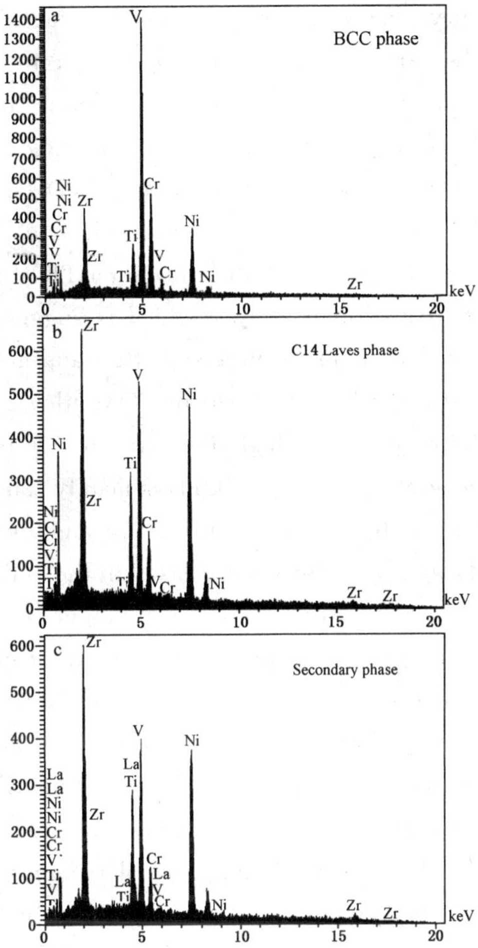

Fig. 3　EDS analysis of COM alloy: (a) BCC phase; (b) C14 Laves phase; (c) secondary phase

Where in S_n is the capacity retention at n cycles, C_n the discharge capacity at n cycles and C_{max} the maximum discharge capacity. It can be seen that the cyclic stability of COM alloy electrode is superior to that of TVS alloy electrode, for example, S_{100} of COM alloy electrode is 96.00%, which is 7.85% higher than that of TVS alloy electrode. In addition, the curve measured is above the curve calculated, which indicates that the real discharge capacity of COM alloy electrode is higher than the sum of all the discharge capacity of the constituent alloys in cyclic process. It is suggested that distinct synergistic effect appears in the cyclic process of COM alloy electrode. According to our previous work [12], the dissolution of V, Zr and Ti elements from COM alloy electrode in KOH electrolyte is greatly restrained after adding $LaNi_5$ alloy in TVS alloy, which may result in the distinct synergistic effect in the cyclic process and improved cyclic stability for COM alloy electrode.

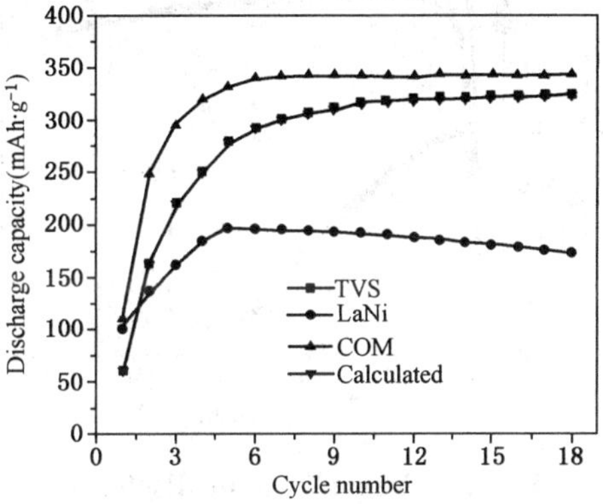

Fig. 4　Activation performance of COM, TVS and $LaNi_5$ alloy electrode

3.5　Temperature properties and synergistic effect

The dischargeability of COM, TVS and $LaNi_5$ alloy electrode at different temperature is shown in Fig. 6. The dischargeability at different temperature is defined as the ratio of the discharge capacity C_T at a certain temperature to the discharge capacity C_{303} at temperature of 303 K. It is obvious that the dischargeability is very sensitive to temperature. Composite alloy electrode reaches maximum discharge capacities at 293 K, while TVS alloy electrode reaches its maximum discharge capacity at 303 K. It can be seen that though the high temperature dischargeabilities (HTD) of COM alloy electrode is a little lower than that of TVS alloy, whereas the low temperature dischargeability (LTD) of COM alloy electrode is distinctly higher than that of TVS alloy electrode, for example, LTD of COM alloy electrode at 233 K is 18.13% higher than that of TVS alloy electrode, which indicates that addition of $LaNi_5$ alloy is beneficial for improving LTD of TVS alloy electrode.

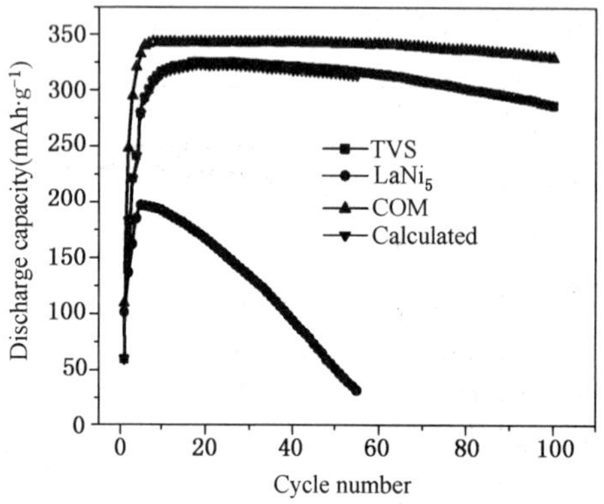

Fig. 5 Dependence of discharge capacity on cycle number for COM, TVS and $LaNi_5$ alloy electrode

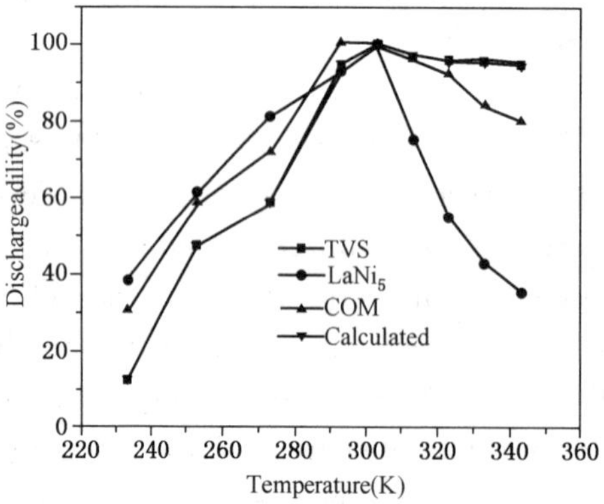

Fig. 6 Dischargeability of COM, TVS and $LaNi_5$ alloy electrode at different temperature

In addition, it is found that the curve measured is at a position higher than that calculated in low temperature range and the circumstance is opposite in high temperature range for COM alloy electrode, namely, the factual HTD (or LTD) of COM alloy electrode is not equal to the sum of all HTD (or LTD) of the constituent alloys, which is suggested that distinct synergistic effect appears in the discharge process of COM alloy electrode at low/high temperature. It is generally known that LTD is mainly controlled by hydrogen diffusion, and hydrogen can diffuse more easily in the bulk of alloys with a larger cell volume and more grain boundaries having an open structure than that in grain. Thus, the distinct synergistic effect in the discharge capacity of COM alloy electrode in low temperature range is probably ascribed to the formation of the secondary phase which becomes the active sites [15] and pathways for hydrogen diffusion. These microsized particles in the composite sample, which increase the phase boundaries and vices in composite alloy particles, not only result in enhanced hydrogen atomic diffusivities in the composite alloy, but also promote the dissociation and recombination of hydrogen in COM alloy. However, HTD is perhaps related to the equilibrium hydrogen pressures of desorption [19]. The hydrogen desorption plateau pressure increases with increasing temperature, the hydrogen desorption plateau pressure of COM alloy electrode is higher than that of TVS alloy electrode [12], and thereby the rates of dehydriding of COM alloy and of diffusion of hydrogen through COM alloy electrode increase, which inevitably increases the reversible capacity loss and decreases HTD. In conclusion, the distinct synergistic effect in the discharge capacity of COM alloy electrode in high temperature range is probably ascribed to the formation of the secondary phase with micro-sized particles resulting in the increase of the electro-catalytic activity of COM alloy electrode.

3.6　High-rate dischargeability and synergistic effect

High-rate dischargeability (HRD) is important kinetic properties for a metal hydride electrode. HRD can be calculated in the following equation:

$$HRD(\%)=(C_i/C_{60})\times 100\% \quad (2)$$

Wherein C_{60} is discharge capacity at both the charge/discharge current density of 60 mA g^{-1}, and C_i is the discharge capacity at certain discharge current density (60—1 500 mA g^{-1}). High-rate dischargeability as a function of discharge current density for COM, TVS and $LaNi_5$ alloy electrode is shown in Fig. 7. It is evident that HRD of COM alloy electrode is improved after adding 1.0 wt.% $LaNi_5$ alloy, for example, HRD of COM alloy electrode is 17.67% bigger than that of TVS alloy electrode at discharge current density of 1500 mA g^{-1}. It can also be seen that the real HRD is obviously higher than that calculated with increasing discharge current density for COM alloy electrode, for example, the real HRD of COM alloy elec-trode is 17.61% higher than that calculated at discharge current density of 1 500 mA g^{-1}. It is suggested that distinct synergistic effect exists in the discharge process of COM alloy electrode at different current density, which is possibly ascribed to the increase of the active sites and the volume fraction of C14 Laves phase [12] resulting in the increase of the electro-catalytic activity of COM alloy electrode.

3.7　Charge-transfer resistance, exchange current density and synergistic effect

Fig. 8 represents the electrochemical impedance spectra of COM, TVS and $LaNi_5$ alloy electrode at 50% DOD at 303 K. On the basis of the model proposed by Kuriyama et al. [20], the charge-transfer resistance R_{ct} are obtained by means of the fitting program Z-View, the exchange current density I_0 is calculated by the following equation when overpotential is very small:

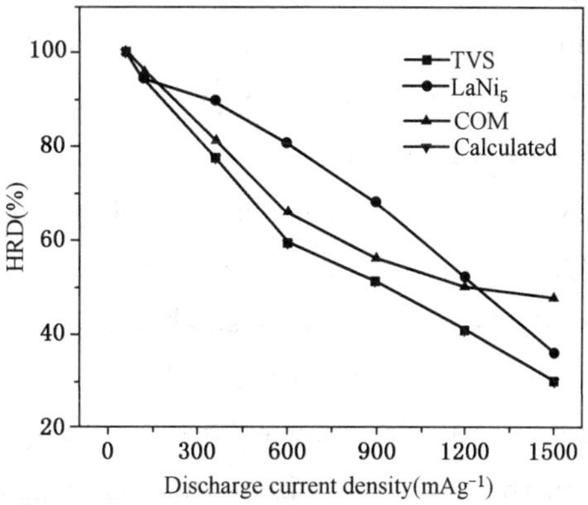

Fig. 7　High-rate dischargeability as a function of exchange current density for COM, TVS and $LaNi_5$ alloy electrode

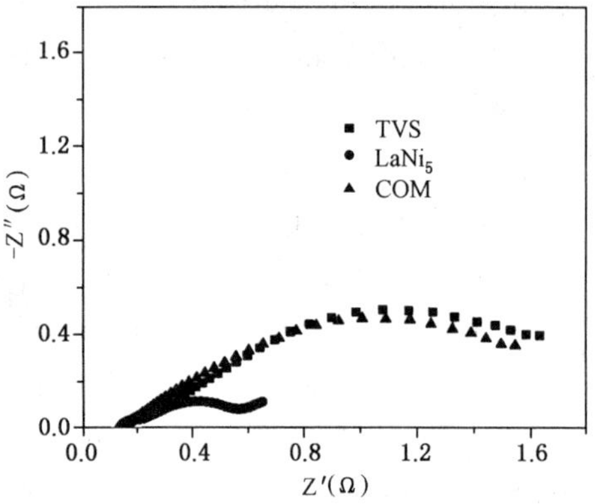

Fig. 8　Electrochemical impedance spectra of COM, TVS and $LaNi_5$ alloy electrode

$$I_0=(RT/F)(1/R_{ct}) \quad (3)$$

Wherein R is the gas constant, T is the absolute temperature and F is the Faraday constant. Table 2 also gives R_{ct} and I_0. First, R_{ct} of COM alloy electrode is 31.33 mΩ smaller than that of TVS alloy, and I_0 of COM alloy electrode is 90.00 mA g^{-1} higher than that of TVS alloy, which implies COM alloy electrode has higher electrochemical activity than that of TVS alloy electrode, and then results in its superior HRD of COM alloy electrode. Second, it shows that the real Rct is 32.74 mΩ smaller than that calculated and the real I_0 is 91.29 mA g^{-1} higher than that calculated for COM alloy electrode, namely, R_{ct} of COM alloy electrode is smaller than the sum of all R_{ct} of TVS and COM alloy, and I_0 of COM alloy electrode is bigger than the sum of all I_0 of the constituent alloys, which means COM alloy electrode has higher electro-catalytic activity than that of TVS alloy electrode. This indicates that distinct synergistic effect occurs in the charge-transfer resistance and the exchange current density for COM alloy electrode. According to the concept of synergetic systems of composite proposed by O. Savadogo [14], the characteristics of a synergetic system may be arranged according to the variations of the exchange current density with the parameters of the electrocatalyst (i. e. concentration, electro-chemically active surface area, etc.). Here, the exchange current density is determined with charge-transfer resistance. In addition, XRD and SEM morphologies indicate that the secondary phase is formed during composite process. As a result, it is proposed that the secondary phase is assumably a good electrocatalyst for charge-transfer reaction on the alloy electrodes, which would result in distinct synergetic effect in the charge transfer resistance and in the exchange current density.

Table2　Kinetic parameters for TVS, $LaNI_5$ and COM alloy electrode

Sample	R_{ct} (mΩ)	I_0 (mA g^{-1})
COM	80.97	322.61
TVS	112.30	232.61
$LaNi_5$	253.28	103.14
Calculated	113.71	231.32

4　Conclusions

(1) The main phase of COM alloy is composed of V-based solid solution phase with a BCC structure and C14 Laves phase with hexagonal structure, while the secondary phase also exists in COM al-

loy.

(2) The real maximum discharge capacity of COM alloy electrode is higher than the sum of all the discharge capacity of the constituent alloys. It is suggested that distinct synergistic effect exists in the composite process.

(3) The activation performance, the cyclic stability and LTD of COM alloy electrode are obviously superior to that of TVS alloy. It is suggested that distinct synergistic effect appears in the activation process, in the cyclic process and in the discharge process at low/high temperature for COM alloy electrode.

(4) Dynamic performances of the composite alloy electrode have remarkably been improved. COM alloy electrode has higher HRD, lower R_{ct}, higher I_0 than that of TVS alloy electrode, respectively. It is suggested that distinct synergistic effect appears in the discharge process at different current density, in the charge-transfer resistance and in the exchange current density for COM alloy electrode.

References

[1] Akiba E, Iba H. Hydrogen absorption by Laves phase related BCC solid solution. Intermetallics 1998;6(6):461-70.

[2] Tsukahara M, Takahashi K, Mishima T, Isomura A, Sakai T. Vanadium-based solid solution alloys with three-dimensional network structure for high capacity metal hydride electrodes. J Alloys Compd 1997;253:583-6.

[3] Kuriyama N, Tsukahara M, Takahashi K, Yoshinaga H, Takeshita HT, Sakai T. Deterioration behavior of a multi-phase vanadium-based solid solution alloy electrode. J Alloys Compd 2003;356:738-41.

[4] Pei P, Song XP, Liu J, Zhao M, Chen GL. Improving hydrogen storage properties of Laves phase related BCC solid solution alloy by SPS preparation method. Int J Hydrogen Energy 2009; 34:8597-602.

[5] Kuriiwa T, Maruyama T, Kamegawa A, Okada M. Effects of V content on hydrogen storage properties of V-Ti-Cr alloys with high desorption pressure. Int J Hydrogen Energy 2010; 35:9082-7.

[6] Miao H, Wang WG. Mechanisms of improving the cyclic stability of V-Ti-based hydrogen storage electrode alloys. J Alloys Compd 2010;508:592-8.

[7] Hang Z, Xiao X, Yu K, Li S, Chen C, Chen L. Influence of Fe content on the microstructure and hydrogen storage properties of $Ti_{16}Zr_5Cr_{22}V_{57-x}Fe_x$ (x=2-8) alloys. Int J Hydrogen Energy 2010;35:8143-8.

[8] Massicot B, Latroche M, Joubert J-M. Hydrogenation properties of Fe-Ti-V bcc alloys. J Alloys Compd 2011;509: 372-9.

[9] Cho S-W, Yoo J-H, Chang H-K, Kim W-B, Kil D-S, Ahn J-G. Changes in the microstructure and hydrogen storage properties of Ti-Cr-V alloys by ball milling and heat treatment. J Alloys Compd 2011;509:5545-50.

[10] Qiu S-J, Chu H-L, Zhang Y, Sun L-X, Xu F, Cao Z. The electrochemical performances of Ti-V-based hydrogen storage composite electrodes prepared by ball milling method. Int J Hydrogen Energy 2008;33:7471-8.

[11] Kim J-H, Lee H, Lee PS, Seo C-Y, Lee J-Y. A study on the improvement of the cyclic durability by Cr substitution in V-Ti alloy and surface modification by the ball-

milling process. J Alloys Compd 2003;348:293-300.

[12] Wang YZ, Zhao MS, Li SC, Wang LM. Structure and electrochemical characteristics of melted composite $Ti_{0.10}Zr_{0.15}V_{0.35}Cr_{0.10}Ni_{0.30}$-$LaNi_5$ hydrogen storage alloys. Electrochim Acta 2008;53:7831-7.

[13] Chai YJ, Yin WY, Li ZL, Zhang XB, Zhao MS. Structure and electrochemical characteristics of $Ti_{0.25-x}Zr_xV_{0.35}Cr_{0.1}Ni_{0.3}$ (x=0.05-0.15) alloys. Intermetallics 2005; 13:1141-5.

[14] Savadogo O. On the concept of synergetic systems of composite or modified materials and their electrocatalytic properties: (1) General approach. Int J Hydrogen Energy 2002; 27(2):157-69.

[15] Seo C-Y, Choi S-J, Choi J, Park C-N, Lee J-Y. Effect of V and Zr on the electrochemical properties of La-based AB_5-type metal hydride electrodes. J Alloys Compd 2003; 351:255-63.

[16] Park HY, Chang I, Cho WI, Cho BW, Jang H, Lee SR, et al. Electrode characteristics of the Cr and La doped AB_2-type hydrogen storage alloys. Int J Hydrogen Energy 2001;26:949-55.

[17] Kwo Y, Taihei O, Michael A, Fetcenko WM, Benjamin R. Structural and electrochemical properties of $Ti_{1.5}Zr_{5.5}V_xNi_{10-x}$. Int J Hydrogen Energy 2009;34:8695-706.

[18] Guo ZP, Huang ZG, Konstantinov K, Liu HK, Dou SX. Electrochemical hydrogen storage properties of nonstoichiometric amorphous $MgNi_{1+x}$-carbon composites (x=0.05－0.3). Int J Hydrogen Energy 2006;31(14):2032-9.

[19] Iwakura C, Kajiya Y, Yoneyama H, Sakai T, Oguro K, Ishikawa H. Self-discharge mechanism of nickel-hydrogen batteries using metal hydride anodes. J Electrochem Soc 1989;136:1351-5.

[20] Kuriyama N, Sakai T, Miyamura H, Uehara I, Ishikawa H, Iwasaki T. Electrochemical impedance and deterioration behavior of metal hydride electrodes. J Alloys Compd 1993; 202:183-97.

Structure and Electrochemical Characteristics of $Ti_{0.10}Zr_{0.15}V_{0.35}Cr_{0.10}Ni_{0.30}$-$LaNi_4Al_{0.4}Mn_{0.3}Co_{0.3}$ Composite Hydrogen Storage Alloy①

Yanzhi Wang[a,b], Minshou Zhao [a,b]

([a] College of Environmental and Chemical Engineering, Yanshan University, Qinhuangdao 066004, PR China)

([b] State Key Laboratory of Metastable Materials Science and Technology, Yanshan University, Qinhuangdao 066004, PR China)

Abstract: Structure and electrochemical characteristics of $Ti_{0.10}Zr_{0.15}V_{0.35}Cr_{0.10}Ni_{0.30}$ (matrix alloy)—1 mass% $LaNi_4Al_{0.4}Mn_{0.3}Co_{0.3}$ composite hydrogen storage alloy have been investigated systematically. The main phase of composite alloy is composed of V-based solid solution phase with a BCC structure and C14 Laves phase with hexagonal structure, while secondary phase which has a composition close to Zr (Ti, V, Ni, Cr, Al, Co, La)$_{1.8}$ also exists in the composite alloy. The real maximum discharge capacity of the composite alloy electrode is 354.9 mAh g^{-1}, and distinct synergetic effect appears during composite process. Comparing with the matrix alloy, the thermodynamic performances, electrochemical characteristics, dynamic performances for the composite alloy electrode have been improved. The secondary phase is probably responsible for the improvement of electrochemical characteristics of the matrix alloy.

Key words: V-based solid solution; Composite alloy; Hydrogen storage alloy; Electrochemical characteristics Ni/MH battery

1 Introduction

With the expected increase in demand for hydrogen energy in the future, investigation of hydrogen storage materials has received more and more attention in recent years [1-3]. As one kind of metal-based hydrogen storage alloys, vanadium-based solid solution alloys have exhibited highly attractive proper ties for practical application because of their higher hydrogen storage capacity and lower hydrogen absorption/adsorption temperature [4,5]. For example, $TiV_{2.1}Ni_{0.3}$ alloy [6] has potentiality of high discharge capacity of 1 055 mA h g^{-1} and the real maximum discharge capacity of 540 mAh g^{-1}, and $V_{2.1}TiNi_{0.4}Zr_{0.06}$ alloy [7] has a high discharge capacity of 468.5 mAh g^{-1} and a poor capacity re-

① International Journal of Hydrogen Energy, 2010(35): 8268-8274.

tention of 22.34% after 30 charging-discharging cycles. But because of their poor properties of dehydriding kinetics and lower effective hydrogen absorption capacity, they are still unacceptable for commercial use [8,9]. How to deal with these problems is the subject of much current investigation. Many studies on the bcc solid solution alloys for hydrogen storage have been carried out to improve kinetic properties and electrochemical properties by adding various alloying elements [10-13], annealing [14] and quenching [15] treatment and surface modification by ball-milling process [16,17].

It has been proved that AB_5-type phase has a catalytic effect to magnesium [18] and AB_5-type alloy has some advantages such as easy initial activation, long cycle life and low cost [19]. It is reported [20] that the discharge capacity and the cycle life of Ti-30V-15Mn-15Cr alloy have been markedly improved after 30 min ball-milling with 20 wt% AB_5. This could be due to the presence of AB_5 alloy particles on the surface of the composite sample, which gives the alloy the electrochemical activity and decreases the amount of dis solved V in the KOH electrolyte.

In our previous work [21, 22], the $Ti_{0.10}Zr_{0.15}V_{0.35}Cr_{0.10}Ni_{0.30}$ alloy was served as matrix alloy, $LaNi_5$ and La-Mg-based alloy were served as additive alloy, respectively, and composite alloys were prepared by melting the mixture of both alloys. The result showed that additive alloy has a great effect on microstructure and electrochemical properties of matrix alloy such as the activation performance, the maximum discharge capacity, P-C-T characteristics, cyclic stability, the low temperature dischargeability, and especially on the kinetic performance of the alloy electrodes. The improvement of the electrochemical characteristics caused by composite process seems to be related to formation of the secondary phase.

Proceeding from the above results, $LaNi_4Al_{0.4}Mn_{0.3}Co_{0.3}$ alloy of commercial AB_5-type alloy was served as additive alloy, the $Ti_{0.10}Zr_{0.15}V_{0.35}Cr_{0.10}Ni_{0.30}$ alloy was served as matrix alloy, and the structure and electrochemical characteristics of $Ti_{0.10}Zr_{0.15}V_{0.35}Cr_{0.10}Ni_{0.30}$ — 1 mass% $LaNi_4Al_{0.4}Mn_{0.3}Co_{0.3}$ compo site hydrogen storage alloy were investigated systematically.

2 Experimental details

$Ti_{0.10}Zr_{0.15}V_{0.35}Cr_{0.10}Ni_{0.30}$ (represented as TVS hereafter) alloy and $LaNi_4Al_{0.4}Mn_{0.3}Co_{0.3}$ (represented as AB_5 hereafter) alloy and composite alloy TVS-1 mass% AB_5 (represented as COM hereafter) were prepared by arc-melting, respectively. The sample alloys were crushed mechanically in air and ground to powder within an agate mortar. The sample powders with a size of 300 meshes for electrochemical measurements, and those with a size of 400 meshes were used for XRD analysis utilizing with CuKα radiation on D/Max-rB X-ray diffractometer using Jade 5 software, respectively. The morphology of COM alloy was observed using KYKY2800-type scanning electron microscopy (SEM) and composition of the phases was analyzed by a Kevex-sigma Level 4 energy-dispersive spectrometer (EDS), respectively. The detailed technique for preparation of the alloys, the analysis of the phase structure, the preparation of the disk-type electrodes, the setup of the electrochemical cell and the measurement of electrochemical properties were similar to those described in our previous paper [21].

P-C-T curve was obtained by converting equilibrium electrode potential of the metal hydride to equilibrium hydrogen pressure on basis of Nernst Equation at 303 K as followings:

$$E_{eq} = -0.9291 - 0.0300 \lg p_{H_2} \quad (1)$$

wherein E_{eq} is the equilibrium electrode potential (vs. Hg/HgO), V, and p_{H_2} is the equilibrium hydrogen pressure, atm. The equilibrium potential curve was obtained according to our previous paper [22].

The electrochemical impedance spectroscopy (EIS) measurements were conducted at 50% depth of discharge (DOD) at 303 K using a Solartron 1287 Potentiostat/Galvanostat and a Solartron 1 255 frequency response analyzer with Z-POLT software after the test electrodes were completely activated. The EIS spectra were obtained in the frequency range of 0.1 Hz—1 MHz with an ac amplitude perturbation of 5 mV under open-circuit condition.

The potentiostatic discharge technique was used to evaluate the diffusion coefficient of hydrogen in the bulk of the alloy. After being fully charged followed by 30 min opencircuit lay-aside, the test electrodes were discharged with +500 mV potential-step for 2500 s on the EG&G PARC Model 273 Potentiostat/Galvanostat.

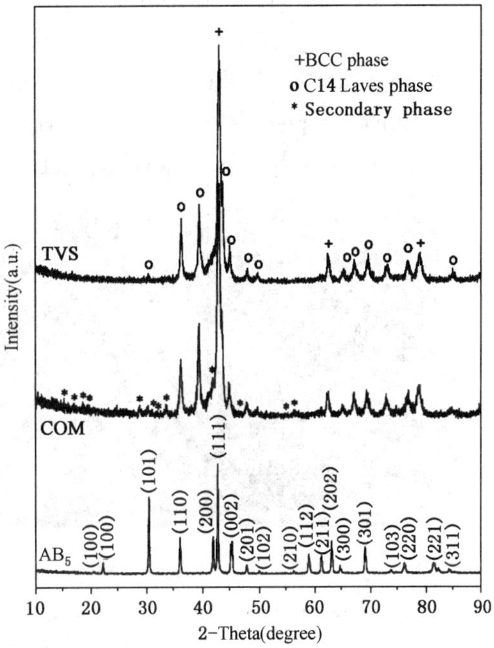

Fig. 1 XRD patterm of COM, TVS and AB_5 as-cast alloy

3 Results and discussion

3.1 Structure characteristics

The XRD diffraction pattern of COM, TVS and AB_5 as-cast alloy is shown in Fig. 1. The result shows that the main phase of COM alloy is composing of V-based solid solution phase with a BCC structure and C14 Laves phase with hexagonal structure, which is as same as that of TVS as-cast alloy. However, the secondary phase is exhibited as small additional peaks and the $CaCu_5$ phase of AB_5 alloy can not be detected in COM alloy. The lattice parameter and cell volume of the BCC phase and C14 Laves phase are calculated with Jade 5 software, respectively, and the result is summarized in Table 1. It is found that the lattice parameter and cell volume of the BCC phase and C14 Lave phase in COM alloy are both larger than that of TVS alloy, respectively, and the larger cell volume would be beneficial for a larger hydrogen storage capacity.

Table 1　Lattice parameters of BCC phase and C14 Laves phase in COM alloy

Sample	Phase	Lattice parameter (nm)		Cell volume (nm^3)
		a	c	
TVS alloy	BCC	0.2969		0.02617
	C14Laves	0.4948	0.8093	0.1716
COM alloy	BCC	0.2973		0.02629
	C14 Laves	0.4959	0.8113	0.1728

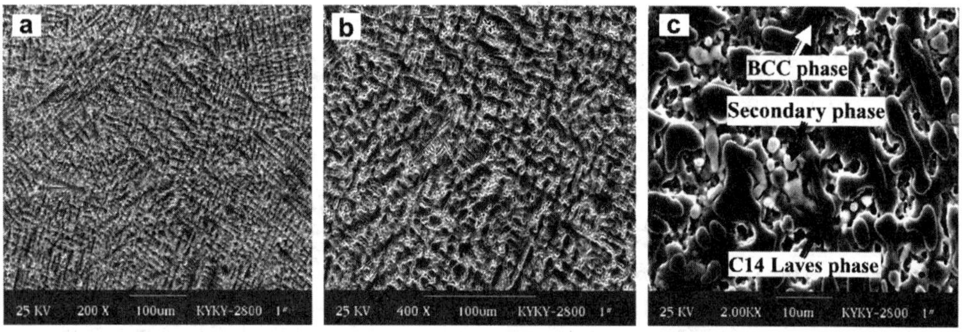

Fig. 2　SEM morphology of COM alloy

The SEM morphology of COM alloy is shown in Fig. 2. The compositions of different phases in COM alloy have been semi-quantitatively with EDS as summarized in Table 2. It is obvious that COM alloy is composed of V-based solid solution phase with a dendritic shape and a continuous C14 Laves phase with a network shape. Comparing to the SEM morphology of TVS alloy [12], it can be easily found that the white lard phase embedded in C14 Laves phase with irregular shape is the secondary phase formed during composite process. The EDS analysis indicates that the V-based solid solution phase is mainly composed of V, Cr and Al, and the C14 Laves phase is mainly composed of Zr, V and Ti, and the secondary phase has a composition close to $Zr(Ti,V,Ni,Cr,Al,Co,La)_{1.8}$. The result shows that the additive AB_5 alloy is decomposed during composite process, and La can be only detected in the secondary phase of the composite alloy.

3.2　P-C-T curve

The P-C-T curve of the alloy electrode after 100 charge-discharge cycles at

303 K is shown in Fig. 3. First, it shows that the maximum hydrogen absorption capacity $[H/M]_{max}$ of COM alloy electrode is 1.52 mass%, which is about 1.14 times as high as that of TVS alloy. The reason is that the V-based solid solution phase is main hydrogen storage phase, and the unit cell volume of the BCC phase in COM alloy is larger than that of TVS alloy, as resulted in XRD. Second, the hysteresis of hydrogen absorption-desorption plateau of COM alloy is distinctly smaller than that of TVS alloy. In general, it is accepted that the hysteresis in metal-hydrogen system resulted from the transformation strain due to cell volume expansion and contraction during both hydride formation and decomposition [23]. That is to say, larger change of cell volume during hydrogen absorption and desorption might lead to larger hysteresis effect between the absorption and desorption equilibrium pressures. Consequently, it can be believed that, in the present study, the diminution of the hysteresis for hydrogen absorption-desorption equilibrium pressures results mainly from the decrease of the expansion and the total change of cell volume with adding AB_5 alloy to TVS alloy. Third, the plateau pressure of hydrogen desorption of COM alloy is evidently higher than that of TVS alloy, which implies that the dehydriding kinetics of COM hydride is perhaps better than that of TVS hydride. Generally speaking, the plateau pressure of a hydrogen storage alloy decreases with the increase in the cell volume. In the present work, it is not the case for COM alloy. COM alloy has three phases, of which the V-based solid solution phase and C14 Laves phase are the hydrogen storage phase, and the C14 Laves phase and the secondary phase may work as the catalyst or the micro-current collector. Therefore, this abnormality is probably related to formation of the secondary phase.

Table 2　Phase composition of COM alloy

Phase	Composition (atom %)								
	Zr	Ti	V	Cr	Ni	Al	Mn	Co	La
BCC	7.05	4.91	49.21	17.43	6.57	11.29	0.94	2.61	—
C14 Laves	29.93	18.54	26.13	6.61	9.50	7.32	1.34	0.64	—
Secondary phase	34.70	7.95	31.63	8.14	12.89	2.20	—	0.67	1.82

3.3　Activation

Fig. 4 illustrates the activation performance of COM and TVS alloy electrode. It can be found that the activation of COM alloy electrode needs only 7 cycles that is fewer 12 cycles than that of TVS alloy electrode, which implies that additive AB_5 alloy is beneficial for improving the electrochemical activity of TVS matrix alloy. Generally, diffusion through grain boundary having an open-structure is easier than that in grain having a perfect lattice [24]. As mentioned above, there are three phases in COM alloy, namely BCC phase, C14 Laves phase and the secondary phase. It is presumed that the phase boundaries in COM alloy are more than that in TVS alloy. Furthermore, the secondary phase may become the active sites [13, 23] and pathways for hydrogen diffusion. Thus, the activation performance of COM alloy is evidently better than that of TVS alloy, which is coincided well with the result of the P-C-T curve.

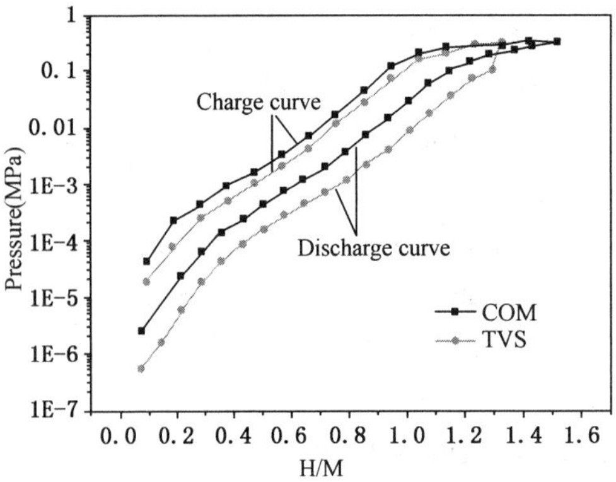

Fig. 3 P-C-T curve of COM and TVS alloy electrode

3.4 Maximum discharge capacity and synergetic effect

Fig. 4 also indicates that the real maximum discharge capacity of COM, TVS and AB_5 alloy electrode is 354.9 mAh g^{-1}, 323.6 mAh g^{-1}, 329.5 mAh g^{-1}, respectively. First, it can be found that the real maximum discharge capacity of COM alloy electrode is 31.3 mAh g^{-1} bigger than that of TVS alloy electrode, which is coincided well with that of the P-C-T curve. As mentioned above, the cell volume of COM alloy is larger than that of TVS alloy. Therefore COM alloy has the larger interstitial position in the lattice, which will be more beneficial to the hydrogen storage process. Second, according to composite ratio of TVS and AB_5 alloy, it can be calculated that the maximum discharge capacity of COM alloy electrode is 323.7 mAh g^{-1}. The above results illuminate that the real maximum discharge capacity (354.9 mAh g^{-1}) of COM alloy electrode is not equal to the sum of all the discharge capacity (323.7 mAh g^{-1}) of the constituent alloys, which implies that distinct synergetic effect appears during composite process.

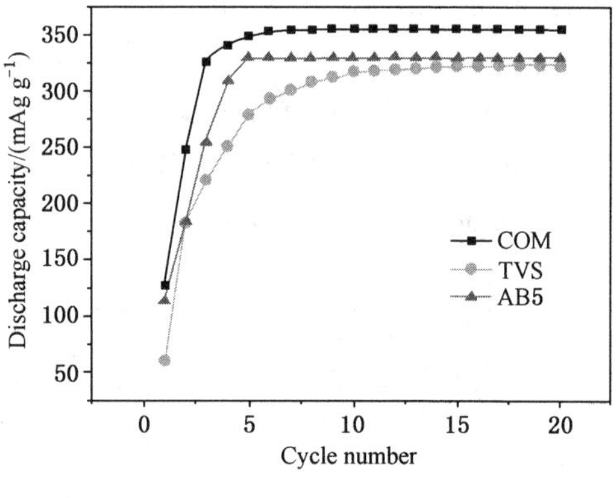

Fig. 4 Activation performance of COM and TVS alloy electrode

3.5 Cyclic stability

The dependence of discharge capacity on cycle number for COM and TVS alloy electrode is shown in Fig. 5. The capacity retention used to represent the cycling stability can be calculated in the following equation:

$$S_n(\%)T=(C_n/C_{max})\times 100 \qquad (2)$$

wherein S_n is the capacity retention at n cycles, C_n the discharge capacity at n cycles and C_{max} the maximum discharge capacity, the capacity retention of COM and TVS alloy electrode after 100 cycles (S_{100}) is listed in Table 3. The results indicate that the capacity retention of COM alloy electrode is 10.55% higher than that of TVS alloy electrode. To examine the capacity degradation behavior of the alloy electrode during cycling in alkaline electrolyte, the concentration of the constituent element dissolved in KOH electrolyte is analyzed with ICP-OES (iCPA6000, Thermo Scientific, USA) measurement at 50th and 100th cycles, and the result is tabulated in Table 4. It indicates that the dissolution of V, Zr, Ti elements for COM alloy electrode is distinctly smaller than that for TVS alloy electrode, respectively. It has been reported that the dissolution of V element being the main hydrogen absorbing element is essentially responsible for the capacity degradation of the alloy, and the dissolution of Zr element being a main element in C14 Laves phase would result in a decrease of the electro-catalytic activity in the alloy, which would affect the activation of the alloy electrode [25]. As a result, it can be proposed that adding AB_5 is helpful for restraining the dissolution of V, Zr, Ti elements and improving charge-discharge cyclic stability of TVS matrix alloy.

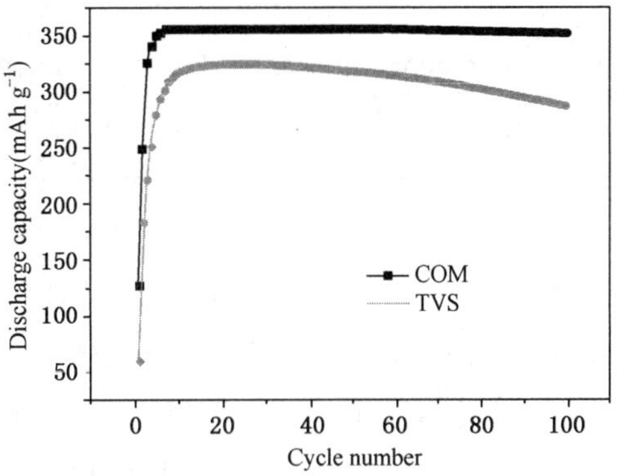

Fig. 5　The dependence of discharge capacity on cycle number for COM and TVS alloy electrode

Table 3　Capacity retention and concentration of main constiuent element dissolved in KOH electroyte at different cycle for COM and TVS alloy electrode

Sample	S_{100}[a] (100%)	Concentration in KOH (mg L^{-1})					
		50 Cycles			100 Cycles		
		Ti	Zr	V	Ti	Zr	V
COM alloy	98.93	0.018	12.65	26.10	0.081	18.14	52.14
TVS alloy	88.50	0.034	13.57	31.11	0.088	27.43	74.14

a The capacity retention after 100 cycles.

3.6　Temperature effect

Fig. 6 shows dischargeability of COM and TVS alloy electrode at different temperature. The dischargeability at different temperature is defined as the ratio of the discharge capacity C_T at a certain temperature to the discharge capacity C_{303} at temperature of 303 K. It can be seen that the dischargeability is very sensitive to temperature. Composite alloy electrode reaches maximum discharge capacities at 293 K, while TVS alloy electrode reaches its maximum discharge capacity at 303 K. It can also be observed that though the high temperature dischargeability (HTD) of COM alloy electrode is a little lower than that of TVS alloy, whereas the low temperature dischargeability (LTD) of COM alloy electrode is remarkably higher than that of TVS alloy electrode, for example, the LTD of COM alloy electrode at 233 K is 27.71% higher than that of TVS alloy electrode, which indicates that addition of AB_5 alloy is beneficial for improving the LTD of TVS alloy electrode. It is generally known that the LTD is mainly controlled by hydrogen diffusion, and hydrogen can diffuse more easily in the bulk of alloys with a larger cell volume and more grain boundaries having an open structure than that in grain. Thus, the increase of cell volume and grain boundaries of composite alloy doubtlessly results in its superior LTD. However, the HTD is perhaps related to the equilibrium hydrogen pressure of desorption [26]. The hydrogen desorption plateau pressure of COM alloy electrode is higher than that of TVS alloy electrode, and the hydrogen desorption plateau pressure increases with increasing temperature, and thereby the rates of dehydriding of COM alloy and of diffusion of hydrogen through COM alloy electrode increase, which inevitably increases the reversible capacity loss and decreases the HTD.

Table 4　Electrochemical kinetic parameters for COM and TVS alloy electrode

Sample	R_{ct} (mΩ)	I_0 (mA g^{-1})	D ($\times 10^{-10}$ cm^2 s^{-1})
COM alloy	83.74	311.94	18.29
TVS alloy	112.3	232.61	12.28

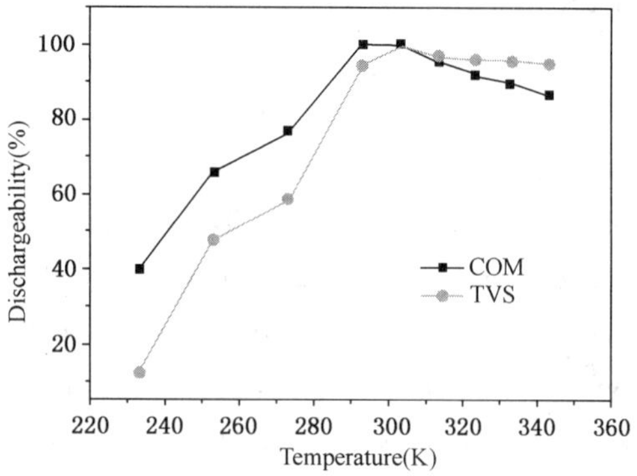

Fig. 6　Dischargeabillity of COM and TVS alloy electrode at different temperatures

3.7　Kinetic properties

High-rate dischargeability (HRD) is important kinetic properties for a metal hydride electrode. The HRD can be calculated in the following equation

$$HRD(\%) = (C_j / C_{60}) \times 100 \qquad (3)$$

wherein C_{60} discharge capacity at both the charge/discharge current density of 60 mA g^{-1}, and C_i is the obtained discharge capacity at certain discharge current density (60 – 1 500 mA g^{-1}). Fig. 7 shows high-rate dischargeability as a function of exchange current density for COM and TVS alloy electrode. It is evident that the HRD of TVS alloy electrode is improved significantly after adding 1 mass% AB_5 alloy, for example, the HRD of COM alloy electrode at discharge current density of 1 500 mA g^{-1} is 23.50% bigger than that of TVS alloy electrode. It is generally thought that exchange current density (I_0) and hydrogen diffusion coefficient (D) are crucial issues for the HRD of an electrode alloy [27].

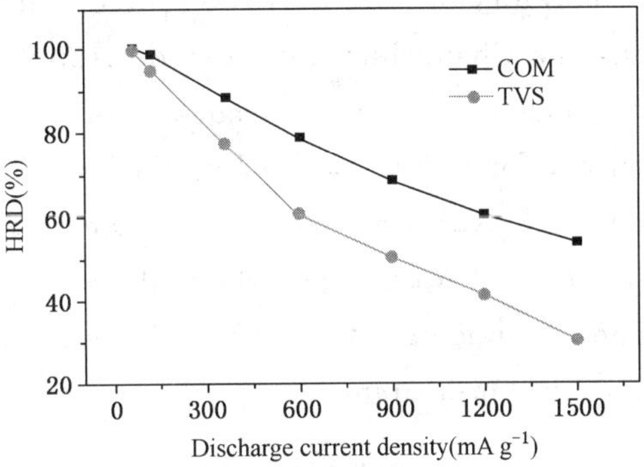

Fig. 7 Hig-hrate dischargeability as a function of exchange current density for COM and TVS alloy electrode

Fig. 8 shows the electrochemical impedance spectra of COM and TVS alloy electrode at 50% DOD at 303 K. On the basis of the model proposed by Kuriyama et al. [28], the charge-transfer resistance R_{ct} is obtained by means of the fitting program Z-View, the exchange current density I_0 is calculated by the following equation when overpotential is very small:

$$I_0=(RT/F)(I/R_{ct}) \quad (4)$$

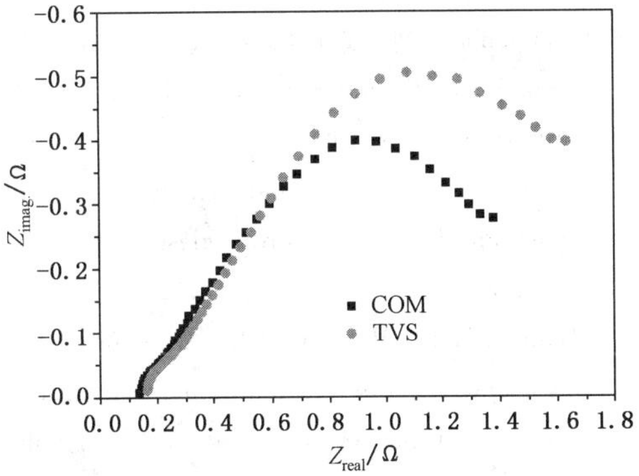

Fig. 8 Electrochemical impedance spectra of COM and TVS alloy electrode

wherein R is the gas constant, T is the absolute temperature and F is the Faraday constant. Table 4 gives R_{ct} and I_0. First, it shows that the R_{ct} of COM alloy electrode is 28.56 mΩ smaller than that of TVS alloy, and the I_0 of COM alloy electrode is 79.33 mA g^{-1} higher than that of TVS alloy, which implies COM alloy electrode has higher electrochemical activity than TVS alloy electrode, and then results in its superior HRD of COM alloy electrode.

According to the model of Zheng et al. [29], the hydrogen diffusion coefficient in the alloy's bulk is estimated and also listed in Table 4. It indicates that the D value in composite alloy's bulk is 1.49 times as high as that in TVS alloy's bulk, which implies adding AB_5 alloy is favorable to hydrogen diffusion in the bulk of TVS alloy. The reason of the increase may be ascribed to following factor: abundant defects and grain boundaries resulted from the multiphase composite alloy can provide good channels for the hydrogen diffusion and make hydrogen diffusion avoid the long-range diffusion through an already formed hydride.

4 Conclusions

Structure and electrochemical characteristics of COM hydrogen storage alloy have been investigated systematically. The conclusions are as followings:

(1) The main phase of COM hydrogen storage alloy is composed of V-based solid solution phase with a BCC structure

and C14 Laves phase with hexagonal structure, while the secondary phase also exists in COM alloy. The lattice parameter and cell volume of the BCC phase and C14 Lave phase in COM alloy are both larger than that of TVS alloy, respectively. BCC phase is mainly composed of V, Cr and Al, and the C14 Laves phase is mainly composed of Zr, V and Ti, and the secondary phase has a composition close to $Zr(Ti,V,Ni,Cr,Al,Co,La)_{1.8}$.

(2) COM alloy electrode has bigger $[H/M]_{max}$, smaller hysteresis and higher plateau pressure than that of TVS alloy electrode, respectively.

(3) The real maximum discharge capacity of COM alloy electrode is 354.9 mAh g^{-1}, and distinct synergetic effect appears during composite process.

(4) The activation cycle number, the S_{100} and the LTD at 233 K of COM alloy electrode is 12 cycles fewer, 10.55% higher and 27.71% bigger than that of TVS alloy electrode, respectively.

(5) COM alloy electrode has higher HRD, lower R_{ct}, higher I_0 and bigger D than that of TVS alloy electrode, respectively, and adding AB_5 alloy is beneficial to improving electro-chemical activity and hydrogen diffusion coefficient of TVS alloy.

Acknowledgments

This work is supported by Foundation of State Key Laboratory of Rare Earth Resource Utilization, Changchun Institute of Applied Chemistry, Chinese Academy of Sciences. And we also wish to thank Dr. Taicheng Duan of State Key Laboratory of Rare Earth Resource Utilization, Changchun Institute of Applied Chemistry, Chinese Academy of Sciences, for ICP test, and Dr. Wentao Hu and Ms. Xuemei Yang of State Key Laboratory of Metastable Materials Science and Technology, Yan-shan University for XRD measurement.

References

[1] Wu CL, Yan YG, Chen YG, Tao MD, Zheng X. Effect of rare earth (RE) elements on V-based hydrogen storage alloys. Int J Hydrogen Energy 2008;33:93-7.

[2] Zhong K, Liu YF, Gao MX, Wang JH, Miao H, Pan HG. Electrochemical kinetic performance of V-Ti-based hydrogen storage alloy electrode with different particle sizes. Int J Hydrogen Energy 2008; 33: 149-55.

[3] Yoo J-H, Shim G, Cho S-W, Park C-N. Effects of desorption temperature and substitution of Fe for Cr on the hydrogen storage properties of $Ti_{0.32}Cr_{0.43}V_{0.25}$ alloy. Int J Hydrogen Energy 2007;32:2977-81.

[4] Tsukahara M, Takahashi K, Mishima T, Sakai T, Miyamura H, Kuriyama N, et al. Phase structure of V-based solid solutions containing Ti and Ni and their hydrogen absorption-desorption properties. J Alloys Compd 1995;224(1):162-7.

[5] Song XP, Pei P, Zhang PL, Chen GL. The influence of alloy elements on the hydrogen storage properties in vanadium-based solid solution alloys. J Alloys Compd 2008;455: 392-7.

[6] Iwakura C, Choi WK, Miyauchi R, Inoue

H. Electrochemical and structural characterization of Ti-V-Ni hydrogen storage alloys with BCC structure. J Electrochem Soc 2000;147:2503-6.

[7] Chen LX, Li L, Wang XH, Dai FB, Zheng FP, Lei YQ. Phase structures and electrochemical properties of $V_{2.1}TiNi_{0.4}Zrx$ ($x=0-0.06$) hydrogen storage electrode alloys. Acta Phys Chim Sin 2006;22(5):523-7.

[8] Tsukahara M, Takahashi K, Mishima T, Isomura A, Sakai T. Vanadium-based solid solution alloys with three-dimensional network structure for high capacity metal hydride electrodes. J Alloys Compd 1997;253:583-6.

[9] Kuriyama N, Tsukahara M, Takahashi K, Yoshinaga H, Takeshita HT, Sakai T. Deterioration behavior of a multi-phase vanadium-based solid solution alloy electrode. J Alloys Compd 2003;356:738-41.

[10] Zhang QA, Lei YQ, Yang XG, Du YL, Wang QD. Phase structure and electrochemical properties of Cr-added $V_3TiNi_{0.56}Hf_{0.24}Mn_{0.15}$ alloys. Int J Hydrogen Energy 2000;25: 977-81.

[11] Chai YJ, Zhao MS. Structure and electrochemical properties of $Ti_{0.25}V_{0.35}Cr_{0.40-x}Ni_x$ ($x=0.05-0.40$) solid solution alloys. Int J Hydrogen Energy 2005;30:279-83.

[12] Chai YJ, Yin WY, Li ZL, Zhang XB, Zhao MS. Structure and electrochemical characteristics of $Ti_{0.25-x}Zr_xV_{0.35}Cr_{0.1}Ni_{0.3}$ ($x=0.05-0.15$) alloys. Intermetallics 2005;13:1141-5.

[13] Qiao YQ, Zhao MS, Zhu XJ, Cao GY. Microstructure and some dynamic performances of $Ti_{0.17}Zr_{0.08}V_{0.34}RE_{0.01}Cr_{0.1}Ni_{0.3}$ (RE=Ce, Dy) hydrogen storage electrode alloys. Int J Hydrogen Energy 2007;32:3427-34.

[14] Zhang QA, Lei YQ, Yang XG, Du YL, Wang QD. Effects of annealing treatment on phase structures, hydrogen absorption-desorption characteristics and electrochemical properties of a $V_3TiNi_{0.56}Hf_{0.24}Mn_{0.15}Cr_{0.1}$ alloy. J Alloys Compd 2000;305:125-9.

[15] Jia Y, Chen L, Xiao X, Yu K, Ying T, Lei Y. Effect of quenching treatment on the phase structure and electrochemical properties of $V_{2.1}TiNi_{0.4}Zr_{0.06}Mn_{0.05}$ alloy. Int J Hydrogen Energy 2009;34:7756-60.

[16] Kim J-H, Lee H, Lee PS, Seo C-Y, Lee J-Y. A study on the improvement of the cyclic durability by Cr substitution in V-Ti alloy and surface modification by the ball-milling process. J Alloys Compd 2003;348:293-300.

[17] Qiu SJ, Chu HL, Zhang Y, Sun LX, Xu F, Cao Z. The electrochemical performances of Ti-V-based hydrogen storage composite electrodes prepared by ball milling method. Int J Hydrogen Energy 2008;33:7471-8.

[18] Terzieva M, Khrussanova M, Peshev P, Radev D. Hydridng and dehydridng characteristics of mixtures with a high magnesium content obtained by sintering and mechanical alloying. Int J Hydrogen Energy 1995;20:53-8.

[19] Seo C-Y, Choi S-J, Choi J, Park C-N, Lee J-Y. Effect of vanadium content on electrochemical properties of La-based AB_5-type metal hydride electrodes. Int J Hydrogen Energy 2003;28:967-75.

[20] Yu XB, Li F, Wu Z, Xia BJ, Xu NX. Enhanced electrochemical properties of ball-milled Ti-30V-15Mn-15Cr + 20 wt% $La(NiMnCoAl)_5$ alloy electrodes. Phys Lett A 2004;320:312-7.

[21] Wang YZ, Zhao MS, Wang LM. Effect of La-Mg-based alloy addition on structure and electrochemical characteristics of $Ti_{0.10}$

$Zr_{0.15}V_{0.35}Cr_{0.10}Ni_{0.30}$ hydrogen storage alloy. Int J Hydrogen Energy 2009;34:2646-53.

[22] Wang YZ, Zhao MS, Li SC, Wang LM. Structure and electrochemical characteristics of melted composite $Ti_{0.10}Zr_{0.15}V_{0.35}Cr_{0.10}Ni_{0.30}$-$LaNi_5$ hydrogen storage alloys. Electrochim Acta 2008;53:7831-7.

[23] Seo C-Y, Choi S-J, Choi J, Park C-N, Lee J-Y. Effect of V and Zr on the electrochemical properties of La-based AB_5-type metal hydride electrodes. J Alloys Compd 2003;351:255-63.

[24] Park HY, Chang I, Cho WI, Cho BW, Jang H, Lee SR, et al. Electrode characteristics of the Cr and La doped AB_2-type hydrogen storage alloys. Int J Hydrogen Energy 2001;26: 949-55.

[25] Qiao YQ, Zhao MS, Li MY, Zhu XJ, Cao GY. Microstructure and electrochemical performance of $Ti_{0.17}Zr_{0.08}V_{0.34}Pd_{0.01}Cr_{0.1}Ni_{0.3}$ electrode alloy. Scr Mater 2006;55:279-82.

[26] Iwakura C, Kajiya Y, Yoneyama H, Sakai T, Oguro K, Ishikawa H. Self-discharge mechanism of nickel-hydrogen batteries using metal hydride anodes. J Electrochem Soc 1989;136:1351-5.

[27] Liu YF, Pan HG, Gao MX, Zhu YF, Lei YQ. Hydrogen storage and electrochemical properties of the $La_{0.7}Mg_{0.3}Ni_{3.825-x}Co_{0.675}Mn_x$ hydrogen storage alloys. J Alloys Compd 2004; 365(1):246-51.

[28] Kuriyama N, Sakai T, Miyamura H, Uehara I, Ishikawa H, Iwasaki T. Electrochemical impedance and deterioration behavior of metal hydride electrodes. J Alloys Compd 1993; 202:183-97.

[29] Zheng G, Popov BN, White RE. Electrochemical determination of the diffusion coefficient of hydrogen through an $LaNi_{4.25}Al_{0.75}$ electrode in alkaline aqueous solution. J Electrochem Soc 1995;142:2695-8.

Effect of La-Mg-based Alloy Addition on Structure and Electrochemical Characteristics of $Ti_{0.10}Zr_{0.15}V_{0.35}Cr_{0.10}Ni_{0.30}$ Hydrogen Storage Alloy①

Yanzhi Wang[a], Minshou Zhao[a,b], Limin Wang[b]
([a] College of Environmental and Chemical Engineering, Yanshan University, Qinhuangdao 066004, China)
([b] State Key Laboratory of Rare Earth Resources and Application, Changchun Institute of Applied Chemistry, CAS, 5625 Renmin Street, Changchun 130022, China)

Abstract: Effect of La-Mg-based alloy (AB_5) addition on Structure and electrochemical characteristics of $Ti_{0.10}Zr_{0.15}V_{0.35}Cr_{0.10}Ni_{0.30}$ hydrogen storage alloy has been investigated systematically. XRD shows that the matrix phase structure is not changed after adding AB_5 alloy, however, the amount of the secondary phase increases with increasing AB_5 alloy content. The electrochemical measurements show that the plateau pressure $Ti_{0.10}Zr_{0.15}V_{0.35}Cr_{0.10}Ni$ $0.30+x\%La_{0.85}Mg_{0.25}Ni_{4.5}Co_{0.35}Al_{0.15}$ ($x=0, 1, 5, 10, 20$) hydrogen storage alloys increase with increasing x, and the width of the pressure plateau first increases when x increases from 0 to 5 and then decreases as x increases further, and the maximum discharge capacity changes in the same trend. The activation performance, the low temperature dischargeabilities, high-rate dischargeability and cyclic stability of composite alloy electrodes increase greatly with increasing x. The improvement of the electrochemical characteristics caused by adding AB_5 alloy seems to be related to formation of the secondary phase.

Key words: Melted composite; Hydrogen storage alloys; Ti-Zr-V-Cr-Ni solid solution alloy; Secondary phase; Electrochemical characteristics

1 Introduction

Hydrogen storage alloys used as the negative electrode materials of the nickel-metal hydride (Ni/MH) batteries have been extensively researched and developed [1-3]. As one kind of metal-based hydrogen storage alloys, vanadium-based solid solution alloys have exhibited highly attractive properties for practical application because of their higher hydrogen storage capacity and lower hydrogen absorption/adsorption temperatures [4, 5]. But because of their poor properties of initial activation and effective hydrogen absorption capacity, they are still

① International Journal of Hydrogen Energy, 2009(34): 2646-2653.

unacceptable for commercial use [6,7]. Many studies on the bcc solid solution alloys for hydrogen storage have been carried out to improve kinetic properties and electrochemical properties, especially charge-discharge cycling stability of them by adding various alloying elements, annealing treatment and surface modification by the ball-milling process [8-13].

Recently, it was suggested that additional La-based alloy particles with better electrochemical hydrogen storage capacity is helpful to improve both the hydrogen reaction kinetics and the discharge capacity by composing treatment [14-16]. It was reported that Mg-added AB_5 based alloys are capable of performing high-rate discharge and have very excellent electrochemical properties as negative electrode materials in Ni-MH battery at low temperature [17]. In this paper, the $Ti_{0.10}Zr_{0.15}V_{0.35}Cr_{0.10}Ni_{0.30}$ alloy was served as matrix alloy, La-Mg-based alloy $La_{0.85}Mg_{0.25}Ni_{4.5}Co_{0.35}Al_{0.15}$ was served as additive alloy and the composite was prepared by melting the mixture of both alloys. Effect of La-Mg-based alloy addition on Structure and electrochemical characteristics of $Ti_{0.10}Zr_{0.15}V_{0.35}Cr_{0.10}Ni_{0.30}$ hydrogen storage alloy has been investigated systematically.

2 Experimental details

$Ti_{0.10}Zr_{0.15}V_{0.35}Cr_{0.10}Ni_{0.30}$ alloy (represented as TVS hereafter) and La-Mg-based alloy $La_{0.85}Mg_{0.25}Ni_{4.5}Co_{0.35}Al_{0.15}$ (represented as AB_5 hereafter) were prepared by arc-melting from pure metals, with a purity of better than 99.5 mass%, under purified argon atmosphere on the water-cooled copper hearth, respectively. The ingots were turned over and re-melted 3 times to ensure the homogeneity. Then, composite TVS$+x\%$ AB_5 ($x=0,1,5,10,20$) alloys were prepared by arc-melting of compressed mixture which consisted of TVS and AB_5 alloy powder in the mass ratio of 9.9 : 0.1, 9.5 : 0.5, 9.0 : 1.0, 8.0 : 2.0 under 0.06 MPa Ar atmosphere, respectively. To make the composition homogeneous, the samples were re-melted 4 times. The melted composite TVS$+x\%$ AB_5 ($x = 0, 1, 5, 10, 20$) alloys were crushed mechanically in air and ground to powder with an agate mortar. The sample powders with a size of 300 meshes for electrochemical measurements, and those with a size of 400 meshes were used for XRD analysis utilizing with Cu Kα radiation on D/Max-rB X-ray diffractometer using JAD5 software, respectively. The morphologies of the composite alloys were observed by using XL30 ESEM FEG scanning electron microscope (FESEM). The distribution of the alloy composition was analyzed by a Kevex-sigma Level 4 energy-dispersive spectrometer (EDS).

The pressure-composition isotherms (P-C-T) curves were electrochemically obtained. The fully charged electrodes were discharged at 60 mA g^{-1} for 0.333 h, followed by a rest period of 0.5 h before the equilibrium potential (E_{eq}) was recorded and then the discharge and rest procedure was repeated until the electrodes reached the cut-off potential of 0.6 V vs. Hg/HgO reference electrode. The relationship between equilibrium electrode potential and equilibrium hydrogen pressure at 303 K can be expressed as

$$E_{eq}(\text{vs. Hg/HgO}) = -0.9291 - 0.03 \lg P_{eq}, \quad (1)$$

Electrochemical properties were then measured in a standard three electrode cell system consisting of working electrode (the metal hydride electrode), a counter electrode ($Ni(OH)_2$/NiOOH electrode) with excess capacity and a reference electrode (Hg/HgO). The electrolyte in the cell was 6 mol/L KOH solution. The metal hydride electrode was prepared by mixing the alloy powder with carbonyl nickel powder in a weight ratio of 1 : 5 and cold-pressing the mixture to form pellets under a pressure of 15 MPa with 10 mm in diameter and about 1.5 mm in thickness. The charge/discharge tests were carried out with DC-5 battery testing instrument under computer control. The low temperature dischargeability (LTD) was measured after being fully charged at constant temperature using a low-temperature-equipment (WGD701). During the charge/discharge tests, the electrodes were fully charged (the over-charged ratio approximately 30%) at current density of 60 mA g^{-1}, and then discharged to −0.6 V vs. Hg/HgO at 60 mA g^{-1}.

After the test electrodes were completely activated, the electrochemical impedance spectroscopy (EIS) measurements were conducted at 50% depth of discharge (DOD) using a Solartron 1287 Potentiostat/Galvanostat and a Solartron 1255 frequency response analyzer with Z-POLT software in the frequency range of 0.1 Hz—1 MHz with an ac amplitude perturbation of 5 mV under open circuit condition.

For potentiostatic discharge, After being fully charged followed by 30 min open-circuit lay-aside, the test electrodes in the fully charged state were discharged with +500 mV potential-step for 2 500 s on the EG&G PARC Model 273 Potentiostat/Galvanostat.

3 Results and discussion

3.1 Structure characteristics

The XRD diffraction patterns of AB_5 and TVS+x%AB_5 (x=0,1,5,10,20) alloys are shown in Fig. 1. It is obvious that AB_5 addition does not change matrix phase structure of TVS alloy composing of V-based solid solution phase with a BCC structure and C14 Laves phase with hexagonal structure, however, the amount of secondary phase increases with the amount of AB_5 addition in composite alloys. The diffraction data reveals that the lattice parameters and cell volumes of the BCC phase increase when x increases from 0 to 5 and decrease as x increases further and those of C14 Laves phase increase when x increases from 0 to 1 and decrease as x increases further, and while the lattice parameter c change in the trend of shrinkage simultaneously, respectively. Formation of the secondary phase and changes of the crystal cell would impact on hydrogen storage performances.

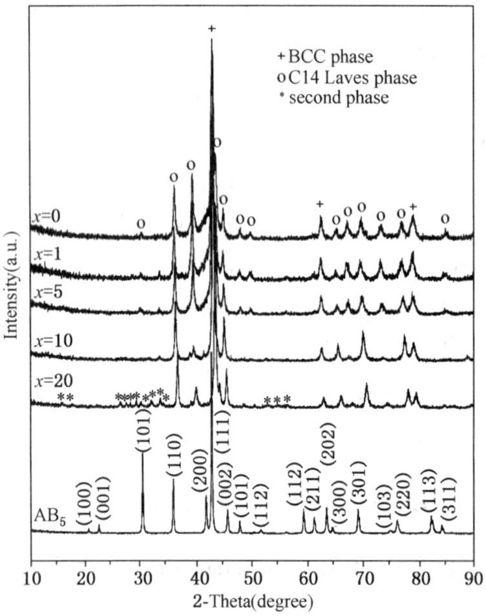

Fig. 1 XRD pattern of AB_5 and TVS $+x\%AB_5$ (x=0,1,5,10,20) alloy

The FESEM morphologies of composite TVS$+x\%AB_5$ (x=0,1,5,10,20) alloys are shown in Fig. 2. It is obvious that the composite alloy is composed of V-based solid solution phase with a dendritic shape and a continuous C14 Laves phase with a network shape. It can be easily found that secondary phase (white lard phase) with irregular shape segregates from the matrix phase and embeds in C14 Laves phase, and the white lard phase increases with increasing AB_5 addition, which is consistent with the results from XRD.

EDS patterns of different phases are shown in Fig. 3, and the compositions are also summarized in Table 1. The results indicate that the V-based solid solution phase is mainly composed of V, Cr and Ti, the C14 Laves phase is mainly composed of Zr, Ni and V, and the white lard phase has a composition close to $(Zr,Ti)(V,Ni,Cr,Al,Mg,Co,La)_2$. The result shows that rare earth La has not been detected in V-based solid solution phase or in original C14 Laves phase for the composite alloy with AB_5 alloy addition.

3.2 P-C-T desorption curves of the alloy electrodes

Fig. 4 exhibits the P-C-T desorption curves of TVS$+x\%AB_5$ (x=0,1,5,10,20) alloy electrodes after 100 charge-discharge circles at 303 K. It is observed that the maximum hydrogen absorption capacity [H/M]max increases from 1.42 to 1.61 mass% when x increases from 0 to 5 and decreases from 1.61 to 1.08 mass% as x increases from 5 to 20, and the width of the pressure plateau changes in the same trend simultaneously. It is noted that the V-based solid solution phase is main hydrogen storage phase, and the unit cell volume of the BCC phase in the composite alloys increases when x increases from 0 to 5 and decrease as x increases further, as resulted in XRD. In addition, with increasing x, the hydrogen desorption plateau flattens and the slope of P-C-T curves decreases while the plateau pressure increases, which indicates that the stability of the composite hydrides decreases with increasing x. Generally speaking, the plateau pressure of a hydrogen storage alloy decreases with the increase in the cell volume. However, in the present work, it is not the case for the composite alloys. The alloys have three phases, in which the V-based solid solution phase and C14 Laves phase are the hydrogen storage phase, and the C14 Laves phase and the secondary phase may work as the catalyst or the micro-current collector. Therefore, the above phenomena and the abnormality can be probably ascribed to the change in the cell volume of C14 Laves phase in the composite alloys showed in Table 1, the increase of amount of the C14 Laves phase and the secondary phase as evidenced in the FESEM morphologies.

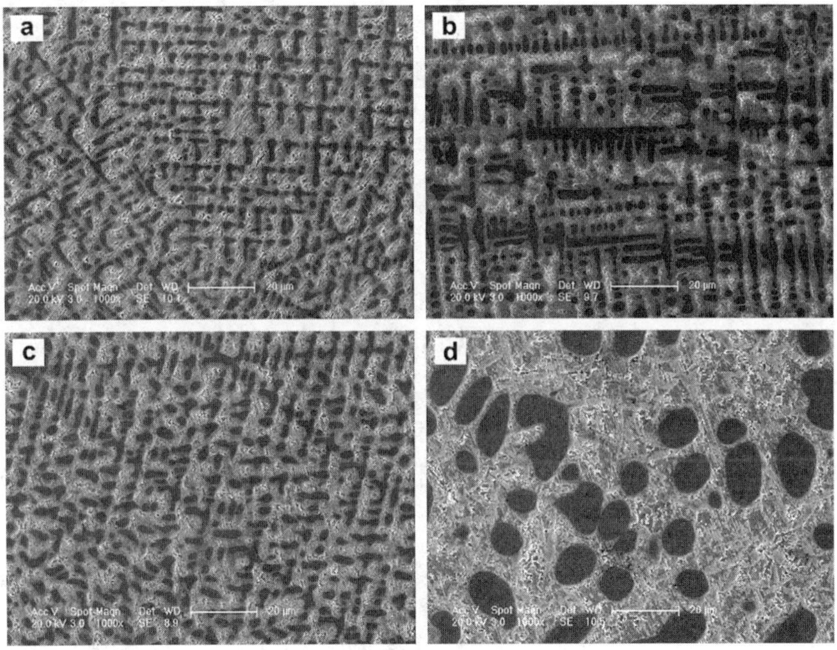

Fig. 2 FESEM morphology of TVS+x%AB_5 (x=0,1,5,10,20) alloy: (a) x=1; (b) x=5; (c) x=10; (d) x=20

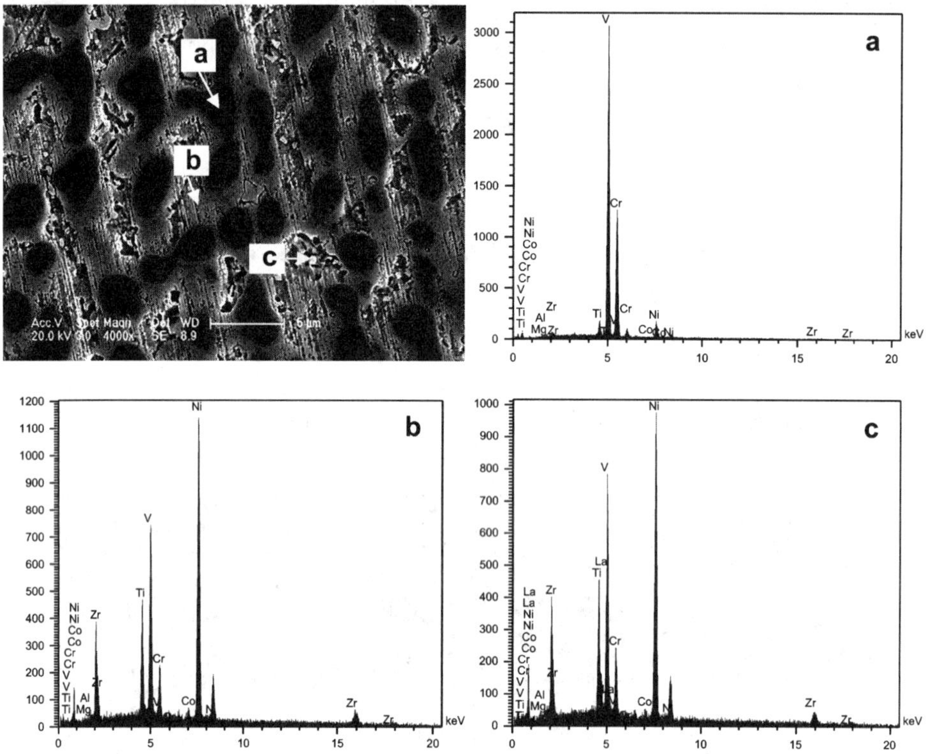

Fig. 3　EDS analysis of TVS+10%AB_5 alloy:
(a) V-based solid solution (b) C14 Laves phase; (c) white lard phase

3.3　Activation and maximum capacity

Fig. 5 illustrates the dependence of discharge capacity on cycle number for TVS+x%AB_5 (x=0,1,5,10,20) alloy electrodes. It can be found that the activation performance is dramatically enhanced by increasing AB_5 alloy content. The activation cycle number decreases with increasing x, for example, it is 19 cycles for x=0, and 3 for x = 20, respectively. Generally, diffusion through grain boundary having an open structure is easier than that in grain having a perfect lattice [18]. The structure characteristics of the composite alloys show that the amount of the secondary phase increases with increasing x, which is presumed that the phase boundaries in the composite alloys increase with increasing x. Furthermore, the white lard phase may become the active sites [13,19] and pathways for hydrogen diffusion.

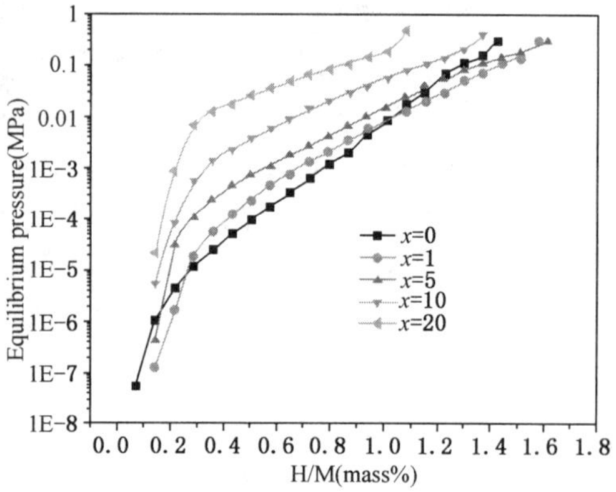

Fig. 4　Electrochemical PCT curve of TVS+x%AB_5 (x=0,1,5,10,20) alloy electrode

Thus, the activation performance of the composite alloys is gradually improved with increasing x. It can also be seen that the maximum discharge capacity of the composites increases first from 323. 6 mAh g^{-1}($x=0$) to 361. 8 mAh g^{-1}($x=5$), then decreases to 235. 8 mAh g^{-1} ($x=20$), which is consistent with the change of the width of the hydrogen desorption pressure plateau. This is probably attributed to the increase of the cell volume of the BCC phase when x increases from 0 to 5 and the decrease of the cell volume as x increases further, as shown in Table 1. It is shown that cell volume of TVS+5% AB_5 alloy is larger than that of other alloys in Table 1, therefore it has the largest interstitial position in the lattice, which will be beneficial to the hydrogen storage process. However, the discharge capacity decreases when the amount of AB_5 is too much in the composites.

Table 1 Phase composition, the lattice parameters of BCC phase and C14 Laves phase in the composite

x	Phase	Lattice parameter(nm)		Cell Volume (nm^3)	Composition(atom%)									
		a	c		Phase	Ti	Zr	V	Cr	Ni	Al	Mg	Co	La
0	BCC	0. 296 9		0. 0261 7	BCC	5. 6	5. 7	44. 4	16. 3	5. 56	9. 9	10. 9	1. 5	—
	C14 Laves	0. 494 8	0. 809 3	0. 171 6										
1	BCC	0. 297 3		0. 026 28	C14 Laves	18. 2	16. 7	28. 8	5. 6	14. 1	6. 0	6. 6	3. 8	—
	C14 Laves	0. 495 9	0. 808 6	0. 172 2										
5	BCC	0. 297 4		0. 026 30	White lard	15. 9	17. 8	26. 3	6. 8	12. 2	7. 6	6. 7	1. 9	4. 8
	C14 Laves	0. 494 3	0. 806 9	0. 170 7										
10	BCC	0. 297 1		0. 026 24										
	C14 Laves	0. 493 0	0. 807 7	0. 170 0										
20	BCC	0. 295 0		0. 025 67										
	C14 Laves	0. 488 6	0. 797 1	0. 164 8										

3. 4 Cyclic stability

The cyclic stability of TVS + x% AB_5(x=0,1,5,10,20) alloy electrodes is shown in Fig. 5. The capacity retention used to represent the cycling stability can be calculated in the following equation:

$$S_n(\%)=(C_n/C_{max})\times 100 \qquad (2)$$

wherein S_n is the capacity retention at n cycles, C_n the discharge capacity at n cycles and C_{max} the maximum discharge capacity. It is calculated that the capacity retention of TVS+x%AB_5(x=0,1,5,

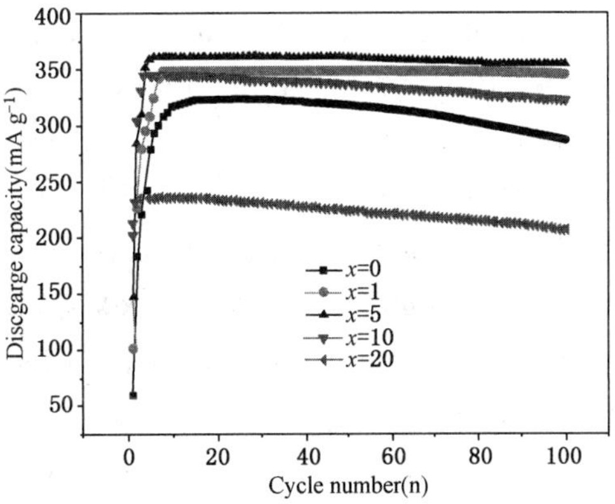

Fig. 5 Charge-discharge cycle curve number of TVS+x%AB_5(x=0,1,5,10,20)alloy electrode

10,20) alloy electrodes after 100 circles increases is 88.50%, 99.05%, 98.00%, 93.67% and 87.62%, respectively, which first increases when x increases from 0 to 1 and then decreases as x increases further. To examine the capacity degradation behavior of the alloy electrode during cycling in alkaline electrolyte, the concentrations of the constituent elements dissolved in KOH electrolyte are analyzed with ICP-OES (iCPA6000, Thermo Scientific, USA) measurement at 50th and 100 th cycles, and the results are tabulated in Table 2. It is indicated that the dissolution of Ti, Zr, V, Cr and Ni elements first decreases when x increases from 0 to 1 and then increases when x increases further, respectively. It has been reported that the dissolution of V element being the main hydrogen absorbing element is essentially responsible for the capacity degradation of the alloy, and the dissolution of Zr element being a main element in C14 Laves phase would result in a decrease of the electro catalytic activity in the alloy, which would affect the activation of the alloy electrode [20]. As a result, it can be proposed that a small amount (1—10%) of additional AB_5 is helpful for restraining the dissolution of Ti, Zr, V, Cr and Ni elements and improving charge - discharge cyclic stability of TVS alloy, but when more AB_5 alloy (>10%) is added, the dissolution of Ti, Zr, V, Cr and Ni elements will be accelerated and the cyclic stability of the composite alloy electrodes will be deteriorated.

3.5 Temperature effects

Negative electrode material used in Ni-MH battery should be capable of working over a wide temperature range. The dischargeability at different temperature is defined as the ratio of the discharge capacity C_T at a certain temperature to the discharge capacity C_{303} at temperature of 303 K. Fig. 6 shows the dischargeability of TVS+x%AB_5 (x=0, 1, 5, 10, 20) alloy electrodes at different temperatures. It can be seen that the dischargeability is very sensitive to temperature. The TVS alloy electrode reaches its maximum discharge capacity at 303 K and all composite alloy electrodes reach their maximum discharge capacities at 293 K, and then decrease sharply with the decrease or increase of temperature. It can also be observed that the high temperature dischargeabilities (HTDs) of the composite alloy electrodes are lower than that of TVS alloy from 303 K to 343 K, whereas the low temperature discharge-ability (LTD) of the composite alloy electrodes increases with increasing x. For example, it is 12.25% for x=0 and 73.47% for x=20 at 233 K, respectively, indicating that AB_5 addition is beneficial for the increase of the LTD of the composite alloy electrodes. It is generally known that the LTD is mainly controlled by hydrogen diffusion, and hydrogen can diffuse more easily in the bulk of alloys with a larger cell volume and more grain boundaries having an open structure than that in grain. Thus, the increase of cell volume and grain boundaries of composite alloy with increasing x doubtlessly results in its superior LTD. However, the HTD is related to the equilibrium hydrogen pressures of desorption [21]. The hydrogen desorption plateau pressure increases with increasing temperature and x, and thereby the rates of dissociation of the composite alloys and of diffusion of hydrogen through the alloy electrodes increase, which inevitably increases the reversible capacity loss and decreases the HTD.

Table 2　Dissolution of constituent elements at different cycles in KOH electrolyte for TVS+x%AB_5 (x=0,1,5,10,20) alloy

Constituent element	Concentration in KOH (mgL^{-1})									
	50 cycles					100 cycles				
	x=0	x=1	x=5	x=10	x=20	x=0	x=1	x=5	x=10	x=20
Ti	0.031	0.016	0.025	0.029	0.056	0.084	0.079	0.117	0.216	0.238
Zr	13.52	12.09	12.69	13.47	14.01	27.39	16.76	17.76	25.34	39.15
V	31.05	25.05	26.96	29.28	31.93	74.09	49.74	54.26	60.51	68.48
Cr	0.023	0.013	0.014	0.016	0.025	0.150	0.022	0.033	0.039	0.042
Ni	0.128	0.070	0.085	0.124	0.131	0.220	0.021	0.053	0.151	0.239

3.6　High-rate dischargeability and electrochemical kinetic

High-rate dischargeability (HRD) is important kinetic properties for the metal hydride electrode. To evaluate the HRD, the charging current density was kept constant at 60 mA g^{-1} and the obtained discharge capacity was denoted as C_i. Then HRD can be calculated in the following equation:

$$HRD(\%)=(C_j/C_{60})\times 100 \qquad (3)$$

wherein C_{60} is the discharge capacity at both the charge-discharge current density of 60 mA g^{-1}. The effect of discharge current density (60—1 500 mA g^{-1}) on discharge capacity of TVS+x%AB_5 (x=0,1,5,10,20) alloy electrodes is shown in Fig. 7. It is obvious that the HRD of TVS alloy electrode is improved significantly after adding AB_5 alloy, and they increase with increasing x. For example, the HRD increases from 30.19% (x=0) to 75.96% (x=20) at discharge current density of 1 500 mA g^{-1}, respectively. It is well known that the HRD of the metal hydride electrodes is influenced mainly by the charge-transfer kinetics at the electrode/electrolyte interface and hydrogen diffusion rate in the bulk of alloy [22]. The exchange current density I_0 of alloy electrode is commonly used to characterize the catalytic activity for charge-transfer reaction at the electrode/electrolyte interface, and hydrogen diffusion coefficient D is used to characterize hydrogen diffusion rate in the bulk of alloy. In order to obtain I_0 and D, electrochemical impedance and potential-step experiment are performed on these alloy electrodes.

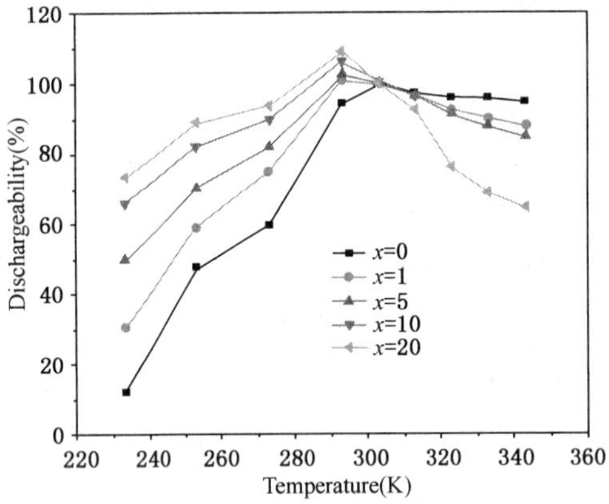

Fig. 6　The dependence of dischargeability on temperature for TVS+x%AB_5 (x=0, 1, 5, 10, 20) alloy electrode

Fig. 8 presents the electrochemical impedance spectra of TVS+x%AB_5(x=0, 1, 5, 10, 20) alloy electrodes at 50% DOD. It is shown that all the electrochemical impedance spectrum consists of two semicircles at high frequency and a short straight line at low frequency. The smaller semicircle in the high frequency region is attributed to the contact resistance between the alloy powder and conductive material, while the larger semicircle in the low frequency region is attributed to the charge-transfer resistance on the alloy surface. On the basis of the model proposed by Kuriyama et al. [23], the charge-transfer resistances R_{ct} are obtained by means of the fitting program Z-View, exchange current density I_0 is calculated by the following equation when overpotential is very small:

$$I_0=(RT/F)(1/R_{ct}) \qquad (4)$$

wherein R is the gas constant, T is the absolute temperature and F is the Faraday constant. Table 3 gives R_{ct} and I_0. The R_{ct} decreases with increasing x. For example, the R_{ct} decreases from 112.3 mΩ(x=0) to 57.71 mΩ(x=20) and accordingly the I_0 increases from 232.61 mA g^{-1}(x=0) to 452.64 mA g^{-1}(x=20) with increasing x, which means that HRD are inevitably increased with the increase of AB_5 alloy content in the composites, as shown in Fig. 7. In addition, XRD shows that the amount of the secondary phase increases with increasing x. As a result, it is proposed that the white lard phase is assumably a good electrocatalyst for charge-transfer reaction on the alloy electrodes.

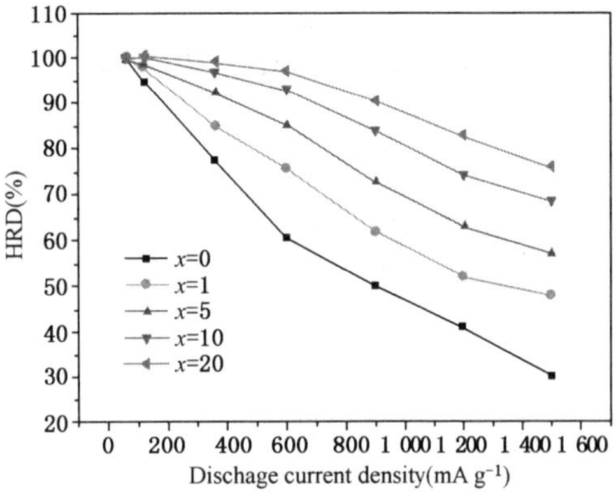

Fig. 7　HRD(%) of TVS+x%AB_5 (x=0, 1, 5, 10, 20) alloy electrode

The diffusion coefficient of hydrogen in the bulk of TVS+x%AB_5(x=0, 1, 5, 10, 20) alloy electrodes is determined with the potential-step method. According to the model of Zheng et al. [24], the hydrogen diffusion coefficient D in the bulk of alloys is estimated and also listed in Table 3. It shows that the hydrogen diffusion coefficient increases with increasing x. For example, the D increases from 11.31×10^{-10} cm^2 s^{-1} ($x=0$) to 26.29×10^{-10} cm^2 s^{-1} ($x=20$). The increase of the hydrogen diffusivity coefficient may be ascribed to the following factors: First, abundant defects and grain boundaries resulted from the formation of the secondary phases can provide good channels for the hydrogen diffusion. Second, the multiphase structure of V-based solid solution phase, C14 Laves phase and the secondary phase containing La avoid the long-range hydrogen diffusion through an already formed hydride and make the hydrogen diffusion easy.

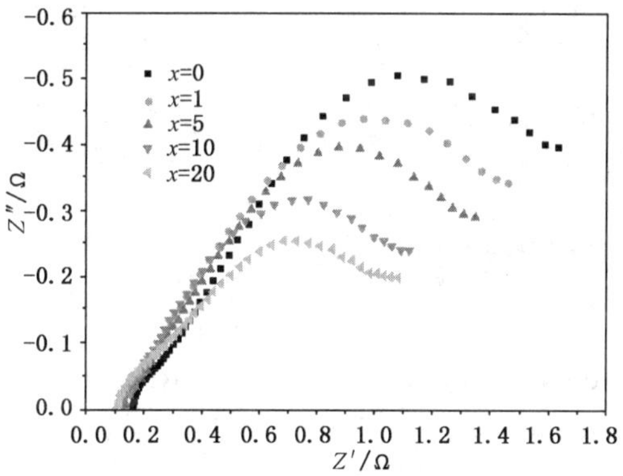

Fig. 8　Electrochemical impedance spectrum of TVS+x% AB_5 (x=0,1,5,10,20) alloy electrode

Iwakura et al. [25] have reported that if the electrochemical kinetics at the electrode/electrolyte interface is rate-determining factor, a linear dependence of HRD on the exchange current density should be observed. In contrast, if the diffusion of hydrogen in the bulk alloy is rate-determining factor, the high-rate chargeability/dischargeability should be constant, irrespective of exchange current density I_0. Fig. 9 illustrates the variation of exchange current density I_0 value with the HRD at the discharge current density of 1 500 mA g^{-1} for melted TVS $+x\%AB_5$ ($x=0,1,5,10,20$) alloy electrodes. The HRD shows a linear relationship with I_0, which implies that in the present study the HRD is essentially controlled by the charge-transfer reaction of hydrogen at electrode/electrolyte interface at a discharge current density of 1 500 mA g^{-1}.

Table 3　Electrochemical kinetic parameters of TVS+x%AB_5 (x=0,1,5,10,20) alloy electrode

Sample	charge-transfer resistance, R_{ct} (mΩ)	Exchange current density, I_0 (mA g^{-1})	Hydrogen diffusion coefficient D ($\times10^{-10}$ cm^{2}s^{-1})
$x=0$	112.3	232.61	11.31
$x=1$	91.47	285.58	16.10
$x=5$	75.05	348.06	17.44
$x=10$	63.86	409.05	19.83
$x=20$	57.71	452.64	26.29

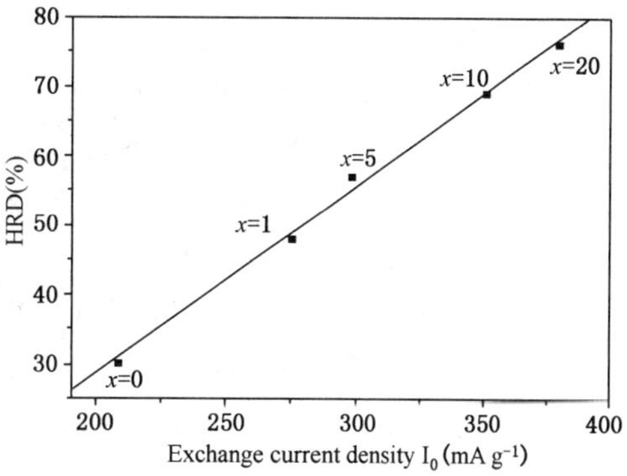

Fig. 9　High-rate dischargeability (HRD) at 1 500 mA g^{-1} as a function of exchange current density (I_0) for the composite electrode

4 Conclusions

Structure and electrochemical characteristics of melted composite TVS + x% AB_5 (x = 0, 1, 5, 10, 20) hydrogen storage alloys have been investigated systematically. The conclusions are as follows:

(1) AB_5 addition does not change matrix phase structure of TVS alloy composing of V-based solid solution phase with a BCC structure and C14 Laves phase with hexagonal structure, however, the amount of secondary phase increases with the amount of AB_5 alloy addition in composite alloys. The lattice parameters and cell volumes of the BCC phase increase when x increases from 0 to 5 and decrease as x increases further, and those of C14 Laves phase increase when x increases from 0 to 1 and decrease as x increases further, and while the lattice parameter c changes in the trend of shrinkage simultaneously. The secondary phase has a composition close to $(Zr,Ti)(V,Ni,Cr,Al,Mg,Co,La)_2$.

(2) The maximum hydrogen absorption capacity [H/M]max increases from 1.42 to 1.61 mass% when x increases from 0 to 5 and decreases from 1.61 to 1.08 mass% as x increases from 5 to 20, and the width of the pressure plateau changes in the same trend simultaneously. With increasing x, the hydrogen desorption plateau flattens and the slope of PCT curves decreases, while the plateau pressure increases, which indicates that the stability of the composite hydrides decreases with increasing x.

(3) The electrochemical measurements show that with increasing AB_5 alloy content, the activation performance, the HRD and LTD of the composite alloys are significantly enhanced. The activation circle number decreases from 19 cycles (x=0) to 3 cycles (x=20). The HRD increases from 30.19% (x=0) to 75.96% (x=20) at discharge current density of 1 500 mAg^{-1}. The LTD increases from 12.25% (x=0) to 73.47% (x=20) at 233 K. The maximum discharge capacity increases from 323.6 mAh g^{-1} (x=0) to 361.8 mAh g^{-1} (x=5), then decreases to 235.8 mAh g^{-1}. The capacity retention after 100 circles first increases from 88.50% (x=0) to 99.05% (x=1) and then decreases to 87.62% (x=20).

Acknowledgments

This work is supported by Foundation of Key Laboratory of Rare Earth Chemistry and Physics, Chinese Academy of Sciences. And we also wish to thank Dr. Taicheng Duan and Ms. Meiye Li of Key Laboratory of Rare Earth Chemistry and Physics, Chinese Academy of Sciences, for ICP and FESEM-EDS test, and Dr. Wentao Hu and Ms. Xuemei Yang of State Key Laboratory of Metastable Materials Science and Technology, Yanshan University for XRD test.

References

[1] Feng F, Geng M, Northwood DO. Electrochemical behaviour of intermetallic-based metal hydrides used in Ni/metal hydride (MH) batteries: a review. Int J Hydrogen Energy 2001; 26:725-34.

[2] Guo R, Chen LX, Lei YQ, Liao B, Ying T, Wang QD. The effect of Ni content on the phase structures and electrochemical properties of $V_{2.1}TiNi_x$ ($x=0.1$—0.9) hydrogen storage alloys. Int J Hydrogen Energy 2003; 28:803-8.

[3] Kohno T, Yoshida H, Kanda M. Hydrogen storage properties of $La(Ni_{0.9}M_{0.1})_3$ alloys. J Alloy Comp 2004;363:249-52.

[4] Tsukahara M, Takahashi K, Mishima T, Sakai T, Miyamura H, Kuriyama N, et al. Metal hydride electrodes based on solid solution type alloy TiV_3Ni_x ($0\leqslant x\leqslant 0.75$). J Alloys Compd 1995; 226(1):203-7.

[5] Tsukahara M, Takahashi K, Mishima T, Sakai T, Miyamura H, Kuriyama N, et al. Phase structure of V-based solid solutions containing Ti and Ni and their hydrogen absorption-desorption properties. J Alloys Compd 1995;224(1):162-7.

[6] Tsukahara M, Takahashi K, Mishima T, Isomura A, Sakai T. Vanadium-based solid solution alloys with three-dimensional network structure for high capacity metal hydride electrodes. J Alloys Compd 1997;253:583-6.

[7] Kuriyama N, Tsukahara M, Takahashi K, Yoshinaga H, Takeshita HT, Sakai T. Deterioration behavior of a multi-phase vanadium-based solid solution alloy electrode. J Alloys Compd 2003;356:738-41.

[8] Zhang QA, Lei YQ, Yang XG, Du YL, Wang QD. Phase structure and electrochemical properties of Cr-added $V_3TiNi_{0.56}Hf_{0.24}Mn_{0.15}$ alloys. Int J Hydrogen Energy 2000; 25: 977-81.

[9] Kim J-H, Lee H, Lee PS, Seo C-Y, Lee J-Y. A study on the improvement of the cyclic durability by Cr substitution in V-Ti alloy and surface modification by the ball-milling process. J Alloys Compd 2003; 348: 293-300.

[10] Zhang QA, Lei YQ, Yang XG, Du YL, Wang QD. Effects of annealing treatment on phase structures, hydrogen absorption-desorption characteristics and electrochemical properties of a $V_3TiNi_{0.56}Hf_{0.24}Mn_{0.15}Cr_{0.1}$ alloy. J Alloys Compd 2000;305:125-9.

[11] Chai YJ, Zhao MS. Structure and electrochemical properties of $Ti_{0.25}V_{0.35}Cr_{0.40-x}Ni_x$ ($x=0.05-0.40$) solid solution alloys. Int J Hydrogen Energy 2005;30:279-83.

[12] Chai YJ, Yin WY, Li ZL, Zhang XB, Zhao MS. Structure and electrochemical characteristics of $Ti_{0.25-x}ZrxV_{0.35}Cr_{0.1}Ni_{0.3}$ ($x=0.05-0.15$) alloys. Intermetallics 2005;13:1141-5.

[13] Qiao YQ, Zhao MS, Zhu XJ, Cao GY. Microstructure and some dynamic performances of $Ti_{0.17}Zr_{0.08}V_{0.34}RE_{0.01}Cr_{0.1}Ni_{0.3}$ (RE = Ce, Dy) hydrogen storage electrode alloys. Int J Hydrogen Energy 2007; 32: 3427-34.

[14] Chu HL, Zhang Y, Sun LX, Qiu SJ, Qi YN, Xu F, et al. Structure and electrochemical properties of composite electrodes synthesized by mechanical milling Ni-free $TiMn_2$-based alloy with La-based alloys. J Alloys Compd 2007;614:446-7.

[15] Bououdina M, Sun D-L, Enoki H, Akiba E. Improved kinetics by the multiphase alloys prepared from Laves phases and $LaNi_5$. J Alloys Compd 1999;288:229-37.

[16] Han SM, Zhang Z, Zhao MS, Zheng YZ. Electrochemical characteristics and micro-

structure of $Zr_{0.9}Ti_{0.1}Ni_{1.1}Mn_{0.6}V_{0.3}$-$LaNi_5$ composite hydrogen storage alloys. Int J Hydrogen Energy 2006;31:563-7.

[17] Zhang XB, Chai YJ, Yin WY, Zhao MS. Crystal structure and electrochemical properties of rare earth non-stoichiometric AB_5-type alloy as negative electrode material in Ni-MH battery. J Solid State Chem 2004;177:2373-7.

[18] Park HY, Chang I, Cho WI, Cho BW, Jang H, Lee SR, et al. Electrode characteristics of the Cr and La doped AB_2-type hydrogen storage alloys. Int J Hydrogen Energy 2001;26:949-55.

[19] Seo C-Y, Choi S-J, Choi J, Park C-N, Lee J-Y. Effect of V and Zr on the electrochemical properties of La-based AB_5-type metal hydride electrodes. J Alloys Compd 2003;351:255-63.

[20] Qiao YQ, Zhao MS, Li MY, Zhu XJ, Cao GY. Microstructure and electrochemical performance of $Ti_{0.17}Zr_{0.08}V_{0.34}Pd_{0.01}Cr_{0.1}Ni_{0.3}$ electrode alloy. Scripta Mater 2006;55:279-82.

[21] Iwakura C, Kajiya Y, Yoneyama H, Sakai T, Oguro K, Ishikawa H. Self-discharge mechanism of nickel-hydrogen batteries using metal hydride anodes. J Electrochem Soc 1989;136:1351-5.

[22] Liu YF, Pan HG, Gao MX, Zhu YF, Lei YQ. Hydrogen storage and electrochemical properties of the $La_{0.7}Mg_{0.3}Ni_{3.825-x}Co_{0.675}Mn_x$ hydrogen storage alloys. J Alloy Comp 2004;365(1): 246-51.

[23] Kuriyama N, Sakai T, Miyamura H, Uehara I, Ishikawa H, Iwasaki T. Electrochemical impedance and deterioration behavior of metal hydride electrodes. J Alloy Comp 1993;202: 183-97.

[24] Zheng G, Popov BN, White RE. Electrochemical determination of the diffusion coefficient of hydrogen through a $LaNi_{4.25}Al_{0.75}$ electrode in alkaline aqueous solution. J Electrochem Soc 1995;142:2695-8.

[25] Iwakura C, Oura T, Inoue H, Matsuoka M. Effects of substitution with foreign metals on the crystallographic, thermodynamic and electrochemical properties of AB_5-type hydrogen storage alloys. Electrochim Acta 1996;41(1):117-21.

Structure and Electrochemical Characteristics of Melted Composite $Ti_{0.10}Zr_{0.15}V_{0.35}Cr_{0.10}Ni_{0.30}$-$LaNi_5$ Hydrogen Storage Alloys①

Yanzhi Wang[a], Minshou Zhao[a,b], Shucun Li[a], Limin Wang[b]
([a] College of Environmental and Chemical Engineering, Yanshan University, Hebei Street, Qinhuangdao 066004, China)
([b] State Key Laboratory of Rare Earth Resources and Application, Changchun Institute of Applied Chemistry, CAS, 5625 Renmin Street, Changchun 130022, China)

Abstract: The structure and electrochemical characteristics of melted composite $Ti_{0.10}Zr_{0.15}V_{0.35}Cr_{0.10}Ni_{0.30}+x\%$ $LaNi_5$ (x=0,1,5 and 10) hydrogen storage alloys have been investigated systematically. XRD shows that the matrix phase structure of V-based solid solution phase with a BCC structure and C14 Laves phase with hexagonal structure is not changed after adding $LaNi_5$ alloy. However, the amount of the secondary phase increases with increasing $LaNi_5$ content. Field emission scanning electron microscopy-energy dispersive spectroscopy (FESEM-EDS) shows that the C14 Laves phase contains more Zr and the white lard phase has a composition close to $(Zr,Ti)(V,Cr,Ni,La)_2$. The electrochemical measurements show that the hysteresis effect decreases dramatically with increasing x. The activation performance, the low temperature dischargeability, high rate dischargeability and cyclic stability of composite alloy electrodes increase greatly with increasing x. The maximum discharge capacity first increases as x increases from 0 to 5 and then decreases when x increases further from 5 to 10. The improvement of the electrochemical characteristics caused by adding $LaNi_5$ seems to be related to formation of the secondary phase.

Key words: Melted composite; Hydrogen storage alloys; Ti-Zr-V-Cr-Ni solid solution alloy Secondary phase; Electrochemical characteristics

1 Introduction

Nickel-metal hydride (Ni/MH) secondary batteries are used extensively as the power source in various portable electronic devices such as notebook computers and cellular phones, elec-tric hand tools and hybrid electric vehicles because of their good electrochemical performance and environment compati bility [1,2]. Since a novel dual phase hydride electrode alloy $V_3TiNi_{0.56}$ was reported, vanadium-based solid solution alloys containing titanium and nickel have attracted

① Electrochimica Acta, 2008(53): 7831-7837.

considerable research interest due to higher hydrogen storage capacity and high hydrogen diffusivity in the alloys [3,4]. However, remarkable hysteresis, poor electro catalytic activity and high rate of degra dation of vanadium keep them from industrialization [5,6]. Many investigations have been carried out to improve kinetic proper ties and electrochemical properties, especially charge-discharge cycling stability of them by adding various alloying elements, annealing treatment and surface modification by the ball-milling process [7-9]. Structure and electrochemical characteristics of $Ti_{0.25}V_{0.35}Cr_{0.40-x}Ni_x$ ($x=0.05-0.40$), $Ti_{0.25-x}Zr_xV_{0.35}Cr_{0.1}Ni_{0.3}$ ($x=0.05-0.15$) and $Ti_{0.17}Zr_{0.08}V_{0.34}RE_{0.01}Cr_{0.1}Ni_{0.3}$ (RE = Ce, Dy). Hydrogen storage electrode alloys have been investigated by adding new elements in our research group [10-12].

It has been proved that $LaNi_5$-based alloys have some advantages such as easy initial activation, long cycle life and low cost, despite the shortcoming of low hydrogen storage capacity [13]. The discharge capacity and the cycle life of Ti-30V-15Mn-15Cr alloy has been markedly improved after 30 min ball-milling with 20 wt% AB_5 [14]. This could be due to the presence of AB_5 alloy particles on the surface of the composite sample, which gives the alloy the electrochemical activity and decreases the amount of dissolved V in the KOH electrolyte. It is reported that both the maximum hydrogen capacity and the reversible hydrogen amount are reduced for 80% $TiCr_{1.1}V_{0.9}$-20% $LaNi_5$ composite by melting, and hydrogenation/dehydrogenation properties are enhanced for the composite by mechanical alloying. In the both cases of alloying, comparing with the starting $TiCr_{1.1}V_{0.9}$ compound, the equilibrium plateau pressure is reduced [15]. Composite alloys consisting of $Zr_{0.5}Ti_{0.5}Cr_{1.5}Ni_{0.5}$ and 5-20wt% $LaNi_5$ were synthesized and its hydrogen storage properties in solid state were investigated. The absorbing-desorbing hydrogen kinetic properties were improved due to the segregation of pure Cr phase and existence of a small amount of $LaNi_5$ phase, but electrochemical properties were not reported yet [16].

In our research group, it was found that $LaNi_5$ addition greatly improves the electrochemical characteristics of $Zr_{0.9}Ti_{0.1}Ni_{1.1}Mn_{0.6}V_{0.3}$ alloy (AB_2 type alloy), such as activation property, high-rate dischargeability (HRD) and charge-discharge cycling stability. These improvements seem to be related to forma-tion of the secondary phases [17]. Therefore, the addition of $LaNi_5$ to $Ti_{0.10}Zr_{0.15}V_{0.35}Cr_{0.10}Ni_{0.30}$ alloy (solid solution alloy) could probably improve the kinetics and electrochemical performances of it. In this paper, the $Ti_{0.10}Zr_{0.15}V_{0.35}Cr_{0.10}Ni_{0.30}$ alloy was served as matrix alloy, $LaNi_5$ was served as additive alloy and the composite was prepared by melting the mixture of both alloys. The structure and electrochemical characteristics of $Ti_{0.10}Zr_{0.15}V_{0.35}Cr_{0.10}Ni\ 0.30+x\%\ LaNi_5$ ($x=$

0,1,5,10) hydrogen storage alloys were investigated systematically.

2 Experimental details

$LaNi_5$ alloy and $Ti_{0.10}Zr_{0.15}V_{0.35}Cr_{0.10}Ni_{0.30}$ alloy (represented as TVS hereafter) were prepared by arc-melting the constituent elements (the purity of each metal was over 99.5%) according to stoichiometric ratio under argon atmosphere on the water-cooled copper hearth, respectively. The ingots were turned over and re-melted three times to ensure the homogeneity. Then the mixture of TVS alloy and $LaNi_5$ alloy in the mass ratio of 9.9 : 0.1, 9.5 : 0.5, 9.0 : 1.0 were arc-melted four times under 0.06 MPa Ar atmosphere, respectively. The melted composite TVS+x% $LaNi_5$ (x=0,1,5,10) alloys were crushed mechanically in air and ground to powder within an agate mortar. The composite alloy powders with a size of 400 meshes were used for XRD, and those with a size of 300 meshes for electrochemical measurements, respectively.

Structure of each sample was examined by XRD analysis utilizing with Cu Kα radiation on D/Max-rB X-ray diffractometer using JAD5 software. The morphologies and the phase compositions of the composite alloys were measured by using field emission scanning electron microscopy-energy dispersive spectroscopy (FESEM-EDS) analysis on XL30 ESEM FEG scanning electron microscope, respectively.

Electrochemical measurements were performed in a standard three electrode cell system. The metal hydride electrode was used as the working electrode which was prepared by mixing the alloy powder with carbonyl nickel powder in a weight ratio of 1 : 5 and cold-pressing the mixture to form pellets under a pressure of 15 MPa with 10 mm in diameter and about 1.5 mm in thickness, a sintered $Ni(OH)_2$/NiOOH electrode with excess capacity was used as the counter electrode, and Hg/HgO electrode was used as the reference electrode in 6 mol/L KOH electrolyte solution. The charge/discharge tests were carried out with DC-5 battery testing instrument under computer control. The low temperature dischargeability (LTD) was measured after being fully charged at constant temperature using a low temperature equipment (WGD701). During the charge/discharge tests, the electrodes were fully charged (the over-charged ratio approximately 30%) at current density of 60 mA g^{-1}, and then discharged to −0.6 V vs. Hg/HgO at 60 mA g^{-1}.

The pressure-composition isotherms (P-C-T) curves were obtained by electrochemical method. The equilibrium potential (Eeq) was obtained by alternating the following processes. (1) The electrodes were charged at 60 mA g^{-1} for 25 min, followed by a rest period of 30 min, and subsequently the Eeq of the electrodes were recorded. Such a charge and rest procedure was repeated continuously until the alloy electrodes were fully charged. (2) The electrodes were discharged at 60 mA g^{-1} for 20 min, followed by a rest period of 30 min before recording the E_{eq}, and then the discharge and rest procedure was repeated until the electrodes reached the cut-off potential of −0.6 V vs. Hg/HgO reference electrode. The relationship between equilibrium electrode potential and equilibrium hydrogen pressure at 303 K can be expressed as:

$$E_{eq} = -0.9291 - 0.03 \lg P_{H2} \quad (1)$$

wherein E_{eq} is the equilibrium electrode potential (vs. Hg/HgO), V, and P_{H2} is the equilibrium hydrogen pressure, atm.

The electrochemical impedance spectroscopy (EIS) measure-ments were conducted at discharge current density of 60 mA g^{-1} and 50% depth of discharge

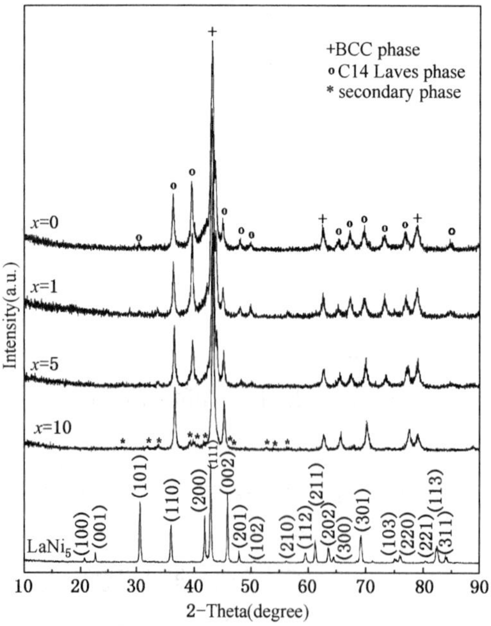

Fig. 1　XRD patterns of $LaNi_5$ and TVS+x% $LaNi_5$ (x=0, 1, 5, 10) alloys

(DOD) using a Solartron 1287 Potentiostat/Galvanostat and a Solartron 1255 frequency response analyzer with Z-POLT software after the test electrodes were completely activated. The EIS spectra were obtained in the frequency range of 0.1 Hz to 1 MHz with an ac amplitude perturbation of 5 mV under open-circuit condition.

The potentiostatic discharge technique was used to evaluate the diffusion coefficient of hydrogen in the bulk of the alloy. After being fully charged followed by 30 min open-circuit lay-aside, the test electrodes were discharged with +500 mV potential-step for 3000 s on the EG&G PARC Model 273 Potentiostat/Galvanostat.

3　Results and discussion

3.1　Structure characteristics

The XRD patterns of $LaNi_5$ and TVS+x% $LaNi_5$ (x=0, 1, 5, 10) alloys are shown in Fig. 1. It is clearly seen that $LaNi_5$ addition does not change matrix phase structure of TVS alloy composing of V-based solid solution phase with a BCC structure and C14 Laves phase with hexagonal structure, however, the amount of secondary phase increases with the amount of $LaNi_5$ addition in composite alloys. But $LaNi_5$ phase is not detected, it is deduced that $LaNi_5$ decomposes in the melt [15]. The diffraction data analysis reveals that the main peaks for individual are slightly different. Based on XRD data analysis, the lattice parameters and cell volumes of the BCC phase and the C14 Laves phase for each alloy are calculated with JAD5 software, respectively, and the results are summarized in Table 1. It can be found that the lattice parameters and cell volumes of the BCC phase increase when x increases from 0 to 5 and decrease as x increases further, but those of C14 Laves phase change in the trend of shrinkage simultaneously. Formation of the secondary phase and changes of the crystal cell must impact on hydrogen storage performances.

Table 1 Phase composition, the lattice parameters of BCC phase and C14 Laves phase in the composites

x	Phase	Lattice parameter (nm)		Cell volume (nm^3)	Composition (atm%)						
		a	c		Phase	Ti	Zr	V	Cr	Ni	La
0	BCC	0.296 9		0.026 17	BCC	3.7	10.7	61.6	20.1	4.8	—
	C14 Laves	0.494 8	0.809 3	0.171 6							
1	BCC	0.297 0		0.026 20	C14 Laves	9.1	40.7	16.5	3.0	30.7	—
	C14 Laves	0.494 8	0.806 6	0.171 0							
5	BCC	0.297 9		0.026 44	White lard	12.3	16.0	17.2	2.9	47.8	3.8
	C14 Laves	0.491 9	0.805 1	0.168 7							
10	BCC	0.296 4		0.026 03							
	C14 Laves	0.490 7	0.804 8	0.167 8							

Fig. 2 shows the FESEM morphologies of composite TVS+x% $LaNi_5$ (x=1, 5, 10) alloys. It is obvious that the composite alloy is composed of V-based solid solution phase with a dendritic shape and a continuous C14 Laves phase with a network shape. It can also be seen that secondary phase (white lard phase) with irregular shape segregates from the matrix phase and embeds in C14 Laves phase, and the white lard phase increases with increasing $LaNi_5$ addition. This is consistent with the results from XRD.

The composition of different phases has been semiquantitatively analyzed with EDS, as shown in Fig. 3 and the results are also summarized in Table 1. The results indicate that the V-based solid solution phase is mainly composed of V, Cr and Ti, the C14 Laves phase is mainly composed of Zr, Ni and V, which is Zr-rich, and the white lard phase has a composition of $Ti_{0.123}Zr_{0.160}V_{0.172}Cr_{0.029}Ni_{0.478}La_{0.038}$ close to $(Zr,Ti)(V,Cr,Ni,La)_2$. The result shows that rare earth La does not exist in V-based solid solution phase or in original C14 Laves phase for the composite alloy with $LaNi_5$ addition and distributes in the white lard phase. It can be believed that $LaNi_5$ has been broken down in the melt. This is disagreement with the result reported that La is not soluble in alloying elements of AB_2-type metal hydride except Ni [18].

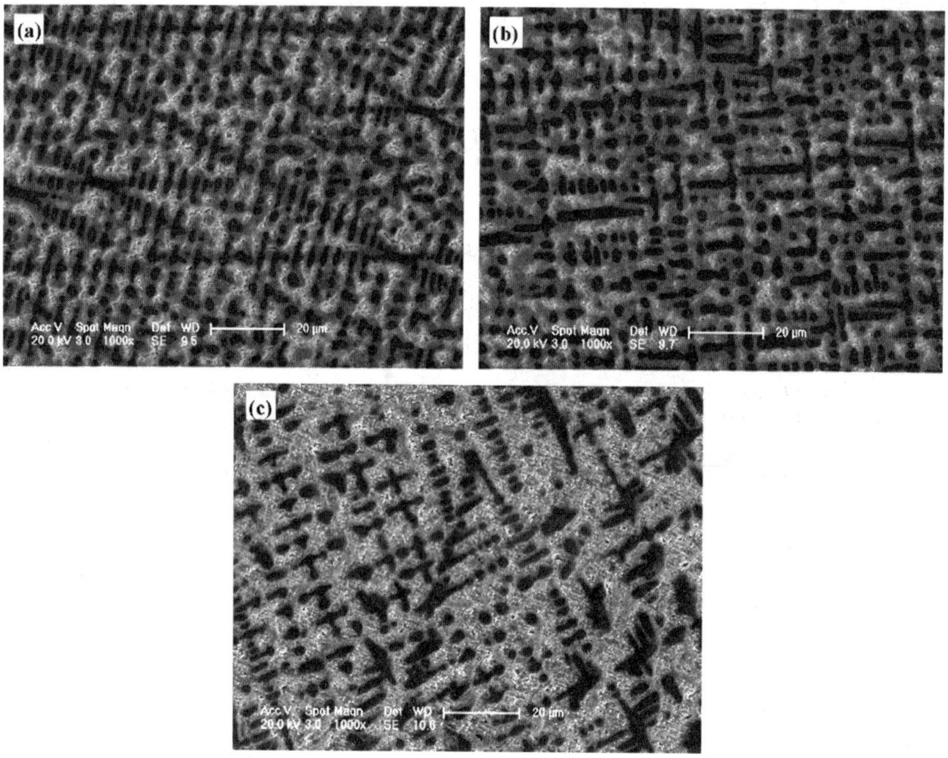

Fig. 2　FESEM morphologies of TVS+x% $LaNi_5$ (x=1,5,10) alloys: (a) x=1; (b) x=5; (c) x=10

3.2　The PCT curves of the alloy electrodes

The P-C-T curves of TVS+x% $LaNi_5$ (x=0,1,5,10) alloy electrodes after 100 charge-discharge circles at 303 K are shown in Fig. 4. First, it is shown that the maximum hydrogen absorption capacity $[H/M]_{max}$ increases from 1.33 to 1.51 mass% when x increases from 0 to 5 and decreases from 1.51 to 1.23 mass% as x increases further from 5 to 10. This is because of the V-based solid solution phase is main hydrogen storage phase, and the unit cell volume of the BCC phase in the composite alloys increases when x increases from 0 to 5 and decrease as x increases further, as resulted in XRD. Second, comparing to the plateau characteristics of the composites with different content of $LaNi_5$ alloy, the hysteresis of hydrogen absorption-desorption plateau is greatly reduced when x increases. In general, it was accepted that the hysteresis in metal-hydrogen systems resulted from the transformation strains due to cell volume expansion and contraction during both hydride formation and decomposition [19]. That is to say, larger change of cell volume during hydrogen absorption and desorption might lead to larger hysteresis effect between the absorption and desorption equilibrium pressures. Consequently, it can be believed that, in the present study, the diminution of the hysteresis for hydrogen absorption-desorption equilibrium

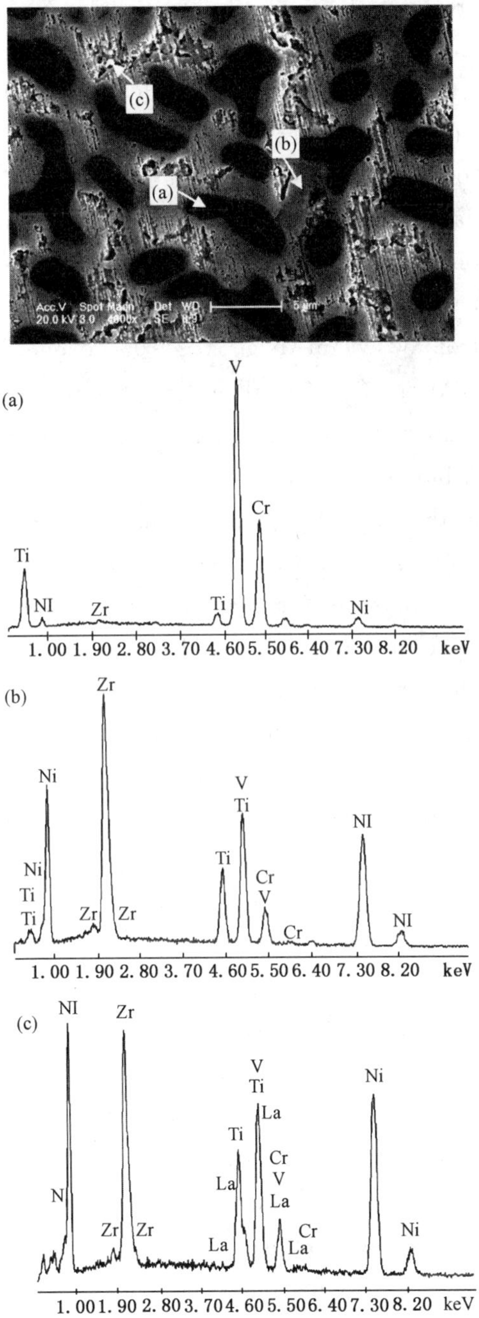

Fig. 3　EDS analyses of TVS+5%$LaNi_5$ alloy: (a) V-based solid solution; (b) C14 Laves phasw; (c) the white lard phase

pressures results mainly from the decrease of the expansion with increasing the $LaNi_5$ alloy content in the composites. The total change of cell volume also decreases with the increasing content of $LaNi_5$ alloy in the composite during the process of hydrogen absorption and desorp-tion. Therefore, the hysteresis effect of the composite is decreased with increasing content of $LaNi_5$ alloy. In addition, the plateau pressure for hydrogen absorption-desorption of these composite alloys increases monotonously with the increasing content of $LaNi_5$ alloy, which indicates that the stability of the composite hydrides decreases with increasing x. Generally speaking, the plateau pressure of a hydrogen storage alloy decreases with the increase in the cell volume. In the present work, it is not the case for the composite TVS-$LaNi_5$ alloys. The alloys have three phases, of which the V-based solid solution phase and C14 Laves phase are the hydrogen storage phase, and the C14 Laves phase and the secondary phase may work as the catalyst or the micro-current collector. Therefore, this abnormality is probably due to the decrease in the cell volume of C14 Laves phase in the composite alloys showed in Table 1 and the increase of a significant amount of secondary phase as evidenced in the FESEM morphologies.

3.3　Activation and maximum capacity

Fig. 5 shows the dependence of discharge capacity on cycle number for TVS $+x\%$ $LaNi_5$ ($x=0,1,5,10$) alloy

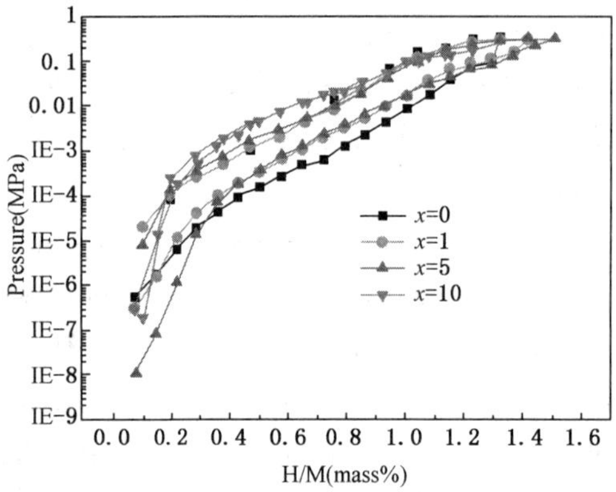

Fig. 4　Electrochemical PCT curves of TVS+x% $LaNi_5$ (x = 0, 1, 5, 10) alloys

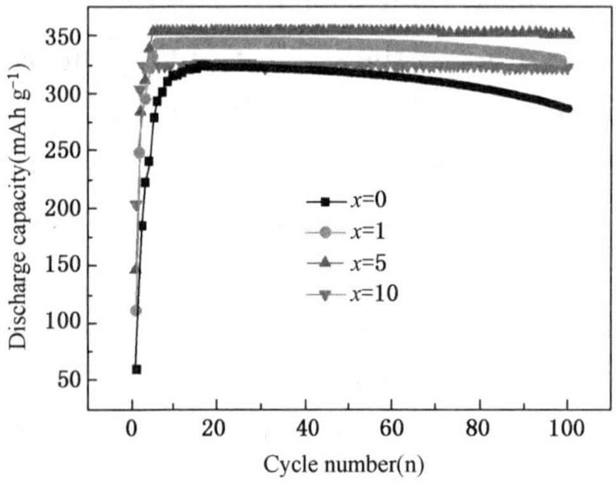

Fig. 5　Charge-discharge cycle curves number of TVS+x% $LaNi_5$ (x=0,1,5,10) alloy electrodes

electrodes. It can be seen that the activation performance is dramatically enhanced by increasing $LaNi_5$ content and the activation cycle number decreases with increasing x. For example, it is 19 cycles for $x=0$, and 4 for $x=10$. Generally, diffusion through grain boundary having an open structure is easier than that in grain having a perfect lattice [20]. The structure characteristics of the composite alloys show that the amount of the secondary phase increases with increasing x. It is presumed that the phase boundaries in the composite alloys increase with increasing x. Furthermore, the white lard phase may become the active sites and pathways for hydrogen diffusion. As a result, the activation performance of the composite alloys is gradually improved with increasing x. It is obvious that the max-imum discharge capacity of the composites increases first from 324.9 mAh g^{-1} ($x=0$) to 353.9 mAh g^{-1} ($x=5$), then decreases to 324.2 mAh g^{-1} ($x=10$). This is probably attributed to the increase of the cell volume of the BCC phase when x increases from 0 to 5 and the decrease of the cell volume as x increases further, as shown in Table 1. Because the V-based solid solution phase plays a more important role on storing hydrogen, and the C14 Laves phase and the secondary phase enhance the electrochemical reaction kinetics of the V-based solid solution main phase. It is shown that cell volume of TVS+5% $LaNi_5$ alloy is larger than that of other alloys in Table 1, therefore it has the largest interstitial position in the lattice, which will be beneficial to the hydrogen storage process. However, the discharge capacity decreases when the amount of $LaNi_5$ is too much in the composites.

3.4　Cyclic stability

The cyclic stability of TVS + x% $LaNi_5$ ($x=0,1,5,10$) alloy electrodes is shown in Fig. 5. The capacity retention used to represent the cycling stability can be calculated in the following equation:

$$S_n(\%)=100\times\frac{C_n}{C_{max}} \quad (2)$$

wherein S_n is the capacity retention at n cycles, C_n the discharge capacity at n cycles and C_{max} the maximum discharge capacity. It is observed that the capacity retention of TVS+x% $LaNi_5$ (x=0,1,5,10) alloy electrodes after 100 circles increases with increasing x. For example, it is 88.15% for x=0 and 99.48% for x=10, respectively. To elucidate the capacity degradation behavior of the alloy electrode during cycling in alkaline electrolyte, the concentrations of the constituent elements dissolved in KOH electrolyte are analyzed with ICP (iCPA6000, USA) measurement at 50th and 100th cycles, and the results are summarized in Table 2. It is shown that the dissolution of Zr, V, Cr and Ni elements decrease and the dissolution of Ti and La elements increase with increasing x. It has been reported that the dissolution of V element being the main hydrogen absorbing element is essentially responsible for the capacity degradation of the alloy, and the dissolution of Zr element being a main element in C14 Laves phase would result in a decrease of the electrocatalytic activity in the alloy, which would affect the activation of the alloy electrode [21]. It has also been reported that segregation of Zr-rich phase can restrain the lattice expansion of metal hydride and decrease the micro-rigidity of the alloy, which has greatly decreased the pulverization rate, and as a result, charge-discharge cycling stability of AB_2 type Laves phase alloy has been greatly improved [22]. As a result, it can be concluded that addition of $LaNi_5$ is helpful in improving charge-discharge cyclic stability of TVS alloy, and the cyclic stability of the composite alloy electrodes increases with increasing x.

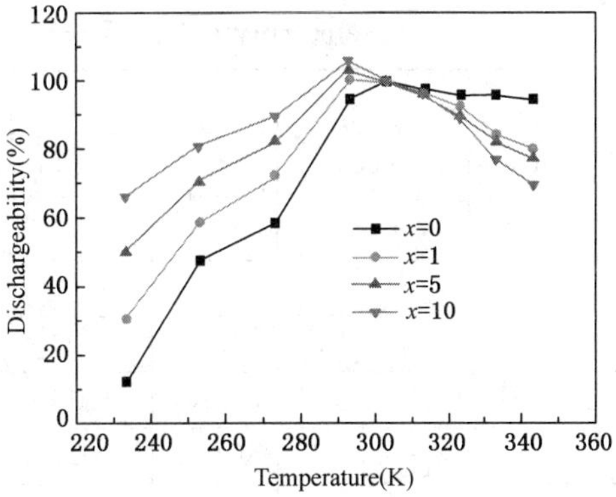

Fig. 6　The dependence of dischargeability on temperature for TVS+x% $LaNi_5$ (x=0,1,5,10) alloy electrodes

3.5　Temperature effects

Negative electrode material used in Ni-MH battery should be capable of working over a wide temperature range. The dischargeability at different temperature is defined as the ratio of the discharge capacity C_T at certain temperature to the discharge capacity C_{303} at the temperature of 303 K. Fig. 6 shows the dischargeability of TVS+x% $LaNi_5$ (x=0, 1,5,10) alloy electrodes at different temperatures. It is clearly shown that the dischargeability is very sensitive to temperature. The TVS alloy electrode reaches its maximum discharge capacity at 303 K and all composite alloy electrodes reach their maximum discharge capacities at 293 K, and then decrease sharply with the decrease or increase of temperature. It can also be found that the high temperature dischargeabilities (HTD) of the composite alloy electrodes are lower than that of TVS alloy from 303 to 343 K, whereas the LTD of the composite alloy electrodes increases with increasing x. For example, it is 12.30% for $x=0$ and 65.74% for $x=10$ at 233 K, respectively. It indicates that $LaNi_5$ addition is beneficial to the increase of the LTD of

Table 2　The dissolution of constituent elements at different cycles in KOH electrolyte for TVS+x% $LaNi_5$ (x=0,1,5,10) alloys

Constituent element	Concentration in KOH (mg L^{-1})							
	50 cycles				100 cycles			
	$x=0$	$x=1$	$x=5$	$x=10$	$x=0$	$x=1$	$x=5$	$x=10$
Ti	0.034	0.063	0.071	0.091	0.088	0.0909	0.1149	0.2141
Zr	13.59	12.92	12.61	10.97	27.43	24.76	19.64	17.34
V	31.107	28.65	25.9	24.88	74.14	72.07	56.14	50.5
Cr	0.026	0.015	0.013	0.012	0.1508	0.0388	0.0306	0.0244
Ni	0.134	0.132	0.083	0.067	0.2206	0.0306	0.0222	0.0212
La	—	—	—	—	—	0.0046	0.0123	0.1286

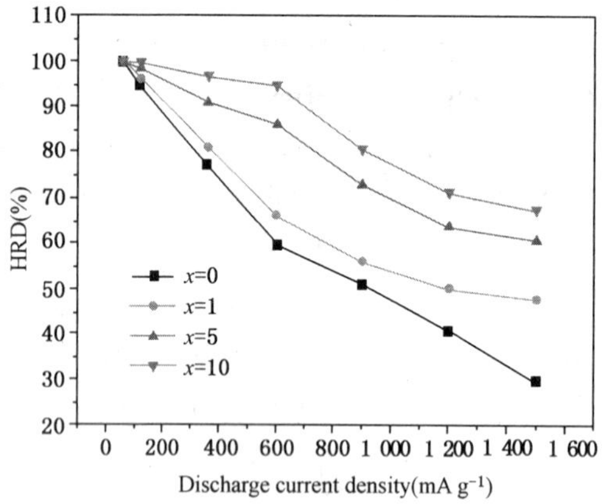

Fig. 7　High rate dischargeability (HRD) of TVS+x% $LaNi_5$ (x=0,1,5,10) alloy electrodes

the composite alloy electrodes. It is generally known that the LTD is mainly controlled by hydrogen diffusion, and hydrogen can diffuse more easily in the bulk of alloys with a larger cell volume and more grain boundaries having an open structure than that in grain. Thus, the increase of cell volume and grain boundaries of composite alloy with increasing x doubtlessly results in its superior LTD. However, the HTD is probably explained in the terms of the equilibrium hydrogen pressures of desorption [23]. The desorption hydrogen plateau increases with increasing temperature and x, and thereby the rates of dissociation of the composite alloys and of diffusion of hydrogen through the electrode alloy increase, which inevitably increase the reversible capacity loss and decrease the HTD.

3.6　High-rate dischargeability and electrochemical kinetic

HRD is important kinetic properties for the metal hydride electrode. To evaluate the HRD, the charging current density was kept constant at 60 mA g^{-1} and the obtained discharge capacity was denoted as C_j. Then HRD can be calculated in the following equation:

$$HRD(\%) = 100 \times \frac{C_j}{C_{60}} \tag{3}$$

wherein C_{60} is the discharge capacity at both the charge/discharge current density of 60 mA g^{-1}. Fig. 7 shows the HRD for TVS+x% $LaNi_5$ (x=0,1,5,10) alloy electrodes as a function of discharge current densities. It can be observed that the HRD of all the alloy electrodes decrease with increasing discharge current density. It can also be easily found that the HRD values are significantly improved by adding $LaNi_5$ alloy, and they increase with increasing x. For example, the HRD increases from 30.19% (x=0) to 7.73% (x=10) at discharge current density of 1 500 mA g^{-1} The improvements are perhaps related to the formed lard phase which accelerates the hydriding/dehydriding on the alloy surface.

It is well known that the HRD of the metal hydride electrodes is influenced mainly by the charge-transfer kinetics at the electrode/electrolyte interface and hydrogen diffusion rate in the bulk of alloy [24]. The exchange current density I_0 of alloy electrode is commonly used to characterize the catalytic activity for charge-transfer reaction at the electrode/electrolyte interface, and hydrogen diffusion coefficient D is used to characterize hydrogen diffusion rate in the bulk of alloy. In order to obtain I_0 and D, electrochemical impedance and potential-step experiment are performed on these alloy electrodes.

Fig. 8 shows the electrochemical impedance spectra of TVS+x% $LaNi_5$ (x=0,1,5,10) alloy electrodes at 50% DOD.

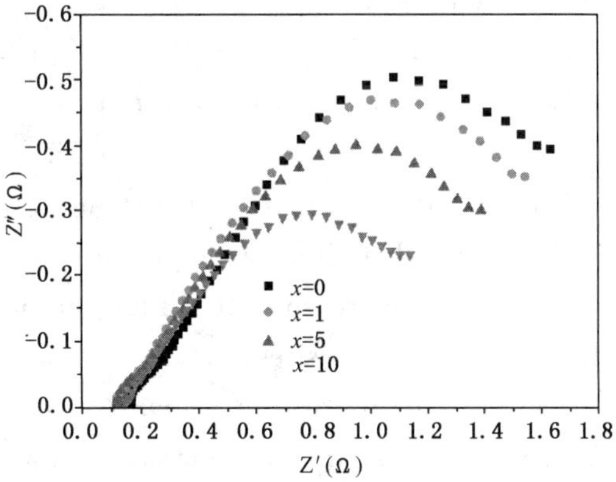

Fig. 8　Electrochemical impedance spectra of TVS+x%$LaNi_5$ (x=0,1,5,10) alloy electrodes

On the basis of the model proposed by Kuriyama et al. [25], the charge transfer resistance R_{ct} is obtained by means of the fitting program Z-View, exchange current density I_0 is calculated by the following equation when overpotential is very small:

$$I_0 = \left(\frac{RT}{F}\right)\left(\frac{1}{R_{ct}}\right) \tag{4}$$

wherein R is the gas constant, T is the absolute temperature and F is the Faraday constant. Table 3 gives R_{ct} and I_0. On the one hand, it is clearly shown that all the electrochemical impedance spectrum consists of two semicircles at high frequency and a short straight line at low frequency. The smaller semicircle in the high frequency region is attributed to the contact resistance between the alloy powder and conductive material, while the larger semi-circle in the low frequency region is attributed to the charge transfer resistance on the alloy surface. Both the radius of the larger semicircle in the low frequency region and the R_{ct} decrease with increasing x. For example, the R_{ct} decreases from 112.3Ω($x=0$) to 63.15 m($x=10$) and accordingly the I_0 increases from 232.61 mA g^{-1}($x=0$) to 413.65 mA g^{-1}($x=10$) with increasing x. This means that HRD is inevitably increased with increasing the addition of LaNi5 in the composites, which is in accordance with the results shown in Fig. 7. This indicates that the increasing $LaNi_5$ content is beneficial to the decrease in the charge transfer resistance and the increase in the exchange current density. On the other hand, XRD showed that the amount of the secondary phase increases with increasing $LaNi_5$ content. As a result, it is proposed that the white lard phase containing La element is assumably a good electrocatalyst for chargetransfer reaction on the alloy electrodes. Of course, the proposed hypothesis needs to be investigated in detail further.

Table 3　Electrochemical kinetic parameters of TVS-x%$LaNi_5$ (x=0,1,5,10) alloy electrodes

Sample	Charge-transfer resistance, (mΩ)	Exchange current density, I_0 (mA g^{-1})	Hydrogen diffusion coeffcient, D($\times 10^{-10}$ $cm^2 s^{-1}$)
$x=0$	112.3	232.61	10.39
$x=1$	80.97	322.61	12.76
$x=5$	71.60	364.83	15.31
$x=10$	63.15	413.65	20.38

The diffusion coefficient of hydrogen in the bulk of TVS+x% $LaNi_5$(x=0,1,5,10) alloy electrodes is determined with the potential-step method. According to the model of Zheng et al. [26].

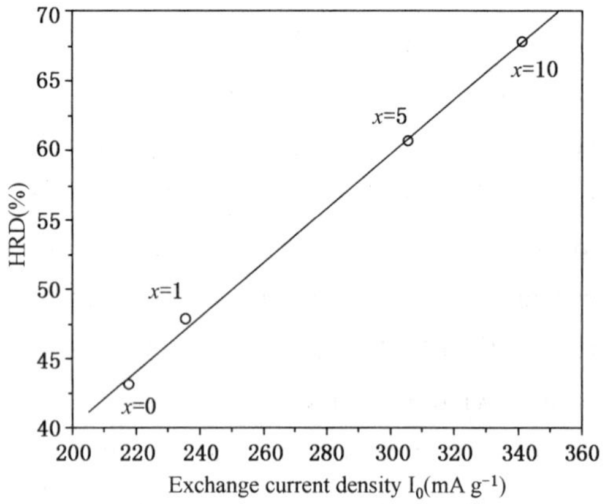

Fig. 9　High rate dischargeability (HRD) at 1 500 mA g^{-1} as a function of exchange current density (I_0) for TVS+x% $LaNi_5$ (x=0,1,5,10) alloy electrodes

The hydrogen diffusion coefficient D in the bulk of alloys is estimated and also listed in Table 3. It can be seen that the hydrogen diffusion coefficient increases with increasing x. For example, it is 10.39×10^{-10} cm^2/s for $x=0$ and 20.38×10^{-10} cm^2/s for $x=10$. The improvement may be attributed to the following factors: first, abundant defects and grain boundaries resulted from the formation of the secondary phases can provide good channels for the hydrogen diffusion. Second, the mixed structure of V-based solid solution phase, C14 Laves phase and the white lard phase containing La makes hydrogen diffusion avoid the long-range diffusion through an already formed hydride. Third, the content of the white lard phase at the surface increases with increasing x, which causes the hydrogen diffusion through the alloy surface more easily.

Iwakura et al. [27] have reported that if the electrochemical kinetics at the electrode/electrolyte interface is rate-determining factor, a linear dependence of HRD on the exchange current density should be observed. In contrast, if the diffusion of hydrogen in the bulk alloy is rate-determining factor, the high rate dischargeability should be constant, irrespective of exchange current density I_0. For melted TVS+x% $LaNi_5$ (x=0,1,5,10) alloy electrodes, the variation of exchange current density I_0 value with the HRD at the discharge current density of 1 500 mA g^{-1} is shown in Fig. 9. The HRD shows a linear relationship with I_0. This implies that in the present study, the HRD is essentially controlled by the charge transfer reaction of hydrogen at electrode/electrolyte interface at a discharge current density of 1 500 mA g^{-1}.

4 Conclusions

Structure and electrochemical characteristics of melted composite TVS + x% $LaNi_5$ (x=0,1,5,10) hydrogen storage alloys have been investigated systematically. The conclusions are as follows:

(1) The composite alloys have special multiphase microstructure, the matrix phase structure of V-based solid solution phase with a BCC structure and C14 Laves phase with hexagonal structure of TVS alloy is not changed after adding $LaNi_5$ alloy. However, the amount of the secondary phase increases with increasing $LaNi_5$ content. The lattice parameters and cell volumes of the BCC phase increase when x increases from 0 to 5 and decrease as x increases further, but those of the C14 Laves phase changes in the trend of shrinkage simultaneously after compositing treatment. The secondary phase has a composition of $Ti_{0.123}Zr_{0.160}V_{0.172}Cr_{0.029}Ni_{0.478}La_{0.038}$ close to $(Zr,Ti)(V,Cr,Ni,La)_2$.

(2) Compared with the matrix alloy, the hysteresis effect of the composite alloy electrodes is greatly decreased with increasing $LaNi_5$ content. The maximum hydrogen absorption capacity $[H/M]_{max}$ after 100 circles increases from 1.33 to 1.51 mass% as x increases from 0 to 5 and decreases from 1.51 to 1.23 mass% when x increases from 5 to 10.

(3) The electrochemical measurements show that the activation performance, the HRD and LTD of the composite alloys are dramatically enhanced, which increase with increasing $LaNi_5$ content. The maximum discharge capacity and cyclic stability of composite alloy electrodes are both improved. The activation circle number decreases from 19 cycles (x=0) to 4 cycles for(x=10). The HRD increases from 30.19% (x=0) to 67.73% (x=10) at discharge current density of 1 500 mA g^{-1}. The LTD increases from 12.30% (x = 0) to 65.74% (x=10). The maxi mum dis-

charge capacity increases from 324.9 mAh g^{-1} ($x=0$) to 353.9 mAh g^{-1} ($x=5$). The capacity retention after 100 circles increases from 88.15% ($x=0$) to 99.48% ($x=10$) due to the decrease of the dissolution of Zr, V, Cr and Ni.

Acknowledgments

This work is supported by Foundation of Key Laboratory of Rare Earth Chemistry and Physics, Chinese Academy of Sciences. And we also wish to thank Dr. Taicheng Duan and Ms. Meiye Li of Key Laboratory of Rare Earth Chemistry and Physics, Chinese Academy of Sciences for ICP and FESEM-EDS test, and Dr. Wentao Hu and Ms. Xuemei Yang of State Key Laboratory of Metastable Materials Science and Technology, Yanshan University for XRD test.

References

[1] T. Kohno, H. Yoshida, M. Kanda, J. Alloys Compd. 363(2004)249.

[2] R. Guo, L.-X. Chen, Y.-Q. Lei, B. Liao, T. Ying, Q.-D. Wang, Int. J. Hydr. Energy 28 (2003)803.

[3] M. Tsukahara, K. takahashi, T. Mishima, T. Sakai, H. Miyamura, N. Kuriyama, I. Uehara, J. Alloys Compd. 224(1995)162.

[4] M. Tsukahara, K. takahashi, T. Mishima, T. Sakai, H. Miyamura, N. Kuriyama, I. Uehara, J. Alloys Compd. 226(1)(1995)203.

[5] N. Kuriyama, M. Tsukahara, K. takahashi, H. Yoshinaga, H. T. Takeshita, T. Sakai, J. Alloys Compd. 356(2003)738.

[6] M. Tsukahara, K. takahashi, T. Mishima, A. Isomura, T. Sakai, J. Alloys Compd. 253 (1997)583.

[7] Q. A. Zhang, Y. Q. Lei, X. G. Yang, Y. L. Du, Q. D. Wang, Int. J. Hydr. Energy 25 (2000)977.

[8] Q. A. Zhang, Y. Q. Lei, X. G. Yang, Y. L. Du, Q. D. Wang, J. Alloys Compd. 305 (2000)125.

[9] J.-H. Kim, H. Lee, P. S. Lee, C.-Y. Seo, J.-Y. Lee, J. Alloys Compd. 348(2003)293.

[10] Y. J. Chai, M. S. Zhao, Int. J. Hydr. Energy 30(2005)279.

[11] Y. J. Chai, W. Y. Yin, Z. Y. Li, X. B. Zhang, M. S. Zhao, Intermetallics 13(2005)1141.

[12] Y. Q. Qiao, M. S. Zhao, X. J. Zhu, G. Y. Cao, Int. J. Hydr. Energy 32(2007)3427.

[13] C.-Y. Seo, S.-J. Choi, J. Choi, C.-N. Park, J.-Y. Lee, Int. J. Hydr. Energy 28 (9) (2003)967.

[14] X. B. Yu, F. Li, Z. Wu, B. J. Xia, N. X. Xu, Phys. Lett. A 320(2004)312.

[15] D. S. dos Santos, M. Bououdina, D. Fruchart, Int. J. Hydr. Energy 28(2003)1237.

[16] M. Bououdina, D.-L. Sun, H. Enoki, E. Akiba, J. Alloys Compd. 288(1999)229.

[17] S. M. Han, Z. Zhang, M. S. Zhao, Y. Z. Zheng, Int. J. Hydr. Energy 31(2006)563.

[18] C.-Y. Seo, S.-J. Choi, J. Choi, C.-N. Park, J.-Y. Lee, J. Alloys Compd. 351(2003)255.

[19] R. Balasubramaniam, J. Alloys Compd. 253 (1997)203.

[20] H. Y. Park, I. Chang, W. I. Cho, B. W. Cho, H. Jang, S. R. Lee, K. S. Yun, Int. J. Hydr. Energy 26(2001)949.

[21] Y. Q. Qiao, M. S. Zhao, M. Y. Li, X. J. Zhu, G. Y. Cao, Scripta Mater. 55(2006)279.

[22] C.-Y. Seo, S.-J. Choi, J. Choi, C.-N. Park, P. S. Lee, J.-Y. Lee, Int. J. Hydr. Energy 28 (2003)317.

[23] C. Iwakura, Y. Kajiya, H. Yoneyama, T. Sakai, K. Oguro, H. Ishikawa, J. Electrochem. Soc. 136(1989)1351.

[24] Y. F. Liu, H. G. Pan, M. X. Gao, Y. F. Zhu, Y. Q. Lei, J. Alloys Compd. 365(2004)246.

[25] N. Kuriyama, T. Sakai, H. Miyamura, I. Uehara, H. Ishikawa, T. Iwasaki, J. Alloys Compd. 202(1993)183.

[26] G. Zheng, B. N. Popov, R. E. White, J. Electrochem. Soc. 142(1995)2695.

[27] C. Iwakura, T. Oura, H. Inoue, M. Matsuoka, Electrochim. Acta 41(1996)117.

Structure and Electrochemical Property of Ball-milled $Ti_{0.26}Zr_{0.07}Mn_{0.1}Ni_{0.33}V_{0.24}$ Alloy ①

Shucun Li[a,c], Minshou Zhao[a,b], Yanzhi Wang[a], Jing Zhai[a]
([a] College of Environment and Chemical Engineering, Yanshan University, Qinhuangdao, 066004, PR China)
([b] State Key Laboratory of Rare Earth on Advanced Materials and Valuable Utilization of Resources, Changchun Institute of Applied Chemistry, Chinese Academic of Science, Changchun, 130022, PR China)
([c] State Key Laboratory of Metastable Material Science and Technology, Yanshan University, Qinhuangdao, 066004, PR China)

Abstract: In present study, high-energy ball-milling (HEBM) is used in order to improve the cyclic stability and other electrochemical properties of $Ti_{0.26}Zr_{0.07}Mn_{0.1}Ni_{0.33}V_{0.24}$ alloy. The effect of the milling time on crystallographic and electrochemical characteristics of the alloy has been investigated systematically. From X-ray diffraction (XRD) patterns, it can be found that the ball-milled alloys retain their respective phase structures with increasing the ball-milling time from 30 min to 180 min. Electrochemical studies show that the cyclic stability of the ball-milled alloys is noticeably improved after charge-discharge cycles. The capacity retention rate C_{40}/C_{max} after 40 cycles increases from 46.3% ($t=30$ min) to 78.3% ($t=180$ min), although the maximum discharge capacity of the ball-milled alloys decreases moderately. Both electrochemical impedance spectra (EIS) and Potentiostatic discharge technique studies indicate that the electrochemical kinetics of the ball-milled alloys is improved with increasing the ball-milling time.

Key words: Ti-Zr-V-Mn-Ni alloy; Bal-milling; Electrochemical property; Kinetic property

1 Introduction

Hydrogen storage alloys have been extensively studied for use as the negative electrode material in nickel-metal hydride (Ni-MH) battery due to several acknowledged advantages over the existing batteries, including Ni-Cd battery, lead-acid battery [1-3]. AB_2 type, Ti-V or Zr-based Laves phase hydrogen storage alloys have attracted the attention of investigators for their higher electrochemical capacities than that of the prevailing rare earth-based hydrogen storage alloys

① Materials Chemistry and Physics, 2009(118):51-56.

[4,5]. The Ti-V based multiphase hydrogen storage alloys are paid much attention, which generally consist of a C14 Laves phase and a V-based solid solution phase. The synergistic effect of the two phases benefits to improve electrochemical performance of the alloy. However, the Ti-V based alloys suffer from insufficient cyclic stability, which are limited in developing high-capacity and high-performance Ni-MH battery [6,7]. Although some electrochemical properties have been greatly improved by the formation of several new phases by favorable multi-component alloying, the cyclic stability the new alloys are still too low for the practical applications [8,9]. It is well known that the processing of materials by high-energy ball-milling is an attractive new method in preparing novel materials [10,11], which decreases the crystallite and particle size and induces the continuous formation of the structural defects through the cycling cut and deformation of large crystallites. In this paper, the effect of HEBM on the structures and electrochemical performances of $Ti_{0.26}Zr_{0.07}Mn_{0.1}Ni_{0.33}V_{0.24}$ alloy is investigated.

2 Experimental details

The base alloy was prepared by arc-melting carefully the constituent elements or master alloy on a water-cooled copper hearth under argon atmosphere. The purity of the metal, i. e., Ti, Zr, V, Mn, and Ni is higher than 99. 9 mass%, respectively. The ingots were remelted for 3—4 times to ensure homogeneity and then mechanically crushed into powders of 200 mesh size.

This powder was employed in the ball-milling process. The ball-milling process was performed with a SPEX model 8000 Mixer/mill for different ball-milling time in Ar atmosphere. The mass ratio of hardened steel balls to alloy powers is 10 : 1. For the electrochemical measurement, the well-mixed alloy powder and carbonyl nickel powder in weight ratio of 1 : 5 were pressed into the tablets with the diameter of 10 mm, thickness of 1 mm and the weight of 0. 9 g as a metal hydride electrode.

The electrochemical properties were performed on DC-5 battery testing instrument using a half-cell system which consists of a metal hydride electrode as a negative electrode and a sintered $Ni(OH)_2$/ NiOOH positive electrode with excessive capacity and 6 mol L^{-1} KOH as electrolyte solution. The MH electrode was charged at a constant current density (60 mA g^{-1}) until the hydrogen concentration reached its saturated value followed by 5 min resting time and then was discharged at a constant current density of 60 mA g^{-1} to a cut-off potential of 0. 8 V. The experimental cell was set in a water bath at controlled (±0. 5 K) temperature ranging from 303 K to 343 K.

In evaluating the high-rate dischargeability (HRD), discharge capacity of the alloy electrode at different discharge current densities was measured. The HRD (%) is defined as

$$\mathrm{HRO}=\frac{C_n}{C_{\max}} \quad (1)$$

where $C_{\max}$ represents the maximum discharge capacity at a discharge current density of 60 mA g^{-1}, C_n is the discharge capacity at a discharge current density of n = 60 mA g^{-1}, 120 mA g^{-1}, 240 mA g^{-1}, 360 mA g^{-1}, 480 mA g^{-1}, and 600 mA g^{-1}, respectively.

The phase structure of the alloy powders was determined by X-ray diffraction (XRD) using a Rigaku D/max 2500 PC powder diffractometer with Cu Kα radiation, and field emission scanning electron microscopy (FESEM) was used to study the images of the alloy powder by XL30 ESEM FEG scanning electron microscope. Electrochemical impedance spectroscopy (EIS) was used for determining the charge transfer resistance (R_{ct}) and the exchange current density (I_0) to clarify the kinetic properties of dehydrating action. After the test electrodes were completely activated, EIS measurements were conducted at 50% depth of discharge (DOD) and the frequency range was from 0. 1 Hz to 1 MHz, using a Solartron 1287 Potentiostat/Galvanostat and a Solartron 1255 B frequency response analyzer with Z-POLT software for WINDOWS. The Potentiostatic discharge technique was used to evaluate the diffusion coefficient of hydrogen in the bulk of the alloys. After being fully charged followed by 30 min open-circuit lay-aside, the test electrodes were discharged with +500 mV potential-step for 3600 s on the EG&G PARC Model 273 Potentiostatic/Galvanostat.

3 Results and discussion

3.1 Alloy structure characteristics

Fig. 1 shows the X-ray diffraction patterns of $Ti_{0.26}Zr_{0.07}Mn_{0.1}Ni_{0.33}V_{0.24}$ ball-milled alloys. It is clear that the alloys are mainly composed of V-based solid solution phase with BCC structure and C14 Laves phase with hexagonal structure. We can find that no new phase forms in the alloys after ball-milling treatment according to the XRD detection. However, as the milling time increases from 30 min to 180 min, the originally diffraction sharp peaks of the ball-milled alloys are gradually broadened and their intensities are gradually decreased. The milled alloy powders lost their crystalline character owing to partial amorphization occurred during the process of ball-milling. The XRD results have shown that the ball-milling time increasing from 30 min to 180 min does not change the main structure and phase composition of the alloys although the relative intensity of corresponding diffraction peaks has changed to some a degree.

Fig. 2 shows FESEM images of the ball-milled alloys. It is found that the ball-milled particles of the alloys are pulverized to the size of less than 20 μm, and the surfaces of the ball-milled alloys particles become rough, which means some fresh surfaces have been generated during the process of ball-milling.

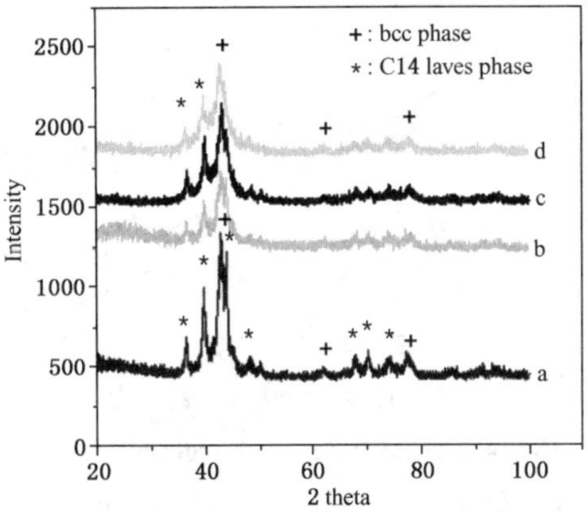

Fig. 1　XRD pattern of $Ti_{0.26}Zr_{0.07}V_{0.24}Mn_{0.1}Ni_{0.33}$ alloy after different milling time. a, 30 min; b, 60 min; c, 120 min; d, 180 min

3.2　Electrochemical property

3.2.1　Discharge capacity and cycling stability

Fig. 3 exhibits cyclic stability curves of $Ti_{0.26}Zr_{0.07}V_{0.24}Mn_{0.1}Ni_{0.33}$ ball-milled alloys at 303 K. It is obvious that the cyclic stability of the ball-milled alloys is greatly enhanced, though their maximum discharge capacity decreases with ball-milling time increasing. For example, after 40 charge-discharge cycles, the discharge capacity retention rate is expressed as $S_{40}(\%) = (C_{40}/C_{max}) \times 100$, where C_{max} is the maximum discharge capacity, C_{40} is the discharge capacity at the 40th cycle, and are 46.3%, 58.9%, 67.3%, 78.3%, respectively. It is indicated that HEBM is an effective method to improve the cyclic stability of $Ti_{0.26}Zr_{0.07}V_{0.24}Mn_{0.1}Ni_{0.33}$ alloy.

The excellent cycling stability is mainly attributed to the amorphous phase in the electrodes. In general, the fundamental reason for capacity decay of the electrode is the pulverization and corrosion in process of the charge/discharge cycles [12]. Zhang et al. [13] pointed out the anti-pulverization capability depended mainly on the strength and toughness of the electrodes. As commonly considered, amorphous phase is beneficial to the increase of the strength and toughness. In-

Fig. 2　Filed emission scanning electron micrograph of $Ti_{0.26}Zr_{0.07}V_{0.24}Mn_{0.1}Ni_{0.33}$ alloy after different milling time. (a) t=60 min, and (b) t=180 min

creasing milling time causes the increase of the amorphous phase, and thereby improves the anti-pulverization capability. Moreover, increasing amorphous phase will also enhance the anti-corrosion ability of the electrodes [14]. However, the alloy surface resulted from a long milling time may have much less sites suitable for hydrogen storage due to amorphization as detected by XRD analysis and that is the reason why increasing ball-milling time decreases the discharge capacity [15].

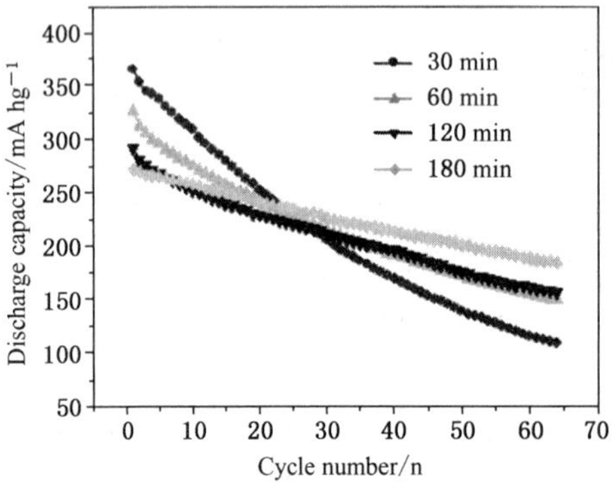

Fig. 3　Relation between discharge capacity and cycle number for $Ti_{0.26}Zr_{0.07}V_{0.24}Mn_{0.1}Ni_{0.33}$ alloy at current density of 60 mA g^{-1} and 303 K

3.2.2　High-rate dischargeability and electrochemical kinetics

Fig. 4 shows the relationship between the high-rate dischargeability and the discharge current density of the alloy electrode after different milling time. It is indicated that the high-rate dischargeability of the ball-milled alloy electrode increases with the increasing of the milling time. The tests show that properly controlling the ball-milling time is effective in improving the HRD of $Ti_{0.26}Zr_{0.07}V_{0.24}Mn_{0.1}Ni_{0.33}$ alloy.

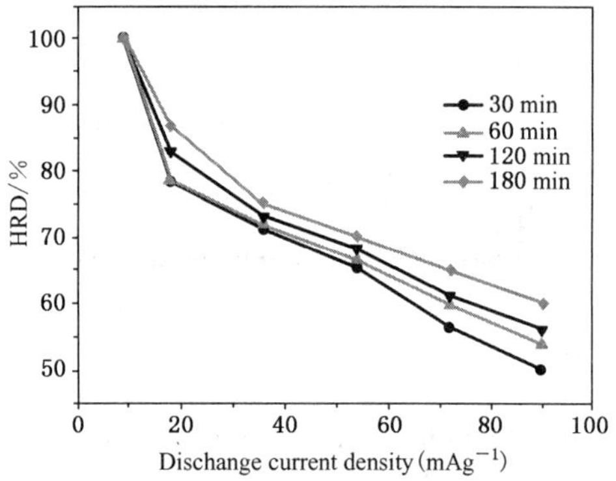

Fig. 4　High-rate dischargeability of $Ti_{0.26}Zr_{0.07}V_{0.24}Mn_{0.1}Ni_{0.33}$ alloy electrode after different milling time

High-rate dischargeability of the alloy electrode is influenced mainly by the charge transfer reaction occurring at the electrode/electrolyte interface and the diffusion rate of hydrogen in the bulky electrode alloy [16]. In general, the charge transfer reaction is dominated by the charge transfer resistance (R_{ct}) at the electrode/electrolyte interface and/or the exchange current density (I_0), and the diffusion rate of hydrogen in the electrode alloy is determined by hydrogen diffusion coefficient (D). In order to examine the effect of the ball-milling time on the kinetic properties, electrochemical impedance and potential-step experiment are performed on the alloy electrodes.

Fig. 5 illustrates the electrochemical impedance spectra for the ball-milled alloys at 50% DOD and 303 K. The EIS curves for these alloy electrodes consist of a smaller semicircle in the high-frequency region and a larger semicircle in the low-frequency region followed by a straight line. The EIS data are analyzed using an equivalent circuit as that proposed by Kuriyama et al. [17]. On the basis of the circuit the charge transfer resistances R_{ct} are obtained by means of fitting program Z-VIEW. The exchange current density I_0 is calculated using the following formula [18] when overpotential is very small, and the results are listed in Table 1:

$$I_0 = \frac{RT}{FR_{ct}} \tag{2}$$

where R is the gas constant, T is the absolute temperature and F is the Faraday constant.

The results show that the R_{ct} for ball-milled alloy electrodes decreases from 0.211 Ω (t = 30 min) to 0.158 Ω (t=180 min). Accordingly, the I_0 increases from 124 mA g^{-1} (t = 30min) to 165 mA g^{-1} (t=180 min). This indicates that increasing ball-milling time is beneficial to the charge transfer reaction at the electrode/electrolyte interface of the ball-milled alloy electrodes.

The diffusion coefficient of hydrogen

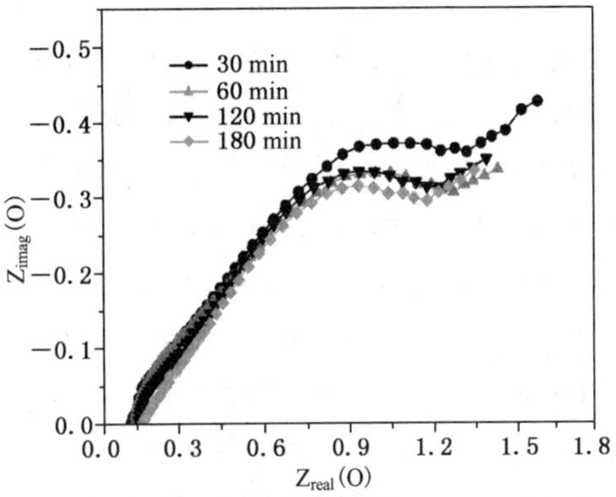

Fig. 5 Electrochemical impedance spectroscopy for $Ti_{0.26}Zr_{0.07}V_{0.24}Mn_{0.1}Ni_{0.33}$ alloy electrode measured at 50% DOD and 303 K after different milling time

in the bulky alloy is determined with the potential-step method. Fig. 6 shows the semi-logarithmic plots of the anodic current vs. the time response of the electrodes. It can be seen that under the operation of a potential-step, the current-time responses in the semi-logarithmic plot (log$i$ vs. t) can be divided into two time regions as proposed by Nishina et al. [19]. In the first region, the current declines abruptly due to the fast consumption of hydrogen on the surface of

Table 1 Electrochemical kinetic parameter of $Ti_{0.26}Zr_{0.07}V_{0.24}Mn_{0.1}Ni_{0.33}$ alloy electrode

Sample	R_{ct} (Ω)	Exchange current density, I_0 (mA g^{-1})	Hydrogen diffusion coefficient, D ($\times 10^{-11}$ $cm^2 s^{-1}$)	
			303 K	333 K
30 min	0.211	124	6.44	15.8
60 min	0.188	139	6.84	14.9
120 min	0.169	154	7.45	13.3
180 min	0.158	165	7.66	13

the alloy particles. In the second region, the current declines relatively slowly in a linear manner. In this case, the current is mainly controlled by the hydrogen diffusion velocity, which is proportional to the concentration gradient of hydrogen in the bulk of the alloys. Therefore, the linear response in the second region can be treated as the finite diffusion of hydrogen atoms inside the alloy particles according to the spherical diffusion model. The hydrogen diffusion coefficient D can be estimated by the following formulas [20] and the calculated values are also listed in Table 1:

$$\log i=\log\left(\pm\frac{6FD}{da^2}(C_0-C_s)\right)-\frac{\pi^2}{2.303}\frac{D}{a^2}t \tag{3}$$

$$D=\frac{2.303a^2}{\pi^2}\frac{\mathrm{d}\log i}{\mathrm{d}t} \tag{4}$$

where i denotes the diffusion current density ($\mathrm{A\ g^{-1}}$), D denotes the hydrogen diffusion coefficient ($\mathrm{cm^2\ s^{-1}}$), C_0 denotes the initial hydrogen concentration ($\mathrm{mol\ cm^{-3}}$) inside the alloy particles, C_s denotes the hydrogen concentration ($\mathrm{mol\ cm^{-3}}$) at the surface of the alloy particles, a denotes the radius of alloy particles (cm), d denotes the density of the hydrogen storage alloy ($\mathrm{g\ cm^{-3}}$) and t denotes the discharge time (s).

It is found that the diffusion coefficient D for the ball-milled alloys increases with increasing the milling time at 303 K. The diffusion coefficient D increases from $6.44\times10^{-11}\ \mathrm{cm^2\ s^{-1}}$ to $7.66\times10^{-11}\ \mathrm{cm^2\ s^{-1}}$ with increasing the milling time from 30 min to 180 min. The results

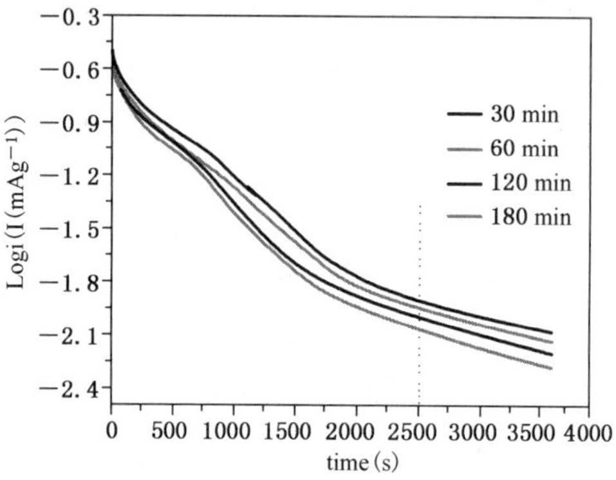

Fig. 6 Anodic current-time responses of $Ti_{0.26}Zr_{0.07}V_{0.24}Mn_{0.1}Ni_{0.33}$ alloy electrode after different milling time

show that ball-milling is effective for increasing the D value. The higher D for the milled electrodes may be ascribed to the following factors: refined grains, abundant defects and grain boundaries caused by ball-milling are beneficial to the hydrogen diffusion, which is due to the fact that refined grains, shortened diffusion length, and abundant defects and grain boundaries can provide good channels for the hydrogen diffusion [21]. More abundant defects, gain boundaries and amorphous phase are generated with increasing ball-milling time, which causes the increase of D value.

It is very difficult to explain which factor caused this effect because there are too many factors influencing the hydrogen diffusion, including the phase composition, components of alloy, the interaction between hydrogen and metal, the volume of lattice, etc. In the practical measurement of diffusion coefficient, the discharge current could be set up as small as possible.

It is noted that a longer ball-milling time is unfavorable for increasing the diffusion process of hydrogen in the alloy, which may be due to the following: a proper concentration of defects in the alloy is good for improving the diffusion process of hydrogen in alloy, but when its concentration is too high, which can be caused by lengthy ball-milling, the thin surface phase can not store hydrogen and hydrogen can not pass through this thin layer, which is similar to an amorphous phase. Thus, it was considered that little change of D with increasing milling time should be attributed to the synthesized effect of advantageous and disadvantageous factors.

From the viewpoint of dynamics, the nature of the increase in the dischargeability at a large current is the increase in the exchange current and the diffusion coefficient, i. e., the electrocatalytic ability and the hydrogen diffusion rate in the bulk alloy. As a result, in order to improve the high-rate dischargeability, two methods should be used: increase the electrocatalytic capability of the alloy surface or accelerate the diffusion process of hydrogen.

Iwakura et al. [22] have reported that a linear dependence of the HRD on the exchange current density should be observed if the electrochemical reaction kinetics at the electrode/electrolyte interface was rate-determining step. In contrast, if the diffusion of hydrogen in the electrode alloy was rate-determining step, the high-rate dischargeability should be irrespective of exchange current density. Fig. 7 shows the HRD at 240 mA g^{-1} as a function of exchange current density for the electrodes. It is evident that the HRD shows a linear relationship with I_0. This implies that the charge transfer reaction at the electrode/electrolyte interface is rate-determining step for the high-rate dischargeability at a discharge current density is 240 mA g^{-1}.

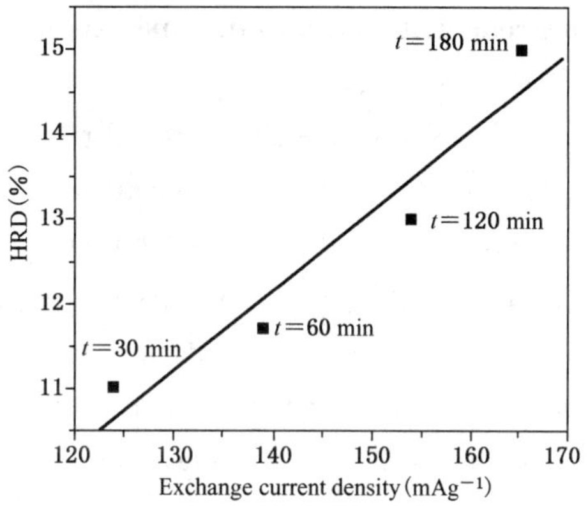

Fig. 7　HRD at 240 mA g^{-1} as a function of exchange current density for the alloy electrode

The apparent activation energy (E_a) of the hydrogen diffusion in the bulk of the alloy is another important kinetic parameter and can be determined by the following formula:

$$\mathrm{Ln}D=-\frac{E_a}{RT+A} \qquad (5)$$

where A is a constant, D is the hydrogen diffusion coefficient at different temperature. The D values are used to plot the $1/T$ dependence of Ln D as shown in Fig. 8. The straight line of Ln D vs. $1/T$ in Fig. 8 gives the apparent activation energy of 44. 8 kJ mol^{-1} with $t=120$ min.

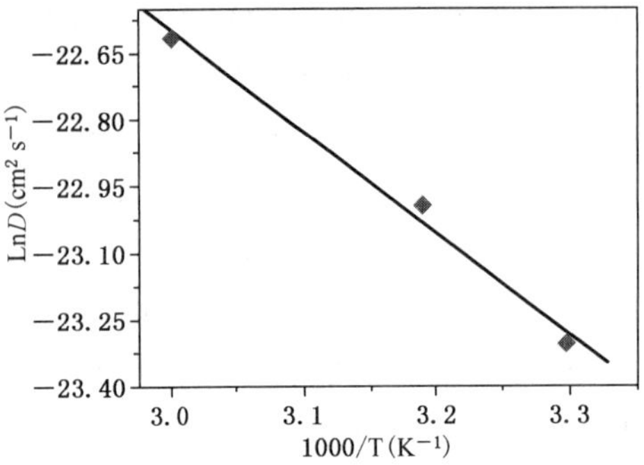

Fig. 8　Relation between Ln *D* and $1/T$ for $Ti_{0.26}Zr_{0.07}V_{0.24}Mn_{0.1}Ni_{0.33}$ alloy electrode with ball-milling time 120 min

3.2.3　Discharge curves

Fig. 9 shows the discharge curves of the first cycle for the alloy electrodes at 60 mA g^{-1} and 303 K. It is noted that each curve has a wide discharge voltage plateau based on the oxidation of desorbed hydrogen from the hydride. With increasing ball-milling time, the initial voltage decreases and the platform is even short. That is to say, increasing ball-milling time leads to a decrease in discharge capacity. It should be noted that the discharge plateau shifts towards a more positive potential as ball-milling time increases, indicating that increasing ball-milling time leads to an increase in discharge overpotential of the alloy electrodes at different extent.

3.2.4　High temperature discharge capacity

Alloys used as negative electrode material in Ni-MH battery should be capable of working at wide temperature range. The discharge capacity as a function of temperature is shown in Fig. 10. It can be easily found that the discharge capacities are sensitive to temperature. The discharge capacity of each sample alloy increases with increasing temperature. Moreover, with increasing the ball-milling time, the high temperature discharge capacity of the alloys increases first and then decreases. $Ti_{0.26}Zr_{0.07}V_{0.24}Mn_{0.1}Ni_{0.33}$ alloy with 30 min ball-milled has higher discharge capacity than other ones.

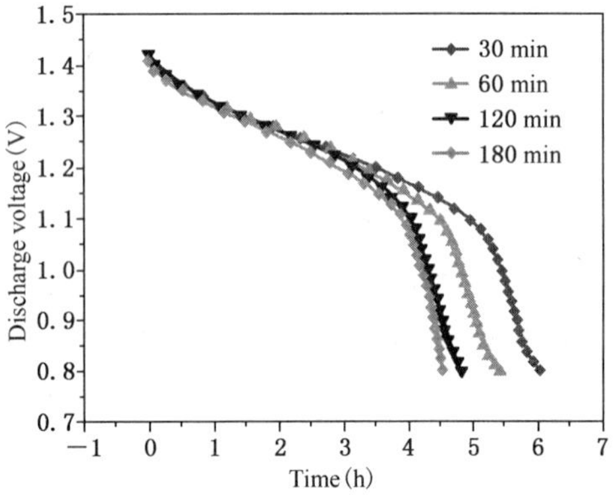

Fig. 9　Discharge curve of $Ti_{0.26}Zr_{0.07}V_{0.24}Mn_{0.1}Ni_{0.33}$ alloys electrode at 303 K after different milling time

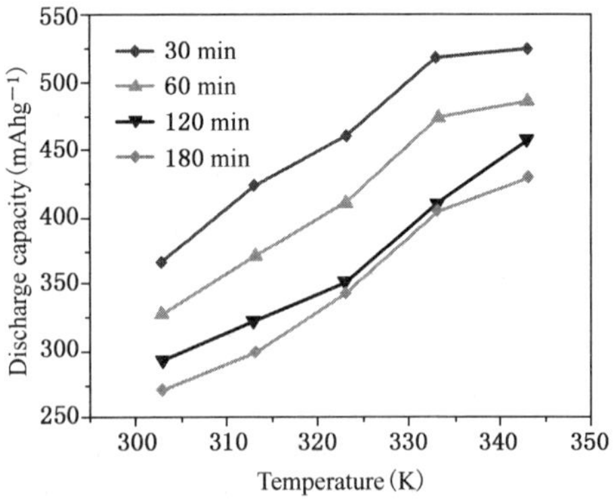

Fig. 10　Relation between discharge capacity and temperature of $Ti_{0.26}Zr_{0.07}V_{0.24}Mn_{0.1}Ni_{0.33}$ alloy electrode after different milling time

The dischargeability of the negative electrodes at relative high temperature is mainly influenced by the hydrogen diffusion and charge transfer process occurring at the metal electrolyte interface [23]. The D for the alloy electrodes at 303 K and 333 K are also tabulated in Table 1. It can found that the D for the ball-milled alloys at 333 K is higher than that at 303 K. Moreover, the D for the ball-milled alloys at 333 K decreases gradually with increasing the ball-milling time, which explains why the high temperature discharge capacity of the alloy electrode increases with increasing temperature.

Fig. 11 shows the high temperature discharge capacity as a function of D for the alloy electrodes. The discharge capacity of each sample alloy increases with increasing temperature. Those are mostly because of the increase of electrolyte activity at high temperature which reasonably leads to the decrease of hydrogen diffusion resistance and thus the obviously increase of the charge efficiency and discharge efficiency, and then inevitably the increase of the discharge capacity of the electrodes.

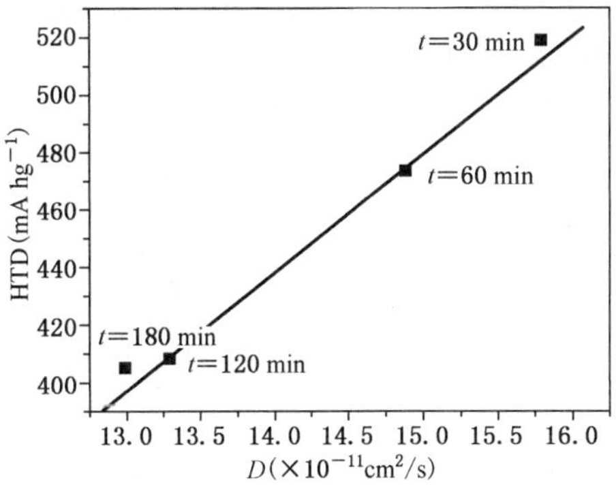

Fig. 11 High temperature discharge capacity as a function of D for the alloy electrode at 333 K after different milling time

4 Conclusion

The effect of HEBM on the structures and electrochemical performances of $Ti_{0.26}Zr_{0.07}Mn_{0.1}Ni_{0.33}V_{0.24}$ alloy is investigated. It is found that the ball-milling treatment do not change the phase structures in the ball-milled alloys. The average particle sizes of ball-milled alloys are less than 20 μm according to the FESEM micrograph. The experimental results show that HEBM is an effective method to improve the electrochemical performances of the alloys such as cycle performance. The capacity retention rate C_{40}/C_{max} of composite electrode increases significantly from 46.3% (t=30 min) to 78.3% (t=180 min). Furthermore, the kinetics of the electrochemical hydrogen reaction is also investigated. The results of electrochemical impedance spectroscopy, Potentiostatic discharge technique and powder X-ray diffraction indicate the improvement of the performances of the ball-milled alloys. Application of HEBM produces the decrease of the crystallite and particle size and the increase of the interlayer spacing. These structural changes lead to the reduction of the charge transfer resistance (R_{ct}) and increase of the diffusion coefficient (D).

Acknowledgements

This work was financially supported by the National Natural Science Foundation of China (Grant No. 20171042).

References

[1] Y. Q. Lei, Y. M. Wu, Q. M. Yang, J. Wu, Q. D. Wang, Z. Phys. Chem. 183 (1994) 379.

[2] Deying Song, Xueping Gao, Yunshi Zhang, Jie Yan, Panwen Shen, J. Alloys Compd. 206 (1994) 43.

[3] C. Khaldi, H. Mathlouthi, J. Lamloumi, A. Percheron-Guégan, Int. J. Hydrogen Energy 29 (2004) 307.

[4] H. -H. Lee, K. -Y. Lee, J. -Y. Lee, J. Alloys Compd. 239 (1996) 63.

[5] D. -M. Kim, S. -W. Jeon, J. -Y. Lee, J. Alloys Compd. 279 (1998) 209.

[6] P. H. L. Notten, P. Hokkeling, J. Electrochem. Soc. 138 (1991) 1877.

[7] H. H. Lee, J. Y. Lee, J. Alloys Compd. 253 (1997) 601.

[9] M. Tsukahara, K. Takahashi, T. Mishima, A. Isomura, T. Sakai, J. Alloys Compd. 243 (1996) 133.

[8] M. Tsukahara, K. Takahashi, T. Mishima, A. Isomura, T. Sakai, J. Alloys Compd. 236 (1996) 151.

[10] L. Zhaolin, Y. Aishui, J. Y. Lee, J. Power Sources 74 (1998) 228.

[11] M. Stubicar, Z. Blazina, A. Tonejc, N. Stubicar, D. Krumes, Physica B 304 (2001) 304.

[12] D. Chartouni, F. Meli, A. Zuttel, K. Gross, L. Schlapbach, J. Alloys Compd. 241 (1996) 160.

[13] Y. H. Zhang, G. Q. Wang, X. P. Dong, S. H. Guo, X. L. Wang, J. Power Sources 137 (2004) 309.

[14] Hai-Liang Chua, Shu-Jun Qiu, Li-Xian Sun, Yao Zhang, Fen Xu, Tao Jiang, Wei-Xue Li, Min Zhu, Wang-Yu Hu, Electrochim. Acta 52 (2007) 6700.

[15] Yan-hui Xu, Chang-pin Chen, Xiao-lin Wang, Qi-dong Wang, Solid State Ionics 146 (2002) 157.

[16] T. Sakai, H. Miyamura, N. Kuriyama, A. Kato, K. Oguro, H. Ishikawa, J. Less-Common Met. 159 (1990) 127.

[17] N. Kuriyama, T. Sakai, H. Miyamura, I. Uehara, H. Ishikawa, T. Iwasaki, J. Electrochem. Soc. 139 (1992) L72.

[18] N. Kuriyama, T. Sakai, H. Miyamura, I. Uehara, H. Ishikawa, J. Alloys Compd. 202 (1993) 183.

[19] T. Nishina, H. Ura, I. Uchida, J. Electrochem. Soc. 144 (1997) 1273.

[20] G. Zheng, B. N. Popov, R. E. White, J. Electrochem. Soc. 142 (1995) 2695.

[21] T. Spassov, L. Lyubenova, U. Köster, M. D. Baŕo, Mater. Sci. Eng. A375-377 (2004) 794.

[22] C. Iwakura, T. Oura, H. Inoue, M. Matsuoka, Electrochim. Acta 41 (1996) 117.

[23] T. Sakai, H. Miyamura, N. Kuriyama, A. Kato, K. Oguro, H. Ishikawa, J. Electrochem. Soc. 137 (1990) 7.

Structures and Electrochemical Characteristics of $Ti_{0.26}Zr_{0.07}V_{0.24}Mn_{0.1}Ni_{0.33}Mo_x$ ($x=0-0.1$) Hydrogen Storage Alloys ①

Shucun Li[a,b], Minshou Zhao[a,b], Limin Wang[b], Yan Liu[a], Yanzhi Wang[a]
([a] College of Environment and Chemical Engineering, Yanshan University, Qinhuangdao 066004, PR China)
([b] State Key Laboratory of Application of Rare Earth Resources, Changchun Institute of Applied Chemistry, Chinese Academic of Science, Changchun 130022, PR China)

Abstract: Microstructures and electrochemical properties of $Ti_{0.26}Zr_{0.07}V_{0.24}Mn_{0.1}Ni_{0.33}Mo_x$ ($x=0, 0.025, 0.05, 0.075, 0.10$) electrode alloys have been investigated. The results of XRD analysis show that the alloys are mainly composed of V-based solid solution phase with body centered cubic (bcc) structure and C14 Laves phase with hexagonal structure. The addition of Mo element can improve the activation characteristics, maximum discharge capacity and cyclic durability for the electrode alloys. The discharge capacity of the electrode alloys increases with changing x from 0.025 to 0.10 within temperature region from 303 to 343 K. The results show that the discharge property of $Ti_{0.26}Zr_{0.07}V_{0.24}Mn_{0.1}Ni_{0.33}Mo_{0.075}$ electrode alloy at high temperature is the best, and its maximum discharge capacity is 633 mAh g^{-1} at 343 K. However, the high-rate dischargeability decreases and the self-discharge rate increases for $Ti_{0.26}Zr_{0.07}V_{0.24}Mn_{0.1}Ni_{0.33}Mo_x$ ($x=0-0.10$) electrode alloys with increasing Mo content. Electrochemical impedance spectroscopy (EIS) shows that the charge transfer resistance at the surface of the alloy electrodes increases obviously with increasing Mo content.

Key words: Ni/MH battery; Mo addition; Metal hydride electrode; Electrochemical property

1 Introduction

Hydrogen storage alloys are a group of new functional materials which can be used in heat pumps, catalysts, hydrogen sensors and Ni/MH batteries. The development of Ni/MH battery based on MH electrodes has been considerable activity in recent years. Batteries based on such hydride materials have some major advantages over the more conventional lead-acid and nickel-cadmium systems. These advantages include high reversible energy storage density, fast electrochemical activation, long cyclic stability, good charge/discharge kinetics and environmental

① Material Science and Engineering B, 2008(150): 168-174.

compatibility [1-3].

The small size Ni/MH batteries (AA size) have been commercialized for portable electronic appliances while the large size Ni/MH batteries are under development for electric vehicles. The Ni/MH batteries for electric vehicles require higher energy density and power density. The energy density of the Ni/MH battery mainly depends on the discharge capacities of the MH electrode. The hydrogen storage capacity of the metal hydride can be increased by developing light high-capacity alloys [4]. These characteristics can be changed by designing the composition of the hydrogen storage alloy to provide optimum performance of the Ni/MH batteries. It has already been noted that Ni/MH battery performance is often better when the metal hydride electrode is a multi-phase material. As many as five phases have been reported in some hydride electrodes, with specific roles (e. g. hydrogen storage capacity, electrocatalysis, and corrosion protection) attributed to each phase [5]. There are several requirements for the electrochemical properties of MH electrode and all these properties must be balanced for practical use. Therefore, multiple elements are needed in "commercial" alloys for their different characteristics. The use of multi-component alloys and non-stoichiometric compositions can readily lead to a multi-phase microstructure. Ti-Zr-V-Mn-Ni-based multi-component alloys have very high initial electrochemical discharge capacities, and can be activated very easily [6]. However, their discharge capacities decrease dramatically within several charging-discharging cycles, which impede their acceptance as practical electrode materials in Ni/MH battery industry.

Much effort has been devoted to search for a more cost-effective substitute element with high reliability to meet the requirements of applications of electric vehicles. Besides Fe [7] and Cu [8], it is believed that Mo is one of the best candidates for substitution element. Some researchers have studied the influence of Mo additive in AB_5-type alloy, but the study of influence of Mo additive in Ti-Zr-V-Mn-Ni-based multi-component alloys is seldom. The motivation for this study is to search for the influence of Mo additive in Ti-Zr-V-Mn-Ni-based multi-component alloys. The reason is that the increase of hydrogen absorption capacity seems related to the increase of atomic number Z of the substituted element[9].

In present study, $Ti_{0.26}Zr_{0.07}V_{0.24}Mn_{0.1}Ni_{0.33}$ alloy is selected as an original alloy and the addition of Mo is expected to improve the Ti-Zr-V-Mn-Ni-based alloy electrodes performance and to develop a high-capacity MH electrode material. The crystal structures and electrochemical properties of the alloys are investigated.

2 Experimental details

All samples were prepared by arc-melting the constituent elements or master alloy on a water-cooled copper hearth under argon atmosphere. The purity of the metals, i. e. Ti, Zr, V, Mn, Ni and Mo is higher than 99.9 mass%, respectively. The samples were all inverted and remelted three to four times to ensure good homogeneity. Thereafter, these alloy samples were mechanically crushed into fine powders of 300-mesh in mortar. Crystallographic characteristics of the alloys were investigated by X-ray diffraction on Rigaku D/Max 2500 PC X-ray diffractometer (Cu Kα, monochromator) using JADE5 software. Field emission scanning electron microscopy (FESEM) was used to study the images of the solid solution alloys by XL30 ESEM FEG scanning electron microscope. Electrochemical impedance spectroscopy (EIS) measurements were conducted at 50% depth of discharge (DOD) and the frequency range was from 0.1 Hz to 1 MHz, using a Solartron 1287 Potentiostat/Galvanostat and a Solartron 1255 B frequency response analyzer with Z-POLT software for WINDOWS.

The well-mixed alloy powder and carbonyl nickel powder in weight ratio of 1 : 5 were pressed into the tablets with the diameter of 10 mm, thickness of 1 mm and the weight of 0.9 g as a metal hydride electrode.

The electrochemical properties were performed on DC-5 battery testing instrument using a half-cell system which consists of a metal hydride electrode as a negative electrode, a sintered $Ni(OH)_2/NiOOH$ positive electrode with excessive capacity and a reference electrode ($Hg/HgO, OH^-$). The electrolyte in the cell was 6 mol L^{-1} KOH aqueous solution. The MH electrode was charged at a constant current density (60 mA g^{-1}) until the hydrogen concentration reached its saturated value followed by 5 min resting time and then was discharged at a constant current density (60 mA g^{-1}) to a cut off potential of 0.8 V. The experimental cell was set in a water bath at controlled (±0.5 K) temperature ranging from 303 to 343 K.

To evaluate the high-rate dischargeability (HRD) (in the range of 60 − 600 mA g^{-1}), discharge capacities of the alloy electrode at different discharge current densities were measured. The high-rate dischargeability (%) is defined as

$$HRD = \frac{C_n}{C_{max}} \tag{1}$$

where C_{max} represents the maximum discharge capacity at a discharge current density of 60 mA g^{-1}, and C_n is the discharge capacity at a discharge current density of n = 60, 120, 180, 240, 360, 480 and 600 mA g^{-1}, respectively.

The charge retention (CR) is one of the major parameters for estimating a battery performance. The charge retention of the negative electrode could be evaluated using the following equation:

$$CR=\left\{\frac{1-2C_2}{C_1+C_3}\right\}\times\frac{100}{\text{day}}(\%\text{day}) \quad (2)$$

where C_1 represents the discharge capacity measured after the activation, C_2 is the discharge capacity measured after the open-circuit condition for a given period of time, and C_3 is the discharge capacity measured in the charge-discharge cycle immediately after the measurement of C_2.

3 Results and discussion

3.1 Alloy structure characteristic

The typical X-ray diffraction patterns are shown in Fig. 1 From the patterns, two distinct crystallographic phases, namely C14 Laves phase with hexagonal structure and V-based solid solution phase with body centered cubic (bcc) structure are found to coexist in all the alloy samples, which are confirmed by SEM in Fig. 2(A). The energy dispersion X-ray spectroscopy (EDS) analysis is shown in Fig. 2(B) and the results are listed in Table 2.

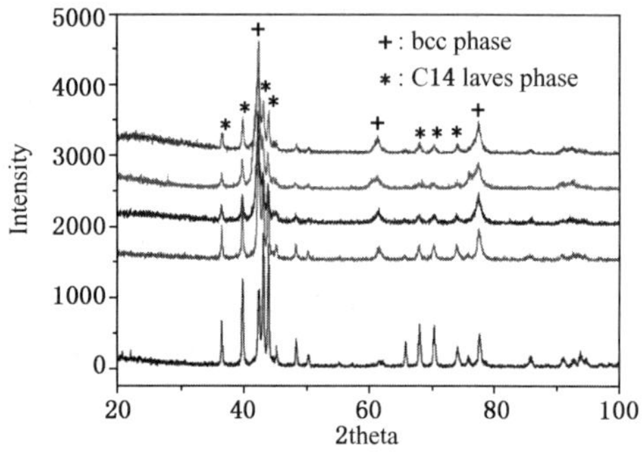

Fig. 1 XRD pattern of $Ti_{0.26}Zr_{0.07}V_{0.24}Mn_{0.1}Ni_{0.33}Mo_x$ (x=0—0.10) alloy. (a) x=0.0; (b) x=0.025; (c) x=0.05; (d) x=0.075; (e) x=0.10

Table 1 Lattice parameter and cell volume of $Ti_{0.26}Zr_{0.07}V_{0.24}Mn_{0.1}Ni_{0.33}Mo_x$ (x=0, 0.025, 0.05, 0.075, 0.10) alloy

Sample	Phase	Lattice parameter (nm)		Cell volume (nm³)
		a	*c*	
x=0.0	bcc	0.3014		0.02738
	C14	0.4903	0.7983	0.1662
x=0.025	bcc	0.3019		0.02752
	C14	0.4904	0.8020	0.1670
x=0.05	bcc	0.3020		0.02756
	C14	0.4911	0.8035	0.1678
x=0.075	bcc	0.3021		0.02757
	C14	0.4918	0.8034	0.1683
x=0.10	bcc	0.3022		0.02758
	C14	0.4918	0.8039	0.1684

With increasing the content of Mo, the diffraction peak intensity of C14 Laves phase decreases as shown in Fig. 1, indicating that the fraction of C14 Laves phase decreases while the fraction of V-based solid solution phase increases in the alloys. When $x=0-0.025$, the diffraction peaks of C14 Laves phase are sharp. However, with changing x from 0.05 to 0.10, the alloys are composed of a main phase with a bcc structure and a little C14 Laves secondary phase, and the fraction of C14 Laves phase decreases gradually.

(A)

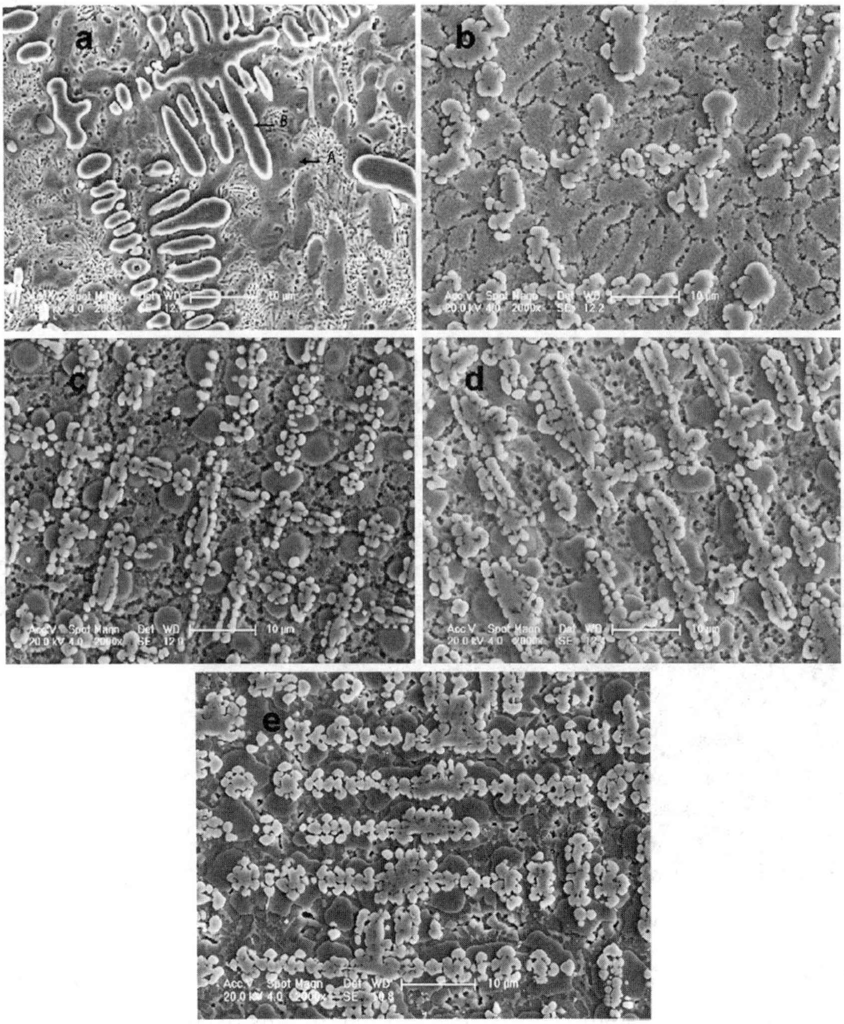

Fig. 2 (A) Scanning electron micrographs of $Ti_{0.26}Zr_{0.07}V_{0.24}Mn_{0.1}Ni_{0.33}Mo_x$ ($x=0-0.10$) alloy. (a) $x=0.0$; (b) $x=0.025$; (c) $x=0.05$; (d) $x=0.075$; (e) $x=0.10$. (B) Energy spectra of bcc phase and C14 Laves phase and elements distribution images on surface of $Ti_{0.26}Zr_{0.07}V_{0.24}Mn_{0.1}Ni_{0.33}Mo_x$ ($x=0.075$) alloy

(B)

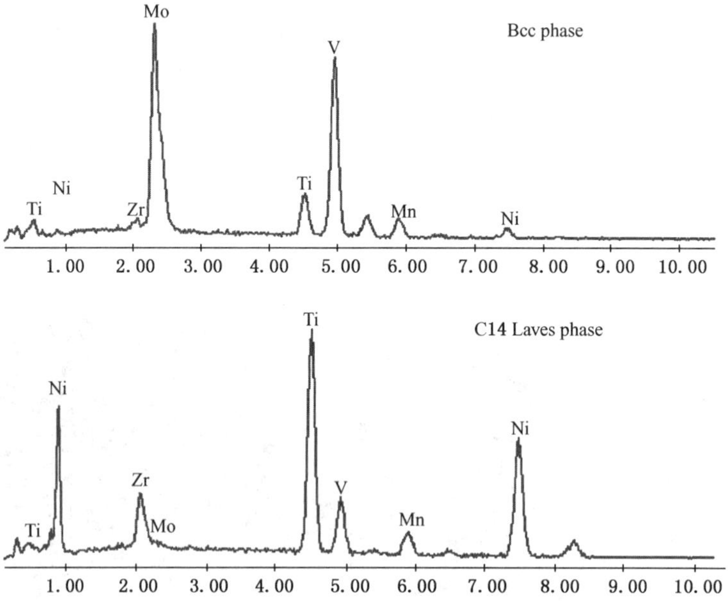

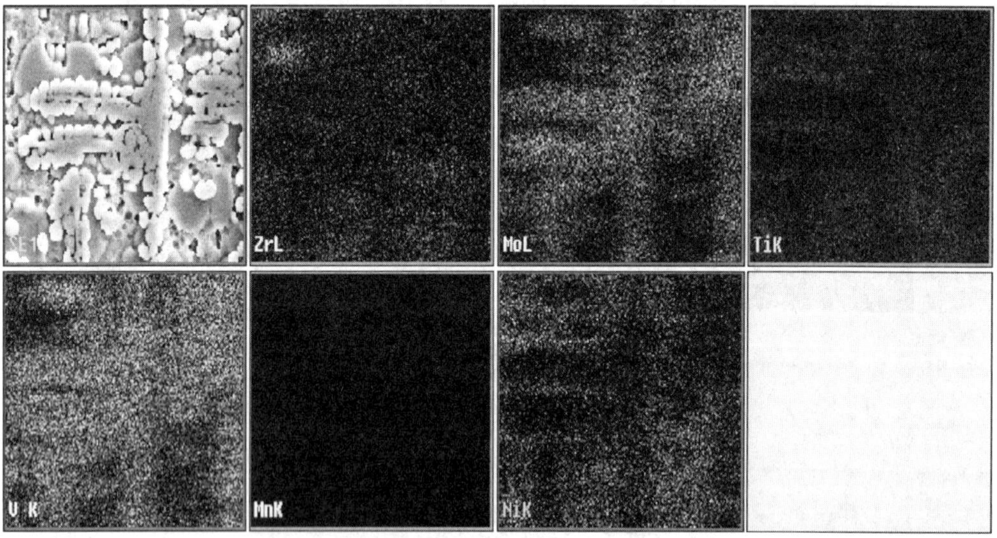

Fig. 2　(Continued)

The calculated lattice parameter and cell volume of the alloys are shown in Table 1. It can be clearly seen that both the lattice parameter and the cell volume of bcc phase monotonically increase with increasing x value in the alloys, which is mainly attributed to the fact that the atomic radius of Mo is larger than that of other elements. It can be concluded that the addition of Mo has a pronounced effect on the structure of the solid solution alloy.

Fig. 2 gives the scanning electron micrographs of $Ti_{0.26}Zr_{0.07}V_{0.24}Mn_{0.1}Ni_{0.33}Mo_x$ (x=0—0.10) alloys. It is obvious that all the alloy samples are mainly composed of two distinct crystallographic phases: one is C14 Laves phase (identified as A), and the other is V-based solid solution phase (identified as B) as confirmed by EDS analysis, which is in agreement with the XRD results. The V-based solid solution phase is in the form of dendritic structures. From the images, it can be easily seen that, with increasing Mo content, bcc phase increases and finally forms a three-dimensional phase structure. The compositions of the solid solution phase and C14 Laves phase are examined semi-quantitatively by EDS and are listed in Table 2.

The results show that the Mo element exists mainly in V-based solid solution. With increasing of stoichiometry x from 0.0 to 0.10, the atomic percentage of Mo in V-based solid solution increases markedly from 0 to 25.69 at.%, while it slightly increases in C14 phase from 0 to 0.94 at.%. This is in good accordance with the increase of cell volume of the two phases, which is related to the relatively large radius of Mo among the constituent elements.

3.2 Electrochemical property

3.2.1 Discharge capacity and cycling stability

The curves of the discharge capacity vs. the cycle number at 303 K for the $Ti_{0.26}Zr_{0.07}V_{0.24}Mn_{0.1}Ni_{0.33}Mo_x$ (x=0—0.10) alloy electrodes are shown in Fig. 3. It is noted that compared with the electrode without Mo addition requiring two to three cycles to be activated, the ones with Mo addition reach their maximum capacity in the first cycle, which means that activation of the alloy electrodes is easy and Mo addition is of benefit to the activation property of the alloy

Table 2 Phase composition of $Ti_{0.26}Zr_{0.07}V_{0.24}Mn_{0.1}Ni_{0.33}Mo_x$ (x=0, 0.025, 0.05, 0.075, 0.10) alloy

Sample	Phase	Composition (at. %)					
		Ti	Zr	V	Mn	Ni	Mo
x=0.0	bcc	13.12	0.98	59.28	13.59	13.03	0
	C14	29.15	7.63	18.57	7.73	36.93	0
x=0.025	bcc	10.94	3.12	58.31	13.23	7.76	6.64
	C14	28.84	8.23	15.03	9.0	38.43	0.47
x=0.05	bcc	8.17	21.39	42.48	9.25	5.25	13.45
	C14	22.57	27.5	10.65	7.86	30.73	0.69
x=0.075	bcc	7.3	23.88	40.01	6.37	3.68	18.77
	C14	21.77	26.08	10.07	7.25	34.07	0.76
x=0.10	bcc	8.36	23.34	34.34	4.85	3.42	25.69
	C14	21.89	30.53	9.01	8.17	29.47	0.94

electrodes. Moreover, the discharge capacity of the alloys increases with Mo addition. The rates of increase in discharge capacity are 5.8, 3.6, 6.9 and 2.9% with x changing from 0.025 to 0.10, respectively.

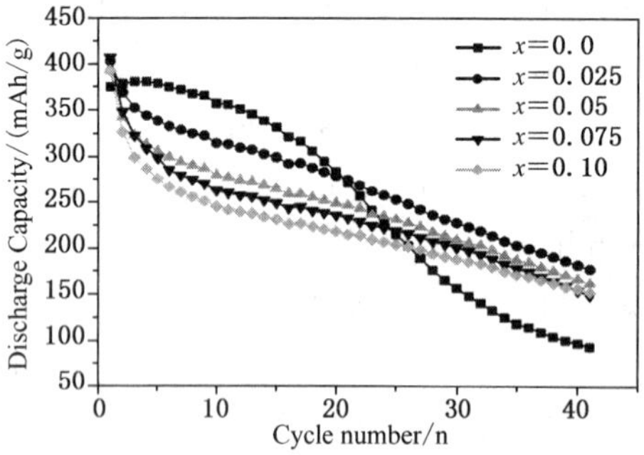

Fig. 3　Relation between discharge capacity and cycle number for $Ti_{0.26}Zr_{0.07}V_{0.24}Mn_{0.1}Ni_{0.33}Mo_x$ ($x=0-0.10$) alloys at current density of 60 mA g^{-1} at 303 K

As mentioned above, increasing Mo content leads to cell volume increase of both C14 Laves and V-based solid solution phase in the alloys, which could result in the increase of discharge capacity. The maximum discharge capacity is 407 mAh g^{-1} at 303 K when $x=0.075$. The discharge capacities of Ti-Zr-V-Mn-Ni-based alloys are sharply decreased within more than 10 charging-discharging cycles, although they have very high electrochemical discharge capacities and are easily activated. The rate of the capacity retention S_{30} of the alloys at 30th cycle (S_{30} is defined as $S_{30}=C_{30}/C_{max}\times100\%$, where C_{30} presented the discharge capacity measured at the 30th cycle and C_{max} is the maximum capacity) is 41.1, 56.4, 53.1, 49.3 and 48% with x changing from 0.0 to 0.10, respectively, which means Mo addition is of benefit to the cyclic durability of the alloys. Mo addition is benefit to the cyclic durability of the alloys maybe it resists the dissolution of alloy element and increases the anti-corrosion of the alloy. To elucidate the capacity degradation behavior of the alloy electrode during cycling in alkaline electrolyte, the concentrations of the constituent elements dissolved in KOH electrolyte are analyzed with ICP-MS measurement for 30 cycles. The results show that only three elements (V, Ti and Zr) are detected and the amount of other elements may be too lower to be detected. As the main hydrogen-absorbing element, the dissolution of V is so important that it is about 72.3 mg L^{-1} with $x=0.0$ and 90.4 mg L^{-1} with $x=0.075$ and the dissolved V element is essentially responsible for the capacity degradation of the alloy.

Tsukahara et al. [10,11] pointed that the V-based solid solution phase alone had very little electrochemical discharge capacity in the KOH electrolyte due to the lack of electrocatalytic activity. However, it could be activated to absorb and desorbs a large amount of hydrogen with the presence of a secondary phase, such as C14 Laves phase, which was considered to act both as a microcurrent collector and as an electrocatalyst. In current study, it is believed that both the two phases are the hydrogen storage phases. V-based solid solution phase is the major hydrogen-absorbing phase while C14 Laves phase not only absorbs hydrogen, but also works as a catalyst and micro-current collector. The increase in unit cell volumes of both C14 Laves phase and V-based solid solution phase here is believed to be the first reason for the increase in discharge capacities of the alloys. Secondly, C14 Laves phase can absorb and desorbs hydrogen reversibly in 6 mol L^{-1} KOH aqueous solution, and the hydrogen atoms in the secondary phase are considered to diffuse into the V-based solid solution main phase after C14 secondary phase is saturated with hydrogen. So it is believed that C14 Laves phase precipitated in the alloys mainly plays the role of providing electrocatalytic activity for the hydrogen absorption of the alloy and also participates in the hydrogen storage [12]. In addition, V-based solid solution phase is known to be the structure of hydrogen storage alloy with very large discharge capacity. Therefore, the increase of the fraction of V-based solid solution phase in the alloys and the increase of Mo content in V-based solid solution phase are also responsible for the increase in discharge capacity.

3.2.2 High-rate dischargeability

It is very important to restrain the decrease of the discharge capacity even at the high discharge current density for practical application of metal hydride electrode. The study of substitution of the host element in RE-based AB_5-type alloy or addition by Mo is extensive [13,14]. Our group also studied the influence of Mo additive in AB_5-type alloy [15], but this study used in Ti-Zr-V-Mn-Ni-based multi-component alloys is seldom. The aim of this study is to evaluate the influence of Mo additive in Ti-Zr-V-Mn-Ni-based multi-component alloys. Fig. 4 gives the high-rate dischargeability for $Ti_{0.26}Zr_{0.07}V_{0.24}Mn_{0.1}Ni_{0.33}Mo_x$ ($x=0-0.1$) alloy electrodes. The HRD of all the alloy electrodes decrease with increasing Mo content and discharge current density. It is generally accepted that the high-rate dischargeability of a metal hydride electrode is mainly determined by the charge transfer process occurring at the metal electrolyte interface and/or the hydrogen diffusion process in the hydride bulk [16,17]. To further investigate the kinetics of the alloy electrodes, the electrochemical impedance spectroscopy has been employed.

Fig. 5 shows the EIS for $Ti_{0.26}Zr_{0.07}$

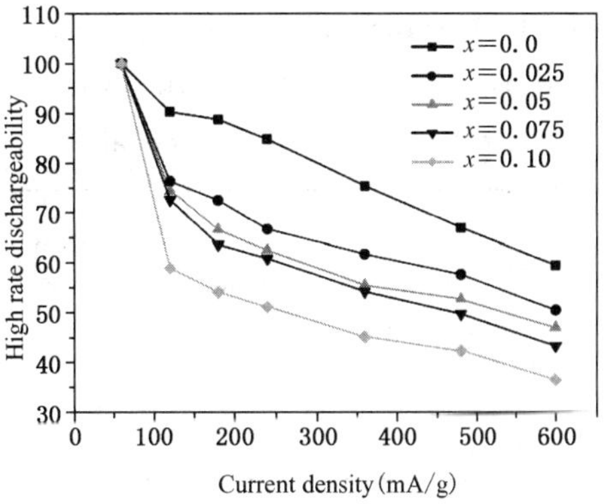

Fig. 4　High-rate dischargeability (HRD) of $Ti_{0.26}Zr_{0.07}V_{0.24}Mn_{0.1}Ni_{0.33}Mo_x$ ($x=0-0.10$) alloy electrode

$V_{0.24}Mn_{0.1}Ni_{0.33}Mo_x$ (x=0.0－0.10) alloy electrodes at 50% DOD. It can be found that all the EIS curves consist of two semicircles followed with a straight line. According to the analysis model proposed by Kuriyama et al. [18], the smaller semicircle in the high frequency region represents the resistance and capacitance between the alloy particles and the current collector, the larger semicircle region represents the charge transfer resistance for electrochemical reaction at the surface, while the straight line is attributed to the Warburg impedance. On the basis of the circuit the charge transfer resistances R_{ct} are obtained by means of fitting program Z-VIEW. The exchange current density I_0 is calculated using the following formula when an overpotential is very small, and the results are listed in Table 3:

$$I_0=\frac{RT}{FR_{ct}} \tag{3}$$

where R is the gas constant, T is the absolute temperature and F is the Faraday constant.

Table 3　Electrochemical kinetic parameters of $Ti_{0.26}Zr_{0.07}V_{0.24}Mn_{0.1}Ni_{0.33}Mo_x$ (x=0－0.10) alloy electrode

Sample	R_{ct} (Ω)	Exchange current density, I_0 (mA g^{-1})
x=0.0	0.154	169.5
x=0.025	0.269	97.0
x=0.05	0.283	92.2
x=0.075	0.373	70.0
x=0.10	0.475	54.9

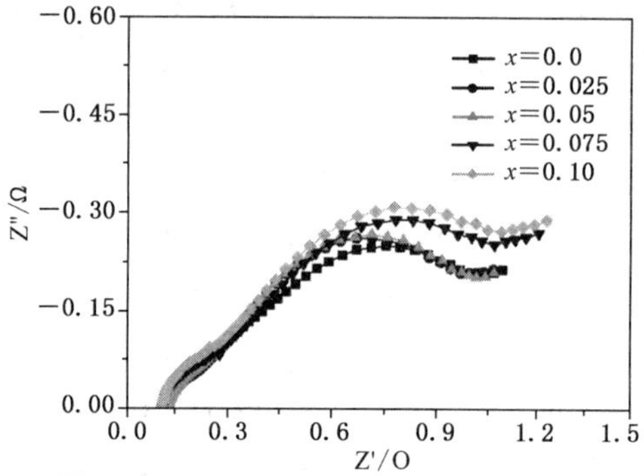

Fig. 5　Electrochemical impedance spectroscopy for $Ti_{0.26}Zr_{0.07}V_{0.24}Mn_{0.1}Ni_{0.33}Mo_x$ (x=0－0.10) alloy electrode measured at the 50% DOD at 303 K

It is obvious that the radius of the larger semicircle increases with increasing x, which indicates that the charge transfer resistance for the alloy electrode increases from 0.154 Ω (x=0.0) to 0.475 Ω (x=0.10) with increasing Mo content. Accordingly, the I_0 decreases from 169.5 mA g^{-1} (x=0.0) to 54.9 mA g^{-1} (x=0.10). Results of the impedance experiments indicate that the charge transfer resistance increases and exchange current density decreases with Mo addition, which explains why the HRD of the alloy electrode decreases with increasing Mo content.

3.2.3　Discharge curves

The discharge curves of the $Ti_{0.26}Zr_{0.07}V_{0.24}Mn_{0.1}Ni_{0.33}Mo_x$ (x=0－0.1) alloy electrodes at 303 K are shown in Fig. 6. It can be seen that the curves show two obvious voltage plateaus with Mo addition. It is strongly presumed that the appearance of the two voltage plateaus on the discharge curves of the $Ti_{0.26}Zr_{0.07}V_{0.24}Mn_{0.1}Ni_{0.33}Mo_x$ (x=0－0.1) alloys is related to their multi-phase composition and multi-phase hydride formation, as Xu et al. [19] indicated. The appearance of the first fastigiated plateau is the result of together releasing hydrogen of two phases. The secondary flat represents releasing hydrogen process of only the second phase. At the initial stage of discharge, the main storage hydrogen phase firstly release the stored hydrogen, at the same time, the part of hydrogen stored in second phase has a possibility to take part in discharge process. Because more than two phase had taken part in the discharge process, therefore, the first plateau at its discharge curve is very fastigiated. The existence of the second discharge plateau is related to the second phase. The increase of the discharge capacity can be explained by the existence of the second phase. With cycling, the width of each plateau become smaller and the total discharge capacity decreases. The main reason is the corrosion, i. e. the decrease of the relative content of the effective phase being storing hydrogen.

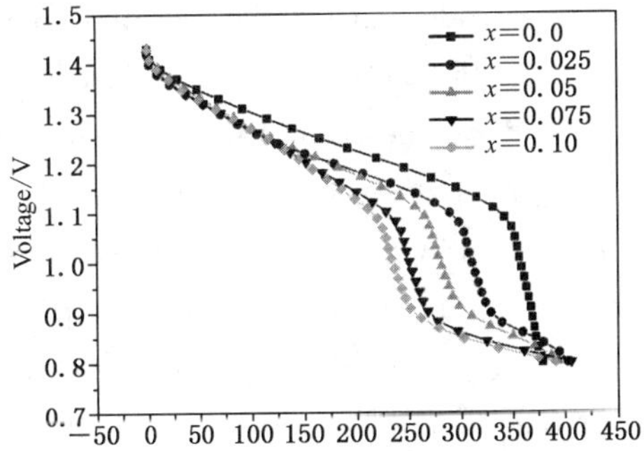

Fig. 6　Discharge curves of $Ti_{0.26}Zr_{0.07}V_{0.24}Mn_{0.1}Ni_{0.33}Mo_x$ (x=0−0. 10) alloy electrodes at 303 K

Zhang et al. [20] have reported that two voltage plateaus are indisputably related to dehydriding reaction. From Fig. 6, we suggested that the first voltage plateau is contributed to the reaction of dehydriding. The second voltage plateau may be dehydriding transition reactions from hydride to β phase. Further researches are being processed.

3. 2. 4　Temperature effect

Negative electrode material used in Ni/MH battery should be capable of working over a wide temperature range. Discharge capacity of $Ti_{0.26}Zr_{0.07}V_{0.24}Mn_{0.1}Ni_{0.33}Mo_x$ (x=0−0. 1) alloy electrodes as a function of temperature is shown in Fig. 7. It can be easily seen that the dischargeability is very sensitive to temperature. The discharge capacity of $Ti_{0.26}Zr_{0.07}V_{0.24}Mn_{0.1}Ni_{0.33}Mo_x$ (x=0−0. 1) alloys increases dramatically with increasing temperature. Moreover, Mo addition is beneficial to the dischargeability of the alloy electrode at high temperature, and $Ti_{0.26}Zr_{0.07}V_{0.24}Mn_{0.1}Ni_{0.33}$

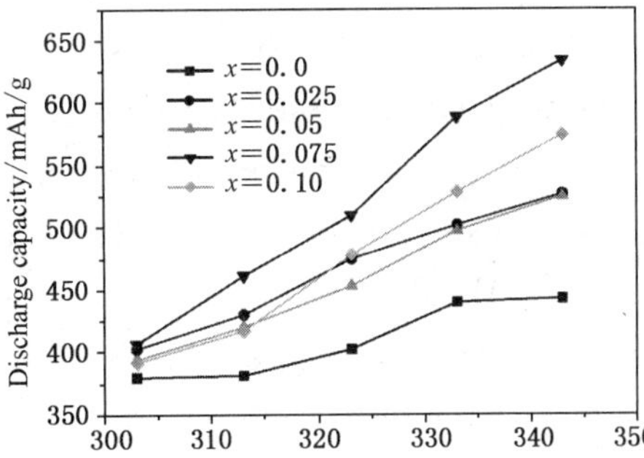

Fig. 7　Relation between discharge capacity and temperature for $Ti_{0.26}Zr_{0.07}V_{0.24}Mn_{0.1}Ni_{0.33}Mo_x$ (x=0−0. 10) alloy electrode

$Mo_{0.075}$ has higher discharge capacity than other ones. Its maximum discharge capacity is increased from 407 mAh g^{-1} at 303 K to 633 mAh g^{-1} at 343 K. The discharge curves of the $Ti_{0.26}Zr_{0.07}V_{0.24}Mn_{0.1}Ni_{0.33}Mo_{0.075}$ alloy electrode at different temperature are shown in Fig. 8. It is obvious that the curves show two obvious voltage plateaus and the initial voltage decreases with increasing temperature. The second plateau voltage increases and is 0.9 V or more when temperature goes beyond 323 K. Moreover, the platform is even plat with increasing temperature. The results indicate that the discharge capacity at a higher temperature is higher than that at a lower temperature.

The discharge capacity of each sample alloy increases with increasing temperature. Those are mostly because of the increase of electrolyte activity at high temperature which reasonably lead to the decrease of hydrogen diffusion resistance and thus the obviously increase of the charge efficiency and discharge efficiency, and then inevitably the increase of the discharge capacity of the electrodes [21]. It seems to be mentioned that the corrosion of the constituent elements (such as V, Mn) of the alloy would affect the discharge capacity at higher temperature. The loss of the discharge capacity is calculated to be about 16 mAh g^{-1} per charging-discharging cycle for the alloys, considering amount of electrochemical dissolution of V and Mn. Fortunately, this value is very small, comparing with the discharge capacity of the alloy at higher temperature.

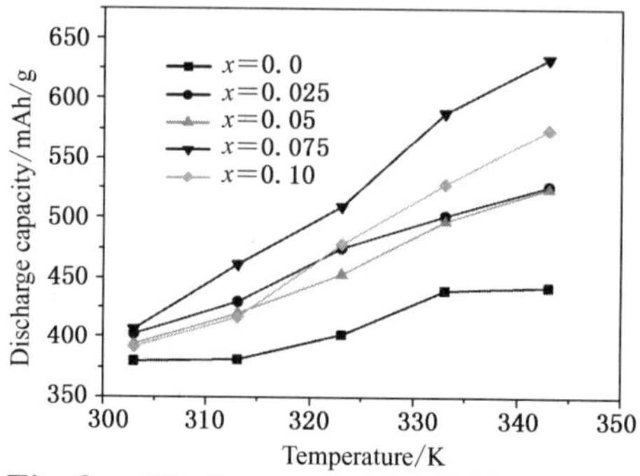

Fig. 8　Discharge curves of $Ti_{0.26}Zr_{0.07}V_{0.24}Mn_{0.1}Ni_{0.33}Mo_x$ ($x=0.075$) alloy electrode at different temperature

3.2.5　Self-discharge behavior

Iwakura et al. [22] have investigated the self-discharge behavior of the alloy electrodes and have divided the capacity loss into two parts, reversible one and irreversible one. The reversible capacity loss is attributed to the chemical desorption of hydrogen from the MH anode and the irreversible capacity loss is attributed to the degradation of the MH anode itself. The self-discharge values of the $Ti_{0.26}Zr_{0.07}V_{0.24}Mn_{0.1}Ni_{0.33}Mo_x$ ($x=0-0.1$) electrodes after the circuit open stands for 8 days are summarized in Table 4. It can be seen that the reversible and irreversible losses increase with increasing x in the alloys and therefore the self-discharge rate is increased. These results imply that Mo addition is unbeneficial to the charge retention of the alloy electrodes.

4　Conclusion

In order to improve the electrochemical properties of Ti - V - based hydrogen

Table 4 Summary of the self-discharge data for $Ti_{0.26}Zr_{0.07}V_{0.24}Mn_{0.1}Ni_{0.33}Mo_x$ (x=0−0.1) alloy

x	C_1 (mAh g^{-1})	C_2 (mAh g^{-1})	C_3 (mAh g^{-1})	C_3-C_2 (mAh g^{-1})	C_1-C_3 (mAh g^{-1})	Self-discharge rate (%day)
0.0	380.8	311.0	360.1	49.1	20.7	2.00
0.025	402.9	298.2	368.8	70.6	34.1	2.84
0.05	394.4	277.0	342.5	65.5	51.9	3.10
0.075	407.0	270.0	348.3	78.3	58.7	3.56
0.10	391.9	244.1	324.2	80.1	67.7	3.98

storage alloy, the non-stoichiometric composition with added Mo to Ti-Zr-V-Ni-Mn system alloys have been studied. As the amount of added Mo increases, the fraction of V-based solid solution phase increases gradually, the diffraction peak intensity and fraction of C14 Laves phase decrease. With increasing Mo content, the abundance, distribution and lattice parameters of V-based phase and C14 Laves phase change markedly and thus affect the synergism of the two phases. The alloy electrodes show easier activation behavior and higher discharge capacity. With increasing x from 0.0 to 0.10, the discharge capacity increases first and then decreases, however, all of them are higher than that of the original alloy and the maximum discharge capacity reaches 407 mAh g^{-1} at 303 K and 633 mAh g^{-1} at 343 K with $x=0.075$. The discharge capacity of the alloys increases with increasing temperature and dischargeability is very sensitive to temperature. However, Mo addition is detrimental to both of the charge retention characteristics and the high-rate dischargeability. The discharge curves show two obvious voltage plateaus with Mo addition owing to their multi-phase composition and multi-phase hydride formation. The EIS results show that the charge transfer resistance increases with increasing x from 0.0 to 0.10.

Acknowledgement

This work was financially supported by the National Natural Science Foundation of China (Grant No. 20171042).

References

[1] T. Kohno, H. Yoshida, F. Kawashima, T. Inaba, I. Sakai, M. Yamamoto, M. Kanda, Journal of Alloys and Compounds 31 (2000) L5-L7.

[2] P. Gifford, J. Adams, D. Corrigan, S. Venkatesan, Journal of Power Sources 80 (1999) 157-163.

[3] Y. F. Zhu, H. G. Pan, M. X. Gao, Y. F. Liu, Q. D. Wang, Journal of Alloys and Compounds 345 (2002) 201-209.

[4] H.-H. Lee, K.-Y. Lee, J.-Y. Lee, Journal of Alloys and Compounds 239 (1996) 63-70.

[5] F. Fenga, M. Genga, D. O. Northwoodb, International Journal of Hydrogen Energy 26 (2001) 725-734.

[6] H.-H. Lee, K.-Y. Lee, J.-Y. Lee, Journal of Alloys and Compounds 239 (1996) 63-67.

[7] K. Yasuda, Journal of Alloys and Compounds 253 (1997) 621.

[8] F. Lichtenberg, U. Kohler, A. Fohzer, N. G. E. Adkins, A. Zuhttel, Journal of Alloys and Compounds 253 (1997) 570.

[9] M. Bououdina, P. D. Rango, D. Fruchart, J. L. Soubeyroux, Journal of Alloys and Compounds 253 (1997) 221.

[10] M. Tsukahara, K. Takahashi, T. Mishima, A. Isomura, T. Sakai, Journal of Alloys and Compounds 236 (1996) 151-155.

[11] M. Tsukahara, K. Takahashi, T. Mishima, A. Isomura, T. Sakai, Journal of Alloys and Compounds 243 (1996) 133-138.

[12] N. Kuriyama, D. Chartouni, M. Tsukahara, K. Takahashi, H. T. Takeshita, H. Tanaka, L. Schlapbach, T. Sakai, I. Uehara, Electrochemical and Solid-State Letters 1 (1998) 37-42.

[13] C. Jeong, W. Chung, C. Iwakura, I. Kim, Journal of Power Sources 79 (1999) 19-24.

[14] M. T. Yeh, V. M. Beibutian, S. E. Hsu, Journal of Alloys and Compounds 293/295 (1999) 721-723.

[15] X. Zhang, D. Sun, W. Yin, Y. Chai, M. Zhao, Journal of Power Sources 154 (2006) 290-297.

[16] C. Iwakura, M. Matsuoka, K. Asai, T. Kohno, Journal of Power Sources 38 (1992) 335-343.

[17] C. Iwakura, T. Oura, H. Inoue, M. Matsuoka, Electrochimica Acta 41 (1996) 117-121.

[18] N. Kuriyama, T. Sakai, H. Miyamura, I. Uehara, H. Ishikawa, T. Iwasaki, Journal of Alloys and Compounds 202 (1993) 183-197.

[19] Y. H. Xu, C. P. Cheng, X. L. Wang, Q. D. Wang, Journal of Power Sources 112 (2002) 105-108.

[20] Q. A. Zhang, Y. Q. Lei, L. X. Chen, Q. D. Wang, Materials Chemistry and Physics 71 (2001) 58-61.

[21] T. Sakai, H. Miyamura, N. Kuriyama, A. Kato, K. Ogura, H. Ishikawa, Journal of the Electrochemical Society 137 (1990) 795-799.

[22] C. Iwakura, Y. Kajiya, H. Yoneyama, T. Sakai, K. Oguro, H. Ishikawa, Journal of the Electrochemical Society 134 (1989) 1351-1356.

Effect of Substitution of Chromium for Nickel on Structure and Electrochemical Characteristic of $Ti_{0.26}Zr_{0.07}V_{0.24}Mn_{0.1}Ni_{0.33}$ Multi-phase Hydrogen Storage Alloy ①

Li Shucun[a,c], Zhao Minshou[a,b], Zhai Jing[a], Wang fengyan[a]

([a] College of Environment and Chemical Engineering, Yanshan University, Qinhuangdao 066004, PR China)

([b] State Key Laboratory of Rare Earth on Advanced Materials and Valuable Utilization of Resources, Changchun Institute of Applied Chemistry, Chinese Academic of Science, Changchun 130022, PR China)

([c] State Key Laboratory of Metastable Material Science and Technology, Yanshan University, Qinhuangdao 066004, PR China)

Abstract: Ti-Zr-V-Mn-Ni-based multi-component alloys demonstrate high discharge capacity in KOH electrolyte. However, the drastic decrease in their discharge capacities makes them unsuitable for use as negative electrode material in the Ni/MH battery. In present work, Ni is partially replaced by Cr in the Ti-Zr-V-Mn-Ni-based alloys to improve their cycle life. The effects of Cr substitution on microstructures and the electrochemical characteristics of the alloys are investigated. It is found that Cr substitution is very effective to improve the cyclic durability of the alloys although the discharge capacity decreases with changing x from 0.05 to 0.20. Some kinetic performances have been also investigated using electrochemical impedance spectroscopy (EIS) and potentiostatic discharge technique. Hydrogen diffusion is a rate-limiting factor at higher discharge current, while exchange current density is the rate-limiting factor at lower discharge current, both hydrogen diffusion and exchange current density are responsible for the poor high-rate dischargeability of the alloy in this case.

Key words: Ni/MH battery; Electrochemical property; Kinetic property; Metal hydride electrode

1 Introduction

Hydrogen storage alloys are a group of new functional intermetallics which can be used in heat pumps, catalysts, hydrogen sensors and Ni/MH battery. Hydrogen storage alloys used as the negative electrode materials of the Ni/MH

① Materials Chemistry and Physics, 2009(113): 96-102.

batteries are being widely and extensively studied. Ni/MH battery has gained much recognition for its higher energy density and less environmental contamination than the Ni/Cd battery. However, researchers are still striving to search for new alloys with higher discharge capacity and lower cost as negative electrode material in order to make the Ni/MH battery more competitive for the application of electric vehicle battery [1-3].

Ti-Zr-V-Mn-Ni-based alloys have very high electrochemical discharge capacities, cost-effectiveness and are easily activated [4]. However, the drastic decrease in their discharge capacities within tens of charging-discharging cycles makes them unsuitable for use as negative electrode material in the Ni/MH battery. The rapid degradation in their capacities of these alloys is due to the deterioration of the surface properties [5].

It has been reported that Cr is very effective to improve the cycle life of solid solution alloy [6]. In present work, Ni is partially replaced by Cr in Ti-Zr-V-Mn-Ni-based alloys in order to improve their cyclic durability. The microstructures, electrochemical properties and especially the cycle life of these Cr-substituted alloys are investigated.

2 Experimental details

All samples were prepared by arc-melting carefully the constituent elements or master alloy on a water-cooled copper hearth under argon atmosphere. The purity of the metal, i. e., Ti, Zr, V, Mn, Ni and Cr is higher than 99.9 mass%, respectively. The ingots were remelted for three to four times to ensure homogeneity and then mechanically crushed into powders of 300 mesh size.

The well-mixed alloy powder and carbonyl nickel powder in weight ratio of 1 : 5 were pressed into the tablets with the diameter of 10 mm, thickness of 1 mm and the weight of 0.9 g as a metal hydride electrode.

The electrochemical properties were performed on DC-5 battery testing instrument using a half-cell system which consists of a metal hydride electrode as a negative electrode and a sintered $Ni(OH)_2$/NiOOH positive electrode with excessive capacity and 6 mol L^{-1} KOH as electrolyte solution. The MH electrode was charged at a constant current density (60 mA g^{-1}) until the hydrogen concentration reached its saturated value followed by 10 min resting time and then was discharged at a constant current density of 60 mA g^{-1} to a cut off potential of 0.8 V. The experimental cell was set in a water bath at controlled ($\pm$0.5 K) temperature ranging from 303 to 343 K.

The microstructures of the alloys were characterized by X-ray diffraction (XRD), field emission scanning electron microscopy (FESEM) and energy dispersive X-ray spectroscopy (EDS).

Potentiostatic discharge technique [7] was used to evaluate the hydrogen diffusion coefficient (D) within the bulk of the alloy. After being fully charged followed by a 30-min open-circuit to reach a stable state, the test electrodes were discharged with +500 mV potential step for 3 600 s on the EG&G PARC Model 273 Potentio-static/Galvanostat. Hydrogen diffusion coefficient D can be obtained from the slope of the linear section at long-time region.

Electrochemical impedance spectroscopy (EIS) was used for determining the charge transfer resistance (R_{ct}) and the exchange current density (I_0) to clarify the kinetic properties of dehydrating action. After the test electrodes were completely activated, EIS measurements were conducted at 50% depth of discharge (DOD) using a Solartron SI1287 Electrochemical Interface with 1255 B Frequency Response Analyzer and ZPLOT electrochemical impedance software. The EIS spectra for the electrodes were obtained in the frequency range of 100 kHz to 10^{-1} Hz with alternating current amplitude of 5 mV under open-circuit conditions. According to the analysis model proposed by Kuriyama et al. [8], an equivalent circuit for the metal hydride electrode was used and the parameters in the equivalent circuit were fitted using least-square method with Z-VIEW electrochemical impedance software; I_0 is calculated from following equation [9] when an over potential is very small:

$$I_0 = \frac{RT}{FR_{ct}} \tag{1}$$

where R is the gas constant, T is the absolute temperature and F is the Faraday constant.

3 Result and discussion

3.1 Alloy structure characteristic

The X-ray diffraction patterns of multi-component $Ti_{0.26}Zr_{0.07}V_{0.24}Mn_{0.1}Ni_{0.33-x}Cr_x$ ($x=0.0-0.20$) alloys are shown in Fig. 1. From the patterns, it is obvious that all the alloys are composed of a C14 Laves phase with hexagonal structure and a V-based solid solution phase with bcc structure, which are confirmed by FESEM (Fig. 2) and EDS analysis (Table 1). The lattice parameters and compositions of the two main phases of the alloys are listed in Table 1.

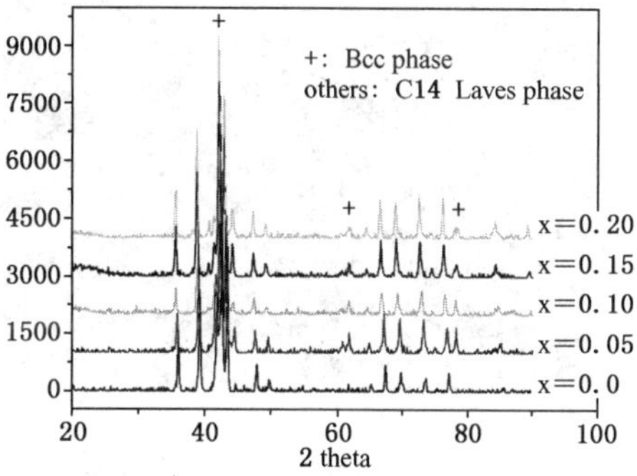

Fig. 1 XRD pattern of $Ti_{0.26}Zr_{0.07}V_{0.24}Mn_{0.1}Ni_{0.33-x}Cr_x$ ($x=0.0-0.20$) alloy

It can be seen that the lattice parameters and unit cell volumes of both phases tend to become a bit larger as the amount of Cr increases. This results from the fact that the atomic radius of chromium is slightly larger than that of nickel. Moreover, it can be found that C14 Laves phase contained all the six component elements, while V-based solid solution phase contains only five ones, Zr being absent (except when $x=0.0$).

Fig. 2 shows FESEM micrographs of $Ti_{0.26}Zr_{0.07}V_{0.24}Mn_{0.1}Ni_{0.33-x}Cr_x$ ($x=0.0-0.20$) alloy samples. It can be seen that all the alloys contain a continuous C14 Laves phase (identified as A) and a dendritic V-based solid solution phase (identified as B), as confirmed by EDS analysis (Fig. 3).

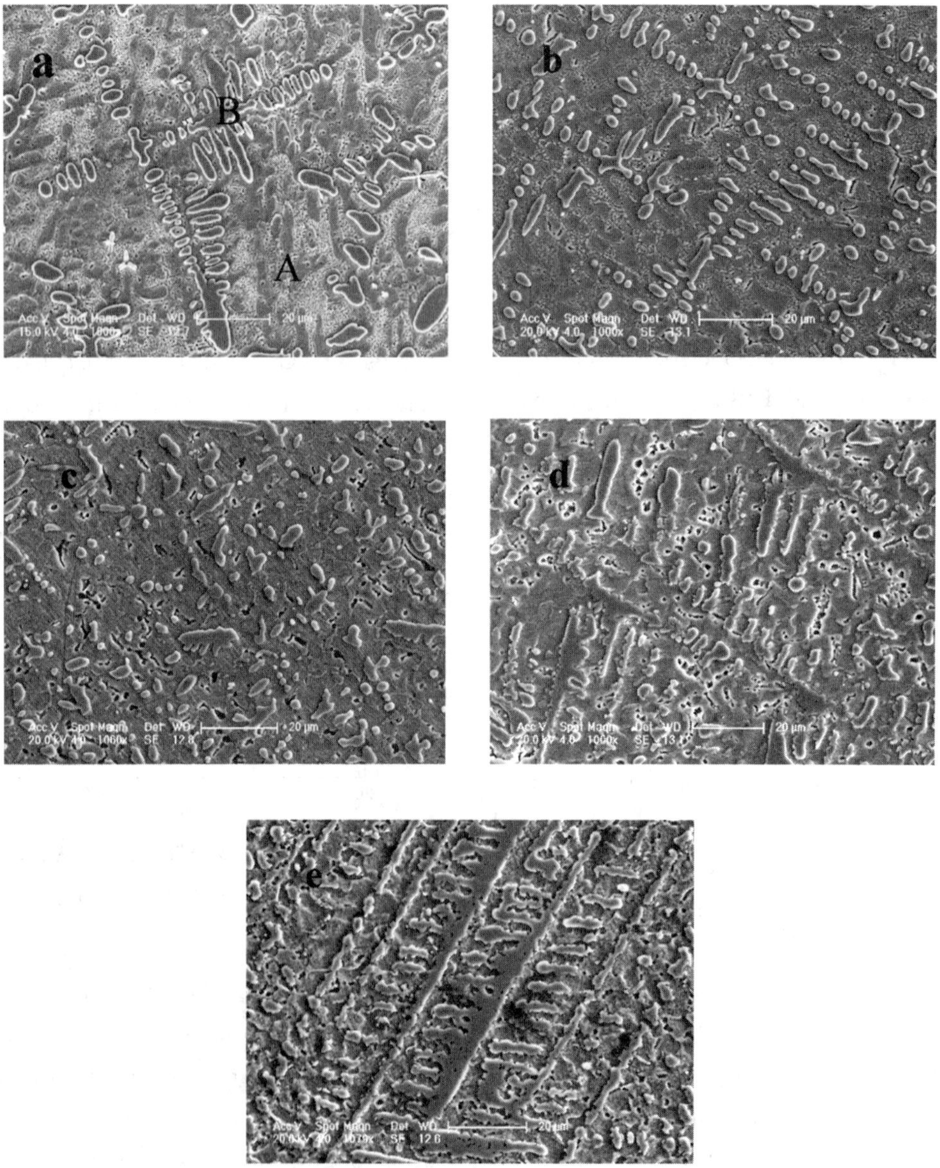

Fig. 2　Field emission scanning electron micrographs of $Ti_{0.26}Zr_{0.07}V_{0.24}Mn_{0.1}Ni_{0.33-x}Cr_x$ alloy: (a) $x=0.0$, (b) $x=0.05$, (c) $x=0.10$, (d) $x=0.15$ and (e) $x=0.20$

Table 1 Phase composition and lattice parameter of $Ti_{0.26}Zr_{0.07}V_{0.24}Mn_{0.1}Ni_{0.33-x}Cr_x$ (x=0.0—0.20) alloy electrode

Sample (x)	Phase	Composition (at. %)						Lattice parameter (nm)		Cell volume (nm^3)
		Ti	Zr	V	Mn	Ni	Cr	a	c	
0.0	bcc	13.12	0.98	59.28	13.59	13.03		0.3014		0.0273
	C14	29.15	7.63	18.57	7.73	36.93		0.4903	0.7983	0.1662
0.05	bcc	10.12	0	58.65	13.07	6.18	11.98	0.3009		0.0272
	C14	27.78	9.34	19.19	11.12	30.53	2.04	0.4906	0.8040	0.1676
0.10	bcc	10.28	0	51.84	10.82	3.84	23.21	0.30219		0.0276
	C14	32.38	8.50	16.63	6.99	31.42	4.08	0.4890	0.8096	0.1677
0.15	bcc	12.83	0	48.58	10.11	3.48	25	0.30250		0.0277
	C14	28.2	8.67	20.55	11.26	20.42	10.9	0.4921	0.8013	0.1680
0.20	bcc	16.73	0	45.17	7.47	2.89	28.11	0.30308		0.0278
	C14	25.04	10.68	18.72	12.74	12.85	19.97	0.4920	0.8032	0.1684

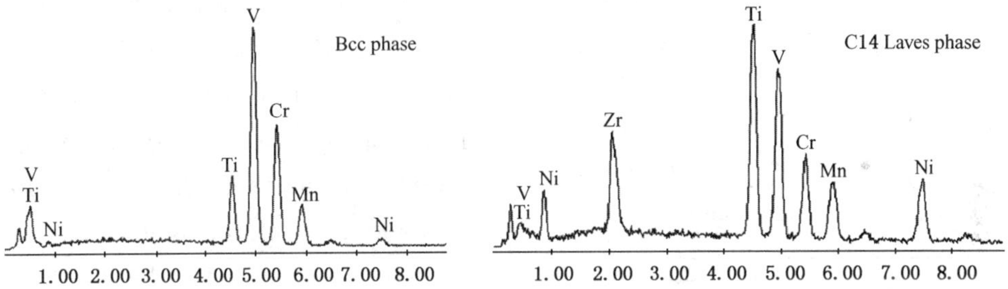

Fig. 3 Energy spectra of bcc phase and C14 Laves phase in $Ti_{0.26}Zr_{0.07}V_{0.24}Mn_{0.1}Ni_{0.33-x}Cr_x$ (x=0.15) alloy

The energy spectra of C14 Laves phase and bcc phase in $Ti_{0.26}Zr_{0.07}V_{0.24}Mn_{0.1}Ni_{0.33-x}Cr_x$ (x = 0.15) alloys are shown in Fig. 3. It is can be seen that the content of V in bcc phase is the highest. From Table 1, it can be found that with increasing the content of Cr, Ni content decreases in V-based solid solution phases. However, Cr content increases in V-based solid solution phase and C14 Laves phase, while V and Mn content decreases in V-based solid solution. In addition, Zr has not been detected in V-based solid solution phase (except when x = 0.0) and its content increases slightly in C14 Laves phase. Hence, it can be concluded that the Zr almost entirely exists in C14 Laves phase.

3.2 Electrochemical property

Fig. 4 shows the discharge capacity at a discharge current of 60 mA g^{-1} vs. cycle number for $Ti_{0.26}Zr_{0.07}V_{0.24}Mn_{0.1}Ni_{0.33-x}Cr_x$ (x = 0.0 — 0.2) alloy electrodes at 303 K. It can be seen that $Ti_{0.26}$

$Zr_{0.07}V_{0.24}Mn_{0.1}Ni_{0.33}$ alloy electrode has the maximum capacity (C_{max} = 380.8 mAh g^{-1}) and can be activated to reach its maximum capacity within 2—3 cycles, which means that activation of the alloy electrode is easy, but the cyclic durability of the alloy electrode is rather poor. The capacity retention rate C_{25}/C_{max} at the 25th cycle is about 56%. However, the cyclic durability of the alloy is improved dramatically as the stoichiometry x increases. For the sample x=0.15, the capacity retention rate C_{25}/C_{max} at the 25th cycle is 88%. Meanwhile, the maximum discharge capacity decreases with increasing x from 0.05 to 0.20. It is generally thought that Cr can not form stable hydride. The increasing Cr content could lead to a decrease of V content which is the main hydrogen storage element in bcc phase and thus reduce the capacity of the alloy electrodes.

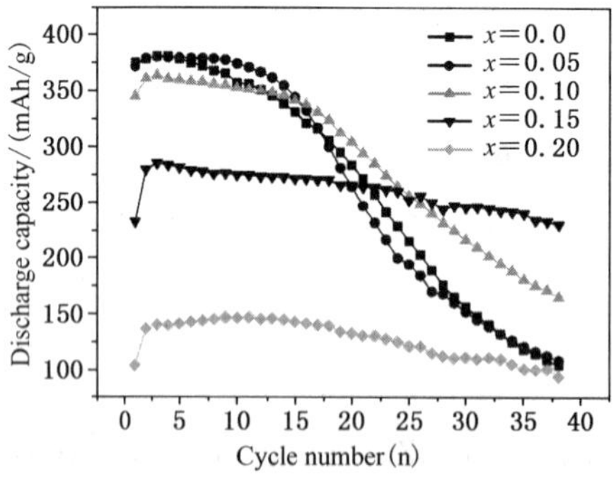

Fig. 4　Relation between discharge capacity and cycle number for $Ti_{0.26}Zr_{0.07}V_{0.24}Mn_{0.1}Ni_{0.33-x}Cr_x$ (x=0.0—0.20) alloy electrode at current density of 60 mA g^{-1} at 303 K

Li et al. [10] pointed out that the most important factors to the TiV-based two phase alloy's hydrogen storage capacity were the phase composition, abundance and distribution of the phase in the alloys. V-based solid solution phase is the major hydrogen-absorbing phase while C14 Laves phase not only absorbs hydrogen, but also works as a catalyst and micro-current collector for V-based phase. Appropriate proportion of the two phases and fine equiaxed microstructures are favorable for C14 phase to take the catalyzing and micro-current collecting effect while insufficient C14 Laves phase and thick dendrite microstructures may debase the catalyzing effect and thus diminish the capacity.

In addition, Mn and V are very unstable in KOH electrolyte, so Mn or V dissolves easily in KOH electrolyte. This phenomenon makes the surface to be micro-porous and then promotes the formation and growth of Ti-oxide. This surface condition is expected to be inferior in electric conductivity because the Ti-oxide film is passive and semi-conductive. Ti-oxide film makes for interior of the electrode with cycling and thus the capacity degrades. However, when Ni is partially replaced by Cr, a passive film is formed on the surface of the electrode which resists the oxidation of Ti and Zr. The passive film becomes thicker with increasing Cr content which promotes the cyclic durability [11].

It has been reported [12] that Cr improves the cyclic durability of Ti-based alloy electrodes due to its good corrosion resistance in an alkaline electrolyte by forming a passive oxide film on the electrode surface, which then retards the oxidation and dissolution of other elements.

To elucidate the capacity degradation behavior of the alloy electrode during cycling in alkaline electrolyte, the concentrations of the constituent elements dissolved in KOH electrolyte for $Ti_{0.26}Zr_{0.07}V_{0.24}Mn_{0.1}Ni_{0.33-x}Cr_x$ (x=0.0; 0.15) alloy electrode are analyzed with ICP-MS measurement for 15 cycles, and the results are also summarized in Table 2. The results show that the main three elements (V, Ti and Zr) are detected and the amount of other elements may be too lower to be detected. As the main hydrogen absorbing element, the dissolved V element is essentially responsible for the capacity degradation of the alloy. From Table 2, we can find that the dissolution of V element content decrease with Cr substitution. So we believe that the increase in Cr content in the alloy when x increases here is responsible for the improved cyclic of the alloy electrodes.

Table 2 Concentration of element dissolved in KOH electrolyte for $Ti_{0.26}Zr_{0.07}V_{0.24}Mn_{0.1}Ni_{0.33-x}Cr_x$ (x=0.0; 0.15) alloy electrode after 15 cycles by ICP-mass analysis

Samples (x)	Concentration (mg L^{-1})					
	Ti	Zr	V	Mn	Ni	Cr
0.0	0.167	4.35	144.3	0.013	—	—
0.15	0.143	4.03	73.1	0.01	—	—

Fig. 5 shows discharge curves after activation of $Ti_{0.26}Zr_{0.07}V_{0.24}Mn_{0.1}Ni_{0.33-x}Cr_x$ (x=0.0—0.20) alloys at a discharge current density of 60 mA g^{-1}. It can be seen that the curves show an obvious voltage plateaus, which can be indisputably considered as a dehydriding one. Moreover, these curves exhibit significant differences according to the amount of chromium. With increasing Cr content, the width of the plateau becomes smaller which indicates the discharge capacity decreases. The main reason is as mentioned previously. From Fig. 5, it is also found that the plateau voltage of alloys is a little decrease with increasing Cr content. This demonstrates that the reaction overpotential increases with increasing Cr content.

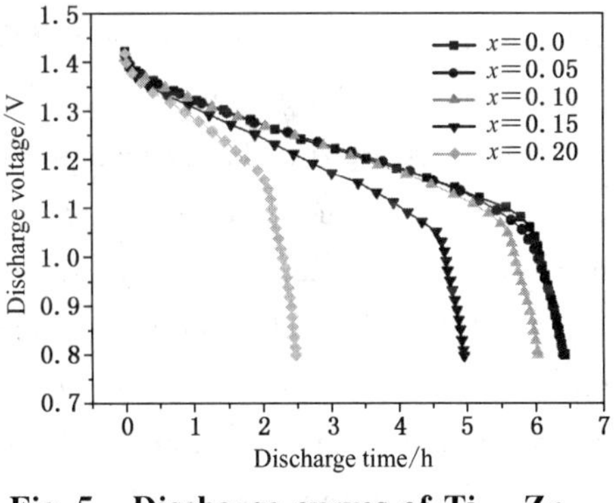

Fig. 5 Discharge curves of $Ti_{0.26}Zr_{0.07}V_{0.24}Mn_{0.1}Ni_{0.33-x}Cr_x$ (x=0.0—0.20) alloy electrode at 303 K

Fig. 6 shows the high-rate dischargeability (HRD) for $Ti_{0.26}Zr_{0.07}V_{0.24}Mn_{0.1}Ni_{0.33-x}Cr_x$ (x = 0.0 — 0.20) alloy electrodes. With increasing Cr content, the HRD of the alloy electrode declines. At the discharge current density of 600 mA h g^{-1}, the HRD of the alloy electrode decreases from 59.5% ($x=0.0$) to 15.5% ($x=0.20$).

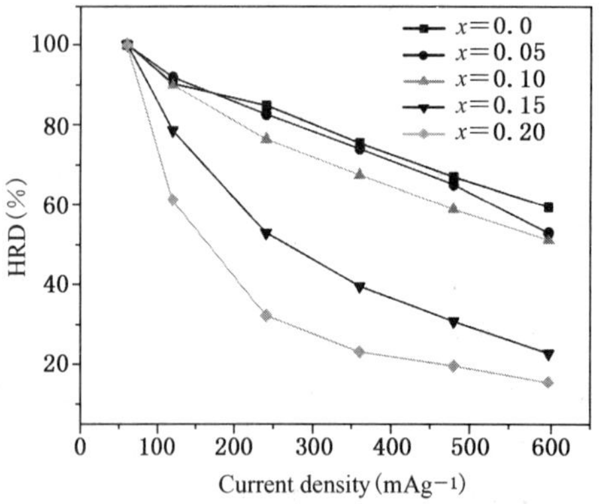

Fig. 6　HRD of $Ti_{0.26}Zr_{0.07}V_{0.24}Mn_{0.1}Ni_{0.33-x}Cr_x$ ($x=0.0-0.20$) alloy electrode at 303 K

It is generally accepted that the high-rate dischargeability of a metal hydride electrode is mainly determined by the charge transfer process occurring at the metal electrolyte interface and/or the hydrogen diffusion process in the hydride bulk [13]. The charge transfer reaction was dominated by the charge transfer resistance (R_{ct}) at the electrode/electrolyte interface and/or the exchange current density (I_0), and the diffusion rate of hydrogen in the electrode alloy was determined by hydrogen diffusion coefficient (D). To further investigate the kinetics of the alloy electrodes, electrochemical impedance spectroscopy and potential-step experiment were performed on the alloy electrodes.

Fig. 7 shows the EIS for $Ti_{0.26}Zr_{0.07}V_{0.24}Mn_{0.1}Ni_{0.33-x}Cr_x$ ($x=0.0-0.20$) alloy electrodes at 50% DOD. It can be found that all the EIS curves consist of two semicircles followed with a straight line. According to the analysis model proposed by Kuriyama et al. [8], the smaller semicircle in the high frequency region represents the resistance and capacitance between the alloy particles and the current collector, the larger semicircle region represents the charge transfer resistance for electrochemical reaction at the surface, while the straight line is attributed to the Warburg impedance.

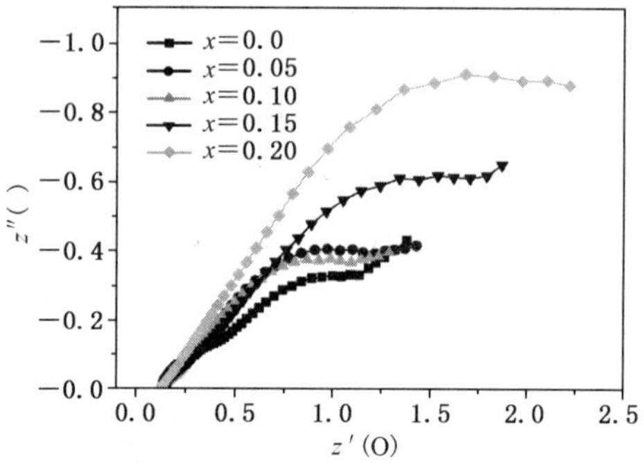

Fig. 7　Electrochemical impedance spectroscopy for $Ti_{0.26}Zr_{0.07}V_{0.24}Mn_{0.1}Ni_{0.33-x}Cr_x$ ($x=0.0-0.20$) alloy electrode measured at the 50% DOD and 303 K

On the basis of the circuit the charge transfer resistances R_{ct} are obtained by means of fitting program Z-VIEW. The exchange current density I_0 is calculated and the results are listed in Table 3. It is obvious that the radius of the larger semicircle increases with increasing Cr content, which indicates that the charge transfer resistance for the alloy electrode increases from 0.154 Ω ($x=0.0$) to 0.734 Ω ($x=0.20$) with increasing Cr content, accordingly, the I_0 decreases from 169.5 mA g^{-1} ($x=0.0$) to 35.6 mA g^{-1} ($x=0.20$), which explains why the HRD of the alloy electrode decreases with increasing Cr content.

Table 3 Electrochemical kinetic parameters of $Ti_{0.26}Zr_{0.07}V_{0.24}Mn_{0.1}Ni_{0.33-x}Cr_x$ (x=0.0—0.20) alloy electrode

Samples (x)	R_{ct} (Ω)	I_0 (mA g^{-1})	D ($\times10^{-11}$ cm^2 s^{-1})
0.0	0.154	169.5	7.44
0.05	0.161	162	7.38
0.10	0.173	151	5.84
0.15	0.288	90.5	4.28
0.20	0.734	35.6	2.95

The diffusion coefficient of hydrogen in the electrode alloy is determined with the potential-step method. Fig. 8 shows the semi-logarithmic plots of the anodic current versus the time response of the electrodes. It can be seen that under the operation of a potential step, the current-time responses in the semi-logarithmic plot (log i vs. t) can be divided into two time regions as proposed by Nishina et al. [14]. In the first region, the current declines abruptly due to the fast consumption of hydrogen on the surface of the alloy particles. In the second region, the current declines relatively slowly in a linear manner. In this case, the current is mainly controlled by the hydrogen diffusion velocity, which is proportional to the concentration gradient of hydrogen in the bulk of the alloy. Therefore, the linear response in the second region can be treated as the finite diffusion of hydrogen atoms inside the alloy particle according to the spherical diffusion model. The hydrogen diffusion coefficient D can be estimated by the following formulas [15] and the calculated values are listed in Table 3:

$$\log i = \log\left(\pm\frac{6FD}{da^2}(C_0 - C_s)\right) - \frac{\pi^2}{2.303}\frac{D}{a^2}t \tag{2}$$

$$D = -\frac{2.303a^2}{\pi^2}\frac{d\log i}{dt} \tag{3}$$

where i is the responding current (A), C_0 is the initial hydrogen concentration in the electrode alloys (mol cm^3), and C_s is hydrogen concentration on the electrode surface after a potential step (mol cm^3), F is Faraday constant (96,485 C mol^{-1}), t is time (s), D is diffusion coefficient (cm^2 s^{-1}) and r is the sphere radius of the alloy particle (cm).

It is found that the diffusion coefficient D decreases from 7.44×10^{-11} cm^2 s^{-1} (x=0) to 2.95×10^{-11} cm^2 s^{-1} (x=0.20). Therefore, we suggest that the hydrogen diffusion resistance for the electrode alloy is increased with increasing Cr content in $Ti_{0.26}Zr_{0.07}V_{0.24}Mn_{0.1}Ni_{0.33-x}Cr_x$ (x=0.0—0.20) alloy electrode.

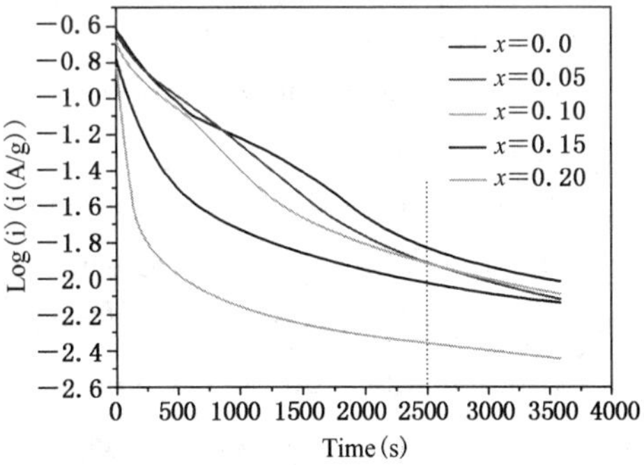

Fig. 8 Anodic current-time responses of $Ti_{0.26}Zr_{0.07}V_{0.24}Mn_{0.1}Ni_{0.33-x}Cr_x$ (x=0.0—0.20) alloy electrode

According to electrochemical theory [16], the process of discharging of hydrogen storage alloy electrodes includes three steps: absorbed hydrogen diffuses from the bulk to the surface of the alloy particles; absorbed hydrogen transforms into adsorbed hydrogen at the surface of the alloy particles; adsorbed hydrogen undergoes charge transfer reactions at the surface of the alloy particles. So the performance of a hydrogen storage alloy electrode is determined by both the kinetics of the processes at the alloy/electrolyte interface and the rate of hydrogen diffusion in the bulk alloy. The exchange current density I_0 and the hydrogen diffusion coefficient D are two important parameters for charactering the kinetics of the alloy electrodes. In the present study, I_0 and D both decrease with the increasing amount of Cr substitution for Ni in the alloys, which is consistent with the variation of HRD.

Iwakura et al. [17,18] have reported that a linear dependence of the HRD on the exchange current density should be observed if the electrochemical reaction kinetics at the electrode/electrolyte interface was rate-determining step. In contrast, if the diffusion of hydrogen in the bulk electrode alloy was rate-determining step, a linear dependence of the HRD on the hydrogen diffusion coefficient should be observed. Fig. 9 shows the HRD at 240 mA g^{-1} as a function of exchange current density and hydrogen diffusion coefficient for the electrodes, respectively. It is clear that the HRD at the current density of 240 mA g^{-1} increases with the increase of the exchange current density and hydrogen diffusion coefficient. The linear dependence of the high-rate dischargeability on both the exchange current density and the hydrogen diffusion coefficient can be observed, which implies that both charge transfer reaction at the electrode/electrolyte interface and the hydrogen diffusion in the bulk electrode alloy should be responsible for the improvement of high-rate dischargeability in present work.

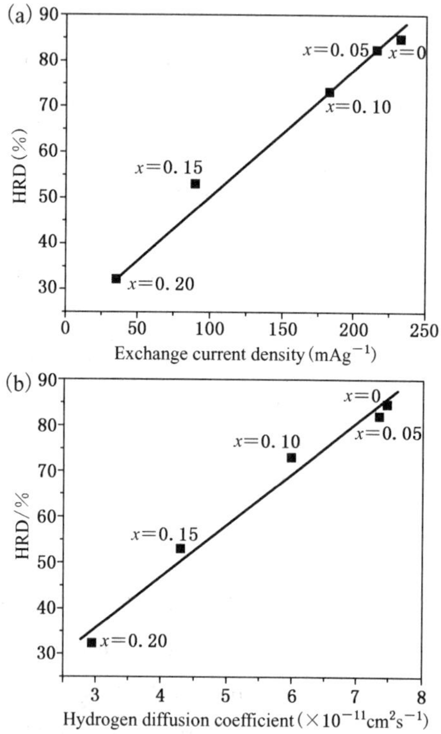

Fig. 9　HRD at 240 mA g^{-1} as a function of exchange current density (a) and hydrogen diffusion coefficient (b) for $Ti_{0.26}Zr_{0.07}V_{0.24}Mn_{0.1}Ni_{0.33-x}Cr_x$ (x= 0.0—0.20) alloy electrode

Negative electrode material used in Ni/MH battery should be capable of working over a wide temperature range.

The discharge capacity as a function of temperature is shown in Fig. 10. The discharge capacity increases with increasing temperature first and then decreases slightly. Moreover, the high-rate dischargeability increases with increasing temperature (Fig. 11). Those are mostly because of the increase of electrolyte activity at high temperature, which reasonably lead to the decrease of hydrogen diffusion resistance and the obviously increase of charge efficiency and discharge efficiency, and then inevitably increase the discharge capacity of the alloy electrodes at high temperature.

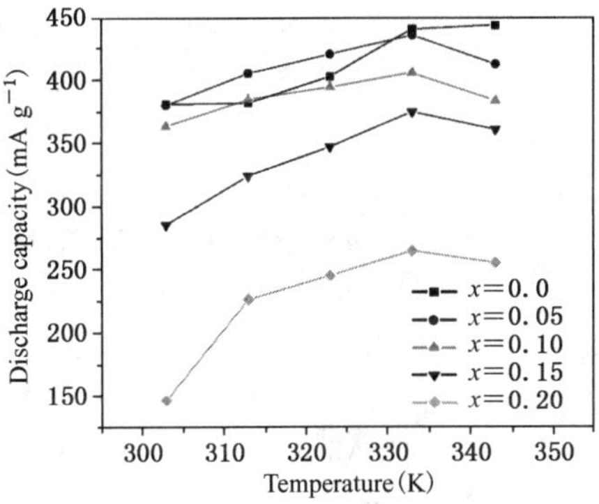

Fig. 10　Relation between discharge capacity and temperature for $Ti_{0.26}Zr_{0.07}V_{0.24}Mn_{0.1}Ni_{0.33-x}Cr_x$ (x=0.0—0.20) alloy electrode

Fig. 12 shows the semi-logarithmic plots of the anodic current vs. the time response of the $Ti_{0.26}Zr_{0.07}V_{0.24}Mn_{0.1}Ni_{0.33-x}Cr_x$ (x=0.15) alloy electrode at different temperature. The hydrogen diffusion coefficient D at different temperatures are estimated by Eq. (2). With increase of the temperature from 303 to 333 K, the D increases from 4.28×10^{-11} to 5.41×10^{-11} $cm^2\ s^{-1}$, which implies increasing temperature is favorable to hydrogen diffusion in the bulk of the electrode alloy.

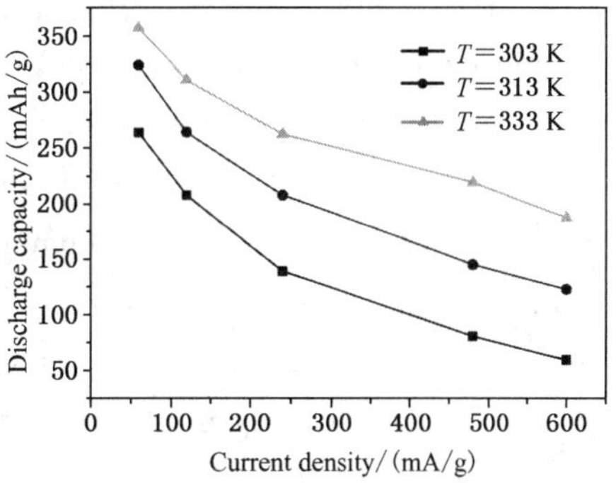

Fig. 11　Dependence of discharge capacity on current density for $Ti_{0.26}Zr_{0.07}V_{0.24}Mn_{0.1}Ni_{0.33-x}Cr_x$ (x=0.15) alloy electrode at different temperature

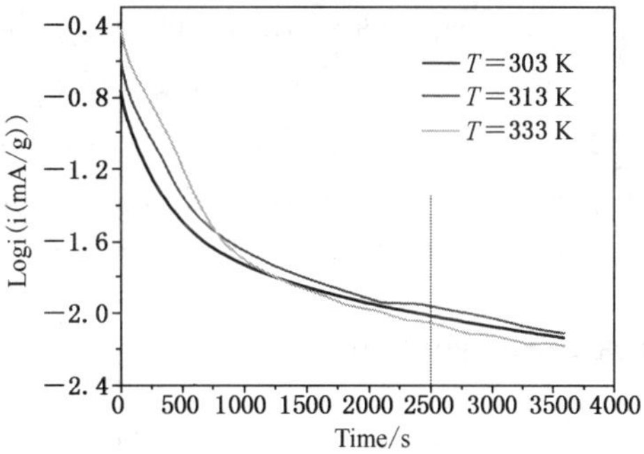

Fig. 12　Anodic current-time responses of $Ti_{0.26}Zr_{0.07}V_{0.24}Mn_{0.1}Ni_{0.33-x}Cr_x$ (x=0.15) alloy electrode at different temperature

4　Conclusion

(1) $Ti_{0.26}Zr_{0.07}V_{0.24}Mn_{0.1}Ni_{0.33-x}Cr_x$ (x=0.0—0.20) alloy electrodes are composed of a V-based solid solution phase with dendritic shape and a continu-

ous C14 Laves phase with network shape. V-based solid solution phase is mainly composed of V and Cr, while C14 Laves phase is mainly composed of Ti, Zr and Ni.

(2) The discharge capacity just after activation decreases with the increase of the Cr content but the cycling performance is improved. The high-rate dischargeability decreases when x changes from 0.0 to 0.20. The discharge capacity is dependent on temperature and is enhanced with increasing temperature from 303 to 343 K.

(3) Hydrogen diffusion is a rate-limiting factor at higher discharge current, while exchange current density is the rate-limiting factor at lower discharge current, the results of EIS and potentiostatic discharge tests show that both the exchange current density and hydrogen diffusion coefficient for the electrode alloy decrease markedly with increasing Cr content.

Acknowledgement

This work was financially supported by the National Natural Science Foundation of China (Grant No. 20171042).

References

[1] T. Kohno, H. Yoshida, F. Kawashima, T. Inaba, I. Sakai, M. Yamamoto, M. Kanda, J. Alloys Compd. 311 (2000) L5.

[2] S. Deying, G. Xueping, Z. Yunshi, Y. Jie, S. Panwen, J. Alloys Compd. 206 (1994) 43.

[3] P. Gifford, J. Adams, D. Corrigan, S. Venkatesan, J. Power Sources 80 (1999) 157.

[4] H.-H. Lee, K.-Y. Lee, J.-Y. Lee, J. Alloys Compd. 239 (1996) 63.

[5] H.-H. Lee, K.-Y. Lee, J.-Y. Lee, J. Alloys Compd. 253/254 (1997) 601.

[6] Q. A. Zhang, Y. Q. Lei, X. G. Yang, Y. L. Du, Q. D. Wang, Int. J. Hydrogen Energy 25 (2000) 977.

[7] X. B. Zhang, Y. J. Chai, W. Y. Yin, M. S. Zhao, J Solid State Chem. 177 (2004) 2373.

[8] N. Kuriyama, T. Sakai, H. Miyamura, I. Uehara, H. Ishikawa, T. Iwasaki, J. Alloys Compd. 202 (1993) 183.

[9] N. Kuriyama, T. Sakai, H. Miyamura, I. Uehara, H. Ishikawa, J. Alloys Compd. 202 (1993) 183.

[10] R. Li, H. Pan, M. Gao, Y. Zhu, Y. Liu, Q. Jin, Y. Lei, J. Alloys Compd. 373 (2004) 223.

[11] Z. Yunfeng, P. Hongge, M. Jianxin, L. Shouquan, G. Hongwei, Y. Tiao, W. Qidong, Chin. J. Acta Metall. Sin. 37 (2001) 1018.

[12] J. S. Yu, B. H. Liu, K. Cho, J. Y. Lee, J. Alloys Compd. 278 (1998) 283.

[13] T. Sakai, H. Miyamura, N. Kuriyama, A. Kato, K. Oguro, H. Ishikawa, J. Less-common Met. 159 (1990) 127.

[14] T. Nishina, H. Ura, I. Uchida, J. Electrochem. Soc. 144 (1997) 1273.

[15] G. Zheng, B. N. Popov, R. E. White, J. Electrochem. Soc. 142 (1995) 2695.

[16] J. K. Chang, D. S. Shong, W. T. Tsai, J. Power Sources 103 (2002) 280.

[17] C. Iwakura, M. Miyamoto, H. Inoue, M. Matsuoka, Y. Fukumoto, J. Alloys Compd. 259 (1997) 132.

[18] C. Iwakura, T. Oura, H. Inoue, M. Matsuoka, Electrochim. Acta 41 (1996) 117.

Enthalpy Change (ΔH^0) and Entropy Change (ΔS^0) Measurement of $CeMn_{1-x}Al_{1-x}Ni_{2x}$ (x=0.00, 0.25, 0.50 and 0.75) Hydrides by Electrochemical P-C-T Curve①

Chun-ping Hou[a,b] Min-shou Zhao[a,*], Jia Li[a], Liang Huang[a], Yan-zhi Wang[a], Min Yue[b]
([a]State Key Laboratory of Metastable Material Science and Technology, Yanshan University, Qinhuangdao, Hebei 066004, China)
([b]Shenzhen BTR New Energy Materials Inc., Shenzhen, Guangdong 518106, China)

Abstract: The thermodynamic properties of $CeMn_{1-x}Al_{1-x}Ni_{2x}$ (x = 0.00, 0.25, 0.50 and 0.75) hydrides have been investigated in this paper. With increasing Ni substitution content, the hydrogen concentration (H/M) in $CeMn_{1-x}Al_{1-x}Ni_{2x}$ (x = 0.00, 0.25, 0.50 and 0.75) hydride increases from 0.129 wt% for x = 0.00 to 0.421 wt% for x = 0.75 at 293 K. The pressure-concentration isotherm (*P-C-T*) curves show that no hydrogen equilibrium pressure plateau has been observed for CeMnAl hydride while the slope of the plateau become flatter and longer with increasing Ni content. Meanwhile, the enthalpy change (ΔH^0) and the entropy change (ΔS^0) of the hydrides for dehydrogenization shift from −67.44 kJ mol^{-1} (x = 0.00) to 21.16 kJ mol^{-1} (x= 0.75) and from −0.24 kJ $mol^{-1}K^{-1}$ (x = 0) to −0.03 kJ $mol^{-1}K^{-1}$ (x = 0.75), respectively. With increasing Ni content, both ΔH^0 and ΔS^0 for dehydrogenization shift to the positive direction and make alloy hydrides more stable and hydrogen desorption much easier.

Key words: Metal hydride electrode; Thermodynamic properties; Rare earth-based; AB_2-type alloy *P-C-T* curve; Equilibrium hydrogen pressure

1 Introduction

Metal hydride-nickel (MH-Ni) secondary batteries have attracted much more attention because of their high energy density, high rate dischargeability, long charge-discharge cycle life, safety and environmental compatibility[1-5].

AB_2-type hydrogen storage alloy and vanadium-based solid solution hydrogen storage alloy are considered as promising negative electrode materials due to their higher hydrogen storage capacities than that of AB_5-type alloy [6,7]. However,

① Interbational Journal of Hydrogen Energy, 2008(33):3762-3766.

titanium or zirconium-based AB_2-type alloys have the disadvantages of being difficultly activated and poor high rate dischargeability, while vanadium-based solid solution alloys have the problems of high cost, poor kinetics of hydrogenation/dehydrogenation and easier corrosion in alkaline electrolyte.

It has been reported that rare earth-based AB_2-type $Ce(Mn_{1-x}Al_x)_2$ ($x = 0.1-0.5$) series alloy hydrides have the advantages of higher hydrogen capacity with a maximum capacity of 4.4 H/f. u. at near ambient conditions and lower cost [8-11]. However, they can not be used as negative electrode materials of MH-Ni batteries for lack of electrochemical activity at near room temperature. It should be a key issue to improve their electrochemical activities of the alloys. In our previous work [12], the electrochemical characteristics of $CeMn_{1-x}Al_{1-x}Ni_{2x}$ ($x = 0.00$, 0.25, 0.50 and 0.75) alloys have been improved greatly by Ni substitution and the formation of a multiphase structure. In this work, the dehydrogenizations for $CeMn_{1-x}Al_{1-x}Ni_{2x}$ ($x= 0.00$, 0.25, 0.50 and 0.75) alloy hydrides were studied from a thermodynamic perspective.

The research on thermodynamic property is one important evaluation to hydrogen storage alloys. Tran et al. [13] investigated multi-component Mg-x wt% Mm alloys synthe sized by the mechanical ball-milling technique and found that the hydrogen desorption activation energy of Mg-x wt% Mm hydrides is much lower than that of MgH_2, and seldom attains an equilibrium state, thus leading to poor reversibility. Yuan et al. [14] reported that the absolute values of ΔH^{des} decrease with increasing Ce content in $La_{0.8(1-x)}Ce_{0.6-x}(PrNd)_{0.2}B_5$ alloy and the thermodynamic stability of the alloy hydride decreases. Tang et al. [15] studied $Ml_{0.8}Mg_{0.2}Ni_{3.2}Co_{0.6}Al_x$ ($x=0-0.6$) hydrogen storage alloys and concluded that the absolute values of ΔH and ΔS of the hydrides increase with increasing Al substitution content and therefore enhance the stability of alloy hydrides. Iwakura et al. [16] investigated $MmNi_{5-x}Al_x$ alloys by *P-C-T* curve method and found that ΔH value increased with an increase in x-value of the alloys. Ye et al. [17] reported that the hydrogen desorption pressure and enthalpy of $MmNi_xCo_{0.75}Mn_{0.40}Al_{0.30}$ alloy hydride increase with increasing Ni content. Moreover, the plateau region of *P-C-T* curves becomesflatter and the stability of hydride decreases as Ni content increases. However, most of the above works were performed by Sievelts gas-solid method. Feng et al. [18] obtained the enthalpy (ΔH) and entropy (ΔS) by fitting the curve of the equilibrium potential vs. hydrogen concentration. Wang et al. [19] introduced a new method of determining the thermodynamic parameters of metal hydride electrode materials.

In this study, the thermodynamic parameters are measured by the electrochemical *P-C-T* curve method. When solid solution and hydride phases coexist, there is a plateau in the isotherms, the length of which determines the amount of stored hydrogen. The equilibrium hydrogen pressure, PH_2, is related to the enthalpy change (ΔH^0) and the entropy change (ΔS^0) respectively. The enthalpy change and the entropy change of the hydrogenation/dehydrogenation reaction of the hydrogen storage alloys have the valuable significances not only in theory, but also in practice for the research and development of hydrogen storage materials. The enthalpy change has more important meaning for metal hydrides. When used as a hydrogen storage material, the enthalpy change value of the hydride should be smaller for the purpose of energy efficiency, whereas when used as a heat storage material, the value should be larger [20].

2 Experimental

2.1 Synthesis of alloys

$CeMn_{1-x}Al_{1-x}Ni_{2x}$ (x = 0.00, 0.25, 0.50 and 0.75) alloys with nominal composition were synthesized from high purity elements (Ce: 99.9%; Mn: 99.6%; Al: 99.9%; Ni: 99.9%) at a small excess of manganese (1 wt%). Surface oxides were mechanically removed from Ce ingots and Al foils. The samples were prepared by arc-melting in a water cooled copper crucible in an argon (purity: 99.999%) atmosphere of 0.03 MPa. To improve homogeneity, the samples were remelted three times, and the button ingot was turned upside down for each time.

2.2 Experimental details

Electrochemical tests (including equilibrium electrode potential and discharge capacity measurement) were conducted with computer-controlled DC-5 battery testing instrument (Made by Shanghai Zhengfang electric-electrical appliances Co., Ltd.). The alloy was ground to fine powders of 200 mesh. The alloy electrodes were prepared as follows: 0.15 g alloy powder was uniformly mixed with carbonyl Ni powder of 0.75 g. The mixture was cold pressed to a pellet with a diameter of 10 mm and a thickness of about 2 mm at a pressure of 15 MPa for 3 min. This round pellet was welded with a Ni pole, which was used as a current conductor. A three-electrode system was employed to measure the equilibrium electrode potential with Hg/HgO electrode as the reference electrode, sintered $Ni(OH)_2/NiOOH$ as the counter electrode and alloy electrode as the working electrode. The alloy electrodes were discharged at a current density of 60 $mA \cdot g^{-1}$ and a resting time of 20 min. The cut-off voltage of the test was −0.6V (vs. Hg/HgO). All experiments were conducted in a controllable temperature chamber (WGD701).

3 Results and discussion

3.1 *P-C-T* curves for $CeMn_{1-x}Al_{1-x}NiM_{2x}$($x$= 0.00, 0.25, 0.50 and 0.75) alloy hydrides

P-C-T curve is the isotherm of equilibrium hydrogen pressure and hydrogen concentration of metal hydride during its reversible hydrogen absorption/desorption process, and it is an important curve to characterize the thermodynamic properties of hydrogen storage material. The *P-C-T* curve is measured by the relationships between the electrode potential and equilibrium hydrogen pressure at different temperatures, electrochemical capacity and hydrogen capacity. The plateau pressure, plateau length, slope and hysteresis effect are not only key indices to evaluate the hydrogen absorption/desorption properties of hydrogen storage alloys, but also the foundation for the development of new hydrogen storage alloys. Meanwhile, the thermodynamic functions of the hydrides can be obtained from *P-C-T* curves[18,21].

The equilibrium hydrogen pressure (P_{H2}) of the hydride can be calculated by the Nernst equation as follows:

$$E_{eq}=E^0(H_2O/H_2)-E^0(Hg/HgO)+\frac{RT}{2F}\ln\frac{\alpha(H_2O)}{\gamma(H_2)P(H_2)} \quad (1)$$

where α is the activity, γ the fugacity coefficient, E_{eq} the equilibrium potential (vs. HgO/Hg 6M KOH), R the gas constant and F the Faraday constant. According to Sakai [22],

$$E^0(H_2O/H_2)-E^0(Hg/HgO)=-1.18041+(4.4666\times10^{-3}-6.693606\times10^{-4}\ln T)T+1.0788\times10^{-6}T^2-4.512\times10^{-10}T^3+5.232/T \quad (2)$$

$$\log\alpha(H_20)=-0.0225m+0.001434m^2+\frac{1.38m-0.9254m^2}{T} \quad (3)$$

where m is the molality of solute KOH, which is 4.75 mol kg^{-1} corresponding to 6M KOH. The relationships between equilibrium electrode potential (E_{eq}) and equilibrium hydrogen pressure (P_{H2}) at different temperatures can be obtained by substituting Eqs. (3) and (2) into Eq. (1)[23]. The relationships between equilibrium electrode potential and equilibrium hydrogen pressure at 293, 303 and 313K can be expressed as Eqs. (4)—(6), respectively.

$$E_{eq}=-0.9324-0.0291\lg P_{H_2}(293\ K) \quad (4)$$

$$E_{eq}=-0.9291-0.0300\lg P_{H_2}(303\ K) \quad (5)$$

$$E_{eq}=-0.9270-0.0311\lg P_{H_2}(313\ K) \quad (6)$$

where E_{eq} is the equilibrium electrode potential (vs. Hg/HgO), V, and P_{H_2} is the equilibrium hydrogen pressure, Pa. The *P-C-T* curves of $CeMn_{1-x}Al_{1-x}Ni_{2x}$ (x = 0.00, 0.25, 0.50and 0.75) alloy hydrides measured by electrochemical methodat 293 K are shown in Fig. 1 [12]. It is apparent that no hydrogen equilibrium pressure plateau has been observed for CeMnAl hydride while the slope of the plateau becomes flatter and longer with increasing Ni content. The hydrogen concentration of the alloy hydride is 0.129, 0.313, 0.406, 0.421 wt%, respectively. It is also seen that the equilibrium hydrogen pressure plateau for $CeMn_{1-x}Al_{1-x}Ni_{2x}$ (x = 0.25, 0.50, 0.75)

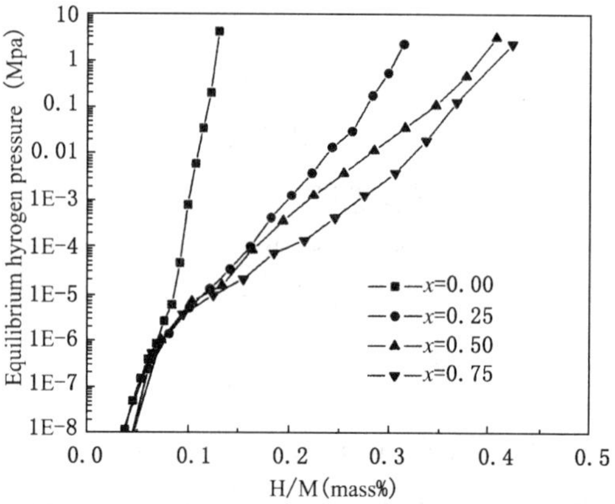

Fig. 1 *P-C-T* curve for $CeMn_{1-x}Al_{1-x}Ni_{2x}$ (x=0.00, 0.25, 0.50 and 0.75) alloy hydride at 293 K.

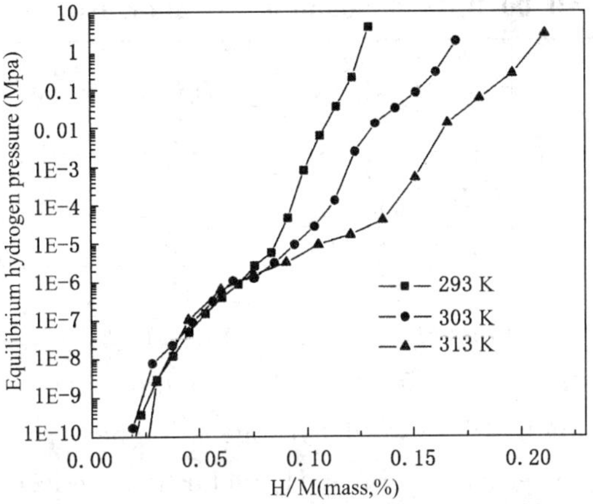

Fig. 2　*P-C-T* curve for CeMnAl hydride at 293,303,313 K.

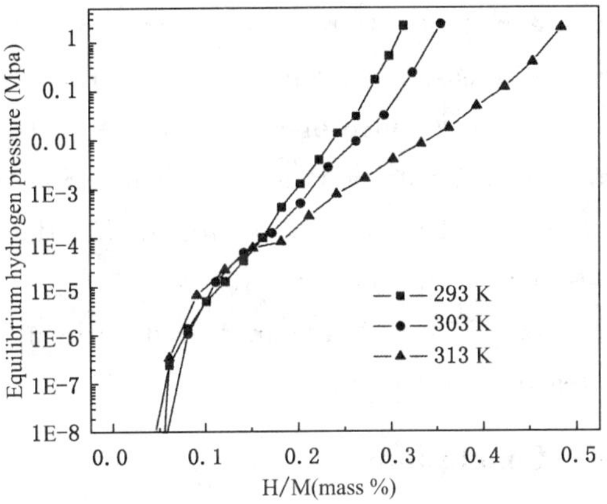

Fig. 3　*P-C-T* cure for $CeMn_{0.75}Al_{0.75}Ni_{0.5}$ at 293,303,313 K.

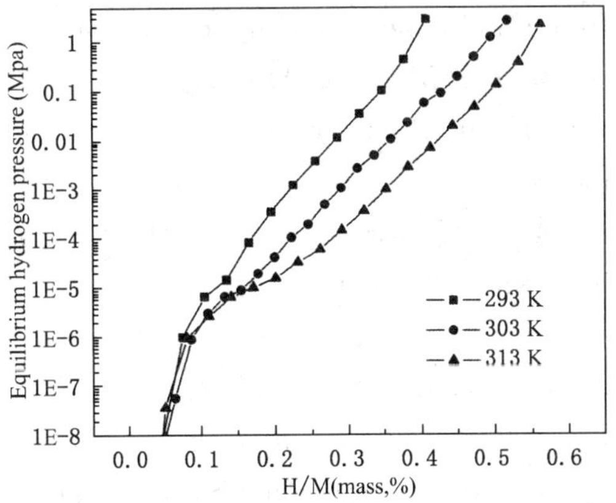

Fig. 4　*P-C-T* cure for $CeMn_{0.50}Al_{0.50}Ni_{1.0}$ at 293,303,313 K.

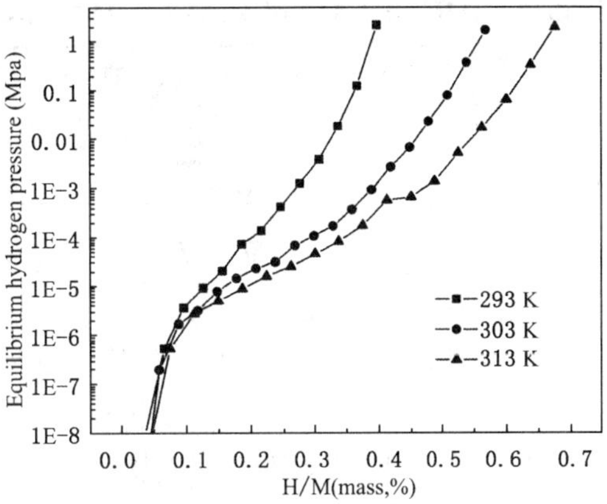

Fig. 5　*P-C-T* curve for $CeMn_{0.25}Al_{0.25}Ni_{1.5}$ hydride at 293,303,313 K.

alloy hydride by Ni substitution is still lower, and even for the alloy at $x = 0.75$, the equilibrium pressure plateau is still lower than 0.01 MPa. Therefore such electrode alloys do not satisfy the requirement of plateau pressure of 0.01—0.5 MPa for hydrogen storage electrode alloys. This fact implies that only a small amount of hydrogen has been desorbed from the metal hydrides at 293 K, which is in accordance with its lower electrochemical capacity.

3.2　Enthalpy change and entropy change of the alloy hydrides

The *P-C-T* curves of $CeMn_{1-x}Al_{1-x}Ni_{2x}$ (x=0.00, 0.25, 0.50 and 0.75) alloys at different temperatures (293, 303, 313 K) are shown in Figs. 2—5, respectively. The thermodynamic parameters can be determined from the Vant Hoff plots of In P_{H2} versus 1/T (see Eq. (7)). The enthalpy change (ΔH^0) and entropy change (ΔS^0) for the alloy hydride can be calculated from the slope and intercept of the plot and are listed in Table 1.

Table 1 ΔH^0 and ΔS^0 of $CeMn_{1-x}Al_{1-x}Ni_{2x}$ (x=0.00, 0.25, 0.50and 0.75) alloy hydrides

x	Equilibrium hydrogen pressure (MPa)			ΔH^0 (kJ mol^{-1})	ΔS^0 (kJ $mol^{-1}K^{-1}$)
	293 K	303 K	313 K		
0.00	2.43×10^{-6}	1.05×10^{-5}	1.41×10^{-5}	−67.44	−0.24
0.25	3.60×10^{-4}	6.57×10^{-4}	1.51×10^{-3}	−54.65	−0.24
0.50	1.37×10^{-3}	8.26×10^{-4}	2.27×10^{-4}	68.04	−0.17
0.75	2.71×10^{-4}	1.42×10^{-4}	1.57×10^{-4}	21.16	−0.03

$$In\ P_{H2}=\Delta H^0/(RT)-S^0/R \quad (7)$$

where P_{H2} is the equilibrium hydrogen pressure, Pa; T istemperature, K; and R is the gas constant.

It can be seen in Table 1 that the enthalpy change of the $CeMn_{1-x}Al_{1-x}Ni_{2x}$ (x=0.00, 0.25, 0.50 and 0.75) hydride is−67.44, −54.65, 68.04, 21.16 kJ mol^{-1}, respectively, which increases firstly and then decreases with increasing Ni substitution content. Meanwhile, the entropy change of the hydrides increases along with increasing Ni content.

It has been shown that CeMnAl hydride for dehydrogenation has both the most negative ΔH^0 and ΔS^0 among these four hydrides, and they are −67.44 kJ mol^{-1} and −0.24 kJ $mol^{-1}K^{-1}$, respectively. For $CeMn_{1-x}Al_{1-x}Ni_{2x}$ (x=0.25, 0.50, 0.75) alloy hydrides, $CeMn_{0.25}Al_{0.25}Ni_{1.5}$ alloyhydride has more appropriate ΔH^0 value, 21.16 kj mol^{-1}, locating between −29 and 46 kJ mol^{-1}, which is more suitable for the hydrogen storage material [20].

When their hydrides are at x= 0.50 and 0.75, the enthalpy change values are positive, and the alloys are heat absorbing type hydrogen storage alloys. Therefore, the hydrogen desorption capacity increases as the temperature increases.

The ΔH^0 and ΔS^0 of $CeMn_{1-x}A_{1-x}Ni_{2x}$ (x=0.00, 0.25, 0.50 and 0.75) alloy hydrides for dehydrogenation have revealed that $CeMnAlH_x$ metal hydride has both the most negative ΔH^0 and ΔS^0 and can not release hydrogen at near ambient conditions, whereas Ni substitution has made it more stable and hydrogen desorption easier. Kwon et al. [24] reported that the added or substituted Ni acts as the catalyst for theelectrochemical reaction and Chai et al. [7] found that the discharge capacity of $Ti_{0.25}V_{0.35}Cr_{0.40-x}Ni_x$ (x=0.05−0.40) increased with increasing Ni content.

4 Conclusions

(1) Ni substitution makes the slope of the hydrogen pressure plateau become flatter and longer. The hydrogen concentration (H/M) in $CeMn_{1-x}Al_{1-x}Ni_{2x}$ (x=0.00, 0.25, 0.50 and 0.75) hydride increases from 0.129 wt% for x = 0.00 to0.421 wt% for x=0.75 at 293 K with increasing Ni substitution amount.

(2) Both the enthalpy change and entropy change of the $CeMn_{1-x}Al_{1-x}Ni_{2x}$ (x = 0.25, 0.50 and 0.75) alloy hydridesfor dehydrogenation have been shifted to the positive direction as the Ni substitution amount increases. The en-

thalpy change and entropy change of the hydrides have revealed that CeMnAlH metal hydride has both the most negative ΔH^0 and ΔS^0 and can not release hydrogen at near ambient conditions, whereas Ni substitution has made it more stable and hydrogen desorption easier.

Acknowledgments

This work is supported by the Foundation of CAS State Key Laboratory of Rare Earth Resources Utilization, Chinese Academy of Sciences.

References

[1] Metzger W, Westfall R, Hermann A. New fabrication method for nickel metal hydride electrodes by sintering alloy onto a foam substrate. Int J Hydrogen Energy 1998; 23: 1179-83.

[2] Feng F, Geng M, Northwood DO. Electrochemical behaviour of intermetallic-based metal hydrides used in Ni/metal hydride (MH) batteries: a review. Int J Hydrogen Energy 2001;26:725-34.

[3] Ziittel A. Materials for hydrogen storage. Mater Today 2003;9:24-33.

[4] Hong K. The development of hydrogen storage electrode alloys for nickel hydride batteries. J Power Sources 2001;96:85-9.

[5] Zavalii IYu, Saldan IV Investigation of Ti (Zr-Ni) hydrogen-sorbing alloys as electrode materials for nickel-metal-hy-dride storage batteries. Mater Sci 2002;38:526-33.

[6] Peretti HA, Visintin A, Mogni IV, Corso HL, Andrade Gamboa J, Serafini D, et al. Hydrogen absorption behavior of multicomponent zirconium based AB2 alloys with different chromium-vanadium ratio. J Alloys Compd 2003;354:181-6.

[7] Chai Y, Zhao M. Structure and electrochemical properties of $Ti_{0.25}V_{0.35}Cr_{0.40-x}Ni_x$ ($x=0.05—0.40$) solid solution alloys. Int JHydrogen Energy 2005;30:279-83.

[8] Spatz P, Gross KJ, Ziittel A, Schlapbach L. Hydriding properties of $Ce(Mn, Al)_2$ and $Ce(Fe, Al)_2$ intermetallic compounds. J Alloys Compd 1997;260:211-6.

[9] Spatz P, Gross K, Zuttel A, Fauth F, Fischer P, Schlapbach L. $CeMnAlH_X$, a new metal hydride. J Alloys Compd 1997; 261: 263-8.

[10] Gross KJ, Chartouni D, Fauth F A new hexagonal Laves phase deuteride $CeMn_{1.5}Al_{0.5}D_x$ ($0<x<4$) investigated by in situneutron diffraction. J Alloys Compd 2000; 306:203-18.

[11] Filinchuk YE, Sheptyakov D, Hilscher G, Yvon K. Hydrogenation induced valence change and metal atom site exchange at room temperature in the C14-type substructure of $CeMn_{1.8}Al_{0.2}H_{4.4}$. J Alloys Compd 2003;356-357:673-8.

[12] Hou C, Zhao M, Qiao Y, Li J, Huang L, Wang Y, et al. Structure and electrochemical characteristics of $CeMn_{1-x}Al_{1-x}Ni_{2x}$ ($x=0.00$, 0.25, 0.50 and 0.75) alloys. Int J Hydrogen Energy 2007;32:4209-14.

[13] Tran NE, Lambrakos SG, Imam MA. Analyses of hydrogen sorption kinetics and thermodynamics of magnesium-misch metal alloys. J Alloys Compd 2006;407:240-8.

[14] Yuan X, Liu H, Ma Zi, Xu N. Characteristics of LaNi5-based hydrogen storage alloys modified by partial substituting La for Ce. J Alloys Compd 2003;359:300-6.

[15] Tang R, Liu Y, Zhu C, Zhu J, Yu G. Effect of Al substitution for Co on the hydrogen storage characteristics of $Ml_{0.8}Mg_{0.2}Ni_{3.2}Co_{0.6-x}Alx$ ($x=0-0.6$) alloys. Intermetallics 2006;14:361-6.

[16] Iwakura C, Oura T, Inoue H, Matsuoka M. Effects of substitution with foreign metals on the crystallographic, thermodynamic and electrochemical properties of AB_5-type hydrogen storage alloys. Electrochim Acta 1996;41:117-21.

[17] Ye H, Zhang H, Cheng JX, Huang TS. Effect of Ni content on the structure, thermodynamic and electrochemical properties of the non-stoichiometric hydrogen storage alloys. J Alloys Compd 2000;308:163-71.

[18] Feng F, Ping X, Zhou Z, Geng M, Han J, Northwood DO. The relationship between equilibrium potential during discharge and hydrogen concentration in a metal hydride electrode. IntJ Hydrogen Energy 1998;23:599-602.

[19] Wang C, Wang X, Lei Y, Chen C, Wang Q. A new method of determining the thermodynamic parameters of metal hy dride electrode materials. Int J Hydrogen Energy 1997;22:1117-24.

[20] Hu Z. Hydrogen storage materials[M]. Beijing: Chemical Industrial Publishing House; 2002. p. 51[in Chinese].

[21] Mani N, Ramaprabhu S. Effect of substitutional elements on hydrogen absorption properties in Mm-based AB5 alloys. J Alloys Compd 2004;363:275-91.

[22] Sakai S, Takaoku T, Matsui H, Kotani T. In: 14th International electric vehicle symposium, Orlando, FL, December 1997. p. 15.

[23] Sakai T, Miyamura H, Kuriyama N, Kato A, Oguro K, Ishikawa H. Metal hydride anode for nickel-hydrogen secondary battery. J Electrochem Soc 1990;137:781-95.

[24] Kwon I, Park H, Song M. Electrochemical properties of $ZrMnNi_{1+x}$ hydrogen storage alloys. Int J Hydrogen Energy 2002; 27:171-6.

Structure and Electrochemical Characteristics of $CeMn_{1-x}Al_{1-x}Ni_{2x}$ (x=0.00, 0.25, 0.50 and 0.75) Alloys①

Chun-Ping Hou[a,b], Min-Shou Zhao [a], Yu-Qing Qiao[a], Jia Li[a],
Liang Huang[a] Yan-Zhi Wang[a], Xu Liu[b], Shy-Zhou Liu[b], Min Yue[b]
([a]College of Environmental and Chemical Engineering,
Yanshan University, Qinhuangdao 066004, China)
([b]Shenhen BTR Energy Materials Co. Ltd., Shenzhen 518106, China)

Abstract: The structure and electrochemical characteristics of Ni substitution for Mn and Al in AB_2-type CeMnAl intermetallic compounds are studied. XRD and SEM reveal that Ni partial substitution leads to a phase change of the alloys and new phase to be formed. The electrochemical activity of $CeMn_{1-x}Al_{1-x}Ni_{2x}$ (x = 0.00, 0.25, 0.50 and 0.75) alloy is greatly improved and the discharge capacity can increase from 17.93 mAh g^{-1} (x=0.00) to 118.3 mAh g^{-1} (x=0.75) at 298 K and from 68.42 mAh g^{-1} (x=0.00) to 216.1 mAh g^{-1} (x=0.75) at 328 K, respectively. The electrochemical *P-C-T* curve shows that no hydrogen equilibrium pressure plateau is observed for CeMnAl alloy while the slope of the plateau becomes flatter and longer with increasing Ni content.

Key words: Hydrogen storage alloy; Electrochemical characteristics; MH-Ni secondary battery; Laves phase

1 Introduciton

Metal hydride-nickel (MH-Ni) secondary batteries have attracted much more attention because of their higher energy density, long charge-discharge cycle life, good tolerance to over-charge and over-discharge and environmental compatibility. The negative electrode materials of MH-Ni secondary batteries being studied at present mostly include: rare earth-based AB_5-type alloy (represented as $LaNi_5$), zirconium-or titanium-based AB_2-type alloy (represented as $ZrCr_2$ and $TiMn_2$), AB-type alloy (represented as TiFe), A_2B-type Mg-based alloy (represented as Mg_2Ni), $PuNi_3$-type alloy (represented as $(La, Mg)_3Ni_9$) and vanadium-based solid solution alloy [1, 2]. Among these hydrogen storage alloys, the aims of the research are to enhance the discharge capacity, improve

① Internatoonal Journal of Hydrogen Energy, 2007(32):4209-4214.

the integrated electrochemical characteristics and down cost of the alloys.

Spatz et al. [3, 4] first found that AB_2-type C15 Laves phase CeMnAl intermetallic compound is a good gas-solid hydrogen storage material and it has a hydrogen capacity of about 1.2 H/formula unit (f. u.) at pressures $< 10^{-3}$ MPa while hydrogen is absorbed up to 2.4 H/f. u. at pressures $> 10^{-3}$ MPa (at 300 K). Gross et al. [5] adjusted Mn/Al ratio and synthesized C 14 (P_{63}/mmc) hexagonal Laves phase compound $CeMn_{1.5}Al_{0.5}$ with a maximum capacity of 4.0 H/f. u. Filinchuket al. [6] discovered that $CeMn_{1.8}Al_{0.2}$ alloy can absorbs more than 4.4 hydrogen atoms at near ambient conditions, thereby undergoing a volume expansion ($\Delta V/V \sim 43\%$) that is the largest known among metal hydrides. Among $Ce(Mn_{1-x}Al_x)_2$ series alloys, different Mn/Al ratios give rise to different crystal structures: $0.15 < x < 0.35$, hexagonal C14-type structure; $x > 0.35$ or $x < 0.1$, cubic C15-type structure; $x = 0.1$, Mn/Al atom distribution tends to become disordered during hydro genation.

Ni is a very important element to improve the electrocatalytic activity of the intermetallic compounds and Ni addition plays a major role in the application of hydrogen storage alloys used as negative electrode materials in MH-Ni batteries. Chartouni et al. [7] investigated the electrochemical properties of $Zr(V_xNi_{1-x})_3$ as electrode material in MH-Ni batteries and discovered that the exchange current density of the alloy electrode increases with increasing nickel content, and the activation becomes faster. Chai et al. [8] revealed that a TiNi secondary phase, which acts as an electrocatalyst and micro-current collector, has been formed in $Ti_{0.25}V_{0.35}Cr_{0.40-x}Ni_x$ ($x = 0.05-0.40$) V-based solid solution alloys, and then improves greatly the electrochemical property of the alloy. Notten et al. [9] reported that the $MoCo_3$ second-phase of a double-phase-hydride has a high electrocatalytic activity, which increases the exchange current density and appreciably advances the electrochemical characteristics of the alloy.

Kondo et al. [10] studied the effect of nickel addition and the microstructure of the alloy on absorption and desorption behavior of hydrogen in $LaNi_5$. It has been concluded that the network of Ni phase in $LaNi_5$-Ni eutectic alloy makes the $LaNi_5$ hydride unstable, and the proper microstructure and additional amount of nickel can distinctly improve the hydrogen absorption and desorption properties of the $LaNi_5$-Ni eutectic alloy.

In this paper the stoichiometric electrode alloy of $CeMn_{0.25}Al_{0.25}Ni_{1.5}$ was prepared by Ni partial substitution for Mn and Al in B-side of the AB_2-type CeMnAl intermetallic compound, and its electrochemical activity is distinctly improved and has a faster activation process, lower and flatter charge curve. Furthermore, this kind of alloy has the discharge capacity of 216.1 mAh g^{-1} at 328 K, and therefore it is a prospective candidate for negative electrode material in MH Ni batteries with further optimizing compositions.

2 Experimental

$CeMn_{1-x}Al_{1-x}Ni_{2x}$ (x=0.00, 0.25, 0.50 and 0.75) alloys with designed nominal composition were melted in WS-3 non-self-consumable vacuum arc — melting furnace (made by Physcience Opto-electronics Co., Beijing) under an argon atmosphere. The purity of material is: Ce 99.9% (mass, here-after), Mn 99.6%, Al 99.9%, Ni 99.9% and Ar 99.999%, respectively. To improve homogeneity, the samples were remelted three times, each time the pellet was turned upside down.

The phase structure analysis of the alloys was conducted with Rigaku D/max-2500/pc X-ray diffractometer using Cu-K α radiation. Sampling was continuous, scanning rate was4°/ min, and the power was 40 kV × 200 mA. After its being polished and etched, the ingot sample was used to investigate the surface morphology and phase composition of the alloys through KYKY-2800 scanning electron microscope equipped with Kevex-Sigma level4 EDS analyzer.

Electrochemical tests were conducted with computer-controlled DC-5 battery testing instrument (made by Shanghai Zhengfang electric-electrical appliances Co. Ltd.). The alloy was ground to fine powders of 180 mesh and then was uniformly mixed with carbonyl nickel powder at a mass ratio of 1 : 5. The mixture was cold pressed to a pellet with a diameter of 10 mm and a thickness of about 2 mm at a pressure of 15 MPa using Tablet Press (769YP-type). The round electrode pellet was welded with a nickel pod which was used as a current collector using P 103-3D Spot Welding Machine, and then the negative electrode was assembled to a stimulant cell with sintered $Ni(OH)_2$/NiOOH positive electrode in a 6 M KOHelectrolyte. For the electrochemical tests, the electrodes were charged/discharged at a current density of 60mA g^{-1} under constant current condition after a resting time of 5 min and thecut-off voltage was 0.8V. For *P-C-T* curve measurements, a three electrode system was employed, and Hg/HgO electrode was used as reference electrode and the cut-off voltage was 0.6 V (vs. Hg/HgO).

3 Results and discussion

3.1 Phase-structure analysis of the alloys

Fig. 1 shows the X-ray diffraction patterns of $CeMn_{1-x}Al_{1-x}Ni_{2x}$ (x=0.00, 0.25, 0.50 and 0.75) alloys. It can be seen that with increasing Ni substitution content, the phase structure change of $CeMn_{1-x}Al_{1-x}Ni_{2x}$ (x=0.00, 0.25, 0.50 and 0.75)

alloys has taken place from an almost single cubic C15 Laves

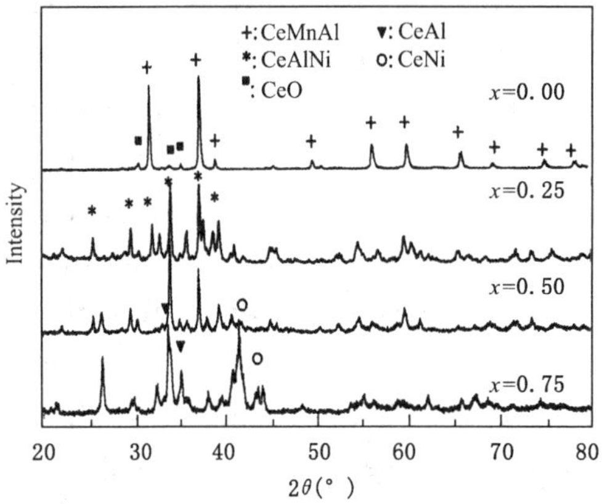

Fig. 1 XRD pattert of $CeMn_{1-x}Al_{1-x}Ni_{2x}$ (x=0. 00, 0. 25, 0. 50 and 0. 75) alloy

phase (exception of less oxide) for x=0. 00 to multi-phase structure for x=0. 25, 0. 50 and 0. 75. When x=0. 25 and 0. 50, the alloys mainly contain hexagonal CeAlNi phase and a little secondary phase, which needs further confirmation; whereas when x= 0. 75, the alloy mainly consists of a cubic CeNi phase and a hexagonal CeAl phase. There is no Mn-containing phase to be observed from the XRD patterns, but EDS semi-quantitative analysis confirm the existence of Mn element in the alloys (see Table 1), and it may be explained by dissolving Mn into other phases.

The SEM images of $CeMn_{1-x}Al_{1-x}Ni_{2x}$ (x=0. 00, 0. 25, 0. 50 and 0. 75) alloys have been shown in Fig. 2. It has been seen distinctly that with creasing Ni substitution content, the phase structures of CeMn $1-x$ $Al_{1-x}Ni_{2x}$ (x=0. 00, 0. 25, 0. 50 and 0. 75) alloys have changed gradually from an almost single Laves phase to a multi-phase structure. A gray, long and narrow secondary phase has appeared clearly on the surface of the alloy at x=0. 50, and this secondary phase is confirmed to be composed of Ce, Mn, Al and Ni elements, as shown in Table 1.

Table 1 Phase compostions for $CeMn_{1-x}Al_{1-x}Ni_{2x}$ (x=0. 00, 0. 25, 0. 50 and 0. 75) alloy

x	Phase	Compostition (atom %)			
		Ce	Mn	Al	Ni
0. 00	Single	35. 23	20. 05	44. 72	-
0. 25	A phase	52. 18	6. 41	38. 54	2. 87
	B phase	42. 40	29. 66	15. 99	11. 94
0. 50	A phase	68. 22	13. 62	8. 56	12. 62
	B phase	38. 27	33. 62	16. 50	11. 62
0. 75	C phase	56. 45	4. 03	16. 39	23. 13
	D phase	28. 14	17. 01	30. 59	24. 26

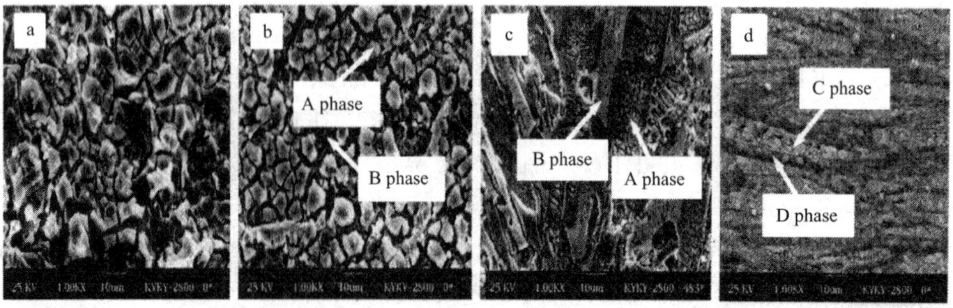

Fig. 2 SEM image of $CeMn_{1-x}Al_{1-x}Ni_{2x}$ (x=0. 00, 0. 25, 0. 50 and 0. 75) alloy
(a) x=0. 00; (b) x=0. 25; (c) x=0. 50; (d) x=0. 7

3.2 *P-C-T* curves for $CeMn_{1-x}Al_{1-x}Ni_{2x}$ (x=0.00, 0.25, 0.50 and 0.75) alloys

Sievelts gas-solid method and electrochemical method are two common methods to measure *P-C-T* curve. The electro-chemical method is based on that electrochemical hydrogen absorption/desorption process of hydrogen storage alloys is as same as that of gas-solid reaction, and the *P-C-T* curve is measured by the relationships between the electrode potential and equilibrium hydrogen pressure, electrochemical capacity and hydrogen capacity, respectively. The electrochemical method has an advantage of easy operating, and the hydrogen concen- tration in metal hydride electrode measured by this method is its reversible hydrogen absorption/desorption capacity. With this method, it is very convenient to study the enthalpy change and entropy change of reversible hydrogen absorption/desorption of alloy electrodes at near room temperature. The relationship between equilibrium electrode potential and equilibrium hydrogen pressure at 298 K can be expressed as

$$E_{eq} = -0.9324 - 0.0296 \lg P_{H_2} (298\ K), \quad (1)$$

where E_{eq} is the equilibrium electrode potential (vs. Hg/HgO), V, and P_{H_2} is the equilibrium hydrogen pressure, Pa.

The *P-C-T* curves of $CeMn_{1-x}Al_{1-x}Ni_{2x}$ (x=0.00, 0.25, 0.50 and 0.75) alloys measured by the electrochemical method have been shown in Fig. 3. It is apparent that no hydrogen equilibrium pressure plateau is observed for CeMnAl alloy while the slope of the plateau become flatter and longer with increasing Ni content. It is also can be seen from Fig. 3 that hydrogen equilibrium pressure plateau of $CeMn_{1-x}Al_{1-x}Ni_{2x}$ (x = 0.25, 0.50 and 0.75) alloy hydrides by Ni substitution is lower, and this phenomena reveal that only small amount of hydrogen can be desorbed from the metal hydride at 298 K, which is in accordance with its lower electrochemical capacity.

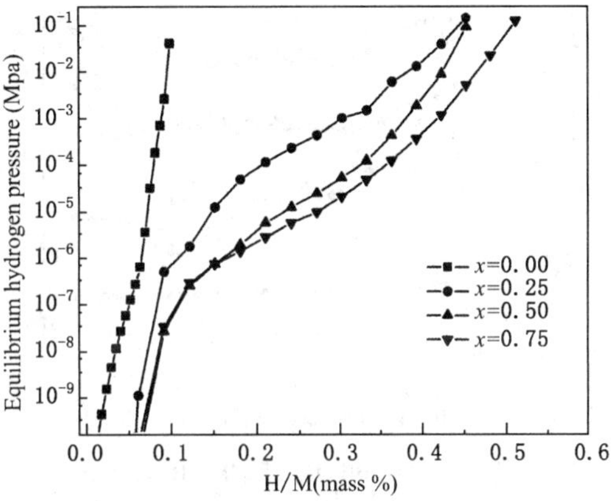

Fig. 3 Electrochemical *P-C-T* curve for $CeMn_{1-x}Al_{1-x}Ni_{2x}$ (x=0.00, 0.25, 0.50 and 0.75) alloy electorde at 298 K

3.3 Activation process and maximum discharge capacity

Fig. 4 shows the discharge capacity of $CeMn_{1-x}Al_{1-x}Ni_{2x}$ alloy electrodes as a function of cycle number at 298 K. It can be see that $CeMn_{1-x}Al_{1-x}Ni_{2x}$ (x=0.00, 0.25, 0.50 and 0.75) alloy electrodes show excellent activation process and they need only two cycles to reach their maximum discharge capacities at 298 K. As x value increases, the maximum discharge capacity ranges from 17.93 mAh g^{-1} for x

=0.00 to 118.3 mAh g^{-1} for $x=0.75$. The enhancement of discharge capacity of these metal hydrides has been ascribed to the improvement of alloy electrochemical activity caused by the electrocatalytic Ni partial substitution and the formation of a secondary phase, which acts as an electrocatalyst and micro-current collector. What the second phases are in a multiphase system and how they act are under investigation.

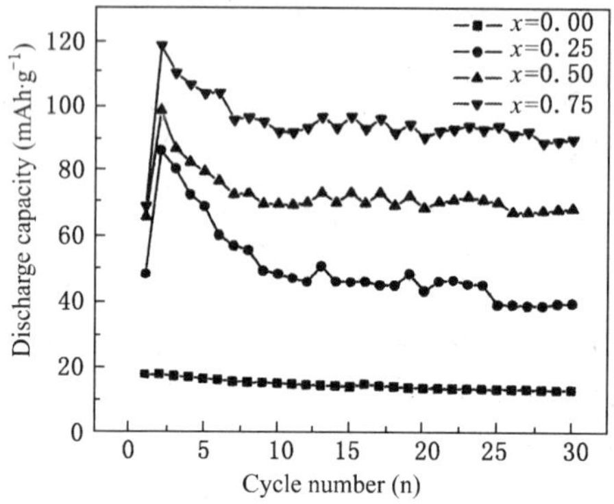

Fig. 4 Discharge capaction of $CeMn_{1-x}Al_{1-x}Ni_{2x}$ ($x=0.00$, 0.25, 0.50 and 0.75) alloy electrode as a function of cycle number at 298 K

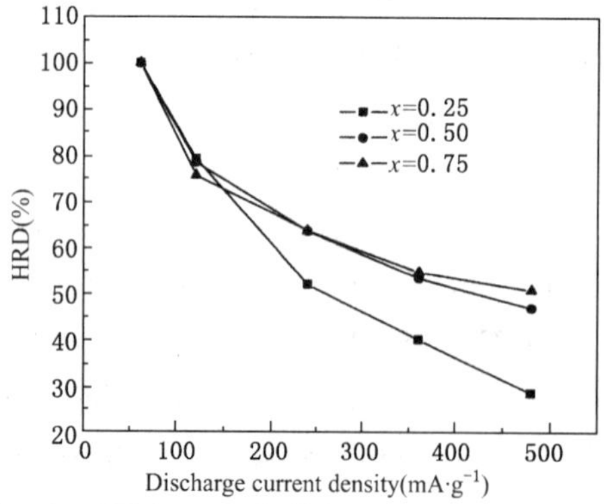

Fig. 5 High-rate dischargeability of $CeMn_{1-x}Al_{1-x}Ni_{2x}$ ($x=0$, 0.25, 0.50 and 0.75) alloy electrode as a function of discharge current density at 298 K

3.4 High-rate dischatgeability

The high rate dischargeabiity (HRD) can be defined as

$$\mathrm{HRD}\ (\%) = C_i/C_{max} \times 100\%,$$

where C_i is the discharge capacity at different discharge current densities ($i=60$, 120, 240, 360 and 480 mA g^{-1}), and C_{max} is the maximum discharge capacity at the discharge currentdensity of 60 mA g^{-1}.

The HRD of $CeMn_{1-x}Al_{1-x}Ni_{2x}$ ($x=0.25$, 0.50 and 0.75) alloy electrodes was shown in Fig. 5. It can be seen that all the discharge capacities decrease with increasing discharge current density, whereas the HRD of $CeMn_{1-x}Al_{1-x}Ni_{2x}$ ($x=0.25$, 0.50 and 0.75) is increased always from 28.54% for $x=0.25$ to 50.73% for $x=0.75$ at 480 mA g^{-1} discharge current density with creasing Ni content. Ni substitution improves the hydrogen absorption/desorption kinetics of these alloys due to catalytic activity of Ni and formation of a secondary phase with catalytic activity [8,9]. It has been found that Ni has a high catalytic activity for the charge transfer reaction in the electrochemical hydrogenation of the metal hydride electrode and leads to increasing exchange current density on the electrode surface [11]. For its lack of electrochemical activity it is of no significance to concern the HRD for CeMnAl.

3.5 Effect of temperature on discharge capacity

Fig. 6 shows the effect of temperature on the discharge capacity of the alloys. The maximum discharge capacities of the alloys increase as temperature increases, and the activation become faster and they need only one cycle to come to their maximum discharge capacities when temperature reaches 308 K. Except for the alloy electrode at $x=0.25$, the other three alloy electrodes achieve their maximum discharge capacities when temperature reaches 328 K, then the maximum discharge capacities decrease as temperature continues to raise. At 328 K, the maximum discharge capacities of $CeMn_{1-x}Al_{1-x}Ni_{2x}$ ($x=0.00$, 0.25, 0.50 and 0.75) alloy electrodes range from 68.42 mAh g^{-1} for $x=0.00$ to 216.1 mAh g^{-1} for $x=0.75$ with increasing Ni content. The increase of maximum discharge capacity is probably ascribed to the decrease of the reaction activation energy of alloy electrode as temperature is elevated, and after 328 K the decrease of discharge capacity is due to much more serious corrosion to the alloy electrodes in a high-temperature alkali electrolyte. Li et al. [12] investigated the high temperature characteristics of $(MmY)_1(NiCoMnAl)_5$ hydrogen storage alloys by ICP-AES analysis and found that at elevated temperature the decrease of discharge capacity of the alloy electrode is owing to the dissolution of Ni, Mn and Al in alkaline electrolyte. Qiao et al. [13] analyzed the KOH electrolyte in which $Ti_{0.17}Zr_{0.08}V_{0.34}Nb_{0.1}Cr_{0.1}Ni_{0.0}$ hydride electrode alloy underwent 100 cycles by ICP-MS method and revealed the capacity decay of the alloy is caused by the dissolution of V and Zr elements.

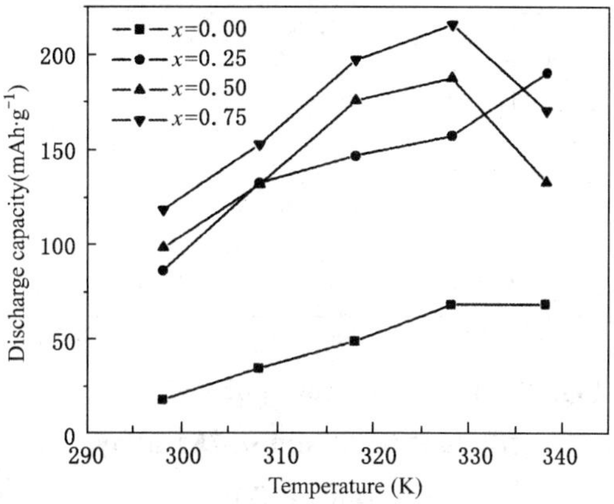

Fig. 6 Discharge capacity of $CeMn_{1-x}Al_{1-x}Ni_{2x}$ ($x=0.00$, 0.25, 0.50 and 0.75) alloy electrode as a function of temperature

3.6 Discharge curves

Fig. 7 shows the discharge curves of $CeMn_{1-x}Al_{1-x}Ni_{2x}$ ($x=0.00$ and 0.75) alloy electrodes at 338 K, and it can be seen that the discharge curve plateau of $CeMn_{1-x}Al_{1-x}Ni_{2x}$ ($x=0.00$ and 0.75) alloy electrodes becomes longer, higher and flatter with increasing x value. Fig. 8 shows the discharge curves of $CeMn_{0.25}Al_{0.25}Ni_{1.5}$ alloy electrodes at 298 and 338 K, respectively. It is seen that the discharge curve of $CeMn_{0.25}Al_{0.25}Ni_{1.5}$ alloy electrode shows two plateaus at elevated temperature (338 K), whereas only one plateau at low temperature (298 K). This indicates that the negative alloy hydride release hydrogen step by step at elevated temperaure, which correlates with different hydrogen phase states of the hydrides. As the reported result by Spatz et al. [3,4], CeMnAl can absorb different amount of hydrogen under different pressures.

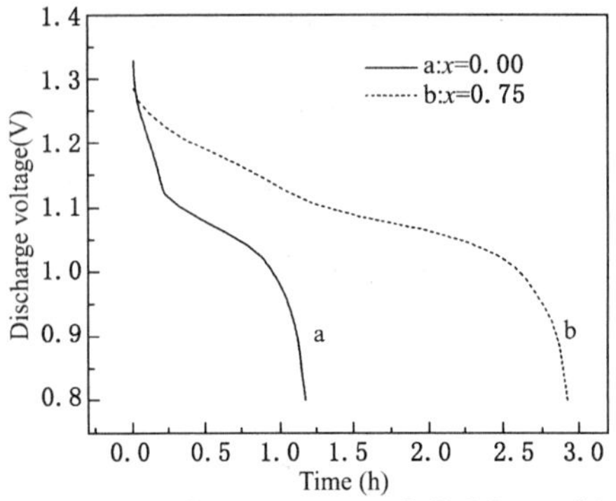

Fig. 7 Discharge curve of $CeMn_{1-x}Al_{1-x}Ni_{2x}$ (x=0.00 and 0.75) alloy electrode at 338 K

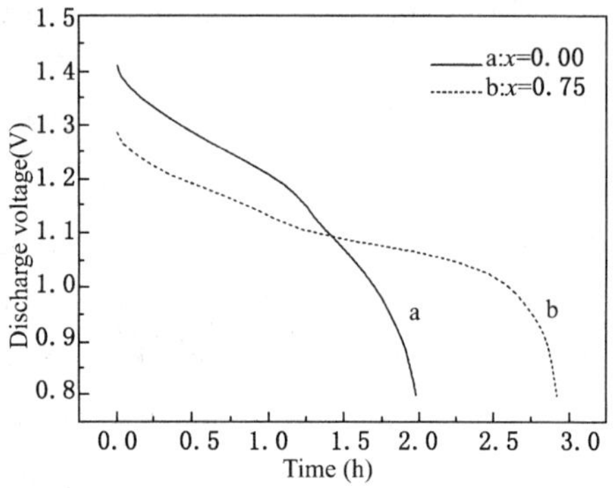

Fig. 8 Discharge curve of $CeMn_{0.25}Al_{0.25}Ni_{1.5}$ alloy electrode at 298 and 338 K

4 Conclusions

(1) Ni partial substitution improves the electrochemical activity of $CeMn_{1-x}Al_{1-x}Ni_{2x}$ (x = 0.00, 0.25, 0.50 and 0.75) and the discharge capacity of $CeMn_{0.25}Al_{0.25}Ni_{1.5}$ alloy electrode amounts to 216.1 mAh g^{-1} at 328 K. The alloy electrode is very easy to be activated and need only two cycles to reach the maximum discharge capacity at 298 K. The HRD of the alloy has been improved appreciably with increasing Ni substitution content.

(2) The improvement of the electrochemical characteristics of $CeMn_{1-x}Al_{1-x}Ni_{2x}$ (x=0.00, 0.25, 0.50 and 0.75) alloys is due to the electrocatalytic Ni partial substitution and the formation of a multi-phase structure of alloy.

(3) The *P-C-T* curves measured by electrochemical method indicate that the slope of the plateau of $CeMn_{1-x}Al_{1-x}Ni_{2x}$ (x=0.00, 0.25, 0.50 and 0.75) alloys become flatter and longer with increasing Ni content.

(4) The hydrogen desorptions of the $CeMn_{1-x}Al_{1-x}Ni_{2x}$ (x=0.00, 0.25, 0.50 and 0.75) alloy hydrides are carried out step by step. When at a hydrogen pressure of less than 10^{-3} MPa the hydrides desorb only a small amount of hydrogen and then as the temperature rises, the amounts of hydrogen desorption of metal hydrides increases.

Acknowledgments

This work is supported by Foundation of Key Laboratory of Rare Earth Chemistry and Physics, Chinese Academy of Sciences. And we also wish to thank Dr. Wentao Hu and Ms. Yan Wang of State Key Laboratory of Metastable Materials Science and Technology, Yanshan University for XRD analysis and SEM-EDS analysis.

References

[1] Hu Z. Hydrogen storage materials [M]. Beijing: Chemical Industrial Publishing House; 2002. p. 45 [in Chinese].

[2] Yan Y, Yan K, Chen Y Progress in research

of V-based solid solution hydrogen storage alloy. Chin J Rare Met 2004;28:738-43 [in Chinese].

[3] Spatz P, Gross KJ, Zuttel A, Schlapbach L Hydriding, properties of $Ce(Mn, Al)_2$ and $Ce(Fe, Al)_2$ intermetallic compounds. J Alloys Compd 1997;260:211-6.

[4] Spatz P, Gross K, Zuttel A, Fauth F, Fischer P $CeMnAlH_x$, a new metal hydride. J Alloys Compd 1997;261:263-8.

[5] Gross KJ, Chartouni D. Fauth F A new hexagonal Laves phase deuteride $CeMn_{1.5}Al_{0.5}D_x$ $(0<x<4)$ investigated by in situ neutron diffraction. J Alloys Compd 2000;06:203-18.

[6] Filinchuk YE, Sheptyakov D, Hilscher G, Yvon K. Hydrogenation induced valence change and metal atom site exchange at room temperature in the C14-type substructure of $CeMn_{1.8}Al_{0.2}H_{4.4}$. J Alloys Compd 2003;356-357:673-8.

[7] Chartouni D, Zuttel A, Nutzenadel C, Gross K, Schlapbach L, Guther V, Otto A. Electrochemical properties of $Zr(V_xNi_{1-x})_3$ as electrode material in nickel-metal hydride batteries. Int J Hydrogen Energy 1999;24:229-33.

[8] Chai Y, Zhao M. Structure and electrochemical properties of $Ti_{0.25}V_{0.35}Cr_{0.40-x}Ni_x$ (x=0. 05—0. 40) solid solution alloys. Int J Hydrogen Energy 2005;30:279-83.

[9] Notten PHL, Hokkeling P Double-phase hydride forming compounds: a new class of highly electrocatalytic materials. J Electrochem Soc 1991;138:1877-85.

[10] Kondo M, Asano K, Iijima Y Effect of nickel addition and microstructure on absorption and desorption behavior of hydrogen in $LaNi_5$. J Alloys Compd 2005;393:269-73.

[11] Lee H-H, Lee K-Y, Lee J-Y The Ti-based metal hydride electrode for Ni-MH rechargeable batteries. J Alloys Compd 1996;239:63-70.

[12] Li R, Wu J, Qi Y, Zhou S. Study of the high temperature characteristics of hydrogen storage alloys. J Alloys Compd 2005;388:138-44.

[13] Qiao Y -Q, Zhao M-S, Li M-Y, Zhu X-J, Cao G-Y Microstructure and electrochemical characteristics of $Ti_{0.17}Zr_{0.08}V_{0.34}Nb_{0.01}Cr_{0.1}Ni_{0.3}$ hydride alloy. Chin J Inorg Chem 2006;22(3):415-20 [in Chinese].

二、熔融盐化学和电化学

Research on Chemical Metallurgy of AI-LI Master Alloy in Molten Salt①

M. Zhao, Y. Zhang, K. Chang, D. Tang
(Changchun Institute of Applied Chemistry
Academia Sinica. Changchun 130 022. P. R. China)

Abstract: The chlorination process of Li_2CO_3 by NH_4Cl has been studied by two thermal analysis methods: DTA and DSC, and has been used in the determination of the ternary phase diagram of LiCl-KCL-LiF successfully. Transformation yield of Li_2CO_3 is 98.87%. The X-ray diffraction analysis of the product clearly shows that only LiCl is formed in the chlorination reaction. Seven vertical cross-sections of LiCl-KCl-LiF ternary system have been measured respectively. The ternary phase diagram of LiCl-KCl-LiF is obtained. The minimum eutectic point of this system is 348 ℃, with the composition of 41.4 KCl+57.3 LiCl+1.3 LiF (mol%). The deposition potential differce between Li(Ⅰ) and Na(Ⅰ) on aluminum electrode from the experiment is +0.27 V(E_{Li}-E_{Na}), while the potential difference of −0.17 V is obtained on inert molybdenum cathode. The difference of deposition potential results from the depolarization caused by the alloying of lithium with aluminium cathode. As a sequence, lithium ion can deposit before sodiumion. And this is a ground for the electrodeposition of hiqh purity Al-Li master alloy on aluminium electrode.

The co-deposition of process of Li(Ⅰ) with RE(Ⅲ) has been studied by linear scan voltammetry, cyclic voltammetry and current reversal chronopotentiometry. Both the electrochemical study and the electrolytic results clearly show that Li(Ⅰ) and RE(Ⅲ) can co-deposit on the aluminium-copper electrode.

Introduction

Aluminium-lithium alloy has been used by a number of aerospace companies and it shows an evergrowing application prospect in the future. But due to the technical problemsencountered in the physical metallurgy process, such as the problem associated with the high active lithium metal and the large spcific weight difference between lithium and aluminium. The Al-Li master alloy with lithium content of 8—10 wt%, as a substitute for lithium metal, is being paid close attentions to in the recent years. The study of physicochemical properties of the electro-

① Materials Science Forum, 1991(73-75): 637-642.

lytic melt, the depolarization on molten aluminium electrode and the co-deposition of lithium with rare earth have been carried out in our laboratory for chemical metallurgy of Al-Li master alloy. A brief summary is given here.

EXPERIMENT AND DiSCUSSION

1 Chlorination of Li_2CO_3 by NH_4Cl

A binary chloride or ternary chloride-fluoride is widely used in the preparation of Al-Li master alloy. But LiCl absorbs moisture very easily, causing troubles in the electrolysis process. The chlorination reaction of Li_2CO_3 by NH_4Cl has been studied by thermal analysis and has been used in the determination of ternarv phase diagram containing LiCl Successfully.

1.1 Determination of Transformation Yield of Li_2CO_3 by Dta

When the mole ratio of NH_4Cl to Li_2CO_3 equals 4, only LiCl peaks are observed on the DTA curve.

1.2 X-ray Diffraction Analysis

The X-ray diffraction diaqram of the chlorination product clearly shows that only the LiCl peaks are observed.

1.3 Determination of Conversion Yielld of Li_2CO_3 by Dsc

Having been heated up to 400 ℃ in thermal balance, the mixture of NH_4Cl and Li_2CO_3 (4 : 1 mole) is transfered to DSC analyser, then DSC curve is plotted and VANTHOFF curve is plotted automaticaily. The purity of LiCl Product, calculated from the VAN ' THOFF curve, is 98.87%. Result of ion chromatography shows that carbonate content in LiCl is lower than 1%, agreeing with the DSC result very well. The purity of Li_2CO_3 used in this experiment is 98%, therefore it can be included that Li_2CO_3 is completely converted into LiCl.

2 Ternary Phase Diagram of LiCl-KCl-LiF

2.1 Application of Chlorination of Li_2CO_3 by NH_4Cl in Binary Phase Diagram Containing LiCl

The binary phase diagrams of LiCl-KCl, LiCl-LiF and LiCl-NaCl determined by the chlorination reaction have been drawn. The characterization data from the phase diaqrams agree with those of literatures very well.

2.2 Ternary Phase Diagram of LiCl-KCl-LiF

This ternary phase diagram has not been yet reported in literatures. In order to gain a full view of the ternary phase diagram, seven vertical cross-sections have been drawn. Eutectic temperature and composition of the each cross-section are listed in Table 1. The projection diagram of liquidus isothermal lines is shown in Fig. 1.

The phase transformation temperatures of various compositions located in the triangle formed by point 9 LiF+27 KCl +64 LiCl, point 6.5 LiF+32.5 KCl +61.0 LiCl and point 58 LiCl+42 KCl (mole %) are listed in Table 2.

The minimum eutectic temperature of the system is 348 ℃, the corresponding composition is nearly 41.4 KCl+57.3 LiCl

+1.3 LiF (mole %), just lying around the intersect of three-phase lines in Fig. 1.

3 Deposition Potentials of Li (Ⅰ) and Na (Ⅰ) on Liquid Cathode and Depolarization

Deposition potentiala of Li(Ⅰ) and Na(Ⅰ) on various liquid cathodes are listed in Table 3 and 4. The deposition potential differences calculated from table 3 and 4 are presented in Table 5. The electrode potential difference of lithium and sodinum in chloride is −0.18 V in literature(1). The experimental value got by Cambi(2) is −0.02 V. In the paper, the value is around −0.17 V in the binary chloride melt at 700 ℃. It can be concluded that deposition of Li (Ⅰ) occures after Na (Ⅰ) in terms of normal elec-trochemical series in pure or mixed chlorides. However, while depositing on aluminium electrode, lithium can strongly alloy with the cathode, which will lead to a strong depolarization, and therefore move the deposition potential difference from −0.17 V to +0.27 V. This is the reason why lithium ion can deposit before sodium ion.

4 Co-deposition of Lithium With Rare Earth in Molten Chloride

4.1 Potential Sweep Voltammetry

Linear scan voltammograms of LiCl (70%)-KCl (29%)-$LaCl_3$ (1wt%) on aluminium-copper electrode are shown in Fig. 2. only mixed deposition potential is obtained on curve 3 in Fig. 2. In order to determine the substances deposited at mixed deposition potential, electrolysis was performed for 15 minutes at the mixed potential. Analysis of the cathode proves the deposition of lithium by XPS and rare earth element in the cathode can be demonstrated by SEM. Fig. 3 is cyclic voltammogram of LiCl(70%)-KCl(29%)-$PrCl_3$(1 wt%) on Al-Cu electrode.

4.2 Current Reversal Chronopotentiommetry

Fig. 4 presents a current reversal chronopotentiogram on Al-Cu electrode in LiCl-KCl-$LaCl_3$. Only one plateau at −2.1 V was observed during cathodic pulse, while two plateaus were observed on reversal of the current. One corresponds to dissolution of lithium and the other one stands for dissolution of rare earth element, agreeing with that from potential scan voltammetry.

4.3 Electrolytic Result

Four constant-current electrolysis have been taken in laboratory scale, with lithium content of 0.18% and rare earth content of 0.2%—0.35% in cathode product, which gives a further verification of the co-deposition of lithium with rare earth element.

References

[1] W. Hamer et al, J. Electrochem. Soc. 103(1), 8(1956).

[2] Cambi et al, Gazz. Chim. Ital. 57, 836(1927).

Table 1 Eutectic Temperature and Composition at Each Cross-section

	cross-section	composition(mol %)	eutectic temperature(℃)
Ⅰ	LiCl:KCL+LiF	6.5LiF	436
Ⅱ	LiCl:3KCL+LiF	14.0LiF	620
Ⅲ	5KCL:LiF+LiCl	15.0LiCl	700
		61.0LiCl	375
Ⅳ	3KCl:LiF+LiCl	64.0LiCl	410
Ⅴ	KCl:LiF+LiCl	69.0LiCl	442
Ⅵ	KCL:3LiF+LiCl	70.5LiCl	465
Ⅶ	LiCl:LiF+KCl	72.5KCl	700

Table 2 Phase Transformation Temperatures of Various Compositions near Minimum Eutectic Composition

Composition (mol %)			1st transition point(℃)	2nd transition point(℃)	3rd transition point(℃)
KCL+LiCl+LiF					
40.9	56.6	2.6	375	375	348
40.6	56.0	3.4	406	352	348
41.4	57.3	1.3	350	350	348
42.2	53.8	4.0	395	355	348
38.4	57.7	3.9	410	410	348
38.7	58.1	3.2	382	382	348

Table 3 Deposition Potential of Li(Ⅰ) in LiCl-KCl System (VS · Ag/AgCl, x=0.1)

cathode	potential(v)						
	660 ℃	680 ℃	700 ℃	720 ℃	740 ℃	760 ℃	780 ℃
Mo	−2.64	−2.60	−2.56	−2.53	−2.48	−2.44	−2.42
Cu	—	—	—	−2.54	−2.50	−2.49	−2.46
Al	—	−2.16	−2.12	−2.11	−2.06	−2.03	−2.00
Al-Cu(20Wt%)	−2.10	−2.08	−2.07	−2.06	−2.03	−2.00	−1.98
Al-Cu(15Wt%)	−2.12	−2.09	−2.07	−2.06	−2.04	−2.01	−1.98
Al-Cu(10Wt%)	−2.14	−2.10	−2.09	−2.07	−2.04	−2.01	−1.98
Al-Cu(6Wt%)	−2.16	−2.12	−2.10	−2.08	−2.05	−2.01	−2.00
Al-RE(6Wt%)	—	—	—	−2.06	−2.04	−2.02	−2.00

Table 4　Deposition Potential of Na(Ⅰ) in NaCl-KCl Melt(VS. Ag/AhCl　$x=0.1$)

potential(v)						
cathode	680 ℃	700 ℃	720 ℃	740 ℃	760 ℃	780 ℃
Mo	−2.44	−2.39	−2.35	−2.30	−2.26	−2.20
Cu	—	—	−2.35	−2.29	−2.24	−2.20
Al	−2.43	−2.39	−2.36	−2.33	−2.30	−2.27
Al-Cu(20wt%)	−2.43	−2.39	−2.36	−2.33	−2.30	−2.26
Al-RE(6wt%)	—	—	−2.36	−2.33	−2.30	−2.27

Table 5　Deposition Potential Difference* Between Li (Ⅰ) and Na (Ⅰ) from Table (3) and Table (4)

potential(v)						
cathode	680 ℃	700 ℃	720 ℃	740 ℃	760 ℃	780 ℃
Mo	−0.16	−0.17	−0.18	−0.18	−0.18	−0.22
Al	0.27	0.27	0.25	0.27	0.27	0.27
Al-Cu(20wt%)	0.35	0.32	0.30	0.30	0.30	0.28
Al-RE(6wt%)	—	—	0.30	0.29	0.28	0.27

* $=E_{LI}-E_{Na}$

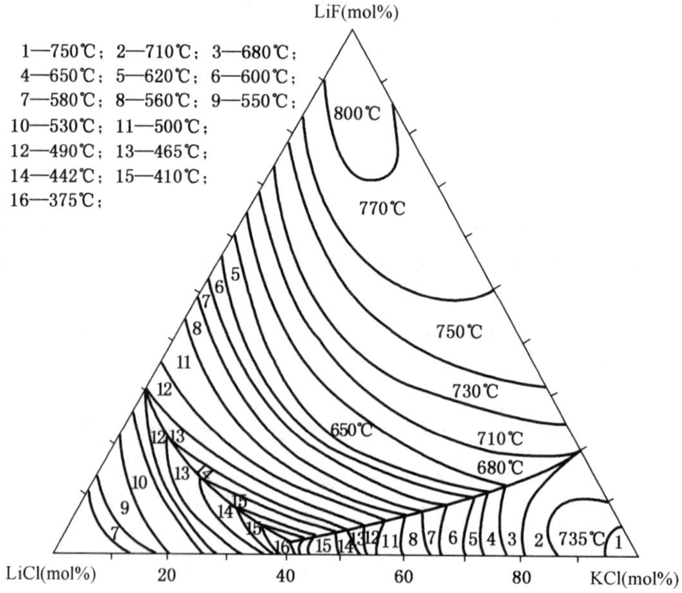

Fig. 1　Projection diagram of liquidus isothermal lines of LiCl-KCl-LiF ternary system

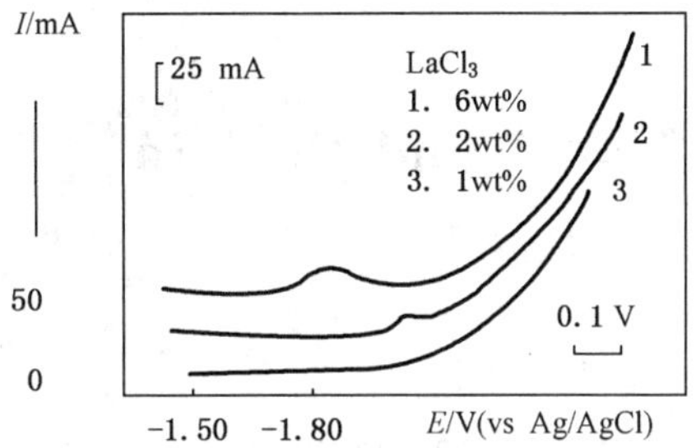

Fig. 2 Polarization curve of Al-Cu cathode in LiCl-KCl-$LaCl_3$ at 1033 K with scanning rate of 0. 25 V/min

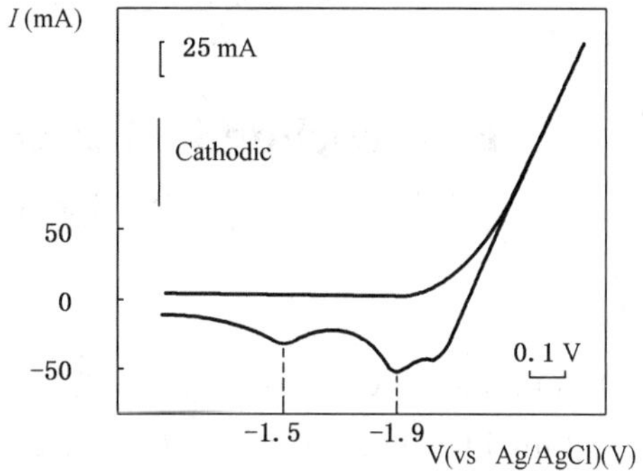

Fig. 3 Typicel volammogram of LiCl-KCl-$PrCl_3$ on Al-Cu electrode at 1033 K with san rate of 0. 3 V/min

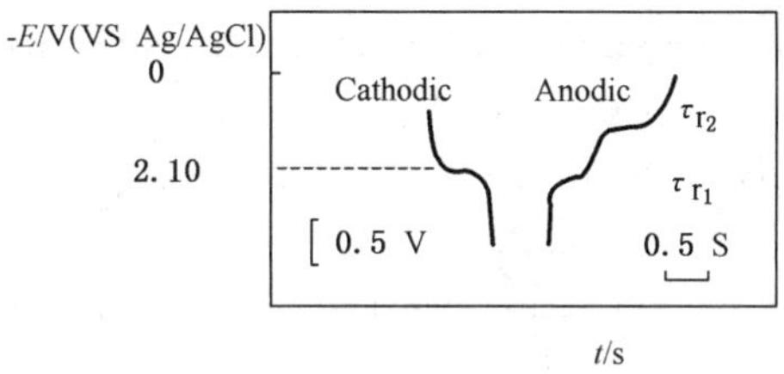

Fig. 4 Typical current reversal chronopotentiogram of LiCl-KCl-$LaCl_3$ on Al-Cu at 1033 K

Electrochemical Behavior of Nd^{3+} and Ho^{3+} in LiCl-KCl Eutectic Melt①

Zhao Minshou, Lu Xiangping, Liang Jin

(Laboratory of Rare Earth Chemistry and Physics, Changchun Institute of Applied Chemistry, Chinese Academy of Sciences, Changchun 130022, China)

Abstract: The electrochemical behavior of Nd^{3+} and Ho^{3+} ions on molybdenum electrode in the LiCl-KCl eutectic melts has been studied by cyclic voltammetry and open-circuit potentiometry. The results show that the reduction process of Nd^{3+} and Ho^{3+} ions on molybdenum electrode is one-step three electron reversible reaction. The diffusion coefficients of Nd^{3+} and Ho^{3+} ions are $1.13 \times 10^{-6}\ cm^2 \cdot s^{-1}$ (450 ℃) and $2.142 \times 10^{-5}\ cm^2 \cdot s^{-1}$ (450 ℃), respectively. The measured standard electrode potential of Ho^{3+}/Ho is 2.987 V(vs. Cl/Cl^-), being more negative than the theoretical one, the reason of which is also discussed.

Key words: Rare earths; Neodymium; Holmium; Diffusion coefficient; Electrode potential

The electrochemical behavior of rare earth elements in molten chloride has been an interesting project for many years [1-7]. The reason is that chloride melt has been usually used for the preparation of most light rare earth metals and mixed rare earth metal, and the interest is also on the alloying on the electrode surface or the research on the electrochemical behavior of synthesizing intermetallic compounds in molten salts system [8-12]. Its electrochemical perspective is very wide and other molten systems such as the low-temperature molten system can not match with it. This paper reports the latest results of the electrochemical behavior of Nd^{3+} and Ho^{3+} ions in LiCl-KCl eutectic melt as a part of the research project on the electrochemical process of lanthanide elements in molten salt system.

1 Experimental Procedure

The experiment procedure, apparatus and preparation of the rare earth chloride were described in our earlier reported paper [13]. Here, we only emphasized the preparation of LiCl-KCl eutectic melts. For LiCl salt has stronger hygroscopicity than other alkaline chlorides, so it was predehydrated under vacuum at 120 ℃ ~ 180 ℃ for at least 48 h. Then the prepared LiCl-KCl salts were molten under argon atmosphere. After addition of RCl_3, dry HCl gas was bubbled through the melt for 30 min to eliminate the water-insoluble substances. Residual

① Journal of Rare Earths, 1997, 15(2): 103-106.

HCl was removed from the melt by bubbing with pure argon gas. One hour later, experiment was performed under argon atmosphere. Ag/AgCl ($x=0.1$) was used as reference electrode, a spectral pure graphite rod as counter electrode and a molybdenum wire as the working electrode .

2 Results and Discussion

2.1 Electrochemical reduction of Nd^{3+} ion

To avoid the disturbance caused by the reduction of Li^{+} ion, reversal scanning was carried out as soon as the current peak occurs. The cyclic voltammogram of Nd^{3+} ion with different scanning rates is shown in Fig. 1 with starting cathodic potential=2.0 V. It is obvious that both the cathodic and anodic peak potentials do not depend on the scanning rate. There is a very good linear relationship between the cathodic peak currentsip and the square root of scanning rate $v^{1/2}$ (as shown in Fig. 2). The solubility of Nd metal in its chloride is the largest among the rare earth elements, so considering its product soluble is rational. In addition, as shown in Fig. 3, a good line would be obtained by plotting E against $\ln[(i_p-i)/i]$. These are the typical features for the reversible reaction with soluble product . From the slop of the Fig. 3, the calculated number of electron transfered is 2.86, close to 3. So the reaction $Nd^{3+}+3e=Nd$ would follow the equation [14].

$$i_p = 0.4463\, nFAc(nF/RT)^{1/2} v^{1/2} D_0^{1/2} \tag{1}$$

Where, A is electrode area ; c the concentration of the electroactive species; v scanning rate; D_0 ion diffusion coefficient, and so is below .

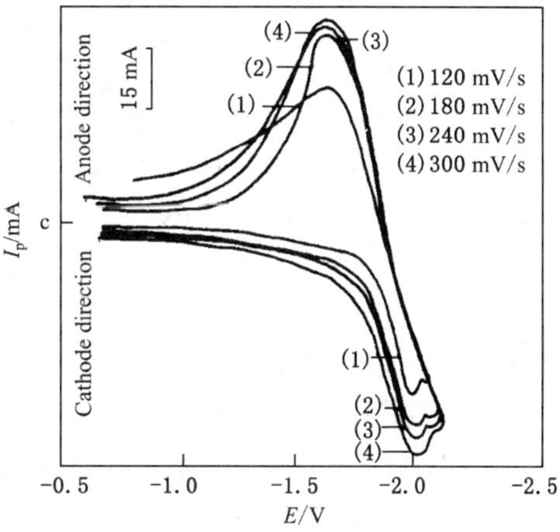

Fig. 1 Cyclic voltammogram of Nd^{3+} on molybdenum electrode in LiCl-KCl eutectic at 450 ℃

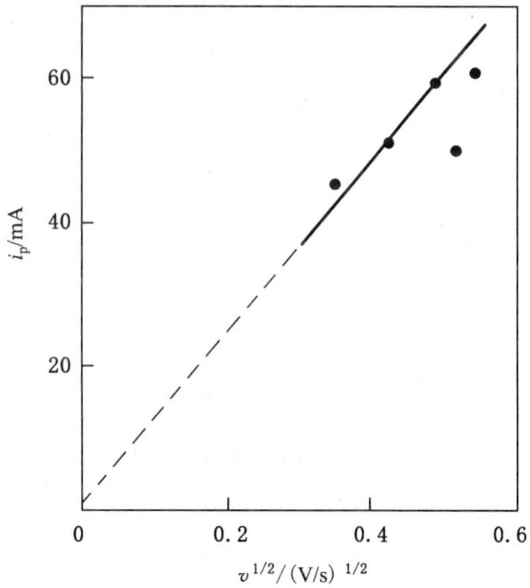

Fig. 2 Relation between i_p and $v^{1/2}$

The diffusion coefficient of Nd^{3+} in the melt calculated from the slop of Fig. 3 and the equation(1) is 1.13×10^{-6} $cm^2\cdot s^{-1}$ (450 ℃).

2.2 Electrochemical reduction of Ho^{3+} ion

A typical cyclic voltammogram of

Ho^{3+} ion is shown in Fig. 4. It is apparent that the cathodic peak potential almost does not shift with scanning rate: Very good linear relationship is obtained for cathodic peak current as a function of the square root of scanning rate $v^{1/2}$. All these prove that the electrochemical reduction reaction is reversible.

As shown in Fig. 4, there is only one reduction peak of Ho^{3+} ion on the molybde-num electrode, so $Ho^{3+} + 3e = Ho$ is a one-step three electron reaction in which is in accordance with the conclusion drawn from the chronopotentiomogram of Ho^{3+} ion.

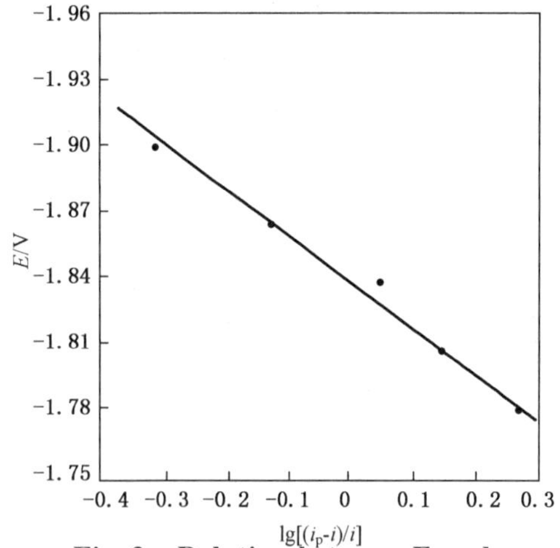

Fig. 3　Relation between E and $\lg[(i_p - i)/i]$

The products of electrochemical reaction of most heavy rare earth ions in their own chloride melts can be regarded as insoluble.

For the reversible electron transfer reaction in which product is insoluble, it's peak current i_p would follow below equation:

$$i_p = 0.6105(nF)^{3/2}(Dv)^{1/2}(RT)^{-1/2}Ac \tag{2}$$

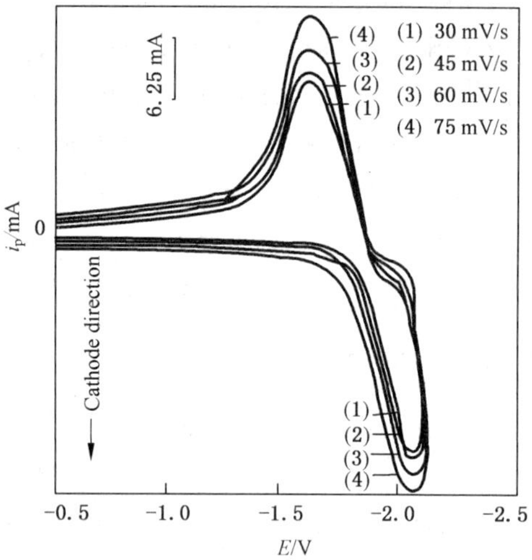

Fig. 4　The cyclic voltammogram of Ho^{3+} on molybdenum electrode in LiCl-KCl eutectic at 450 ℃

The diffusion coefficient of Ho^{3+} ion calculated from the slop of the line (i_p against $v^{1/2}$) is 2.142×10^{-5} cm^2 s^{-1} (450 ℃). The D value of Ho^{3+} ion is bigger than that of Y^{3+} ion. The reason may be that the complexbility of Y^{3+} is stronger than that of Ho^{3+} ion, which leads to larger complex ion .

2.3　Standard electrode potential measurement of Ho^{3+}/Ho couple

Table 1　Standard potentical of Ho^{3+}/Ho at different temperature (vs. Ag/Ag^-Cl, V)

ln x	Equilibrium		Potential
	450 ℃	500 ℃	550 ℃
−6.91	−2.025	−2.004	−1.998
−6.21	−2.021	−1.996	−1.972
−5.81	−2.019	−1.989	−1.961
−5.52	−2.001	−1.980	−1.958
The st andard potential E^0	−1.928	−1.891	−1.837

Open-circuit potentiometry was carried out with different concentrationof Ho^{3+} ion at various temperature to determine its equilibrium potential E. Extraploating the line of E against $\lg x$ to $x=1$, then the standard electrodepotential E^0 at various temperatures can be calculated as listed in Table 1.

The E^0 of Ho^{3+}/Ho at 450 ℃ obtainedin the present work and those of Dy^{3+}/Dy, Y^{3+}/Y measured in our earlier works were presented vs. Cl^-/Cl reference electrode and listed in Table 2 .

Table 2　Experimental and theorctical values of Dy^{3+}/Dy, Y^{3+}/Y and Ho^{3+}/Ho (vs. Cl^-/Cl)

	Theoreti cal values/V	Experimental values/V	Differences/V	Reference
Dy^{3+}/Dy	−2.902	−3.139	0.239	[2]
Y^{3+}/Y	−2.858	−3.174	0.316	[3]
Ho^{3+}/Ho	−2.830	−2.987	0.157	This work

The measured values E^0 of Dy^{3+}/Dy, Y^{3+}/Y and Ho^{3+}/Ho are all more negative than the theoretical ones,it may relate to the molten salts salts solvation . The difference between experimental value and the theoretical one may be regarded as an index of solvation degree.

References

[1] Zhang Xiaolian, Zhao Minshou. J. Rare Earths,1991,9(3):177.

[2] Chang Kaiguo,Zhao Minshou. Chinese Journal of Chemistry,1991,1:27.

[3] Zhao Minshou,Hikino S,Xie Gang,Ema K, Ito Y. J. Electrochem. Soc., 1992, 39 (7):1820.

[4] Duan Shuzheng,Zhou Chungeng,Qiao Zhiyu, Zhai Qing,Wu Siming. Journal of the Chinese Rare Earth Society (Chin.), 1992, 10 (2):116.

[5] Yang Qiqin, Hong Huijuan, Wu Zherong. Journal of the Chinese Rare Earth Society (Chin.),1989,7(1):1.

[6] Lu Qintao,Ye Yunw ei,Li Guoxun,Ye Shangyun. Journal of the Chinese Rare Earth Society (Chin.),1991,9(1),17.

[7] Qiao Z Y,Duan S,Inman D. J. Appl. Eletrochem.,1989,19:937.

[8] Xie G,Ema K,Ito Y,Zhao Minshou. J. Applied Electrochem.,1993,23:753.

[9] Yang Qiqin, Qiu Kairong, Liu Guankun, Zheng Ruiguang. Journal of the Chinese Rare Earth Society(Chin.),1994,12(2):116.

[10] Liu Guankun, Hun Huijuan, Yang Qiqin, Huang Taidou. Journal of the Chinese Rare Earth Society(Chin.),1994,12(4):309.

[11] Yang Qiqin,Liu Guankun,Shu Yuzhi. Electrochemistry.,1994,1(1):44.

[12] Zhou Chungen, Duan Shuzheng. Electrochemistry,1995,1(1):94.

[13] Tateiwa K,Tada M,Ito Y. Surface Technology(in Japanese).,1995,46(7):672.

[14] Zhao Minshou,Tang Ding xiang. The Collected Papers of Changchun Insitute of Applied Chemistry,Chinese Academy of Sciences(in Chin.),1981,20:91 .

[15] Bard A J,Faulkner L R . Editors Electrochemical Methods,Fundamental and Applications,New York:John Wiley and Sons, 1980,218.

[16] Berzins T,Delahay P. J. Am. Chem. Soc., 1953,75:555.

熔融氯化物中钕和钇在液体阴极上析出电位的研究①

赵敏寿　赵奇金　唐定骧
（中国科学院长春应用化学研究所）

摘　要：用线性扫描伏-安法研究了等摩尔 KCl · NaCl 熔体中钕和钇离子在锑、铋、铝、镓、锡、锌、铅、铟八种液体阴极和固体钼阴极上析出电位，求出了析出电位差 $\Delta\varphi$。产生 $\Delta\varphi$ 的原因是稀土在液体阴极中的活度比在固体阴极上低，使析出电位向正移，同时也由于稀土与液体阴极合金化产生去极化作用的结果。稀土金属和液体阴极材料的电负性差越大，$\Delta\varphi$ 也越大，还研究了稀土氯化物浓度和熔体温度对稀土离子析出电位和 $\Delta\varphi$ 的影响，给出了相应的关系式。

Investigation of Deposition Potential of Neodymium and Yttrium Ions on Liquid Cathodes in Molten Chloride

Zhao Minshou　Zhao Qijin　Tang Dingxiang
(Changchun Institute of Applied Chemistry, Academia Sinica)

Abstract: Deposition potentials of neodymium and yttrium ions on liquid Sb, Bi, Al, Ga, Sn, Zn, Pb and In cathodes and Solid Mo cathode in equimolar KCl · NaCl have been studied using technique of potential sweep voltammetry. The deposition potential differences between liquid cathodes and Mo cathode $\Delta\varphi$ have been calculated. These differences are not only due to decreased activity of neodynium and yttrium in liquid cathodes, shifting deposition potentials to oppositive direction but also the depolarization effect caused by alloying neodymium and yttrium with liquid cathode. The greater electronegativity differences between rare earth metals and liquid cathode materials, the greater is $\Delta\varphi$. Effects of $NdCl_3$ and YCl_3 concentrations and temperature of the melt on deposition potentials of neodymium and yttrium ions and $\Delta\varphi$ have been studied as well. Corresponding equations are given.

一、前言

随着液体阴极制取稀土中间合金工作的发展，液体阴极化过程研究已有一些报道[1-3]。钕和铒在铅阴极上的极化过程研究[4]，镧系和钇十五种稀土离子在液体铝阴极上的析出电化序工作，都取得了可喜的结果[5]。

① 中国稀土学报，1983，1(2)：41-46.

本工作研究碱金属氯化物熔体中，钕和钇在液体阴极上的极化过程，并测定钕和钇离子的析出电位。探讨钕和钇在液体阴极上析出电位较在惰性阴极上明显偏正的原因，是稀土熔盐化学的基础研究课题之一，也为制取稀土中间合金寻找适宜的阴极材料和选择工艺参数提供依据。

二、实验程序和装置

电解槽结构和实验装置见文献[5]。实验在氩气保护下进行，用上升线性波电位扫描，扫描范围 0～2.5 伏，周期 10 分钟。用银一氯化银参比电极。固体钼电极 $S_{固}=0.225$ 厘米^2，最大电流密度 $d_{max}=4.55$ 安/厘米^2，液体阴极面积 $S_{液}=1.31$厘米^2，最大电流密度 $d_{max}=0.76$ 安/厘米^2。

三、实验结果和讨论

（一）钕和钇在钼和液体阴极上的析出电位

800 ℃下等摩尔 KCl・NaCl 熔体中，钕和钇在固体钼及液体阴极上析出电位和两者之间的电位差 $\Delta\varphi$，列于表 1。

由表 1 得知：钕和钇离子在各种液体阴极上的析出电位较在固体钼上分别偏正 0.86～1.23 伏和 0.66～1.13 伏。这与钕和钇在液体阴极中的活度降低有关。由 $\varphi=\varphi_o+\dfrac{RT}{nF}\ln\dfrac{a_{L_n^{3+}}}{a_{L_n^o}}$ 知，当 $a_{L_n^o}<1$ 时，较之固体钼阴极 $a_{L_n^o}=1$ 的情况下，φ 要向正方向偏移。若阴极中稀土金属的浓度（活度）低至 10^{-11}（摩尔分数）数量级以下，可使 φ 偏正 0.8 伏以上（$t=800$ ℃），这在稀土离子开始析出的瞬间是完全可能达到的。

表 1　钕和钇在钼和液体阴极上的析出电位

（$t=800$ ℃，$\varphi_{cl^-/cl_2}=0$，$X_{NdCl3}=X_{NYCl_3}=1.75\times10^{-2}$）

Table1　Deposition potentials of neodymium ion and yttrium ion on liquid cathodes at 800 ℃

Nd								
阴极金属	Mo	Sb	Bi	Ga	Sn	Zn	Pb	In
析出电位(φ)，伏	−3.28	−2.05	−2.21	−2.23	−2.25	−2.38	−2.40	−2.42
电位差($\Delta\varphi$)，伏		1.23	1.07	1.05	1.03	0.90	0.88	0.86
Y								
阴极金属	Mo	Sb	Bi	Sn	Al	Pb	In	Zn
析出电位*(φ)伏	−3.31	−2.18	−2.29	−2.40	−2.43	−2.59	−2.59	−2.65
电位差($\Delta\varphi$)，伏		1.13	1.02	0.91	0.88	0.72	0.72	0.66

误差按 $\delta=\sqrt{\sum \varepsilon i^2/n}$计算，范围为±0.02 伏。

钕离子在各种液体阴极上析出电位依锑、铋、镓、钖、锌、铅、铟的顺序变负。在固、液体阴极上析出电位差 $\Delta\varphi$ 的顺序为：锑＞铋＞镓＞钖＞锌＞铅＞铟。将此顺序和元素周期表对照发现：同一周期的金属做阴极时，$\Delta\varphi$ 从左向右递增（锑＞钖＞铟；铋＞铅；镓＞锌）；同一族金属做阴极时，$\Delta\varphi$ 自上而下减小（锑＞铋；镓＞铟；钖＞铅）。显然，这样的顺序和阴极金属的电负性规律基本一致[6]。也就是说，随着液体阴极金属电负性的增大，$\Delta\varphi$ 也变大。

钇离子在各种液体阴极上析出电位大小的顺序基本上与钕离子析出时一致，

只有锌阴极例外，这可能和锌阴极的特殊极化过程有关。

在所研究的阴极上，钇离子的析出电位均较钕离子偏负，与纯氯化钇和氯化钕理论分解电位序相反。这是由于钇离子（离子半径 0.88Å）的熔剂化作用较钕离子（离子半径 0.99A）强所致。钕离子在钼和各种液体阴极析出电位差 $\Delta\varphi$ 较钇离子在相应阴极析出电位差大，这与钕较钇和液体阴极金属电负性差值更大相一致[6]。

为了进一步研究钕和钇在液体阴极上析出电位较在固体钼阴极上向正偏移的原因，我们对钕在锑阴极，钇在锡和锌阴极上电沉积后的样品进行了 *X* 射线衍射分析，见图 1，衍射图表明：钕和钇与液体阴极生成了多种金属间化合物。这有力地揭示了合金化作用是钕和钇在液体阴极上较在固体钼阴极上的析出电位向正方向偏移的重要原因。

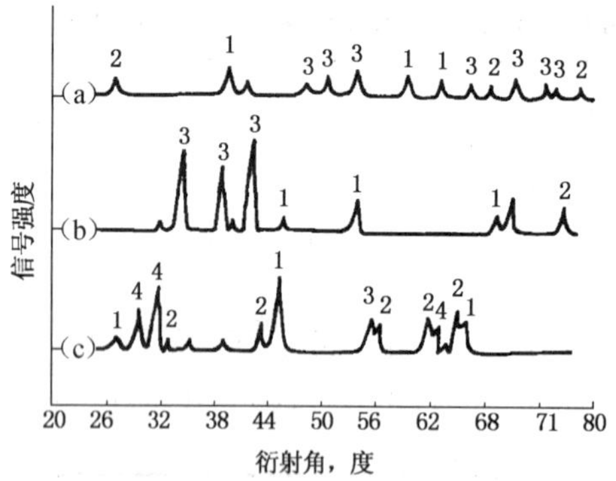

图 1　沉积在锑阴极上的钕和沉积在锡和锌阴极上的钇的 X 射线衍射图

Fig. 1　X-ray diffraction diagram of neodymium deposited on Sb cathode and yttrium deposited on Sn and Zn cathodes

(a) 1—NdSb；2—Nd；3—Sb(b) 1—YZn5；2—Y_2Zn_{17}；3—Zn(c) 1—$Sn_{10}Y_5$；2—$Sn_{10}Y_{11}$；3—Sn_4Y_5；4—Sn

（二）YCl_3-KCl. NaCl 熔体中锌阴极的极化过程

YCl_3-KCl · NaCl 熔体中，锌阴极的伏-安曲线如图 2 所示，这在所研究的液态阴极极化过程中是特殊的。

图 2 中 a 区是锌阴极在熔体中腐蚀溶解的 Zn^{2+} 放电，b 区可能是钇离子在 ZnO 上析出，这与锂离子在锌阴极上析出相似；c 区相应为钇离子在锌上析出。由 d 区可见，当电流密度＞0.46 安/厘米^2 时，碱金属开始析出。

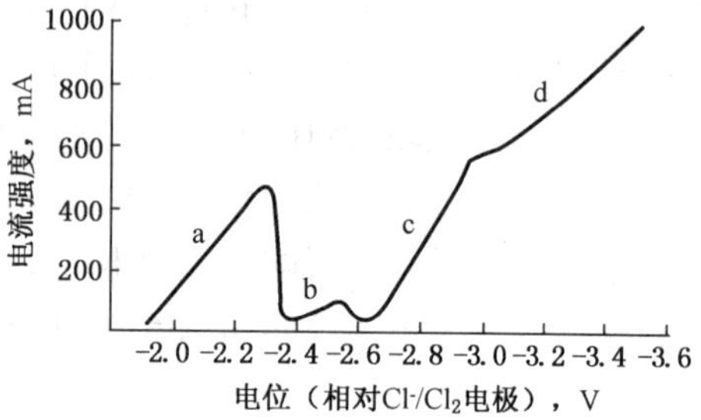

图 2　YCl_3－KCl · NaCl 熔体中锌阴极的极化曲线（X_{YCl_3}＝1.75×10^{-2}）

Fig. 2　Polarization curve of Zn cathode in YCl_3-KCl · NaCl melt at 800 ℃

（三）温度对钕和钇析出电位的影响

不同温度下，钕在钼、铅和锑阴极，钇在钼和锡阴极上析出电位的实验结果列于表 2，并用线性回归法给出了析出电位与温度（700～850 ℃）的关系式。

钕和钇在钼或液体阴极上的析出电位，都是随着温度升高向正向偏移，而温度对 $\Delta\varphi$ 的影响较小。

（四）稀土氯化物浓度对钕和钇析出电位的影响

氯化钕和氯化钇浓度分别对钕在钼和锑阴极，钇在钼和锡阴极析出电位影响的实验结果列于表 3，并给出了钕和钇在钼阴极上析出电位与它们氯化物浓度的关系式。

表 2 不同温度下钕和钇在阴极上的析出电位

（$\varphi_{cl/cl_2}=0$，$X_{NdCl_3}=X_{YCl_3}=1.75\times10^{-2}$）

Table 2 Deposition potentials of neodymium and yttrium on the cathods at different temperatures

温度 ℃	钕的析出电位，伏					钇的析出电位，伏		
	Mo	Pb		Sb		Mo	Sn	
	ϕ	ϕ	$\Delta\phi$	ϕ	$\Delta\phi$	ϕ	ϕ	$\Delta\phi$
700	−3.35	−2.46	0.89	−2.14	1.21	−3.51	−2.46	1.05
750	−3.33	−2.42	0.91	−2.10	1.23	−3.44	−2.43	1.01
800	−3.28	−2.40	0.88	−2.05	1.23	−3.31	−2.40	0.91
850	−3.26	−2.37	0.89	−2.00	1.26	−3.27	−2.35	0.92
析出电位与温度的关系（700～850 ℃）	$\varphi_{Mo}=-3.80\pm0.01+6.4\times10^{-4}t$ $\varphi_{Pb}=-2.86\pm0.01+5.8\times10^{-4}t$ $\varphi_{Sb}=-2.80\pm0.01+9.4\times10^{-4}t$					$\varphi_{Mo}=-4.70\pm0.03+1.7\times10^{-3}t$ $\varphi_{Sn}=-2.970\pm0.01+7.2\times10^{-4}t$		

表 3 $NaCl_3$ 和 YCl_3 浓度对钕和钇在阴极析出电位的影响（$\varphi_{cl^-cl_2}=0$，t=800 ℃）

Table 3 Influence of $NdCl_3$ and YCl_3 concentrations on deposition potentials of neodymiumion and yttrium ion on the cathods

$NdCl_3$ 浓度 （X）	阴极析出电位，伏		电位差 $\Delta\varphi$，伏	YCl_3 浓度 （X）	阴极析出电位，伏		电位差 $\Delta\varphi$，伏
	Mo	Sb			Mo	Sn	
0.59×10^{-2}	−3.43	−2.04	1.39	1.00×10^{-2}	−3.43	−2.39	1.04
1.15×10^{-2}	−3.35	−2.04	1.31	1.75×10^{-2}	−3.31	−2.40	0.91
1.75×10^{-2}	−3.28	−2.05	1.23	4.35×10^{-2}	−3.27	−2.39	0.88
3.98×10^{-2}	−3.23	−2.03	1.20	7.44×10^{-2}	−3.20	−2.35	0.85
7.18×10^{-2}	−3.17	−1.99	1.18				
$\varphi_{MO}=-2.90\pm0.02+0.23\lg x$				$\rho_{MO}=-2.94\pm0.03+0.23\lg x$			

$NdCl_3$ 浓度对钕离子在钼阴极析出电位影响的实验关系式与从 Nernst 方程得出的 $\varphi=-2.86+0.213\lg x$（$t=800$ ℃）较好地符合。外推法得到纯 $NdCl_3$（$x=1$）的分解电位（−2.90±0.02 伏）与热力学计算值（−2.86 伏）相近，而在锑阴极上呈现出较复杂的情形。

YCl_3 浓度对钇离子在钼和钖阴极析出电位影响，呈现和 $NdCl_3$ 浓度对钕离子在钼和锑阴极析出电位影响相类似的情况。

我们在实验中发现等摩尔 KCl·NaCl 体系较 YCl_3-KCl·NaCl（$X_{YCl_3}=1.75\times10^{-2}$）在锑和铋阴极上呈现出稍偏正的放电电位。为此，将 YCl_3-KCl·NaCl 体系中锑和铋阴极极化后的样品进行了原子吸收光谱和发射光谱分析。结果表明，阴极中同时含有钾、钠和钇。这说明当 $X_{YCl_3}=1.75\times10^{-2}$ 时，钾，钠和钇能在锑和铋阴极上共同析出，这在稀土中间合金的制备过程中是应当加以避免的。

四、小结

（1）测定了 $NdCl_3$-KCl·NaCl 和 YCl_3-KCl·NaCl 熔体、800 ℃下钕和钇在固体钼以及液体锑、铋、镓、铝、锡、锌、铅和铟阴极上的析出电位。钕和钇在上述液体阴极上析出电位均较在固体钼上明显偏正。其原因是钕和钇在液体阴极中的活度较固体钼上大大降低，以及合金化作用形成金属间化合物所致。在液、固体阴极上析出电位差 $\Delta\varphi$ 随着钕和钇与阴极金属电负性差的增大而增大。

（2）钇在钼和上述各种液体阴极上析出电位较钕为负，这是钇离子的熔剂化作用较钕离子强造成的。钕在液、固体阴极上析出电位差 $\Delta\varphi$ 较钇大，与钕和液体阴极金属电负性差较钇大是一致的。

（3）YCl_3-KCl · NaCl 熔体中，YCl_3 含量低时，锑和铋做阴极易发生钾、钠、钇共析。即锑和铋做为电沉积钇的阴极是不理想的。钇在锌阴极上的极化曲线形状比较复杂。

（4）研究了温度，$NdCl_3$ 和 YCl_3 浓度对钕及钇在钼、铅、锑和锡阴极析出电位的影响，给出了相应的关系式。

参加本工作的还有崔秀珍，杜富英和路连清同志。赵奇金同志现在有色金属研究总院工作。

参考文献

[1] Кокорин, М. Nилр., Изв. ВУЗ, Цветная метаппургия,1969,(4),42.

[2] Голъгштейн, С. Л. и др., Изв. ВУЗ. Цветнаяметаллургня,1976,(6),57.

[3] Буторов. В. П. и др., Изв. ВУЗ. Цвтная металлургня,1971,(3),85.

[4] Баяяов. А. Л., Изв. ВУЗ. Цвтная металлургня, 1969,(2),98.

[5] 赵敏寿、唐定骧等，中国科学院长春应用化学研究所集刊，1983,(20),91.

[6] 尹敬执，申泮文编，基础无机化学，人民教育出版社，1980,52.

Electrochemical Behavior of Yttrium Ion in LiCl-KCl-NaCl Eutectic Melt①

S. Hikino, Gang Xie, K. Ema, Y. Ito
(Department of Nuclear Engineering, Faculty of Engineering,
Kyoto University, Sakyo-ku, Kyoto 606, Japan)
Zhao Min Shou
(Changchun Institute of Applied Chemistry,
Academia Sinica, Changchun 130022 China)

Abstract: The electrochemical reduction of yttrium ion on a molybdenum electrode in a LiCl-KCl-NaCl eutectic melt at 723 K was found to be almost reversible and to proceed by a one-step three electron reaction. The diffusion coefficient *D* of the Y(Ⅲ) ion was measured to be $(3.3\pm0.4)\times10^{-6}\,cm^2\,s^{-1}$ by cyclic voltammetry, $(5.0\pm0.9)\times10^{-6}\,cm^2\,s^{-1}$ by the rotating disk electrode method, and $(7.1\pm0.7)\times10^{-6}\,cm^2\,s^{-1}$ by chronopotentiometry. The *D* values obtained by the latter two methods are in fairly good agreement with each other. The rather low *D* value obtained by cyclic voltammetry might be attributed to the fact that yttrium metal can dissolve slightly in the chloride melt. The standard potential of Y(Ⅲ)/Y(0) couple was determined to be (-3.174 ± 0.006) V (*vs.* Cl_2/Cl^-) by open-circuit potentiometry, (-3.15 ± 0.02) V (*vs.* Cl_2/Cl^-) by the rotating disk electrode method and (-3.16 ± 0.02) V (*vs.* Cl_2/Cl^-) by chronopotentiometry. These three values are in good agreement with each other. Several types of Ni-Y intermetallic compounds were found to be formed on a nickel electrode.

Yttrium is widely used as an alloying element [1]. The preparation of a yttrium containing master alloy, which is the dominant type used in practice, is mainly performed by electrolysis in molten chlorides [2]. However, few papers have dealt with the electrochemical properties of Y(Ⅲ) ion in chloride melt [3-5]. Thus, the present work has been conducted to elucidate the electrochemical behavior of yttrium ion in a 55LiCl-36KCl-9NaCl mole percent (m/o) eutectic at 723 K by cyclic voltammetry, the rotating disk electrode (RDE) method, chronopotentiometry and open-circuit potentiometry at molybdenum and nickel electrodes. The formation of several types of Ni-Y intermet-allic compounds is demonstrated by x-ray diffraction spectra.

---

① J. Electrochem Soc., 1992, 139(7): 1820-1824.

Experimental

LiCl, KCl, and NaCl were all of reagent grade (Wako Chemical Co., Ltd). The anhydrous YCl_3 was obtained by slowly heating a mixture of $YCl_3 \cdot 6H_2O$ and NH_4Cl under vacuum. Molybdenum or nickel wire of 1 mm diam and a molybdenum disk of 7 mm diam were used as the working electrode and RDE, respectively. To measure the electrode potential, a stabilized zirconia-air electrode was used as a quasi-reference electrode [6] for convenience, and the measured values are presented in the figures relative to the M^+/M electrode potential. Here, M represents an alkali metal (Li and Na), and the potential of M^+/M remains constant value, (-3.627 ± 0.006) V *vs.* Cl_2/Cl^-, though the exact composition of M is not defined. A glassy-carbon rod of 5 mm diam was used as the counter electrode. The LiCl-KCl-NaCl eutectic melt was contained in a high purity alumina crucible (99.5% Al_2O_3, SSA-S Nippon Kagaku Togyo Co., Ltd) and heated to be fused under dry argon atmosphere. After anhydrous YCl_3 was added to the eutectic, dry HCl gas was passed through the eutectic for 30 min to eliminate any yttrium oxychloride that may exist in the anhydrous YCl_3 or may be produced during the process of dissolving anhydrous YCl_3. Then dry argon gas was bubbled through the electrolyte for 1 h to purge away residual HCl gas from the melt. All experiments were performed at 723 K. The experimental apparatus was almost the same as previously described [7].

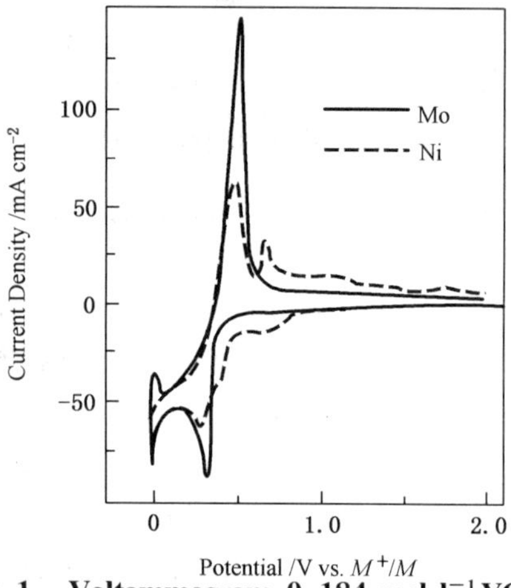

Fig. 1 Voltammogram: 0.184 mol l^{-1} YCl_3, Scan rate: 100 mV/s

Results and Discussion

Electrochemical reduction of Y(Ⅲ) ion. — Figure 1 shows typical cyclic voltammograms obtained for electrochemical reduction of Y(Ⅲ) ion at molybdenum and nickel electrodes. A sharp reduction wave with a peak potential of 0.35 V(*vs.* M^+/M) is observed at a molybdenum electrode; on the other hand, several reduction waves are observed at a nickel electrode. These cathodic peaks all have their corresponding anodic peaks. From the cyclic voltammograms with different scan rates at the Mo electrode, it is found that the cathodic peak potentials hardly change with scan rate. This means that the electrochemical reduction of Y(Ⅲ) ion is actually a reversible process at a molybdenum electrode. In the case where the product, yttrium metal, is hardly soluble, the following formula is preferred for calculating the number of electrons involved in the electrode reaction [8,9]

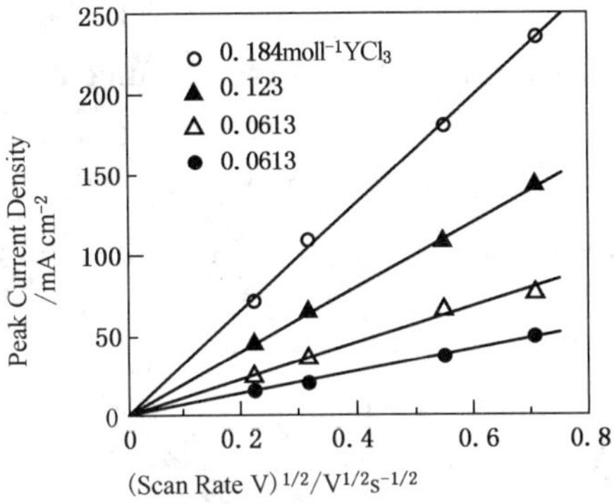

Fig. 2 Peak cerrent density vs. square root of scan rate

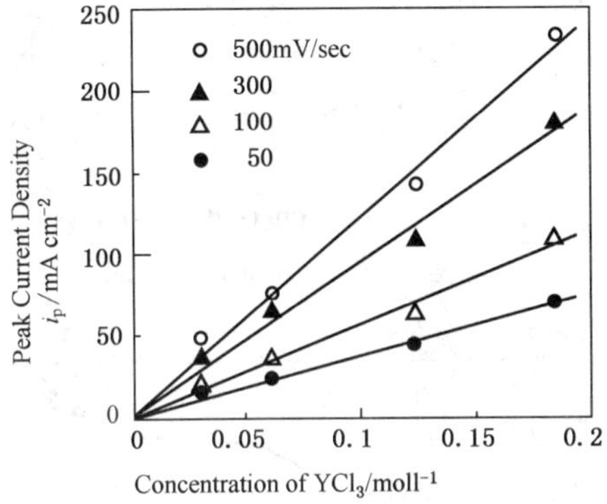

Fig. 3 Peak current density vs. concentration of YCl_3

$$E_p^c - E_{p/2}^c = -0.774RT/nF \qquad (1)$$

After correcting for ohmic drop, n, the number of electrons involved in the electrode reaction, can be estimated to be 2.8±0.4, which is smaller than but close to 3. Here, E_p^c; and $E_{p/2}^c$ are the cathodic peak potential and half peak potential, respectively. R, F, and T have their general significance. Thus, the electrochemical reduction of Y(Ⅲ) ion at a molybdenum electrode can be concluded to be a one-step three electron reaction: Y(Ⅲ)+3e−Y. As shown in Fig. 2 and Fig. 3, the plot of cathodic peak current density, i_p, against the square root of scan rate is linear, and i_p increases linearly with increasing YCl_3 concentration. These results show that the reduction is diffusion controlled and the following equation is applicable [8]

$$i_p = 0.6105(nF)^{3/2}(RT)^{-1/2}D^{1/2}CV^{1/2} \qquad (2)$$

Here, i_p is the peak current density (mA cm^{-2}), C, the bulk concentration of active species (mol l^{-1}), V, scan rate (vs^{-1}), D, diffusion coefficient (cm^2 s^{-1}). Figure 4 shows the linear dependence of normalized $i_p C^{-1}$ on the square root of the scan rate. From the slope of Fig. 4, the diffusion coefficient of the Y(Ⅲ) ion is estimated to be (3.3±0.4)×10^{-6}cm^2 s^{-1}.

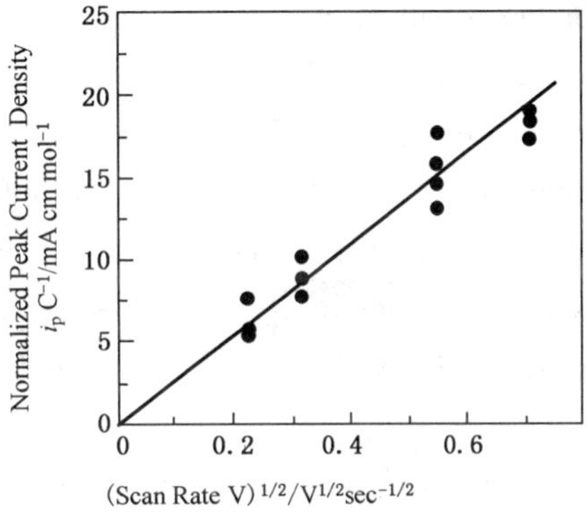

Fig. 4 Normalized peak current density vs. square root of scan rate

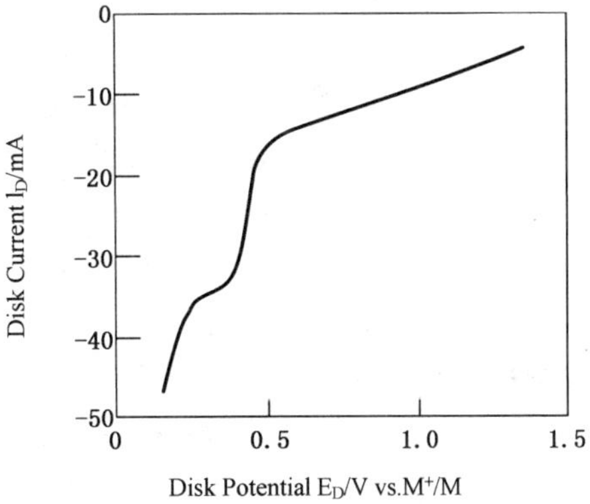

Fig. 5 $I_D \sim E_D$ curve at rotating Mo disk electrode: 0.184 mol l^{-1} YCl_3, ratating velocity of disk: 100 rpm

As described below, this value is rather low compared to the values obtained by other methods. One of the possible reasons is that yttrium metal can dissolve slightly in the chloride melt. In fact, if the equation for the reversible deposition of a soluble substance [13]

$$i_p=0.4463(nF)^{3/2}(RT)^{-1/2}D^{1/2}CV^{1/2} \quad (3)$$

is used instead of Eq. (2), D can be estimated to be $(6.1\pm0.8)\times10^{-6}$ cm^2 s^{-1}. The situation is the same regarding the electron number, n. Considering the slight dissolution of yttrium metal, the true electron number n will be larger than the value calculated by Eq. (1). When D is calculated using a rotating disk electrode or chronopotentiome-try method, this slightly soluble nature of the yttrium metal does not affect the determination of D values as seen in the theoretical derivations of Eq. (4) and (9) [8,11].

RDE method. — The experiment was carried out at a rotating disk electrode with the electrode rotation velocity between 25 and 1000 rpm to determine the standard potential of Y(Ⅲ)/Y(0) and the diffusion coefficient of Y(Ⅲ). A typical disk current-disk potential curve is shown in Fig. 5. Only one plateau was observed, which corresponds to the reduction of Y(Ⅲ) ion at a molybdenum electrode. Figure 6 shows a linear relationship between the limiting current density i_L and the square root of the rotation velocity $\omega^{1/2}$. It means that the Levich equation (10) is applicable and the reduction is diffusion controlled

$$i_L=0.62nFD^{2/3}v^{1/6}w^{1/2}C \quad (4)$$

Here, i_n is the diffusion limiting current density ($mA\cdot cm^{-2}$), v, the kinematic viscosity (a value of 0.0148 cm^2 s^{-1} for LiCl-KCl is used as an approximation), w, the angular velocity of the disk ($rads^{-1}$).

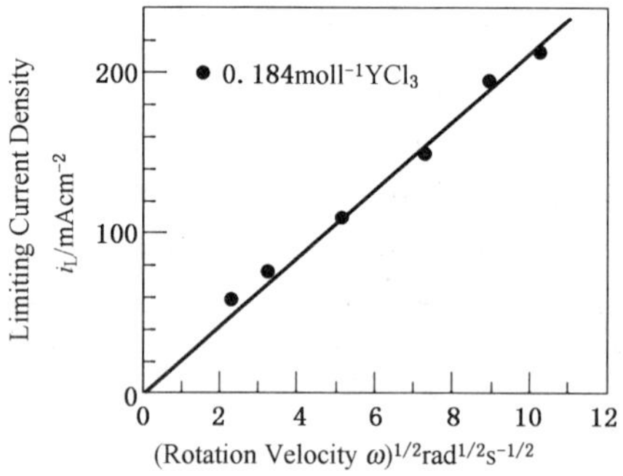

Fig. 6　Limiting current density vs. square root of rotating velocity

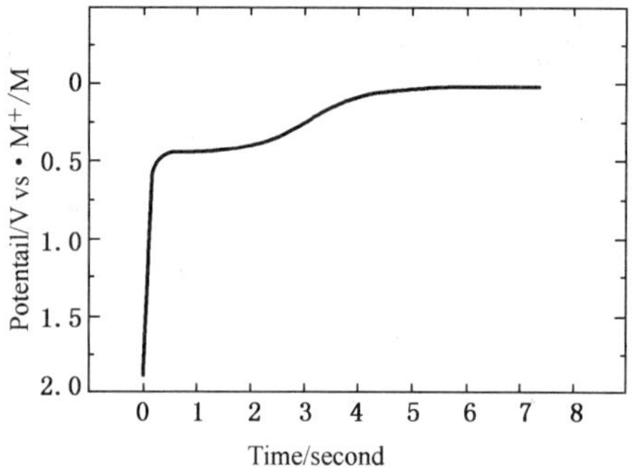

Fig. 7　Chronopotentiogram at Mo electrode: 0.368 mol l^{-1} YCl_3, $i=168.15$ mA cm^{-2}

From the slope of Fig. 6, D is estimated to be $(5.0\pm0.9)\times10^{-6}$ cm^2 s^{-1}.

For the reversible deposition of an insoluble substance, the formula

$$E=E^{\circ}+RT/nF\ln C+Rt/nF\ln(i_L-i)/i_L \quad (5)$$

can be derived [8]. At one half the limiting current value

$$Ei_{L/2}=E^{\circ}+RT/nF\ln C/2 \quad (6)$$

Here, E° is the standard potential (V).

From Fig. 5, $E_{iL/2}$ is (0.43 ± 0.01) V *vs.* M^+/M. E° is thus estimated to be (0.48 ± 0.01) V *vs.* M^+/M, or (−3.15 ± 0.02) V *vs.* Cl_2/Cl^-.

Chronopotentiometry. —A chronopotentiogram of Y(Ⅲ) ion in the melt at a molybdenum electrode is shown in Fig. 7. Only one plateau appears, giving further proof for a one-step electrochemical reduction of Y(Ⅲ) ion.

For the reversible deposition of an insoluble substance, the following formula can be derived [8,11]

$$E=E^\circ+RT/nF\ln C+RT/nF\ln(\tau^{1/2}-t^{1/2})/\tau^{1/2} \quad (7)$$

Here, E° is the standard potential (*V*). When $t=\tau/4$

$$E=E^\circ+RT/nF\ln C/2 \quad (8)$$

E° can thus be estimated to be (0.47 ± 0.01) V *vs.* M^+/M, or (−3.16 ± 0.02) V *vs.* Cl_2Cl^- from Fig. 7. Straight lines for plots of $i_\tau^{1/2}$ *vs.* i are obtained, as shown in Fig. 8 on various concentrations of Y(Ⅲ). Figure 9 shows the linear relationship between $i_T^{1/2}$ and C. The line goes through the origin of coordinates which further verifies that the electrochemical reduction of Y(Ⅲ) ion is reversible and diffusion-controlled. These results imply that Sand equation [11]

$$i_\tau^{1/2}=85.5nD^{1/2}C \quad (9)$$

is applicable.

Here, i is current density ($mAcm^{-2}$), τ, transition time (s). From the slope of Fig. 9, D can be calculated to be $(7.1\pm0.7)\times10^{-6}$ $cm^2\ s^{-1}$.

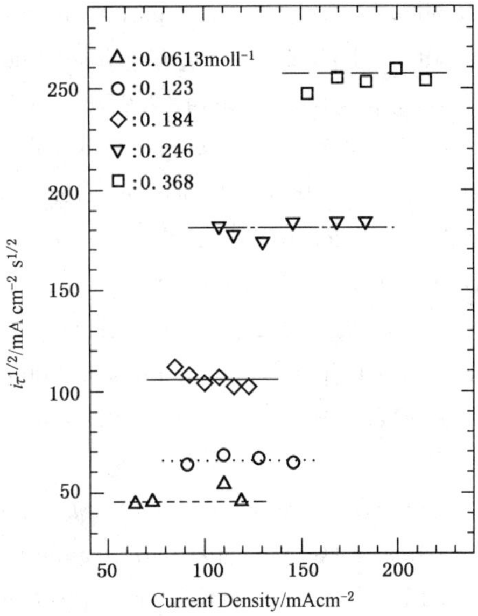

Fig. 8 Relation between $i_\tau^{1/2}$ and i

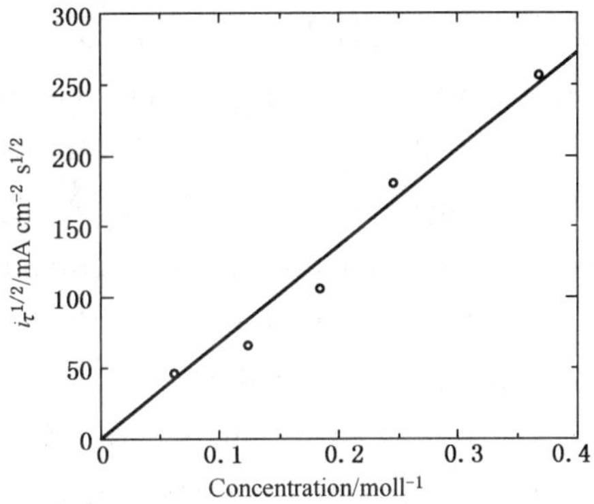

Fig. 9 Relation between $i_\tau^{1/2}$ and C

Open-circuit potentiometry. -Pure yttrium deposits are formed on a molybdenum electrode by constant current electrolysis with cathodic current densities of 70—145 $mAcm^{-2}$. The deposits are sufficiently stable to present the same characteristics as pure yttrium. A typical potential decay obtained after electrolysis is shown in Fig. 10. A potential plateau remains stably at 0.437 V (*vs.* M^+/M) for more than 5 min, then slowly shifts toward the positive potential and finally arrives at the rest potential of molybdenum in the melt. A plot of the plateau potential E against log C gives a linear relationship with a slope of (0.053±0.003) V $decade^{-1}$, which is very close to the Nernst slope of 0.048 V $decade^{-1}$ for a reversible transfer of three electrons at this temperature, as shown in Fig. 11. A least squares calculation gives the molarity-scale standard potential E^{o} as (0.453±0.006) V *vs.* M^{+}/M, or (−3.174±0.006) V *vs.* Cl_2/Cl^{-}.

Comparison between present results and the earlier work. —Y(Ⅲ)/Y(0) couple was studied in the 59LiCl-41KCl (m/o) eutectic earliest by Yang and Hudson [14], from whose data Plambeck [15] calculated the standard molarity-scale potential of this couple to be −2.859 V against the standard molar platinum electrode (S. M. P. E.). This value was obtained by extrapolating the data taken at temperatures higher than 723 K to 723 K. The standard molarity-scale potential of this couple in the 59 LiC1-41 KC1 (m/o) eutectic was redetermined as −2.831 V(*vs.* S. M. P. E.) by Hoshino and Plambeck [4]. Although the eutectic composition of the present study is different from those used in previous works, a comparison between the results of those works and the result of our study will give a better appreciation of the electrochemistry of yttrium and yield insights into the factors affecting the reduction reaction and the re-duction potentials. Such a comparison is summarized in Table 1, and the standard molarity-scale potentials given by the previous works are translated into potentials *vs.* Cl_2/Cl^{-} to make the comparison more clearly. Unfortunately, diffusion coefficient of Y(Ⅲ) ion was not given by those authors, it is impossible to make a direct compari-son. It can be seen from Table 1 that in all the cases, the reduction of Y(Ⅲ) is determined to be a one-step three elec-tron reaction without regard to the electrolyte used, and the standard molarity-scale potentials of the present study are very similar to those given by the previous authors, it seems that the sodium ion does not interfere with the reduction of Y(Ⅲ) under the experimental conditions. The difference in composition of the electrolyte used between present study and the previous works is not significant.

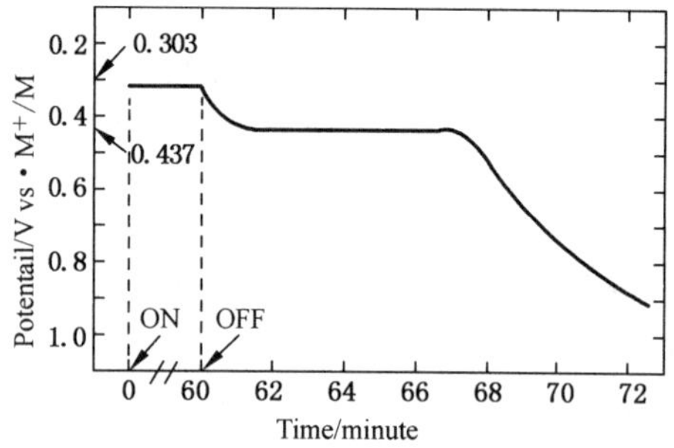

Fig. 10　Open-circuit potential decay curve of Mo electrode after polarization at 145 mA cm^{-2}, 0.368 mol l^{-1} YCl_3.

Table 1　A comparison between present results and the earlier works

	Present study	Yang *et al* (14,15)	Hoshino *et al* (4)	Duan *et al* (3)
Eutectic (mol%)	Li:K:Na (55:36:9)	Li:K (59.41)	Li:K (59.41)	Li:K (59.41)
n	3	3	3	3
E^{o} (vs Cl_2/Cl^{-})	−3.174 −3.15 −3.16	−3.181	−3.153	no data

Formation of Ni-Y alloy on nickel, disk electrode. —It is well known that nickel can form several types of interme-tallic compounds with yttrium [12]. On the other hand, several reduction-oxidation waves are observed in the voltammogram obtained with a nickel electrode in Fig. 1. In order to correlate these phenomena, electrodeposition of yt-trium on a Ni-disk electrode was carried out by constant current electrolysis in the melt between 723 and 873 K. Figure 12 shows a typical x-ray diffraction pattern for the deposit prepared under these conditions. The existence of NiY and Ni_2Y can be observed, which corresponds to the appearance of more than one reduction-oxidation wave in Fig. 1. Depending on the electrolytic conditions (current density, temperature and so on) Ni_2Y_3 can be formed also. Details of this electrochemical intermetallic compound formation reaction will be presented by the authors in due course.

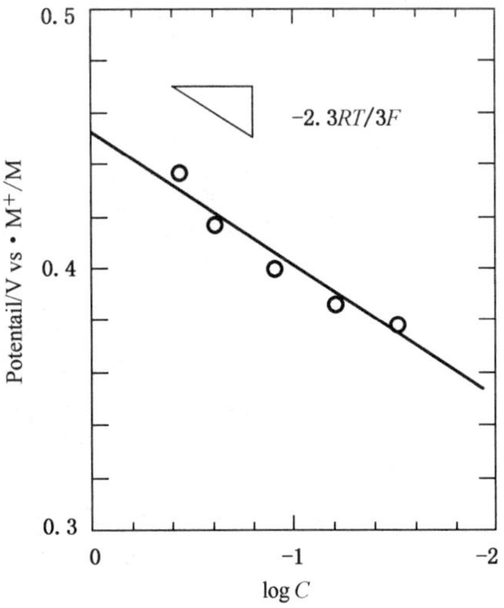

Fig. 11 *E* vs. log *C*

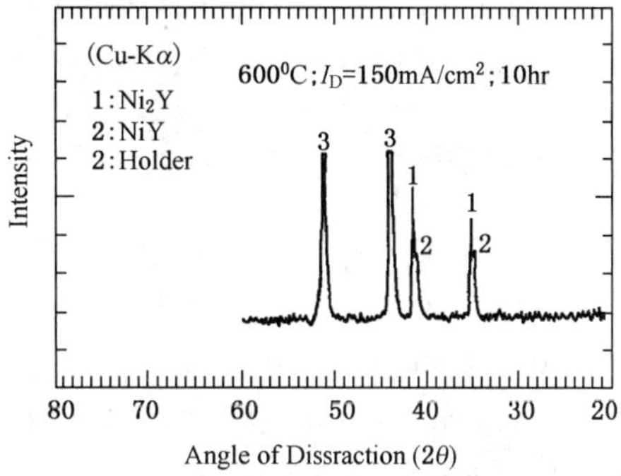

Fig. 12 X-ray diffraction spectrum of Ni-y alloy

Conclusion

The results described above show that the electrochemi-cal reduction of Y(Ⅲ) ion is almost reversible and proceeds by a one-step three electron reaction on a molybdenum electrode in LiCl-KCl-NaCl eutectic at 723 K, *i. e.* Y(Ⅲ)+3e=Y(0). The diffusion coefficient of Y(Ⅲ) ion was determined to be $(3.3\pm0.4)\times10^{-6}$ cm^2 s^{-1} by cyclic voltammetry, $(5.0\pm0.9)\times10^{-6}$ cm^2 s^{-1} by a rotating disk electrode method and $(7.1\pm0.7)\times10^{-6}$ cm^2 s^{-1} by chronopotentiometry. The value of *D* obtained by cyclic voltam-metry is different from those by the other two methods. One of the possible reasons is that yttrium metal can dissolve slightly in the chloride melt. The standard molarity-scale potential was estimated to be (-3.174 ± 0.006) V (*vs.* Cl_2Cl^{-1}) by open-circuit potentiometry, (-3.15 ± 0.02) V (*vs.* Cl_2/Cl^-) by the rotating disk electrode method, and (-3.16 ± 0.02) V (*vs.* Cl_2/Cl^-) by chronopotentiometry. These values are in good agreement with each other. Depending on electrolytic conditions, several types of Ni-Y alloy are formed at a nickel electrode, which was demonstrated by x-ray diffraction spectra.

Acknowledgment

This work was supported by a Grant-in-Aid from the Japanese Ministry of Education, Science and Culture.

Manuscript submitted Oct. 4, 1991; revised manuscript received March 9, 1992.

Kyoto University assisted in meeting the publication costs of this article.

References

[1] E. Mortice and M. M. Wong, *Miner. Sci. Eng.*, 11, 3, 125(1979).

[2] Zhang Xiou Lian and Zhao Mm Shou, *Rare Earth*, to be published.

[3] Shuzhen Duan and Linzhong Zhao, in "Proceedings of the Seventh international Symposium on Molten Salts," C. V. Hussey, J. S. Wilkes, S. N. Flengas, and Y. Ito, Editors, PV 90-17, p. 525, The Electrochemical Society Softbound Proceedings Series, Pennington, NJ(1990).

[4] Y. Hoshino and J. A. Plambeck, Cana. J. Chem., 48, 685(1970).

[5] Zhao Minshou, Zhao Qijien, and Tang Dingxiang, *J. Rare Earth*, 1, 41 (1983).

[6] Y. Ito, H. Yabe, T. Nakai, K. Ema, and J. Oishi, *Electro-chimica Acta*, 31, 1579 (1986).

[7] H. Yabe, K. Ema and Y. Ito, ibid., 34, 1479 (1989).

[8] T. Berzins and P. Delahay, *J. Am. Chem. Soc.*, 75, 555(1953).

[9] T. Shimada, M. iizuka and Y. Ito, *Denki Kagaku*, 60, 200 (1992).

[10] A. J. Bard and L. R. Faulkner, Editors, "Electrochemi-cal Methods, Fundamentals and Applications," p. 288, John Wiley and Sons, New York (1980).

[11] *Ibid.*, p. 253.

[12] W. W. Scott, Jr., in "Binary Alloy Phase Diagrams," T. B. Massalski, Editor, *Vol.* 2, p. 1175, ASM (1987).

[13] A. J. Bard and L. R. Faulkner, Editors. "Electrochemi-cal Methods, Fundamentals and Applications," p. 218, John Wiley and Sons, New York (1980).

[14] L. Yang and R. G. Huson, *Trans. Met. Soc. A. I. M. E.*, 215, 589 (1959).

[15] J. A. Plambeck, *J. Chem. Eng. Data*, 12, 77 (1967).

二元氯化物熔体中锂和钠离子析出电位的测定及去极化作用的研究①

张英珊　赵敏寿　唐定骧
（中国科学院长春应用化学研究所，长春，130022）

摘要：本文利用 *I-V* 曲线法测定了锂和钠离子在二元混合氯化物体系（LiCl-KCL；NaCl-KCl）中的析出电位，为利用熔盐电解法制备低钠高纯铝-锂合金提供了理论依据。根据锂离子在铝阴极上产生的去极化值求出铝和锂发生合金化反应的热力学意义，提出二元合金类型与极化类型之间的经验关系。首次通过研究锂离子在铝合金电极上的去极化行为，发现某些第三合金元素的存在可以加强锂离子的去极化作用，为进一步制取低钠高纯三元铝-锂-M 合金系列提供了参考，还研究了在氯化钾-氯化锂体系中，氯化锂浓度对锂离子在铝阴极上析出电位的影响，求出了氯化锂的平均活度系数。

Study on Deposition Potentials of Lithium and Sodium Ions and Depolarization in Binary Chloride

Zhang，Ying-Shan Zhao，Min-Shou，Tang，Ding-Xiang
（Changchun Institute of Applied Chemistry，Academia Sinica，
Changchun，130022）

Abstract：Deposition potentials of Lithium and Sodium ions have bsen measured in binary cohloride systems（LiCl-KCl，NaCl-KCl）by *I-V* curve method，to provide a theoretical base for preparing high purity A1-Li alloy by eleebrolysis in molten salt. The changes of free energy and enthalpy were ealeulabed in，terms of depolarization values on Al cathode. Thermodynamic meaning of depolarization was discussed in details and the empirical relation between binary alloy type and depolarization type was proposed. It is shown for the first time that the presence of a third elemenb in Al-Li alloy can strengthen depolarization of Li ion at Al alloy cathode and give foundation for preparing high purity Al-Li-M ternary alloy. The effect，of LiCl concentraltion on deposition potentials of Li ion at Al cathode in KCl-LiCl melt was studied and average active coeffioien of LiOl was obtained.

对熔盐电解法制备铝-锂合金的研究结果表明：利用锂离子在铝阴极上析出时产生的去极化作用可以生产低钠、高纯铝-锂合金，显示出了广阔的发展前景。

① 化学学报，1991(49)：382-388.

但在所用的氯化物体系中，锂离子的析出电位、在铝阴极上析出时产生的去极化值以及与钠离子析出电位的定量比较等重要数据迄今未见报道。本文详细研究了锂和钠两种离子的电化学行为，测定它们在氯化锂-氯化钾、氯化钠-氯化钾体系中，在各种阴极上的析出电位，并就有关热力学问题进行了较详细的讨论。

实验

仪器和试剂　DHZ-1 型电化学综合测试仪（三明无线电厂生产），参比电极：Ag/AgCl；对电极：光谱纯石墨棒；工作电极[1]：一、液态电极面积：0.58 cm^2，二、固态电极面积：0.70 m^2，按文献[1]对 LiCl 进行脱水干燥，并做 KCl-LiCl 体系的伏安曲线，检测纯化结果。*I-V* 曲线上的残余电流很小，且无其他干扰峰存在，说明经干燥处理过的盐可以直接用于测定，毋需再进行预电解处理。

实验方法和实验条件　利用 *I-V* 曲线法完成全部析出电位的测定。每次测量均从开路电位开始起扫，扫速为 0.25 V/min。

结果与讨论

析出电位的测定　在测定析出电位之前，首先研究 KCl-LiCl，NaCl-KCl 体系的电极反应。测绘以上二体系在 Mo，Al 和 Cu 电极上的循环伏安曲线（图 1，图 2），在扫描范围电位最负处恒电位电解 3 min，取出电极，用正己烷清洗掉电解液后，用能谱作表面分析（图 3，图 4），结果说明：在各电极上发生电极反应的离子分别为锂离子和钠离子，在所研究的电位范围内钾离子均不析出。在此基础上利用 *I-V* 曲线测定锂和钠离子在多种电极上的析出电位，结果列于表 1 和表 2 中。

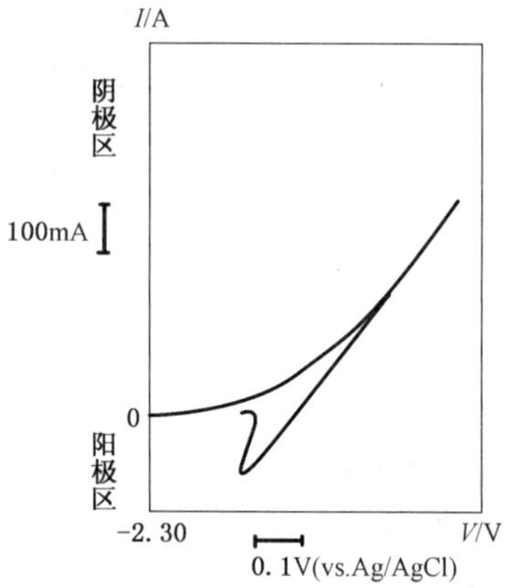

图 1　循环伏安图

KCl：LiCl=1：1(mol)；Mo 阴极；*T*=720 ℃

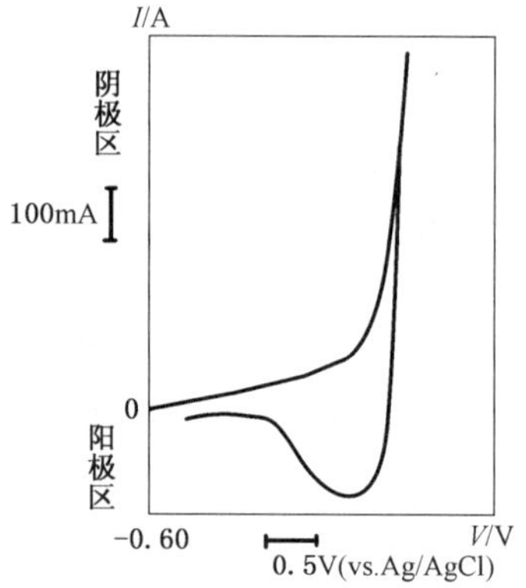

图 2　循环伏安图

KCl：NaCl=1：1(mol)；Mo 阴极；*T*=720 ℃

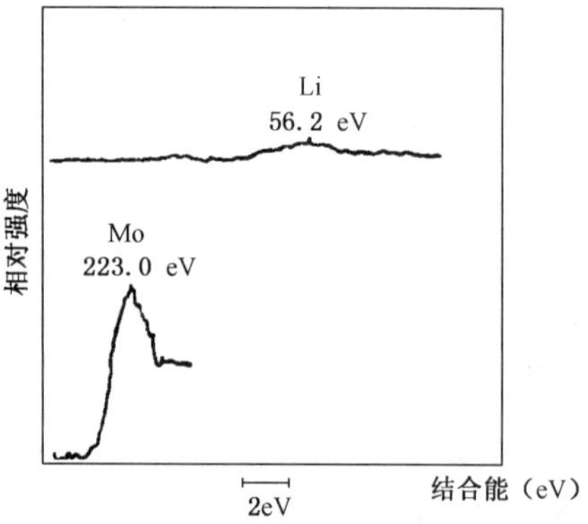

图 3　Mo 电极能谱图(Li)

KCl：NaCl=1：1(mol)；Mo 阴极；*T*=720 ℃

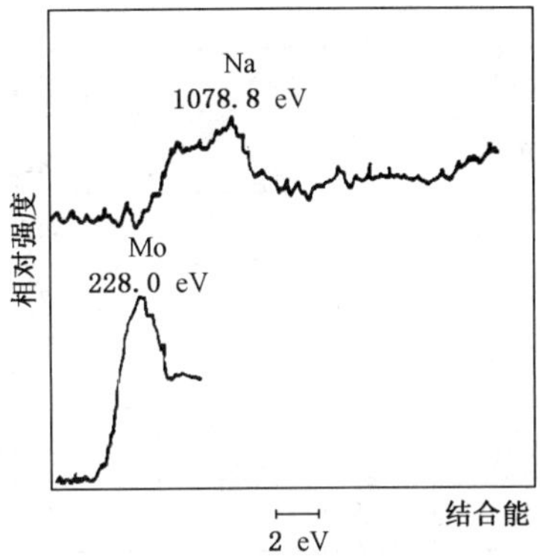

图 4　Mo 电极能谱图(Na)

去极化作用的热力学讨论

合金化反应的自由焓变化与去极化作用　对于完全惰性电极，电极反应 $M^{+}+e\rightleftharpoons M$ 的自由焓变化与析出电位之间满足热力学关系 $\Delta G=-nFE$。若析出金属与电极材料形成合金时，离子析出电位的去极化值 ΔE 与合金化反应的自由焓变化之间的关系为：

$$\Delta G_x+\Delta G_m=-nF\Delta E,$$

其中，ΔG_m 是形成理想合金溶液时，由于金属浓度降低而产生的混合自由焓变化；ΔG_x 是由于合金偏离理想状态而产生的过剩偏摩尔自由焓的变化。设 ΔG_E 对去极化的贡献在各电极上均相同，可得去极化值与过剩偏摩尔自由焓之间的关系为：

$$\Delta E=-\frac{1}{nF}\Delta G_x-c,$$

因此，去极化作用直接反映了所测金属在阴极材料中产生过剩偏摩尔自由焓的大小，即与合金结构的类型密切相关。前人已总结出熔盐结构类型与偏摩尔过剩自由焓之间的关系[2]，如将此经验关系应用于合金，则合金类型与电极极化之间应有如下关系(表 3)。

所以，可从待测离子的金属与阴极材料的合金相图上得到离子在此电极上是否有去极化作用以及去极化作用大小的信息。在本实验中，根据有关合金相图[3-5]，依照表 3 可作出如下判断：Cu 和 Mo 均为钠离子的惰性电极；Mo 为锂离子的惰性电极；锂离子在铝阴极上会出现去极化，在铜阴极上可能会出现极化。

表 1　KCl-LiCl 体系中 Li^{+} 的析出电位(vs. Ag/AgCl)

电极	析出电位(V)						
	温度(℃)						
	660	680	700	720	740	760	780
Mo	−2.64	−2.60	−2.56	−2.53	−2.48	−2.44	−2.42
Cu	—	—	—	−2.54	−2.50	−2.49	−2.46
Al	—	−2.14	−2.12	−2.11	−2.06	−2.03	−2.00
Al-Cu(20%wt)	−2.10	−2.08	−2.07	−2.06	−2.03	−2.00	−1.98
Al-Cu(15%wt)	−2.12	−2.09	−2.07	−2.06	−2.04	−2.01	−1.98
Al-Cu(10%wt)	−2.14	−2.10	−2.09	−2.07	−2.04	−2.01	−1.98
Al-Cu(6%wt)	−2.16	−2.12	−2.10	−2.08	−2.05	−2.01	−2.00
Al-RE(6%wt)	—	—	—	−2.06	−2.04	−2.02	−2.00

表 2　KCl-NaCl 体系中 Na 的析出点位(vs. Ag/AgCl)

电极	析出电位(V)						
	温度(℃)						
	660	680	700	720	740	760	780
Mo	—	−2.44	−2.39	−2.35	−2.30	−2.26	−2.20
Cu	—	—	—	−2.35	−2.29	−2.24	−2.20
Al	—	−2.43	−2.39	−2.36	−2.33	−2.30	−2.27
Al-Cu(20%,wt)	—	−2.43	−2.39	−2.36	−2.33	−2.30	−2.26
Al-RE(6%,wt)	—	—	—	−2.36	−2.33	−2.30	−2.27

表 3　合金类型与极化类型之间的关系

二元合金相图类型	连续固溶体		简单共晶体	化合物
过剩偏摩尔自由焓 ΔG_x	$>\|\Delta G_m\|$	$<\|\Delta G_m\|$	$\leqslant 0$	$\leqslant 0$
极化类型	极化	去极化	去极化	去极化

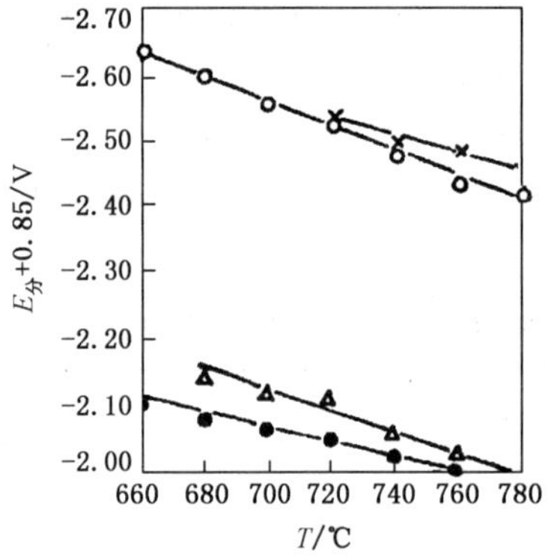

图 5　LiCl-KCl(1∶1 mol)体系中 LiCl 分解电压与温度的关系

○—Mo 电极；×—Cu 电极；△—Al 电极；●—Al-Cu(20wt%)电极

根据析出电位数据求去极化值 ΔE 及自由焓变化 ΔG，分别列于表 4 中，显然，根据相图作出的判断是正确的。

合金化反应的热效应与去极化作用

将 KCl-LiCl(1∶1 mol)体系中 LiCl 在各电极上的分解电压* 与温度的关系示于图 5，按照线性方程 $E_{分}=a+bT$ 进行归一化，求出归一化因子 a，b。根据 Gibbs-Helmholtz 方程：

$$E_{分}=-\Delta H/nF+T\cdot \mathrm{d}E_{分}/\mathrm{d}T$$

归一化因子具有明确的物理意义：

$$a=-\Delta H/nF;b=\mathrm{d}E/\mathrm{d}T,$$

求出 LiCl 分解反应的热效应 ΔH 及分解电压的温度系数 $\mathrm{d}E/\mathrm{d}T$(表 5)。

对于惰性固体电极分解反应的热效应是以下两反应的和：

$$2Cl^- -2e=Cl_2;2Li^+ +2e=2Li$$

表 4　Li 在各电极上发生合金化反应的自由焓变化($\Delta G=\Delta G_x+\Delta G_m$)

电极	热力学函数	温度(℃)						
		660	680	700	720	740	760	780
Al-Cu(20%)	ΔE(V)	0.53	0.51	0.48	0.47	0.45	0.44	0.44
	$\Delta G_x+\Delta E_m$ (kJ/mol)	−51.6	−49.7	−46.8	−45.8	−43.4	−42.9	−42.9

* 在氯化物熔体中分解电压在数值上等于金属离子相对 Cl_2/Cl^{-1} 电极的析出电位。

续表

电极	热力学函数	温度(℃)						
		660	680	700	720	740	760	780
Al-Cu (15%)	ΔE(V) $\Delta G_x+\Delta G_m$ (kJ/mol)	0.452 −50.2	0.50 −48.7	0.48 −46.3	0.46 −44.9	0.44 −42.5	0.44 −42.5	0.44 −42.5
Al-Cu (10%)	ΔE(V) $\Delta G_x+\Delta G_m$ (kJ/mol)	0.50 −48.2	0.48 −48.8	0.47 −45.7	0.46 −44.9	0.47 −47.6	0.44 −42.8	0.43 −41.4
Al-Cu (6%)	ΔE(V) $\Delta G_x+\Delta G_m$ (kJ/mol)	0.48 −46.3	0.47 −45.3	0.46 −44.3	0.44 −42.3	0.44 −42.4	0.43 −41.5	0.42 −40.5
Al	ΔE(V) $\Delta G_x+\Delta G_m$ (kJ/mol)		0.44 −42.9	0.44 −42.5	0.44 −42.5	0.42 −40.5	0.41 −39.6	0.41 −39.6
Al-RE (6%)	ΔE(V) $\Delta G_x+\Delta G_m$ (kJ/mol)				0.46 −44.4	0.44 −42.4	0.43 −41.4	0.41 −39.6
Cu	ΔE $\Delta G_x+\Delta G_m$ (kJ/mol)				−0.01 0.965	−0.2 1.93	0.04 3.76	−0.05 4.92

表 5　LiCl 的分级反应热效应及分解电压的温度系数

电极	温度范围(℃)	阀一化方程	相关因子[a]	整体偏差	温度系数	反应热效应(kJ/mol)
Mo	660—780	$E=4.70+0.0018T$	0.997	0.0068	0.0018	453.6
Al	680—780	$E=-4.02+0.0014T$	0.977	0.014	0.0014	387.9
Al-Cu(20%)	660—780	$E=-3.69+0.0011T$	0.989	0.0079	0.0011	356.1
Al-Cu(15%)	660—780	$E=-3.73+0.0011T$	0.985	0.0094	0.0011	359.9
Al-Cu(10%)	660—780	$E=-3.83+0.0013T$	0.989	0.0090	0.0013	369.6
Al-Cu(6%)	660—780	$E=-3.89+0.0013T$	0.991	0.0085	0.0013	375.4
Al-RE(6%)	720—780	$E=-3.67+0.0010T$	0.995	0.032	0.0010	354.1

但对于可以发生去极化作用的电极，热效应 ΔH 中还包括析出金属与电极材料发生合金化反应的热效应 $\Delta H'$，由此可求出合金化反应的热效应 $\Delta H'$(表 6)。

表 6　Li 在 Al 系列电极上发生合金化反应的热效应 $\Delta H'$

电极	适度范围(℃)	反应热效应 $\Delta H'$(kJ/mol)
Al	680—780	−65.7
Al-Cu(20%)	660—780	−97.5
Al-Cu(15%)	660—780	−93.7
Al-Cu(10%)	660—780	−84.6
Al-Cu(5%)	660—780	−78.2
Al-RE(6%)	720—780	−99.5

因此，我们认为对于 $\gamma<1$ 的合金（形成低共晶点及化合物的合金），利用合金化反应的热效应亦可估计去极化作用的大小。

第三合金元素对去极化作用的影响　将锂在 Al-Cu 合金电极上发生合金化反应的自由焓变化与合金电极中含铜量的关系示于图 6。显然，在电极中加入某些第三元素可以加强与析出金属的合金化趋向，增大去极化作用。实验结果表明：除铜外，稀土亦属此类第三合金元素。这对熔盐电解直接生产 Al-Li-M 三元合金是很有意义的。

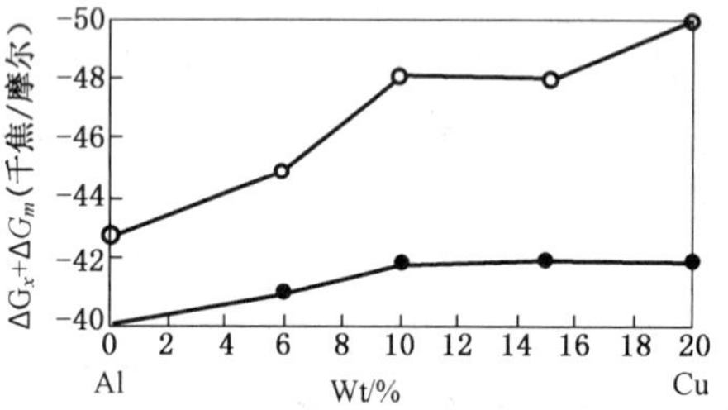

图 6　合金化反应自由焓变化与 Al 电极中 Cu 含量关系

○—680℃；×—760℃

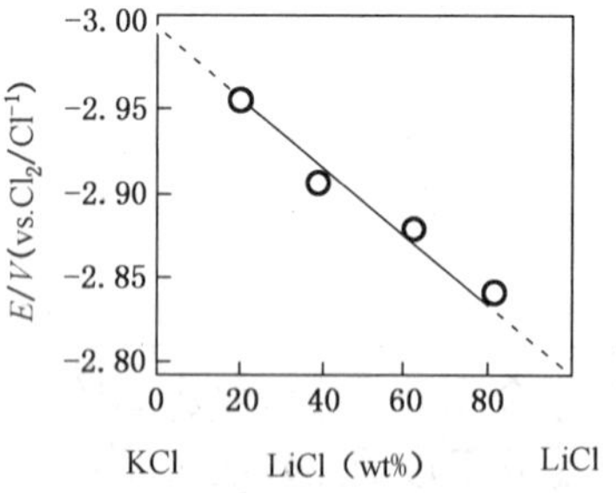

图 7　LiCl-KCl 体系中 Li^+ 析出电位与 LiCl 浓度的关系

Al 阴极；$T=740$ ℃

LiCl 浓度对 Li^+ 在液体 Al 阴极上析出电位的影响及 LiCl 在 LiCl-KCl 体系中活度系数的近似估算　在 740 ℃下分别测定 LiCl 浓度为 20、37、60 和 80wt%时锂离子在液态铝阴极上的析出电位，结果列于表 7，同时做出析出电位随 LiCl 浓度变化的函数曲线（图 7）。

表 7　不同 LICl 浓度时 Li^+ 在液体 Al 阴极上的析出电位（vs. Cl_2/Cl^-）

LiCl 浓度（wt%）	20	37	60	80
析出电位（V）	−2.95	−2.91	−2.88	−2.85

对数据进行归一化处理，得到归一化方程：$E=-2.96+0.16c$，外推至 $c=1$，求出单一 LiCl 熔体中锂离子在液体铝阴极上析出电位为 -2.79 V（vs. Cl_2/Cl^-）。设 KC1-LiC1 体系中 LiCl 的离子活度为 $a_\pm$，平均活度系数为 $\gamma_\pm$，则有：$a_\pm=c\cdot\gamma_\pm$。用活度代替 Nernst 方程中的浓度，得到实际溶液中 LiCl 分解电压的热力学表达式：

$$E=E^\circ+\frac{RT}{nf}\ln a_{Cl^-}^2\cdot a_{Li^+}^2/P_{Cl_a}\cdot a_{Li}^2$$

$$=E^\circ+\frac{2RT}{nF}\ln a_\pm+\frac{RT}{nf}\ln(1/P_{cl2}\cdot a_{Li}^2)$$

$$=E'+\frac{2RT}{F}\ln\gamma_\pm+\frac{2RT}{F}\ln c_{LiCl}\qquad(1)$$

其中　$E'=E^\circ+\frac{RT}{F}\ln(1/P\cdot a_{Li}^2)$

是纯 LiCl 在铝阴极上的分解电压，$E'=-2.79$V。将此值代入式（1），得

$$E=-2.79+\frac{2RT}{F}\ln\gamma_\pm+\frac{2RT}{F}\ln c_{LiCl}\quad(2)$$

将实验数据［LiCl 的浓度 c，$\ln c$ 与对应的析出电位（vs. $Cl_2/C1^-$）］列于表 8 中，依此表做出 E-1nc 曲线（图 8），读出纵轴截距 $b\approx-2.85$，由式（2）可知：

$$b=-2.79+\frac{2RT}{F}\ln\gamma_\pm=-2.85,$$

求出 $\gamma_\pm\approx0.71$，因此，在 KCl-LiCl 体系中当温度为 $T=740$ ℃时，LiCl 的离子平均活度系数 $\gamma_\pm=0.71$，对理想溶液产生负偏差。

锂离子、钠离子析出电位的比较　将不同温度下 KCl-LiCl，NaCl-KCl（1：1 mol）中测出的锂离子-钠离子的析出电位之差列于表 9。

由热力学数据计算得到：在 $T=700$ ℃时，单一氯化物中 Li^+ 与 Na^+ 的电极电位之差，$\Delta E=-0.18$ V[6]，实验值为 $\Delta E=-0.02$ V[7]。本实验测出：在二元混合氯化物体系中 $\Delta E=-0.17$ V。说明无论在单一盐还是混合盐中，如果按正常的电化顺序，Li^+ 均应在 Na^+ 之后析出。但在铝阴极上，由于 Li^+ 产生了很强的去极化作用，改变了正常的电化顺序，使得 ΔE 由 $=0.17$ V 变到 0.27 V，导致 Li^+ 在 Li^+，Na^+ 共存时亦可优先选择析出。

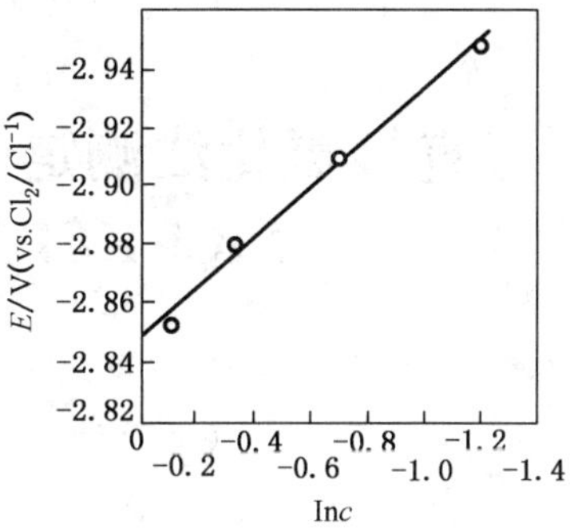

图 8　*E*-ln*c* 关系

表 8　c_{LiCl}, $\ln c_{LiCl}$, E 数据表

c_{LiCl}（摩尔分数）	0.30	0.50	0.72	0.88
$\ln c_{LiCl}$	−1.20	−0.69	−0.33	−0.13
E	−0.95	−2.91	−2.88	−2.85

表 9　Li^+，Na^+ 析出电位差值（V）

电极	$\Delta E=E_{Li}-E_{Na}$					
	温度（℃）					
	680	700	720	740	760	780
Mo	−0.16	−0.17	−0.18	−0.18	−0.18	−0.21
Al	0.28	0.27	0.24	0.28	0.27	0.26
Al-Cu(20%)	0.33	0.31	0.30	0.31	0.30	0.29
Al-Re(6%)	—	—	0.30	0.30	0.27	0.26

结论

（1）测定了 Li^+，Na^+ 在二元氯化物中的析出电位，阐明了 Li^+ 在 Al 阴极上产生很强的去极化作用是利用熔盐电解法制备低钠高纯 Al-Li 合金的理论基础。

（2）根据发生合金化反应的自由焓变化与去极化作用的热力学意义，提出二元合金类型与极化类型之间相互对应的经验关系，并根据去极化值求出合金化反应的热效应。

（3）测定了 Li^+ 和 Na^+ 在 Al-Cu，Al-RE 合金电极上的析出电位，指出某些第三合金元素的存在可以加强 Li^+ 在 Al 阴极上的去极化作用。

参考文献

[1] 张英珊，硕士论文，中国科学院长春应用化学研究所，长春，1988.

[2] Делйарский，Ю. К.；Mapkos，Б. Ф. 著，彭瑞伍译，“熔盐电化学”，上海科学技术出版社，上海，1994.

[3] Fink，W. L.；Willoy，L. A.；Stamp，H. C.，Trans. Atme.，1948，175.

[4] Pastorells，S.，Gazz，Chirn. ItaL，1930，60，988.

[5] Grube，G.；Mohr，L.；Breuning，W.，Z. Elektrochem.，1935，41.

[6] Hamer，W.；Malmberg，M.；Rubin，B.，J. Elektrochem. Soc.，1956，103，8.

[7] Oambi，L.；Devote，G.，Gazz. Chirn. Ital.，1927，57，836.

直接氯化法测定 LiCl 熔盐体系相图的研究及 LiCl-KCl-LiF 三元相图的制作①

张英珊　赵敏寿*　唐定骧　李　平
（中国科学院长春应用化学研究所，长春）

摘　要：首次成功地将 NH_4Cl 直接氯化 Li_2CO_3 的反应引入热分析，制作含 LiCl 的二元、三元作系熔盐图，避免 LiCl 吸收性给相图绘制带来的困难，三个二元体系 LiCl-KCl、NaCl-LiCl 和 LiCl-LiF 的测定结果与文献吻合很好。并在此基础上制作了 LiCl-KCl-LiF 三元相图。

Study on Fusibility Diagrams Containing LiCl and Phase Diagram of LiCl-KCl-LiF Ternary by Direct Chlorination

Zhang, Ying-Shan Zhao, Min-Shou* Tang, Ding-Xiang Li, Ping
(Changchun Institute of Applied Chemistry, Academia Sinica, Changchun)

Abstract: In order to avoid the hygroscopicity of LiCl specimem, the method of directly chlorinating Li_2CO_3 with NH_4Cl was successfully introducing into the thermal analysis of the system containing LiCl. The three fusibility diagram of LiCl-KCl, LiCl-NaCl, LiCl-LiF were determined using the method. The results are in agreement with the values reported in the literature, and phase diagram of: LiCl-KCl-LiF ternary system was constructed based on these results. Temperature of the ternary eutectic, composed of 57.3 mol% LiCl, 41.4 mol% KCl, 1.3 mol% LiF, was found to be 348 ℃.

LiCl 具有强烈的吸水性，给 LiCl 熔盐体系性质的研究带来很大的困难。过去研究 LiCl 体系的相图，一般均需事先脱水干燥，然后在惰性气体保护下的手套箱内完成称量、混合等制样过程。操作周期长。工作量大，而且样品在转移过程中很难避免水份的影响。本工作将 NH_4Cl 完全定量氯化 Li_2CO_3 生成 LiCl 的反应，直接引入热分析方法制作 LiCl 熔盐体系的相图研究中，从根本上解决了由于 LiCl 的吸水性给相图制作带来的困难，获得了满意的结果，并利用直接氯化法制作了迄今尚未见报道的 LiCl-KCl-LiF 三元相图。

实验

仪器和样品　本工作进行 DTA 测量所用的仪器是北京光学仪器厂生产的 P-2 型差热分析仪。Li_2CO_3 为光谱纯，

① 化学学报，1990(48)：644-647.

NH_4Cl 为优级纯，NaCl、KCl、Li_2Cl 均为分析纯。将 NaCl、KCl、LiF、Li_2CO_3 在 200 ℃下加热至衡重。按 $NH_4Cl:Li_2CO_3=4:1$(mol)及其计第量准确称量各样品，研细使其充分混合后备用。NH_4Cl 完全定量氯化 Li_2CO_3 的工作我们将另文报告。

实验步骤　按最终产物为 20 mg 计算称取样品，将样品装入白金坩埚内压实后放置在坩埚架上，以另一个相同大小的白金坩埚作为对照物。刚玉均热器加盖后放置钟罩。在钟罩夹层内通冷却水，充入干燥 Ar 气 5 min 后，开始程序升温。控制 Ar 气流量为 0.2 L/min，以 20 ℃/min 的速度程序升温。当温度升至高于样品熔化温度 50 ℃左右时，以 10 ℃/min 的速度开始程序降温，同时记录样品温度及差热信号，并取降温曲线的外推始点所对应的温度为相变温度。

结果与讨论

直接氮化法用于差热分析　将 $Li_2CO_3:4NH_4Cl$(mol)的混合样品的差热曲线示于图 1。结果说明：在 190 ℃时氯化铵发生晶型转变；继续加热至 198 ℃开始发生碳酸锂的氯化反应，当温度升高至 393 ℃氯化反应及剩余氯化铵的分解反应完全结束，体系中只剩下 LiCl。测出其熔点为 607 ℃。与经过严格脱水干燥的分析纯 LiCl[1] 的差热测量结果(608 ℃)相比(图 2)，吻合得很好。

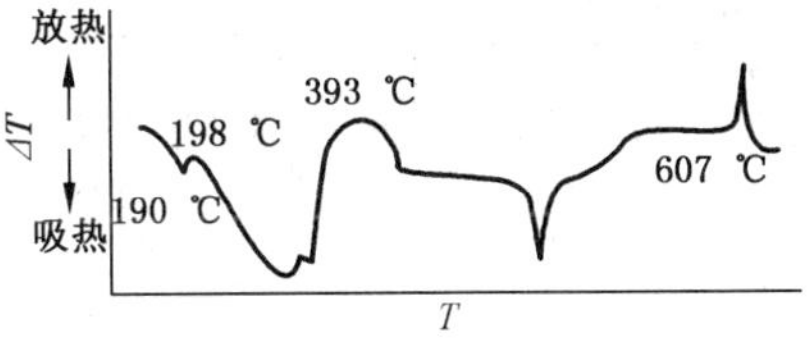

图 1　$Li_2CO_3:NH_4Cl=1:4$(mol)混合样品的 DTA 曲线

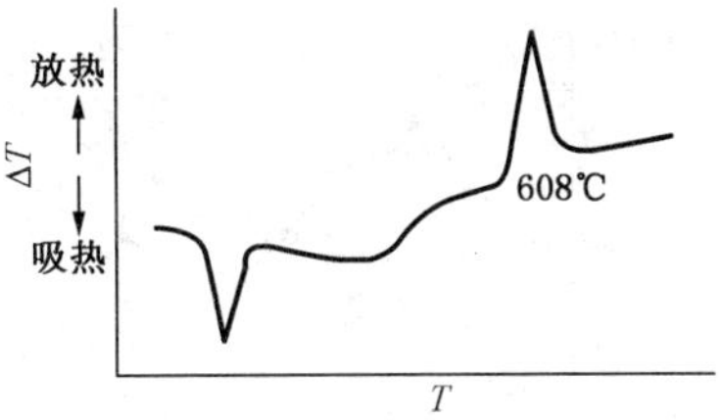

图 2　LiCl 的 DTA 曲线

用直接氯化法测定二元体系相图的研究　为考察将直接氯化法引入热分析测定氯化锂体系相图的可靠性，我们首先将此法用于测定一些二元体系的相图：KCl-LiCl；LiCl-LiF；LiCl-NaCl。所测出的相图分别示于图 3、图 4、图 5。将测得结果列于表 1，与大量文献值比较[1]说明将直接氯化法引入热分析测定含氯化锂熔盐体系的相图所得结果是可靠的。

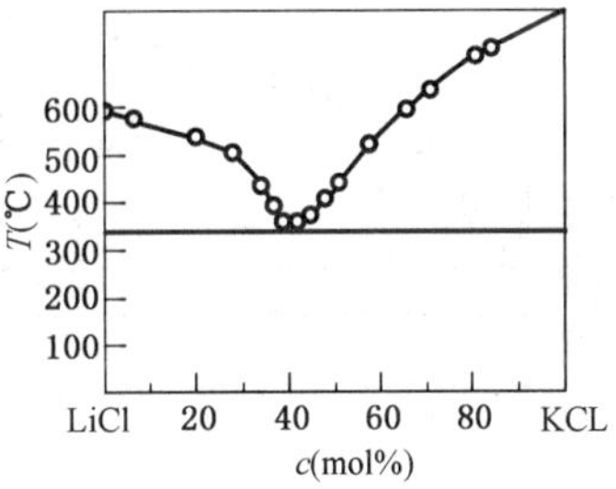

图 3　LiCl-KCl 相图

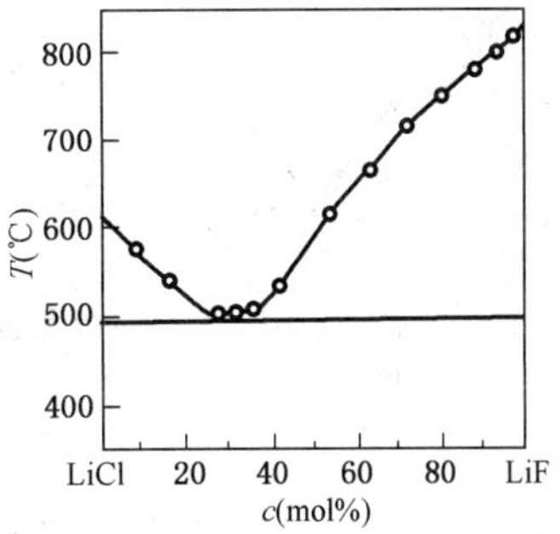

图 4　LiCl-LiF 相图

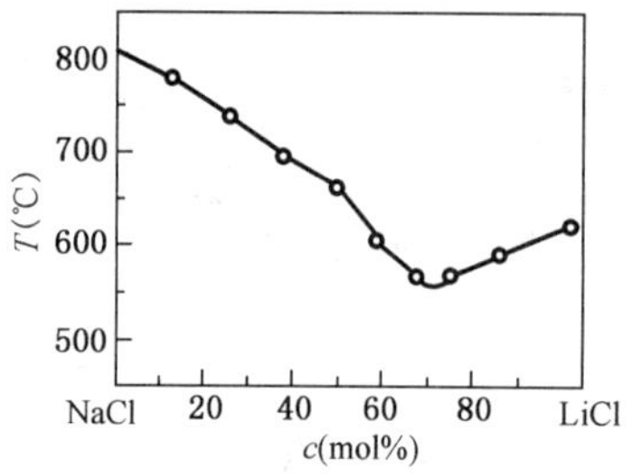

图 5　LiCl-NaCl 相图

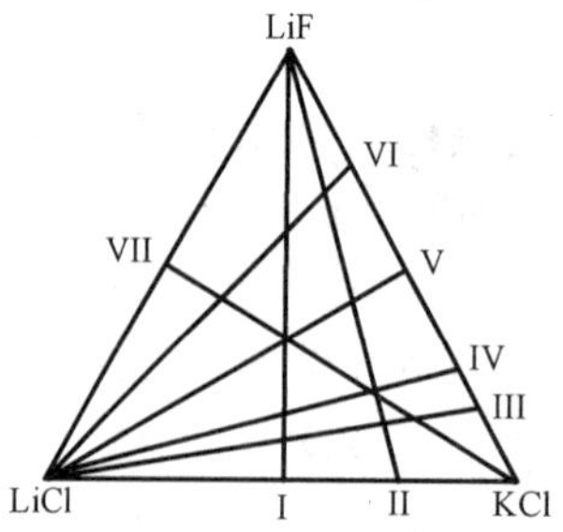

图 6　LiCl-KCl-LiF 垂直截面分布图

表 1　二元相图的测定结果

相图	最低共晶点温度(℃)	最低共晶点组成(mol%)
LiCl-KCl	352	42(KCl)
LiCl-LiF	496	30(LiF)
LiCl-NaCl	550*	72(LiCl)

* 最低点。

利用直接氯化法测定 LiC-KCl-LiF 三元相图　在测定 LiCl-KCl，LiCl-LiF 二元相图的基础上，引用文献[2]测定的 KCl-LiF 相同，用直接氯化法测定 LiCl-LiF-KCl 三元体系相图，为准确反映三元相图的全貌，本文设计测量了 7 个垂直截面，其分布情况如图 6 示。7 个垂直截面的测定结果示于图 7。各截面上最低共晶点的温度及组成列于表 2。

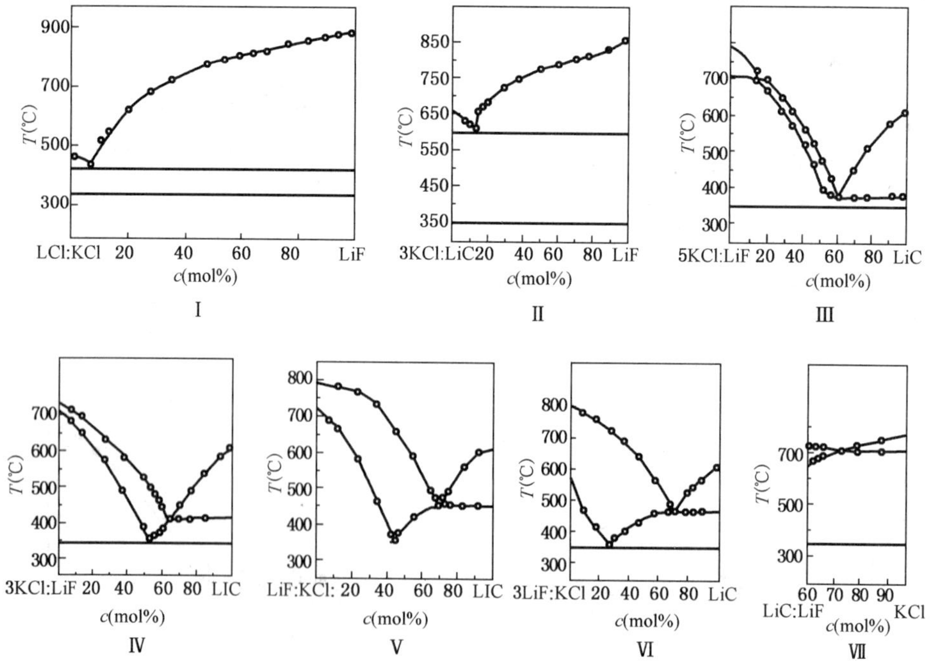

图 7　LiCl-KCl-LiF 体系的七个垂直截面

表 2　各垂直截面上最低共晶点的组成与温度

截止	组成(mol)	温度(℃)
(Ⅰ) LiCl-KCl-LiF	6.5%(LiF)	436
(Ⅱ) LiCl:3KCl-LiF	14.0%(LiF)	620
(Ⅲ) 5KCl:LiF-LiCl	15%(LiCl)	700
	61%(LiCl)	375
(Ⅳ) 3KCl:LiF-LiCl	64%(LiCl)	410
(Ⅴ) KCl:LiF-LiCl	69%(LiCl)	442
(Ⅵ) KCl:3LiF-LiCl	70.5%(LiCl)	465
(Ⅶ) LiCl:LiF-KCl	72.5%(KCl)	700

表 3　体系最低共晶点附近几个点组成与相变温度

组成　mol/L	第一相变点温度(℃)	第二相变点温度(℃)	第三相变点温度(℃)
40.9KCl+56.5LiCl+2.6LiF	375	375	348
40.6KCl+56.0LiCl+3.4LiF	406	352	348
41.4KCl+57.3LiCl+1.3LiF	350	350	348
42.2KCl+53.8LiCl+4.0LiF	395	355	348
38.4KCl+57.7LiCl+3.9LiF	410	410	348
38.7KCl+58.1LiCl+3.2LiF	382	382	348

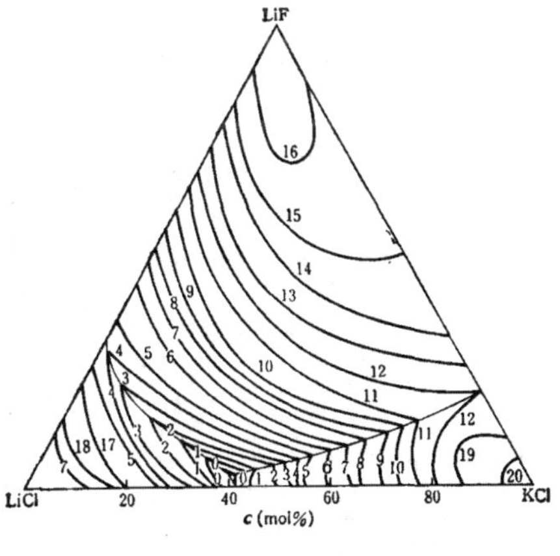

0—375 ℃;1—410 ℃;2—442 ℃;3—465 ℃;4—490 ℃;5—500 ℃;6—560 ℃;7—580 ℃;8—600 ℃;9—620 ℃;10—650 ℃;11—680 ℃;12—710 ℃;13—730 ℃;14—750 ℃;15—770 ℃;16—800 ℃;17—530 ℃;18—550 ℃;19—735 ℃;20—758 ℃

图 8　LiCl-KCl-LiF 三元体系液相线投影图

从各垂直截面上读出等温条件下的相界点投影到浓度三角形中,得到液相等温线投影图(图 8)。为尽可能准确地指出体系的最低共晶点(四相点)的组成,在组成分别为 9LiF + 27KCl + 64LmoCl(mol,6.5LiF+32.5KCl+61.0

LiCl(mol)和 58LiCl＋42KCl(mol)三点组成的三角形之中选择一系列不同组成的体系测定其相变情况，结果列予表 3。得到体系的最低共晶点温度为 348 ℃，组成近似为41.4KCl＋57.32LiCl＋1.3LiF(mol%)，在图 8 中三条三相线的交点处。

参考文献

[1] 张英珊，硕士论文，中国科学院长春应用化学研究所. 长春，1988.

[2] HaendlerJ H. M.,；Sennett，P. S.，Wheeler，C. M. Jr.，J. Electrochem. Soc.，1959，106，264.

Li 在液态 Al 中扩散系数的测定研究①

张英珊　赵敏寿*　唐定骧

（中国科学院长春应用化学研究所，长春）

摘　要：首次尝试利用开路电位-浓度曲线法测定合金的浓度，并用阳极计时电位法快速测定 Li 在液态 Al 中的扩散系数。720 ℃下 Li 在液态 Al 中的扩散系数 $D_{Li/Al}=4.94\times10^{-5}$ $cm^2\cdot s^{-1}$。与根据 Smkes-Einstein 方程计算得到的理论值 $D_{Li/Al}=4.85\times10^{-5}$ $cm^2\cdot s^{-1}$ 相吻合。

Study on Measurement of Diffusion Coefficient of Li Atom in Liquid Aluminium

Zhang, Ying-Shan Zhao, Min-Shou* Tang, Ding-Xiang

(Changehun Institute of Applied chemistry, Academia Sinica, Changchun)

Abstract: The rest potential-concentration curve was first applied to measure the concentration of an alloy. Attempt to use the *V-c* curve of Al-Li alloy in measuring the diffusion coefficient of Liatom in liquid aluminium with anode chronopotentiometry at 720 ℃, was made and $D_{Li/Al}=4.94\times10^{-5}$ $cm^2\cdot s^{-1}$ was obtained. The value is well conaistent with the theoretical value, $D_{Li/Al}=4.85\times10^{-5}$ $cm^2\cdot s^{-1}$ in terms of Stokes-Einstein equation.

合金中某一组分的扩散系数在熔盐化学中具有很重要的意义，为选择电流密度、分离金属时选择时间和温度等可提供参考。电流密度的大小不仅影响着电流效率，而且还直接影响到合金的纯度[1]。

利用电化学方法，对不同组成的固态 Al-Li 合金中的扩散系数已进行了大量的研究[2,3]，但 Li 在液态 Al 中的扩散系数迄今未见报道。本文利用阳极计时电位法测定 720 ℃下 Li 在液态 Al 中的扩散系数。

国内有人利用阳极计时电位法测定了 Dy 在液态 Al，La 在液态 Al-Si 合金中的扩散系数[4,5]。但所用方法，合金浓度不易控制，实验周期也较长。

本文尝试利用浓度-开路电位曲线法测定 Al-Li 合金的浓度。用此方法，不仅合金浓度容易控制，而且只需一个样品即可在不同浓度下进行连续阳极计时电位测量，大大缩短了实验周期。

实验

实验设备与实验药品

三电极电解池系统 阳极计时电位测量的电解池系统如图 1 所示。工作电极为液态 Al-Li 合金。Mo 丝作为导电棒，

① 化学学报，1990(48)：690-693.

电极面积 0.58 cm^2。对电极为光谱纯石墨棒。参比电极为将银丝插入熔融的 0.45 NaCl-0.45 KCl-0.1 AgCl(mol)混合熔体中，密封制成。

电化学则量仪器　用 DEZ-1 型电化学综合测试仪。

药品　NaCl，KCl 和 LiCl 均为分析纯，A1 纯度 99.99%。

LiCl 的脱水干燥　将块状 LiCl 研细后，在 140 ℃下真空干燥脱水 18 h，然后在干燥 HCl 气氛中缓慢加热至熔化，继续用 HCl 气体鼓泡 1 h 后，换纯净、干燥 Ar 气鼓泡 30 min，驱赶残留的 HCl 气体。

实验步骤　在一定温度和确定电解质组成的条件下，液态 Al-Li 合金相对 Ag/AgCl 参比电极的开路电位值只取决于 Al-Li 合金的组成。因此，若测出 Al-Li 合金浓度与其开路电位之间的关系曲线，即可由开路电位值求出 Al-Li 合金样品的浓度。

首先用冲稀法配制一系列不同含 Li 量的 Al-Li 合金，并由原子吸收光谱仪准确测出各样品中 Li 的浓度在 1∶1 mol KCl-NaCl 加 2%(w.t)LiCl 的熔体中，720 ℃下测定 Al-Li/Li^+ 电极相对 Ag/AgCl 参比电极的开路电极电位。根据测量结果作出浓度(c)-开路电位(V)曲线(图 2)。在相同条件下，用任一较高浓度的 Al-Li 合金为工作电极，记录其开路电位值，然后进行阳极计时电位测量，得到计时电位图(图 3)。求出过渡时间 τ_1；待电极稳定后记录 Al-Li/Li^+ 的开路电位，再进行阳极计时电位测量，求出过渡时间 τ_2。从 c-V 曲线上查出各开路电位所对应 Al-Li 合金中 Li 的浓度。如此可得到一系列不同浓度所对应的 $J\tau^{1/2}$ 值，从而根据 Sand 方程求出 Li 在液体 Al 中，在 720 ℃下的扩散系数。

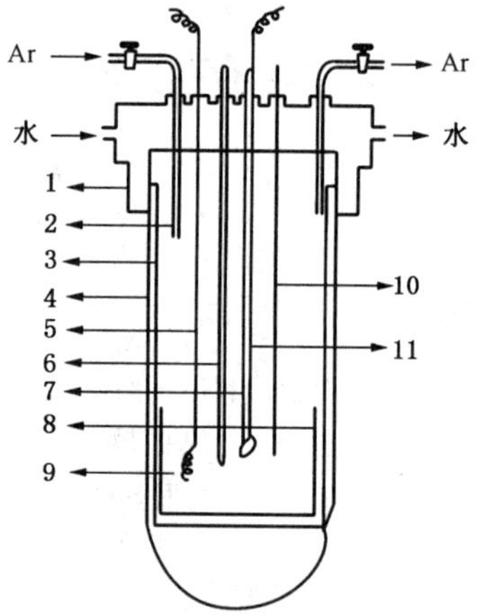

1—水套管，2—Ar 气进口管，
3—刚玉内衬，4—石英外套，
5—参比电极，6—热电偶，
7—工作电极(容器)，8—刚玉坩埚，
9—熔盐，10—石墨电极，
11—工作电极(Mo 导电棒)

图 1　三电极电解池系统

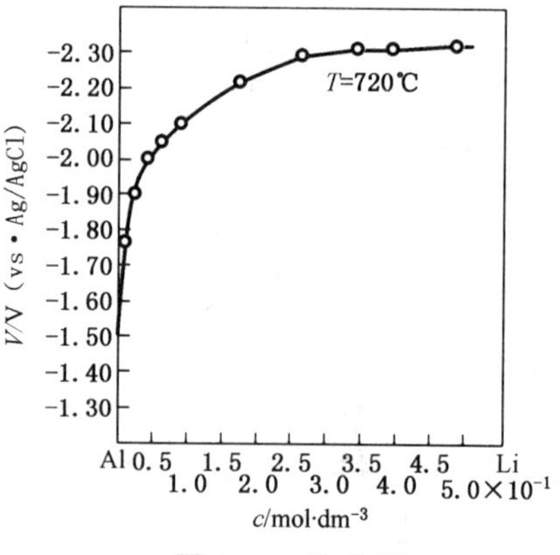

图 2　c-V 曲线

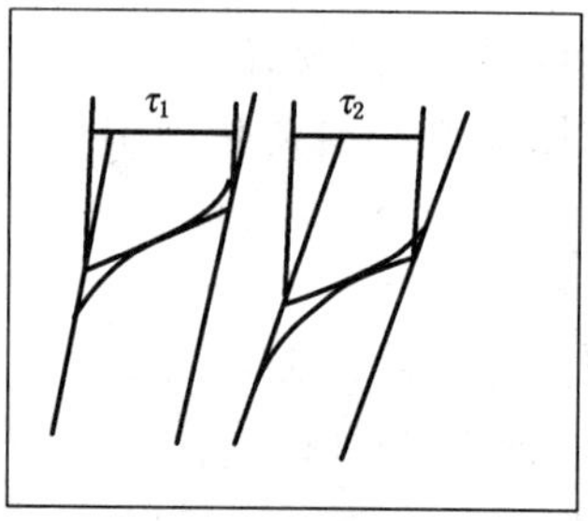

图 3　在 720 ℃ Li 氧化的计时电位曲线

结果与讨论

为确定在测量的样品浓度范围内 Li 的阳极氧化过程的控制步骤，在每一浓度下均选择不同的电流密度进行阳极计时电位测量，所得结果列于表 1. $J\tau^{1/2}$-J 曲线（如图 4 示）均为平行于横轴的直线，说明在所选条件下的 Li 阳极氧化过程是半无限扩散控制过程，满足 Sand 方程：

$$J\tau^{1/2} = \frac{1}{2}nF\pi^{1/2}cD^{1/2}$$

J—通过电极的电流密度（A/cm^2）；F—法拉第常数；τ—过渡时间（s）；D—扩散系数（$cm^2\cdot s^{-1}$）；c—Li 的浓度（$mol\cdot dm^{-3}$）。

因此可以利用 Sand 方程计算 Li 在液体 A1 中的扩散系数。

表 1　阳极计时电位法的测量结果

开路电位，V（VS，Ag　AgCl）	Li 浓度 $c/mol\cdot dm^3$	电流密度，$J/A\cdot cm^{-2}$	过渡时间，τ/s	$J\tau^{1/2}A\cdot cm^2\cdot s^{1/2}$
−2.08		0.69	0.35	0.41
−2.07	8.0×10^{-1}	0.86	0.25	0.43
−2.07		1.03	0.20	0.46
−2.00		0.43	0.30	0.24
−2.00	4.0×10^{-1}	0.52	0.25	0.26
−2.01		0.67	0.12	0.23
−1.84		0.17	0.38	0.10
−1.84	2.0×10^{-1}	0.21	0.26	0.11
−1.84		0.26	0.24	0.13
−1.74		0.17	0.28	0.09
−1.75	1.5×10^{-1}	0.22	0.20	0.19
−1.75		0.26	0.15	0.10

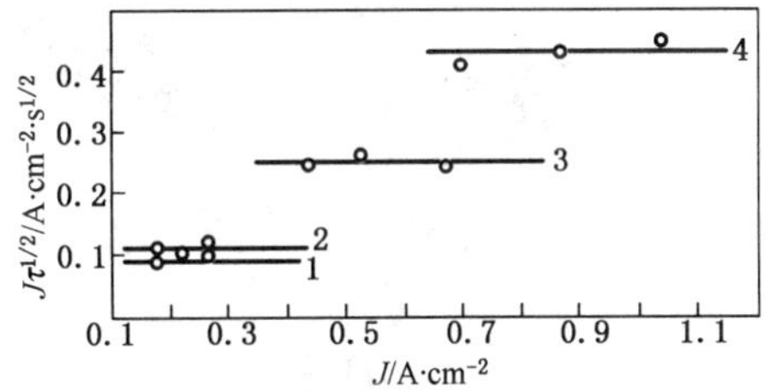

图 4　$J\tau^{1/2}$-J 曲线

T=720 ℃

1—$c=1.5\times10^{-1}$ $mol\cdot dm^{-3}$，

2—$c=2.0\times10^{-1}$ $mol\cdot dm^{-3}$，

3—$c=4.0\times10^{-1}$ $mol\cdot dm^{-3}$，

4—$c=8.0\times10^{-1}$ $mol\cdot dm^{-3}$

按照表 1 中数据作图 $J\tau^{1/2}$-c 曲线（图 5），求出直线斜率 $k=600$。根据 Sand 方程有：$k=\frac{1}{2}nF\pi^{1/2}D^{1/2}=600$，求出 Li 在液态 Al 中的扩散系数 $D_{Li/Al}=4.94\times10^{-5}$ $cm^2\cdot s^{-1}$。

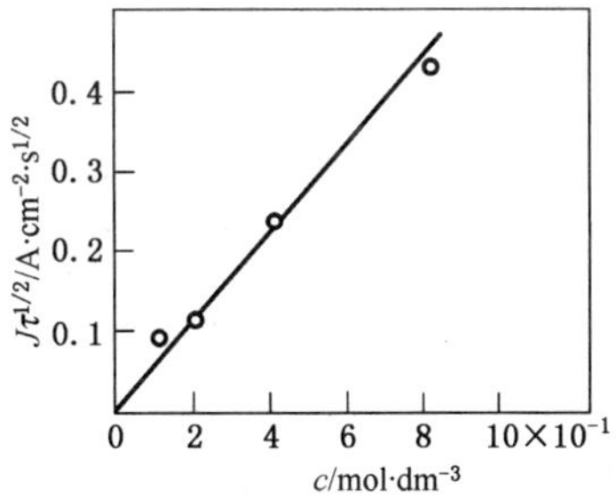

图 5　$J\tau^{1/2}$-c 曲线

根据 Stokes-Einstein 方程 $D=\frac{KT}{6\pi r\eta}$。式中，K-Boltzmann 常数，T—绝对温度，r—Li 的金属半径 1.5×10^{-8} cm，η—Al-Li 合金的粘度，此处用 Al 的粘度代替，计算出 720 ℃下 Li 在液态 Al 中的理论扩散系数 $D_{Li/Al}=4.85\times10^{-5}$ $cm^2\cdot s^{-1}$，与

实验测定值极为相近。测定结果说明：Li 在液态 Al 中的扩散速度远大于在固态 Al 中的扩散速度（$D\simeq10^{-10}\ cm^2\cdot s^{-1}$），这对于利用液态 Al 阴极电解制备 Al-Li 合金的研究具有重要参考价值。

参考文献

[1] 渡过吉章，豊嶋雅康，伊藤勝久，加藤荣，日本金属学会会报，1987，26，(4)，308.

[2] Wen，C. J.；Boukamp，B. A.；Huggins，R. A.；Weppner，W.，*J. Electrochem. Soc.*，1979，126，2258.

[3] Melendres，C. A.，*J. Electrochem. Soc.* 1977，124，650.

[4] 苏明忠，杜森林. 唐定骧，中国稀土学报，1988，6(2)，81.

[5] 杨振国，杜维玺，杜森林，金属学报，1989，25(2)，B92.

YCl_3-NaCl·KCl熔体中 Y^{3+} 在钼和镍电极上的电极过程

张小联　赵敏寿　官素珍
（中国科学院长春应用化学研究所，长春 130022）

摘　要：用循环伏安法和计时电位法研究了 YCl_3－KCl·NaCl熔体中 Y^{3+} 在钼和镍电极上的电极过程。Y^{3+} 的还原是分步反应过程：$Y^{3+}+e=Y^{2+}$，$Y^{2+}+2e=Y$。Y^{3+} 在镍电极上还原后能与镍形成合金，对不同条件下形成的合金组成进行了X射线分析。

关键词：钇；钼电极；镍电极；电极过程

Y-Ni合金主要用于电热合金、镍基超合金和某些特殊钢及部分有色金属中作添加剂。钇能明显改善这些合金的高温抗氧化性能和耐腐蚀性能，同时还能改善合金的加工性能。熔盐体系中有关钇的电化学性质研究不多，钇在电极上还原的电化学过程研究还未见报道。本文用循环伏安法和计时电位法研究了 YCl_3-NaCl·KCl熔体中 Y^{3+} 在钼和镍电极上还原的电化学过程，并借助X射线分析对镍电极上形成的Y-Ni合金成分进行了研究。

一、实验部分

参照文献(1)的制备方法，在瓷蒸发皿中用 Y_2O_3(99.99%)和 NH_4Cl(优级纯)作为原料，在加热条件下“干法”制得 YCl_3，其中水不熔物含量小于1 wt%，用等摩尔NaCl·KCl作溶剂，合成具有一定浓度的 YCl_3 熔体，电解槽结构和实验装置参见文献[2]。

实验前向熔体中通入干燥的HCl气体15～20 min以除去氯化稀土中少量的水不溶物，再向熔体中通入干燥、纯净的氩气15 min，以驱除剩余的HCl气体。静止30 min后在氩气保护下进行实验。文中所给电位均为相对 Cl_2/Cl^- 标准电极的电位。

二、实验结果和讨论

（一）Y^{3+} 在钼电极上的电极过程

在不同熔体温度(1023～1123K)、不同 YCl_3 浓度(1.5～7 wt%)和不同扫描速度(120～480 mV/s)下，用循环伏安法研究了 Y^{3+} 在钼电极上的电极过程。

图1(a)是典型的 Y^{3+} 在钼电极上不同扫描速度下的循环伏安曲线。在向阴极方向扫描中出现了两个较为明显的转折 I_c 和 II_c，它们分别出现在－2.42～－2.58 V和－2.58～－2.75 V之间，相应的氧化峰 I_a 和 II_a 峰电位则分别出现在－2.42和－2.58 V左右。从图中可看出各峰电位基本上不随扫描速度变化而改变，因而可将各反应按可逆反应过程处理。各阴极峰电流 I_{pc} 对 $V^{1/2}$ 作图，都能得到较好的直线，且直线的延长线偏离原点

① 中国稀土学报，1991，9(4)：302-305.

都很小，可近似认为 Y^{3+} 在钼电极上的还原是受扩散控制的可逆反应过程。

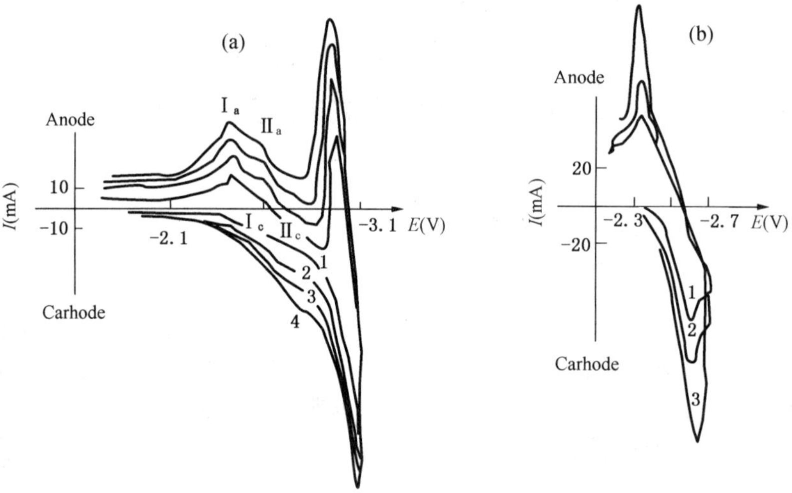

图 1　Y^{3+} 在钼电极上的循环伏安曲线(a)和 I_c 反应的循环伏安曲线(b)

T：1123 K；c_{YCl_3}：(a)7wt%，(b)5wt%；A_{Mo}；(a)0.094 cm^2，(b)0.095 cm^2；

1. V=120 mVs^{-1}，2. V=240 mVs^{-1}，3. V=360 mVs^{-1}，4. V=480 mVs^{-1}

在研究还原波 I_c 时，为了避免还原波 $Ⅱ_c$ 的影响，扫描到刚出现 $Ⅰ_c$ 的电流峰便回扫。图 1(b)是从 $E=-2.10$ V 扫描到 -2.70 V 后再回扫，在不同扫描速度下 Y^{3+} 在钳电极上极化的循环伏安曲线。从图中可看出，阴极峰电位 E_{pc} 和阳极峰电位 E_{pa} 基本不随 V 变化而变化，且峰电流和 $V^{1/2}$ 大致成正比，这都符合可逆电极反应的特征。对于原料和产物均可溶的可逆电极反应，$\Delta E_p=E_{pa}-E_{pc}=2.22RT/nF$[3]，由图 1(b)中各扫描速度下的 ΔE_p 计算出 I_c 反应的得电子数分别为 1.02、1.01和 0.95，可近似认为 I_c 反应为得一个电子的可逆过程：$Y^{3+}+e=Y^{2+}$。

对原料和产物均可溶的可逆反应过程，在电流为 35～70%i_p 时，E 对 $\ln(i_p-i)/i$ 作图能得一直线，且直线斜率等于 $0.744RT/nF$[4]。高温时钇易与熔体作用，将$Ⅱ_c$ 反应作产物可溶的反应处理，对图 1(a)中 V=360 mV/s 的 $Ⅱ_c$ 反应的 E 对 $\ln(i_p-i)i$ 作图，如图 2，从所得直线斜率可求得电子转移数，$n_2=2.2$。对不同 V、c_{YCl_3} 和不同熔体温度下的 $Ⅱ_c$ 反应按 $E\sim\ln(i_p-i)i$ 处理，从直线斜率求得 $Ⅱ_c$ 反应的平均得电子数 $\bar{n}_2=2.1$，标准偏差 $S=0.19$，因而可认为 $Ⅱ_c$ 反应为得两个电子的过程：$Y^{2+}+2e=Y$。

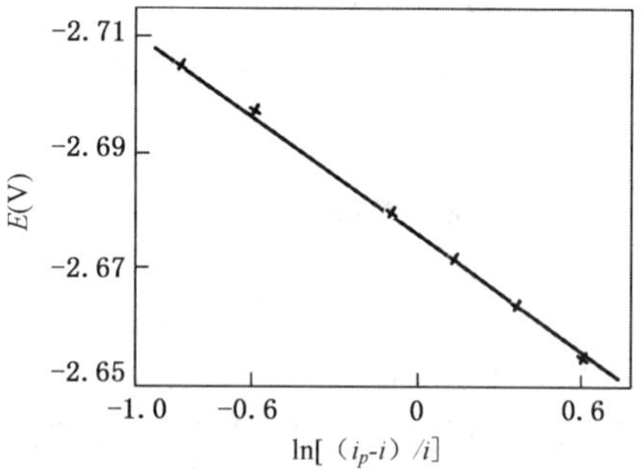

图 2　$Ⅱ_c$ 反应的 $E\sim\ln[(i_p-i)/i]$

V=360 mVs^{-1}，T=1123 K，

c_{YCl_3}=7wt%，A_{mo}=0.094 cm^2

为进一步验证所得到的结论，做了 Y^{3+} 在钼电极上的计时电位曲线，如图 3。从图 3 可看出，在 -2.53 和 -2.64 V 左右分别开始出现平台，它们分别与循环伏安曲线中的 I_c 和 II_c 反应起始电位相对应。由曲线的平台测出过渡时间 τ[5]，得出 $\tau_1=0.085$ s，$\tau_2=0.60$ s。据 Delahay[6] 导出的扩散方程，对于可逆反应及产物可溶的情况，对稀溶液有：$E=E_{\tau/4}+(RT/nF)\ln[(\tau^{1/2}-t^{1/2})/t^{1/2}]$，对于一种组分的分步反应有：$\tau_2=\tau_1[2(n_2/n_1)+(n_2/n_1)^2]$，当，$n_2=2n_1$ 时有：$\tau_2/\tau_1=8$，而实验结果 $\tau_2/\tau_1=7.06$，考虑到 YCl_3 的浓度偏离稀溶液及试验误差，可认为 τ_2/τ_1 值近似为 8，说明 I_c 和 II_c 反应分别为得一个和两个电子的过程。

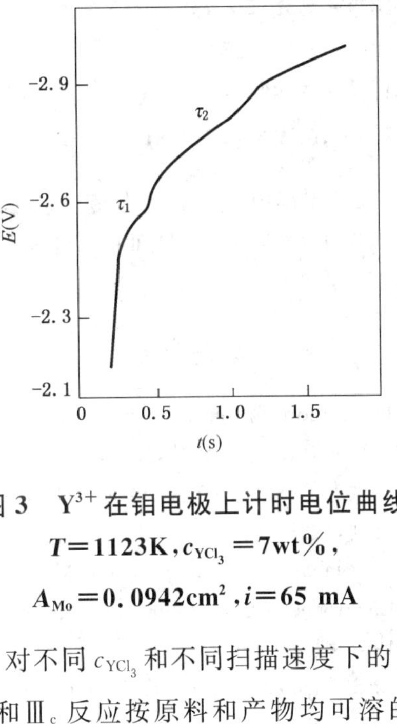

图 3　Y^{3+} 在钼电极上计时电位曲线

$T=1123$K，$c_{YCl_3}=7$wt%，

$A_{Mo}=0.0942cm^2$，$i=65$ mA

对不同 c_{YCl_3} 和不同扫描速度下的 I_c、II_c 和 III_c 反应按原料和产物均可溶的可逆反应处理，可得到 I_c、II_c 和 III_c 反应的平均电子数分别为 1.21、2.18 和 2.86，标准偏差分别为 0.10、0.15 和 0.15，因而可近似认为它们分别是得一、二和三个电子的反应。Y^{3+} 在镍电极上的电极过程与在钼上的相似，如图 4。不同处在于，在镍电极上析出的钇能与镍合金化，X 射线分析结果证实了 Ni-Y 合金的生成，这也许是 Y^{3+} 可接受三个电子而被还原的原因。

图 5(a)是 850 ℃、$c_{YCl_3}=3$wt%时，在镍片电极（1.55 cm^2）上从 $E=-1.101$ V，以 240 mV/s 的扫描速度扫至 -2.053 V(vs AgCl/Ag)后，再继续电解 30 s 取样分析的 X 射线图。从中分析出镍片电极表面有 Ni_5Y、Ni_4Y、Y_2O_3 和少量的 Ni_2Y_3。Y_2O_3 是由生成的金属钇或 Ni-Y 合金氧化的结果，当钇的沉积速度大于钇与镍合金化速度时，金属钇就在 Ni-Y 合金表面析出。

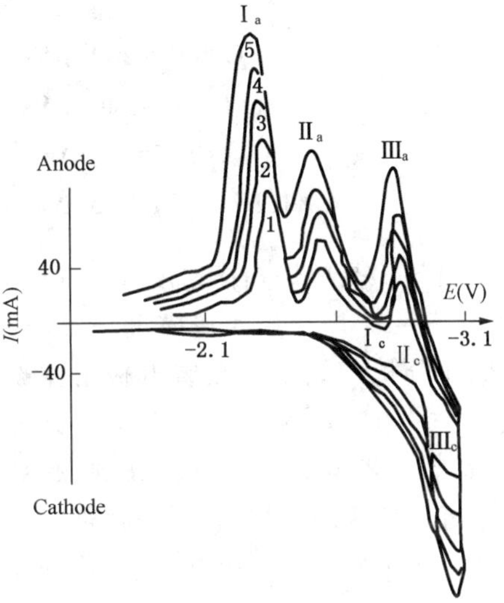

图 4　Y^{3+} 在镍电极上的循环伏安曲线

$T=1123$K，$c_{YCl_3}=5$wt%，$A_{Ni}=0.113cm^2$，

1. $V=120mVs^{-1}$，

2. $V=240mVs^{-1}$，3. $V=360mVs^{-1}$，

4. $V=480mVs^{-1}$，5. $V=600mVs^{-1}$

图 5(b)是相同条件下，从 $E=-1.101$ V扫描到 -2.48 V 再继续电解 30 s 取样分析的结果。从中可看出有大量 Ni_5Y 生成，Ni_4Y 的量也很显著，生成的合金量明显比图 5(a)多，同样也有少量 Y_2O_3 和 Ni_2Y_3。这说明电解电位越负，即阴极电流密度越大，越有利于 Ni-Y 合

金生成。

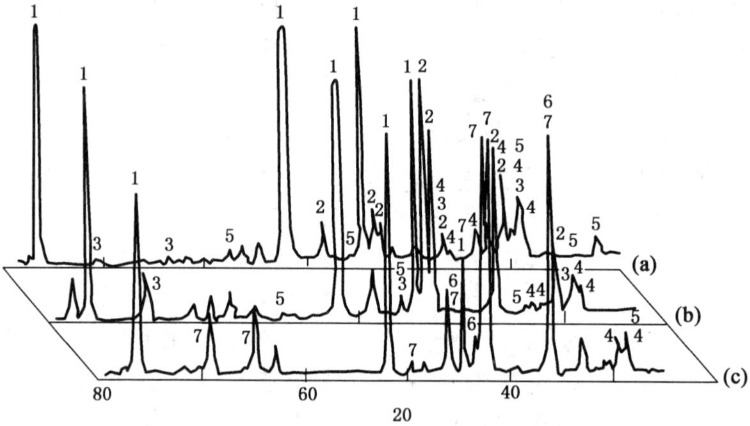

图 5　镍电极 X 射线分析

(a) $V=240\ mVs^{-1}$, $E=-1.101\sim-3.154$ V;

(b) $V=240\ mVs^{-1}$, $E=-1.101\sim-3.583$ V;

(c) $V=5\ mVs^{-1}$, $E=-1.101\sim-3.583$ V;

1. Ni, 2. Ni_5Y, 3. Ni_4, 4. Ni_2Y_3, 5. Y_2O_3, 6. YNi_2, 7. YNi

图 5(c)是放慢扫描速度至 5.0 mV/S 时，从 $E=-1.101$ V 扫描至 -3.583 V 后取样分析的结果。在镍电极上主要生成 Ni_3-Y，还有 Ni_2-Y、Y_2O_3 和少量的 Ni_2Y_3。主要生成含钇量较高的 Y-Ni 合金是可以理解的。扫描放慢时，部分在快扫描时来不及与镍合金化的钇，有充足的时间与镍合金化。这说明钇与镍合金化需要一定时间，电解制备 Y-Ni 合金时必须控制钇的析出速度，即控制一定的阴极电流密度是十分必要的。

三、结论

(1) YCl_3-KCI・NaCl 熔体中在钼和镍电极上 Y^{3+} 的还原都存在分步反应：$Y^{3+}+e=Y^{2+}$，$Y^{2+}+2e=Y$；当电位足够负时，在镍电极上一步还原也可实现：$Y^{3+}+3e=Y$。

(2) 在镍电极上析出的钇能与镍合金化，阴极电流密度高，有利于 Y-Ni 合金的生成。

参考文献

[1] H. S. Booth 著，龚毅生、申泮文译，《无机合成》，北京，科学出版社，1959，1，23.

[2] 赵敏寿等，中国科学院长春应用化学研究所集刊，1983，20，91.

[3] P. Delahay, "New Instrumental Merthod s in Electrochemistry", Interscience, New York, 1954. Chapt. 6.

[4] R. S. Nicholson, I. Shain, Anal. Chem. Soc., 1956, 103, 8.

[5] W. W. Reimuth, Anal. Chem., 1960, 32, 1514.

[6] P. Delahay, T. Berzins, J. Am. Chem. Soc., 1953, 75, 4205.

Determination of the Apparent Standard Potential of the Dy/Dy(Ⅲ) System in the LiCl-KCl Eutectic ①

CHANG Kai-Guo LU Xiang-Ping DU Fu-Ying ZHAO Min-Shou
(Changchun Institute of Applied Chenistry, chinese Academy of science changchun, Jilin 130022 China)

Abstract: The apparent standard potential of Dy/Dy(Ⅲ) system in the LiCl-KCl eutectic has been determined by the logarithmic analysis of the semi-integrals of voltammograms, logarithmic analysis of chronopotentiograms and the open circuit potentiometry. The dysprosium equilibrium potentids for various concentration of dysprosium chloride in the LiCl-KCl eutectic melt between 400—500 ℃ were determined experimentally, and the apparent standard potential of this system and its temperature dependance have been calculated.

Key words: Rare earth; standard potential; electrochemistry of dysprosium; molten salt.

Introduction

The physical and electrochemical properties of rare earth elements in the molten salt media are of great importance to the electrolytic production and purification of rare earth metals and their alloys. Although the standard potentials of several rare earth metal and its metal ion couple in the chloride melt have been published, [1-3] no relevant data about the Dy/Dy(Ⅲ) system was found in literature. The objective of this work was to determine the apparent standard potential of Dy/Dy(Ⅲ) system in the LiCl-KCl eutecic melt.

Experimental

The eutectic mixture of 41% potasium chloride and 59% (molar percent) lithium chloride was used as solvent system. The solvent was purified by the method described in literature. [4]

The dysprosium chloride was prepared from dysprosium oxide (of purity 99. 9%) by the improved chlorination method introduced in our previous work. [5]

The cell used in this work has been described previously. [6] The working electrode was 1 mm diameter molybdenum wire, the counter electrode was 6 mm diameter graphite rod, all electrode potentials were measured vs the Ag/AgCl (10 mol%) reference electrode. All the electrochemical measurements were performed by using a Model DCG function generator, a DHZ-1 model potentiostat/

---

① Chinese Journal of Chemistry, 1994, 12(6): 509-515.

Galvanostat and a LZ3-200X-Y recorder.

Before the electrochemical measurements, a constant flow of dry'HC1 gas is introduced to the cell for about fifteen minutes to eliminate the possibl oxychloride residue existing in the melt. Also, pre-electrolysis at cathodic current density of 10 rnA/cm [2], using a molybdenum rod, was made to eliminate metallic impurities. An atmosphere of pure argon(of 99.99% purity) is maintained throughout the experiment. The argon gas is purified by a system described elsewhere. [6]

Results and discussion

Equibrium potential measurement by voltammetry

The characteristic voltammogram obtained on molybdenum electrode in the dys prosium chloride melt at 450 ℃ is shown in Fig. 1. We limit our attention to the cathodic peak A of reduction of Dy(Ⅲ) ion and the cathodic limit of B of the solvent corresponding to the formation of the metallic lithium. It can be seen from Fig. 1 that the cathodic peak A lies nearly at constant potential as the scan rate changes, which shows the Nernst behaviour. [7] It has been found that the reduction of the trivalent dysprosium ion on molybdenum electrode is reversible and according to the mechanism [8,9] in chloride melt.

$$DyCl_6^{3-} + 3e = Dy + 6Cl^-$$

This process is controlled by the diffusion of the electroactive species in the electrolyte solution. Due to the ohmic drop between the working electrode and the reference electrode, measurement of equilibrium potentials from the conventional interpretation of voltammograms is difficult. The semi-integration technique is more satisfactory for these systems, because the semi-integrals are independent of the potential sweep rate and the ohmic drop can be corrected easily. [10] Fig. 2 shows the semi-integrals curve of the voltammograms presented in Fig. 1.

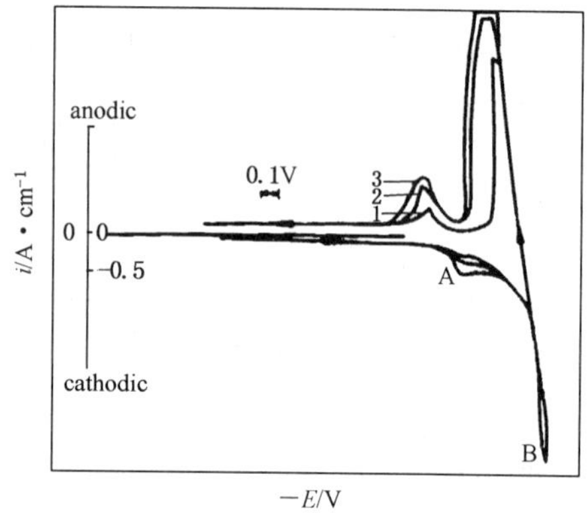

Fig. 1 Voltammogram for Dy(Ⅲ) reduction on molybdenum at 450 ℃. $DyCl_3$ concentration: 2×10^{-3} mol/L; Scan rate: 0.25, 0.45, 0.60 V/s

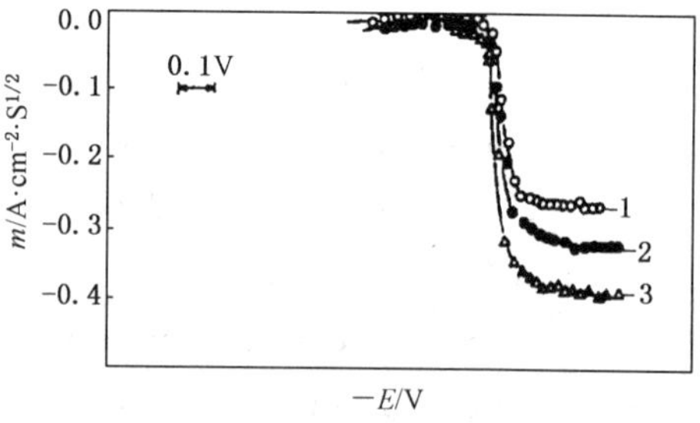

Fig. 2 Semi-integrals of the voltammograms plotted in Fig. 1. scan rate: ○ —0.25; ×—0.45; △—0.60 V/s

For a diffusion controlled process, the semi-integral constant, m, leads to a limit value of m^* for the highest negative overpotential. In case of a reversible system with formation of an insoluble product [10] the semi-integral m is related to the electrode potential by the equation:

$$E = E_{th} + (RT/nF)\ln(m^* - m)/m^*)$$

where E_{th} represents the equilibrium potential of the system and n is the number of exchanged electrons.

The logarithmic analysis of the semi-integrals in Fig. 2 is shown in Fig. 3. Appearance of the linear relation confirms the reversibility of this system. [10] The intersection of the linear part of the curves with the E-axis corresponds to the equilibrium potential of dysprosium metal in dysprosium ion solution. For dysprosium chloride concentration of 2×10^{-3} mol/L at 450 ℃, the equilibrium potential is −2.14 V (vs Ag/AgCl).

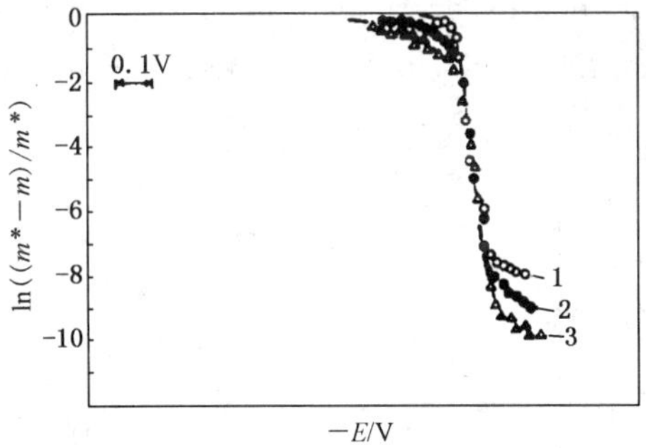

Fig 3.　Logarithmic analysis of the semi-integrals plotted in Fig. 2. Scan rate: ○—0.25; ×—0.45; △—0.60 V/s

Equilibrium potential measurement by chronopotentiometry

A reverse chronopotentiogram obtained on molybdenum in a $DyCl_3$-LiCl-KCl solution at 450 ℃ for a 1.2 A/cm^2 current density is presented in Fig. 4.

Logarithmic analysis of the chronopotentiogram in Fig. 4 by using the following equation shows a linear part in the potential domain of dysprosium ion reduction (Fig. 5). This confirms the reversibility of this system.

$$E = E_{th} + (RT/nF)\ln((\sqrt{\tau} - \sqrt{t}/\sqrt{\tau})$$

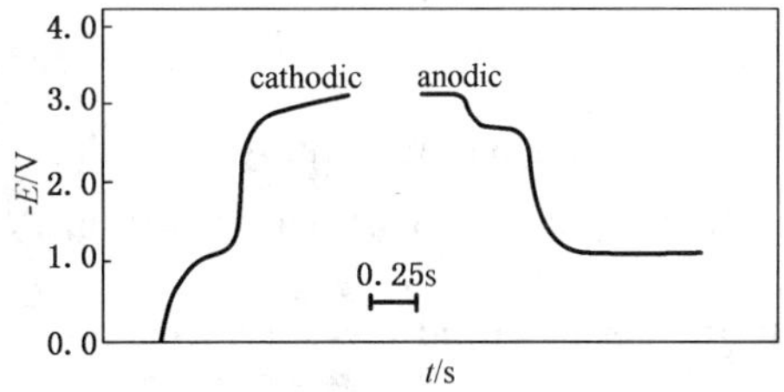

Fig. 4　Reverse chronopotentiogram on molybdenum in $DyCl_3$-LiCl-KCl melt at 450 ℃. $DyCl_3$ concentration: 2×10^{-3} mol/L; current density: 1.2 A/cm^2

where E_{th} is the equilibrium potential of the system, n is the number of exchanged electrons and τ is the cathodic transition time. The intersection of the straight line in Fig. 5 with the E-axis allows to determine the equilibrium potential of dysprosium ion in the melt. In this case, when the dysprosium chloride concentration is 2×10^{-3} mol/L and at temperature of 450 ℃, the equilibrium potential of this system is −2.13 V.

Pure dysprosium deposit was formed on molybdenum electrode surface by constant cathodic polarization around −2.40 V at current density of 0.64 A/cm^2 during 1 to 8 min. The deposits are thick, and sufficiently continuous to present the same characteristics as pure dysprosium metal.

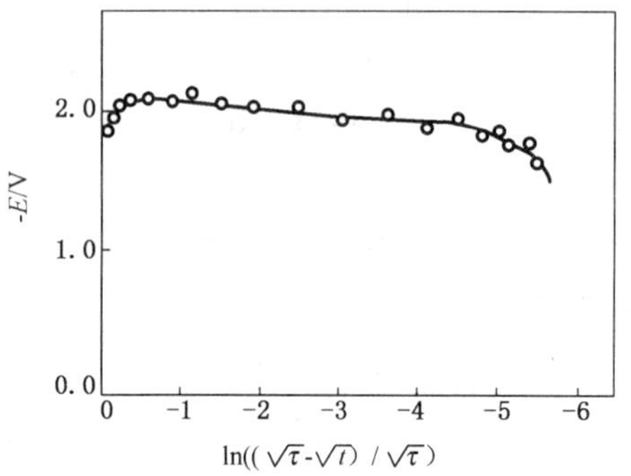

Fig. 5 Logarithmic analysis of the cathodic chronopotentiogram in Fig. 4

Equlibrium potential measurement by open circuit potentiometry

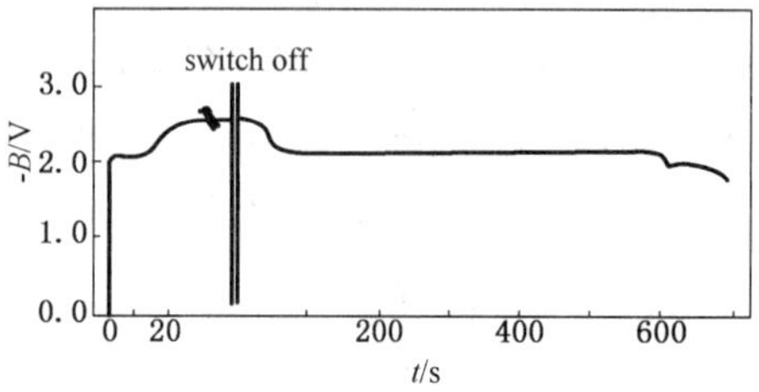

Fig. 6 Open circuit potential evolution of the dysprosium deposit with time after cathodic polarization for 3 min. $DyCl_3$ concentration: 2×10^{-3} mol/L

Fig. 6 shows the potential plateau during cathodic polarization and the open circuit potential evolution with time. The curve presents a potential plateau around −2.40 V and a slow open circuit potential evolution toward the transition, after a period of time, to the equilibrium potential of this system. The potential measured during 10—100 s could be considered to be equal to the equilibrium potential of this system. In the experimental condition as Fig. 6, the equilibrium potential was found to be −2.13 V.

Determination of the apparent standard potential and its temperature dependence

The equilibrium potentials of the Dy/Dy(Ⅲ) system were determined as a function of the dysprosium chloride concentration. The results are shown in Fig. 7.

Results obtained by cyclic voltammetry and open circuit potentiometry are in good agreement. But due to the ohmic drop and poor precision of resistance measurement, a constant error is observed with the result obtained by chronopotentiometry.

Because the experimental concentration is very dilute, by equalizing the molar concentration to the activity, the equilibrium potential can be written as:

$E_{th} = E^{o} + (RT/3F)\ln X$, here X is mole fration of dysprosium chloride. The apparent standard potential, E^{o}, can be obtained by extrapolation of the straight line $E_{th} - \ln X$, to $X = 1$. The experimental value of E^{o} is −2.08 V at 450 ℃.

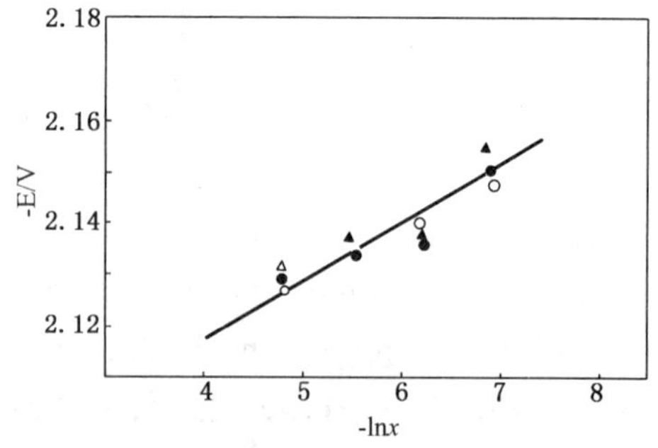

Fig. 7 Relation of Dy/Dy(Ⅲ) equlibriumpotential with Dy(Ⅲ) ion concentration at 450 ℃. Determined by: ○—Open circuit potentiometry; □—Chronopotentiometry; △—Cyclic wltammetry

The equilibrium potential and corresponding apparent standard potential determined at different temperature are given in Table 1.

The temperature dependence of the apparent standard potential of this system between 450-500 ℃ can be described by the equation:

$$E^{o}(T) = -2.30 + 5.0 \times 10^{-4} T,$$
$$(T/℃ ; \gamma = 0.94)$$

Table 1　Equilibrium potential and corresponding apparent standard potential at different temperatures. ○—Open Circuit Potentiometry; △—Cyclic Voltam-metry; □—Chronopotentiometry

$\ln x$		T(℃)		
		450	500	550
−6.91	○	2.15	2.14	2.13
	△	2.16	2.15	2.14
	□	2.14	2.14	2.13
−6.22	○	2.14	2.13	2.12
	△	2.14	2.13	2.12
	□	2.14	2.12	2.12
−5.52	○	2.13	2.11	2.11
	△	2.14	2.12	2.11
	□	2.13	2.12	2.11
	○	2.13	2.11	2.10
−4.83	△	2.13	2.11	2.10
	□	2.13	2.10	2.10
E^{o}		2.08, $\gamma=1$	2.04, $\gamma=1$	2.03, $\gamma=1$

· γ-linear regression coefficient.

Conclusion

The equilibrium potentials of Dy/Dy(Ⅲ) system in LiCl-KCl eutectic melt were determined by cyclic voltammetry, chronopotentiometry and the open circuit poteniometry. The apparent standard potential of this system is found to be −2.08 V (vs Ag/AgCl 10 mol%) at 450 ℃, the temperature dependence of the apparent standard potential can be described by:

$$E^{o}(T) = -2.30 + 5.0 \times 10^{-4} T$$

The reduction mechanism of Dy(Ⅲ) ion on molybdenum electrode is further confirmed as a reversible transfter of three electrons in this study.

References

[1] Yang, L.; Houson, R. G., Trans. *Met. Soc. A. I. M. E.*, 215, 589(1959).

[2] Zhao, M.-S., Hikino, S.; Ito, Y., *J. Electrochem. Soc.*, 139, 1820(1992).

[3] Hoshino, Y.; Plambeck, J. A., *Can. J. Chem.*, 48, 685(1970).

[4] Pov, B.; Laitinen, *H. A.*, *J. Electrochem. SOC.*, 117, 644(1970).

[5] Zhao, M.-S., Tamg, D.-X., *Collected papers of the Changchun institute of applied chemistry*, Chineae Academy of Sicnecea, 1983, p. 91.

[6] Chang, K.-G., *Master these*, Changchun Inetitute of Applied Chemistry, Chinese Academy of sciences, Changchun, 1989.

[7] Su, M.-Z.; Du, S.-L.; Tang, D.-X., *Xiyou Jinshu*, 9, 166(1990).

[8] Panchinko, I. D.; Penkalo, I. I., Delimarskii, U. K., *Electrokhimiya*, 2, 529(19GG).

[9] Picard, G.; Moto, Y., 168*th Meeting*, *The electrochemical Society*, Las Vog, Nevada, October, 1985, Caesars Palace.

[10] Robin, A.; Lepinary, J. D. E.; Barbier, M. J., *J. Electroanal. Chem.*, 230, 125(1987).

三、金属间化合物和合金

Magnetic and Magnetotransport Properties of Intermetallic $SmMn_2Si_2$ ①

M. Zhao, C. Sun, L. Wang, W. Li, Q. Su
(Changchun Institute of Applied Chemistry, Chinese Academy of sciences, Changchun 130022, People's Republic of China)
W. Zhao, J. Tang
(Department of Physics, University of New Orleans, New Orleans, Louisiana 70148)

Abstract: The magnetic properties of naturally layered intermetallic compound $SmMn_2Si_2$ with textured structure have been studied. There exist a ferromagnetic transition at 35 K and two antiferromagnetic transitions at 120 and 230 K. The antiferromagnetic state below 230 K exhibits different magnetoresistance, with a negative magnetoresistance of 3%—4% for current I applied perpendicular to the c axis and with a positive magnetoresistance effect of about 4%—6% for current I parallel to the c axis. The observed magnetoresistance is likely to be related to magnetovolume effects. In the ferromagnetic state, a positive magnetoresistance with a maximum increase of 22% under an applied field of 5 T is observed at 4 K, and both $H \perp I$ and $H \parallel I$ configurations show positive magnetoresistance. [S0021－8979(97)73808－8]

I Introduction

Naturally layered intermetallic ternary compounds, RMn_2X_2 (R = rare earth and X = Si, Ge), have become of renewed interest recently because of the large magnetoresistance (MR) effect [1—3] which quite resembles that of the artificially layered magnetic thin film. [2,4] The crystal structure of the compounds is of body-centered tetragonal $ThCr_2Si_2$ type. The structure is formed by the stacking of atomic layers perpendicular to the c axis with the sequence -Mn_2-X-R-X-. In this system, much attention has been paid to $SmMn_2Ge_2$ because it has been shown to undergo several magnetic phase transitions at high and low temperatures [1—3,5,6] and exhibits interesting magnetotransport behavior. [1—3] For the Si containing system, little work has been done on $SmMn_2Si_2$ (Ref. 6) or Si-substituted $SmMn_2(Ge_{1-x}Si_x)_2$. [7] The study by Szytula and Szott [6] indi-

① Journal of Applied Physics, 1997, 4(1): 5534-5536.

cated that $SmMn_2Si_2$ is an antiferromagnet with $T_N=398$ K. However, the low-temperature magnetic properties were not reported. The Si-substituted $SmMn_2(Ge_{1-x}Si_x)_2$ was studied over the composition range $x=0-0.15$ only. [7] Thus the low-temperature magnetic and magnetotransport behaviors of $SmMn_2Si_2$ have not been well studied. In this study, $SmMn_2Si_2$ has been prepared and its low-temperature magnetic phase transitions and magnetoresistive effects have been investigated.

Ⅱ Experimental Details

$SmMn_2Si_2$ samples were prepared by arc melting of stoichiometric mixture of starting materials (purity > 99.9%) in an Ar atmosphere. The melting procedure was first to form Mn-Si alloy and then to form the final products by adding Sm metal. The samples were subsequently sealed into evacuated quartz tubes and annealed at 800 ℃ for a week. The resulting samples were of textured structure in which the *c* axis is easy to identify based on the layered structure. X-ray diffraction analysis indicated that the samples were single phase with body-centered tetragonal $ThCr_2Si_2$ structure of lattice parameters $a=0.3990$ and $c=1.0509$ nm. Composition analysis by x-ray photoemission spectroscopy (XPS) also verified that the stoichiometry of the samples was in 1 : 2 : 2.

Magnetization measurements as a function of temperature between 4 and 300 K, and as a function of applied field up to 5 T, were carried out by means of a SQUID magnetometer (Quantum Design). Measurements of the resistance without or with an applied field up to 5 T were taken by the standard four-lead method.

Ⅲ Results and Discussion

The magnetic properties of RMn_2X_2 are sensitive to Mn-Mn intralayer distance with a critical value 0.2865 nm. The compounds with the distance less than 0.2865 nm are antiferromagnetic while those are ferromagnetic for the distance larger than the critical value. [7] The Mn-Mn intralayer distance in $SmMn_2Ge_2$ is 0.2873 nm, larger than the critical value. It is ferromagnetic with a Curie temperature of 340 K. [6] As it is cooled below 340 K, the ferromagnetic phase persists down to 150 K, then it orders antiferromagnetically, which is retained down to 100 K. As the sample is further cooled to below 100 K, a ferromagnetic phase reenters. [1] For $SmMn_2Si_2$, its Mn-Mn intralayer distance is 0.2821 nm, less than the critical value of 0.2865 nm. This compound is antiferromagnetic with a Néel temperature of 398 K. [6] However, the low-temperature magnetic properties of this compound have not been well studied. Figure 1 gives the first detailed view of the magnetic properties of $SmMn_2Si_2$ at low temperatures.

The temperature dependence of the magnetic susceptibility of the sample

$SmMn_2Si_2$ in an applied field of 100 G is shown in Fig. 1. The sample was cooled down from room temperature in an applied field before magnetization measurement. As seen from Fig. 1, the compound undergoes several magnetic phase transitions at low temperatures. These transitions occur at about 35, 120, and 230 K, which correspond to a ferromagnetic phase transition at ~35 K, and two antiferromagnetic phase transitions at ~120 and ~230 K, respectively.

It is known that at the transition point of antiferromagnetic state and the ferromagnetic state (see Fig. 1), a corresponding anomaly in the resistance is observed. [1—3] The temperature dependence of the resistance of $SmMn_2Si_2$, measured when cooling from room temperature to 4 K, is shown in the inset of Fig. 1, which shows corresponding transitions at those transition temperatures indicated by arrows, ~35, ~100, and ~230 K. In addition to the transitions at about 35, 100 (120 K), and 230 K, an anomaly of the resistance at about 165 K was observed with a drop of the resistance. It is unclear what caused this anomaly at 165 K. From the magnetic susceptibility data shown, it does not appear that the anomaly is of magnetic origin.

Figure 2 shows the magnetic field dependence of magnetization at temperatures 4.2, 220, and 300 K. At 4.2 K, the magnetization increases sharply up to about 0.5 T, and then increases linearly up to the maximum applied field of 5.0 T without saturation. For the magnetization at 220 K, a linear relationship between the magnetization and the applied field is found. The magnetization at 300 K also changes linearly with applied field, both consistent with antiferromagnetic states.

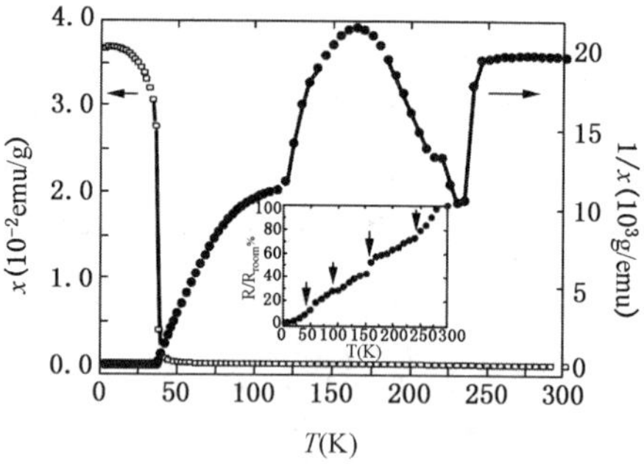

Fig. 1 Temperature dependence of the magnetic susceptibility and reciprocal susceptibility for $SmMn_2Si_2$. The inset shows the temperaturedependent resistance at zero field. The arrows mark the temperature where anomalies in the resistance were observed

The magnetoresistance measurements were performed at 220 and 4 K as a function of applied field up to 5 T. Because the samples are of textured structure, two configurations $H \parallel c$ and $H \perp c$ were employed when the applied current was perpendicular to the c axis. Figure 3 shows the field dependence of the resistance at 220 K, plotted as $(R-R_0)/R_0\%$ versus applied field H. At this temperature, the sample is in the antiferromagnetic state. A negative magnetoresistance was observed for $H \parallel c$ with a value of -3% and for $H \perp c$ with a value of -4.2% in the field up to 5 T applied for the first time. Thereafter, the MR value changes within a small range between -4.2% and -5.4% with field cycling between -5 and 5 T and does not come back to 0 at $H=0$ (not shown here). The inset of Fig. 3 shows the field dependence of the resistance at 220 K, measured with a configuration of $H \perp c$ when applied current was parallel to the c axis. A positive magnetoresistance of about 6% at 5 T was observed. Resembling the negative MR behavior, the positive MR value shifts between 4% and 6% with further field cycling and does not go back to 0 at $H=0$. This behavior that the MR changes monotonically initially with the applied field and does not go back to zero at $H_0=0$ upon further cycling was also observed in other layered systems, for example, AgSn/Co multilayer film. [8] While such behavior in the multilayer systems, for example in AgSn/Co, is understood in that Co has a remanent moment, the cause for such behavior in $SmMn_2Si_2$ cannot be explained. As shown in Fig. 2(b), no observable remanence can be seen in its magnetization. Further investigation is needed in order to understand the mechanism for such hysteretic behavior in the magnetoresistance of $SmMn_2Si_2$.

In the antiferromagnetic state, the resistance is higher than in the ferromagnetic state and a negative magnetoresistance effect has been observed in the polycrystalline $SmMn_2Ge_2$ related compounds, [1,3] which can be understood on the basis of a spin-valve mechanism. [4] However, in Fig. 3, both positive and negative magnetoresistance effects are observed when the current is applied along different directions (perpendicular or parallel to the c axis of the textured sample). Therefore the above mechanism can not explain the observed results here. Similar results have been found by van Dover *et al.* who revealed that the antiferromagnetic state has a lower resistance than the ferromagnetic state when the current is along the a direction of a single crystal $SmMn_2Ge_2$ (Ref. 2) and it has a higher resistance when the current is along the c direction. [9] A mechanism related to bandstructure effects has been used to explain the observed results. [2,3]

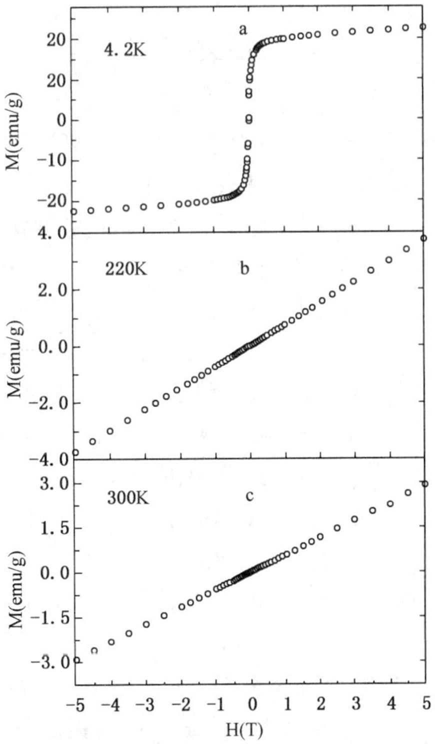

Fig. 2 Magnetization of $SmMn_2Si_2$ as a function of applied field at 4.2 K (a), 220 K (b), and 300 K (c)

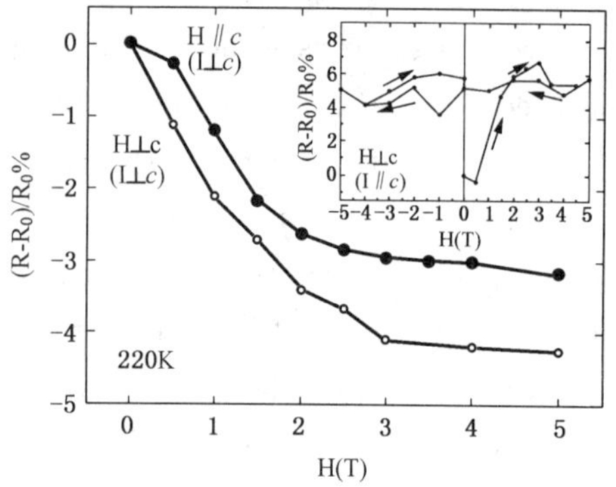

Fig. 3　Field dependence of the resistance of textured $SmMn_2Si_2$ at 220 K. Applied current was perpendicular to the *c* axis. The inset shows the field-dependent resistance where applied current was parallel to the *c* axis

The sample enters the ferromagnetic state when cooled below 35 K. Figure 4 shows the resistance-field dependence of the sample at 4 K. With $H \parallel c$, an increase in MR of about 22% is observed at 5 T [Fig. 4(a)]. For $H \perp c$ [Fig. 4(b)], an increase in MR of 11% at applied field up to 5 T is found. Thereafter, the MR cycles reproducibly with field, with a subsequent minimum 2.3% at $H=0$. The inset of Fig. 4(a) is the field dependence of the resistance at 4 K, measured with the same configuration as that of the inset of Fig. 3. A positive MR with an increase of 18% at 5 T is found. The MR cycles reproducibly with field and does not saturate with applied field up to 5 T. The MR observed in the ferromagnetic state is believed to be the anisotropic magnetoresistance.[10]

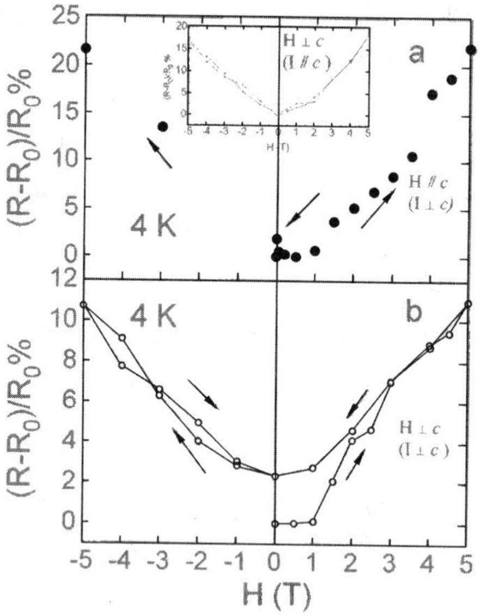

Fig. 4　Resistance as a function of applied field for textured $SmMn_2Si_2$ at 4 K. Applied current was perpendicular to the *c* axis. The inset shows the field-dependent resistance where applied current was parallel to the *c* axis

Ⅳ　Conclusions

Magnetization measurements between 4 and 300 K for the compound $SmMn_2Si_2$ indicated a ferromagnetic transition at 35 K, two antiferromagnetic transitions at 120 and 230 K, consistent with the resistance-temperature dependence. MR measurements in the antiferromagnetic state of 220 K revealed different magnetoresistive behaviors for different directions of the applied current with respect to the *c* axis of the textured samples. For $I \perp c$, a negative MR effect was observed with a decrease of about $-3\% \sim -4\%$ in the resistance at an applied field of 5 T. For $I \parallel c$, a positive MR effect was found with an increase of about 4% - 6% in the resistance. These MR effects can not be explained in terms of a spin-valve mechanism. [4] The observed MR is likely to be related to band-structure effects, [2] probably related to magneto-volume effects as proposed recently. [3] Further research using a single crystal of $SmMn_2Si_2$ is needed in order to obtain data for comparison with those of a $SmMn_2Ge_2$ single crystal. For MR in the ferromagnetic state of 4 K, a positive MR effect was always observed, with a maximum increase of 22% at 5 T. This MR behavior is similar to that of the anisotropic magnetoresistance found in ordinary ferromagnets.

Acknowledgments

Acknowledgment is made to the National Natural Science Foundation of China, K. C. Wang Education Foundation of Hong Kong, U. S. DOE, NSF, Louisiana Education Quality Support Fund, and Research Corporation.

References

[1] J. H. V. J. Brabers, K. Bakker, H. Nakotte, F. R. de Boer, S. K. J. Lenc-zowski, and K. H. J. Buschow, J. Alloys Compd. 199, L1 (1993).

[2] R. B. van Dover, E. M. Gyorgy, R. J. Cava, J. J. Krajewski, R. J. Felder, and W. F. Peck, Phys. Rev. B 47, 6134 (1993).

[3] J. H. V. J. Brabers, A. J. Nolten, F. Kayzel, S. K. J. Lenczowski, K. H. J. Buschow, and F. R. de Boer, Phys. Rev. B 50, 16410 (1994).

[4] M. N. Baibich, J. M. Broto, A. Fert, F. Nguyen van Dau, F. Petroff, P. Etienne, G. Creuzet, A. Friederich, and J. Chazeles, Phys. Rev. Lett. 61, 2472 (1988).

[5] H. Fujii, T. Okamoto, T. Shigeoka, and N. Iwata, Solid State Commun. 53, 715 (1985).

[6] A. Szytula and I. Szott, Solid State Commun. 40, 199 (1981).

[7] S. Saha and N. Ali, J. Appl. Phys. 79, 5233 (1996).

[8] W. P. Pratt, Jr., S.-F. Lee, Q. Yang, P. Holody, R. Loloee, P. A. Schroeder, and J. Bass, J. Appl. Phys. 73, 5326 (1993).

[9] R. B. van Dover, E. M. Gyorgy, and R. J. Cava, J. Appl. Phys. 73, 5332 (1993).

[10] C. L. Chien, J. Q. Xiao, and J. S. Jiang, J. Appl. Phys. 73, 5309 (1993).

稀土元素在 6063 合金中的分布及其作用机理①

赵敏寿 党 平 吕翔平
（中国科学院长春应用化学研究所）

摘 要：用金相观察、扫描电镜的波谱和能谱分析结果表明，稀土在 6063 铝合金铸态组织中富集于晶界，稀土促进了 Si 和 Fe 向晶界偏聚，减少了针状铁相，铸态组织均匀、细化，强度提高。过量稀土会形成 Al-La 类稀土夹杂物，分布在晶界和晶内，使铸态组织粗化，合金强度下降。含稀土的铝合金型材中铁相有所细化，稀土化合物呈球团状，强度及硬度有所提高。

Studies on Distribution and Function of Rare Earth Metal in 6063 Aluminium Alloy

Zhao Minshou Dang Ping Lu Xiangping
(Changchun Institute of Applied Chemistry, Academia Sinica)

Abstract: Metallogaph and scanning electron microscope studies of the distribution and function of a small quantity of rare earth metal in 6063 aluminium alloy show that rare earth metal is concentrated at the grain boundary of the as-cast 6063 aluminium alloy, and also promotes Si and Fe to be concentrated at the grain boundary . The needle phase containing Fe are redueed, and the as-cast microstructure is homogeneous and modified, thus the as-cast strength is increased obviously. But excess rare earth in the as-cast alloy will lead to the formation of some rare earth compounds like Al-La distributed in the cells and at the grain boundary, which makes the as-cast microstructure coarsen and the stre-ngth of the alloy fall. In the deformed 6063 aluminium alloy containing Fe are modified to a certain extent, and there are some spherical compounds containing rare earth metal, whieh leads to enhancing the strength and hardness of the deformed 6063 Aluminium alloy.

6063 合金（AL-Mg-Si 系）是一种应用非常广泛的型材合金。而稀土元素在 6063 合金中的应用也取得良好效果，如合金机械性能、耐腐蚀性能、表观质量及着色效果等均得到明显提高。但由子合金中稀土含量较少，检验其分布及存在状态十分困难，所以有关稀土在 6063 合金中的分布及作用机理方面的研究工作报道很少。文献[1，2]研究了 Ce 在工业纯铝中的作用机理。本文在扫描电镜上用波谱和能谱分析测定了稀土在 6063 合金中的分布及其对 Fe、Si 和 Mg 分布的影响，初步对稀土元素在合金中的作用机理进行了探讨，以期对稀土 6063 合金的应用提供理论依据。

① 中国稀土学报，1989，7(3)：59-64.

1　实验方法

用熔盐电解法添加铈族混合稀土，制备稀土6063合金。铸态试样为ϕ20×100 mm的圆棒，成分见表1。在圆棒底部截取金相试样，磨抛后用0.5%HF水溶液浸蚀，为了清晰地显示其晶界，一般需擦蚀1 min左右。型材试样为热挤压时效状态（RCS），挤压温度为470±10℃，挤压速度为10 m/S，挤压后17 h内进行人工时效处理。使用卧式金相显微镜观察和拍摄金相组织，在JXA-840型扫描电镜上进行波谱和能谱分析。

表1　实验合金的成分

Table 1　Composition of the alloy(wt%)

试样号	Mg	Si	Fe	RE	Cu	Mn	Cr	Al
2	0.61	0.45	0.28	0	0.008	0.0064	0.0056	余量
3	0.69	0.45	0.19	0.12	0.007	0.0040	0.0060	余量
4	0.60	0.45	0.20	0.22	0.006	0.0048	0.0064	余量
5	0.64	0.55	0.19	0.25	0.007	0.0052	0.0056	余量
6	0.60	0.46	0.16	0.29	0.007	0.0028	0.0064	余量
7	0.64	0.55	0.14	0.36	0.006	0.0044	0.0060	余量
9	0.60	0.43	0.12	0.34	0.005	0.0028	0.0064	余量

2　实验结果及分析

2.1　稀土在铸态组织中的分布及其对组织性能的影响

图1显示未加入稀土的2#样中合金元素Mg、Si和杂质元素Fe的分布结果。Mg和Si基本上均匀分布在铝基体上，Si在晶界处稍有富集，而杂质Fe在晶界明显富集。铁一般以针状化合物形式沿晶界析出（图1d），这对合金的强度和塑性十分有害。

图2是稀土含量为0.29wt%的6#样中Mg、Si、Fe和Ce的波谱分析结果。Mg基本上仍均匀分布，少量的富集点可能是Mg_2Si析出的结果。与图1 c相比，Si较多地富集于晶界，说明稀土促进了Si向晶界偏聚。Fe和RE在晶界富集。从Fe的面分布看，针状铁相减少，球团状铁相增加。对照Fe、Si和Ce的面分布，发现Fe、Si和Ce在晶界处的偏聚情况是一致的，晶界上可能存在由这些元素组成的某些金属间化合物，因而促使Si向晶界偏聚，而含稀土的铁相化合物呈球团状，减少了针状铁相的危害。

对不同稀土含量的多个试样的检测结果表明，稀土元素一般都与Si和Fe一起偏聚于晶界，但过量的稀土除与Si和Fe等偏聚在晶界外，还可能与铝形成金属间化合物。

对含0.36wt%RE的7#样品观察发现，在合金基体中（晶界、晶内）分布有大量的稀土相（见图3）。

图4是不同稀土含量的6063铝合金铸态组织。由图可见，稀土含量为0.25wt%时，晶粒均匀、细化（图4b）。稀土含量为0.34wt%时，晶粒反而粗大（图

4c)，这说明稀土含量对铸态组织影响较大。

表 2 是稀土含量对铸态机械性能的影响。可以看出，适量稀土元素可以提高合金的抗拉强度和屈服强度，但稀土含量过高(大于 0.30wt%)，强度值又开始下降。对照图 4 的铸态组织发现，晶粒均匀、细化者(图 4b)强度就高，二者吻合得非常好。又从表 2 的延伸率值可以看出，合金的塑性虽略有降低，但仍保持在较高的水平。可见，稀土元素在提高合金强度的同时，并不明显降低合金塑性。

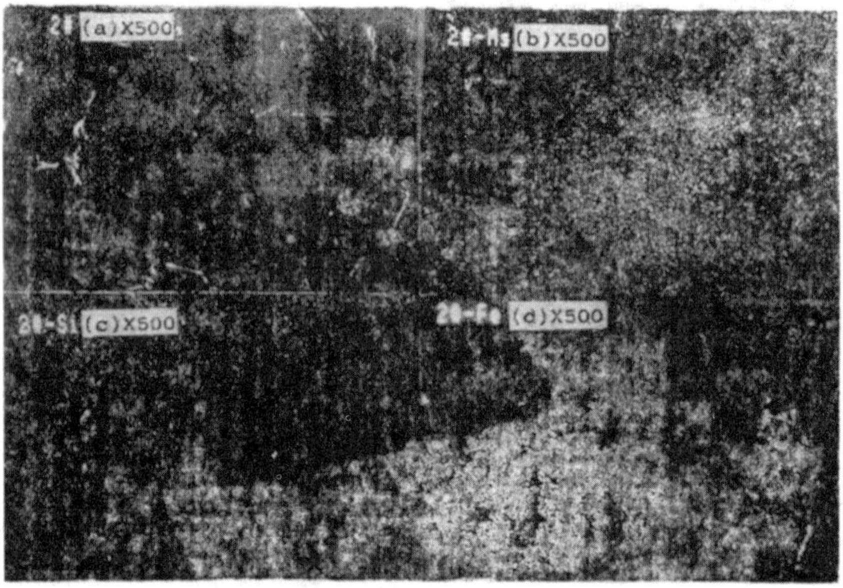

图 1　未加稀土的 2 号样中 Mg、Si 、Fe 元素的分布

Fig. 1　Distribution of Mg, Si and Fe in speeimen 2 without RE, 500X

(a) Secondary electronimage　(b) Mg K_α image

(c) Si K_α image　(d) Fe K_α image

从上述实验结果看，在铸态组织中稀土主要分布在晶界上，而在晶内的溶解量很小，这是因为稀土原子半径比铝的大，若进入铝晶格内，势必引起较大的晶格畸变，使系统的能量增加，为保持系统的自由能最低，稀土原子只能向原子排列不规则的晶界上富集。在 a-Al 结晶时，由于溶质再分配，进入固相中的稀土量很小，而大量聚集在固-液界面前沿，使合金在凝固过程中的成分过冷增大，a-Al 相以树枝方式凝固生长倾向明显增加，同时在分枝交接处产生缩颈、熔断，增加了 a-Al 相结晶的活的晶种，促进了 a-Al 相的动力学成核，从而细化了晶粒[3]。在一定范围内，稀土加入量越高，成分过冷倾向越大，a-Al 相枝晶越发达，枝晶间距越小，组织越细化，合金完全凝固后，稀土元素大部分被排挤在晶界或枝晶界。

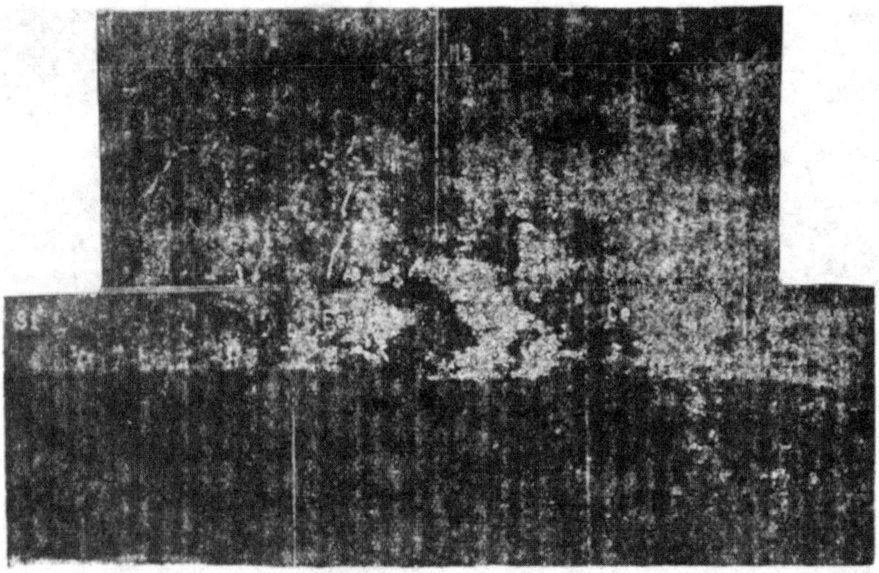

图 2　含 0.29wt%RE 的 6 号样中 Mg、Si、Fe、Ce 的分布

Fig. 2　Distribution of Mg, Si, Fe and Ce in speeimen 6 containing 0.29wt%RE, 500X

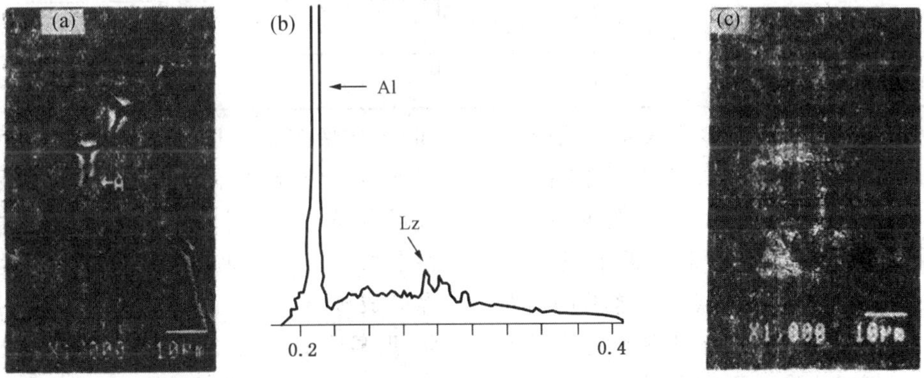

图 3　含 0.36wt%RE 的 7 号样中的稀土相

Fig. 3　RE compounds in speeimen 7 containing 0.36wt%RE

(a) Seeondary electron image　(b) Composition of compound "A"

(c) Distribution of La

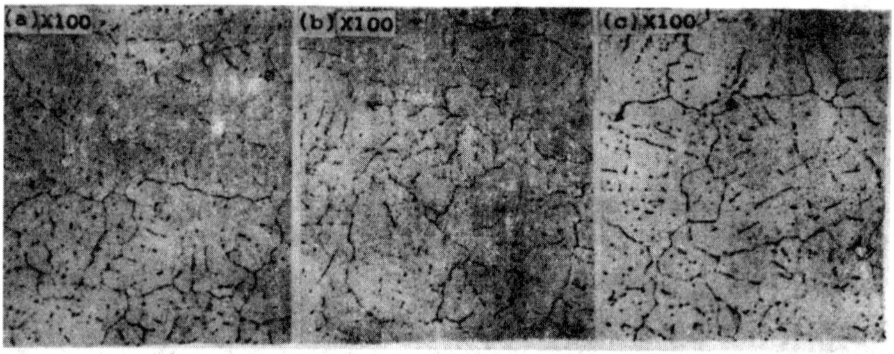

图 4　稀土对 6063 铝合金铸态组织的影响

Fig. 4　Effect of RE of on as-cast microstructure of 6063 aluminium alloy

(a) O wt% RE (specimen 2)　(b) 0.25 wt% RE(specimen 5)

(c) 0.34 wt% RE(specimen 9)

表 2　稀土含量对铸态机械性能的影响

Table 2　Effect of RE content on the mechanical properties of as-cast 6063 aluminium alloy

稀土含量,wt%	0	0.12	0.22	0.25	0.29	0.36	0.34
抗拉强度,N/mm^2	236	245	242	257	248	243	240
屈服强度,N/mm^2	202	213	205	221	218	214	210
延伸率,%	14.1	14.8	12.2	13.1	14.4	14.2	12.9

过量的稀土由于形成大量稀土化合物,减少了稀土原子的成分过冷作用,合金组织逐渐粗化。文献[1,2]也曾报道,在稀土含量较高的工业纯铝中发现有 $CeAl_4$ 和 $Al_{2.12}$-$La_{0.88}$ 化合物,这不仅消耗一定量的稀土,对合金组织和性能也十分不利,所以稀土含量不宜高于 0.3wt%。

稀土元素提高合金强度的原因很多,从本文结果看,稀土有细化晶粒的作用,根据 Hall-Petch 关系 $\sigma=\sigma_0+Kd^{-1/2}$,强度($\sigma$) 与晶粒尺寸($d$)有对应关系,所以稀土对金相组织和强度的影响是一致的,晶粒越细,强度越高。另外,稀土的加入改善了 Si 和 Fe 的分布及存在状态,Si、Fe 和 Ce 偏聚在晶界上,强化了晶界,并使针状铁相减少,球状化合物增加,这也是合金强度提高的一个原因。文献[2]报道,在未加稀土的工业纯铝中,Fe 与 Al 在晶界形成 α-Al + Al_3Fe 共晶。Al_3Fe 呈针状,明显降低晶界强度,而添加稀土之后,Si、Fe 和 Ce 一起偏聚,形成球状物,减少了针状的 Al_3Fe,从而改善了铝的性能。本文的结果也说明了这一点。

2.2　稀土在型材合金中的分布及作用

该合金型材试样为不含稀土和含 0.12wt%稀土的两种,状态均为 RCS。其机械性能如下:

试样号	稀土含量,wt%	抗拉强度,N /mm²	硬度,HV	延伸率%
A-30	0	200	65.9	10.4
B-30	0.12	242	70.8	9.8

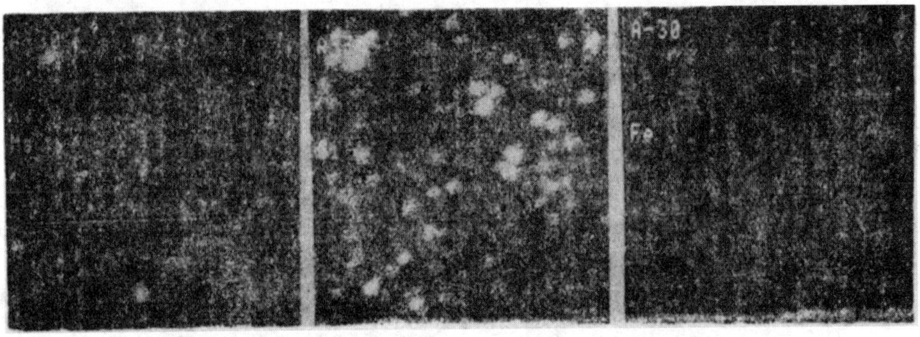

图 5　型材合金中 Mg、Si、Fe 的分布(不含 RE)

Fig. 5　Distribution of Mg,Si and Fe in the deformed 6063 aluminium alloy without RE

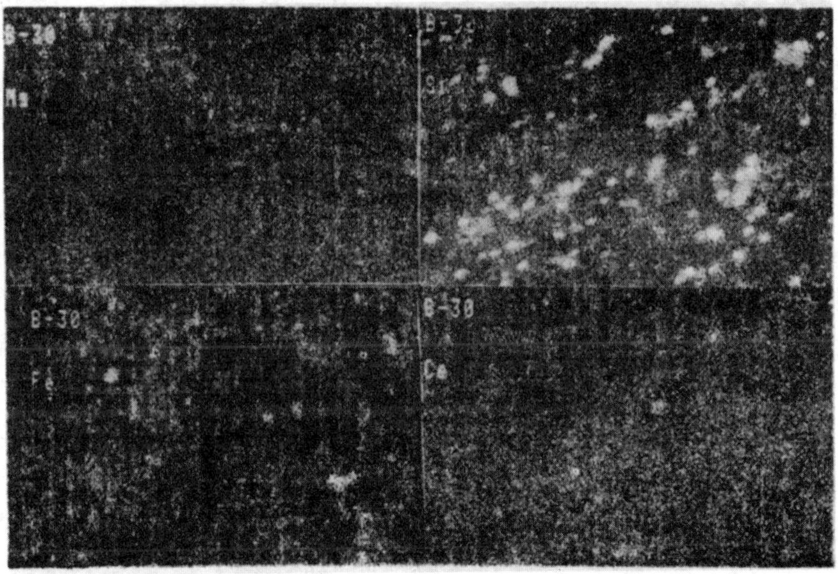

图 6　含 0.12wt%RE 的型材合金中 Mg、Si、Fe、Ce 的分布

Fig. 6　Distribution of Mg,Si,Fe and Ce in the deformed 6063 alloy with 0.12 wt%RE

图 5 和图 6 分别为两种试样中各元素分布的波谱测定结果。

对照两种试样相应元素的面分布,可以看出,A-30 样中 Mg 分布有明显的较为粗大的富集区,Si 的富集点也较为粗大,Fe 的富集点较。B-30 样中 Mg 分布比较均匀,无明显的富集点,Si 的富集点有所减少,并沿挤压主变形方向排列,Fe 的富集点为球团状并稍有减少，Ce 有少量富集点。对照 Si 和 Fe 的面分布，发现在 Ce 富集的区域也有 Si 和 Fe 的富集，很可能是存在有球团状的含 Si、Fe 和 Ce 的多元化合物。Fe 相是合金中的杂质相。铸态分析表明，稀土有减少针状铁相的作用。不含稀土的 A-30 样中，铁相在挤压前多为针状，而含稀土的 B-30 样中铁相在挤压前多为球团状。热挤压时，铁相均被破碎为颗粒状，但 B-30 样中的铁相挤压后较为圆整细小。B-30 样中的稀土相也为细球状，这些细质点弥散分布在合金基体上，增加合金变形阻力，促进位错增殖，使合金强度和硬度有所提高。由于稀土相很小，均匀分布，对合金塑性影响不大，仍保持在较高的水平上。

3　结论

（1）稀土在 6063 铝合金铸态组织中主要分布在晶界上，稀土促进了 Si 向晶界偏聚，减少了针状铁相。但过量稀土会形成 Al-La 类稀土化合物。

（2）适量稀土对 6063 铝合金铸态组织有均匀、细化作用，强度也有所提高。但过量稀土使铸态组织粗化，强度下降。稀土含量不宜高于 0.30wt%。

（3）在 6063 型材合金中，稀土促进硅相和铁相细化，稀土相呈球状，合金强度及硬度有所提高。

对吉林工大金彩凤和吴秀珍老师，本所张伯兰和葛辽海同志和沈阳黎明铝材厂同志的热情帮助，在此谨致谢意。

参考文献

[1] 霍成章等，金属学报，1985，21(5)，B272.

[2] 韩其勇等，中国稀土学报，1986，4(2)，84.

[3] 李庆春主编，《铸件形成理论》，北京，机械工业出版社，1982，P. 154.

[4] Livak R. J. ，Metal. Trans. 1982，13A，1318.

Electrochemical Formation of Ni-Y Intermetallic Compound Layer in Molten Chloride

G. XIE, K. EMA, Y. ITO
(Department of Nuclear Engineering, Faculty of Engineering, kyoto University, Sakyo-Ku, Kyoto GOG, Japan)
Zhao Min shou
(Changchun Institute of Applied Chemistry, Academia Sinica, Changchun 130022, China)

Abstract: The reduction of Y(Ⅲ) ions in molten chloride is known to be a one-step three electron reaction [1,2,3], but a voltammogram of YCl_3 in molten LiCl-KCl-NaCl at a nickel electrode shows at least two reduction peaks of Y(Ⅲ) ions, indicating the possibility of formation of Ni-Y intermetallic compounds. Using a galvanostatic electrolysis method, samples were prepared at several current densities at 450, 500, 600 and 700 ℃, respectively, and were identified with X-ray diffraction (XRD) and electron probe microanalysis (EPMA) methods. The results show that Ni_2Y, Ni_2Y_3 and NiY can be produced by electrolysis and Ni_2Y is found to be the predominant Ni-Y intermetallic compound under the experimental conditions. Nickel appears to diffuse in Ni_2Y faster than yttrium, and the diffusion process is the rate determining step during Ni_2Y formation.

1 Introduction

Rare earth metals are well known as effective catalysts, and they are also excellent alloying elements. For example, Cr-Ni-Y, Fe-Cr-A1-Y and nickel-basesuperalloy have been developed as anticorrosive, heat resistant, long service life alloy materials. Considering the good mechanical properties of intermetallic compounds and effective catalytic characteristic of rare earth metals, as well as the existence of many kinds of intermetallic compounds of nickel and yttrium [4], it is not difficult to imagine the possibility of Ni-Y intermetallic compounds as surface functional materials. In this study, an attempt is made to produce Ni-Y intermetallic compound films on nickel surfaces by an electrochemical process in molten chloride.

2 Experimental details

For the experiments carried out at 450—600 ℃, 55LiCl-36KCl-9NaCl (mol %) eutectic mixture was used as a sol-

① Journal of Applied Electrochemistry, 1993(23):753-759.

vent electrolyte. 50KCl-50NaCl mixture was used for experiments at 700 ℃. LiCl, KCl and NaCl were all of reagent grade (Wako Chemical Co., Ltd). The anhydrous YCl_3 was obtained by slowly heating a mixture of $YCl_3 \cdot 6H_2O$ and NH_4Cl under vacuum. A molybdenum wire 1 mm in diameter and a nickel disc of 7 mm in diameter were used as the working electrodes. To measure the electrode potential, a stabilized zirconia-air electrode was used as a quasi-reference electrode for convenience [5], and the measured values are presented in the figures relative to the M^+/M electrode potential. Here, M represents an alkali metal (Li and Na), and the potential of M^+/M remains constant, (-3.627 ± 0.006) V (Cl_2/Cl^-), at 450 ℃, which is the decomposition potential of the solvent [3], though the exact composition of M is not defined. A glassy carbon rod of 5 mm in diameter was used as the counter electrode. The salt mixture was contained in a high purity alumina crucible (99.5% Al_2O_3, Nippon Kagaku Togyo Co., Ltd SSA-S) and was melted under dry argon atmosphere. After anhydrous YCl_3 was added to the eutectic, dry HCl gas was passed through the eutectic for 2 h. Finally, the cell was kept under a slight positive pressure of dry argon gas to keep out atmospheric moisture.

3 Results and discussion

3.1 Voltammetry

A typical cyclic voltammogram of Y(Ⅲ) ion at a nickel electrode obtained at 450 ℃ in the solvent electrolyte with addition of 1.2 mol % YCl_3 is shown in Fig. 1. There are at least two clear reduction peaks at about 300 mV and 400 mV, respectively. Near 0 mV, cathodic breakdown of the electrolyte occurs. However, previous work [3] revealed that the electrochemical reduction of Y(Ⅲ) in molten 55LiCl-36KCl-9NaCl (mol %) system is a one-step three electron reaction. According to the Ni-Y phase diagram [4], several intermetallic compounds can be formed between nickel and yttrium. The two reduction peaks may be associated with the formation of yttrium and a Ni-Y intermetallic compound, respectively. For comparison, the cyclic voltammogram of the Y(Ⅲ) ion at a molybdenum electrode, obtained under the same conditions, is also plotted as dashed line in Fig. 1.

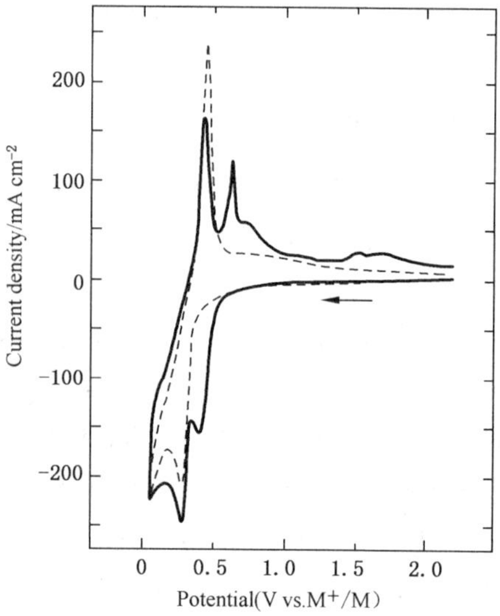

Fig. 1 Voltammograms of Ni (——) and Mo (----) electrodes. (1.2 tool % YCl_3; scanning rate: 100 mV s^{-1}, 450 ℃)

Because no alloys or intermetallic compounds can be formed between molybdenum and yttrium, only the reduction peak of Y(Ⅲ) appears. Considering the result for the molybdenum electrode, it seems that the reduction peak at 300 mV, which is just the deposition potential of yttrium at the molybdenum electrode, corresponds to the electrodeposition of yttrium metal, and the other peak corresponds to the direct formation of an Ni-Y intermetallic compound. On the reversal sweep, in addition to the two sharp oxidation peaks, which correspond to the two reduction peaks, there are two other oxidation peaks (shoulders) at about 0.7 V and 1.5 V, though there are no corresponding reduction peaks. These indicate the possibility of formation of more than one kind of Ni-Y intermetallic compounds. The cyclic voltammograms of Y(Ⅲ) ion at the nickel electrode at 500, 600 and 700 ℃ are all very similar to that obtained at 450 ℃.

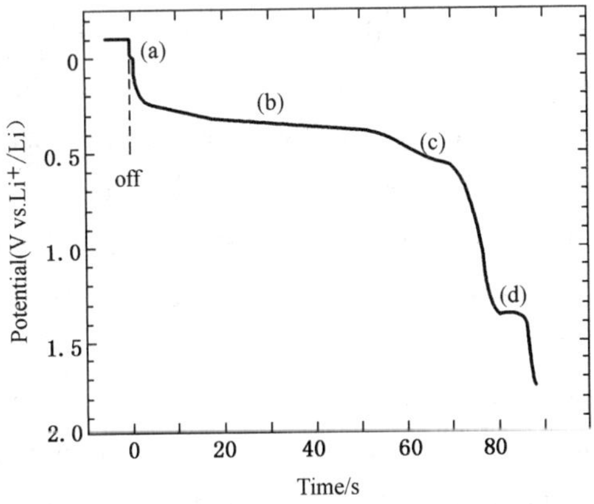

Fig. 2 Open-circuit potential decay curve of Ni electrode after electrolysis at 800 mAcm^{-2} for 30 s. (1.2 mol % YCl_3, 450 ℃)

3.2 Open-circuit potentiometry

Open-circuit potentiometry was also carried out to confirm the results for the cyclic voltammetry. After galvanostatic electrolysis for 30 s at an electrolysis current density of 800 mA cm^{-2}, the current was interrupted, and the open-circuit potential decay curve of the nickel electrode was measured. The result is shown in Fig. 2. Plateau (a) represents the cathodic breakdown of the electrolyte, and the two plateaus, (b) and (c), correspond to the two sharp oxidation peaks in Fig. 1. Plateau (d), which corresponds to the peak at about 1.5 V, is still not understood. No plateau corresponding to the oxidation peak at about 0.7 V in Fig. 1 appears.

3.3. Potentiostatic electrolysis

In order to confirm the inference concerning the two reduction peaks in Fig. 1, potentiostatic electrolysis was conducted near the two peak potentials, i. e. 400 and 310 mV, respectively, at 450 ℃, with 700 C charge. It should be noted that the charging times are different in these two experiments, since the current densities are different. After electrolysis, the samples were taken out from the bath, and the surfaces of the samples were investigated. A black mud-like deposit was found on the surfaces. The amount of this deposit on the sample prepared at 310 mV was much more than that on the sample prepared at 400 mV. The samples were washed with distilled water and then cleaned in alcohol using an ultrasonic cleaner. Weight increases of these two samples were also measured, as 12 and 0 mg, respectively. The XRD patterns of the two samples are shown in Figs 3 and 4. From the results, it can be seen that the surface of the sample prepared at 400 mV is composed of Ni_2Y and Ni_2Y_3. The cross-section of the sample prepared at 400 mV was analysed quantitatively by EPMA with atomic number (Z)-adsorption-fluorescence (ZAF) correction. The result shows that the bulk product is Ni_2Y. In contrast, nothing was left on the surface of the sample prepared at 310 mV. Judging from the above results, the black mud-like deposit is likely to be yttrium metal. Because of the reactive properties of yttrium metal, the deposited yttrium metal on the samples will react with water and oxygen in the air, when taken out from the bath, and washed out by distilled water after electrolysis. That is why nothing is detected on the surface of the sample prepared at 310 mV. Of course, deposited yttrium can form Ni-Y intermetallic compounds by thermal diffusion, but the total period of the experiment in this case was too short for its formation.

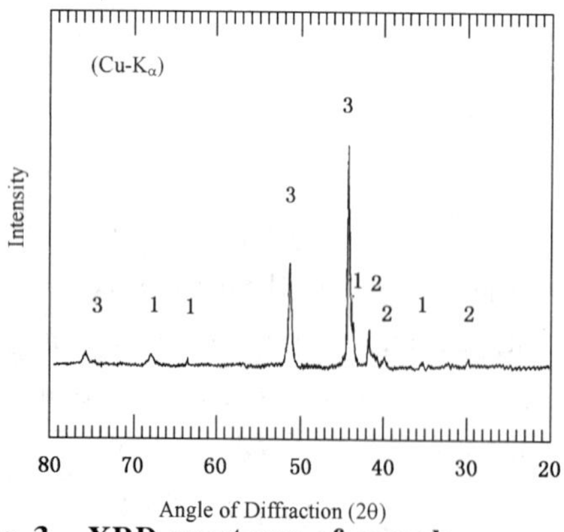

Fig. 3　XRD spectrum of sample prepared at 400 mV for 40 h. (1.2 tool % YCl_3, 700 C charge, 450 ℃). (1) Ni_2Y, (2) Ni_2Y_3 and (3) Holder (Monel)

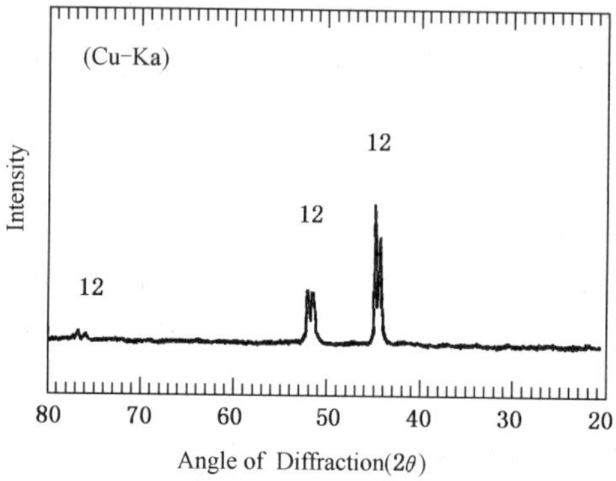

Fig. 4　XRD spectrum of sample prepared at 310 mV for 2.5 h. (1.2 mol% YCl_3, 700 C charge, 450 ℃). (1) Ni and (2) Holder (Monel)

3.4　Thermal diffusion effect

To discuss the effect of thermal diffusion, a sample was prepared by potentiostatic electrolysis at 310 mV. In this experiment, however, after passing 1420 C charge, instead of being taken out of the bath immediately, the sample was kept in the bath until the total period was as long as the experiment period for preparation of the sample prepared at 400 mV, and then washed and cleaned in the same way as above. The surface and the cross-section of the sample were then investigated by XRD and EPMA, respectively. The XRD pattern of the sample is shown in Fig. 5: the result reveals that the surface product is NiY. EPMA measurement indicates that the bulk product is Ni_2Y. But the weight increase of the electrode was only 4 mg, which was much smaller than that of the electrode prepared at 400 mV, i. e. 12 mg, though the quantity of charge passed at the former was twice that of the latter. The different weight increases result from the different formation mechanisms.

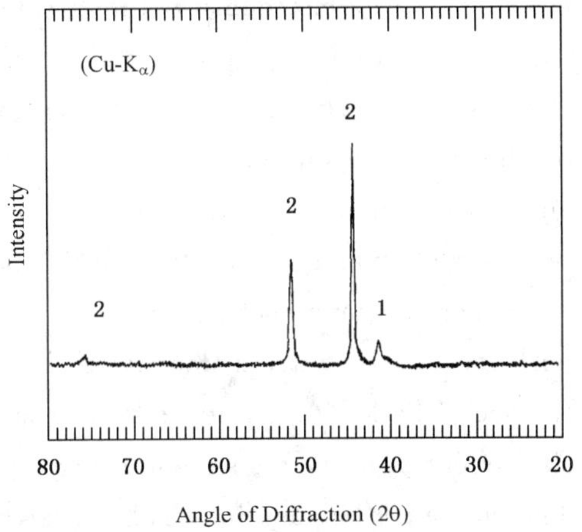

Fig. 5 XRD spectrum of sample prepared at 310 mV and kept in the bath until total experimental period being 40 h. (1.2 mol% YCl_3, 1420 C charge, 450 ℃)
(1) NiY and (2) Holder (Monel)

3.5 The influence of electrolysis current density and bath temperature

In order to investigate the effects of electrolysis current densities and bath temperatures, samples were prepared by galvanostatic electrolysis at various current densities at 450, 500, 600 and 700 ℃. The samples were washed and cleaned in the same way as above. The surfaces were analyzed with XRD, and the crosssections with ZAF correction EPMA. The results are summarized in Table 1. It can be seen that at 450 ℃, NiY and Ni_2Y_3 are formed at the surface and the fraction of NiY decreases with increase in current density. On the other hand, Ni_2Y was found as bulk product with no dependence on the current density. At 500, 600 and 700 ℃, both surface and bulk products are Ni_2Y, being independent of current density, except in the case of 500 ℃ at 200 mA cm^{-2}. It seems that both bath temperature and current density can affect the product composition to some extent, but only in the surface region. Ni_2Y is found to be the predominant Ni-Y intermetallic compound under the experimental conditions.

SEM images of cross-sections of the sample were also taken. Figures 6-9 show the SEM images of cross-sections of the samples prepared at 600 ℃ at electrolysis current densities of 50, 100, 150 and 200 mA cm^{-2}, respectively. In this current density range, the electrode potential stays between the deposition potential of yttrium and the direct formation potential of Ni-Y intermetallic compound, and moves closely to the deposition potential of yttrium with increase of current density. It can be seen from the photos that in all these cases, adhesive uniform Ni_2Y layers were formed. Line analysis of the cross-sections were implemented to identify the existence of Ni_2Y layers. The concentration profiles of Y and Ni are also shown in Figs 6-9. The results of line analysis also prove that the Ni_2Y layers formed are uniform. An adhesive uniform Ni_2Y layer can also be obtained at 500, 600 and 700 ℃. But the situation at 450 ℃ is different; the deposit layer has a double-layer structure (Fig. 10). The inner layer is only composed of Ni_2Y, but the surface layer seems to be a mixture of

NiY and Ni_2Y_3 and inside this layer there are numerous cracks, which may be caused by the different stresses from the different intermetallic compounds.

Table 1　The effects of electrolytic current density and bath temperature

Current density /mAcm^{2}	Analysis method	Bath temperature			
		450 ℃	500 ℃	600 ℃	700 ℃
50	XRD	NiY, Ni_2Y_3	Ni_2Y	Ni_2Y	Ni_2Y
	EPMA	Ni_2Y	Ni_2Y	Ni_2Y	Ni_2Y
100	XRD	NiY, Ni_2Y_3	Ni_2Y	Ni_2Y	Ni_2Y
	EPMA	Ni_2Y	Ni_2Y	Ni_2Y	Ni_2Y
150	XRD	NiY, Ni_2Y_3	Ni_2Y	Ni_2Y	Ni_2Y
	EPMA	Ni_2Y	Ni_2Y	Ni_2Y	Ni_2Y
200	XRD	Ni_2Y_3	Ni_2Y, Ni_2Y_3	Ni_2Y	Ni_2Y
	EPMA	Ni_2Y	Ni_2Y	Ni_2Y	Ni_2Y

Electrolytic current efficiencies were also investigated. When taken out from the bath after electrolysis, the samples were washed and then weighed. The apparent current efficiency was calculated as the ratio of electrode weight increase during the electrolysis to the theoretical weight increase corresponding to all the charge passed through the electrode. Clearly, the real current efficiency will be much larger, since the deposition of yttrium does not contribute to the apparent current efficiency. If there is no electrochemical side reaction here, that is, all the charge passed through the electrode is used for the direct formation of Ni-Y intermetallic compounds and the deposition of yttrium, the real current efficiency will be 100%. The results of experiments conducted at 500 ℃ are shown in Fig. 11. It can be deduced that interdiffusion of yttrium and nickel atoms is the rate determining step in the formation of Ni_2Y. When the yttrium deposition rate is larger than the diffusion rate, the larger the electrolysis current density, the greater the accumulation of yttrium on the electrode surface. The accumulated yttrium on the electrode surface reacts with water and oxygen in the air and is washed out by distilled water after electrolysis. So the apparent current efficiency decreases with increase in current density. The influence of bath temperature on electrolysis current efficiency is shown in Fig. 12. The current efficiency increases with increase in bath temperature, since interdiffusion of yttrium and nickel is accelerated as the temperature is raised.

3.6　Interdiffusion of yttrium and nickel

In order to investigate the interdiffusion of yttrium and nickel during Ni_2Y formation, the following experiment was designed: a tungsten marker, a halfcircle shaped film of 0.1 mm in thickness, was fixed on a nickel disc surface by spot welding. Through this film diffusion of both yttrium and nickel could be completely prevented. A sketch of such an electrode before electrolysis is shown in Fig. 13. Using this electrode, galvanostatic electrolysis was carried out for 20 h at a current density of 50 mA cm^{-2} at 500 ℃. An SEM image of the cross-section of the sample after electrolysis is shown in Fig. 14. Part A in the figure indicates the original position of the tungsten marker. Since the interface between nickel and Ni_2Y is quite hard to see on the micrograph, both being shades of grey, a simple sketch is used to make the point better (Fig. 15). Clearly, the Ni_2Y-Ni interface has moved in the direction of the nickel base. The thickness of the Ni_2Y layer is about 290 μm, and the distance between the Ni_2Y-Ni interface and the original nickel surface is about 210 μm. On the other hand, the left edge of the Ni_2Y layer moved outside by 80 μm from the original nickel surface. Ni_2Y has a fcc crystal structure, which is the same crystal structure as Ni. It appears that nickel diffuses in Ni_2Y faster than yttrium. A quantitative consideration of the intermetallic diffusion phenomenon will constitute a future research subject.

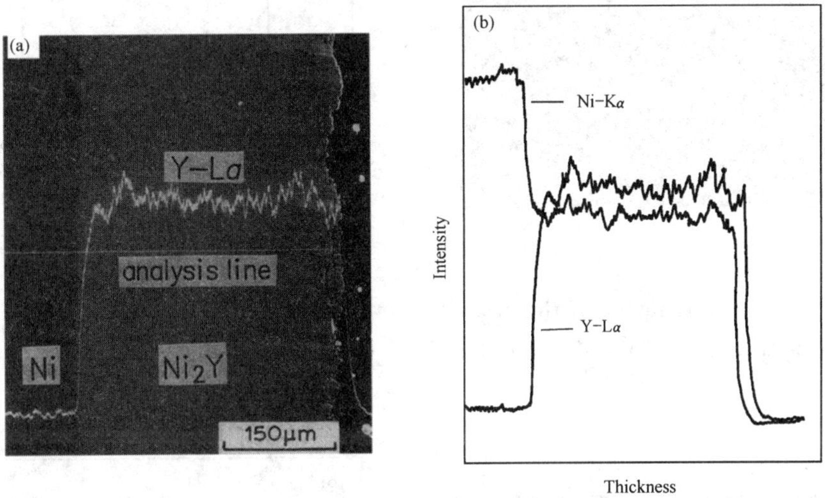

Fig. 6 (a) SEM image of the cross-section of sample prepared at 50mAcm^{-2} (b) Concentration profiles of Y and Ni of the cross-section. (1.2 mol % YCl_3, 600 ℃)

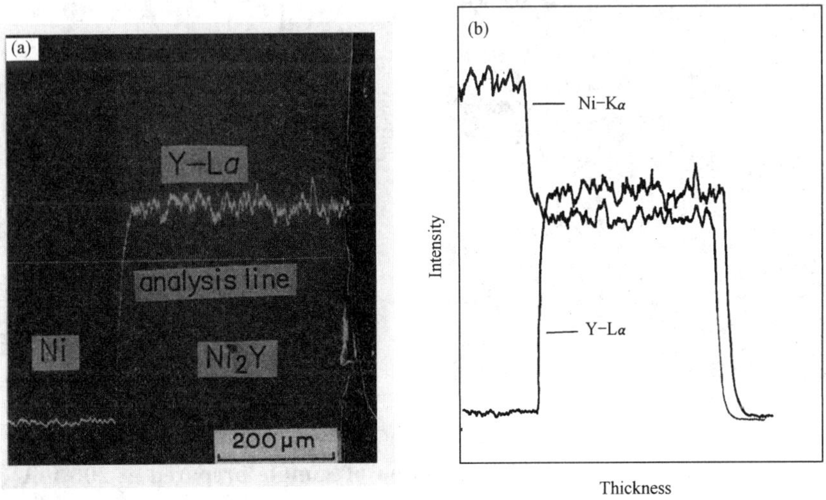

Fig. 7 (a) SEM image of the cross-section of sample prepared at 100 mA cm^{-2} (b) Concentration profiles of Y and Ni of the cross-section. (1.2 mol % YCl_3, 600 ℃)

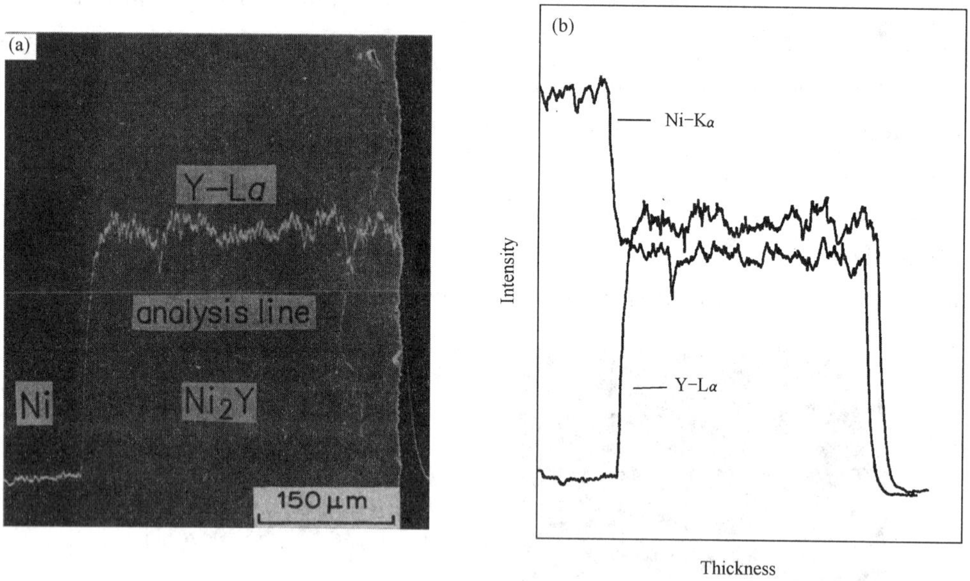

Fig. 8 (a) SEM image of the cross-section of sample prepared at 150 mA cm^{-2} (b) Concentration profiles of Y and Ni of the cross-section. (1.2 mol % YCl_3, 600 ℃)

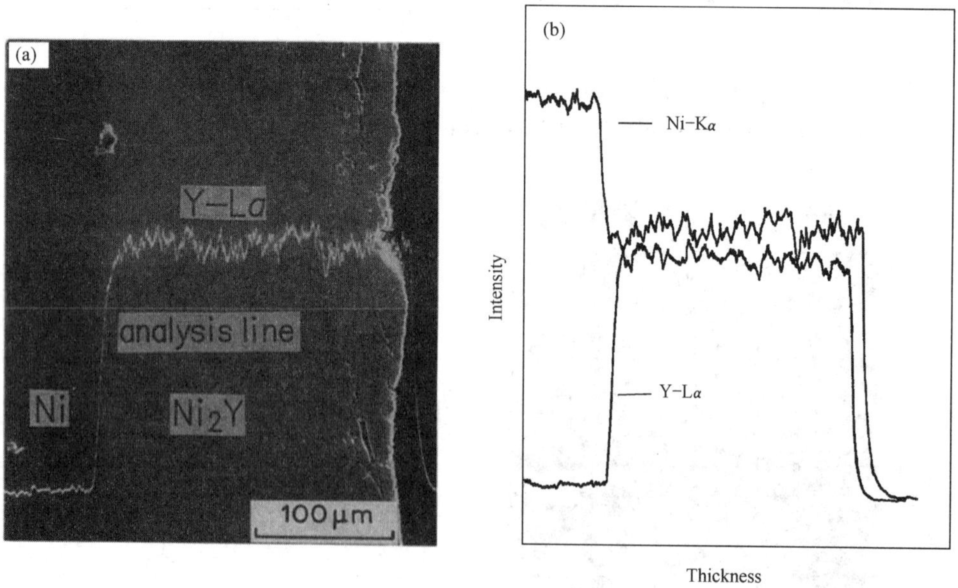

Fig. 9 (a) SEM image of the cross-section of sample prepared at 200 mA cm^{-2} (b) Concentration profiles of Y and Ni of the cross-section. (1.2 mol % YCl_3, 600 ℃)

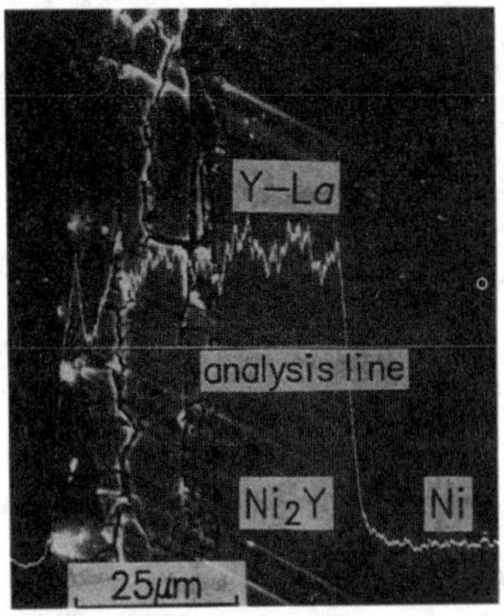

Fig. 10　SEM image of the cross-section of sample prepared at 200 mAcm^{-2} (1.2 mol% YCl_3, 450 ℃)

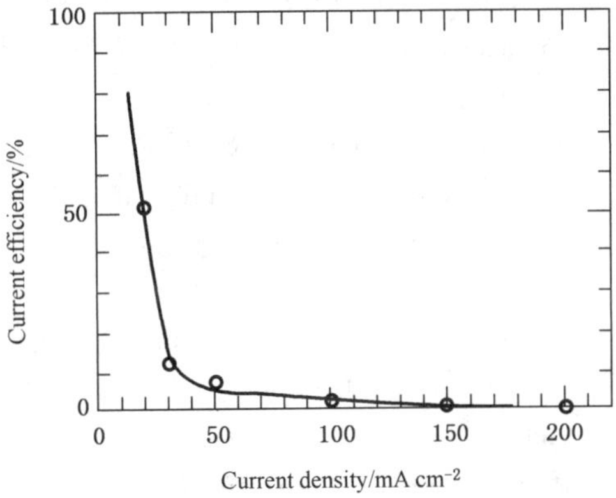

Fig. 11　Electrolytic current effciency (1.2 mol % YCl_3, 500 ℃)

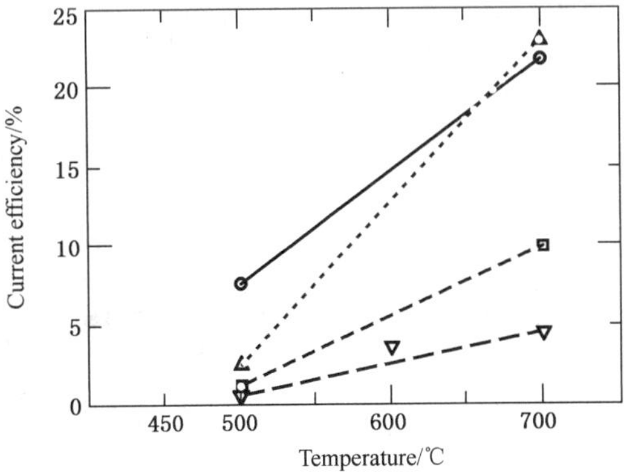

Fig. 12　The influence of bath temperature on electrolytic current efficiency. (1.2 mol% YCl_3). Current density/mA cm^{-2}; (O) 50, (△)100, (□)150 and (▽)200

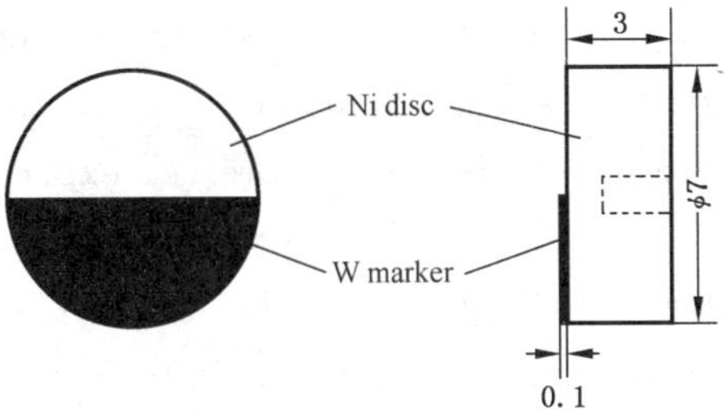

Fig. 13　A sketch of a nickel electrode with a tungsten marker

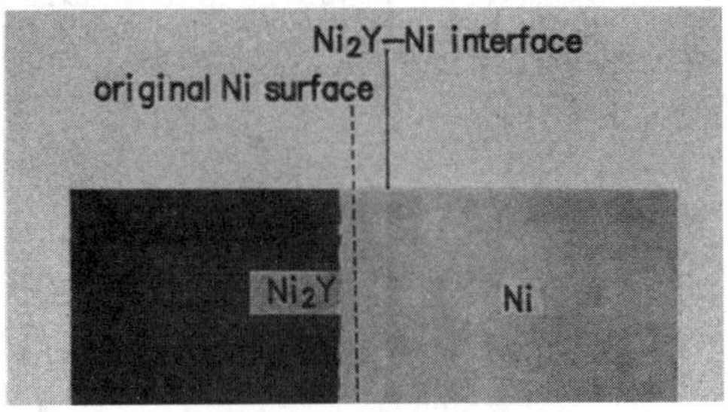

Fig. 14　SEM image of the cross-section of the sample with a tungsten marker after electrolysis. (1.2 mol% YCl_3, 500 ℃, 50 mAcm^{-2}, 24 h)

4　Conclusion

The voltammogram of YCl_3 in molten LiCl-KClNaCl at a nickel electrode showed the possibility of formation of Ni-Y intermetallic compounds. Using galvanostatic electrolysis, samples were prepared at several electrolytic current densities at 450, 500, 600 and 700 ℃, respectively, and were identified with XRD and EPMA. The results show that Ni_2Y, Ni_2Y_3 and NiY can be produced by electrolysis and Ni_2Y, which is formed in bulk independent of bath temperature and current density, is found to be the predominant Ni-Y intermetallic compound. Bath temperature and current density affect the composition of the product to some extent, but only in the surface region under the present experimental conditions. Rather thick adhesive uniform Ni_2Y layers can be obtained in the bath temperature range 500—700 ℃ at all the experimental current densities investigated. Nickel appears to diffuse in Ni_2Y faster than yttrium, and the diffusion process is the rate determining step in Ni_2Y formation.

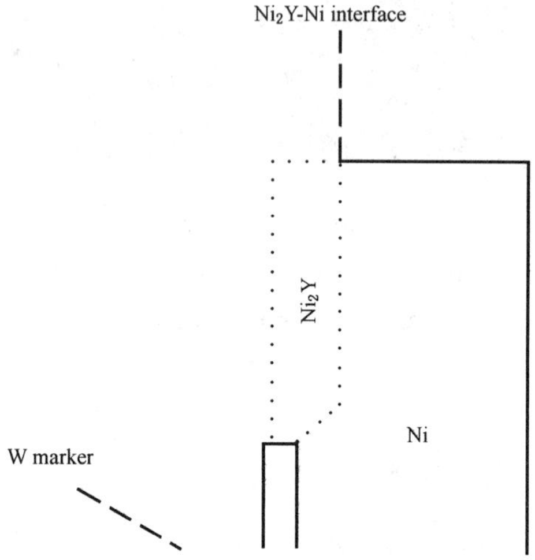

Fig. 15　A sketch of the micrograph of Fig. 14

Acknowledgement

The work was supported by a grant-in-aid from the Japanese Ministry of Education, Science and Culture. The authors thank Mr Teruyoshi Unezaki of Kyoto University for the measurements of SEM and EPMA. The authors also thank Mr Koji Yoshida of Kyoto University for his help and support of this work.

References

[1] L. Yang and R. G. Hudson, Trans. Metall. Soc. AIME 215 (1959) 589.

[2] Y. Hoshino and J. A. Palmbeck, Can. J. Chem. 48 (1970) 685.

[3] Z. M. Shou, S. Hikino, G. Xie, K. Ema and Y. Ito, J. Electrochem. Soc. , in preparation.

[4] O. Izumi, 'Intermetallic Compound' (in Japanese), Sangyo-Toshyo Inc. (1988).

[5] J. Shiokawa, Denki Kagaku 58 (1990) 702.

[6] T. B. Massalski, J. L. Murray, L. H. Bennett and H. Baker, 'Binary Alloy Phase Diagrams', American Society for Metals (1987) p 1775.

[7] Y. Ito, H. Yabe, T. Nakai, K. Ema and J. Oishi, Electrochimica Acta 31 (1986) 1579.

Extended Solubility and Spin-glass Behavior in a Ag-Gd Solid Solution Prepared by Mechanical Alloying①

J. Tang, W. Zhao, C. J. O' Connor, and C. Tao
(Departments of Physics and of Chemistry, University of New Orleans, New Orleans, Louisiana 70148, USA)
M. Zhao and L. Wang
(Changchun Institute of Applied Chemistry, Chinese Academy of Sciences, Changchun 130022, People's Republic of China)

Abstract: The effects of mechanical alloying on the solubility in a Ag-Gd solid solution have been investigated. The study shows that the solubility of Gd in Ag can be extended to about 5 at. % Gd by mechanical alloying from the equilibrium solubility of less than 0. 95 at. % Gd. $Ag_{85}Gd_{15}$. prepared by mechanical alloying exhibits a spin-glass-type transition at ~5 K. A Curie-Weiss behavior at higher temperatures and x-ray patterns of the material indicate that Gd atoms are either dissolved in the Ag matrix or in the form of small clusters of diameters of a few nanometers.

Ⅰ Introduction

It has been demonstrated that extended solubility in two originally immiscible elements can be achieved by mechanical alloying in transition metals [1-3]. For example, a solubility of 60 at. % of Fe in fcc Cu was found in the as mechanically alloyed samples [4], while Fe and Cu are virtually insoluble in each other at equilibrium. The study of metastable solid solution formation by mechanical alloying in intermetallic systems containing rare earths, however, has been scarce. Decomposition of La-Ni, La-Co, and La-Ag intermetallic compounds into the elements by ball milling was reported by Loeff, Bakker, and de Boer [5], and no observable solid solution was found in the systems. On the other hand, ball milling of crystalline La-Au alloys resulted in an amorphous alloy [6]. In this paper, we report the observation of extended solid solution (~5 at. % Gd in Ag) induced by mechanical alloying of the starting powder elements. A spin-glass transition at ~5 K is observed in this binary Ag-Gd system.

Ⅱ Experimental Details

Samples were prepared by mechanical alloying using a high-energy Spex

① Phys Rev B Condens Matter, 1995, 11(1): 829-832.

8000 mixer/mill. The starting materials were fine powders of silver and gadolinium of 99.9% purity. The starting composition of the Ag-Gd mixture was $Ag_{85}Gd_{15}$, which was sealed in a grinding vial made of hardened steel under argon atmosphere. Also sealed in the vial were hardened steel balls. The sticking of metal powders to the walls of vial and balls, which often occurs during milling, was avoided by the addition of small amount of ethanol to the initial mixture. Samples were obtained after 2.5, 15, and 35 h of mechanical alloying. They were dried under vacuum at room temperature. The vacuum dried samples contained no ethanol as indicated from their spectroscopy. The weight of the balls was measured before and after mechanical alloying, and there was no weight loss of the balls (less than 0.01 g), which indicated that the samples (~7 g) were essentially Fe free (less than 0.1 wt% Fe). X-ray diffraction was conducted on a Rigaku x-ray powder diffractometer with Cu $K\alpha$ radiation. During the experiments, samples were sealed underneath an Al_2O_3 foil in order to prevent any possible oxidation of the samples. Magnetic susceptibility of the 35-h mechanically alloyed sample was measured as a function of temperature under both zero-field-cooled (ZFC) and fieldcooled (FC) conditions using a Quantum Design superconducting quantum interference device susceptometer (model MPMS-5S).

Ⅲ Results and Discussion

Shown in Fig. 1 are the x-ray-diffraction patterns of samples ground for 2.5, 15, and 35 h. Also shown in Fig. 1 is the x-ray pattern of the 35-h mechanically alloyed sample, which was subsequently heat treated at 550 ℃ for 10 min. The pattern for the 2.5-h mechanically alloyed sample was essentially that of a mixture of Ag and Gd. As the grinding time increased, the intensities of the Gd peaks decreased and became very broad at 35 h, and, at the same time, the intensities of the Ag peaks increased, which might be caused by the presence of heavier Gd atoms in the fcc Ag matrix. A more direct evidence for the formation of a solid solution of Gd in Ag was that the positions of the Ag peaks were shifted toward lower angles for the 15- and 35-h mechanically alloyed samples because of the substitution of the larger Gd atoms for Ag.

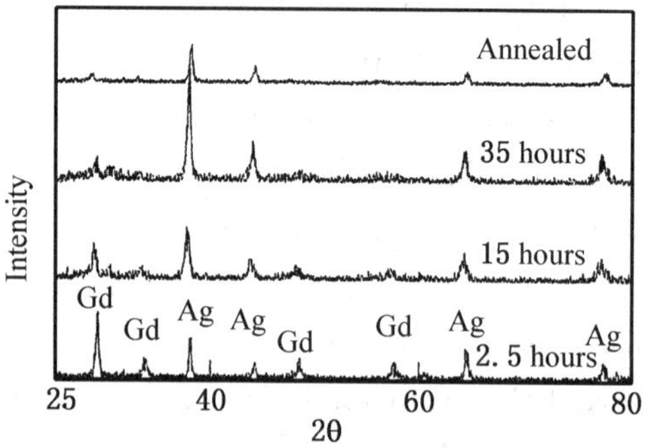

Fig. 1 X-ray-diffraction patterns of samples mechanically alloyed for 2.5, 15, and 35 h and that of the 35-h sample that was subsequently annealed at 550 ℃. The intensity is in arbitrary units and 2θ in degrees

As a matter of fact one can estimate the number of Gd atoms dissolved in the Ag matrix by determining the lattice constants of the samples. The lattice constant of pure fcc Ag $a=4.086$ Å was determined from the Ag powders used in this study. The lattice constant of the 35-h mechanically alloyed sample had a lattice constant a of 4. 100 Å. If one assumes that the linear relation between the lattice constant and Gd^T concentration in fcc Ag under equilibrium conditions for concentrations less than the maximum solubility of 0. 95 at. % Gd is valid in our case, a lattice constant $a=4.100$ Å of the mechanically alloyed sample corresponds to a solubility of ~5 at. % Gd in fcc Ag. This extended solubility was a direct result of mechanical alloying, in which intimate contacts between Gd and Ag and subsequent imbedding of Gd into Ag might have been brought by the high-energy ball sample-container collisions. [1,8] It should be noted that the reported maximum equilibrium solubility of 0. 95 at. % Gd is at a eutectic temperature of 805 ℃, the equilibrium solubility at room temperature is even lower (~0. 1 at. % Gd)[7]. This is not hard to understand if one considers the fact that the metallic radius of Gd is 25% larger than that of Ag. The 15-h mechanically alloyed sample showed a lattice constant that is very close to the 35-h sample, which suggested that much of the 5 at. % of Gd atoms were already dissolved in the Ag matrix at 15 h and the solubility of Gd in fcc Ag may not be extended much further by simply extending the grinding time. The Gd atoms in the 35-h mechanically alloyed "$Ag_{85}Gd_{15}$ sample were either dissolved in the Ag-Gd solid solution (~5 at. % Gd), or in the form of small clusters of average diameter of 2-3 nm as determined from the broadening of Gd x-ray peaks using the Scherrer formula. [9]

After 10 min of annealing at 550 ℃, the metastably dissolved Gd atoms in the 35-h sample precipitated out of the fcc lattice, and the fcc Ag peaks in the x-ray pattern returned to their original positions of pure Ag (Fig. 1).

Magnetic susceptibility of the 35-h mechanically alloyed sample was measured as a function of temperature under both ZFC and FC conditions. Shown in Fig. 2 is the ZFC and FC susceptibilities measured with magnetic fields of $H=20$, 100, 1 000 G. The spin-glass transition at $T_f=5$ K is clearly seen in the ZFC and FC susceptibilities at a measuring field of $H=20$ G. T_f was reduced to 3. 5 K for $H=100$ G and further reduced to below 2 K, which is the lowest temperature our instrument can reach, for $H=1\ 000$ G. A spin glass transition was observed in a Ag-Gd solid solution.

The magnetic properties of Ag-Gd, mostly amorphous, have been studied extensively. [10-14] Amorphous Gd_xAg_{100-x}, for $x>20$ were prepared and exhibited ferromagnetic ordering with a transition temperature proportional to the Gd concentration, although alloys for $x<30$ displayed some of the features normally associated with spin glass. The amorphous Ag-Gd system for smaller Gd concentration was difficult to prepare, and Y was used to dilute the Gd concentration by Mohammed and Lanchester. [15]Their study indicated that amorphous $Gd_{10}Y_{20}Ag_{70}$ and $Gd_{20}Y_{10}Ag_{70}$ are spin glasses with freezing temperatures of ~6 and ~13 K, respectively. The spin-glass behavior observed in our study is of significance in that the Ag-rich fcc Ag-Gd (5 at. %) system is a true binary alloy and is crystalline rather than amorphous. As far as we know, the only other study on the crystalline fcc Ag-Gd alloy was that of Sugawara *et al.* , where a sharp maximum in resistivity and change of slope in magnetic susceptibility were found at about 3 K in quenched dilute Ag-Gd alloys between 0. 3 and 0. 5 at. % Gd. [16]However, no anomaly was found in the heat capacity of these alloys, which was expected for either a spin glass or for other magnetic phase transitions. [17]The extended solubility of ~5 at. % Gd in Ag achieved by mechanical alloying has made possible the direct observation of the spin-glass behavior in this true binary system. Experiments are being planned to prepare samples with varying initial Gd concentration near 5 at. % to obtain complete alloying. Magnetic study on such a pure solid solution sample will shed more light on the nature of the spin-glass transition and Ruderman-Kittel-Kasuya-Yosida interaction.

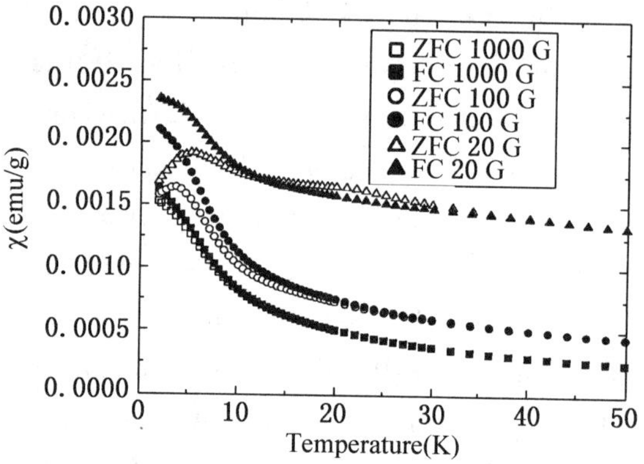

Fig. 2　Zero-field-cooled(ZFC) and field-cooled (FC) susceptibilities of the 35-h sample measured with magnetic fields of *H*=20, 100, and 1 000 G

In the 35-h mechanically alloyed sample, about one-third of the Gd atoms were dissolved in the Ag-Gd solid solution(5 at. % Gd) and two-thirds of the Gd atoms were in the form of nanoparticles 2~3 nm in size. It should be pointed out that superparamagnetisrn arising from these Gd nanoparticles can not be accountable for the peak in susceptibility at 5 K. The blocking temperature T_B of superparamagnetic particles is proportional to KV, where K is anisotropy constant and V the particle volume. [18]The anisotropy constants K are $\sim 5\times10^5$ and $\sim 1\times10^6$ erg/cm^3 for Fe and Gd, respectively. [19] The blocking temperatures of systems containing Fe particles of a few nanometers have been found to have a typical value of $T_B>10$ K, which suggests that the T_B of the Gd nanoparticles of similar size should be at least twice that (>20 K). In addition, a recent study on small Gd clusters has suggested that the blocking temperature of Gd clusters containing 10~35 atoms has typical values between 100 K and room temperature. [20] Thus the peak at ~5 K could not be associated with the blocking temperature of Gd nanoparticles. However a broad maximum between 15 and 30 K in low-field susceptibility (ZFC and $H=20$ G) might be related to the blocking of the Gd superparamagnetic nanoparticles. Compared to the nanoparticles of transition metals (Fe, Co, and Ni), the magnetic behavior of Gd nanoparticles is far less understood and needs to be further investigated. Additional experiments will be conducted in order to study the superparamagnetic properties of Gd nanoparticles produced by mechanical milling.

Figure 3 shows the inverse susceptibility $1/(\chi-\chi_0)$ measured at 1 000 G, where constant $\chi_0=0.000058$ emu/g. It follows the Curie-Weiss law, with a small and negative $\theta=-0.5$ K. If one assumes that the Gd atoms dissolved in the Ag-Gd solid solution have effective moment $\mu_{eff}=7.9\ \mu_B$ (expected for a free-Gd ion), the saturation magnetization M_s of the Gd nanoparticles can be calculated from $\chi=M_s^2V/3k_B(T-\theta)$, where V is the average Gd particle volume. $\theta=-0.5$ K and $V=(4-14)\times10^{-27}$ m^3 (particle diameter $d=2$—3 nm) were used in the calculation. Such a calculation resulted in an average saturation magnetization of M_s between 3 and 5 μ_B per Gd atom for Gd particles. The reduced magnetization (compared to 7 μ_B) in small Gd particles has been observed in a few cases and may be attributed to the possible presence of antiferromagnetic coupling within the particle. [13,20] The reduced moment can also be seen in the magnetization curve (Fig. 4), which shows that the magnetization does not saturate at 2 K and a field of 5 T. The highest value obtained was 4.9 μ_B/Gd. The inset of Fig. 4 shows the hysteresis normally associated with spin glass or superparamagnetic particles below the critical temperature. The low field susceptibilities ($H=20$ and 100 G) could not be fitted into a Curie-Weiss law, which is attributed to the enhanced effect at low fields by residual ferromagnetic Gd existing in the sample. This is also seen as the difference in susceptibilities between different measuring fields (Fig. 2) at high temperatures.

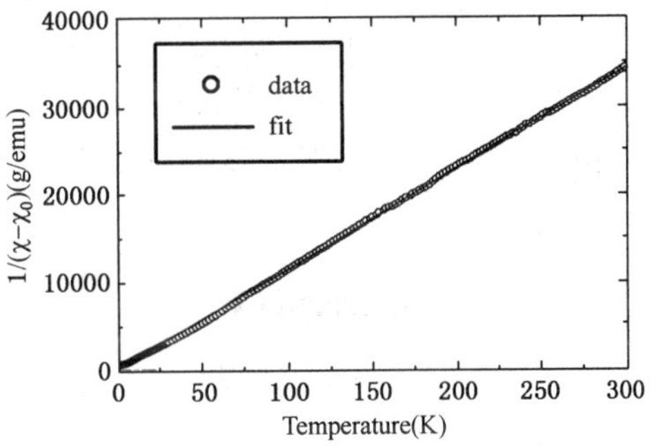

Fig. 3　Inverse susceptibility $1(\chi-\chi_0)$ of the 35-h sample measured at 1000 G, where $\chi_0=0.000058$ emu/g

IV　Conclusions

An extended solubility (5 at.% Gd) was induced by mechanical alloying in an Ag-rich fcc solid solution. A spin glass freezing temperature of 5 K was observed in this system. A Curie-Weiss behavior at higher temperatures and x-ray patterns of the material indicate that Gd atoms are either dissolved in the Ag matrix or in the form of small clusters of diameters of a few nanometers.

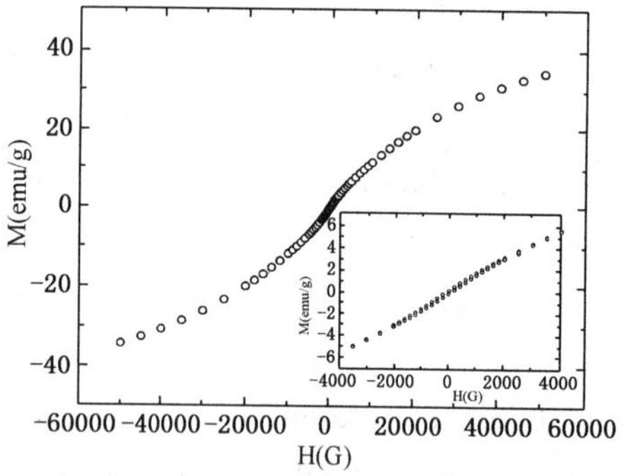

Fig. 4 Magnetization and hysteresis loop for the 35-h sample. The inset shows the region of smaler fields ($H<4\,000$ G)

Acknowledgments

Acknowledgment is made to the NSF, the U. S. DOE, Louisiana Education Quality Support Fund, Research Corporation, and the K. C. Wong Education Foundation.

References

[1] A. R. Yavari, P. J. Desre, and T. Benameur, Phys. Rev. Lett. **68**, 2235 (1992).

[2] J. Eckert, J. C. Holzer, C. E. Krill III, and W L. Johnson, J. Appl. Phys. **73**, 2794 (1993).

[3] R. Bruningk, K. Samwer, C. Kuhrt, and L. Schultz, J. Appl. Phys. **72**, 2978 (1992).

[4] E. Ma, M. Atzmon, and F. E. Pinkerton, J. Appl. Phys. **74**, 955(1993).

[5] P. I. Loeff, H. Bakker, and F. R. de Boer, New Materials by *Mechanical Alloying Techniques*, edited by E. Arzt and L. Schultz (DGM, Oberursel, Germany, 1989), p. 119.

[6] P. I. Loeff and H. Bakker, Scr. Metall. **22**, 401 (1988).

[7] K. A. Gschneidner, Jr., O. D. McMasters, D. G. Alexander, and R. F. Venteicher, Metall. Trans. **1**, 1961 (1970).

[8] C. C. Koch, Annu. Rev. Mater. Sci. **19**, 121 (1989).

[9] A. Guinier, Theoric et Technique de la Radiocristallographie (Dunod, Paris, 1964).

[10] J. J. Hauser, Phys. Rev. B **12**, 5160 (1975).

[11] K. H. J. Buschow, Solid State Commun. **27**, 275 (1978).

[12] S. W. Charles, J. Popplewell, and P. A. Bates, J. Phys. F **3**, 664 (1973).

[13] R. J. Begum, C. A. Cornelius, E. W. Lee, and V. Samadian, J. Phys. F **14**, 2739 (1984).

[14] C. D. Fuerst, J. F. Herbst, R. K. Mishra, and R. D. McMichael, J. Appl. Phys. **76**, 6301 (1994).

[15] K. A. Mohammed and P. C. Lanchester, Solid State Commun. **70**, 367 (1989).

[16] T. Sugawara, R. Soga, and I. Yamase, J. Phys. Soc. Jpn. **19**, 780 (1964).

[17] G. R. Pickett, Phys. Lett. **21**, 618 (1966).

[18] E. M. Logothetis, W. J. Kaiser, H. K. Pluammer, and S. S. Shinozaki, J. Appl. Phys. **60**, 2548 (1986).

[19] E. P. Wohlfarth, Ferromagnetic Materials, edited by E. P. Wohlfarth (North-Holland, New York, 1980), Vol. 1, p. 1; S. Legvold, ibid., Vol. 1, p. 183.

[20] D. C. Douglass, A. J. Cox, J. P. Bucher, and L. A. Bloomfield, Phys. Rev. B **47**, 12 874 (1993).

Formation and Structure of $LaNi_2$ Intermetallic Compound Under High Pressure①

Jin Liang[a], Xianfeng Ma[a], Jinkui Tang[a], Xuewei Yan[a], Wei Zhao[a], Minshou Zhao[a,*], Joan A. Wiemann[b], Jinke Tang[b]

([a] Changchun Institute of Applied Chemistry, Chinese Academy of Sciences, Changchun, 130022, PR China)

([b] Department of Physics, University of New Orleans, New Orleans, LA 70148, USA)

Abstract: The cubic $LaNi_2$ Laves phase has been synthesized under high pressure. The effects of temperature and pressure on the stability of the Laves phase have been studied. High pressure also induces the phase transitions from intermetallic compounds La_2Ni_3 and $LaNi_{2.286}$ to the Laves phase.

Key words: A. Laves phase; F. Diffraction (electron, neutron and x-ray); Phase transformations

1 Introduction

The $LaNi_2$ Laves phase is of particular interest since its hydrogen absorption capacity is higher than that of $LaNi_5$ [1]. However, many efforts to prepare pure $LaNi_2$ phase have failed [2-7]. A stable tetragonal phase with composition $LaNi_{2.286}$ exists in the multiphase samples when the compound is prepared according to the stoichiometry of $LaNi_2$. This is because of the large disparity between the metallic radii (CN=12) of lanthanum and nickel ($r_{La}/r_{Ni}=1.506$). The ratio expected for the ideal AB_2 cubic Laves phase is $r_A/r_B=1.225$. $LaNi_2$ is believed to be a metastable phase which can be obtained by rapid quenching or stabilized by certain impurities [7].

It is well known that compounds may undergo phase transitions into denser phases and often into new phases under high pressure [8]. Frequently new compounds form from two phase regions under high pressure, and many of these new dense phases can be preserved as metastable phases at ambient pressure and temperature. High-pressure technique is thus a powerful tool for the synthesis and characterization of new and metastable materials.

In this paper, the synthesis of pure $LaNi_2$ cubic Laves phase under high pressure and high temperature is reported. The phase transition and stability of La-Ni intermetallic compounds are also studied and discussed.

① Intermetallics, 2003(11): 875-878.

2 Experimental details

$LaNi_x$ samples (x=1.5, 2.0, 2.286) were prepared by arc melting of constituent elements, lanthanum (3 N) and nickel (4 N), in a 4 N argon atmosphere. The sam-ples were remelted at least five times for homogenization, then they were placed in an anvil cell with a graphite sleeve heater, as shown in Fig. 1. The cell and its contents were held at various pressures in the range of 4.0—5.0 GPa and temperatures between 900 and 1500 ℃. The temperature was then lowered to ambient by shutting off the power to the cell. The pressure was later released, and the sample was taken out.

In the experiments, the pressure was measured with the phase transformation of bismuth, thallium and barium under the known pressure, which has been described in previous papers [9-11], the temperature was measured with a Pt6%Rh-Pt13%Rh thermocouple without correction for the effect of the pressure.

The phases in the synthesized samples were deter-mined by X-ray diffraction (XRD) with CuKa radiation and a diffractometer scanning rate of 2°(2θ) min^{-1} was employed.

3 Results and discussion

3.1 Formation of $LaNi_2$ intermetallic compound

A sample with stoichiometric composition was synthesized by arc melting under argon atmosphere. The XRD pattern of the sample [Fig. 2(a)] shows that the pure $LaNi_2$ phase could not be obtained at normal pressure, which is consistent with other studies [3,6,12].

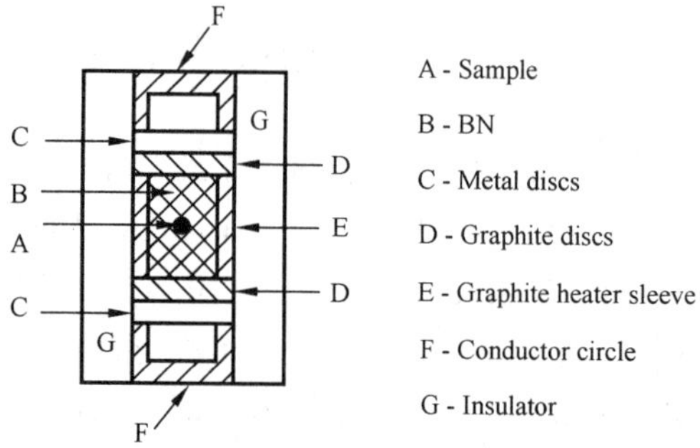

Fig. 1 Schematic diagram of the high pressure cell

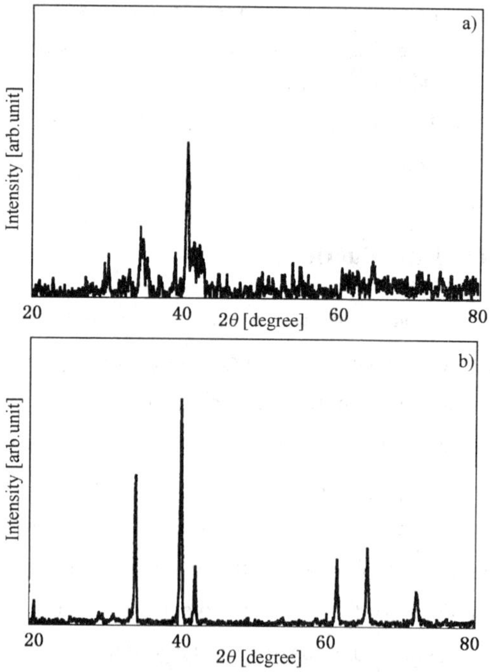

Fig. 2 (a) XRD pattern of the asarcmelted $LaNi_2$ sample. (b) XRD pattern of the same sample after it was heat treated at P=4.0 GPa, T=1200 ℃ and t=30 min

However, the pure $LaNi_2$ phase could form when the sample was heat treated under high pressure. The XRD pattern of the sample after heat treatment at $P=4.0$ GPa and $T=1200$ ℃ for 30 min is shown in Fig. 2 (b), which matches that of $LaNi_2$ Laves phase. Data obtained from the XRD pattern are listed in Table 1 along with the calculated values for the $LaNi_2$ Laves phase. Obviously, the experimental values agree well with the calculated ones. The lattice constant a, deter－mined from a least squares fit, is 0.73906 nm.

The cubic C15 unit cell (space group Fd3m) is presented in Fig. 3. There are 24 atoms in each cubic cell (8 La atoms and 16 Ni atoms). Each La atom is close to four other La atoms and 12 Ni atoms. Therefore the coordination number of La is 12+4, while the coordination number of Ni is 12. In the cubic unit cell, the La-La and Ni-Ni distances are 3a/4and 2a/4, respectively. The ideal ratio of radii r_A/r_B for the C15 AB_2 Laves phase is 1.225, which is much smaller than the actual ratio of radii $r_{La}/r_{Ni}=1.506$. This is the reason that the pure cubic Laves phase does not exist in the equilibrium La-Ni phase diagram. It is, instead, replaced by a more stable compound $LaNi_{2.286}$.

The tetragonal unit cell of the compound $LaNi_{2.286}$, which could be more reasonably written as $La_{0.875}Ni_2$, can be viewed as being formed via doubling of the cubic C15 unit cell of $LaNi_2$ in the c-direction with two of the lanthanum atoms missing. As shown in Fig. 4, there are 46 atoms (14 La atoms, 32 Ni atoms) in each tetragonal unit cell, and two lanthanum atoms are missing from the center of the basal plane and the edges of the unit cell at $z=0.5$. Applied pressure favors the formation of the phase that is more closely packed. In our case, the cubic $LaNi_2$ Laves phase is formed as a result of the applied high pressure.

Table 1 Comparison of the experimental XRD data of $LaNi_2$ with the calculated ones

$d_{exp.}$ (nm)	$d_{cal.}$ (nm)	I/I_0	h,k,l
0.4271	0.4267	10	1,1,1
0.2616	0.2613	64	2,2,0
0.2229	0.2228	100	3,1,1
0.2133	0.2133	26	2,2,2
0.1846	0.1848	3	4,0,0
0.1692	0.1696	4	3,3,1
0.1509	0.1509	29	4,2,2
0.1422	0.1422	34	3,3,3
0.1306	0.1306	16	4,4,0

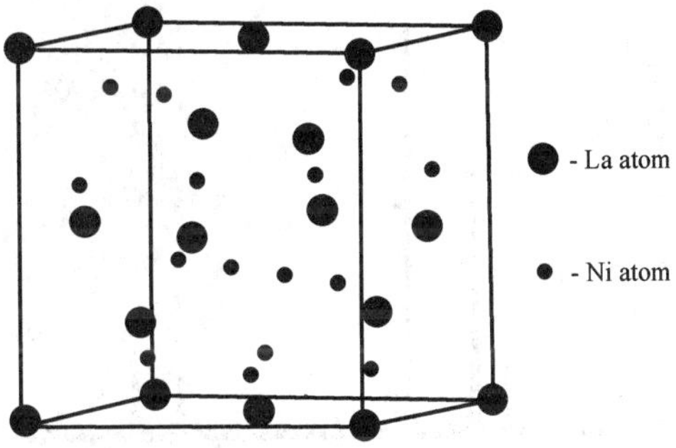

Fig. 3 Unit cell of cubic Laves phase $LaNi_2$

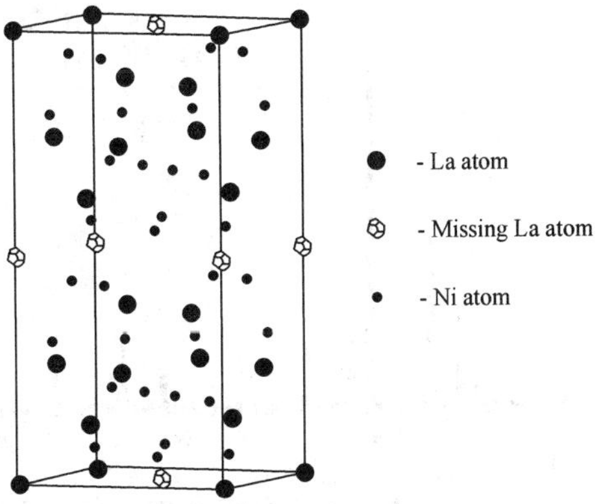

Fig. 4 Tetragonal unit cell of $LaNi_{2.286}$.

3.2 Stability of La-Ni compounds at high pressure

3.2.1 Influence of pressure and temperature on the structure of $LaNi_2$

The XRD patterns of samples synthesized under two different pressures are shown in Fig. 5(a) and (b) for $P=4.5$ and 4.0 GPa, respectively. No significant effect of pressure on the XRD patterns of the cubic $LaNi_2$ Laves phase is observed, which suggests that the structure of cubic $LaNi_2$ is stable at high pressure when the pressure exceeds a certain value.

Keeping the pressure constant, samples were heat treated at different temperatures under the pressure. The XRD patterns are shown in Fig. 5(b)—(d). The results indicate that when the temperature is relatively low [$T=1200$ ℃, Fig. 5 (b)], the sample is of high crystalline quality and single phase. As the temperature is raised to a higher value ($T=1300$ ℃) some small peaks from lanthanum appear [Fig. 5 (c)], and when the temperature is raised further ($T=1350$ ℃), peaks from metal nickel and lanthanum are found [Fig. 5 (d)]. The compound decomposes under high pressure when the temperature is too high, which is similar to the observations in some intermetallic compounds that disproportionate into their components under high pressure.

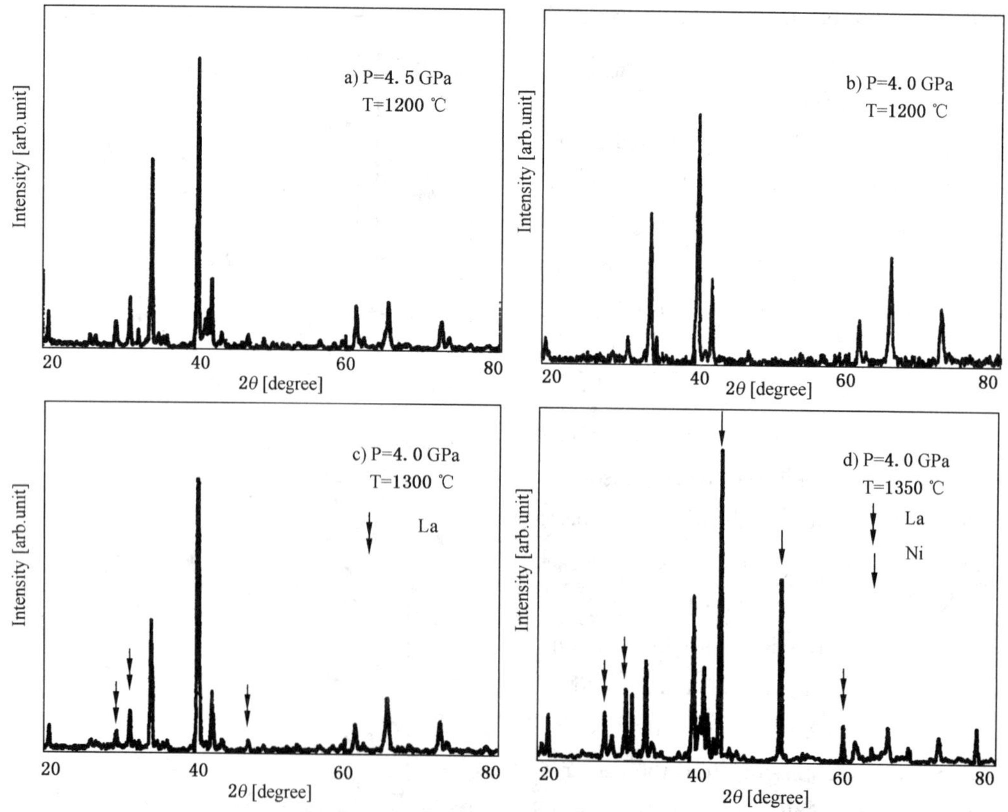

Fig. 5 XRD patterns of $LaNi_2$ samples heat treated under different pressure and temperature ($t=15$ min)

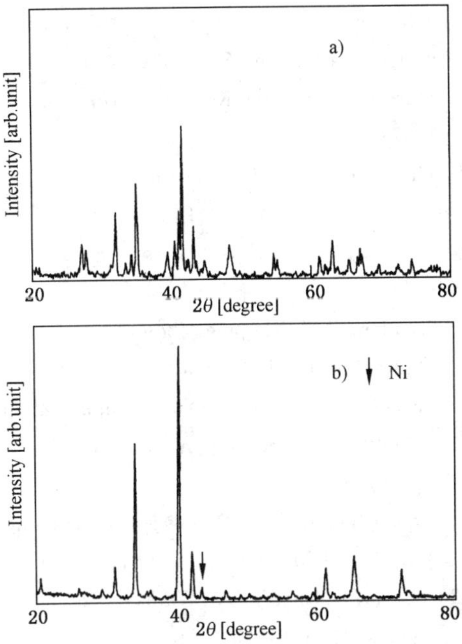

Fig. 6　XRD patterns of $LaNi_{2.286}$. (a) as-arc-melted sample; (b) sample heat treated at P=4.0 GPa and T=1200 ℃

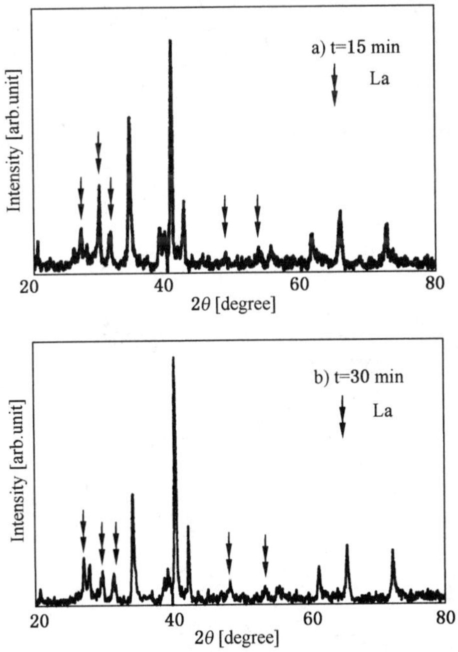

Fig. 7　XRD patterns of La_2Ni_3 heat treated at P=4.0 GPa and T=1200 ℃ for 15 (a) and 30 (b) min, respectively

3.2.2　Stability of $LaNi_{2.286}$ and La_2Ni_3 at high pressure

The effects of pressure on the stability of $LaNi_{2.286}$ prepared by arc-melting has been studied. The as-cast sample of $LaNi_{2.286}$ was heat treated for 30 min under high pressure. The XRD patterns of the samples are shown in Fig. 6. Fig. 6(a) is the pattern of the as-cast sample and Fig. 6(b) is that of the heat treated sample at $P=4.0$ GPa and $T=1200$ ℃. The results indicate that $LaNi_{2.286}$ transforms to the C15 structure under high pressure. A weak nickel peak is observed in Fig. 6(b) suggesting the decomposition of the $LaNi_{2.286}$ phase into $LaNi_2$ and nickel. A similar result is found for the orthorhombic compound La_2Ni_3. Fig. 7 (a) and (b) are the XRD patterns of La_2Ni_3 after it undergoes heat treatment at 4.0 GPa and 1200 ℃ for 15 and 30 min, respectively. These decomposition processes can be expressed by reaction equations $LaNi_{2.286} \Rightarrow LaNi_2 + 0.286Ni$ and $La_2Ni_3 \Rightarrow 1.5\ LaNi_2 + 0.5\ La$, respectively, accompanied by density changes of 4.87 and 4.31%.

4　Conclusions

The cubic $LaNi_2$ Laves phase can be synthesized by heat treating the as arc-melted samples at high pressure and high temperature. No significant effect of pressure on the XRD patterns of the cubic $LaNi_2$ Laves phase is observed for the pressure range applied in this study. However, heat treating under pressure at temperatures above 1300 ℃ results in the decomposition of the Laves phase to lanthanum and nickel. Both tetragonal $LaNi_{2.286}$ and orthorhombic La_2Ni_3 are unstable at high pressure and high temperature, and transform to the $LaNi_2$ Laves phase.

References

[1] Oesterreicher H, Clinton J, Bittner H. Mater Bull 1976;11:1241.

[2] Nassau K, Cherry LV, Wallace WE. J Phys Chem Solids 1960;16:123.

[3] Mansey RC, Raynor GV, Harris IR. J Less-common Met 1968;14:329.

[4] Paul-Boncour V, Percheron Guegan A, Diaf M, Achard JC. J Less-common Met 1987;131:201.

[5] Klimyenko AV, Seuntjents J, Miller LL, et al. J Less-common Met 1988;144:133.

[6] Harries IR, Mansey RC. J Less-common Met 1967;131:591.

[7] Zhang D, Tang J, Gschneidner Jr KA. J Less—common Met 1991;169:45.

[8] Joubert JC, Chenavas J. J Solid State Chem 1979;27:29.

[9] Xianfeng Ma, Yanping Zhou, Xuewei Yan. Chinese Science Bulletin 1996;41:418.

[10] Xianfeng Ma, Xuewei Yan, Yanping Zhou, Shoujing Cui. Science in China (series B) 1996;26:427.

[11] Zhao Tinghe, Yan Xuewei, Cui Shuojing, Niu Wei. J Mater Science 1994;29:1514.

[12] Nassau K, Cherry LV, Wallace WE. J Phys Solids 1960;16:123.

Effect of Rare Earth Metals on Microstructure of Directional Solidified Al-3Li Alloy①

Wang Li-Min, Dang Ping, Du Fu-Ying,
Zhao Min-Shou
(Changchun Institute of Applied Chemistry. Academia Sinica,
Changchun 130022, China)

Abstract: The effect of rare earth metals(La, Ce, Pr, Nd, Mm and Ymm)on microstructure of directional solidified Al-3 Li alloy has been studied. Results show that rare earth metals reduce the distance between primary longitudinal dendrites for Al-3Li, which is related with species, content of rare earth metals and solidification rate of the alloy. RE is mainly segregated at grain boundaries. Constitutional supercooling formed in RE-rich regions during solidification is considered to be the main factor of modification of microstructure.

Key Words: Rare Earth; Al- 3Li alloy; Microstructure

Al-Li alloy is getting great attention in aviation and spaceflight since it has excellent combination of low density and high modulus. To improve the properties of Al-Li alloy. Reduce production costs and develop new Al-Li alloys, primary researches[1-6] have been made on Al-Li alloy containing rare earth metals(RE). This paper studied the microstructure of Al-3Li alloy with small addition of RE (La, Ce, Pr, Nd, Mm and Ymm). The mechanism of the effect of RE on microstructure of Al-3Li alloy is proposed.

1 Experimental

Al-3Li-RE alloys were melted in an alumina crucible heated in a resistance furnace. Al (99. 99wt%), Al-Li and Al-RE master alloys were added in the melt covered by molten salt of KCl + LiCl + LiF and the temperature was kept between 740 and 760 ℃, Stirred with alumina bar and held for 10 min, the melt was then directionally solidified at 720 ℃. Table 1 shows the composition of alloys.

During directional solidification, the molten alloy was poured into a graphite mold(ϕ_{out} 40 mm × ϕ_{in} 15 mm × 100 mm) which had been preheated to 720 ℃ and the mold was moved in directional solidification furnace of 720 ℃. After molten alloy turned to be still, cooling water flowed through bottom of the mold at certain rate to develop alloy a directional solidification. Meanwhile the cooling

① Journal of Rare Earths, 1994, 12(3): 198-201.

curves were measured by NiCr-NiAl thermocouple at the distance of 10, 35 and 60 mm from the bottom of molten alloy. The mean cooling rates were calculated to be 8.7, 4.2 and 2.8 ℃/S at 10, 35 and 60 mm, respectively.

After directional solidification, sample were taken from the central part at 35, 10 and 60 mm from the bottom and polished and etched with 0.5% HF. The distances between longitudinal dendrites were measured by intersecting line method. Every mean value was taken from six measurements. The distribution of RE in alloy was detected by JXA-840 scanning electron microscope.

Table 1　Composition of specimens(wt%)*

No.	Al-Li - La		Al-Li - Ce		Al - Li - Pr		Al-Li - Nd		Al - Li - Mm		Al-Li -Ymm		
	Li	La	Li	Ce	Li	Pr	Li	Nd	Li	Mm**	Li	Ymm	Al
0#	2.88	0	2.88	0	2.88	0	2.88	0	2.88	0	2.88	0	bal
1#	2,91	0.03	2.81	0.03	2.94	0.02	2.94	0.03	2.97	0.03	2.95	0.04	bal
2#	2.84	0.06	2.90	0.07	2.89	0.06	2.90	0.06	2.84	0.06	2.82	0.10	bal
3#	2.87	0.11	2.72	0.10	2.81	0.10	2.85	0.12	2.82	0.11	2.75	0.21	bal
4#	2.82	0.15	2.95	0.16	2,92	0.14	2.92	0.16	2.78	0.17	2.83	0.35	bal
5#	2.85	0.22	2.84	0.22	2.83	0.19	2.87	0.23	2.90	0.21	2.82	0.56	bal
6#	2.90	0.31	2.93	0.32	2.79	0.34	2.85	0.33	2.83	0.35	2.76	0.72	bal
7#	2.86	0.58	2.78	0.61	2.76	0.55	2.80	0.62	2.81	0.64			bal

* Fe<0.05; Si<0.04; Ca<0.02; K<0.6x10^{-4}; Na<0.4x10^{-4}

** Mm(wt%): La 44.8, Ce 2.9 Nd 38.9, Pr 10.5, Eu 1.4, the rest: <1.5; Ymm: (wt%): Y 82.2, Lu 0.60, Yb 5.4, Tm 0.81, Eu 6.42, Ho 2.8, Dy 1.4, the rest: <0.3

2　Results and Discussion

2.1　Macrostructure of directional solidified alloy

All alloys were longitudinally solidified and a similar macrostructure was obtained. Fig. 1 shows the typical macrostructure of sample Al-Li-La(5#) and the area with same colour is a crystalline grain. The longer the distance from cooling terminal the bigger the grain size (as shown in Fig. 1). Since the solidification heat was passed through solidified alloy and brought out by cooling water, with the increase of distance from cooling end, the cooling rate decreased and macrostructure coarsened.

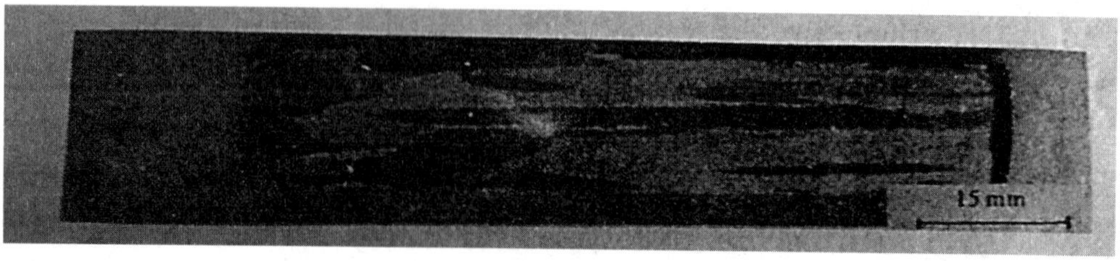

Fig. 1　Macrostructure of the Al-Li-La(5#) alloy

2.2　Microstructure of directional solidified alloy

The distances (d_1) between dendrites for all alloys were measured. Fig. 2 shows the relationship between d1 and contents of RE. It can be seen that a rare earth contents will reduce d1. However, this effect is different RE elements, their contents and cooling rates. When the RE content is less than 0.06 wt%, this effect is not obvious. When they are 0.2wt% or more it is obvious. However, when RE content is more than 0.3wt%, d_1 increases only slightly. Different kind of RE has different effect on d1. When RE content is in the range of 0—0.7wt%, La, Mm and Ce reduce d1 considerably, Pr and Nd do less, and Ymm does only slightly. The effect of RE on d1 is also related to cooling rate. According to F test (variance ratio test), the effect decreases with increasing of cooling rate.

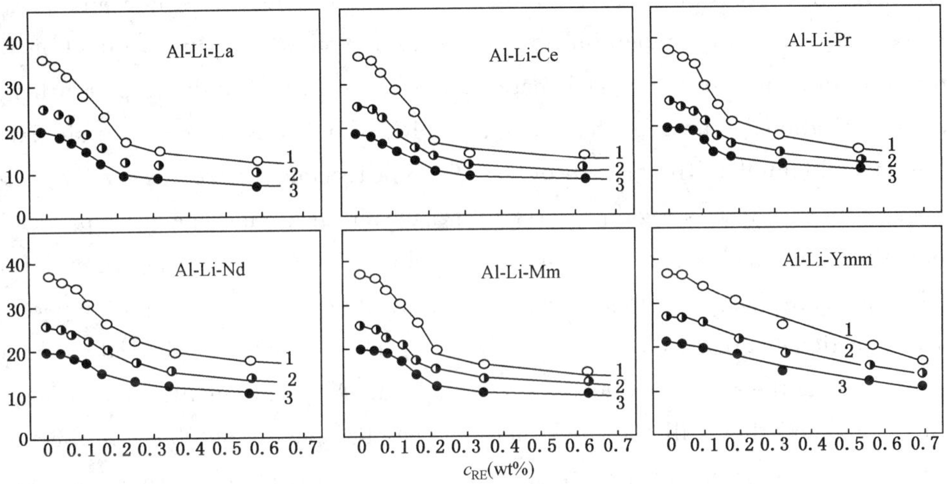

Fig. 2　Relationship between *d*. and RE contents

2.3　Mechanism of effect of RE elements on d_1

To determine the microdistribution of RE in solidified alloy, a liquid quenching experiment was conducted. When the process of directional solidification went on half way, the alloy was quenched to obtain a solid-liquid interface. Wave spectrum analyses were conducted to determine the distribution of La at the interface. The results are shown in Fig. 3 in this secondary electron image on left, the bottom is directional solidified structure and the top is quenched structure. The right side shows the distribution of La. It can be seen that La is rich at grain boundary near solid-liquid interface. Experiments on other samples also show that RE is rich at the grain boundary when RE content is more than 0.1wt%, and it is consist with Ref. 4 and 5. This is due to low solubility of RE in Al-3Li alloy. During solidification, RE is rich in front of solid-liquid interface and segregated at grain boundary on late crystallization.

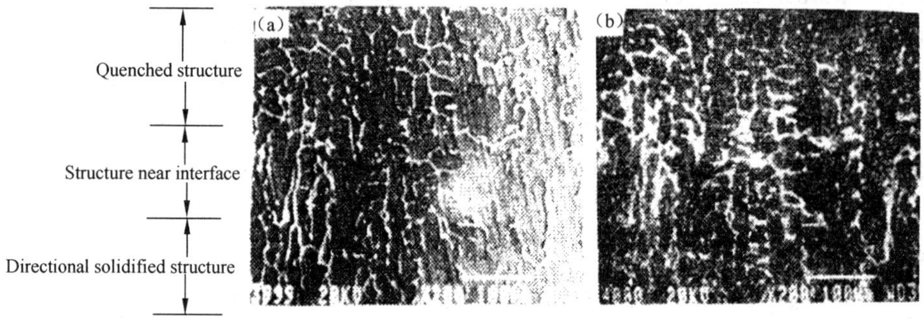

Fig. 3 Element X-ray mapping for Al-Li-La(6[#])alloy

Under our experimental conditions, all alloys grow cellularly. The segregation of RE in process of solidification decreases crystallization temperature of the front of solid-liquid interface and increases constitutional supercooling effect. Thus it will stimulate the growth of secondary dendrites in this region to keep about the same melting temperature at solid-liquid interface. Due to the mandatory directional growth, the secondary dendrites take the same direction as crystalline cells and they will form new dendrites and cells with shorten distances between cells.

When RE content is small, constitutional supercooling effect increases slightly and the effect on d_1 is not obvious. When it is 0. 2wt% or more, adsorption of RE at solid-liquid interface become saturated and supercooling effect is apparent, and d_1 decreases apparently. Due to the formation of RE compounds [5] with further increasing of RE content, the supercooling effect increases very slightly and d1 changes only a little. When cooling rate is too high, supercooling effect would disappear and the effect of RE on d_1 turns to be relatively small.

The effect of single and mixed RE on the microstructure of directional solidified Al-3Li alloy shows that either single RE or mixed RE has almost similar effect on d1. Some differe ences may be related to physical and chemical properties of different RE. Since the effect of RE is mainly due to increasing of supercooling, an element with larger radius (compared with Al) and smaller electronegativity would have low solubility in the alloy and more segregation. Since the atomic radii of La, Ce, Pr, Nd are in the order of decreasing and their electronegativity are in the order of increasing, the effect on these elements on d_1 decreases accordingly. The effect of Mm is obvious since Mm contains more La. Ymm is mainly containing yttrium, Y has similar electronegativity with La, the effect of Ymm on d_1 is less than that of La due to its smaller atomic radius. In addition, diffusion, nucleus charge and valence electrons and other factor of RE may also have some effects on microstructure.

3 Conclusion

(1) RE could have effect on microstructure of directional solidified Al-3Li alloys. When RE content is 0.2wt% or more, distance (d1) between longitudinal dendrites decreases with increasing of RE. The effect decreases with the sequence of La, Ce, Pr, Nd and Ymm.

(2) RE mainly distribute at dendrites boundary. The effect of RE on microstructure is essentially due to increasing of constitutional supercooling effect in the process of solidification.

References

[1] Zhang, B. C; Wang, Z. Z.; Zhu, W. B.; Li, Y. H.; Liang, Y. Aluminum- Lithium V. Birmingham, U. K: MCE Publications Ltd. 1989, 529.

[2] Zhang, Y.; Zhao, H. E.; Gao, G. Z.; Chen, J. Z.; Yao, D. P.; Hu, Z. Q. Aluminum- Lithium V. Birmingham, U. K: MCE Publications Ltd. 1989, 539.

[3] Higashi, K.; Ito, T. Rare Earths (in Jpn.) 1989, 14, 24.

[4] Chen, Z.; Li, M. L.; He, M. Acta metallurgical Sinica. 1991, 27(2), A 153.

[5] Dang, P.; Zhao, M. S.; Chang, k. G.; Lu, X. P.; Du, F. Y. Rare Metals. 1991, 10(4), 272.

[6] Song, S. H.; Zheng, Z. J.; Cui, Q.; Zhang, W. B. Qing Hejin Jiagong jishu (in China). 1987, 15(7), 21.